Why You Need this New Edition

3 good reasons why you should buy this latest edition of *Sociology of Religion*

1. In the Second Edition, 36 of the 46 readings are new

2. Two new sections – Section 11: Religious Violence and Section 12: Religion in a Globalized World – have been added and explore topics such as:
   - The role religion plays in international terrorism
   - Whether religion is the culprit or the victim of terrorism
   - The connections between religion and violence
   - Religious peacemakers, and why religion is sometimes used for violence, but often used for positive dialogue and nonviolent resolution of conflicts
   - How the advancement of communication and transportation technologies influence religion; how religious life has become transnational, and the difference that makes
   - The globalization of religion, and how globalization shapes and is shaped by religion

3. Section 3 has been expanded to include Immigration in its discussion of Race and Religion and now includes articles examining the literature written about post-1965 immigrants to the United States and their religions; the impact of different religions on the same ethnic group; and how members of multiracial congregations come to identify and achieve stable affiliation with their congregation given their disparate ethnic and racial heritages.

PEARSON

SOCIOLOGY OF RELIGION

A Reader

Second Edition

Edited by

Susanne C. Monahan
Montana State University

William A. Mirola
Marian University

Michael O. Emerson
Rice University

Allyn & Bacon

Boston   Columbus   Indianapolis   New York   San Francisco   Upper Saddle River
Amsterdam   Cape Town   Dubai   London   Madrid   Milan   Munich   Paris   Montreal   Toronto
Delhi   Mexico City   Sao Paulo   Sydney   Hong Kong   Seoul   Singapore   Taipei   Tokyo

Publisher: Karen Hanson
Editorial Assistant: Alyssa Levy
Executive Marketing Manager: Kelly May
Marketing Assistant: Janeli Bitor
Production Editor: Karen Mason
Editorial Production and Composition Service: Laserwords Private Limited, Chennai, India
Manufacturing Buyer: Debbie Rossie
Cover Administrator: Kristina Mose-Libon

Library of Congress Cataloging-in-Publication Data

Sociology of religion : a reader / edited by Susanne C. Monahan, William A. Mirola, Michael O. Emerson.—2nd ed.
   p. cm.
Includes bibliographical references.
ISBN 978-0-205-71082-9 (alk. paper)
  1. Religion and sociology—Textbooks. 2. Religion and sociology—United States—Textbooks. I. Monahan, Susanne C. II. Mirola, William A. (William Andrew) III. Emerson, Michael O., 1965-

BL60.S629 2010
306.6—dc22   2010030496

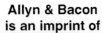

**Allyn & Bacon
is an imprint of**

www.pearsonhighered.com

ISBN-10: 0-205-71082-4
ISBN-13: 978-0-205-71082-9

Contents

Although most people in the United States continue to practice their religion in same-race gatherings, not all do. For those in multiracial congregations, Dr. Marti asks an important question: How do members of disparate ethnic and racial heritages come to identify and achieve stable affiliation with their multiracial congregation? It's an important question, because most theory and research tells us why people find it easier and more rewarding to be in same-race gatherings, yet we do have multiracial congregations. See if you can identify his answers.

Gender and Religion

Woodhead addresses two key issues related to the sociological study of gender and religion. First, shifts in patterns of women's religious affiliation and practice, as well as women's disaffiliation from certain forms of religion, merit more study. Second, these religious changes are related to changes in women's labor force participation, traditional domestic roles, and their efforts to bridge the two. Woodhead highlights how the religious dimensions of men's and women's lives are shaped by the social worlds in which they find themselves.

Sechzer provides an historical look at the status of women within Islam. While you may be familiar with recent controversies related to the veiling of Muslim women, this essay helps us understand how women's status across the Muslim world has changed as interpretations of Islamic religious teachings, traditions, and laws have changed. While many Muslim countries have increased social restrictions on women, Islamic women have organized to fight for their rights and to improve their status.

As Woodhead notes in the opening essay, some women are abandoning traditional forms of organized religion and gravitating to alternative religious traditions which place women's lives and experiences at the center of their spiritual beliefs and practices. Griffin used participant observation and interviews to study feminist witches who belong to the Coven of the Redwood Moon and Womancircle. In examining the rituals and symbols used by each group, Griffin shows how members actively use their religious beliefs and practices to redefine and challenge traditional patriarchal gender relations and power inequalities.

Despite much debate following the Second Vatican Council in 1965, the Roman Catholic Church maintains its traditional view that women cannot be priests: as Wallace notes in her essay, women are "laity" no matter what leadership role they hold. As we learn in this essay, however, a shortage of priests in the U.S. has resulted in more women heading *congregations as pastors. Wallace examines how women's leadership styles differ from their male counterparts and how their long-term presence in leadership roles affects the attitudes of their parishioners regarding women pastors.*

Smith and Faris's essay sparked renewed interest in studying the links between social class, economic inequality, and religion. After decades of neglect, class analysis has been re-united with studies of religious organizations, their beliefs, and practices. While their study is exploratory, its findings raise important questions about how social class differences are reflected in American religious groups.

As suggested by Smith and Faris, social class differences among religious groups are reinforced by the culture that each group expresses through its language, norms for behavior, and values. Using fifteen classic community studies from the 1930s-1960s, Nelson explores how class differences are reflected in the aesthetics, linguistic styles, and physical expression of American congregations and how this contributes to social class segregation among these congregations.

Much research has focused on how social class affects religious beliefs and practices in adults. But what about teenagers? Drawing on survey data from the National Study of Youth and Religion, Philip Schwadel found numerous differences between poor and non-poor adolescents. Social class is associated—sometimes in surprising ways—with aspects of religion including prayer, reading scriptures, attendance at worship services and emotionally charged religious experiences.

Religion can be a force for stability, or a force for change. In this essay, Keister analyzes upward mobility and change within the class structure for white, non-Hispanic Roman Catholics. Prior studies found that Catholics have been economically disadvantaged especially compared to mainline Protestants. Keister's findings, however, suggest that recent generations of Roman Catholics have moved up significantly in their wealth attainment compared to conservative and mainline Protestants.

Hunter argues that religious responses to human sexuality generally and homosexuality specifically are rooted in diverse moral understandings of the family as the appropriate context for sexual behavior. Hunter wrote this piece in 1991. Do you think his observations are still relevant today? Consider especially activism by religious groups in favor of and against granting official rights and protections for gays and lesbians through anti-discrimination laws, recognition of same-sex marriages, and ordination to religious leadership positions.

The Secularization Debate

Within pagan groups, "authenticity" is defined in contrast to "fluffy bunnies:" those whose belief is superficial or tainted by commercialism.

Reviewing reports from a number of ethnographers of new religious movements, Ayella explores the complexities and difficulties inherent in studying "cults."

Religion, Politics, and Social Change

Religion can be seen as a "toolbox" of cultural resources that social change movements draw upon to achieve political goals. Smith's essay remains one of the only exhaustive attempts to categorize the resources available to movements from religious beliefs, practices, and structures. As you will see, religion has the potential to provide the beliefs and ideological support necessary to motivate people to act while also supplying the practical organizational resources that allow a movement to go forward.

Patillo-McCoy documents how African American religion provides a toolbox for mobilizing community political activism. This essay represents a practical application of Smith's theoretical outline of religious resources used by movements trying to achieve social and political change. Here we see the black church as a gate-keeping institution that can channel religious beliefs, meeting space, finances, and other cultural resources to movements whose political efforts in turn, shape church members and the broader African American community.

Studying individual attitudes regarding the separation of church and state has been a common focus in exploring the links between religion and politics in the United States. Using survey data collected in the Washington D.C. area in 1993 and 2000, Wilcox and Goldberg examine changes to and continuities of these attitudes in the face of increasing religious diversity.

Lindsay contributes to our understanding of religious dimensions of politics and policy-making in this study of 360 evangelical elites. In looking behind the scenes at an elite social group we know little about, we see how powerful evangelicals across many sectors of U.S. society use their shared religious identity, social networks, and evangelical groups and initiatives to build cohesion among themselves. It is important to also note the individual and structural challenges facing elite evangelicals who try to use their power and position to achieve desired cultural changes.

called the Catholic Charismatic Renewal movement, that is, Catholic people and organizations that practice "charismatic gifts" such as speaking in tongues. He traces for us the international expansion of this movement, showing a specific case of how globalization occurs.

Focusing on the activities of US congregations and their members, Wuthnow and Offutt provide an expansive view of how religion shapes and is shaped by globalization. Focus on the main argument and ask yourself if you can identify the categories of global influence.

Preface

Much has changed since the First Edition of *Sociology of Religion: A Reader* was published in early 2001.

- Terrorists attacked the World Trade Center and Pentagon in September of 2001; soon after, the U.S. went to war in Afghanistan and Iraq.
- The forces of globalization and technological change accelerated, making our world smaller in some ways but also creating new gulfs and distances.
- Long-building changes due to immigration became highly visible as California became the first U.S. state where whites were no longer the majority.
- Changes driven by immigration were seen around the world, driving increases in ethnic and religious diversity in cities around the world.
- The U.S. saw a presidential election where a white woman was a serious contender, and a black man won.
- There has been a sea-change in attitudes about homosexuality and same sex marriage, not just in the U.S. but in a number of places around the world.

In ten short years, the world seems new. Depending on your perspective, however, it may not be new in a welcome way! None of these changes have been easy or comfortable, and for some they create a sense of dis-ease or disorientation.

What has not changed is the critical role that religion, religious groups, and religious people play in these shifts. The "new atheists" notwithstanding, God (or its equivalents) is not dead. Even those who personally eschew religion admit its influence in our lives: It organizes and motivates people, provides community and meaning, and infuses innumerable aspects of the lives of so many people. Whether the topic is terrorism or war, globalization or immigration, politics or marriage, religious people and groups are right in the middle of it.

This reality—the undeniable importance of religion in our world—motivated us to put together the First Edition of this reader ten years ago. Today, in a new millennium and a changed world, we are more convinced than ever of how important it is that we understand religion and its role in our world.

In this reader, we let the voices of leading and emerging scholars of the sociology of religion speak for themselves. We have lots to say about the role of religion in society: We say much of it in a companion text, *Religion Matters: What Sociology Teaches Us About Religion in Our World* (Allyn and Bacon 2011), along with other writings by each of us individually. But we believe it is important for students of religion to also read original works that inform the thinking of scholars in this field, parse the arguments, and come to their own conclusions. We hope that *Sociology of Religion: A Reader* is the beginning of a rewarding intellectual journey where you are not just filled with knowledge but take part in building that knowledge yourself. Each of the editors of this reader has an abiding fascination with religion—driven both by our intellectual interests and our personal concerns. We hope that this reader sparks a similar fascination with religion in you.

We—Bill Mirola, Mike Emerson, and Sue Monahan—first met in 1997 in Santa Barbara, CA, at a Pew Foundation-funded "Young Scholars of American Religion" seminar series. Through this multiyear seminar series, we found both an intellectual community and good friends: Lori Beaman, Patty Chang, Eric Gormly, Conrad Kanagy, Bill MacDonald, Rich Wood, and Wendy Young. Although this group has since gone in many different directions, we treasure the collegiality, intellectual challenge, and personal support this group has brought us over the years. So, again, we thank those who gave us the chance to know each other: the Pew Foundation, Wade Clark Roof, the Center for the Study of Religion and American Culture at the Indiana University-Purdue University-Indianapolis, Conrad Cherry, Terry Grimm, and Bob Carpenter. We are also grateful to the editorial staff at Allyn and Bacon for bringing this Second Edition of the reader to fruition: Jeff Lasser, Karen Hanson, and Ted Knight. And finally, we thank Jessie Moura and Allysa Levy who gamely pitched in with nitty-gritty details of preparing a Second Edition.

Reading 1

Subject of the Study: Religious Sociology and the Theory of Knowledge

EMILE DURKHEIM

Durkheim argues that religion is eminently social, and made up of beliefs and practices that tie people together into a cohesive moral community. In this excerpt from The Elementary Forms of Religious Life, *Durkheim concludes with his definition of religion.*

. . .

For a long time it has been known that the first systems of representations with which men have pictured to themselves the world and themselves were of religious origin. There is no religion that is not a cosmology at the same time that it is a speculation upon divine things. If philosophy and the sciences were born of religion, it is because religion began by taking the place of the sciences and philosophy. But it has been less frequently noticed that religion has not confined itself to enriching the human intellect, formed beforehand, with a certain number of ideas; it has contributed to forming the intellect itself. Men owe to it not only a good part of the substance of their knowledge, but also the form in which this knowledge has been elaborated.

At the roots of all our judgments there are a certain number of essential ideas which dominate all our intellectual life; they are what philosophers since Aristotle have called the categories of the understanding: ideas of time, space, class, number, cause, substance, personality, etc. They correspond to the most universal properties of things. They are like the solid frame which encloses all thought; . . . for it seems that we cannot think of objects that are not in time and space, which have no number, etc. Other ideas are contingent and unsteady; we can conceive of their being unknown to a man; a society or an epoch; but these others appear to be nearly inseparable from the normal working of the intellect. They are like the framework of the intelligence. . . .

Religion is something eminently social. Religious representations are collective representations which express collective realities; the rites are a manner of acting which take rise in the midst of the assembled groups and which are destined to excite, maintain or recreate certain mental states in these groups. So if the categories are of religious origin, they ought to participate in this nature common to all religious facts; they too should be social affairs and the product of collective thought. . . .

3

Religious phenomena are naturally arranged in two fundamental categories: beliefs and rites. The first are states of opinion, and consist in representations; the second are determined modes of action. Between these two classes of facts there is all the difference which separates thought from action.

The rites can be defined and distinguished from other human practices, moral practices, for example, only by the special nature of their object. A moral rule prescribes certain manners of acting to us, just as a rite does, but which are addressed to a different class of objects. So it is the object of the rite which must be characterized, if we are to characterize the rite itself. Now it is in the beliefs that the special nature of this object is expressed. It is possible to define the rite only after we have defined the belief.

All known religious beliefs, whether simple or complex, present one common characteristic: they presuppose a classification of all the things, real and ideal, of which men think, into two classes or opposed groups, generally designated by two distinct terms which are translated well enough by the words *profane* and *sacred*. . . . This division of the world into two domains, the one containing all that is sacred, the other all that is profane, is the distinctive trait of religious thought; the beliefs, myths,

dogmas and legends are either representations or systems of representations which express the nature of sacred things, the virtues and powers which are attributed to them, or their relations with each other and with profane things. But by sacred things one must not understand simply those personal beings which are called gods or spirits; a rock, a tree, a spring, a pebble, a piece of wood, a house, in a word, anything can be sacred. A rite can have this character; in fact, the rite does not exist which does not have it to a certain degree. There are words, expressions and formulæ which can be pronounced only by the mouths of consecrated persons; there are gestures and movements which everybody cannot perform. . . . The circle of sacred objects cannot be determined, then, once for all. Its extent varies infinitely, according to the different religions. That is how Buddhism is a religion: in default of gods, it admits the existence of sacred things, namely, the four noble truths and the practices derived from them.

Up to the present we have confined ourselves to enumerating a certain number of sacred things as examples: we must now show by what general characteristics they are to be distinguished from profane things.

One might be tempted, first of all, to define them by the place they are generally assigned in the hierarchy of things. They are naturally considered superior in dignity and power to profane things, and particularly to man, when he is only a man and has nothing sacred about him. One thinks of himself as occupying an inferior and dependent position in relation to them; and surely this conception is not without some truth. Only there is nothing in it which is really characteristic of the sacred. It is not enough that one thing be subordinated to another for the second to be sacred in regard to the first. Slaves are inferior to their masters, subjects to their king, soldiers to their leaders, the miser to his gold, the man ambitious for power to the hands which keep it from him; but if it is sometimes said of a man that he makes a religion of those beings or things whose eminent value and superiority to himself he thus recognizes, it is clear that in any case the word is taken in a metaphorical sense, and that there is nothing in these relations which is really religious.

On the other hand, it must not be lost to view that there are sacred things of every degree, and that there are some in relation to which a man feels himself relatively at his ease. An amulet has a sacred character, yet the respect which it inspires is nothing exceptional. Even before his gods, a man is not always in such a marked state of inferiority; for it very frequently happens that he exercises a veritable physical constraint upon them to obtain what he desires.... To have rain, he throws stones into the spring or sacred lake where the god of rain is thought to reside; he believes that by this means he forces him to come out and show himself. Moreover, if it is true that man depends upon his gods, this dependence is reciprocal. The gods also have need of man; without offerings and sacrifices they would die....

But if a purely hierarchic distinction is a criterion at once too general and too imprecise, there is nothing left with which to characterize the sacred in its relation to the profane except their heterogeneity. However, this heterogeneity is sufficient to characterize this classification of things and to distinguish it from all others, because it is very particular: *it is absolute*. In all the history of human thought there exists no other example of two categories of things so profoundly differentiated or so radically opposed to one another. The traditional opposition of good and bad is nothing beside this; for the good and the bad are only two opposed species of the same class, namely morals, just as sickness and health are two different aspects of the same order of facts, life, while the sacred and the profane have always and everywhere been conceived by the human mind as

two distinct classes, as two worlds between which there is nothing in common. The forces which play in one are not simply those which are met with in the other, but a little stronger; they are of a different sort. In different religions, this opposition has been conceived in different ways. Here, to separate these two sorts of things, it has seemed sufficient to localize them in different parts of the physical universe; there, the first have been put into an ideal and transcendental world, while the material world is left in full possession of the others. But howsoever much the forms of the contrast may vary, the fact of the contrast is universal.

This is not equivalent to saying that a being can never pass from one of these worlds into the other: but the manner in which this passage is effected, when it does take place, puts into relief the essential duality of the two kingdoms. In fact, it implies a veritable metamorphosis. This is notably demonstrated by the initiation rites, such as they are practised by a multitude of peoples. This initiation is a long series of ceremonies with the object of introducing the young man into the religious life: for the first time, he leaves the purely profane world where he passed his first infancy, and enters into the world of sacred things. Now this change of state is thought of, not as a simple and regular development of pre-existent germs, but as a transformation *totius substantiae*—of the whole being. It is said that at this moment the young man dies, that the person that he was ceases to exist, and that another is instantly substituted for it. He is re-born under a new form. Appropriate ceremonies are felt to bring about this death and re-birth, which are not understood in a merely symbolic sense, but are taken literally. Does this not prove that between the profane being which he was and the religious being which he becomes, there is a break of continuity?

This heterogeneity is even so complete that it frequently degenerates into a veritable antagonism. The two worlds are not only conceived of as separate, but as even hostile and jealous rivals of each other. Since men cannot fully belong to one except on condition of leaving the other completely, they are exhorted to withdraw themselves completely from the profane world, in order to lead an exclusively religious life. Hence comes the monasticism which is artificially organized outside of and apart from the natural environment in which the ordinary man leads the life of this world, in a different one, closed to the first, and nearly its contrary. Hence comes the mystic asceticism whose object is to root out from man all the attachment for the profane world that remains in him. From that come all the forms of religious suicide, the logical working-out of this asceticism; for the only manner of fully escaping the profane life is, after all, to forsake all life.

The opposition of these two classes manifests itself outwardly with a visible sign by which we can easily recognize this very special classification, wherever it exists. Since the idea of the sacred is always and everywhere separated from the idea of the profane in the thought of men, and since we picture a sort of logical chasm between the two, the mind irresistibly refuses to allow the two corresponding things to be confounded, or even to be merely put in contact with each other; for such a promiscuity, or even too direct a contiguity, would contradict too violently the dissociation of these ideas in the mind. The sacred thing is *par excellence* that which the profane should not touch, and cannot touch with impunity. To be sure, this interdiction cannot go so far as to make all communication between the two worlds impossible; for if the profane could in no way enter into relations with the sacred, this latter could be good for nothing. But, in addition to the fact that this establishment of relations is always a delicate operation in itself, demanding great precautions and a more or less complicated initiation, it is quite impossible,

unless the profane is to lose its specific characteristics and become sacred after a fashion and to a certain degree itself. The two classes cannot even approach each other and keep their own nature at the same time.

Thus we arrive at the first criterion of religious beliefs.... They always suppose a bipartite division of the whole universe, known and knowable, into two classes which embrace all that exists, but which radically exclude each other. Sacred things are those which the interdictions protect and isolate; profane things, those to which these interdictions are applied and which must remain at a distance from the first. Religious beliefs are the representations which express the nature of sacred things and the relations which they sustain, either with each other or with profane things. Finally, rites are the rules of conduct which prescribe how a man should comport himself in the presence of these sacred objects....

4

However, this definition is not yet complete, for it is equally applicable to two sorts of facts which, while being related to each other, must be distinguished nevertheless: these are magic and religion.

Magic, too, is made up of beliefs and rites. Like religion, it has its myths and its dogmas; only they are more elementary, undoubtedly because, seeking technical and utilitarian ends, it does not waste its time in pure speculation. It has its ceremonies, sacrifices, lustrations, prayers, chants and dances as well. The beings which the magician invokes and the forces which he throws in play are not merely of the same nature as the forces and beings to which religion addresses itself; very frequently, they are identically the same....

Then will it be necessary to say that magic is hardly distinguishable from religion; that magic is full of religion just as religion is full of magic, and consequently that it is impossible to separate them and to define the one without the other? It is difficult to sustain this thesis, because of the marked repugnance of religion for magic, and in return, the hostility of the second towards the first. Magic takes a sort of professional pleasure in profaning holy things; in its rites, it performs the contrary of the religious ceremony. On its side, religion, when it has not condemned and prohibited magic rites, has always looked upon them with disfavour. . . . Whatever relations there may be between these two sorts of institutions, it is difficult to imagine their not being opposed somewhere; and it is still more necessary for us to find where they are differentiated, as we plan to limit our researches to religion, and to stop at the point where magic commences.

Here is how a line of demarcation can be traced between these two domains.

The really religious beliefs are always common to a determined group, which makes profession of adhering to them and of practising the rites connected with them. They are not merely received individually by all the members of this group; they are something belonging to the group, and they make its unity. The individuals which compose it feel themselves united to each other by the simple fact that they have a common faith. A society whose members are united by the fact that they think in the same way in regard to the sacred world and its relations with the profane world, and by the fact that they translate these common ideas into common practices, is what is called a Church. In all history, we do not find a single religion without a Church. Sometimes the Church is strictly national, sometimes it passes the frontiers; sometimes it embraces an entire people (Rome, Athens, the Hebrews), sometimes it embraces only a part of them (the Christian societies since the advent of Protestantism); sometimes it is directed by a corps of priests, sometimes it is almost completely devoid of any official directing body. But wherever we observe the religious life, we find that it has a definite group as its foundation. . . .

It is quite another matter with magic. To be sure, the belief in magic is always more or less general; it is very frequently diffused in large masses of the population, and there are even peoples where it has as many adherents as the real religion. But it does not result in binding together those who adhere to it, nor in uniting them into a group leading a common life. *There is no Church of magic.* Between the magician and the individuals who consult him, as between these individuals themselves, there are no lasting bonds which make them members of the same moral community, comparable to that formed by the believers in the same god or the observers of the same cult. The magician has a clientele and not a Church, and it is very possible that his clients have no other relations between each other, or even do not know each other; even the relations which they have with him are generally accidental and transient; they are just like those of a sick man with his physician. The official and public character with which he is sometimes invested changes nothing in this situation; the fact that he works openly does not unite him more regularly or more durably to those who have recourse to his services.

It is true that in certain cases, magicians form societies among themselves: it happens that they assemble more or less periodically to celebrate certain rites in common; it is well known what a place these assemblies of witches hold in European folk-lore. But it is to be remarked that these associations are in no way indispensable to the working of the magic; they are even rare and rather exceptional. The magician has no need of uniting himself to his fellows to practise his art. More frequently, he is a recluse; in general, far from seeking society, he flees it. . . . Religion, on the other hand, is inseparable from the idea of a Church. From this point of view, there is an essential difference between magic and religion. But what is especially important is that when these societies of magic are formed, they do not include all the adherents to magic, but only the magicians; the laymen, if they may be so called, that is to say, those for whose profit the rites are celebrated, in fine, those who represent the worshippers in the regular cults, are excluded.... A Church is not a fraternity of priests; it is a moral community formed by all the believers in a single faith, laymen as well as priests. But magic lacks any such community.

But if the idea of a Church is made to enter into the definition of religion, does that not exclude the private religions which the individual establishes for himself and celebrates by himself? There is scarcely a society where these are not found. Every Ojibway, as we shall see below, has his own personal *manitou*, which he chooses himself and to which he renders special religious services; the Melanesian of the Banks Islands has his *tamaniu*; the Roman, his *genius*; the Christian, his patron saint and guardian angel, etc. By definition all these cults seem to be independent of all idea of the group. Not only are these individual religions very frequent in history, but nowadays many are asking if they are not destined to be the pre-eminent form of the religious life, and if the day will not come when there will be no other cult than that which each man will freely perform within himself.

But if we leave these speculations in regard to the future aside for the moment, and confine ourselves to religions such as they are at present or have been in the past, it becomes clearly evident that these individual cults are not distinct and autonomous religious systems, but merely aspects of the common religion of the whole Church, of which the individuals are members. The patron saint of the Christian is chosen from the official list of saints recognized by the Catholic Church; there are even canonical rules prescribing how each Catholic should perform this private cult. In the same way, the idea that each man necessarily has a protecting genius is found, under different forms, at the basis of a great number of American religions, as well as of the Roman religion (to cite only these two examples).... In a word, it is the Church of which he is a member which teaches the individual what these personal gods are, what their function is, how he should enter into relations with them and how he should honour them. When a methodical analysis is made of the doctrines of any Church whatsoever, sooner or later we come upon those concerning private cults. So these are not two religions of different types, and turned in opposite directions; both are made up of the same ideas and the same principles, here applied to circumstances which are of interest to the group as a whole, there to the life of the individual....

Thus we arrive at the following definition: *A religion is a unified system of beliefs and practices relative to sacred things, that is to say, things set apart and forbidden—beliefs and practices which unite into one single moral community called a Church, all those who adhere to them.* The second element which thus finds a place in our definition is no less essential than the first; for by showing that the idea of religion is inseparable from that of the Church, it makes it clear that religion should be an eminently collective thing.

2

The Sacred Canopy

PETER L. BERGER

Berger argues that religion provides a shield against the terror of chaos, a sacred canopy that infuses human experience with cosmic meaning.

Every human society is an enterprise of world-building. Religion occupies a distinctive place in this enterprise. Our main purpose here is to make some general statements about the relationship between human religion and human world-building....

Society is a dialectic phenomenon in that it is a human product, and nothing but a human product, that yet continuously acts back upon its producer. Society is a product of man. It has no other being except that which is bestowed upon it by human activity and consciousness. There can be no social reality apart from man. Yet it may also be stated that man is a product of society. Every individual biography is an episode within the history of society, which both precedes and survives it. Society was there before the individual was born and it will be there after he has died. What is more, it is within society, and as a result of social processes, that the individual becomes a person, that he attains and holds onto an identity, and that he carries out the various projects that constitute his life. Man cannot exist apart from society. The two statements, that society is the product of man and that man is the product of society, are not contradictory. They rather reflect the inherently dialectic character of the societal phenomenon....

The fundamental dialectic process of society consists of three moments, or steps. These are externalizations, objectivation, and internalization.... Externalization is the ongoing outpouring of human being into the world, both in the physical and the mental activity of men. Objectivation is the attainment by the products of this activity (again both physical and mental) of a reality that confronts its original producers as a facticity external to and other than themselves. Internalization is the reappropriation by men of this same reality, transforming it once again from structures of the objective world into structures of the subjective consciousness. It is through externalization that society is a human product. It is through objectivation that society becomes a reality *sui generis*. It is through internalization that man is a product of society. . . .

The socially constructed world is, above all, an ordering of experience. A meaningful order, or nomos, is imposed upon the discrete experiences and meanings of individuals. To say that society is a world-building enterprise is to say that it is ordering, or nomizing, activity. . . . Man, biologically denied the ordering mechanisms with which the other animals are endowed, is compelled to impose his own order upon experience. Man's sociality presupposes the collective character of this ordering activity. The ordering of experience is endemic to any kind of social interaction. Every social action implies that individual meaning is directed toward others and ongoing social interaction implies that the several meanings of the actors are integrated into an order of common meaning. . . .

The socially established nomos may thus be understood, perhaps in its most important aspect, as a shield against terror. . . . The anthropological presupposition for this is a human craving for meaning that appears to have the force of instinct. Men are congenitally compelled to impose a meaningful order upon reality. This order, however, presupposes the social enterprise of ordering world-construction. To be separated from society exposes the individual to a multiplicity of dangers with which he is unable to cope by himself, in the extreme case to the danger of imminent extinction. Separation from society also inflicts unbearable psychological tensions upon the individual, tensions that are grounded in the root anthropological fact of sociality. The ultimate danger of such separation, however, is the danger of meaninglessness. This danger is the nightmare *par excellence*, in which the individual is submerged in a world of disorder, senselessness and madness. Reality and identity are malignantly transformed into meaningless figures of

horror. To be in society is to be "sane" precisely in the sense of being shielded from the ultimate "insanity" of such anomic terror. Anomy is unbearable to the point where the individual may seek death in preference to it. Conversely, existence within a nomic world may be sought at the cost of all sorts of sacrifice and suffering—and even at the cost of life itself, if the individual believes that this ultimate sacrifice has nomic significance. . . .

Whenever the socially established nomos attains the quality of being taken for granted, there occurs a merging of its meanings with what are considered to be the fundamental meanings inherent in the universe. . . . When the nomos is taken for granted as appertaining to the "nature of things," understood cosmologically *or* anthropologically, it is endowed with a stability deriving from more powerful sources than the historical efforts of human beings. It is at this point that religion enters significantly into our argument.

Religion is the human enterprise by which a sacred cosmos is established. Put differently, religion is cosmization in a sacred mode. By sacred is meant here a quality of mysterious and awesome power, other than man and yet related to him, which is believed to reside in certain objects of experience. This quality may be attributed to natural or artificial objects, to animals, or to men, or to the objectivations of human culture. There are sacred rocks, sacred tools, sacred cows. The chieftain may be sacred, as may be a particular custom or institution. Space and time may be assigned the same quality, as in sacred localities and sacred seasons. The quality may finally be embodied in sacred beings, from highly localized spirits to the great cosmic divinities. The latter, in turn, may be transformed into ultimate forces or principles ruling the cosmos, no longer conceived of in personal terms but still endowed with the status of sacredness. The historical manifestations of the sacred vary widely, though there are certain uniformities to be observed cross-culturally (no matter here whether these are to be interpreted as resulting from cultural diffusion or from an inner logic of man's religious imagination). The sacred is apprehended as "sticking out" from the normal routines of everyday life, as something extraordinary and potentially dangerous, though its dangers can be domesticated and its potency harnessed to the needs of everyday life. Although the sacred is apprehended as other than man, yet it refers to man, relating to him in a way in which other non-human phenomena (specifically, the phenomena of non-sacred nature) do not. The cosmos posited by religion thus both transcends and includes man. The sacred cosmos is confronted by man as an immensely powerful reality other than himself. Yet this reality addresses itself to him and locates his life in an ultimately meaningful order.

On one level, the antonym to the sacred is the profane, to be defined simply as the absence of sacred status. All phenomena are profane that do not "stick out" as sacred. The routines of everyday life are profane unless, so to speak, proven otherwise, in which latter case they are conceived of as being infused in one way or another with sacred power (as in sacred work, for instance). Even in such cases, however, the sacred quality attributed to the ordinary events of life *itself* retains its extraordinary character, a character that is typically reaffirmed through a variety of rituals and the loss of which is tantamount to secularization, that is, to a conception of the events in question as *nothing but* profane. The dichotomization of reality into sacred and profane spheres, however related, is intrinsic to the religious enterprise. . . .

On a deeper level, however, the sacred has another opposed category, that of chaos. The sacred cosmos emerges out of chaos and continues to confront the latter as its terrible contrary. This opposition of cosmos and chaos is frequently expressed in a variety of cosmogonic myths. The sacred cosmos, which transcends and includes man in its ordering of reality, thus provides man's ultimate shield against the terror of anomy. To be in a "right" relationship with the sacred cosmos is to be protected against the nightmare threats of chaos. To fall out of such a "right" relationship is to be abandoned on the edge of the abyss of meaninglessness. It is not irrelevant to observe here that the English "chaos" derives from a Greek word meaning "yawning" and "religion" from a Latin one meaning "to be careful." To be sure, what the religious man is "careful" about is above all the dangerous power inherent in the manifestations of the sacred themselves. But behind this danger is the other, much more horrible one, namely that one may lose all connection with the sacred and be swallowed up by chaos. All the nomic constructions, as we have seen, are designed to keep this terror at bay. In the sacred cosmos, however, these constructions achieve their ultimate culmination—literally, their apotheosis.

Human existence is essentially and inevitably externalizing activity. In the course of externalization men pour out meaning into reality. Every human society is an edifice of externalized and objectivated meanings, always intending a meaningful totality. Every society is engaged in the never completed enterprise of building a humanly meaningful world. Cosmization implies the identification of this humanly meaningful world with the world as such, the former now being grounded in the latter, reflecting it or being derived from it in its fundamental structures. Such a cosmos, as the ultimate ground and validation of human nomoi, need not necessarily be sacred. Particularly in modern times there have been thoroughly secular attempts at cosmization, among which modern science is by far the most important. It is safe to say, however, that originally *all* cosmization had a sacred character. This remained true through most of human history, and not only through the millennia of human existence on earth preceding what we now call civilization. Viewed historically, most of man's worlds have been sacred worlds. Indeed, it appears likely that only by way of the sacred was it possible for man to conceive of a cosmos in the first place.

It can thus be said that religion has played a strategic part in the human enterprise of world-building. Religion implies the farthest reach of man's self-externalization, of his infusion of reality with his own meanings. Religion implies that human order is projected into the totality of being. Put differently, religion is the audacious attempt to conceive of the entire universe as being humanly significant.

RELIGION AND WORLD-MAINTENANCE

All socially constructed worlds are inherently precarious. Supported by human activity, they are constantly threatened by the human facts of self-interest and stupidity. The institutional programs are sabotaged by individuals with conflicting interests. Frequently individuals simply forget them or are incapable of learning them in the first place. The fundamental processes of socialization and social control, to the extent that they are successful, serve to mitigate these threats. Socialization seeks to ensure a continuing consensus concerning the most important features of the social world. Social control seeks to contain individual or group resistances within tolerable limits. There is yet another centrally important process that serves to support the swaying edifice of social order. This is the process of legitimation.

By legitimation is meant socially objectivated "knowledge" that serves to explain and justify the social order. Put differently, legitimations are answers to any questions about the "why" of institutional arrangements. A number of points should be noted about this definition. Legitimations belong to the domain of social objectivations, that is, to what passes for "knowledge" in a given collectivity. This implies that they have a status of objectivity quite different from merely individual cogitations about the "why" and "wherefore" of social events. Legitimations, furthermore, can be both cognitive and normative in character. They do not only tell people what *ought to be*. Often they merely propose what *is*. For instance, the morals of kinship, expressed in a statement such as, "You ought not to sleep with X, your sister," are obviously legitimating. But cognitive assertions about kinship, such as, "You are X's brother and she is your sister," are legitimating in an even more fundamental sense. To put it a little crudely, legitimation begins with statements as to "what's what." Only on this cognitive basis is it possible for the normative propositions to be meaningful. Finally, it would be a serious mistake to identify legitimation with theoretical ideation. "Ideas," to be sure, can be important for purposes of legitimation. However, what passes for "knowledge" in a society is by no means identical with the body of "ideas" existing in the society. There are always some people with an interest in "ideas," but they have never yet constituted more than a rather small minority. If legitimation always had to consist of theoretically coherent propositions, it would support the social order only for that minority of intellectuals that have such theoretical interests— obviously not a very practical program. Most legitimation, consequently, is pretheoretical in character. . . .

It will readily be seen that the area of legitimation is far broader than that of religion, as these two terms have been defined here. Yet there exists an important relationship between the two. It can be described simply by saying that religion has been the historically most widespread and effective instrumentality of legitimation. All legitimation maintains socially defined reality. Religion legitimates so effectively because it relates the precarious reality constructions of empirical societies with ultimate reality. The tenuous realities of the social world are grounded in the sacred *realissimum*, which by definition is beyond the contingencies of human meanings and human activity.

The efficacy of religious legitimation can be brought home by asking an, as it were, recipe question on the construction of worlds. If one imagines oneself as a fully aware founder of a society, a kind of combination of Moses and Machiavelli, one could ask oneself the following question: How can the future continuation of the institutional order, now established *ex nihilo*, be best ensured? There is an obvious answer to the question in terms of power. But let it be assumed that all the means of power have been effectively employed—all opponents have been destroyed, all means of coercion are in one's own hands, reasonably safe provisions have been made for the transmission of power to one's designated successors. There still remains the problem of legitimation, all the more urgent because of the novelty and thus highly conscious precariousness of the new order. The problem would best be solved by applying the following recipe: Let the institutional order be so interpreted as to hide, as much as possible, its *constructed* character. Let that which has been stamped out of the ground *ex nihilo* appear as the manifestation of something that has been existent from the beginning of time, or at least from the beginning of this group. Let the people forget that this order was established by men and continues to be dependent upon the consent of men. Let them believe that, in acting out the institutional programs that have been imposed upon them, they are but realizing the deepest aspirations of their own being and putting themselves in harmony with the fundamental order of the universe. In sum: Set up religious legitimations. There are, of course, wide historical variations in the manner in which this has been done. In one way or another, the basic recipe was followed throughout most of human history. And, actually, the example of Moses–Machiavelli

figuring the whole thing out with cool deliberation may not be as fanciful as all that. There have been very cool minds indeed in the history of religion.

Religion legitimates social institutions by bestowing upon them an ultimately valid ontological status, that is, by *locating* them within a sacred and cosmic frame of reference. The historical constructions of human activity are viewed from a vantage point that, in its own self-definition, transcends both history and man. This can be done in different ways. Probably the most ancient form of this legitimation is the conception of the institutional order as directly reflecting or manifesting the divine structure of the cosmos, that is, the conception of the relationship between society and cosmos as one between microcosm and macrocosm. Everything "here below" has its analogue "up above." By participating in the institutional order men, *ipso facto*, participate in the divine cosmos. The kinship structure, for example, extends beyond the human realm, with all being (including the being of the gods) conceived of in the structures of kinship as given in the society. Thus there may be not only a totemic "sociology" but a totemic "cosmology" as well. The social institutions of kinship then merely reflect the great "family" of all being, in which the gods participate on a higher level. Human sexuality reflects divine creativity. Every human family reflects the structure of the cosmos, not only in the sense of representing but of embodying it. Or, for another crucial case, the political structure simply extends into the human sphere the power of the divine cosmos. The political authority is conceived of as the agent of the gods, or ideally even as a divine incarnation. Human power, government, and punishment thus become sacramental phenomena, that is, channels by which divine forces are made to impinge upon the lives of men. The ruler speaks for the gods, or *is* a god, and to obey him is to be in a right relationship with the world of the gods. . . .

To repeat, the historically crucial part of religion in the process of legitimation is explicable in terms of the unique capacity of religion to "locate" human phenomena within a cosmic frame of reference. All legitimation serves to maintain reality—reality, that is, as defined in a particular human collectivity. Religious legitimation purports to relate the humanly defined reality to ultimate, universal and sacred reality. The inherently precarious and transitory constructions of human activity are thus given the semblance of ultimate security and permanence. Put differently, the humanly constructed nomoi are given a cosmic status.

This cosmization, of course, refers not only to the over-all nomic structures, but to specific institutions and roles within a given society. The cosmic status assigned to these is objectivated, that is, it becomes part of the objectively available reality of the institutions and roles in question. For example, the institution of divine kingship, and the several roles representing it, is apprehended *as* a decisive link between the world of men and the world of the gods. The religious legitimation of power involved in this institution does not appear as an *ex post facto* justification of a few theoreticians, it is objectively present as the institution is encountered by the man in the street in the course of his everyday life. Insofar as the man in the street is adequately socialized into the reality of his society, he cannot conceive of the king *except as* the bearer of a role that represents the fundamental order of the universe—and, indeed, the same assumption may be made for the king himself. In this manner, the cosmic status of the institution is "experienced" whenever men come into contact with it in the ordinary course of events.

The "gains" of this kind of legitimation are readily evident, whether one looks at it from the viewpoint of institutional objectivity or from that of individual subjective consciousness. All institutions possess the character of objectivity and their legitimations, whatever content these may have, must continuously undergird this objectivity. The religious legitimations, however, ground the socially defined reality of the institutions in the ultimate reality of the universe, in reality "as such." The institutions are thus given a semblance of inevitability, firmness and durability that is analogous to these qualities as ascribed to the gods themselves. Empirically, institutions are always changing as the exigencies of human activity upon which they are based change. Institutions are always threatened not only by the ravages of time, but by those of conflict and discrepancies between the groups whose activities they are intended to regulate. In terms of the cosmic legitimations, on the other hand, the institutions are magically lifted above these human, historical contingencies. They become inevitable, because they are taken for granted not only by men but by the gods. Their empirical tenuousness is transformed into an overpowering stability as they are understood as but manifestations of the underlying structure of the universe. They transcend the death of individuals and the decay of entire collectivities, because they are now grounded in a sacred time within which merely human history is but an episode. In a sense, then, they become immortal.

From *Contribution to the Critique of Hegel's Philosophy of Law*

KARL MARX

In perhaps the most widely-quoted and infamous explanation of the purpose of religion, Marx argues that religion is the "opium of the people." That has implications for both believers and society.

The *criticism of religion* is the premise of all criticism.

Man, who looked for a superhuman being in the fantastic reality of heaven and found nothing there but the *reflection* of himself, will no longer be disposed to find but the *semblance* of himself, only an inhuman being, where he seeks and must seek his true reality.

The basis of irreligious criticism is: *Man makes religion*, religion does not make man. Religion is the self-consciousness and self-esteem of man who has either not yet found himself or has already lost himself again. But *man* is no abstract being encamped outside the world. Man is *the world of man*, the state, society. This state, this society, produce religion, an *inverted world-consciousness*, because they are an *inverted world*. Religion is the general theory of that world, its encyclopaedic compendium, its logic in a popular form, its spiritualistic

point d'honneur, its enthusiasm, its moral sanction, its solemn complement, its universal source of consolation and justification. It is the *fantastic realisation* of the human essence because the *human essence* has no true reality. The struggle against religion is therefore indirectly a fight against *the world* of which religion is the spiritual *aroma*.

Religious distress is at the same time the *expression* of real distress and also the *protest* against real distress. Religion is the sigh of the oppressed creature, the heart of a heartless world, just as it is the spirit of spiritless conditions. It is the *opium* of the people.

To abolish religion as the *illusory* happiness of the people is to demand their *real* happiness. The demand to give up illusions about the existing state of affairs is the *demand to give up a state of affairs which needs illusions.* The criticism of religion is therefore *in embryo*

Source: Karl Marx, "From Contribution to the Critique of Hegel's Philosophy of Law." Reprinted with the permission of Cambridge University Press.

the criticism of the value of tears, the *halo* of which is religion.

Criticism has torn up the imaginary flowers from the chain not so that man shall wear the unadorned, bleak chain but so that he will shake off the chain and pluck the living flower. The criticism of religion disillusions man to make him think and act and shape his reality like a man who has been disillusioned and has come to reason, so that he will revolve round himself and therefore round his true sun. Religion is only the illusory sun which revolves round man as long as he does not revolve round himself.

The *task of history*, therefore, once the *world beyond the truth* has disappeared, is to establish the *truth of this world*. The immediate *task of philosophy*, which is at the service of history, once the *holy form* of human self-estrangement has been unmasked, is to unmask self-estrangement in its *unholy forms*. Thus the criticism of heaven turns into the criticism of the earth, the *criticism of religion* into the *criticism of law* and the *criticism of theology* into the *criticism of politics*.

4

Religion and Spirituality: Unfuzzying the Fuzzy

BRIAN J. ZINNBAUER, KENNETH I. PARGAMENT,
BRENDA COLE, MARK S. RYE, ERIC M. BUTFER,
TIMOTHY G. BELAVICH, KATHLEEN HIPP, ALLIE B. SCOTT,
AND JILL L. KADAR

This article explores how ordinary people understand what religion is and how it differs from spirituality. Sociologists use these terms in specific ways that sometimes diverge from how most people think about them.

In the past 20 years, interest in religiousness and spirituality has increased, and a large number of social scientists have attempted to define, study, and theorize about these two terms (e.g., Ingersoll 1994; Shafranske and Gorsuch 1984; Spilka 1993; Turner, et. al 1995). Still, the ways in which the words are conceptualized and used are often inconsistent in the research literature. Despite the great volume of work that has been done, little consensus has been reached about what the terms actually mean. In particular, the term spirituality has [at] times been used so loosely that one researcher has called it a "fuzzy" concept that "embraces obscurity with passion" (Spilka 1993: 1). Not surprisingly, spirituality has been described recently as an obscure construct in need of empirical grounding and operationalization (Hood et al. 1996; Spilka 1993; Spilka and McIntosh 1996).

Current conceptions of religiousness and spirituality in the social scientific study of religion are nothing if not diverse. Definitions of religiousness have ranged from subscription to institutionalized beliefs or doctrines (Vaughan 1991), to "a system of beliefs in a divine or superhuman power, and practices of worship or other rituals directed towards such a power" (Argyle and Beit-Hallahmi 1975: 1), to "the feelings, acts, and experiences of individual men in their solitude, so far as they apprehend themselves to stand in relation to whatever they may consider the divine" (James 1902/1961: 42).

Current definitions of spirituality are equally diverse. Spirituality has been variously defined by theorists as "the human response to God's gracious call to a relationship with himself" (Benner 1989: 20), "a subjective experience of the sacred" (Vaughan 1991: 105), and "that vast realm of human potential dealing with ultimate purposes, with higher entities, with God, with love, with compassion, with purpose" (Tart 1983: 4). Furthermore, the terms spirituality and religiousness have been used interchangeably and inconsistently by some authors. For example, Miller and Martin (1988: 14) frequently interchange the terms even after they explicitly state that spirituality "may or may not include involvement in organized religion."

The finding that researchers define these terms differently is mirrored in the ways that religious and spiritual believers themselves define the terms. For example, Pargament, Sullivan, Balzer, Van Haitsma, and Raymark (1995) used a policy-capturing approach to assess the meanings college students and clergy attribute to the word religiousness. Their findings indicated that different individuals attributed different meanings to religiousness. To some, religiousness meant church attendance, to others it meant acts of altruism, and to others it meant performing religious rituals. Similarly, if popular publications such as Newsweek and Time reflect the views and attitudes of the American public, contemporary spirituality is also defined in diverse ways. Popular references to spirituality have included elements such as interest in angels, New Age interest in crystals and psychic readings, and evangelical or Pentecostal religious experiences.

While this diversity of opinion regarding religiousness and spirituality may enrich our understanding of the constructs, the inconsistency in the definitions can also have some negative implications for social scientific research. First, without a clearer conception of what the terms mean, it is difficult to know what researchers and participants attribute to

these terms. Second, a lack of consistency in defining the terms impairs communication within the social scientific study of religion and across other disciplines interested in the two concepts. Third, without common definitions within social scientific research it becomes difficult to draw general conclusions from various studies.

. . .

Apart from a handful of studies which have explored the meanings that individual believers attribute to religiousness and spirituality (e.g. Clark 1958; Coe 1900; McReady and Greeley 1976; Pargament et al. 1995; Roof 1993, Zinnbauer 1997), precious little research has addressed how individual believers think about and distinguish the terms. Moreover, few investigations have considered whether self-evaluations of religiousness and spirituality are associated with distinctive demographic, religio/spiritual, and psychosocial factors.

. . .

METHOD

Participants

Eleven different samples from Pennsylvania and Ohio were collected for this study. Groups were specifically selected from different churches, institutions, and age groups that were likely to hold different definitions and self-reported levels of religiousness and spirituality. . . . The total number of surveys distributed was 608, and 346 were returned complete (57%).

The entire sample consisted of 112 males (32%) and 234 females (68%), whose ages ranged from 15 to 85 (Arithmetic mean of sample = 40). The sample was predominantly white (95%). The median household income level of this sample was $50,000-$64,000 39% of the participants were married; and the median highest level of education completed was some college.

. . .

Measures

Measures of religiousness and spirituality. Participants' self-definitions and conceptions of religiousness and spirituality were assessed in several ways. First, respondents were asked to write their own definitions of religiousness and spirituality. . . .

. . .

RESULTS

Self-Definitions and Conceptions of Religiousness and Spirituality

. . .

Content analysis. A content analysis was performed on the participants' personal definitions of religiousness and spirituality. Each definition was coded on two dimensions: overall content; and the nature of the sacred. Thirteen content categories and four categories describing the nature of the sacred in participant definitions were created for this study. . . . Three coders initially coded the definitions separately. The statistic Kappa on the content category codings was .65 ($z = 61.08$; $p < .0001$) and on the nature of the sacred category was .67 ($z = 17.41$; $p < .0001$), indicating an acceptable level of agreement among the coders. The three coders then convened to arrive at mutually agreed upon codes for every definition. Three hundred and twenty-five pairs of religiousness and spirituality definitions were coded. Fifty-six spirituality definitions (17% of total) were labeled as uncodable due to poverty of codable content or extreme ambiguity. Forty definitions of religiousness (12% of total) were labeled as uncodable.

Frequencies were calculated for each content category over the entire sample. The most common definitions of spirituality were coded in the following content categories: feeling or experience of connectedness/relationship/oneness with God/Christ/Higher Power/transcendent reality/Nature/[etc]. (36%); personal beliefs such as belief or faith in God/Higher power/the divine/personal values/etc. (34%); uncodable (17%); integrating one's values or beliefs with one's behavior in daily life, following God's will in one's life, demonstrating God's love to others, etc. (5.5%); feeling or aimed at attaining a desirable inner affective state such as comfort, anxiety reduction, security, etc. (3%); and aimed at obtaining personal growth, actualization, mastery, or self-control (2%). In terms of the categories describing the nature of the sacred, the results were as follows: 70% of the definitions referred to traditional concepts of the sacred (God, Christ, higher power, the church); 13% made no reference to the sacred; 10% referred to nontraditional concepts of the sacred (transcendent reality, ground of being, nature); and 7% made reference to the sacred but did not provide enough information to code as traditional or nontraditional.

The most common definitions of religiousness were content coded as follows: personal beliefs such as belief or faith in God/Higher power/the divine/personal values/etc. (22%); organizational practices or activities such as attendance at services, performance of rituals, church membership or allegiance, etc. (21%); commitment to organizational beliefs or adherence to institutionally based belief systems or dogma (16%); integrating one's values or beliefs with one's behavior in daily life, following God's will in one's life, demonstrating God's love to others, etc. (13%); uncodable (12%); personal worship or practices such as prayer, Bible reading, meditation, etc. (8%); negative means or ends such as gaining extrinsic rewards, feeling superior to others, an excuse to avoid personal responsibility, etc. (3%); feeling or experience of connectedness/relationship/oneness with God/Christ/Higher Power/transcendent reality/Nature/[etc]. (3%). In terms of the categories describing the nature of the sacred, the results were as follows: 76% of the definitions referred to traditional concepts of the sacred (God, Christ, higher power, the church); 13% made no reference to the sacred; 10% made reference to the sacred but did not provide enough information to code as traditional or nontraditional; and less than 1% referred to nontraditional concepts of the sacred (transcendent reality, ground of being, nature).

For the entire sample, definitions of religiousness and spirituality were significantly different in content (Chi2 (132) = 198.94; p < .001) but not in the nature of the sacred (Chi2 (9) = 12.94; p = .17). Descriptively, definitions of spirituality most often included references to connection or relationship with a Higher Power of some kind, belief or faith in a Higher Power of some kind, or integrating one's values and beliefs with one's behavior in daily life. As with definitions of spirituality, definitions of religiousness included belief or faith in a Higher Power of some kind and integrating one's values and beliefs with one's behavior in daily life, but they also commonly included references to organized activities such as church attendance and performance of rituals, as well as commitment to organizational or institutional beliefs or dogma. Therefore, both definitions share some features in common, but they diverge in the focus of religiousness definitions on organizational or institutional beliefs and practices, and the focus of spirituality definitions on the personal qualities of connection or relationship with a Higher Power.

. . .

DISCUSSION

. . .

. . . [E]vidence for the distinction between the terms [also] comes from participants' definitions of religiousness and spirituality. As with more recent definitions provided by scholars (see Spilka and McIntosh 1996), spirituality was most often described in personal or experiential terms, such as belief in God or a higher power, or having a relationship with God or a higher power. Definitions of religiousness included both personal beliefs, such as a belief in God or a higher power, and organizational or institutional beliefs and practices such as church membership, church attendance, and commitment to the beliefs system of a church or organized religion.

A second conclusion is that although religiousness and spirituality appear to describe different concepts, they are not fully independent. Self-rated religiousness and spirituality were modestly but significantly correlated (r = .21), and most respondents indicated that they consider themselves both spiritual and religious (S+R, 74%). Also, in line with our hypotheses, both religiousness and spirituality were associated with frequency of prayer. Additionally, both were related to church attendance, intrinsic religiosity, and religious orthodoxy. Finally, definitions of religiousness and spirituality did not significantly differ in the nature of the sacred. Rather, both religiousness and spirituality definitions commonly incorporated traditional concepts of the sacred (e.g., references to God, Christ, the Church).

Although most individuals in our sample appeared to integrate spirituality with traditional organizational beliefs and practices (i.e., "religious and spiritual" group), there was a small proportion of our sample (19%) that identified themselves as solely spiritual (i.e., the "spiritual not religious" group), and this group differed from the majority in several ways. Compared with the S+R group, the SnR group was less likely to evaluate religiousness positively, less likely to engage in traditional forms of worship such as church attendance and prayer, less likely to hold orthodox or traditional Christian beliefs, more likely to be independent from others, more likely to engage in group experiences related to spiritual growth, more likely to be agnostic, more likely to characterize religiousness and spirituality as different and nonoverlapping concepts, more likely to hold nontraditional "new age" beliefs, and more likely to have had mystical experiences. Also, though the difference is modest, the SnR group was more likely than the S +R group to hold a pejorative definition of religiousness, labeling it as a means to extrinsic ends such as feeling superior to others and avoiding personal responsibility.

Interestingly, the "spiritual not religious" group identified in this study matches very closely the description provided by Roof (1993) of the "highly active seekers" in the baby-boomer generation. Both groups identify themselves as "spiritual" but not "religious", both appear to reject [traditional] organized religion in favor of an individualized spirituality that includes mysticism along with New Age beliefs and practices, and compared with their contemporaries both are more individualistic and more likely to come from homes in which their parents attended religious services less frequently.

...

The findings of this study illustrate the necessity for researchers to recognize the many meanings attributed to religiousness and spirituality by different religious and cultural groups, and the different ways in which these groups consider themselves religious and/or spiritual. As indicated by Hood et al. (1996), no single perspective on religion dominates postmodern culture, but rather multiple perspectives exist simultaneously. Whether one considers oneself religious or spiritual depends upon the meaning and relevance of these terms to members of a given religious or ideological group. Thus, to accurately measure religiousness and spirituality it becomes necessary to consider the system of beliefs or worldviews of the individuals or groups studied. Studies employing methodologies such as policy capturing, that go beyond simple self-reports

have documented that many different meanings are attributed to the terms religiousness and spirituality (Pargament et al. 1995; Zinnbauer 1997). Future studies of religiousness and spirituality must go beyond the use of single-item self-report measures and scales that are not sensitive to different group ideologies. Only by explicitly operationalizing religiousness and spirituality in terms that reflect the variety of perspectives of potential research participants can we make generalizations across groups and ideologies, and cumulate findings across studies.

...

APPENDIX: BELIEFS ABOUT GOD ITEMS

Pantheistic: "I believe that [God] is all around us. I look to nature to see God. I see God in every person I [meet]. I believe God is involved in everything we do and touches every person."

Theistic: "I believe God is a personal being who reigns over all creation, who looks after us and listens to our prayers and praise. He responds to our needs and protects us from evil."

Deistic: "I believe God created the world and everything in it and then left us to fend for ourselves. God is no longer involved in the happenings of this world and looks down on us from above without ever intervening in out lives."

Agnostic: "I am not sure what or who God is but I do think that it is beyond our understanding to comprehend such ultimate things. I often wonder if there is a God but I do not think that I will ever know for sure."

Atheistic: "I do not believe there is a God I do not believe that God created the world or controls our affairs. There is no higher power that can intervene in our lives."

...

REFERENCES

ALTEMEYER, B. 1981. Right-wing authoritarianism. Winnepeg, Canada: University of Manitoba Press.

ARGYLE, M., and B. BEIT-HALLAHMI. 1976. The social psychology of religion. London: Routledge & Kegan Paul.

BERGIN, A. E. 1980. Psychotherapy and humanistic values. Journal of Consulting and Clinical Psychology 48: 96–106.

BATSON, C. D., and W. L. VENTIS. 1982. The religious experience: A social psychological perspective. New York: Oxford University Press.

BENNER, D. G. 1989. Toward a psychology of spirituality: Implications for personality and psychotherapy. Journal of Psychology and Christianity 8: 19–30.

CLARK, W. H. 1968. How do social scientists define religion? Journal of Social Psychology 47: 143–47.

COE, G. A. 1900. The spiritual life: Studies in the science of religion. New York: Eaton and Mains.

FALBO, T. and S. S. BELK. 1986. A short scale to measure self-righteousness. Journal of Personality Assessment 49 72–77.

HOGE, D. 1972. A validated intrinsic religious motivation scale Journal for the Scientific Study of Religion 11: 369–76.

HOOD, R. W. 1976. The construction and preliminary validation of a measure of reported mystical experience. Journal for the Scientific Study of Religion, 14: 29–41.

HOOD, R. W., B. SPILKA, B. HUNSBERGER and R. GORSUCH. 1996. The psychology of religion: An empirical approach. New York: Guilford Press.

INGERSOLL, R. E. 1994. Spirituality, religion, and counseling Dimensions and relationships. Counseling and Values 3& 98–111.

JAMES, W. 1961. [1902]. The varieties, of religious experience. New York: Collier.

KELLY, T. A. 1990. The role of values in psychotherapy: A critical review of process and outcome effects. Clinical Psychology Review 10:171–86.

MCREADY, W. C. and A.M. GREELEY. 1976. The ultimate values of the American population. Vol. 23. Beverly Hills, CA Sage.

MILLER, W. R. and J. E. MARTIN 1988. Spirituality and behavioral psychology: Toward integration. In Behavior therapy and religion: Integrating spiritual and behavioral approaches to change, edited by W. R. MILLER and J. E. MARTIN, 13–23. Newbury Park, CA: Sage.

OSGOOD, C. E. and J. G. SNYDER, editors. 1969. Semantic differential technique; A sourcebook. Chicago: Aldine Publishing Co.

PARGAMENT, K 1. 1997. The psychology of religion ant coping. New York: Guilford Press

———. 1996, August. What is the difference between religiousness and spirituality? Symposium conducted at the meeting of the American Psychological Association, Toronto, Canada.

PARGAMENT, K. I., M. S. SULLIVAN, W. K BALZER, K S. VAN HAITSMA, and P. H. RAYMARK. 1995. The many meanings of religiousness: A policy capturing approach Journal of Personality 63: 963–83.

ROOF, W. C. 1993. A generation of seekers: The spiritual journeys of the baby boom generation. San Francisco: Harper.

SCHWEHN, J. and C. G. SCHAU. 1990. Psychotherapy as a process of value stabilization. Counseling and Values 36: 24–30.

SHAFRANSKE, E. P. and R. L. GORSUCH 1984. Factors associated with the perception of spirituality in psychotherapy. Journal of Transpersonal Psychology 16: 231–41.

SPILKA, B. 1993. August. Spirituality: Problems and directions in operationalizing a fuzzy concept. Paper presented at the American Psychological Association annual conference, Toronto, Canada.

SPILKA, B and D. N. MCINTOSH. 1996. August. Religion and spirituality: The known and the unknown. Paper presented at the American Psychological Association annual conference, Toronto, Canada.

TART, C. 1983. Transpersonal psychologies. El Cerrito, CA Psychological Processes Inc.

TRIANDIS, H. C. 1995. Individualism and collectivism. Boulder, CO: Westview press.

TURNER, R. P., D. LUKOFF, R. T. BARNHOUSE and F. G. LU. 1996. Religious or spiritual problem: A culturally sensitive diagnostic category in the DSM-IV. Journal of Nervous and Mental Disease 183: 436–44.

VAUGHAN, F. 1991. Spiritual issues in psychotherapy. Journal of Transpersonal Psychology, 23: 106–19.

ZINNBAUER, B. J. 1997. Capturing the meanings of religiousness and spirituality: One way down from a definitional Tower of Babel. Unpublished doctoral dissertation, Bowling Green Stab University.

Reading  5

The Principal Totemic Beliefs: The Totem as Name and as Emblem

EMILE DURKHEIM

Examining reports of what some call "primitive" religions, Durkheim explores the notion of totemism, including speculation about just what totems represent.

At the basis of most Australian tribes, we find a group that has a dominant place in collective life: That group is the clan. Two essential traits characterize it.

First, the individuals who comprise it consider themselves joined by a bond of kinship but a bond of a particular sort...they are not fathers, mothers, sons or daughters, uncles or nephews... nevertheless they regard themselves as forming a single family . . . solely because they are collectively designated by the same word. And if we say they regard one another as being of the same family, it is because they acknowledge reciprocal obligations identical to those that have been incumbent on kin in all ages: obligations of help, vengeance, not marrying one another and so forth.

What distinguishes the Australian clan is that the name it bears is also that of a definite species of material things with which it thinks it has special relations . . . relations of kinship. The species of things that serves to designate the clan collectively is called its *totem*. The clan's totem is also that of each clan member.

. . . In the great majority of cases, the objects that serve as totems belong to either the plant or animal kingdom, but mainly to the latter.

. . . The totem is ordinarily not an individual but a species or a variety: It is not such and such kangaroo or crow but the kangaroo or the crow in general. Nonetheless it is sometimes a particular object. This is unavoidably the case when a thing that is unique of its kind serves as totem: the sun, the moon, such and such constellation, and so forth.

Sometimes—though rarely—a group of ancestors or a single ancestor is used as a totem. The totem in this case is not named after a real thing or a species of real things but

---

after a purely mythical being. . . . Among the Warramunga and among the Tjingilli is a clan that bears the name of an ancestor called Thaballa, who seems to incarnate gaiety. Another Warramunga clan bears the name of a fabulous giant snake named Wollunqua, from whom the clan is held to be descended.

. . . In all these cases, it is rather easy to see what must have happened. Under the influence of various causes, and through the development of mythological thought itself, the collective and impersonal totem gave way to certain mythical personages who moved to the first rank and became totems themselves.

. . . The totem is not simply a name; it is an emblem, a true coat of arms, and its resemblance to the heraldic coat of arms has often been commented upon.

. . . The nobles of the feudal age sculpted, engraved, and in every way displayed their coats of arms on the walls of their castles, on their weapons and on all kinds of other objects belonging to them. The blacks of Australia and the Indians of North America do the same with their totems. The Indians who accompanied Samuel Hearne painted their totems on their shields before going into battle.

Wherever the society has become sedentary, where the house has replaced the tent and the plastic arts are more developed, the totem is carved on the wood and on the walls. This occurs, for example, among the Haida, the Tshimshian, the Salish, and the Tlingit. . . . [Among the Tlinglit, these] are animal forms combined in certain cases with human forms and sculpted on poles that rise beside the door as high as fifteen meters; they are usually painted in very flashy colors.

. . . But totemic images are not only reproduced on the outsides of houses and canoes, on weapons, instruments, and tombs; they recur on men's bodies. Men do not simply place their emblem on the objects they possess but also wear it on their persons; they imprint it in

their flesh, and it becomes part of them. This mode of representation is in fact, and by far, the most important one.

. . . These totemic decorations suggest that the totem is not merely a name and an emblem. They are used during religious ceremonies and are part of the liturgy. Thus, while the totem is a collective label, it also has a religious character. In fact, things are classified as sacred and profane by reference to the totem. It is the very archetype of sacred things.

. . . This sacredness stems from one cause: It is a material representation of the clan.

. . . The things represented are mainly animals and plants. Since the profane role of plants and certainly that of animals ordinarily is to serve as food, the sacredness of the totemic animal or plant is signified by the prohibition against eating it. Of course, because they are holy things, they can enter into the composition of certain mystic meals, and we will see in fact that they sometimes serve as true sacraments; in general, however, they cannot be used for ordinary eating. Anyone who violates that prohibition exposes himself to extremely grave danger.

. . . A prohibition against killing the totem (or picking it, if it is a plant) is often added to the prohibition against eating it.

. . . In addition to the basic prohibitions, there are examples of a prohibition against contact between a man and his totem.

If we now compare these various prohibitions with those applied to the totemic emblem, it seems . . . that those applied to the totemic emblem are the more numerous, strict, and rigorously imperative. All kinds of figures representing the totem are surrounded with a markedly greater respect than the being itself, whose form the figures imitate.

. . . And since the number and importance of the restrictions that isolate a sacred thing, withdrawing it from circulation, correspond to the degree of sacredness with which it is invested, we arrive at the remarkable result that *images of the totemic being are more sacred than the totemic being itself.*

. . . The totem is above all a symbol, a tangible expression of something else. But of what?

It follows from the same analysis that the totem expresses and symbolizes two different kinds of things. From one point of view, it is the outward and visible form of what I have called the totemic principle or [god]; and from another it is also the symbol of a particular society that is called the clan. It is the flag of the clan, the sign by which each clan is distinguished from the others, the visible mark of its distinctiveness, and a mark that is borne by everything that in any way belongs to the clan: men, animals, and things. Thus, if the totem is the symbol of both the god and the society, is this not because the god and society are one and the same? How could the emblem of the group have taken the form of that quasi-divinity if the group and the divinity were two distinct realities? Thus the god of the clan, the totemic principle, can be none other than the clan itself, but the clan transfigured and imagined in the physical form of the plant or animal that serves as a totem.

Reading 6

Characters in Search of a Script: The Exit Narratives of Formerly Ultra-Orthodox Jews

LYNN DAVIDMAN AND ARTHUR GREIL

Davidman and Greil argue that going into a religious group is a highly structured experience. When adherents leave a group, however, the authors find that those exiting typically have little guidance. As a result, leaving is an especially disorienting experience.

When I made a telephone call on [a Jewish holiday] I felt as though I was tearing apart one of my vital organs. I felt as though I was foolishly opening the door to hell and sending myself into a wilderness where hope for survival was grim. I felt as though I was standing on the tallest bridge and I was jumping off to a sea filled with sharks and deadly fish. I felt as though I was separating myself from a group I had grown to love, which raised and supported me.

INTRODUCTION

These words were spoken by a young formerly Haredi (ultra-Orthodox) Jewish woman who had moved out of her family, although she worked hard to maintain contacts with them. Haredi communities engage in a daily round of life that is immersed in Jewish tradition and that takes place to a large extent within the Haredi community.[1] Haredim try to keep themselves isolated as much as possible from the larger society: they do not send their children for secular education; expose themselves to mass media; or participate to a great extent in the mainstream secular consumer culture. This article is based on the analysis of narratives told by men and women who grew up in Haredi families in the United States and Israel and who, at some point in their lives, left the encapsulated communities in which they were raised (hereafter referred to by the Hebrew term, *yotzi'im*, those who leave, or ex-Haredim).[2]

. . . We argue that narratives of identity change are texts that can shed light on the micro-structural context in which identity change occurs. In the process of converting into a group, individual narratives are shaped according to the key ideas and values of the new community. New members are presented—sometimes in actual texts, more generally by modeling by members—with stories that reflect and support the ideology of the group (Beckford 1978a, 1978b; Snow 1976). For example, when Jewish women convert to Orthodoxy, they learn to tell listeners that they were always interested in Orthodox Judaism, thus suggesting that becoming Orthodox is appropriate for them and does not represent a significant disruption in their biographies (Davidman 1991). With regard to disaffiliation, Bromley (1998a, 1998b) has convincingly argued that different structural settings give rise to different types of exit narratives. We can see how social contexts shape narratives by comparing women who join a modern Orthodox synagogue with those who join a Lubavitch Hasidic community. In keeping with the teachings of that community, the modern Orthodox converts did not emphasize God in their conversion narratives, in contrast to those who became members of the Hasidic group, who were taught to emphasize that they were following God's will.

There is considerably less structured support for leaving religious groups than there is for joining them. Exiters are not provided with scripts in which to formulate their deconversion narratives, giving rise to accounts that emphasize themes of scriptlessness, anomie, and a lack of a readily available language with which to tell one's story (Bromley 1997; Jacobs 1989; Lewis 1986; Solomon 1981; Wright 1984, 1987, 1991). We can further see the relationship between social context and narrative in the comparison between the accounts of those who disaffiliate from new religious movements with the aid of the anti-cult movement and of those who do not. Those whose departure is mediated by the anti-cult movement tell "captivity narratives" that employ metaphors of warfare and hostage rescue (Bromley 1998a, 1998b; Wright 1998). In contrast, those who exit without the involvement of the anti-cult movement often find it difficult to construct viable narratives and have ambivalent feelings about their former group for quite a long time. The accounts of the defectors from Haredi communities cannot rely on language provided by the anti-cult movement, for example. Thus their stories emphasize how they felt lost, anomic, and scriptless. In fact, however, a deeper reading of their stories reveals that these individuals construct narratives that emphasize their individual heroism in surviving departure from a community that emphasized how leaving would involve personal and group danger.

The existence of tightly knit communities in the Haredi world makes it difficult for *yotzi'im* to construct exit narratives: there are neither ready-made organizational nor ready-made society-wide public narratives for *yotzi'im* to draw upon. *Yotzi'im*, like others who leave encapsulated, tightly structured enclaves, must construct their own accounts of identity out of the more general public narratives available to them in the larger society, such as the narrative of the autonomous individual who thinks on his or her own rather than following the dictates of others. The conversion accounts of former Haredim are stories of individual triumph against the odds. The *yotzi'im* present themselves as individuals who have struggled to see the truth behind the ultra-Orthodox "matrix." They portray themselves as "actors without a script," who have had to improvise new identities with a minimum of social support. The narratives *yotzi'im* tell do not convey a sense of progression from chaos to certainty but rather a movement from a false certainty to a more ambiguous and self-constructed reality. The ex-Haredim describe their transition as a long, torturous, process, involving pushes and pulls in both directions. . . .

METHODS

This article is part of a larger project that analyzes the narratives told by people who grew up Orthodox and at some point in their lives moved outside of the religious communities in which they were born and raised. . . . We left respondents free to define "leaving Orthodoxy" for themselves and let our definition evolve from the ground up (Glazer and Strauss 1967); thus, respondents range from those who have continued many or some traditional practices to those who have become entirely secular. . . .

Davidman began this research late in the summer of 2003 and is continuing to interview. So far the sample consists of over 50 interviewees, half in the United States and half in Israel. In the United States, she located her respondents in several ways: word of mouth, snowball sampling, advertisements in Providence, RI and Boston, MA newspapers, an ad in *The Village Voice*, and postings on the website H-Judaic, an Internet list serve for people interested in any aspect of Jewish studies and/or life. . . .

The data for this article are drawn from a subset of Davidman's sample, comprising 22 former Haredim in the United States and in Israel. These 22 respondents are all of the ex-Haredim in our sample. Of the respondents, 13 were living in the United States at the time of the interview; nine were living in Israel. The sample includes 12 men and 10 women. . . .

For this discussion of exiting Haredi communities, we have chosen to highlight the narrative of one former American Hasidic woman. We have chosen to highlight one narrative in order to better capture the back and forth, push and pull, ambivalent and ambiguous nature of the exiting process. *Yotzi'ims'* accounts of the unscripted, unsettled, unstable quality of their lives can be best appreciated by following a detailed narrative of this process. Analyzing an individual narrative in depth yields thick description of how exiters understand and construct the details and parameters of their stories of leaving Orthodoxy. At the same time, however, we have provided numerous quotations from other *yotzi'im* in order to provide evidence that the account we present is not idiosyncratic but rather similar to those of others in the larger group.

THE HAREDI WORLD

. . .Haredi (including Hasidic) Jews, like other highly encapsulated groups, provide environments that are insulated from secular life in a variety of ways. Education, worship, food, dress, and observance are all governed within the community. Rules pertaining to every aspect of life are clearly and strictly outlined by religious texts and reinforced by the rabbis, who lead, teach, and shape their communities. The communities themselves are geographically isolated; haredim generally live within their own distinct neighborhoods and rarely interact with those whose secular lives they disdain. In Greil and Rudy's (1984) article on social cocoons, they refer to the impact of these community boundaries as physical encapsulation.

Kosher laws, rules about appropriate clothing, prescriptions for modest behavior and appearance, and males' necessity to pray in a group of 10 men three times a day all have the effect of focusing members lives within the community and demarcating the boundaries between insiders and outsiders. Fear of the immodest and corrupting influence of the secular world has resulted in prohibitions against watching television, going to the movies, reading secular literature, listening to secular music, use of the Internet, and participation in other secular activities. Another mechanism of physical encapsulation is the provision of separate education for children, ensuring that they are not exposed to secular influences in the public schools. Haredi education is sex-segregated and focused on Jewish law with very limited exposure to science, secular literature, history, or other worldly subjects. Within school, family, and the community in general, children are socialized into every aspect of life throughout their early years: they are shown, by constant example, how to dress, what and when to eat, how to pray, and what their roles are within the family and the world.

Rigid gender separation is a central organizing principle of Haredi existence. From childhood, young boys and men are led down a path of study and worship while girls and young women are encouraged to embrace a role within the home, and limit their attention to family matters. There is much less focus on the importance of worship and study for women; their intellectual curiosity is often dismissed or even discouraged. Modesty is a value instilled within men and women alike, as is manifest in distinctive styles of dress and demeanor; the norms of modesty for women are particularly constraining and involve more aspects of their lives. For example, they are not allowed to sing in public because their voices might be sexually distracting to men. Discussion of sexuality and sexual identity is prohibited. The principles of modesty and the separation of the sexes serve as mechanisms of social encapsulation (Greil and Rudy 1984), which limit interaction not only between the sexes within the community, but also with outsiders, Jewish and Gentile. In some groups, where Yiddish rather than English or Hebrew is the primary language of everyday life, language, too, can contribute to boundary maintenance.

Social encapsulation in this community is accompanied by ideological encapsulation: strong religious beliefs are inculcated and serve to maintain boundaries between insiders and outsiders (Greil and Rudy 1984). Parents and elders encourage Haredi youth to avoid the society around them by stressing the emptiness of secular society. Nonobservant Jews are depicted as living like fools with no future, while Haredim are privileged because they know the truth. The nonobservant are seen as free but living utterly meaningless lives; in contrast, Haredim are taught that their more restricted lives are ultimately more rewarding because their behavior will result in the coming of Moshiach, the Messiah. In Haredi communities, the concept of the fear of God is used both to regulate behavior and to limit the influence of the behavior of those outside the community.

Greil and Rudy (1984) point out that it is quite difficult for groups to build and maintain an encapsulated environment. Even such an enclave community as the Haredim cannot build impervious walls to keep members in. Members of the community can gain exposure to secular society through books (which some would-be defectors sneak out to the library to read), music, movies, or contact with nonreligious relatives.[4] In this way, individuals can come to question the taken-for-granted nature of the Haredi world and its beliefs. Those who find the restrictions in Orthodoxy stifling and/or are attracted to the secular world may decide to undertake the challenges that accompany attempts to leave Orthodoxy and reconfigure their identities. However, would-be defectors often experience a tension between their dissatisfaction with the rigidity of the Haredi lifestyle and their comfort and familiarity with its stable structure. As illustrated in the epigram to this article the dangers of leaving the community can seem great, involving fear of punishment by God, loss of family, community, social support systems, and a secure sense of identity.

LEAH: AN ILLUSTRATIVE NARRATIVE[5]

. . .Leah grew up in a prominent Lubavitcher Hasidic family in a Hasidic enclave in Brooklyn that was insulated from what she called "the real world" and in which secular society was presented as wholly negative and dangerous by her family and schools. Her father was Hasidic, although she noted that, unlike many other members of his community, he loved America. He fought on the American side in World War II and "he was very interested in American ways." Perhaps his affection for the United States already provided a bit more openness for her to see beyond the Hasidic world than might otherwise have been possible for girls in her community. In addition, he married a woman from a more secular background, which Leah suggested resulted in a family structure in which the rituals in the household were not particularly fulfilling. Leah's mother was not able to teach the children to say *brachot*[6] or to sing *zmirot*[7] around the table.[8] We note at the outset here that Leah's narrative reveals that in some ways she was born and raised with "one foot out of the door"; rather than in a totalistic encapsulated environment. This factor, however, does not weaken our case for using her as our exemplar; rather, her account demonstrates how difficult it is for any group in contemporary society to reach a state of full encapsulation, a characteristic that we saw in many other narratives of *yotzi'im*.

Like Leah, other ex-Haredim, especially those who had grown up in Satmar communities, described themselves as having grown up in an encapsulated world. Sherry, who grew up in an American Satmar Hasidic community, reported that Yiddish was her only language until she was six. Yankl, another American Satmar, described life in the Yeshiva as follows: "you study, and study, and study, and know nothing about the outside world. It's like you go into a shelter." Ruthie, another American

Satmar, described the power of the worldview she grew up with in the following terms:

Shabbos[9] was like if I would put on a light, not purposely, you know if I were to walk into my room and put on the light, I would feel very guilty. It was always guilt trips, everything was guilt trips. Shabbos was something—I wouldn't even think about breaking Shabbos because it was so instilled in me that Shabbos is like the foundation of Judaism. If you don't keep Shabbos, it's like you're not a Jew, you know. That's what I was brought up with.

Despite the community's attempts at physical, social, and ideological encapsulation, many *yotzi'im*, like Leah, described themselves as having more exposure to outside influence than one might expect of Haredim. Joel, who grew up in an American, non-Hasidic household, narrated that his father did not fully participate in the Haredi round of life and that "during the week he did not go to synagogue. He always left for work very early and went to sleep very late." Yehuda, an Israeli who was raised in a Belz Hasidic community, said that his father was not raised in a Hasidic family and did not seem as committed to the Haredi lifestyle as his mother was. Avi, an Israeli ex-Haredi from a non-Hasidic background, had a mother who seemed less committed. Although both of D'vorah's non-Hasidic parents were Haredi, her uncle's family was Conservative. Although Yankl was from a Hasidic family, he reported that he grew up with a VCR in his home. Danny, an Israeli citizen who described his family as non-Hasidic but as influenced by Hasidism, grew up in an area of France with few Jews. Danny describes experiencing his life as "running on two parallel tracks," one revolving around his secular high school and the other focusing on the rebbe. Many of these *yotzi'im*, then, lived within an encapsulated world but grew up with one foot out of the door. Dov, an Israeli raised in a Lubavitch community, spoke for many when he said, "we lived in an . . . open yet secluded society."

Leah presented herself as someone who recognized flaws in the Hasidic round of life from an early age. She narrated, "Shabbos was kind of a wash in general. My father was tired. My mother was tired. They were fighting. Shabbos seemed to be just for eating candy and sleeping." Leah felt that perhaps if Shabbos had been more spiritual, communal, and fun, she might have received the proper "brainwashing" that would have kept her in the community. Leah identified this lack of Shabbos warmth in her own household as a key factor in her beginning to search outside of Orthodoxy. Many other respondents expressed a lack of identification with the Haredi way of life at a very early age. Sherry related, "I just couldn't understand my way of life; I couldn't understand the ways they're teaching us, and I had so many questions I knew I couldn't [ask]." Similarly, Joel recounted, "I didn't get it. I felt for years that they cheated me because always in the school they said, 'Talmud is like math. It's very logical, it's rational.' And I never saw what is logical and rational about it." Significantly, most of these respondents do not describe themselves as having become disillusioned after having had a traumatic experience but rather as just being able to see the holes in the worldview that others in their community did not see.

A major lack in her world presented itself in Leah's early education, where she perceived her gender as an intellectual and spiritual impediment in the Orthodox world. While her brothers were sent to male Yeshivas[10] in which they received a very intensive, serious education, Leah, like other ultra-Orthodox girls, went to an all-girls' school where she was taught what she described as "Judaism light." For example, she and her classmates "learned the Torah over and over and over again. There was no Talmud at all. And, they taught us only their particular interpretation of the Torah and did not expose us to the entire real thing."

Leah told Davidman that her ability to see weaknesses in the social structure and culture of her world derived from her early recognition that as a girl she was excluded from the central Orthodox institutions, norms, values, and behaviors. She related that when she reached the age of seven or eight she was told she could no longer go with her father to the little synagogue she so enjoyed. "I loved it there. It was fun. The guys would give us candy and the Rebbetzin[11] would give us food. And so once I was not allowed to go with my father, I did not go at all. My mother would make me set the table or just do stuff in the house, and it was boring and stupid." She explained that at that point there was no more participatory religion for her, "it was over for me, basically." Other ex-Haredi women also reported feeling restricted by the circumscribed roles assigned to women.

Despite Leah's description that she was able to see serious problems with the Orthodox world and her place in it beginning at age five or six, she nevertheless clung on to it, partly because in her youth she felt she had no other place to go. She also attributed her reluctance to rebel to her deep fear of God:

I was much filled with fear. The famous thing that they would tell you is that all your sins go to your father until you are twelve years of age and I loved my father and I thought, "Oh my God. All my sins are going to him and he's going to die."

Despite growing up in a family with several children, and in a tightly knit community, Leah's narrative was permeated with a sense of being alone in her inability to fit in. As she said: "Well, let's see. I'm a woman but I don't want to do that role. I don't want to be like my mother and not go to shul so I can stay home and cook. I just did not feel that there was a place for me in the religious world. There was nobody else like me." Leah stated that from an early age she could no longer rely on her family or community, nor could she find her place within the culture.

At around age eight or nine, Leah started to question outwardly, perhaps hoping to get answers that would satisfy her and help her stay in the community, thus avoiding the anomie and homelessness a radical departure would cause. She reported that when she began asking the rabbis at her school serious questions, they simultaneously complimented and condescended: "You're such a nice girl, such a sweet girl. Why are you going crazy asking all these questions?" Leah explained:

[I] would get confused. He would say complimentary things. So [I] would forget for a minute that he [was] not answering [my] questions and I would feel that perhaps I am the one who is at fault; I just have to try harder.

Her doubts about her questions and the rabbi's responses further reveal how difficult it was for her to trust her doubts, given the closed social system and tightly woven worldview in which she had been raised. Leah's story reveals her sense of a lack of a script for expressing her serious challenges to the ideas and norms and behavioral expectations of her culture. "I did not know even how to speak it. I would be crazed, and it was so frightening." As she recounts her story, her fright was born out of the glimpse of loneliness and displacement that would be the result of her questioning, illustrating how difficult it was for her, as for other Haredim, to make a break from her settled life.

Even though as a young teenager she was still living a relatively established life within the Haredi world, Leah reports that she slowly became exposed to another culture (a secular world where feminism was a legitimate option), which led her to question her own. One powerful stimulus for her exposure to feminism was actually provided in school, where her "English" teacher assigned Ibsen's *A Doll's House*[12] to her class.

I remember reading it then and I loved that book! I found it so unbelievable that I had found my book! I was crazed but in school they just spoke about its literary dimensions and they did not get how deeply and profoundly a book like that could be to someone like me!

Leah's recognition of her own story in *A Doll's House* reveals her sense that her loneliness in and emotional alienation from the Haredi world was deepened by her growing awareness of alternative worldviews. Other interviewees also reported the importance of books in introducing them to the outside world. David, a non-Hasidic American, recounted that he

read like a maniac. . . . I read Bertrand Russell. What was his book? *Why I am an Atheist* or something. And I can remember reading it, in fact, at a funeral for a rabbi. The eulogies were going on and on and I was a rotten little rebel back then. I was sitting there reading. But I still looked like I belonged.

Spending time with secular relatives was mentioned by several *yotzi'im* as a source of their exposure to the secular world. Leah said that the movement back and forth between worlds that characterized her exiting process began when she visited with her secular cousins.

They were introduced in a positive way to us—"they're your cousins and you're supposed to love them"—and they were just normal, suburban kids. Not only did they have more money than we did and did many exciting things, like skiing and going to the Grand Canyon, it was so interesting to see that they were living with sin but without dying or something. They seemed to be doing all this stuff, and there was no sign of illness or death. So I thought that maybe what we had been told was a little wrong or something, or maybe that there is just a delay in the punishment.

Other *yotzi'im* recounted finding a variety of ways through which they were exposed to outside influences. Sherry reported how important it was to her when she first saw a television at a neighbor's house. "[S]o I go to this neighbor's house, and I come back to my mom, and I say, you know what I saw? Something really interesting, a blue box with people playing ball, football or something. It was a game on TV. A blue box. My mom forbid me from ever visiting that friend again." Similarly, Ruthie discovered the Internet:

So I got on to the web, and I started chatting around. I started realizing that there's interesting stuff out there. I started going into chat rooms. I started talking to people, and I felt safe to talk about anything because nobody knows who's sitting behind the screen and talking. And I would talk to people about where I come from, and people would be interested in finding out about me. And I'd be interested in finding out about the outside world. I started talking to gentiles. You know, God forbid you talk to a gentile.

Leah described that as she went through adolescence, she felt caught between two worlds: she saw that what she was told within her tightly knit, strict community was not the only valid way of life, but she did not feel steady enough in a new, different world to entirely discard her past. Other interviewees, too, told of a time when they felt "betwixt and between," no longer satisfied with the world in which they had been raised but not yet ready to venture out. As Danny, an Israeli, exiter, put it: "I tried to find some kind of way to accommodate both my questioning and my desire to stay within the borough or whatever the word is in English, *lehisha'er ba-telem, nu*?" Some experimented with small acts of rebellion. Linda, who grew up in a Satmar community in Brooklyn, recounted: "I must have been fourteen, fifteen, and I went out of the house for the first time with different socks. Socks that were considered very modern (i.e., made of thinner threads) that only people in Flatbush [largely a non-Haredi section of Brooklyn] wore." Yitzhak, a non-Hasidic Israeli, narrated:

One day I'd put on tefillin,[13] one day I wouldn't; one day I'd pray, one day I wouldn't. But then I'd say to myself, like why am I not doing it? It only takes five minutes, like what do I care? Like little by little it was this feeling of like, as if, like, it's like you're riding down a slope and you see ahead of you that the path splits into two and you have time, but you have to choose. And the car's driving, but you have to decide. You have to choose.

Emotionally, socially, and physically, Leah recalls being quite frustrated about her lack of knowledge about and experience with boys: "From the sexuality point of view you are completely repressed. There is just nothing happening. I mean, like even, your vagina is not given a name. . . . You're just like you don't have anything, and the boys have something. And that is it." A lack of acknowledgment of or information about her body and its processes further alienated Leah from her cultural surroundings. She pushed at the boundaries by wearing shorter skirts, spending more time among secular or rebellious young people, and asking more pressing questions about the rules of her community. Men also complained about the Haredi silence concerning sexuality. Like most other Yeshiva-educated male interviewees, Chaim, the son of a Lubavitcher *Ba'al T'shuvah*,[14] reported that as an adolescent he found it difficult to reconcile his natural impulses for sexual self-exploration with the stringent prohibition of masturbation in the religious texts he learned in school. "I'm supposed to feel all guilty about all of this. . . . I had my body, I had my natural urges, and . . . they were telling me that this is wrong."

Leah represented her late teenage years (ages 17 to 19) as the time when she began to learn enough about feminism to have a language with which to express revolutionary ideas concerning women's freedom of choice:

I was talking, you know, liberation. They wanted girls to just shut up, look pretty, and get married. And I was saying stuff like, "but why? Why should we do the dishes?" And this talk became very disturbing to everybody. I did not know if I meant it, but still, I still felt compelled. I felt like I was . . . you know, that I wanted to belong, and I didn't know how and I had no other place to belong. So even though I was saying what I didn't want, I did not know what I wanted.

Such cognitive, social, and emotional questions led to radical changes in her behavior: she stopped observing Shabbos altogether:

It just became claustrophobic and I could not stand it anymore. I just hated, you know . . . the countdown, and when it started. I did really bad things . . . like, I lived in Boro Park [an ultra-Orthodox section of Brooklyn], and on the edge of Boro Park there were these bars. And at some point, I just needed to go to a bar . . . [to] feel like an international adventuress or something. . . . Like in the movies [that she had snuck out to see], Bette Davis or something. That is who I was. Lauren Bacall or Katherine Hepburn. I would tuck some money into a pocket and I would sneak out of my house on a Friday night with pants under my skirt remove my skirt as I approached the bar, and then there would be all these drunken Irishmen or something. Luckily no one ever talked to me because I would have been so dumbfounded. And after I had my drink and paid for it. I left the bar, put my skirt back on, and returned to my house, crept into bed and went to sleep.

Here, Leah is describing the transitional stage of "passing" between two worlds; in essence she is living the contradiction of being in both the Haredi and the secular worlds at once. Both her religious and her secular identities co-existed at this point, accounting for why her struggle was so intense and her narrative so dramatic. Yankl recounted a similar incident of passing:

Now I think when I was like fifteen years old, I and two or three other guys went to like clubs, dancing clubs. I was never really into dancing clubs because we still had the curls [the long side locks Hasidic men and boys wear]. And I mean I always hung out with a lot of my friends, but they had their curls down. So I didn't like the idea of going to a club and people like staring at us. Instead of staring at the girls dancing; they were staring at us. So whenever I went outside the village, I just put my curls behind my ears. I tried to hide them.

Leah was unusual in her community; she refused to have an arranged marriage at age 18 and instead enrolled herself at Brooklyn College. There she had her first experience of daily existence in a social structure and culture that differed from the cocoon in which she had grown up. She reported that she hated Brooklyn College because of the predominance of Orthodox (generally non-Haredi) Jews; most of the young women were concerned about

finding a *shidduch*[15] and less interested in their intellectual development. She subsequently arranged her own transfer to Hunter College in Manhattan. There, Leah began to meet some "cool" people who introduced her to rock music, marijuana, and ideas of radical individualism. She began dating a man she met at Hunter; he was from Brooklyn and he was "also leaving the Orthodox world, but, you know, cheating." Leah's report that her boyfriend was "cheating" suggested that he, too, was passing in both worlds and reveals how the Haredi discourse of prohibitions is so deeply internalized by its members. She described her marriage to this man (notwithstanding their eventual divorce) as her "exit ticket" out of the intensely closed Orthodox world. Her explanation that her way out was with a young man from the same background serves as an example of how hard it is to completely leave the social cocoon that is Orthodoxy. And although she and her new husband were not practicing Jewish traditions and rituals, they remained connected with their families:

We moved to a place in Brooklyn that was far enough from our parents that they could not walk on Shabbos. And that was a key thing. But we could walk to see them on Shabbos, which we did sometimes. . . . At the time it was good for both of us. . . . You know, on my own I wouldn't have known where to go . . . like, it was so hard to make sense of the world.

Although she and her husband lived secular lives, Leah claimed that she nevertheless found it difficult to understand what ordinary people were doing on the weekend and how they spent time in their houses. "I felt I had no commonality; no idea what to say to them." Not only was it still difficult to enter into new social relations, she still felt unsure of her footing in terms of daily life:

I think that the hardest thing to believe is that you have to make up each day as it goes along; there is simply no routine of davening in the morning, and you wash your hands or whatever, and then you say this bracha[16] and then that bracha and you have to keep track of all the brachot and the bathroom and did you eat bread? So did you wash your hands? Did you eat fleishig[17] or did you eat milchig[18] and how long to wait between them. So you're just so busy all day with all these rules that it fills your day and it gives a great structure, which is very comforting to many people, though not to me. But this life is not easy either!

Although Leah had clearly and successfully transitioned out of the Haredi community in which she grew up, she found herself uncertain about how to live a secular life. Her narrative describes the [arc] of her progression into the secular world. When she was in her mid-20s, her marriage failed, and she began traveling around in Europe: "I wanted the world!" she exclaimed and described that through her travels she began to feel more sophisticated and more comfortable in speaking to others. Ironically, her journeys exploring various secular worlds helped her put the Orthodox world of her background into a larger context. Although she had intensely disliked the conformity Orthodoxy required, she found that everywhere she went conformity was the norm. Every society had its own repertoire of values, norms, and behaviors that it expected of its members; recognition of this allowed her to see the intensely regulated Hasidic world as just one among many structured societies and cultures.

Today, Leah has a young daughter and it is important to her parents, and to her, that her daughter has a relationship with her grandparents. Although she has found a place in the "outside world," a significant and successful career, a satisfying marriage with a non-Jewish European man, and does not observe any commandments, cultural elements from her former life continue to influence her post-Orthodox identity. She described her life at the time of the interview as a somewhat precarious balance of some elements of the cultural tool kit of her childhood with a larger percentage of the language, culture, values, and individualism of the secular world. She occasionally

takes her daughter "shul shopping", for example, hoping that perhaps her daughter might be more successful than she was at developing a strong sense of herself as a woman within some Jewish context. Leah still feels enough of a pull from her past, and enough of a sense of the fluidity of the boundaries (something she had not seen as a child), that she maintains contact with her parents, moving back and forth between her secular and their Hasidic worlds. . . .

From a structural perspective, Leah's narrative, as well as the narratives of other *yotzi'im*, demonstrates that encapsulation is much harder to achieve than one might expect. Even in encapsulated communities, it is difficult to prevent individuals from being exposed to outside influences. Leah was, in a sense, born with one foot out the door: her mother was raised in a secular environment, and she had an ongoing relationship with her secular cousins. She may, then, have been more exposed to the secular world than other Haredim, making it easier for her to see pathways out of the community. Nevertheless, every one of our interviewees reported awareness that other lifestyles were available and found ways to expose herself/himself to the secular world.

Other studies of those who leave Orthodoxy, one done in the United States (Uretsky 2002) and one done in Israel (Barzilai 2004), show that those most likely to leave are somehow less embedded in the community in the first place. Nevertheless, the particular details of their families of origin cannot fully account for why these particular people left the community. Leah had several siblings who did not question Orthodoxy and have stayed within the Haredi community. That Leah left and her siblings did not highlights the point that a focus on the structural context of identity change does not take away from the agency of those who seek to change themselves. . . .

Intensive religious communities provide a unifying belief system that members attempt to apply to all aspects of their daily lives. Orthodox Judaism provides a clear set of guidelines, ideals, and practices for the social organization of all aspects of life from one how goes to the bathroom and blesses food, down to the minutest details of permitted and forbidden sexual behaviors. Such groups also provide new members with scripts for expressing to themselves and others how their lives have changed now that they have found the group. Those who are born into such groups and then leave them, like the ex-Haredim discussed here, see themselves [as] having to write their own scripts. The main character in this article, Leah—clearly a very articulate woman—reported that at the time she began questioning, she felt that she was "speechless." This appears to be her way of saying that there were no scripts available to help her learn how to undergo such a radical transformation of self and world, whereas the culture she was brought up in provided scripts for every aspect of her life. By focusing on Leah's account, we have tried to show how both the exiting process and exit narratives are shaped by structural factors. We have also tried to demonstrate the methodological point that narratives are useful for learning about the influence of particular social structures on individual accounts, as well as for what they can tell us about actual social processes.

NOTES

1. Haredi (singular, used as a noun and as an adjective; Haredim in plural) is a term that applies to Hasidic and ultra-Orthodox Jews who live within enclave communities in an attempt to reduce the influence of secular society. Not all Haredi Jews are Hasidic. Hasidism refers to a revitalization movement in Europe in the 18th century that placed an emphasis on piety and joyous celebration instead of the Scholasticism advocated by the elite, educated rabbis who were known as Mitnagdim, Litvaks, or Lithanias. The Hasidic movement is made up of small groups of disciples focusing on a charismatic leader, usually called a rebbe. These groups generally take their name from the town in Eastern Europe where the founding rebbe lived. Lubavitch Hasidim differ from other Hasidic groups in that they are much more focused on outreach to nonreligious Jews in an attempt to attract them to traditional Jewish observance. Belz and Satmar Hasidim are more concerned with maintaining distance from secular society. Belz Hasidim endorse a certain level of engagement with the secular Israeli state, but the more conservative Satmars are staunchly opposed to Zionism.

2. The term *"yotzi'im,"* exiters, is another way of referring to people who in Israel are sometimes referred to as *hozrim be Shealah*, meaning "return with questions." This latter phrase is a spinoff of the earlier term, *hozrim betshuvah*, meaning those who "return" (even if they were not brought up that way) to orthodox religious observance. Another meaning could be "the process of leaving."

3. . . .

4. Within the Haredi and Hasidic communities, the term "nonreligious" refers more to one's level of observance than to the nature of one's beliefs. "Nonreligious" Jews are those who do not maintain the strict levels of observance called for by the Orthodox tradition.

5. This name, like all names that appear in this article, is a pseudonym.

6. Blessings. The Lubavitchers are a Hasidic group, headquartered in Brooklyn, which has become well known in recent years for its outreach to nonreligious Jews. Chabad is the outreach movement associated with the Lubavitchers.

7. Songs.

8. We are not arguing here that her mother's native unfamiliarity with the blessings is causally related to Leah's leaving. After all, she has siblings who do not leave. We are simply reporting on the linkages Leah made herself in her account.

9. The Sabbath.

10. Religious school.

11. Rabbi's wife.

12. A powerful play by Henrik Ibsen about a 19th-century woman rebelling against her husband's dominance.

13. Usually translated into English as "phylacteries." They are small boxes, containing Hebrew prayers, which Orthodox Jewish men attach to their arms and foreheads for morning prayers.

14. "Returnee," or convert to Orthodoxy.

15. Matches for marriage.

16. Blessings.

17. Meat.

18. Dairy.

REFERENCES

BARZILAI, S. 2004. *To storm a hundred gates: A journey into the world of the newly secular.* Tel Aviv: Yediot Aharanot. (Hebrew)

BECKFORD, J. 1978a. Through the looking glass and out the other side: Withdrawal from Reverend Moon's Unification Church. *Archives des sciences socials des religions* 45:95–116.

BROMLEY, D. G. 1978b. Accounting for conversion. *British Journal of Sociology* 29:249–62.

———. 1997. Falling from the new faiths: Toward an integrated model of religious affiliation/disaffiliation. In *Leaving religion and religious life,* edited by M. Bar-Lev and W. Shaffir, pp. 31–60. Vol. 7 of *Religion and the social order,* edited by D. G. Bromley. Greenwich, CT: JAI Press.

———, ed. 1998a. *The politics of religious apostasy: The role of apostates in the transformation of religious movements.* Westport, CT: Praeger.

———. 1998b. Linking social structure and the exit process in religious organizations: Defectors, whistleblowers, and apostates. *Journal for the Scientific Study of Religion* 37:145–60.

DAVIDMAN, L. 1991. *Tradition in a rootless world: Women return to Orthodox Judaism.* Berkeley: University of California Press.

GLAZER, B. and A. STRAUSS. 1967. *The discovery of grounded theory.* Chicago: Aldine.

GREIL, A. L., and D. R. RUDY. 1984b. Social cocoons: Encapsulation and identity transformation. *Sociological Inquiry* 54:260–78.

JACOBS, J. L. 1989. *Divine disenchantment: Deconverting from new religions.* Bloomington: Indiana University Press.

LEWIS, J. 1986. Reconstructing the "cult" experience *Sociological Analysis* 40:197—207.

SNOW, D. 1976. *The Nichiren Soshu movement in America: A sociological examination of its value orientation, recruitment efforts, and spread.* PhD thesis. University of California at Los Angeles.

SOLOMON, T. 1981. Integrating the "Moonie" experience: A survey of ex-members of the Unification Church. In *In gods we trust: New patterns of religious pluralism in America,* edited by T. Robbins and D. Anthony, pp. 275–95. New Brunswick, NJ: Transaction.

URETSKY, A. 2002. *Leaving Orthodoxy: A study of religious and cultural transformation.* Senior Honors Thesis presented to the Department of Sociology, Clark University.

WRIGHT, S. A. 1984. Post-involvement attitudes of voluntary defectors from controversial new religious movements. *Journal for the Scientific Study of Religion* 23:172–82.

———. 1987. *Leaving cults: The dynamics of defection.* Washington: Society for the Scientific Study of Religion.

———. 1991. Reconceptualizing cult coercion and withdrawal: A comparative analysis of divorce and apostasy. *Social Forces* 70:125–45.

———. 1998. Exploring factors that shape the apostate role. In *The politics of religious apostasy: The role of apostates in the transformation of religious movements,* edited by D. G. Bromley, pp. 95–114. Westport, CT: Praeger.

7

From a Community of Believers to an Islam of the Heart: "Conspicuous" Symbols, Muslim Practices, and the Privatization of Religion in France

CAITLIN KILLIAN

Religious communities—their beliefs, rituals and experiences—are shaped by larger social forces. Killian explores how the powerful trend towards secularization affects the beliefs, rituals, and experiences of Muslim women in France.

Waves of immigrant workers, family reunification policies, and children born in France have made Islam the second largest religion in France. Five million Muslims live in a country that has looked at religion with skepticism since the Enlightenment. From the French Revolution on, political battles have been waged to wrest control of the government and the educational system away from members of the largest religion, Roman Catholicism. The most recent battle in the struggle over *laïcité* ("secularism") has affected Muslims directly. In 2004, "conspicuous" religious symbols, including large crosses, Jewish *kippot*,[1] and Muslim headscarves, were banned from French schools. . . .

As Muslims in a secular society, Maghrebin immigrants in France have the choice of resisting, "establishing strong boundaries with the broader culture, resisting cultural encroachments as much as possible, and setting the group up as a radical alternative" or accommodating, "adapting certain features of the religion to make it more consonant with secular

---

[1]*Kippot* are cloth skullcaps worn by observant Jews. The singular is *kippah*. In the United States, they are commonly known by the Yiddish term, "yarmulke."

Source: Caitlin Killian, "From a Community of Believers to an Islam of the Heart: 'Conspicuous' Symbols, Muslim Practices, and the Privatization of Religion in France." Reprinted with permission, from *Sociology of Religion*, Volume 68, © 2007.

ways of life" (Davidman 1991:32). The Algerian, Moroccan, and Tunisian women I interviewed generally practiced accommodation. I thus examine how Muslim immigrant women's religious practices and beliefs about how to be a good Muslim have changed since their arrival in France. I look at holidays and prayer and then focus on the contentious symbol of the veil.[2] Many North African women in France support the ban on the headscarf, but this tends to vary by age, with younger women more likely to accept the veil in school. Throughout the article, I also point out some of the contradictions between France's position on secularism and the maintenance of Catholic traditions and question the importance of ethnicity, immigration, and Islam in shaping the new law banning religious symbols in school.

THE CONTEXT

This article is part of a larger study on North African women's cultural expression, identity negotiation, and general adaptation in France (Killian 2006). France colonized the three central Maghrebin countries, Algeria, Tunisia, and Morocco, and since World War II, these North African countries have been sending male laborers to France. Maghrebin women began arriving in large numbers in the 1970's, thanks in large part to family reunification laws. The majority of North Africans in France are poorly educated and occupy the bottom rungs of the social structure.

I conducted and audio-taped in-depth, semi-structured interviews with 45 women in Paris and the surrounding suburbs between January and June 1999. I refer to respondents by pseudonyms and have changed certain details about them in order to protect their anonymity. All of the participants are first-generation Muslim immigrants from the Maghreb, but they differ on other characteristics such as age, country of emigration, ethnicity (Arab or Berber), education, employment history, marital status, and number of children. The sample consists of 26 Algerians, eleven Moroccans, and eight Tunisians between the ages of 25 and 58, who have resided in France between one and 37 years (see Killian [2006] for more details).

France is often called a *"terre d'accueil,"* a welcoming country. However, the French do not see themselves as a people of immigrants the way Americans do (Horowitz 1998). Immigrants in France are expected to become French and not cling to hyphenated identities like Irish and Italian-Americans. The French method of integration implies a loss of ethnic identity and pressure to conform to a standard civic model. There is no concept of "minority group" in French legal texts; the "ethnic citizen" is not supposed to exist (Feldblum 1993). The French model of integration stands in opposition to the multicultural Anglo-Saxon model, which the French argue causes societal disintegration and ghettoization of minority groups (Feldblum 1993). President Jacques Chirac has said, "We cannot accept that France becomes a pluricultural society in which our historical heritage would be placed on the same level as this or that other recently imported culture" (quoted in Rude-Antoine 1997:89, translation mine). In the past couple of decades, however, the traditional assumption that immigrants would abandon their cultural traditions in favor of French civic culture is increasingly challenged by the growing numbers of visible immigrants and by the influence of the European Union, some of whose members are more tolerant of cultural pluralism.

Warner and Wittner (1998) point out that in the U.S., immigrants actively cling to religious traditions because religion has historically

---

[2]In this article I use "headscarf" and "veil" interchangeably, even though the use of the word veil in French discourse is often politically motivated.

been the one cultural aspect in which they were not expected to gradually assimilate. This is due in part to the U.S.'s celebrated (and sometimes mythic) history of immigrants fleeing religious persecution abroad and finding a safe haven for practicing their beliefs in their new home. Immigrant parents may indeed emphasize religion in their children's training because they view language and other cultural behaviors as already lost (Warner and Wittner 1998). In France, Maghrebin immigrants are also likely to place great emphasis on religion, but unlike the Americans, the French are less encouraging of religious difference and expect religious expression to be confined to the home and places of worship. Césari (2000:93) writes that France's assimilation model "insists that if immigrants seek to become French citizens, they must eschew their foreign cultural, religious, political and ideological alliances. In other words, they must accept the already existing consensus of reality and polity of the prevailing system and assimilate into it, shedding all alien characteristics. The French policy of Gallicization sees the end result of integration as the privatization of religious practice, with the Muslim individuals becoming socially and economically assimilated."

After months of study by the specially-appointed Stasi Commission, the French government passed a law in February of 2004 banning *"ostensible"* (which best translates as "conspicuous") religious symbols—in particular, Muslim head-scarves, Jewish *kippot*, and large Christian crosses—in school starting with the 2004-2005 school year (Stasi Commission Report 2003).[3] This law was passed

after a series of debates in 2003, despite the fact that the number of girls wearing head-scarves to school had been declining for nearly a decade (Geisser 2003). In a poll conducted by CSA for the newspapers *Le Monde* and *La Vie* in January 2004, 76 percent of junior high and high school teachers pronounced themselves in favor of the ban on the headscarf (compared to 69% of French people and 42% of Muslims), yet 91 percent did not have a veiled girl in the school where they taught at the time, and 65 percent admitted that they had never seen a veiled girl in any school during their career. Of the 35 percent who had run across veiled girls in the careers, only five percent said it was a frequent occurrence (CSA 2004). That it was legislated against despite its rarity suggests that the veil has taken on a greater symbolic meaning in French society (Amiraux 2004). Auslander (2000) argues that public reaction against the veil is a way to reassert national identity at a time when France is feeling threatened by globalization, the European Union, and immigration. Geisser (2003:11) believes that "the defensive and punitive policies towards all visible signs of *Islamity*" are a response to fears of an "Arabo-Muslim menace" (translation mine).

The new law sums up the feeling of many French people reflected in statements made by former Prime Minister Alain Juppé: "[I]ntegration which confers rights, all the rights of the French, of course, with naturalization, also implies accepting a certain number of rules for common life, in particular performing national [military] service for France, when one wants to be French; accepting the role of the school as integrator and not multicultural . . . ; and finally, accepting certain modes of social and family organization" (cited in Rude-Antoine 1997:93, translation mine). In an era that has recently made military service optional instead of mandatory, schooling is seen as the primary vehicle for making immigrants French.

---

[3]In previous pronouncements, only *"ostentatoires"* (in English, "ostentatious") symbols that were considered proselytizing by nature were banned. Consequently, some school principals deemed the headscarf ostentatious, and therefore cause for suspension, and others did not. Crosses and *kippot* were not viewed as ostentatious, thus necessitating the change in language from "ostentatious" to "conspicuous" in order to include them in the ban.

The headscarf affair raises several issues for the French including how to interpret *laïcité*. Strong public support for the separation of the church and state, made law in 1905, remains prevalent in France today. *Laïcité* grew out of the Jacobin tradition and the long and hard-fought quest to purge the government and French public schools of Catholic influence. Thus, in the United States, "separation of church and state" means that the state cannot favor a particular religion and should not interfere with religion, a position McClay (2001) calls "negative" secularism. By contrast, in France, religion and religious symbols are simply not permitted in public institutions, a position McClay calls "positive" secularism. According to McClay (2001:59), negative secularism is "an opponent of established belief— including a *nonreligious* establishment—and a protector of the rights of free exercise and free association. On the other hand, [positive secularism is] a proponent of established *unbelief* and a protector of strictly individual expressive rights, a category that includes right of religious expression."[4] Negative secularism in the U.S. allows politicians to proclaim "God Bless America" as long as they do not name a particular God, whereas positive secularism in France makes any public reference to God (e.g., on the currency) anathema. The difference in laws about marriage provides another good example of the contrast. In the U.S., a couple may marry civilly, but if they choose to marry religiously, this wedding is accepted by the state. In France, while many people have a religious ceremony, they must marry civilly in order to be legally recognized. In comparing the two contexts, the question becomes whether all signs of and references to religion must be kept out of the schools entirely or whether there is room for cultural and religious expression on the part of students, if not the teachers.

French politicians argue that the French Republic is under attack by forces antithetical to equality and freedom.[5] Feminist groups and politicians alike believe that banning religious symbols in school will take pressure off Muslim girls who are forced to veil by their parents, by fundamentalist groups, or by peers who call them names and may even threaten violence against girls who do not veil. Given that one of the key arguments is peer pressure, the exact number of girls actually wearing the veil to school is important. Government estimates show a constant decline in the total number of headscarves in school, from 2,000 girls a year ten years ago to a little over 1,000 in 2004, and longtime Department of Education mediator Hanifa Chérifi puts the figure for incidents requiring her intervention at only 150 in 2003 compared to 300 in 1994 (*L'Humanité*, April 29, 2003). Yet members of the Stasi Commission argued that because so many girls were veiling, it was putting tremendous pressure on non-veiled Muslim girls to also adopt a headscarf. This is particularly crucial because the law only conforms to European human rights standards if it can be demonstrated that the religious expression in question must be restricted to protect public order or others' rights and freedoms and that restriction is proportional to the desired goal (Weil 2005). Is it necessary to limit religious expression in order

---

[4]While this distinction is useful, it also downplays some complex manifestations of *laïcité* in France. For example, rather than simply trying to separate church and state, in some respects the state is actually trying to subsume the Roman Catholic Church, to influence its spokesmen, and to control its funding (Bowen 2004). Similarly, the recent creation of the Council of Muslims of France is an attempt by the French government to gain some control over and nationalize "French Islam" (Kastoryano 2002). See also Fetzer and Soper's (2005:73–76) discussion of "soft" vs. "strict" *laïcité* in France.

[5]Amselle (2003:120) points out that "... in the Enlightenment tradition, the philosophy of the rights of man discredits the legitimacy of any public expression of ethnicity or religion on the pretext that they entail fanaticism, despotism, and ignorance."

to protect the several thousands of schoolgirls who do not wear a headscarf from the thousand or so who do? Ultimately, politicians assert that the new law will help students get along with one another and ease ethnic tensions. Yet the law can be viewed as a blow to religious freedom, as constituting, in recently elected French President Nicolas Sarkozy's phrase, "secular fundamentalism" (Sciolino 2003). It may also lead to the creation of more Islamic schools encouraging further "*communitarianisme*" or "ghettoization" and less government oversight of education.

PRACTICING ISLAM IN FRANCE

How does living in a society as secular as France affect Muslims' religious practices? For the majority of the women I interviewed, Islam continues to play a very important role in their lives, even if they have lived in France for several years. Although one-third of the women interviewed do not actively practice Islam, they all self-identify as Muslims. Several of these women noted that they "believe but don't practice." Another third of the respondents are very religious, fasting during the month of Ramadan, observing food restrictions, and praying daily. The other third are also religious, respecting Ramadan, and not consuming pork or alcohol, but do not pray daily. Those participants who are religious talked at length about the challenges of practicing Islam in France and the accommodations they have made.

Keeping the Muslim Holidays

Coming from a Muslim society that follows the Muslim calendar, to a Catholic country that still follows many aspects of the Catholic calendar poses problems. One of the most frequent complaints women mentioned was the difficulties involved in celebrating Muslim holidays in France. Fasting during Ramadan is a uniting experience for the members of the

community all showing their obedience to God in the same manner at the same time. In Muslim countries, the workdays during the month are often cut short. For the celebration of *Eid-el-Kebir*, which commemorates Abraham's sacrifice, Muslims ritually slaughter sheep and then feast with others. Both of these holidays are hard to celebrate in France in the same way they are carried out in the Maghreb. Fatima explains how her work interferes with the holidays:

Ramadan . . . is very tiring here because we work. Because there, in Morocco, when it's Ramadan, we only work half a day. We have to work, but we work a half day, but not the whole day. Here you have to work your whole day without [eating]. As the French say, they don't give a shit. You have to do your day, and that's it. They don't want to know anything. You do your religion, you don't, you do your work, and that's it, no discussion. So I can't leave my job. I have to take care of my children and not find myself in the street, so I prefer to work. It's too tiring, too tiring.

Having to work is not the only factor that makes celebration difficult. When asked about celebrating the holidays, Telja raised other problems she faces:

It's too difficult because we can't make noise as we'd like. We don't have room, space like we'd like to celebrate. If we do a wedding, we have to search a year in advance. And that's what is missing, and it's a shame. Holidays are joy. That gets ruined. Sometimes going I don't know how many kilometers to do a wedding. We have to work when [a holiday] falls during the week. It's a shame that there aren't days like that for us, because the Muslim holidays are sacred.

When the Stasi Report that led to the ban on religious symbols in school was originally submitted to the French government, it also recommended making *Eid-el-Kebir* a national holiday, but this part of the proposal was rejected.

Prayer

In addition to holidays, participants spoke about prayer. Religious Muslims are supposed to pray five times a day, but as respondents pointed out, work, and life in France in general, make the hours of prayer hard to keep. Joumana notes that the "rhythm of life" in France makes prayer difficult, and that the French do not respect the Muslim day of prayer: "Catholics, Catholics don't care.... Have to work on Friday. Normally, Friday is the day of prayer. It's sacred." Although Khadija explains that "for people who work, yes, yes, they can do their prayers by saving up all the prayers for the evening," those who do work full-time, like Fatima, often found this challenging.

No, I don't pray. I don't have time. It's hard.... I'm telling the truth. I don't do it because it's hard.... Prayer you have to stay at home to pray each morning, but you can save them, you do it at night. Me, when I get home at 8:00, it's not at that moment; I have to shower, cook. So I'm totally exhausted, my feet hurt, my head too, so I eat and I sleep, for the next morning and everything. God forgive me. And when I'm retired, if God lets me live until retirement, I'll do it.

Amel agreed:

Prayer, I did it in the beginning, but with my hours and everything it's hard. I remember in the beginning when I came, I already did it in Algeria, when I came, I tried to do it, but sometimes when I got home at 10:00 at night, I had to make it all up. And honestly, I wasn't concentrated on those things. When I was praying, it was 'when am I going to finish and be able to go to bed?" So I said to myself, it's hypocrisy; it would be better to stop. So I stopped. And it's true. I say to myself that God sees what I'm doing, so I don't have to think about praying. Well, maybe I'll do it someday, but the day when I think I can assume it, meaning do it well.

Those participants who do pray, whether five times a day or just occasionally, find that it brings them peace and a sense of well-being. They talked about what Islam means to them and what it gives them. Souad explained why she started to pray:

I do my prayer so that my conscience, I'll be tranquil vis-à-vis God. Later we'll be punished if, it's like a debt, it's a debt to God. If we don't do Ramadan, we don't pray, um, it's a debt, and I'm happy to do it, to be at peace. It's like someone, you owe him money and you don't pay him, your conscience isn't tranquil. This, it's more even, because later you pay more, much more.

Keltouma spoke about prayer and about the role of religion in her life more generally: "I think that religion is an element that helps me ... that helped me surmount difficult moments in my life. For me, it's a moment of peace when I do my prayer, honestly I feel very, very good." Although Warda fluctuates on praying five times daily, she insists:

I don't go to bed without asking God forgiveness for everything I could have done that's not very moral, and where I concentrate a little on essential things. But it's, I mean, it's an individual prayer, profound, that doesn't need any exterior manifestation. I don't put down a rug, no one sees me do it. But I always give myself fifteen minutes to think about what I've done. Is it good? I'm a Muslim, have I conformed to what I believe? It's very important to me. It's a crutch I can't do without.

Warda's focus on an individualized relationship in Islam echoes the feelings of many other respondents who make assertions in France about keeping their religion private. Several women do use a prayer rug and wear a headscarf to pray, but they point out that this is done in the home and is therefore not a public expression of religion. For many older religious women, Islam is between oneself and God. It should be practiced in private and should not interfere with life in French space: on the street, and especially at work or in schools. Chafiqa explains: "You do it for you; you don't do it for others. Me, I do Ramadan, I don't ask others to do it with me, or show others that I do it. If they ask me, okay, I'll say I do it, but if they don't ask me, it's not their business what I do at home.... Intimacy is kept at home. You want to do your prayer, you do it at home."

The Headscarf

Despite the controversy surrounding the law banning religious symbols in school, the majority of French people support it. Many Muslims in France do as well. Recall that in the January 2004 CSA poll, 42 percent of Muslims favored the ban (CSA 2004). This was nearly perfectly replicated in my sample among the 43 respondents asked directly about the veil in school. Among the Muslim immigrants I interviewed who took a clear position for or against the headscarf in school, about 43 percent (12 of 28) were for preventing girls from wearing the headscarf to school, and just under 60 percent (16 of 28) opposed the ban. The other fifteen respondents in my sample made more nuanced arguments and/or had mixed feelings about it (see Killian 2003).

Eleven of the 43 respondents—ten of them among the most religious participants in the sample—argue that the veil is not really required in Islam, that other facets of the religion matter more, that a woman can dress modestly without covering her hair, or that one must not show off or try to stand out. Despite being raised in a society where many women veiled and having often veiled themselves while in the Maghreb, none of this group of respondents believes that to be a good Muslim woman one must veil. They focus on other aspects of their religion, asserting that Islam is "not doing bad things," "helping people," "being tolerant," and "respecting the religion of others." Souad, who prays five times a day, shuns alcohol and pork, and celebrates all the holidays, draws the line at the headscarf:

I am Muslim, and I am against this, against people who dress like this, who wear veils; I can't stand it. Because when you want to follow the religion, as

we say, religion is in the heart. It's not wearing the veil and then behind it doing things that are against the religion. I am Muslim, I practice, I do Ramadan, I do my prayers, and it stops there. It's not worth it that I wear a headscarf, or that I have to go to work like that or to school. That I don't accept.

This response is especially revealing about a whole group of Muslims in France. Many immigrant women, many of whom grew up with the veil in their countries of origin, abandoned it in France to work, to be hired, to fit in. The traditional practice of veiling in Muslim countries demarcates men's space, or public space, from women's space in the home. Thus, in the Maghreb, women put on the veil to go out into the street and take it off at home. In France, where the street is no longer men's space but rather French space, the relegation of headscarves to the home demonstrates a case of cultural adaptation (Killian 2003). In coming to France, these Muslim women have become members of a minority group, and many were cut off from most of their family members. Religion, a communal affair in North Africa, became a private affair in France. As five participants put it, religion is an affair "of the heart."

Discussing Islam and secularization, Babès (2000:32) writes:

[L]et us remain attentive to the evolution that is taking shape within the community. The question of religious practice is inseparable from faith and extends beyond orthodoxy. Canonic rites say nothing (or very little) on the question of deep belief, nor on practice in a broader sense (individual ethics). The relationship between spirituality and the norm is at the heart of the evolution of the relationship between, on one side the normative logic of the community, and on the other the demands of universal faith and spirituality in the middle of secularization. (Translation and italics mine)

This leads to a crucial question. When my interview respondents use the word heart, is it out of a conception of deep individual belief, or is it simply a reaction to trying to practice Islam in a context that shuns it, an instance of making religion internal and private because of external pressures? Amel gave up her prayers at night because she was really thinking about going to bed, but this may be different from the insistence on the heart that comes when one realizes she is not allowed to show on the outside what she feels inside.

Although all religion in France is supposed to be private, the cultural climate and calendar are conducive to practicing Catholicism, while, as we have seen, they are not conducive to practicing Islam. Auslander (2000:288) argues that "[s]ecularism in France, then, is largely accommodating of Christianity but only partially of other religions. . . .The requirement that people bear no distinctive signs of religious belonging and yet that they inhabit an everyday life that is rhythmed by the Christian calendar forces observant Muslims and Jews to make a choice. They can either be good French citizens and bad Muslims or bad Jews, or vice versa." Banning the Jewish *kippah* and the Muslim headscarf is very different from banning large Christian crosses, as many devout Jewish men and Muslim women believe their religion *requires* that they cover their heads outside the home, while few, if any, Christians believe they must wear a cross. Thus, while Christians can effectively choose to put on or take off a religious symbol and be no less Christian for it, the new law forces some Jews and Muslims to "choose" between their religious obligations and going to school. In contrast to the French case, when an American Muslim girl in Oklahoma was suspended for wearing a headscarf to school in 2003, the Assistant Attorney General of the United States filed a complaint against *the school*. The complaint declared, "No student should be forced to choose between following her faith and enjoying the benefits of a public education. We certainly respect local school systems' authority to set dress standards, and otherwise regulate their students, but

such rules cannot come at the cost of constitutional liberties. Religious discrimination has no place in American schools" (United States Department of Justice 2004).

In a society that leaves little room for plural identities and expects immigrants to integrate by taking on French behaviors and values, immigrants who have lived in France for decades have learned to accommodate. When Telja says, "[m]y religion, I keep it inside of me. I don't show anyone, because it belongs to me and God, nobody else," a statement she would not have felt compelled to make in North Africa, she echoes Kastoryano's (2002:50) pronouncement that after the passage of 1905 law in France separating church and state, "Belief in God was now only a private matter." Instead of conforming to the norms they grew up with in the Maghreb, many older immigrant women have redefined what it means to be a good Muslim woman. For example, in discussing her life in Morocco, Najet says that "a real Muslim woman does not meet a man without her brother or husband, or someone from the family. A stranger, she won't sit next to him, talk, discuss, won't say anything." Yet in France, going shopping, riding the bus, and other daily chores necessitate a breakdown of this segregation between the sexes, and Najet feels no less Muslim for it. By focusing on the purity of one's heart and the expression of religion through private acts, this group of respondents has made compromises between their cultural customs and the requirements of French society, but they are compromises with which they feel comfortable.

Many of these women came in an era when immigrants just wanted work and hoped to be overlooked by the French. Although they did not expect to fully belong to French society, they saw little reason to purposely mark themselves as foreign and other. Instead of mixing customs and creating new patterns of behavior no matter where one lives, these women feel that when in North Africa one should follow North African norms, and when in France, one should follow French norms, at least to a certain extent. Oumniya says simply, "Me, here in France, French habits. There I have Algerian habits. Here we live the French way. There we live the Algerian way." Najet agreed: "Yes. Do like there. If we're here, we do like here. That's it."

The participants who voiced this kind of negative reaction to the veil in school were of very similar backgrounds. Eight of the eleven were women over 40 with little or no formal education; of the three younger women, two stopped school before high school, and only one had been to college. All but one were observant Muslims, yet virtually all were against girls wearing the headscarf to school; only two had mixed feelings about the issue, and these two were both younger women. These women's position as immigrants with little education, especially those who came before the 1980's and 1990's, likely affects their views on the issue and their general strategy of accommodation rather than resistance. It is increasingly members of the second generation who choose to resist and criticize the compromises and adaptation of their parents. . . .

REFERENCES

AMIRAUX, VALÉRIE. 2004. "Le Foulard en République: Quinze Ans Déjà." *Les Cahiers de l'Orient* 76(4):73–88.

AMSELLE, JEAN-LOUP. 2003. *Affirmative Exclusion: Cultural Pluralism and the Rule of Custom in France.* Translated by J.M. Todd. Ithaca, NY: Cornell University Press.

AUSLANDER, LEORA. 2000. "Bavarian Crucifixes and French Headscarves: Religious Signs and the Postmodern European State." *Cultural Dynamics* 12:283–309.

BABÈS, LEÏLA. 2000. *L'Islam Intérieur: Passion et Désenchantement.* Beyrouth, Lebanon: Editions Al Bouraq.

BOWEN, JOHN R. 2004. "Does French Islam Have Borders? Dilemmas of Domestication in a Global Religious Field." *American Anthropologist* 106:43–55.

CÉSARI, JOCELYNE. 2000. "Islam in European Cities." Pp. 88–99 in *Minorities in European Cities: The Dynamics of Social Integration and Social Exclusion at the Neighborhood Level,* edited by S. Body-Gendrot and M. Martiniello. New York: St. Martin's Press.

CSA. 2004. "Les Enseignants des Collèges et Lycées et la Laïcité." Retrieved 5 February 2004 (http://www.csa-tmo.fr/dataset/data2004/opi20040124c.htm).

DAVIDMAN, LYNN. 1991. *Tradition in a Rootless World: Women Turn to Orthodox Judaism.* Berkeley: University of California Press.

FELDBLUM, MIRIAM. 1993. "Paradoxes of Ethnic Politics: The Case of Franco-Maghrebis in France." *Ethnic and Racial Studies* 16:52–74.

FETZER, JOEL S., and J. CHRISTOPHER SOPER. 2005. *Muslims and the State in Britain, France, and Germany.* New York: Cambridge University Press.

GEISSER, VINCENT. 2003. *La Nouvelle Islamophobie.* Paris: Editions La Découverte.

HOROWITZ, DONALD L. 1998. "Immigration and Group Relations in France and America." Pp. 320–338 in *The Immigration Reader: America in a Multidisciplinary Perspective,* edited by D. Jacobson. Oxford, UK: Blackwell Publishers Ltd.

KASTORYANO, RIVA. 2002. *Negotiating Identities: States and Immigrants in France and Germany.* Translated by B. Harshav. Princeton: Princeton University Press.

KILLIAN, CAITLIN. 2003. "The Other Side of the Veil: North African Women in France Respond to the Headscarf Affair." *Gender & Society* 17:567–90.

———. 2006. *North African Women in France: Gender, Culture, and Identity.* Stanford: Stanford University Press.

MCCLAY, WILFRED. M. 2001. "Two Concepts of Secularism." *Journal of Policy History* 13:47–72.

RUDE-ANTOINE, EDWIGE. 1997. *Des Vies et des Familles: Les Immigrés, la Loi et la Coutume.* Paris: Editions Odile Jacob.

SCIOLINO, ELAINE. 2003. "Ban Religious Attire in School, French Panel Says." *New York Times.* December 12.

Stasi Commission Report. 2003. "Commission de Réflexion sur l'Application du Principe de Laïcité dans la République: Rapport au Président de la République." Retrieved 13 March 2006 (http://www.ladocumentation francaise.fr/rapports-publics/034000725/ index.shtml).

United States Department of Justice. 2004. *Religious Freedom in Focus,* Volume 3 (April). Retrieved 13 March 2006 (http://www.usdoj.gov/crt/religdisc/ newsletter/ focus_3.htm).

WARNER, R. STEPHEN, and JUDITH G. WITTNER. 1998. *Gatherings in Diaspora: Religious Communities and the New Immigration.* Philadelphia: Temple University Press.

WEIL, PATRICK. 2005. *La République et sa Diversité: Immigration, Intégration, Discriminations.* Paris: Seuil.

Reading 8   Immigration and Religion

WENDY CADGE AND ELAINE HOWARD ECKLUND

This reading is a synthesis reading, reviewing the literature written on post-1965 immigrants to the United States and their religions. It is a fine way to get familiar with what we know about the topic of immigration and religion in the United States. The authors also, in their work on synthesizing previous studies, identify holes in the previous research. What is it that we know, and yet need to know?

INTRODUCTION

Recent estimates suggest that 23% of the American population is an immigrant or the child of an immigrant (Alba & Nee 2003, Lee & Bean 2004, Malone et al. 2003). . . . During the past 15 years, sociologists of religion, immigration, and race and ethnicity have begun to investigate how religion influences the experiences of post-1965 immigrants to the United States (i.e., those who arrived after the Immigration and Naturalization Services Act of 1965) (Carnes & Yang 2004, Diaz-Stevens 2003, Diaz-Stevens & Stevens-Arroyo 1998, Ebaugh 2003, Ebaugh & Chafetz 2000b, Haddad et al. 2003, Leonard et al. 2005, Levitt 2005, Min & Kim 2002, Warner 1998, Warner & Wittner 1998, Yoo 1996). . . . We

selectively synthesize and review these studies to chart patterns in current thinking and to identify blind spots to be addressed in future research. . . .

The recent pilot and first wave of the New Immigrant Survey (NIS), a nationally representative survey of post-1965 legal immigrants to the United States, includes several questions about religion that are just now allowing for analytic comparisons previously not possible. Conducted in 1996, the pilot survey revealed that two-thirds of post-1965 immigrants are Christian and 42% are Catholic (Jasso et al. 2003). Such results confirm the work of other scholars, who argue that new immigrants are increasing the racial and ethnic diversity of American Christianity as well as bringing larger numbers of adherents of non-Christian religions (Smith & Kim 2005, Warner 2005;

Source: Wendy Cadge and Elaine Howard Ecklund, "Immigration and Religion." Reprinted with permission, from the *Annual Review of Sociology*, Volume 33, © 2007 by Annual Reviews www.annualreviews.org.

see also *http://nis.princeton.edu* for the data from the New Immigrant Survey, which is public access). More than four times as many immigrants (17%) as native-born Americans (4%) report religious affiliations that are non-Judeo Christian. Not all immigrants are religious, however, with 15% reporting no religion, compared with 12% of the native born (Jasso et al. 2003). Additional analyses suggest religious patterns related to visa status, marriage partners, religious service attendance, and other issues to be further investigated using the full NIS (Cadge & Ecklund 2006; Jasso et al. 2000, 2003).

The remainder of this article is divided into four sections. First, we briefly review existing case studies focused largely on immigrants' religious gathering places. Second, we consider how religion contributes to identity formation for immigrants, with particular attention to ethnic and gender identities. Third, we focus on research about religion and civic and political participation among immigrants. Fourth, we consider the religious beliefs, practices, and organizations of second-generation immigrants. We conclude by outlining several ways to enrich theoretical thinking in future research, with particular attention to the ways post-1965 immigrants are situated within and changing American religious institutions and social institutions more broadly.

CHANGING AMERICAN RELIGIOUS INSTITUTIONS

. . . Around 1990, sociologists began to conduct research about the religious lives of post-1965 immigrants. This work first emphasized religiously based migration patterns to the United States and then focused almost exclusively on "congregations"[1] or the "local face-to-face religious assemblies" where immigrants gather (Warner & Wittner 1998). Scholars argued that "de facto congregationalism" or the process of

"adopting a congregational form in organizational structure and ritual" is one of the central processes that "contribute to the transformation of immigrant religion in the contemporary United States" (Yang & Ebaugh 2001b, p. 270; see also Bankston & Zhou 2000; Warner 1993, 2000). Studies of individual congregations began in the 1990s. . . .

Subsequent books and articles based on these and other studies clearly show how important religion and religious organizations are in the lives of many immigrants. The majority of studies described facets of the founding, structure, and internal operation of these gatherings. Researchers pointed out that immigrant religions in the United States often operate through a professionalized clergy, increased reliance on lay leadership, and voluntary membership and have changed rituals and worship styles compared with those in immigrants' nations of origin (Yang & Ebaugh 2001b). This scholarship stresses the similarities between rather than differences among immigrant religious centers in various traditions and locales. Ebaugh, O'Brien, and Chafetz are three of the few sociologists to think systematically about variation among different organizations. By combining GIS (geographic information systems) and ethnographic data, they describe differences between parish congregations in which participants live in the geographic area and niche congregations that draw from a broader metropolitan area through strong social networks (Ebaugh et al. 2000). Ebaugh & Chafetz (2000c) also define two ideal-type congregations they call the congregational structure model and the community center model to further chart organizational variation. They find

---

[1]We recognize the Christian connotation in use of the term "congregation." This is the term used in much of the literature on immigration and religion, however, so we employ the term when it is an appropriate reference to a specific scholar's work.

that these two ideal types capture largely unrelated aspects of immigrants' religious organizations and that no clear patterns by religious tradition, ethnicity, membership size, socioeconomic status, or local availability of secular groups emerge.

Within individual religious centers, scholars have also paid attention to internal diversity based on ethnicity, language, region of origin, and even religious tradition. Some centers maintain what Yang has called a tenacious unity, whereas others divide often through schism (Badr 2000; George 2003; Numrich 1996; Yang 1998, 2000b). Many include newcomers, individuals outside of their religious or ethnic group, either in their usual gatherings or in separate gatherings that some scholars call parallel congregations. Language differences are often a key dividing line, with some worship centers deciding to have separate services in different languages and others struggling to maintain single language services (Ebaugh & Chafetz 2000a). In some cases, such as at a Ghanaian Pentecostal church in Chicago, centers decide to use the English language in services rather than traditional languages because they want to include more people as part of their commitment to evangelism (Stevens 2004).

The ways immigrants' religious organizations facilitate their adaptation in the United States remains a central theme in recent studies. Historically, religious centers were viewed as conservative organizations that preserved ethnic customs, language, and group solidarity and as adaptive organizations that helped immigrants adjust to their new environments (Mullins 1987). Within the literature, there is evidence of centers serving all these functions (for example, Ebaugh & Chafetz 2000b, Hurh & Kim 1990, Kim & Kim 2001, Min 1992, Warner & Wittner 1998). Many studies illustrate the range of formal and informal social services immigrants have access to through local religious organizations upon arriving in the United States (Campion 2003, Ebaugh & Pipes 2001, Menjívar 2001, Min 1992). Churches in New York's Chinatown, for example, provide housing, food, employment, and a safe haven to Chinese recently arrived from the Fuzhou region of China (Guest 2003). In addition to direct assistance, religious centers also foster networks that often lead to mortgages, housing, jobs, and business opportunities that facilitate social and economic adaptation (Bankston 1997, Bankston & Zhou 2000, Kwon 1997, Kwon et al. 1997, Zhou et al. 2002).

Despite the sustained attention to religious centers, sociologists have devoted relatively little attention to the relationship between individual centers and their broader religious institutional contexts. Some research suggests that shape of more macro-level religious institutions, such as denominations, may influence whether and how centers schism (George 2003, Shin & Park 1988). Additionally, Yang & Ebaugh (2001b) argue that some immigrant centers actually come together to create broader regional and international religious organizations similar to Protestant denominations. The way this happens in different traditions and its impact have not been investigated, however (Yang & Ebaugh 2001b). Immigrant and second-generation centers, for example Latino Catholic parishes, are also having a profound effect on the shape and direction of their broader religious traditions in the United States (Cadena 1998; Lawson 1998, 1999; Levitt 2002). Through an analysis of the National Catholic Bishops Conference of the United States, Mooney (2006) argues that immigration is changing the shape of the Catholic church and has become a strategic issue on which the "Catholic church has reasserted its prophetic voice in society" (p. 1455). Similarly, Ecklund (2006) argues that some groups of second-generation immigrants are bringing a broader focus on race and ethnicity to the religious institution of American evangelicalism. To understand fully how immigrants participate in local religious life in the United States, it is essential to understand how their organizations are shaped and institutionally embedded in their existing, nonimmigrant and larger denominational and religious bodies.

IDENTITY FORMATION: ETHNIC, RELIGIOUS, AND GENDER IDENTITIES

Individual and group identity formation, or the ways individuals think of themselves and their relationships to groups of others (Cerulo 1997), is a central theme in research about religion and immigration. Scholars of religion and immigration have deepened and expanded the literature on identities by showing how identities are many-sided, fluid (shaped by historical and social contexts), and overlapping (Ajrouch 2004). Some scholars have suggested that religious identities become more salient for immigrants in the United States than in their nations of origin because of the role religions have in preserving ethnic identities, although there is only indirect evidence for this. For example, in a study of two Hindu Indian religious groups, Kurien (1998) shows how Hinduism helps a group of Indian immigrants ease the transition between being Indian and being American by enabling them to "assert pride in their Hindu Indian heritage [as a way] of claiming a position for themselves at the American multicultural table" (p. 37).

Scholars have pushed understanding of religious identity beyond being either achieved or ascribed to show that identities for immigrants, even those who are part of the same religion, might have aspects of both. For example, Cadge & Davidman (2006) examine the narratives of religiosity among third-generation Jews and first-generation Thai Buddhists and demonstrate that the content of religious identities in these groups have both achieved and ascribed aspects. This is an important finding

in light of the fact that both of these religious traditions have a strongly inherited component (Cadge & Davidman 2006). The work of some authors also reflects the theme that agency is an important part of creating religious identities (Ng 2002; Yang 1999a,b). For example, on the basis of evidence of the conversion process for members of a Chinese immigrant church, Ng (2002) argues that the process of converting to a mainstream religion in the United States involves Chinese immigrants' developing their own appropriations of cultural categories, symbols, and practices even though they are converting to Christianity, an institutionally accepted religion in the United States. And in his work, Yang (1999b, 2000a) shows through ethnographic research among Chinese immigrant churches that religious and ethnic identities are not an either/or matter of assimilation or cultural retention. Rather, identities for Chinese are best described as adhesive, allowing for both selective assimilation and selective preservation of ethnicity in the process of negotiating what it means to be Christian, American, and Chinese.

Most of these studies measure religion in terms of participation in religious organizations and the influence this has on ethnic-oriented and gender-based identities and on the relationship between religious, ethnic, and gender identities in religious settings. Immigrants may use religion as part of identity construction in multiple ways. Religion can be used primarily to construct a religious identity, to facilitate development or retention of an ethnic identity, or some combination of these depending on the context or ethnic resources of a particular religious gathering. Most of the current religion and immigration literature focuses on the ways immigrant religious organizations help to reinforce and maintain ethnicity (Ebaugh & Chafetz 2000b, Warner & Wittner 1998). Min's (1992) study of first-generation Korean churches shows that preserving ethnic traditions and customs is a main function of those religious centers. Min's later study of Indian Hindus and Korean Christians additionally shows how religious organizations help both groups preserve their ethnic traditions by making religious and ethnic rituals synonymous and combining ethnic and religious rituals. Min argues that Korean Christians have an easier time using their religion to preserve ethnicity compared with Indian Hindus because of the more organizationally based nature of Korean Christianity (Min 2003, 2005). In work on Latina women, Peña & Frehill (1998) similarly show that women who are more embedded culturally in the Latino ethnic community place a higher importance on their religiosity. . . .

Little research compares differences in identity construction between religious and nonreligious immigrants. In an exception to this, Carnes (2004) shows through a study of Chinese immigrants in New York City's Chinatown that those who are religious are more likely than the nonreligious to fuse religious and ethnic identities. Carnes's work is also unique in his focus on the elderly, many of whom are not able to travel to regular religious services, which enables him to conceptualize religiosity based on rituals that occur outside as well as inside of religious organizations (Carnes 2004). . . .

In addition to religion and ethnicity, scholars of religion and immigration have considered the role of gender in identity construction and maintenance in religious organizations and individuals' lives. . . . For example, through examining an Indian immigrant church, George (1998) shows how religion sometimes acts as an empowering resource for women, taking less patriarchal forms in organizations in the United States than in immigrants' countries of origin. At the same time, religion is contested space over which Indian Christians try to retain traditional cultural characteristics in the face of a more liberal American Christianity (George 1998).

Ebaugh & Chafetz (1999) argue that, in the 13 religious organizations studied in Houston, women reproduce traditional ethnic culture but also have increased access to high-status positions in their congregations to the degree that men are not able or willing to fill them. Men tend to be interested in these positions in direct proportion to the amount of social status they lose in the process of migration (Ebaugh & Chafetz 1999, George 1998).

Numerous other examples show how women create new religious spaces for themselves inside and outside of religious organizations and creatively adapt to their new positions in religious organizations (Abusharaf 1998, Cadge 2004). Chen's (2005) ethnographic work in a Taiwanese Buddhist temple and a Taiwanese evangelical Christian church, for example, shows in detail that both environments offer a space for women to construct a distinct sense of self as separate from the family. Other research shows that how Korean Buddhists use religion to understand the relationship to the homeland happens, in part, in gendered ways, with men asserting an identity through religious activities that construct distinctively male spaces in the temple in response to the degrading aspects of the male immigrant experience (Suh 2003). Research on second-generation Korean Americans further reveals that religion, race, ethnicity, and gender operate differently depending on the social relationships in which these identities are played out. Korean Americans negotiate the place of gender, religion, and ethnicity in relationship to members of the larger U.S. society, to first-generation Koreans, and to other members of the second generation (Park 2001). Other research examines specifically how members of the second generation have views of gender that influence their commitment to their religion in the face of more egalitarian ideas than their parents had (Alumkal 1999, Yang 2004). . . .

RELIGIOUS LIVES AND CIVIC PARTICIPATION FOR IMMIGRANTS

In addition to questions about identity formation, a small number of scholars are beginning to investigate religion and civic life among post-1965 immigrants (Chen 2003, Ecklund 2006). Civic life describes the ways post-1965 immigrants and their families view their responsibility to participate in American society. Civic actions are generally voluntary, not aimed at reaping an economic profit, and are often concerned with improving some version of the common good. Scholars of late nineteenth and early twentieth century European immigration saw religious participation as a centrally important part of developing identities as American citizens. High levels of cultural and religious assimilation were expected to foster large-scale inclusion into the networks and institutions of American society, including adaptation to mainstream American civic life (Gordon 1964). Among post-1965 immigrants, scholars have only begun to examine how religion influences the ways in which civic life for new immigrants is constructed. . . .

The first part of developing an identity as a citizen is actually becoming a citizen. Gaining citizenship involves navigating the application process, language barriers, and other impediments to gaining legal status as an American citizen. There is resource variation among immigrants, and some researchers are studying how religious organizations link immigrants together in ways that help them through this process. Researchers have examined this process in the Korean church (Min 1992) and other immigrant religious organizations, arguing that religious organizations might provide social service resources, such as help with learning the English language and help studying for the U.S. citizenship exam (Ebaugh &

Chafetz 2000b). Scholars have also examined whether religious identity and participation facilitate attaining U.S. citizenship (Lien 2004). In a study of Asian Americans living in the five metropolitan areas with the highest numbers of immigrants, Lien (2004) shows that Catholic immigrants have the highest rate of citizenship attainment.

A second aspect of civic life is related to participatory political incorporation. Lien (2004) also finds that, among Asian Americans, a group that according to the 2000 Census accounted for over 40% of immigration between 1990 and 1999, those who are religiously involved are more likely to vote. Researchers who study religion and immigration are beginning to compare religious and nonreligious immigrants in terms of civic and political participation. One study finds that in a city that is religious and conservative, even nonreligious Latinos find ways to be involved and integrated into local community civic life (Cavalcanti & Schleef 2005). Among immigrants and their children, there is also evidence that religious identities sometimes overlap with racial and ethnic identities to form new types of political coalitions. For example, researchers are finding that Latinos who are either conservative Protestants or traditional Catholics are defying the traditional liberal/conservative allegiances and are more like black Christians in their commitment to economic liberalism in tandem with a conservative social/moral perspective (Espinosa et al. 2003, Leal et al. 2005).

Religion and politics often have different connections in the United States than in countries of origin, leading immigrants to different understandings of their relationships. For example, a study of Hindu and Muslim immigrants in the United States concluded that the relationship between religion and politics depends both on the kinds of political resources an immigrant brings to the United States and on the context into which the immigrant religion is received (Kurien 2001). The nation of origin often continues to have an influence on U.S. religion and politics via the transnational ties that religion facilitates between U.S. immigrants and those in their sending nations (Levitt 2002). Once immigrants do gain access to the American political system through forms of participation such as citizenship, voting, and campaign participation, religion also fosters specific ideological allegiances among existing U.S. political factions (Lien 2004). Many current scholars further argue that involvements in religious organizations lead people to be more involved in their ethnic and nonethnic communities as well as in their home countries (Klineberg 2004, Yang 1999b). Congregations themselves also evolve over time in ways that influence immigrants' levels of engagement (Mullins 1987).

A third aspect, beyond macro political participation, is the ability of religious organizations to provide participating individuals with motives for volunteering, as well as with connections to local forms of community service that may or may not be sponsored by a particular religious organization (Wuthnow 1999). Most of the research on religion and community volunteerism among immigrants has focused almost entirely on the extent to which immigrant congregations provide social services for immigrants, particularly those in their congregations (Ebaugh & Chafetz 2000b, Min 1992). Some research shows that immigrant congregations have a difficult time providing organizationally sponsored volunteer activities (Cnaan 1997, Ebaugh & Pipes 2001). Religion also has the ability to provide a moral narrative for helping others outside an individual's own religious or ethnic communities (Ecklund 2006). Scholars of religion and immigration are just beginning to ask whether and how the religious organizations of first- and second-generation immigrants extend beyond the boundaries of the immigrant community. In

particular, researchers are starting to take into account how differences between specific religious ideologies might influence the connection between religion and community service....

Fourth, in addition to focusing on citizenship status, voting, and community service, a small number of recent scholars consider the cultural aspects of civic identities or the extent to which immigrants view themselves as part of the United States. Some research suggests that as immigrants become more American they may also become more religious, a process that may influence the development of a civic identity (Chen 2002, 2003). Religions that are closely tied to the national identity of a country of origin may contribute to the creation of a civic identity as "other" in the mainstream United States, as Rajagopal (2000) argues about the development of Hindu nationalism in the United States (see also Kurien 2003). The contribution of religion to the development of civic identities not only differs between religions but, as Ecklund (2005a, 2006) shows, between organizations within the same religion. Immigrants also use religion to renegotiate different categories of race and ethnicity, which have implications for how they view their roles as American citizens (Ecklund 2005b)....

Fifth, researchers are just beginning to examine the possibilities of religion to act as a resource for political mobilization. For example, research by Menjívar (2003) shows how a Catholic church encourages Salvadoran immigrants to work collectively to transform their communities, whereas evangelical Christian churches attended by Salvadorans place more stress on individual salvation. And Hondagneu-Sotelo and colleagues (2004) find that religious and nonreligious individuals use moral forms of Mexican Catholicism when engaged in political protest along the United States/Mexico border....

RELIGION AND THE SECOND GENERATION

...Herberg (1955) argued that second-generation immigrants would be less religious than their parents, and that by the third generation individuals would return to their religion as a way of distinguishing themselves from others. There are too few members among the third generation of post-1965 immigrants to have systematic research about their lives, and there is some disagreement about religion in the lives of the second generation. Researchers suggest that, for some ethnic groups, members of the second generation may leave their immigrant religious organizations (Chai 1998, Kwon et al. 2001). We have few systematic survey data, however, about actual religious participation among the immigrant second generation. A rare example is work by Min & Kim (2005), which shows through a small survey ($n = 202$) of Koreans in the New York City area that about two-thirds of the adults surveyed who attended a Korean church as children participate in a church as adults. More than two-thirds of those attend a Korean congregation (Min & Kim 2005).

Other researchers view immigrant religious communities as places where the second generation is present, negotiates their relationship with the first generation, and gathers cultural and social capital that leads to economic and educational success (Bankston & Zhou 1995, 1996). Although some researchers have echoed the sentiments of religious leaders that there may be a movement away from religion in the second generation, what those who study Asian communities have called the "silent exodus" (Chai 2001), there are few national survey data about these issues. In a rare exception to the above, Hunt (1998) uses data from an analysis from the 1984 National Alcohol Survey to show that Latinos in the second and third generations are more likely to switch from Catholicism to Protestantism. . . .

Researchers who study the involvement of second-generation immigrants in immigrant congregations have developed a series of arguments about the protective effects religious communities have in helping young second-generation immigrants adapt to American society. Bankston & Zhou (1995, 1996) argue that participation in an ethnic church provides children with protective social networks with coethnics, which facilitate adolescent success in school and adaptation to American society. Particularly for youth who are at risk for what the authors call "dangerous and destructive behavior," religious communities often serve as beneficial locations of social, financial, and surrogate parental support (Cao 2005; Guest 2003, 2004). On the basis of research in a New York Chinatown church, Cao (2005) argues that, for working-class immigrant youth, churches act as surrogate families that facilitate the process of moving from the working class to the middle class, enlarging Portes & Rumbaut's (2001) argument about segmented assimilation.

In addition to providing social services and protective benefits for members of the second generation, there are intangible resources religious organizations provide for second-generation immigrants to help them maintain an ethnic identity as well as construct new racial and ethnic identities (Cha 2001, Kurien 2005, Yang 1999a). Chong (1998) finds that, for second-generation Koreans, the Korean church helps them retain ethnic identity by legitimizing a core set of Korean values and making those values sacred through their identification with a conservative Christian morality and worldview. Applying Smith's (1998) theories of subcultural identities, Chai (1998, 2001) argues that Korean churches provide a place for members of the second generation to successfully negotiate a religious and ethnic identity that is distinctive from the first generation.

Another set of researchers examines the ways that ethnic religious organizations help members of the second generation negotiate wider American constructs of race and gender. For example, Busto (1996) argues that participation in campus evangelical Christian organizations provides Asian Americans with cultural resources for reinforcing the image of Asian Americans as model minorities. Drawing on a survey and interviews with members of Asian American congregations in the Bay Area (both mainline and evangelical churches), Jeung (2004, 2005) examines how Asian Americans organize religiously around a pan-ethnic identity as Asian. There is very little research that deals with members of non-Christian religions. One exception is a study of a Hindu Student Council Chapter by Kurien (2005) that illustrates the complexity of intersecting identities of race, ethnicity, and religion among this group of Hindu students; although they came to the group to deal with the intersection of race and religion, the intersection of these same two identities also produced conflict....

A key part of developing racial and ethnic identities for members of the second generation involves figuring out their relationship to the first generation.... On the basis of ethnographic research comparing second-generation Koreans and Chinese, Alumkal (2003) argues that members of the second generation must continually legitimize being part of a religious tradition (evangelical Christianity) that is concerned with imparting a religious message that is supposedly open to anyone while worshipping in an ethnic-specific context. He shows how members of the second generation remain distinct from their parents' generation while still worshipping in an ethnic-specific context (Alumkal 2003). Research on Indian Christians shows that members of the second generation sometimes have different ideas about the content of their religion, with the first generation viewing Christianity according to ascribed religious and ethnic criteria and the second generation viewing Christianity according to

the more achieved and individualistic criteria they perceive as evangelical (Kurien 2004). Other research reveals differences by generation in how individuals think about gender. In some immigrant religious communities, the second generation adopts a more conservative view about gender than the first generation as a way of upholding a distinctive religious identity (Alumkal 1999, Yang 2004).

LOOKING FORWARD: DIRECTIONS FOR FUTURE RESEARCH

... In addition to studies of immigrants' religious organizations, many more studies are needed to understand how immigrants live and experience their religions outside of particular religious contexts. A small but growing number of studies, for example, focus on immigrants' interactions with social service organizations and the ways their religious experience is constructed and utilized in both religious and secular organizations (Bruce 2006, Nawyn 2006). As in native-born populations, religion is often a factor in immigrants' health-care access and use, though this is rarely acknowledged in reviews about immigration and health (Kandula et al. 2004). Although some religious organizations foster traditional healing practices (Numrich 2005), others may influence individuals' health outcomes and/or foster interactions with health-care institutions, but additional study is needed (Hurh & Kim 1990). Anecdotal evidence suggests that some hospitals and doctor's offices are increasingly accommodating religion by creating Muslim prayer spaces, for example. Also, some religion-specific health-care organizations such as the University Muslim Medical Association in Los Angeles are beginning (Miller et al. 2001). Although accounts are mainly journalistic at this point, religion also clearly influences how many immigrants consult the mainstream medical community and how they make decisions about health-care concerns (Barnes & Sered 2005 Fadiman 1998, Ong 1995).

Moreover, sociologists rarely consider how religion influences the experiences immigrants have in social spheres that are not thought of as specifically religious, such as workplaces, neighborhoods, local civic and political organizations, childcare centers, recreational facilities, and other aspects of daily life in the United States. The kind of "lived religion" or religion in daily life approach that such inquiries might require is more often utilized by religious studies scholars and anthropologists (for example, Hall 1997, Orsi 1996, Tweed 1997). Sociologists who have used this approach have looked at migration decisions and experiences; for example, Hagan & Ebaugh (2003) describe how religion influences all aspects of the migration of undocumented Mayans from Guatemala, from the decision they make to migrate to Houston to the preparation process, the journey, and the subsequent arrival in the United States. Using such an approach, Smith & Bender (2004) illustrate how South Asian Muslim taxi drivers in New York City pray while working, primarily by stopping in restaurants that have created informal prayer spaces. Thinking more about how religion influences immigrants' lives in nonreligious spheres such as schools, workplaces, and medical facilities is likely to reveal not only the mixing and messiness of religious experience, but the ways in which nonimmigrants are involved in the migration process, the importance of transnational relations, and how immigrants who are not involved in religious organizations experience religion, if at all, a topic about which almost nothing is known. A religion in everyday life approach also raises questions about religion as a conceptual category and facilitates broader analytic thinking about how the sacred is present and influential apart from formal religions and religious spaces. . . .

LITERATURE CITED

ABUSHARAF RM. 1998. Structural adaptations in an immigrant Muslim congregation in New York. See Warner & Wittner 1998, pp. 235–64

AJROUCH KJ. 2004. Gender, race, and symbolic boundaries: contested spaces of identity among Arab American adolescents. *Sociol. Perspect.* 47:371–91

ALBA R, NEE V. 2003. *Remaking the American Mainstream: Assimilation and Contemporary Immigration.* Cambridge, MA: Harvard Univ. Press

ALUMKAL AW. 1999. Preserving patriarchy: assimilation, gender norms, and second-generation Korean American evangelicals. *Qual. Sociol.* 22:127–40

ALUMKAL AW. 2003. *Asian American Evangelical Churches: Race, Ethnicity, and Assimilation in the Second Generation.* New York: LFB Scholarly

BADR H. 2000. The Al-Noor Mosque: strength through unity. See Ebaugh & Chafetz 2000b, pp. 193–227

BANKSTON CL. 1997. Bayou lotus: Theravada Buddhism in southwestern Louisiana. *Sociol. Spectr.* 17:453–72

BANKSTON CL, ZHOU M. 1995. Religious participation, ethnic identification, and adaptation of Vietnamese adolescents in an immigrant community. *Sociol. Q.* 36:523–34

BANKSTON CL, ZHOU M. 1996. The ethnic church, ethnic identification, and the social adjustment of Vietnamese adolescents. *Rev. Relig. Res.* 38:18–37

BANKSTON CL, ZHOU M. 2000. De facto congregationalism and socioeconomic mobility in Laotian and Vietnamese immigrant communities: a study of religious institutions and economic change. *Rev. Relig. Res.* 41:453–70

BARNES LL, SERED SS, eds. 2005. *Religion and Healing in America.* New York: Oxford Univ. Press

BRUCE TC. 2006. Contested accommodation on the meso level: discursive adaptation within Catholic Charities' immigration and refugee services. *Am. Behav. Sci.* 49:1489–508

BUSTO RV. 1996. The gospel according to the model minority? Hazarding an interpretation of Asian American evangelical college students. *Amerasia J.* 22:133–47

CADENA GR. 1998. Latinos and Latinas in the Catholic Church: cohesion and conflict. In *Religion in a Changing World: Comparative Studies in Sociology*, ed. M Cousineau, pp. 109–19. Westport, CT: Praeger

CADGE W. 2004. Gendered religious organizations: the case of Theravada Buddhism in America. *Gender Soc.* 18:777–93

CADGE W, DAVIDMAN L. 2006. Ascription, choice, and the construction of religious identities in the contemporary United States. *J. Sci. Study Relig.* 45:23–38

CADGE W, ECKLUND EH. 2006. Religious service attendance among immigrants: evidence from the New Immigrant Survey-Pilot. *Am. Behav. Sci.* 49:1574–95

CAMPION P. 2003. One nation under God? Religious entrepreneurship and pioneer Latino immigrants in southern Louisiana. *Sociol. Spectr.* 23:279–301

CAO N. 2005. The church as a surrogate family for working class immigrant Chinese youth: an ethnography of segmented assimilation. *Sociol. Relig.* 66:183–200

CARNES T. 2004. Faith, values, and fears of New York City Chinatown seniors. See Carnes & Yang 2004, pp. 223–44

CAVALCANTI HB, Schleef D. 2005. The case for secular assimilation? The Latino experience in Richmond, Virginia. *J. Sci. Study Relig.* 44:473–84

CERULO KA. 1997. Identity construction: new issues, new directions. *Annu. Rev. Sociol.* 23:385–409

CHA PT. 2001. Ethnic identity formation and participation in immigrant churches: second-generation Korean American experiences. See Kwon et al. 2001, pp. 141–56

CHAI KJ. 1998. Competing for the second generation: English-language ministry at the Korean Protestant church. See Warner & Wittner 1998, pp. 295–331

CHAI KJ. 2001. Beyond 'strictness' to distinctiveness: generational transition in Korean Protestant churches. See Kwon et al. 2001, pp. 157–80

CHEN C. 2002. The religious varieties of ethnic presence: a comparison between a Taiwanese immigrant Buddhist temple and an evangelical Christian Church. *Sociol. Relig.* 63:215–38

CHEN C. 2003. Cultivating acceptance by cultivating merit: the public engagement of a Chinese Buddhist Temple in America. See Iwamura & Spickard 2003, pp. 67–85

CHEN C. 2005. A self of one's own: Taiwanese immigrant women and religious conversion. *Gender Soc.* 19:336–57

CHONG K. 1998. What it means to be Christian: the role of religion in the construction of ethnic identity and boundary among second-generation Korean Americans. *Sociol. Relig.* 59:259–86

CNAAN RA. 1997. *Social and Community Involvement of Religious Congregations Housed in Historic Religious Properties: Findings from a Six-City Study.* Philadelphia: Program Study Organ. Relig. Soc. Work, Univ. Penn.

DIAZ-STEVENS AM. 2003. Colonization versus immigration in the integration and identification of Hispanics in the United States. See Haddad et al. 2003, pp. 61–84

DIAZ-STEVENS AM, STEVENS-ARROYO AM. 1998. *Recognizing the Latino Resurgence in U.S. Religion: The Emmaus Paradigm.* Boulder, CO: Westview

DOUGLAS TJ. 2003. The cross and the lotus: changing religious practices among Cambodian immigrants in Seattle. See Iwamura & Spickard 2003, pp. 159–76

EBAUGH HR. 2003. Religion and the new immigrants. In *Handbook of the Sociology of Religion*, ed. M Dillon, pp. 225–39. New York: Cambridge Univ. Press

EBAUGH HR, CHAFETZ JS. 1999. Agents for cultural reproduction and structural change: the ironic role of women in immigrant religious institutions. *Soc. Forces* 78:585–612

EBAUGH HR, CHAFETZ JS. 2000a. Dilemmas of language in immigrant congregations: the tie that binds or the Tower of Babel? *Rev. Relig. Res.* 41:432–52

EBAUGH HR, CHAFETZ JS, eds. 2000b. *Religion and the New Immigrants: Continuities and Adaptations in Immigrant Congregations.* Walnut Creek, CA: AltaMira

EBAUGH HR, CHAFETZ JS. 2000c. Structural adaptations in immigrant congregations. *Sociol. Relig.* 61:135–53

EBAUGH HR, O'BRIEN J, CHAFETZ JS. 2000. The social ecology of residential patterns and membership in immigrant churches. *J. Sci. Study Relig.* 39:107–16

EBAUGH HR, PIPES P. 2001. Immigrant congregations as social service providers: Are they safety nets for welfare reform? In *Religion and Social Policy*, ed. P Nesbitt, pp. 95–110. Walnut Creek, CA: AltaMira

ECKLUND EH. 2005a. Models of civic responsibility: Korean Americans in congregations with different ethnic compositions. *J. Sci. Study Relig.* 44:15–28

ECKLUND EH. 2005b. 'Us' and 'them': the role of religion in mediating and challenging the 'model minority' and other civic boundaries. *Ethn. Racial Stud.* 28:132–50

ECKLUND EH. 2006. *Korean American Evangelicals: New Models for Civic Life.* New York: Oxford Univ. Press

Espinosa G, Elizondo V, Miranda J. 2003. Hispanic churches in American public life: summary of findings. Interim Rep. 2, Univ. Notre Dame, Inst. Lat. Stud., South Bend, Indiana. http://hdl.handle.net/2305/240

FADIMAN A. 1998. *The Spirit Catches You and You Fall Down: A Hmong child, her American doctors and the collision of two cultures.* New York: Noonday

FETZER JS. 1998. Religious minorities and support for immigrant rights in the United States, France, and Germany. *J. Sci. Study Relig.* 37:41–49

GANS H. 1994. Symbolic ethnicity and symbolic religiosity: towards a comparison of ethnic and religious acculturation. *Ethn. Racial Stud.* 17:577–92

GEORGE S. 1998. Caroling with the Keralites: the negotiation of gendered space in an Indian immigrant church. See Warner & Wittner 1998, pp. 265–94

GEORGE S. 2003. Why can't they just get along? An analysis of schisms in an Indian immigrant church. See Iwamura & Spickard 2003, pp. 209–24

GORDON M. 1964. *Assimilation in American Life: The Role of Race, Religion, and National Origins.* New York: Oxford Univ. Press

GUEST KJ. 2003. *God in Chinatown: Religion and Survival in New York's Evolving Immigrant Community.* New York: NY Univ. Press

GUEST KJ. 2004. Liminal youth among Fuzhou Chinese undocumented workers. See Carnes & Yang 2004, pp. 55–75

HADDAD YY, LUMMIS AT. 1987. *Islamic Values in the United States: A Comparative Study.* New York: Oxford Univ. Press

HADDAD YY, SMITH JI, ESPOSITO JL, eds. 2003. *Religion and Immigration: Christian, Jewish, and Muslim Experiences in the United States.* Walnut Creek, CA: AltaMira

HAGAN J, EBAUGH HR. 2003. Calling upon the sacred: migrants' use of religion in the migration process. *Int. Migr. Rev.* 37:1145–62

HALL DD, ed. 1997. *Lived Religion in America: Toward A History of Practice.* Princeton, NJ: Princeton Univ. Press

HAMMOND PE, Warner K. 1993. Religion and ethnicity in late-twentieth century America. *Ann. Am. Acad. Polit. Soc. Sci.* 527:55–66

HANDLIN O. 1951. *The Uprooted: The Epic Story of the Great Migrations that Made the American People.* Boston: Little Brown & Co.

HERBERG W. 1955. *Protestant, Catholic, Few: An Essay in American Religious Sociology.* Garden City, NY: Doubleday & Co.

HIRSCHMAN C. 2004. The role of religion in the origins and adaptation of immigrant groups in the United States. *Int. Migr. Rev.* 38:1206–33

HONDAGNEU-SOTELO P, GAUDINEZ G, LARA H, ORTIZ BC. 2004. There's a spirit that transcends the border: faith, ritual, and postnational protest at the U.S.-Mexico border. *Sociol. Perspect.* 47:133–59

HUISMAN K, HONDAGNEU-SOTELO P. 2005. Dress matters: change and continuity in the dress practices of Bosnian Muslim refugee women. *Gender Soc.* 19:44–65

HUNT LL. 1998. The spirit of Hispanic Protestantism in the United States: national survey comparisons of Catholics and non-Catholics. *Soc. Sci. Q.* 79:828–45

HURH WM, KIM KC. 1990. Religious participation of Korean immigrants in the United States. *J. Sci. Study Relig.* 29:19–34

IWAMURA JN, Spickard P, eds. 2003. *Revealing the Sacred in Asian and Pacific America.* New York: Routledge

JANOWITZ M, ed. 1966. *W.I. Thomas on Social Organization and Social Personality: Selected Papers.* Chicago: Univ. Chicago Press

JASSO G, MASSEY DS, ROSENZWEIG MR, SMITH JP. 2000. The New Immigrants Survey Pilot (NIS-P):overview and new findings about U.S. legal immigrants at admission. *Demography"* 37:127–38

JASSO G, MASSEY DS, ROSENZWEIG MR, SMITH JP. 2003. Exploring the religious preferences of recent immigrants to the United States: evidence from the New Immigrant Survey Pilot. See Haddad et al. 2003, pp. 217–53

JEUNG R. 2004. Creating an Asian American Christian subculture: Grace Community Covenant Church. See Carnes & Yang 2004, pp. 287–312

JEUNG R. 2005. *Faithful Generations: Race and New Asian American Churches.* New Brunswick/London: Rutgers Univ. Press

KANDULA N, KERSEY M, LURIE N. 2004. Assuring the health of immigrants: what the leading health indicators tell us. *Annu. Rev. Public Health* 25:357–76

KIM KC, KIM S. 2001. Ethnic roles of Korean immigrant churches in the United States. See Kwon et al. 2001, pp. 71–94

KLINEBERG SL. 2004. Religious diversity and social integration among Asian Americans in Houston. See Carnes & Yang 2004, pp. 247–62

KURIEN P. 1998. Becoming American by becoming Hindu: Indian Americans take their place at the multicultural table. See Warner & Wittner 1998, pp. 37–70

KURIEN P. 2001. Religion, ethnicity, and politics: Hindu and Muslim Indian immigrants in the United States. *Ethn. Racial Stud.* 24:263–93

KURIEN P. 2003. To be or not to be South Asian: contemporary Indian American politics. *J. Asian Am. Stud.* 6:261–88

KURIEN P. 2004. Christian by birth or rebirth? Generation and difference in an Indian American Christian church. See Carnes & Yang 2004, pp. 160–81

KURIEN P. 2005. Being young, brown, and Hindu: the identity struggles of second generation Indian Americans. *J. Contemp. Ethnogr.* 34:434–69

KWON HY, KIM KC, WARNER RS, eds. 2001. *Korean Americans and Their Religions: Pilgrims and Missionaries from a Different Shore.* University Park: Penn. State Univ. Press

KWON VH, EBAUGH HR, HAGAN J. 1997. The structure and functions of cell group ministry in a Korean Christian church. *J. Sci. Study Relig.* 36:247–56

LAWSON R. 1998. From American church to immigrant church: the changing face of Seventh-Day Adventism in metropolitan New York. *Sociol. Relig.* 59:329–51

LAWSON R. 1999. When immigrants take over: the impact of immigrant growth on American Seventh-Day Adventism's trajectory from sect to denomination. *J. Sci. Study Relig.* 38:83–102

LEAL DL, BARRETO MA, LEE J, DE LA GARZA R. 2005. The Latino vote in the 2004 election. *PS: Polit. Sci. Polit.* 38:41–49

LEE J, BEAN FD. 2004. America's changing color lines: immigration, race/ethnicity, and multiracial identification. *Annu. Rev. Sociol.* 30:221–42

LEONARD K, STEPICK A, VASQUEZ M, HOLDAWAY J, eds. 2005. *Immigrant Faiths: Transforming Religious Life in America.* Walnut Creek, CA: AltaMira

LEVITT P. 2002. Two nations under God? Latino religious life in the U.S. In *Latinos: Remaking America*, ed. MM Suárez-Orozco, MM Páez, pp. 150–64. Berkeley: Univ. Calif. Press

LEVITT P. 2005. Immigration. In *Handbook of Religion and Social Institutions*, ed. HR Ebaugh, pp. 391–410. New York: Springer

LIEN P. 2004. Religion and political adaptation among Asian Americans: an empirical assessment from the Pilot National Asian American Political Survey. See Carnes & Yang 2004, pp. 263–84

MALONE N, BALUJA KF, COSTANZO JM, DAVIS CJ. 2003. *The Foreign-Born Population: 2000. Census 2000 Brief.* Washington, DC: US Census Bur.

MENJÍVAR C. 2001. LATINO immigrants and their perceptions of religious institutions: Cubans, Salvadorans, and Guatemalans in Phoenix, Arizona. *Migr. Int.* 1:65–88

MENJÍVAR C. 2003. Religion and immigration in comparative perspective: Catholic and evangelical Salvadorans in San Francisco, Washington D.C., and Phoenix. *Sociol. Relig.* 64:21–45

MILLER DE, MILLER J, DYRNESS G. 2001. *Immigrant Religion in the City of Angels.* Los Angeles: Cent. Relig. Civic Cult., Univ. South. Calif.

MIN PG. 1992. The structure and social functions of Korean immigrant churches in the United States. *Int. Migr. Rev.* 26:1370–94

MIN PG. 2003. Immigrants' religion and ethnicity: a comparison of Korean Christian and Indian Hindu immigrants. See Iwamura & Spickard 2003, pp. 125–42

MIN PG. 2005. Religion and the maintenance of ethnicity among immigrants: a comparison of Indian Hindus and Korean Protestants. See Leonard et al. 2005, pp. 99–122

MIN PG, KIM DY. 2005. Intergenerational transmission of religion and culture: Korean Protestants in the U.S. *Sociol. Relig.* 66:263–82

MIN PG, KIM JH, eds. 2002. *Religions in Asian America: Building Faith Communities.* New York: AltaMira

MOONEY M. 2006. The Catholic Bishops Conferences of the United States and France: engaging immigration as a public issue. *Am. Behav. Sci.* 49:1455–70

MULLINS MR. 1987. The life-cycle of ethnic churches in sociological perspective. *Jpn. J. Relig. Stud.* 14:321–34

NAWYN SJ. 2006. Faith, ethnicity, and culture in refugee resettlement. *Am. Behav. Sci.* 49:1509–27

NG KH. 2002. Seeking the Christian tutelage: agency and culture in Chinese immigrants' conversion to Christianity. *Sociol. Relig.* 63:195–214

NUMRICH PD. 1996. *Old Wisdom in the New World: Americanization in Two Immigrant Theravada Buddhist Temples.* Knoxville: Univ. Tenn. Press

NUMRICH, P.D. 2005. Complementary and alternative medicine in America's 'two Buddhisms.' See Barnes and Sered 2005, pp. 343-58.

ONG A. 1995. Making the biopolitical subject: Cambodian immigrants, refugee medicine and cultural citizenship in California. *Soc. Sci. Med.* 40:1243–57

ORSI R. 1996. *Thank You, St. Jude: Women's Devotion to the Patron Saint of Hopeless Causes.* New Haven, CT: Yale Univ. Press

PARK S. 2001. The intersection of religion, race, gender, and ethnicity in the identity formation of Korean American evangelical women. See Kwon et al. 2001, pp. 193–207

PEÑA M, FREHILL LM. 1998. Latina religious practice: analyzing cultural dimensions in measures of religiosity. *J. Sci. Study Relig.* 37:620–35

PORTES A, RUMBAUT R. 2001. *Legacies: The Story of the Immigrant Second Generation.* Berkeley: Univ. Calif. Press

RAJAGOPAL A. 2000. Hindu Nationalism in the US: changing configurations of political practice. *Ethn. Racial Stud.* 23:467–96

RUSSO NJ. 1969. Three generations of Italians in New York: their religious acculturation. *Int. Migr. Rev.* 3:3–17

SHIN EH, PARK H. 1988. An analysis of causes of schisms in ethnic churches: the case of Korean-American churches. *Sociol. Anal.* 49:234–48

SMITH C. 1998. *American Evangelicalism: Embattled and Thriving.* Chicago: Univ. Chicago Press

SMITH E, BENDER C. 2004. The creation of urban niche religion: South Asian taxi drivers in New York City. See Carnes & Yang 2004, pp. 76–97

SMITH TW, KIM S. 2005. The vanishing Protestant majority. *J. Sci. Study Relig.* 44:211–23

SOLBERG RW. 1992. *Open Doors: The Story of Lutherans Resettling Refugees.* St. Louis: Concordia

STEVENS WD. 2004. Spreading the word: religious beliefs and the evolution of immigrant congregations. *Sociol. Relig.* 65:121–38

SUH SA. 2003. 'To be Buddhist is to be Korean': the rhetorical use of authenticity and the homeland in the construction of post-immigration identities. See Iwamura & Spickard 2003, pp. 177–92

TWEED T. 1997. *Our Lady of the Exile: Diasporic Religion at a Cuban Catholic Shrine in Miami.* New York: Oxford Univ. Press

WARNER RS. 1993. Work in progress toward a new paradigm for the sociological study of religion in the United States. *Am. J. Sociol.* 98:1044–93

WARNER RS. 1998. Approaching religious diversity: barriers, byways, and beginnings. *Sociol. Relig.* 59:193–215

WARNER RS. 2000. Religion and new (post-1965) immigrants: some principles drawn from field research. *Am. Stud.* 41:267–86

WARNER RS, WITTNER JG, eds. 1998. *Gatherings in Diaspora: Religious Communities and the New Immigration.* Philadelphia: Temple Univ. Press

WUTHNOW R. 1999. Mobilizing civic engagement: the changing impact of religious involvement. In *Civic Engagement in American Democracy*, ed. T Skocpol, MP Fiorina, pp. 331–64. Washington, DC: Brookings Inst. Press

YANG F. 1998. Tenacious unity in a contentious community: cultural and religious dynamics in a Chinese Christian church. See Warner & Wittner 1998, pp. 333–64

YANG F. 1999a. ABC and XYZ: religious, ethnic, and racial identities of the new second generation Chinese in Christian churches. *Amerasia J.* 25:89–114

YANG F. 1999b. *Chinese Christians in America: Conversion, Assimilation, and Adhesive Identities*. University Park: Penn. State Univ. Press

YANG F. 2000a. Chinese Gospel Church: the Sinicization of Christianity. See Ebaugh & Chafetz 2000b, pp. 89–107

YANG F. 2000b. The Hsi-Nan Chinese Buddhist Temple: seeking to Americanize. See Ebaugh & Chafetz 2000b, pp. 67–87

YANG F. 2004. Gender and generation in a Chinese Christian church. See Carnes & Yang 2004, pp. 205–22

YANG F, EBAUGH HR. 2001b. Transformations in new immigrant religions and their global implications. *Am. Sociol. Rev.* 66:269–88

YOO D. 1996. For those who have eyes to see: religious sightings in Asian America. *Amerasia J.* 22:xiii-ii

ZHOU M, BANKSTON CL, KIM R. 2002. Rebuilding spiritual lives in the new land: religious practices among Southeast Asian refugees in the United States. See Min & Kim 2002, pp. 37–70

Reading 9

The Religious Varieties of Ethnic Presence: A Comparison between a Taiwanese Immigrant Buddhist Temple and an Evangelical Christian Church

CAROLYN CHEN

Dr. Chen zeros in on two Taiwanese congregations—one a Buddhist temple and the other an evangelical Christian church. Her intent is to study how, within the same ethnic group, religion makes a difference. In this case she is attempting to understand the paradox she finds: the Buddhist temple (a minority religion in the United States) actually is more publicly engaged with American society than is the evangelical Christian church (a majority religion in the United States). To find out why, she spent over a year attending these congregations' functions and interviewed over fifty people. So, what is the answer to the paradox?

It was the second day of the new millennium, Sunday, January 2, 2000. To inaugurate the beginning of the twenty-first century, Dharma Light Temple,[1] a Chinese Buddhist temple, hosted a "World Peace Day," inviting groups from different religious faiths in the community to share in a ceremony of prayer and blessing. Following the opening welcome delivered by the abbess in Mandarin and translated into English, the American national anthem was played, and the American flag was ceremoniously presented by six Taiwanese men in dark suits and white gloves, and, with proper protocol, raised up the flagpole. With their hands upon their hearts and their amber robes flapping in the wind, three rows of Buddhist monks rose to sing the American national anthem.

---

[1]Pseudonyms have been given to protect the identity of the institutions and individuals referred to in this article.

Source: Carolyn Chen, "The Religious Varieties of Ethnic Presence: A Comparison between a Taiwanese Immigrant Buddhist Temple and an Evangelical Christian Church." Reprinted with permission, from *Sociology of Religion*, Volume 63, © 2002.

The crowd, mostly Taiwanese devotees, followed along, humming with the melody, not quite certain of the lyrics. Peppered among the crowd were whites, Latinos, blacks, and other Asians, who had been invited from the local community to come to celebrate and pray for world peace. Facing the crowd on a raised platform were the distinguished guests, religious leaders who represented the diverse religious and racial mosaic of the local community: a white B'ahái minister, a Chinese Roman Catholic priest, an Indian Hindu priest, a Japanese Buddhist Church of America bishop, an African American Methodist Episcopal minister, and a Chinese Mormon minister, as well as a Latino schoolboard representative and a white judge. It appeared as if they had covered all possible ethnicities and religions—except for one. Curiously missing were any representatives from one of the largest religious groups in the Taiwanese community, the evangelical Christians.

Less than five miles away from the Dharma Light temple, Grace Taiwanese Church, another Taiwanese immigrant religious group, was in the midst of its first Sunday service of the twenty-first century. The pastor, a tall man dressed in a blue power suit, spoke forcefully from the pulpit about Grace's vision for the new millennium. "Press towards the goal," he urged the congregation, quoting a famous passage from the apostle Paul. "By the year 2010 we aspire for Grace Taiwanese Church to have planted fifty churches around the world." He proceeded to outline how church members would participate in this growth through the "1-2-1" plan—each church member was to bring at least two new people into the church in the year 2000. Banners boldly displaying "press towards the goal" in English and Chinese streamed above the entrances to the

sanctuary. The congregation, ranging from teenagers to senior citizens, carefully listened. Some took sermon notes. Others nodded their heads in agreement. Later in the closing prayer the pastor prayed that the church might bring Christ to the local community and that through them others might experience Jesus' salvation, especially given the presence of the Dharma Light temple in such close vicinity. He reminded them of the Great Commission in Acts 1:8[2] where Jesus commanded his disciples to spread the Gospel to the ends of the earth. As twenty-first century disciples they were likewise called to participate in the mission to spread the Gospel around the world. The congregation, however, was homogeneously Taiwanese.

These scenarios shed light on some of the ways that new immigrant religious institutions publicly engage in American society. Dharma Light Temple and Grace Taiwanese Church are both religious institutions serving a predominantly Taiwanese immigrant population in Southern California and both belong to world religions which claim to transcend racial and ethnic boundaries. On the face of it, one might expect that of the two, Grace Taiwanese Church would have greater interactions with those outside of their own immigrant religious community. After all, as Protestant Christians, they are not only "inner-worldly," but also more easily assimilated into the wider American society than Buddhists. Instead, the "other-worldly" Buddhists, whom one would expect to be publicly disengaged and religiously not easily assimilated, extend themselves out to mainstream American society.[3]

---

[2]But you will receive power when the Holy Spirit comes upon you and you shall be witnesses to Me in Jerusalem, and in all Judea and Smaria, and to the end of the earth."

[3]In his essay, "The social psychology of world religions" (1946a). Weber categorized Protestant sects as *inner-worldly,* referring to their tendency to be oriented towards the world in "rationalizing the world ethically in accordance with God's commandments" (291). In contrast, he categorized Buddhists as *other worldly*: "On the other hand, the Buddhist monk was also active, but his activities were withdrawn from any consistent rationalization in this world; his question for salvation was ultimately oriented to the flight from the 'wheel' of the rebirths" (292).

This seeming paradox touches upon a question that is critical to scholars of religion, ethnicity, and migration alike: How do minority groups interact with the larger society? In this case we consider institutions that are guided by distinct religious ideals, Dharma Light Temple and Grace Taiwanese Church, which undoubtedly have different types of interactions with American society. Religions provide unique "maps" of the way the world ought to be and inspire believers to make these ideals a reality. As ethnic immigrants, their interactions with American society are influenced not only by their own limited linguistic and social skills, but also by socially imposed constraints, particularly symbolic constructions of difference and foreignness. As immigrant Taiwanese, both religious communities are deemed racially "other." However, while the Christians are religiously similar to mainstream America, Buddhists are considered foreigners by virtue of both race and religion. By comparing two Taiwanese immigrant religious institutions—an evangelical Christian church and a Buddhist temple—this article demonstrates not only how particular religious ideals guide public engagement, but also how discourses of religious and racial difference shape an immigrant religious institution's interactions with the wider society.

RELIGIOUS INSTITUTIONS AND THE NEW POST-1965 IMMIGRATION

With an increasing number of non-European immigrants since the liberalization of immigration laws in 1965, a growing body of scholarly attention has been given to the religion of these new immigrants (e.g. Warner and Wittner 1998; Yang 1999; Hurh and Kim 1990; Fenton 1988; Min 1992; Christiano

1991). The focus of much of the literature on new immigrant religion, however, has been on the happenings within the religious institution, and little attention has been given to their public presence and relationship to those outside their institutional walls. For example, it has been well-documented that beyond being merely a religious and spiritual resource, immigrant religious institutions often offer a wide array of formal and informal social services facilitating the material, social and psychological adjustment of their members to the United States (Haddad and Lummis 1987; Hurh and Kim 1990; Kashima 1977; Warner and Wittner 1998; Kurien 1998; Leon 1998; Ebaugh and Chafetz 2000).

Much of the literature also speaks to the theme of the immigrant religious institution as an ethnic fortress where immigrants can communally practice, preserve, and pass down their ethnic traditions (Lin 1996; Smith 1978; Kim 1981; Yang 1999; Hurh and Kim 1990; Min 1992; Williams 1988). Pervasive in all this literature is the recognition that immigrant religious institutions undergo changes and develop new congregational forms as they adapt towards American religious life (Warner and Wittner 1998; Kurien 1998; Numrich 1996; Williams 1988; Abusharaf 1998). As Eastern religions have grown increasingly popular in the United States, some non-Christian immigrant religious institutions have moved to make themselves more accessible to those outside of the ethnic community by, for example, using English (Numrich 1996; Chandler 1998; Yang and Ebaugh 2000; Lin 1996). This literature describes shifts within the institutional walls, such as the development of professionalized clergy, Sunday Schools, and weekly meetings, as "natural" adaptive responses to the American environment, rather than analyzing how these immigrant religions connect to the larger society.[4]

This lacuna in the literature misses two important aspects of new immigrant religious institutions that my study brings to light. The first is a consideration of how the unique characteristics of post-1965 immigrants, as well as the contemporary racial climate of multiculturalism, shapes the public interactions of immigrant religious congregations. Reflected in much of the pre-1965 immigrant religion literature is the model of the immigrant church as a withdrawn, sheltered enclave that is disengaged from mainstream American society (Handlin 1952; Herberg 1960).[5] Not only did pre-1965 immigrants lack the material resources and cultural know-how to participate in mainstream American society, they were further beset by rampant racism and xenophobia. While this characterization may be appropriate for the historically-specific, class-bound experiences of most immigrants in pre-1965 America, they do not capture the diversity of experiences of post-1965 immigrants, especially those of the new highly skilled and professional class of immigrants largely from Asia (Ong and Azores 1994; Liu and Cheng,

1994; Fong 1994; Mangiafico 1988; Wong 1987; Zhou 1992; Kim 1981; Hurh and Kim 1984; Min 1996).[6] No longer residing in urban ethnic ghettos, these new immigrants settle in affluent suburbs and come prepared with higher levels of education, income and [English] skills to make the speedy climb up the American ladder of mobility (Fong 1994; Yang 1999; Chen 1992; Ong and Azores 1994).[7]

Hardly shying away from the American political arena, the new immigrants have also proven themselves to be visibly active in the political system (Saito 1998; Wong 1987).[8] Not only distinct class-wise and educationally from earlier immigrant cohorts, they arrive at a period in America where the racial-ethnic ideal of multiculturalism, rather than the "melting pot," reigns supreme (Glazer and Moynihan 1963; Hollinger

---

[4]Interpreting "congregationalism" as a natural adaptive process masks the manner in which power imposed from outside the congregation plays into internal congregational decision-making. Here I am referring to power in a Foucauldian and Granscian sense—the assumptions of power that are embedded in our everyday cultural norms and ways of knowing and being. What may be interpreted as natural processes of assimilation from the outside are regarded as strategic responses from the inside to allay the suspicions of Anglo-Americans of immigrant foreignness and difference. For example, the Japanese-American Buddhist Church of America adopted Protestant forms of worship such as meeting on Sundays, using pews, and having Sunday School to downplay the American perception that they were different and "dangerous" (Kashima 1977; Horinouchi 1973).

[5]In this same defensive posture, immigrant religious institutions frequently sponsored schools for the children of immigrants in hopes of curbing the second-generation's exposure to a godless and foreign America (Ernst 1979; Pozzetta 1991).

[6]Clearly not all Asian immigrants are professional and educated. There are an equally representative proportion of Asian immigrants who are unskilled and semi-skilled as well (Liu and Cheng 1994). While the Asian professional and educated class possess the skills for upward mobility, their incomes and professional status are still not commensurate with equally educated Anglos (Barringer, Takeuchi, and Xenos 1990; Der 1993; Chan 1991; Tuan 1998).

[7]John M. Liu and Lucie Cheng (1994) make the argument that to protect its interests and to prevent the Soviet Union from gaining the upper hand, the United States invested a great deal in the educational, economic and political infrastructures of post-W.W.II Asia. One of the consequences of this is the rise of a professional middle-class who would become the source of skilled and talented immigration to the United States after the liberalization of immigration policies in 1965 (See Committee on the International Migration of Talent 1970; Li 1988; Melendy 1981).

[8]In fact, the political participation of Asians is perceived by some to be "too active," as the recent [indictment] of Chinese immigrants Maria Hsia and John Huang in the Democratic campaign finance scandal may suggest. At the Senate Committee's hearings on Al Gore's infamous fund raising scandal at Hsi Lai Temple, Senator Fred Thompson, chairman of the Senate Panel, told nuns "You are a little more sophisticated than what we might have thought, or else you had some help," suggesting that perhaps as monastics and immigrants the Buddhist nuns should be ignorant about how the American political system really operates.

1995). Furthermore, achievements of the Civil Rights movement have inspired immigrants to mobilize around their collective interests and identity (Espritu 1992). Without neglecting the continuing persistence of racism that immigrants face in American society, it must also be recognized that the climate of multiculturalism minimizes some of the obstacles that difference—racial, ethnic and religious—present to participation in mainstream America, while perhaps simultaneously presenting different obstacles.[9] Specifically regarding the case of post-1965 skilled Asian immigrants, their class and educational advantages, along with the current multicultural climate of the United States, undoubtedly challenge some of the assumptions of immigrant life based upon immigration of a different historical era. Do their religious institutions continue to play the role of the protective ethnic sanctuary disengaged from the concerns of those outside? Or do they make efforts to reach out?

The second issue to which this paper draws attention is how religious ideals shape the public mission of an immigrant religious institution. Like other associations and institutions within the immigrant community, the religious organization provides a space for communal solidarity through the sharing of resources, symbols and traditions. What differentiates religious institutions from other immigrant institutions is that they consider themselves to be the living embodiment of universal and timeless truths. They are, to use Robert Wuthnow's term, the "public expression of the sacred" (1994). As such, they carry a certain weight, a gravity of responsibility, that transcends the concerns of their own congregation and extends into visions of how the world ought to be. How these ideas become publicly manifest is as much a theological question as it is a social question.

Sociological literature has addressed how religious ideals inform a congregation's public presence (Troeltsh 1951; Weber 1946b; Niebuhr 1951; Niebuhr 1929; Wilson 1970; Roozen, McKinney, and Carroll 1988; Wuthnow 1994; Ammerman 1999; Warner 1988). From these a number of competing typologies have been constructed to categorize the different types of communal engagement a congregation might have in the larger society. In addition to theological message, varying factors have been cited as critical determinants, for example, geographic locale, socio-economic class of members, congregational size, authority structure and human and material resources.

For the most part, these congregational typologies have been based upon cases that are both Christian and Anglo-American. Where post-1965 immigrant religious congregations are not Anglo and often not Christian, I argue that these determining factors only partially shed light on the issue.[10] Overlooking these salient characteristics of new immigrant congregations neglects the way

---

[9]Multiculturalism still has not prevented the rise of anti-immigrant sentiment in places like California. For example, campaigns for California propositions that have been detrimental to the welfare of its immigrants simultaneously appeal rhetorically to ideals of pluralism and multiculturalism. No doubt multiculturalism has increased the level of tolerance for difference in our public institutions. On the other hand, the very ubiquity of its presence is evidenced in the multiple ways that it has been reappropriated, even to the disadvantage of those whom it claims to "celebrate." The argument might even be made that the focus on the cultural aspects of difference only diverts attention from the truly subversive issue of material inequiries that continue to persist among different racial groups.

[10]Some scholars argue that the experience of Asian and other non-Anglo immigrants does not fit into the assimilation model of white ethnic immigrants because of the racial factor. Where white ethnics eventually could integrate, non-white immigrants became racialized into an "other" category. Despite the fact that some Asians have achieved middle-class suburban aspirations, scholars argue that Asians will be unable to shed their status "foreigners" in the United States (Tuan 1998; Lowe 1996; Kitano and Daniels 1985).

that difference, whether it be religious and/or racial, will mediate the sort of presence the religious institution will have in society. Religious institutions operate in a dynamic environment whereby they are responding to a larger social context. Regardless of the intentions of a religious institution, the opportunity to enact these religious ideals in the wider society will depend on the degree of access the public grants them. . . .

Using the case studies of two Taiwanese immigrant religious institutions, I will address how religious and social factors shape the public engagement of immigrant religious institutions both inside and outside of the ethnic immigrant community. I suggest that two simultaneous internal and external dynamics influence how an immigrant religious institution interacts with the wider society. First, building upon the sociological literature on congregations, I examine the factors that are internal to the religious institutions: their theological visions and the cultural transferability of the strategies they employ to carry their respective religious missions out into society. Second, I consider the external forces of surrounding racial and religious discourses, specifically the rhetoric of multiculturalism, and how this opens and constrains possibilities for engagement in mainstream society.

METHODS AND SETTING

The data consists of ethnographic fieldwork conducted at Dharma Light Temple and Grace Taiwanese Church between January 1999 and March 2000. Fieldnotes based on participant-observation at church and temple activities were recorded.[12] Furthermore, I conducted fifty-five in-depth interviews with immigrants from both

. . .

[12]At the temple this included volunteer activities, retreats, summer camp, religious ceremonies, religious education classes, and suna study meetings. At the church this included Sunday services, Sunday school, Bible study meetings, weekly visitations, retreats and summer camp.

Dharma Light and Grace. Respondents were recruited through snowball sampling. Interviews were also conducted with religious and lay leaders from both communities. Mandarin, Taiwanese and English were used in the interviews.

Dharma Light and Grace Church are located in suburban Southern California, an area that has had a high influx of immigration from Taiwan in the 1980s and early 1990s. For example, approximately 20 percent of immigrants from Taiwan to the United States have settled in greater Los Angeles county (Gall and Gall 1991). In highly impacted areas of Los Angeles, ethnic Chinese (primarily from Taiwan, Hong Kong and China) can comprise anywhere from 25 percent to 50 percent of the population (Ong and Azores 1994).

Owing to the generous financial donations of their members and forward-looking leadership of their clergy, Dharma Light and Grace Taiwanese Church have been able to command a significant presence in the Southern California Taiwanese community. Both Dharma Light and Grace are branch locations belonging to larger organizations that have churches and temples located throughout the world and serve a predominantly ethnic Chinese diasporic community, the majority from Taiwan. Both local religious congregations have been in existence for a little over ten years, although their larger institutional affiliations have existed in Southern California for over two decades.

Reflecting the socio-economic status of the Taiwanese immigrant community, members of Dharma Light and Grace Taiwanese Church are similar in length of residency and social class. The men are mostly well-educated and hold at least Bachelor's, if not advanced, degrees. . . . A significant minority of the men are skilled professionals who are concentrated in the science, technology and medical industries and work predominantly outside of the ethnic community. Some, however, have experienced professional downward mobility in the process of immigration and have opted to run small businesses in the ethnic community. Immigrant women predominantly help in the family business or are full-time homemakers. A very small minority work outside the ethnic community. Most immigrants have been in the United States for at least ten years, although some, those with more advanced degrees, have been in the United States for twenty years or more. As a whole, Grace members are slightly more educated and have resided in the United States longer than devotees at Dharma Light.

Most immigrants from Taiwan come to America with a weak, if any, sense of religious commitment. While popular religion in Taiwan is a mix of Buddhism, Taoism, and folk religion, it is often deemed superstitious and is not seriously practiced by most immigrants, who tend to come from urban areas. Christians in Taiwan now comprise a mere 2 percent, a figure which is declining, but scholars and religious leaders estimate that 24 percent to 32 percent of the Taiwanese immigrant population in the United States are Christian (Chen 1992; Chao 1995; Dart 1997). Reflecting this difference is the high proportion of Grace members who are converts. About 60 percent of Grace members converted to Christianity in the United States.[13] Similarly, at Dharma Light Temple, approximately the same proportion of the devotees claim to have become "practicing Buddhists" after immigrating to the United States.[14] Both religious communities have a

high proportion of first-generation Christians and Buddhists, respectively.

GRACE TAIWANESE CHURCH: SAVING THE WORLD THROUGH EVANGELISM

Theological Orientation: A Mission to Evangelize

Hanging on the church office wall is a map of the world, titled "Status of Global Evangelization," where different regions of the world are color-coded according to the percentage of the population that is Christian. The map is a visible reminder to those at Grace Taiwanese Church of the areas in the world that are still in need of hearing the gospel. Grace flexes its evangelical muscle through an aggressive [proselytizing] campaign that has resulted in the planting of over forty Grace Taiwanese Church branches in the United States and abroad in its nearly thirty-year existence.

Like other evangelical congregations in the United States, Grace's evangelical orientation is theologically rooted in Jesus Christ's command for the "Great Commission," calling Christians to spread the Gospel "to the end of the earth" (Roozen et al. 1988; Hunter 1983; Smith 1998). Christians have a duty to proselytize as salvation is offered by God only to those who accept Jesus Christ as their personal lord and savior. Through [proselytization], evangelicals bring salvation to the world. . . .

While Jesus Christ's words are certainly to be universally applied, Grace Taiwanese Church practices a selective evangelism as it sees its special mission to evangelize to the Taiwanese and Mandarin-speaking population of the world. And judging from numbers, it seems that Grace Taiwanese Church and other like-minded evangelical Christian organizations have been quite successful in this mission.

---

[13]This figure is based upon the estimates of Grace Taiwanese Church pastors and church leaders.

[14]This figure is based upon my own observations and the estimates of Dharma Light leaders.

Institutionalizing a Strategy of Personal Evangelism

In its public mission to evangelize, Grace's most important resource is its members, who do the evangelizing. Like other religious groups who successfully recruit new members (Stark and Bainbridge 1980; Bainbridge and Stark 1981), the key to Grace Taiwanese Church's evangelization strategy is personal networks and friendships. The "1-2-1" strategy mentioned in the introduction to this piece not only indicates that each person should bring two new people to Grace, but that effective evangelism is based on personal "one to one" relationships. In this environment, evangelization becomes expected, as is evidenced in one respondent's remarks:

You also have to understand that the Buddhists don't evangelize like we Christians. They talk about having a good heart and doing good deeds. That's it. I feel like they provide good guidelines for living like don't do things that hurt others, be a good person. That's it. It's not like Christianity where we are supposed to be good people already, and on top of that share the good news.

All of the Christian respondents that I interviewed told me that they converted to Christianity because they were initially introduced to Grace through friends. Visitors are often encouraged to attend Friday night small-group Bible study meetings or other church social events rather than the Sunday service. These smaller, more intimate, settings are conducive towards meeting others and developing friendships. To attract non-Christians, Grace will frequently sponsor lectures dealing with practical life issues that are of interest to the general population, rather than explicitly religious issues. Popular lectures often feature a professional psychologist who speaks on issues such as dealing with relationships between husband and wife, or parent and child.[15]

Furthermore, Grace Taiwanese Church employs social activities such as ski trips and camping as opportunities to attract non-Christians and share the Gospel with them. Many of the respondents commented that while they initially may not have been interested in Christianity, they continued coming to Grace Taiwanese Church because of the friendly persistence of the members. This was the case even among those respondents who were also at the time regularly attending a Buddhist temple. In contrast, those who were attending a Buddhist temple said that no one there made efforts to reach out to them and that they made very few friends there.

Grace uses several strategies to institutionalize evangelism. At baptism individuals are asked not only if they believe the central tenets of the Christian faith, but also to promise to share their faith with those who are not yet Christian. Pastors and lay leaders are constantly urging church members to bring more friends and create goal-oriented slogans such as "1-2-1" to remind the congregation of the larger Grace Taiwanese Church vision. Another common technique is to have members make commitments or vows to evangelize to a certain number of people or to a certain group within a specified time period. In so doing, Grace cultivates in its members the expectation and obligation to evangelize.

To incorporate new membership, the congregation has a "welcome group" or "caring group" which is in charge of welcoming and "following up" on newcomers. One of the church leaders told me the following about welcoming procedures:

There's a caring group and there's a caring group leader. We have people assigned to care for that person. Of course when we assign we try not to make the person feel like it's just a formality. That person will call the newcomer. We try to make friends with that person. That's the right intention to have when you try to care for somebody ... everybody has to be in a caring group at some point and you take turns.

---

[15]James Davison Hunter (1982, 1983, 1991) has pointed out that this concern for issues dealing with psychology and family is shared among many American conservative Christians.

During services, Grace creates opportunities for conversion through altar calls, which immediately follow the sermon. In my observations at the church, there was never an altar call that went unheeded. When someone comes forward for the altar call, they are always accompanied by friends or "welcome group members" who kneel with them on the floor and pray with them. Those in the welcome group are trained especially to minister to new converts by leading them through the "Sinner's Prayer"[16] and praying for them. New converts learn about the Christian faith through a special class that leads them towards baptism. Those who eventually become baptized are required to give a public testimony. In this environment conversion becomes expected and regular rather than extraordinary—so much so that the testimonies and baptism have become too time consuming in regular Sunday services and have been moved to a separate afternoon service that happens a few times a year.

Consequences of Evangelistic Theology and Strategy

Grace is highly visible in the ethnic community but has very limited interactions with those outside. Two important internal factors shape its public engagement. The first is its evangelical theological orientation which prioritizes public engagement through evangelization. The second is its resources and strategies for outreach. While Grace does not have an explicit agenda of racial or ethnic exclusion, its strategies for evangelism have had ethnic and racial consequences and have

limited its interactions with those outside of the Chinese-speaking community. First, the personal evangelism strategy tends to limit outreach to members' personal networks. As Taiwanese immigrants in a heavily populated Taiwanese immigrant locale, most of their friends are Taiwanese like themselves. This leads to the reproduction of the existing ethnic and class proportions of the church. Second, as immigrants, many do not possess the linguistic or social skills to reach out to the non-Taiwanese or Mandarin speaking. The personal evangelism model is based on first developing a friendship and then leading the person to Christ. Lacking in cultural transferability, this strategy limits engagement to that population whom members have the social and linguistic skills to befriend.[17] Even among those who speak fluent English, there always remains a sense of cultural disconnection between themselves and non-Chinese that prevents them from developing relationships beyond the acquaintance level. In this sense, Grace's most valuable resource for outreach, its members, is simultaneously an obstacle that hinders it from outreach beyond the ethnic immigrant community.

Logically they limit their evangelism to those who can fit into their community—those who are ethnic-linguistically similar. When asked whether the church should open itself up to those of different ethnic groups, the respondents uniformly replied that while this might be possible with the English-speaking second-generation congregation, this would certainly be impossible and even unnecessary with the immigrant congregation. They reasoned that it was not a matter of active exclusion, but that since they had defined themselves as a Taiwanese and Mandarin speaking community it was impossible to accommodate to other linguistic groups. A typical response is as follows:

---

[16]The Sinner's Prayer is as follows: Dear God, I confess that I am a sinner and I am sorry for all the wrongs that I have done. I believe that your Son, Jesus Christ, died on the cross for my sins. Please forgive me and I invite you, Jesus, to come into my heart and life as Lord and Savior. I commit and trust my life to you. Thank you for dying for my sins, for your free pardon, for your gift of eternal life, and for hearing and answering my prayer. Amen.

[17]Daniel V. A. Olson (1989) comes to a similar conclusion that the same forces which may create a tightly knit congregation can limit its potential for growth in membership.

It doesn't matter what race you are. If you understand Taiwanese or Mandarin you're welcome. It's not like we can say, 'oh you're from Hong Kong, we have to speak Cantonese for you, or you're Mexican and we have to speak Spanish.' We can't accommodate to all of them. So it's not that we don't welcome them, it's just if they can understand our language they are welcome to come.

To conduct outreach only to a Taiwanese and Mandarin-speaking population does not contradict the universal injunction of Jesus Christ to evangelize to the world. In fact they are being most faithful to this call by strategically evangelizing those with whom they can most effectively share the Gospel. Ironically, the combination of evangelical mission and linguistically-specific outreach strategies make Grace highly active in the ethnic community. However, these same factors limit it from extending its religious mission to mainstream America.

DHARMA LIGHT TEMPLE: CHARITABLE ENGAGEMENT

Theological Orientation: A Mission of Charity

Despite Weber's categorization of Buddhism as "other-worldly" and withdrawn from the affairs of the world, Dharma Light practices a particular brand of "inner-worldly" Buddhism that it calls "Involved Buddhism," a Buddhism that is highly involved in the human world. Involved Buddhism is the outgrowth of a larger reform movement in Chinese Mahayana Buddhism that was started in China fifty years ago by the monk Venerable Taixu. Where Buddhism in Taiwan was traditionally perceived by the public as superstitious and primarily a medium for praying for the dead, Involved Buddhism is oriented towards individual practice through daily living. Instead of "escaping the world" as Weber claims (1946a: 291), Involved Buddhism teaches

that one truly practices Buddhism by living fully in this world.[18] This is evidenced in a saying from Venerable Taixu, "When you become fully human, you will become a Buddha. That is the living meaning of truth."[19]

Underlying the Buddhist practice of charity is a radically different understanding of "salvation" than evangelical Christianity. Buddhists believe that beings operate in a continual cycle of rebirth whereby one's karma, the culmination of one's actions and deeds, determines the form of one's future life. Salvation for the Buddhist is attaining nirvana, or freedom from the karmic cycle of rebirth altogether. In the state of nirvana one is finally liberated from the illusions of the self and its attachments to this world, which are the ultimate causes of suffering. One works towards attaining nirvana by re-orienting one's thoughts and actions. Through practices of meditation and chanting one learns to empty the mind of illusory thoughts. Through acts of self-giving or charity, one loses the illusion of the separateness of the self.

For those who do not see attaining nirvana in this life as a reality, the more immediate goal is to at least secure rebirth into a higher realm of being. By doing good, one cultivates merit and works towards the assurance of rebirth into a higher realm. By doing bad things in this life one will earn rebirth into a lower realm. One can also accumulate merit through participation in Buddhist rituals and

---

[18]Involved Buddhism's "inner-worldly" orientation is not unique to only Chinese Buddhism but is mirrored in contemporary Buddhist movements around the world. For example, see the writings of Thich Nhat Hanh who calls for an "engaged Buddhism" that is quite similar to Involved Buddhism. For scholarly accounts of socially engaged Buddhism see C. S. Queen and S. King, eds., 1996.

[19]According to an authority at the Dharma Light Temple, this is a quote passed down through popular oral tradition.

practice.[20] Belonging to the Pure Land tradition of Buddhism, most devotees at Dharma Light aspire towards rebirth in Amitahba Buddha's Pure Land, a realm believed to be more conducive towards the attainment of enlightenment.

Given the nature of their salvation message, Buddhists have a very different orientation to the world than evangelical Christians. Buddhists regard the world and their present lives as a temporary realm where they work out their karmic debts and merits. Buddhists may be concerned about propagating the Dharma but they rarely consider it to be their primary mission in the world. Furthermore, because Buddhists believe that individuals have multiple lifetimes to reach enlightenment, there is less urgency to evangelize. Like Christian religious institutions, the temple exists primarily to serve its own community of devotees. As an institution of salvation it offers both the education and ritual services that connect the individual to that which is transcendent and facilitates the cultivation of merit. To the extent that a temple, or a church for that matter, focuses all of its energies on the maintenance of its own community, its engagement with those outside will be limited. But where a temple does extend itself beyond its own community, the world is a place where individuals can work out their own salvation through good thoughts and deeds. Through such acts of charity, Buddhists work for the "salvation" of themselves and others.

Dharma Light's particular practice of Involved Buddhism has challenged the temple's traditional institutional role of merely offering sacred ritual and ceremony, expanding its concerns beyond the temple walls to those of public service and charity. As an institution of salvation which sees its orientation as this life rather than the next, Dharma Light proclaims

---

[20]For example, in the Pure Land tradition a common practice is the recitation of Amitahba Buddha's name.

its public mission to "establish a Pure Land on earth" through the dual process of physically transforming the world through charity and promoting internal purification through Buddhist teachings. Where traditionally the Pure Land is considered a realm one enters after this life, Dharma Light insists that we can establish the Pure Land in the here and now. While giving visitors a tour of the temple, one of the monastics explained to visitors, "We don't just sit in the forest to meditate; to isolate ourselves for our own religious practice would be selfish. We want to be involved in society." Like Grace Taiwanese Church, Dharma Light is also concerned about propagating its own religious message. However, this is not the sole mission of the temple or its devotees. In Taiwan and around the world, the Dharma Light order has made every attempt to engage its temples in the local community through charity and public service. In its mission statement, one of Dharma Light's expressed objectives is "to benefit society through charitable programs." For example, Dharma Light has been involved in local prison outreach, gang intervention, and charitable fund drives with the larger American society. While it was rare for the evangelical pastors to voice concern for worldly affairs that did not affect the church community, it was not uncommon for monastics to pray for events remote from Southern California, such as the war in Kosovo or the shootings at Columbine High School. It even held a special service in October 1996 to honor the servicemen killed in a fire on the Navy carrier USS Oriskany.

Cultivating a Culture of Charity

Just as Grace Taiwanese Church attempts to cultivate an institutional culture of evangelism, Dharma Light attempts to cultivate an institutional culture of charity. To encourage its devotees towards greater charity in 1999, Dharma Light promoted the theme "Three

Good Movements," referring to "say good words, have a good heart, and do good things." Walking through the temple grounds, it is impossible not to notice all of the Dharma Light volunteers in their purple-vested uniforms who are attempting to put the "three good movements" into practice. In fact, at times it seems that there are more volunteers than devotees at the temple. Some are giving tours, some are sweeping the grounds, others are answering phones, working in the kitchen, managing the parking lot or running the gift shop. Dharma Light takes volunteering seriously and volunteers must go through a requisite training course. Furthermore, while volunteering activities might appear to be casual and fun, volunteers are hardworking and diligent in attending to their tasks. Their reasons for volunteering are multiple. Some come for social reasons, others come because they have the leisure time. Some have even admitted that they come for the vegetarian food. Whether consciously articulated or not, devotees associate volunteering with doing good and the accumulation of merit. Volunteering is mutually beneficial for both the temple and the devotee. For the temple, the presence of a readily available, trained volunteer corps is both cost-effective and convenient. At the same time, to the volunteer it offers opportunities for spiritual enhancement and merit cultivation.

Just as Grace Taiwanese Church becomes an institution of salvation through preaching the gospel, Dharma Light becomes an institution of salvation by giving its devotees the opportunity to do good. It is no longer solely through ritual and ceremony that one cultivates merit, but also through actions in one's practical daily life. Dharma Light extends this charity outside of its temple walls to engage in the world. Having cultivated a culture of charity, Dharma Light is able to mobilize this readily available volunteer corps to direct acts of charity towards

the public. For example, when the temple wanted to organize a disaster relief for the victims of Hurricane Mitch, the human apparatus was already in place for a timely and effective response. In a culture where good deeds are a moral imperative, people are quite willing to donate their time and money for the cause, not only within the Taiwanese immigrant community but also the larger local community.

Interreligious dialogue and cooperation

Another important way in which Dharma Light performs good deeds in the world is through interreligious dialogue and cooperation. Dharma Light regards the cultivation of respect and communication between different religious groups as important steps towards world peace. Sponsoring the annual "World Peace Day" and inviting leaders from different religious traditions is one example of Dharma Light initiating interreligious cooperation. In Taiwan, the Dharma Light order has frequently been the initiator of Buddhist-Catholic dialogues. The Dharma Light Temple participates in monthly Roman Catholic-Buddhist dialogues with local Buddhist and Catholic religious leaders. In addition, Dharma Light enjoys a friendly relationship with a local African American Methodist Episcopal Church. Dharma Light monks and the AME gospel choir have performed at each other's communities. Both the temple and church have collaborated in a charity drive in the local area.

Consequences of Theological Orientation and Strategies

Whereas the evangelical mode of engagement through personal evangelism limits the immigrant Taiwanese church's sphere of interaction to other Taiwanese and Mandarin-speaking populations, the Buddhist practice of charity is more easily extended towards other populations.

The Taiwanese church's engagement is more selective because they go out into the world to incorporate others into their own linguistically-specific community. In contrast, practicing charity allows for the possibility of more inter-actions with mainstream America because it does not require the linguistic and social skills that personal evangelizing does. Dharma Light's practices of charity and public service outside of the temple rarely involve extensive interactions between the lay immigrant popula-tion and the recipients of the charity. Most of the acts of generosity are in the form of dona-tions of money or material necessities that are first gathered within the temple. Donations do not require a great deal of interaction with the larger American public. Furthermore, it is a select group of lay and monastic representatives of the temple who present the donations to the receiving party. On the other hand, with the evangelicals, it is not church representatives who engage with the world, but each lay indi-vidual is expected to be a public spokesperson for the faith. While this sort of personal and relationship-based engagement may allow for deeper and more substantial individual transfor-mation of the world, given the linguistic and cultural resources of the immigrant population, this strategy limits the extent of its interactions with main-stream America.[21]

Secondly, Dharma Light has more contact with those outside of the Taiwanese immi-grant community because of its concern for interreligious dialogue and cooperation. While Dharma Light does not actively seek to promote interracial dialogue, its active mis-sion to establish world peace through inter-religious dialogue inadvertently promotes interracial interactions as well. For example, in his 1998 year end message, the Dharma Light Master did not fail to mention that he had vis-ited prominent Catholic and Muslim religious leaders at the Vatican and in Malaysia, respec-tively. The stated significance of these visits in the newsletter is explicitly religious, "We had a religious dialogue that went beyond the cen-tury. In fact world peace is not just a dream. If everyone could understand that all beings are one, and if we know how to be respectful and tolerant, then this human world will be filled with joy and harmony. There would be no war and no injustice." While motivated by religious ideals, the racial and ethnic implications are clear: a Chinese monk having conversations with a white Roman Catholic and a Southeast Asian Muslim demonstrates that world peace will be achieved through the cooperation of not only different religions, but different racial and ethnic groups as well. Particularly in the racially and religiously plural population of the United States, one cannot have interreli-gious dialogue without at the same time engaging other racial and ethnic groups. In comparison, because Grace Taiwanese Church regards Christian salvation as exclusive, it feels no need to interact with other religious groups, and in effect limits its potential inter-action with other racial and ethnic groups.

GETTING ON THE INSIDE BY BEING ON THE OUTSIDE: CHRISTIANS AS RELIGIOUS INSIDERS AND BUDDHISTS AS RELIGIOUS OUTSIDERS

Internal factors such as salvation mission, resources and strategies shed only partial light on the way that immigrant religious institu-tions negotiate their public presence in society.

---

[21]The literature on evangelical Christians shows that in general they are more concerned about individual transfor-mation rather than social transformation. Taiwanese immi-grant evangelicals are similar to other American evangelicals in emphasizing the role of evangelization. However, on social issues such as abortion and school prayer where American evangelicals have traditionally taken public action, Taiwanese immigrant evangelicals have not. Cultural and linguistic barriers have been signif-icant obstacles to Taiwanese immigrant evangelical partic-ipation in the American public in this manner.

External factors and social context need to be taken into account. In the case of Dharma Light and Grace Church, both are located in the same west coast suburb and serve a Chinese immigrant population primarily from Taiwan, and both have members of similar socio-economic background. They differ in how the respective religious ideals of evangelical Christianity and Buddhism inform distinct types of public engagement. But they also differ in how mainstream America perceives and receives a Taiwanese Buddhist temple versus a Taiwanese Christian church. Immigrant religious institutions, and all religious institutions for that matter, are guided not only by their religiously-defined mission, but are shaped by the dynamic interaction with their surrounding religious and social environment. Where the religious group is theologically inclined towards social engagement, I suggest that ironically it is the presence of religious difference that encourages greater engagement in mainstream America.[22]

The disengagement of Taiwanese Christian churches from mainstream American society is reinforced by the fact that in the minds of most Americans, the association of Chinese with Christianity is incongruous and does not fit into typical religio-racial categorization. By not being "sufficiently foreign" as most Americans might expect, the Taiwanese Christian churches are overlooked and rendered nearly invisible. While immigrant churches might advertise themselves to the American public as ethnic institutions, the lack of distinction between the architecture of their buildings and any other Christian church makes them easily overlooked.

On the other hand, the oriental exoticism of the Buddhist temple captures the attention of most Americans and fits into the American imagination of what is Chinese. In the categories of American representation, Dharma Light symbolically represents what is Chinese more adequately than does Grace Taiwanese Church. Being a symbol of difference, Dharma Light must navigate within a dense forest of competing discourses advocating religious pluralism on the one hand and Christian hegemony on the other. The temple, a massive structure built in traditional Chinese architecture, faced severe obstacles from the local community in gaining permission for its construction. When arguments were raised by the local community that the temple would devalue the local property or cause obstructing traffic, both members of the local community and Dharma Light devotees confided to me that these masked the underlying concern for the imposing presence of a non-Christian community in the town. Other arguments stemmed from misunderstandings of Buddhism, such as the unfounded fear of animal sacrifices or local residents' worries that their children would be entrapped by a "religious cult."

Sensing the antagonism from the local community, Dharma Light leaders have taken extra steps to befriend local organizations and to quell any perception of threat. In an interview with the local press the temple Abbot posed the question "What can we do to get the support of the American people?" He promised that the temple would be open for use by the community, including non-Buddhist groups, as well as be a site for running charitable programs. To build a positive image the temple holds an annual "Get to Know Your

---

[22]The presence of religious difference alone will not necessarily encourage engagement with mainstream America unless there exists a theologically oriented foundation towards public engagement. For example, in the vicinity of Dharma Light and Grace Church there are other Taiwanese Buddhist temples whose presence do not extend beyond the ethnic immigrant community despite being "religiously different." Unlike Dharma Light, their missions are primarily to serve the existing temple community through religious education and ritual ceremony rather than through the social services as forwarded by Involved Buddhism.

Neighbors" Banquet where they invite representatives from local organizations and businesses to acquaint them with the temple community. Numerous photographs of non-Chinese people at temple events are proudly displayed in the temple's monthly newsletters and publications, suggesting that they are receptive to Americans. An American flag is not raised in the immigrant Christian church however it is conspicuously present in the temple courtyard leading to the main Buddha hall. Dharma Light is also a frequent financial sponsor of local public events, such as free concerts in the park. In contrast, the immigrant Christian churches do not make the effort to participate in local charity events.

At the same time that their religious difference prevents Dharma Light from being truly "American," in the age of multiculturalism, the presence of "just enough difference" becomes the ticket to recognition and possible acceptance. By virtue of the association of Buddhism with the Far East and Christianity with the West, the Buddhists, rather than the Christians, are the ones to be recruited and courted as the Chinese representatives at the multicultural table. Since more Taiwanese immigrants regularly attend a Christian church than regularly visit the temple, the church would be the more effective venue of the two for political campaigning. However, when local politicians want to court the vote of the Chinese immigrant population or publicize their multicultural platform, photographs with temple monastics are at a premium because the Buddhists are the symbolic representatives for the Chinese immigrant population. Indeed, the temple and local politicians share a symbiotic relationship whereby non-Chinese use the temple to gain the favor of the Chinese immigrant population and the temple uses the attention by local leaders and figures to gain acceptance into mainstream America. From the vantage point of those at Dharma Light,

mainstream American society sends two seemingly conflicting sets of undercurrent messages. On the one hand there is the pressure they feel to conform to American society, and on the other hand is the message to "stay Chinese." Many Taiwanese Buddhists relayed to me how they are frequently pressured by Taiwanese Christians to convert whereas the Anglo Christians are the ones who encourage them to stay Buddhist.

Ironically, because of the public perception of religious difference, those at Dharma Light feel the need to engage in mainstream American society to bargain for acceptance. Having been labeled as different, Dharma Light's acts of charity are simultaneously marks of "cultural citizenship" that are no different from the philanthropic extravagance that has been demonstrated by other new Asian immigrant tycoons to high culture institutions (Ong 1999). To interpret Dharma Light's acts of charity as simply a "natural" process of assimilation into American society misses the point that their public presence is shaped by the stigma of difference and the struggle to find acceptance. Ironically, on the other hand, in an historical era where multiculturalism has taken the moral high ground, those at Dharma Light are courted by mainstream America solely on the basis of their "difference." In comparison, as a Christian institution, Grace Taiwanese Church does not have the burden to engage in public relations work among mainstream Americans to prove its American-ness. But not being perceived "different enough," neither are they invited to participate in mainstream multiculturalism.

CONCLUSION

At the outset of this paper I presented two scenarios of what would appear to be a Weberian paradox—the fact that of two immigrant religious institutions an "other-worldly" Buddhist temple is more publicly engaged in mainstream American society than an "inner-worldly" evangelical Christian church. I have attempted to explain this seeming contradiction by focusing on the religious ideals which drive their public missions, the strategies they employ, and the social context in which these ideals are enacted. I demonstrate that indeed both groups are inner-worldly in that they see this world as a place to work for salvation. Grace's evangelical interpretation of salvation drives it to engage in the world through personal evangelism. In contrast to Weber's characterization of Buddhism as a "flight from the world," Dharma Light's interpretation of Involved Buddhism is an example of an inner-worldly Buddhism that advocates for the path to [enlightenment] both through contemplation and acts of charity.

Common to the case of all immigrant institutions, both Dharma Light and Grace face similar cultural and linguistic obstacles in enacting their religious mission outside of the ethnic community. However, unique to the cases of Dharma Light and Grace are the historically-specific opportunities and constraints on public action that multiculturalism presents in American society today. Where Dharma Light could have limited its outreach to the ethnic community like Grace, or to the homeland, like the mainline Taiwanese church, it chooses to extend its public mission outside of the ethnic community. Herein lies the critical factor of Dharma Light's status as a religious outsider compared to Grace's status as a religious insider. Representations of religious and racial difference as well as discourses of multiculturalism combine forces to pressure Buddhists, as religious outsiders, to engage in acts of public relations to both prove their [Americanness] and yet remain representative Chinese. . . .

While the cases I present are specific in religious orientation and social context, the implications can be extended to understand more generally how ethnic religious institutions interact with the larger American public. In regard to racial and religious minority groups, one needs to consider not only how religious ideals inform public [engagement], but how the cultural transferability of their outreach strategies, as well as surrounding discourses and representations of difference shape the public expressions of their theology.

REFERENCES

ABUSHARAF, R. M. 1998. Structural adaptations in an immigrant Muslim congregation in New York. In *Gatherings in diaspora*, edited by R. S. Warner and J. Wittner, 235–264. Philadelphia: Temple University Press.

AMMERMAN, N. T. 1999. *Congregation and community.* New Brunswick: Rutgers University Press.

BARRINGER, H. R., D. T. Takcuchi, and P. Xenos. 1990. Education, occupational prestige, and income of Asian-Americans. *Sociology of Education*:27–43.

CHAN, S. 1991. *Asian-Americans: An interpretive history.* Boston: Twayne Publishers.

CHANDLER, S. 1998. Chinese Buddhism in America: Identity and Practice. In *The faces of Buddhism in America*, edited by C. S. Prebish and K. K. Tanaka, 13–30. Berkeley: University of California Press.

CHAO, H. 1995. Mobilizing to grow: The persistence and transformation of the Evangelical Formosan Church of Los Angeles. Ph.D. Dissertation, West Lafayette, IN: Purdue University.

CHEN, H. 1992. *Chinatown no more: Taiwan immigrants in contemporary New York.* Ithaca: Cornell University Press.

CHRISTIANO, K. J. 1991. The Church and the new immigrants. In *Vatican II and U.S. Catholicism: Twenty-five years later*, edited by H. R. Ebaugh, 169–186. Greenwich, CT: JAI Press.

Committee on the International Migration of Talent, ed. 1970. *The international migration of high-level manpower: Its impact on the development process.* New York: Praeger.

DART, J. 1997. Poll studies Chinese-Americans, Religion. P. B5 in *Los Angeles Times*.

DER, H. 1993. Asian pacific islands and the 'glass ceiling'. New era of civil rights activism In *The state of Asian Pacific America: Policy issues to the year 2020*, edited by LEAP Asian Pacific American Public Policy Institute, 215–231. Los Angeles: The Editors.

EBAUGH, H. R. and J. S. CHAFETZ. 2000. Structural adaptations in immigrant congregations. *Sociology of Religion* 61:135–153.

ERNST, R. 1979. *Immigrant life in New York City 1825–1863*. New York: Octagon Books.

ESPIRITU, Y. L. 1992. *Asian American panethnicity: Bridging institutions and identities.* Philadelphia: Temple University Press.

FENTON, J. Y. 1988. *Transplanting religious traditions: Asian Indians in America.* New York: Praeger.

FONG, T. P. 1994. *The first suburban Chinatown: The remaking of Monterey Park, California.* Philadelphia: Temple University Press.

GALL, S.B., and T. L. GALL, editors. 1991. Statistical record of Asian Americans. Detroit: Gale Research Inc.

GLAZER, N., and D. P. MOYNIHAN. 1963. *Beyond the melting pot.* Cambridge: M.I.T. Press.

HADDAD, Y. Y., and A. T. LUMMIS. 1987. *Islamic values in the United States: A comparative study.* New York: Oxford University Press.

HANDLIN, O. 1952. *The uprooted.* Boston: Little, Brown and Company.

HERBERG, W. 1960. *Protestant, Catholic, Jew: An essay in American religious sociology.* New York: Anchor Books.

HOLLINGER, D. A. 1995. *Postethnic America: Beyond multiculturalism.* New York: Basic Books.

HORINOUCHI, I. 1973. Americanized Buddhism: A sociological analysis of Protestantized Japanese religion. Ph.D. Dissertation, Davis, CA: University of California, Davis.

HUNTER, J. D. 1982. Subjectivization and the new evangelical theodicy. *Journal for the scientific study of religion* 21: 313–327.

———. 1983. *American Evangelicalism: Conservative religion and the [quandary] of modernity.* New Brunswick, NJ: Rutgers University Press.

———. 1987. *Evangelicalism: The coming generation.* Chicago: University of Chicago Press.

———. 1991. *Culture wars: The struggle to define America.* New York: HarperCollins Publishers.

HURH, W. M., H. C. KIM, and K. C. KIM. 1978. *Assimilation patterns of immigrants in the U.S.: A case study of Korean immigrants in the Chicago Area.* Washington, DC: University Press of America.

HURH, W. M., and K. C. KIM. 1990. Religious participation of Korean immigrants in the United States. *Journal for the Scientific Study of Religion* 29:19–34.

KASHIMA, T. 1977. *Buddhism in America: The social organization of an ethnic religious institution* Westport, CT: Greenwood Press.

KIM, I. 1981. *New urban immigrants: The Korean community in New York.* Princeton: Princeton University Press.

KITANO, H. H. L., and R. DANIELS. 1995. *Asian-Americans: Emerging minorities.* Englewood Cliffs, NJ: Prentice-Hall.

KURIEN, P. 1998. Becoming American by becoming Hindu: Indian Americans take their place at the multicultural table. In *Gatherings in diaspora*, edited by R. S. Warner

and J. Wittner, 37–70. Philadelphia: Temple University Press.

LEON, L. 1998. Born again in East LA: The congregation as border space. In *Gatherings in diaspora*, edited by R. S. Warner and J. Wittner, 163–196. Philadelphia: Temple University Press.

LI, K. 1988. *Economic transformation of Taiwan, R.O.C.* London: Shepheard Walwyn.

LIN, I. 1996. Journey to the Far West: Chinese Buddhism in America. *Amerasia Journal* 22:106–132.

LIU, J. M., and L. CHENG. 1994. Pacific Rim development and the duality of Post-1965 Asian immigration. In *The new Asian immigration in Los Angeles and global restructuring*, edited by P. Ong, E. Bonacich, and L. Cheng, 74–99. Philadelphia: Temple University Press.

LOWE, L. 1996. *Immigrant acts.* Durham, NC: Duke University Press.

MANGIAFICO, L. 1988. *Contemporary American immigrants: Patterns of Filipino, Korean, and Chinese settlement in the United States.* New York: Praeger.

MELENDY, H. B. 1981. *Asians in America: Filipinos, Koreans, and East Indians.* New York: Hippocrene Books.

MIN, P. G. 1992. The structure and social functions of Korean immigrant churches in the United States. *International Migration Review* 26:1370–1394.

———. 1996. *Caught in the middle: Korean communities in New York and Los Angeles.* Berkeley: University of California Press.

NIEBUHR, H. R. 1929. *Social sources of denominationalism.* New York: Henry Holt.

———. 1951. *Christ and culture.* New York: Harper and Row.

NUMRICH, P. D. 1996. *Old wisdom in the new world: Americanization in two immigrant Theravada Buddhist temples.* Knoxville: University of Tennessee Press.

OLSON, D. V. A. 1989. Church friendships. Boon or barrier to church growth? *Journal for the Scientific Study of Religion* 28: 432–447.

ONG, A. 1999. *Flexible citizenship: The cultural logics of transnationality.* Durham: Duke University Press.

ONG, P., and T. AZORES. 1994. Asian immigrants in Los Angeles: diversity and divisions. In *The new Asian immigration in Los Angeles and global restructuring*, edited by P. Ong, E. Bonacich, and L. Cheng, 100–132. Philadelphia: Temple University Press.

POZZETTA, G. E., ed. 1991. *American immigration and ethnicity: A 20-volume series of distinguished essays: Volume 19: The immigrant religious experience.* New York: Garland.

QUEEN, C. S., and S. B. KING. 1996. *Engaged Buddhism: Buddhist liberation movements in Asia.* Albany: State University of New York Press.

ROOZEN, D. A., W. MCKINNEY, J. W. CARROLL. 1988. *Varieties of religious presence: Mission in public life.* New York: Pilgrim Press.

SAITO, L. T. 1998. *Race and politics: Asian Americans, latinos, and whites in a Los Angeles suburb*. Urbana: University of Illinois Press.

SMITH, C. 1998. *American evangelicalism: Embattled and thriving*. Chicago: University of Chicago Press.

STARK, R., and W. S. BAINBRIDGE. 1980. Networks of faith: Interpersonal Bonds and recruitment to cults and sects. *American Journal of Sociology* 85: 1376–1395.

———. 1981. Friendship, religion and the occult: A network study. *Review of Religious Research* 22:313–327.

TROELTSCH, E. 1951. *The social teachings of the Christian church*. New York: Macmillan.

TUAN, M. 1998. *Forever foreigners or honorary whites? The Asian ethnic experience today*. New Brunswick: Rutgers University Press.

WARNER, R. S. 1988. *New wine in old wineskins*. Berkeley: University of California Press.

WARNER, R. S., and J. G. WITTNER, eds. 1998. *Gatherings in diaspora: Religious communities and the new immigration*. Philadelphia: Temple University Press.

WEBER, M. 1946a. The social psychology of world religions. In *From Max Weber*, edited by H. H. Gerth and C. W. Mills, 267–301. New York: Oxford University Press.

———. 1946b. Protestant sects and the spirit of capitalism. In *From Max Weber*, edited by H.H. Gerth and C. W. Mills, 302–322. New York: Oxford University Press.

WILLIAMS, R. B. 1988. *Religions of immigrants from India and Pakistan: New threads in the American tapestry*. Cambridge: Cambridge University Press.

WILSON, B. 1970. *Religious [sects]: A sociological study*. New York: McGraw Hill.

WONG, B. 1987. The Chinese: New immigrants in New York's Chinatown. In *New immigrants in New York*, edited by N. Foner, 243–272. New York: Columbia University Press.

WUTHNOW, R. 1994. *Producing the sacred*. Urbana: University of Illinois Press.

YANG, F. 1999. *Chinese Christians in America: Conversion, assimilation and adhesive identities*. University Park, PA: Pennsylvania State University Press.

YANG, F., and H. R. EBAUGH. 2000. Religion and ethnicity: The impact of majority/minority status in home and host country. *Journal for the Scientific Study of Religion*: forthcoming.

ZHOU, M. 1992. *Chinatown: The socioeconomic potential of an urban enclave*. Philadelphia: Temple University Press.

10 Sacrifice of Praise: Emotion and Collective Participation in an African-American Worship Service

TIMOTHY J. NELSON

In this fascinating reading, Dr. Nelson spends much time in one Pentecostal African American church, a church with highly expressive worship, including dancing and shouting (usually accompanied by several other emotional expressions). In what may appear to be chaos and unscripted behavior, Dr. Nelson finds order and script. Read on to see what he means.

On the corner of a rundown street in Charleston, South Carolina there is a small African Methodist Episcopal church. The modest brick structure sits on a lot entirely enclosed, as are all of the church lots in this poor urban neighborhood, by a substantial fence. Visible through the straight iron bars is a sign that proclaims "Eastside Chapel AME Church. Sunday morning worship 11:00 AM. Thursday Prayer Service 7:00 PM. Rev. R. L. Wright, Pastor."[1] If one were to open the doors of this building on a Sunday morning shortly

after 11:00, step through the tiny narthex and into the red-carpeted sanctuary, the scene would look something like this: James Ravenel, organist and choir director, is seated at his instrument directly behind and slightly above the pulpit. While the worshippers continue to arrive and file into the pews, he quietly plays a gospel song. On the back wall above the choir loft, a computer-generated banner proclaims "WE'VE COME THIS FAR BY FAITH." The adjacent wall holds a similar banner that features a rendition of praying hands and the caption "WHAT A MIGHTY GOD WE SERVE." These banners are the sanctuary's only adornment. As Ravenel plays,

---

[1]The names of the church and all persons have been changed to protect their identity.

Source: Timothy Nelson, "Sacrifice of Praise: Emotion and Collective Participation in an African-American Worship Service." Reprinted with permission, from *Sociology of Religion*, Volume 57, © 1996.

Tony Green sets up his drums on the floor to the side of the pulpit.

After several minutes, as most of the hundred and fifty or so worshippers have settled into their places, Ravenel begins playing the refrain to the Isaac Watts hymn "Alas! and Did My Savior Bleed," more popularly known as "At the Cross." At this cue the congregation stands for the processional, their singing scattered at first but quickly gathering force. . . .

So begins another Sunday morning worship service at Eastside Chapel. Starting off slow and measured, with an opening prayer and hymn, the service rapidly builds in intensity and congregational involvement. By the time the choir sings its first selection, swaying slowly from side to side, many worshippers are standing and clapping to the music. Soon several of the "church mothers," older women in the first row or in the front flanking pews known collectively as the "amen corner," start to "shout" or dance in a stylized way with their heads down and eyes closed, moving across the front of the sanctuary. The choir stops singing but the music continues while several other worshippers begin to shout in the pews, some moving out into the center aisle. Cries of "Glory!" and "Hallelujah!" punctuate the heavy beat and churning bass of the organ and drums. This continues for over ten minutes before the shouters move back to their seats, worshippers begin to sit down, and organist Ravenel plays several closing chords. Service leader Nazarene Simmons steps up to the pulpit and announces the next activity in the order of worship.

The display of enthusiastic response and shouting I have just described (and which is often repeated two or three more times throughout the three-hour service) is a common one at Eastside Chapel. Sociologists, anthropologists, and other observers have labeled this type of worship as "emotional," and it is most characteristic of lower-class African-American congregations. . . .

EMOTION NORMS AND THEIR FULFILLMENT

An "emotional" worship service, like a funeral, carries with it a proper definition of itself. According to the understanding which Eastside Chapel members have of the Sunday morning service, it provides an occasion for God to meet with his people in a time of celebration and praise; it is a party which worshippers give in honor of God for who he is and in gratitude for what he had done in their lives. This definition of the situation carries with it implications for the particular emotions that congregants should feel throughout the service. Hochschild calls these emotional standards "feeling rules" and indicates that these rules not only pressure people into *displaying* the situationally "correct" emotion (what she calls "surface acting") but actually motivates them to try and *experience* appropriate emotions and suppress inappropriate ones (or "deep acting"). From my participant-observation at Eastside Chapel I have identified five particular emotions that operate as normative standards throughout the worship service.

This particular list—praise, gratitude, love, joy, and hope—are the individual feelings which constitute Eastside Chapel's normative constellation of emotion, and through the liturgical discourse worshippers are constantly reminded of these standards. Thus far I have shown how feeling rules are incorporated into an "emotional" service through the discourse within hymns, prayers, sermons, Sunday School lessons, and segments of the liturgy. . . .

Despite the traditional label for this type of ritual there appears to be nothing unique about the emotions generated within an "emotional" worship service. Certainly, "nonemotional" Christian worship services also have feeling rules (which probably involve the same set of particular emotions) and they also have methods for evoking these emotions in the service (perhaps even using many of the same hymns, at least in Protestant congregations). Rather, the observable difference between the two types of services lies in the types of expressive behavior worshippers engage in, and it is to that topic that I now turn.

BEHAVIORAL NORMS

Norms not only operate internally upon the feelings of the congregants but upon their external behaviors as well. These standards of appropriate behavior cannot be reduced to the internal feelings of the participants—as both Goffman's observation on funerals and Durkheim's discussion of mourning rites illustrate quite clearly. Instead, they form a separate but related system of expectations, and these expectations can differ quite markedly from one congregation to another. The following account gives a graphic picture of the kind of behavior that was considered completely appropriate at Eastside Chapel that would be out of place (to put it mildly) during a "nonemotional" worship ritual.

One Sunday morning in mid-November Reverend Wright invited Reverend Rose Drayton an assistant pastor at a nearby AME congregation, to act as guest preacher. The delivery of her sermon started out calm and measured, began to build in intensity and congregational response, and ended with most of the congregation on its feet clapping, while a handful of members engaged in prolonged shouting. Here is how it happened.

She began by reading a portion of scripture from the Old Testament book of Daniel, where the Babylonian king Belshazzar sees a disembodied hand writing on the wall during a banquet. When a Jewish captive named Daniel translates the writing, the King hears a prophecy regarding his impending demise. After reading this passage, Rev. Drayton closed the Bible and announced that her theme was going to be "The Party's Over." The gist of the sermon, which was delivered

in the traditional call-and-response style, was that people should start living right because God was going to come back soon and announce to the world that "the party's over." The congregation was very quiet during the scripture reading and remained quite still for the several minutes it took Rev. Drayton to set out her general theme and establish her rhythm. Then she moved out from behind the pulpit and said, "Pray with me for a little while, now," and people started to come alive.

It happened gradually. At first one person in the choir stood up. Then after about half a minute, another choir member stood up. Then more choir members stood, and then people in the congregation started standing up, until after several minutes almost the whole choir and about half of the congregation was on its feet. The responses to her phrases became louder and more emphatic during this time. Several women choir members in the front started smiling and waving their arms at Rev. Drayton in a "go on now" motion. The drummer tossed a drumstick in the air and caught it again with a flourish. People began clapping and shouting back at her during the response time in the cadence. One young man started running to the front of the center aisle, pointing his finger and shouting at her, then running back to his seat. He did this over and over. The organ and drums started chiming in during the response times, building in volume and emphasis until finally at the end of the sermon they took the congregation immediately into a song. As they started playing several members began to "shout" in earnest, moving out to dance in the unconfined spaces of the aisles and in front of the pulpit.

A close examination of this scene reveals two types of behavior. First there is what I will call "response behavior" which includes both vocal and physical reactions to the music, preaching, prayer, or whatever provides the current focus of attention and stimulus. The response behavior in the above story includes cries of "amen," and "hallelujah" as well as the bodily actions of standing, running, pointing, and clapping.

In nonemotional churches, the norms guiding response behavior are quite simple: none is allowed, not even the polite smattering of applause at the conclusion of a performance which characterizes secular occasions. Contrast those standards with the response behavior exhibited at Eastside Chapel, where those in highly visible positions (in the choir loft behind the pulpit) stood up and waved their arms, where a congregant ran down the aisle pointing and shouting at the preacher, where the musical instruments played loudly during the pauses in the preacher's delivery. If congregants in a "nonemotional" service behaved in this overtly responsive manner they would immediately disrupt the proceedings; the situational order would be completely shattered and all such behavior would have to cease before the service could proceed.

However, in some important respects the norms of behavior at Eastside Chapel are not so different from standards operating in other types of gatherings. For example, the response behaviors at Eastside Chapel bear a resemblance to those at sporting events where it is expected that spectators will cheer a good performance by their team of choice. In fact, a visiting pastor once scolded the congregation for not responding to his point with sufficient enthusiasm by saying, "You should be on your feet and cheering about that. If you had just seen Michael Jordan slam-dunk the ball on the court, you would be up on your feet. Well, the Lord has slam-dunked your sins into the sea of forgetfulness, and that is something to cheer about!"

One fundamental difference, then, between "emotional" and "nonemotional" worship services is simply the set of rules governing congregational response. The range of permitted response behavior sometimes leads a naive observer who is used to "nonemotional" norms to the assumption that there are no holds barred concerning congregational activity. However, it was my observation that at Eastside Chapel and other "emotional" churches, the conduct of worshippers was very tightly monitored.

This is true even of the more sensational behavior known as shouting. On one hand, shouting may be seen as an extreme form of physical response—like clapping, only with the whole body rather than just the hands. Certainly this is true from a behavioral standpoint. One can watch congregants progress from clapping and verbal responses to more vigorous behaviors like swaying and stomping their feet and finally "cutting loose" into a full-blown shout, and from this perspective the transition from clapping to shouting seems to be simply a matter of degree.

Yet from the perspective of the individual undergoing this transition, there is a radical break between clapping and other response behavior and shouting. To get a sense of the internal state of the actor during a shout I interviewed several Eastside members in detail about their experiences while shouting. When a congregant engages in response behavior such as standing, clapping, pointing, waving, and their verbal counterparts, it involves them more completely in the service. Indeed, this behavior is only possible for the congregant who is completely "tuned-in" to the sermon, prayer, song, or testimony that is providing the stimulus (it's hard to clap to the rhythm when you're not listening to the music). But a congregant who is shouting has entered another realm of consciousness; he or she has left the service far behind and is aware only of the presence of God. I asked Darryl Lawson, a teacher's aide in his mid-twenties and active member of the senior choir, about his state of consciousness when he was shouting and if he was aware of his surroundings. He replied:

You would know what's going on—cause I remember bumping into a couple of benches. [But that's not where I am focused] . . . I don't try to figure out who's around me or anything, because I'm just enjoying my Jesus.

This withdrawal of consciousness is taken by Eastsiders as the sign of a genuine shout and is attributed to the work of the Holy Ghost. However, shouts which congregants suspect are simply responses to external stimuli are considered counterfeits. Because music provides such a powerful stimulus, and because much shouting occurs during musical selections, congregants may have reason to suspect that some dancers are simply responding to the music rather than undergoing a true shift of consciousness prompted by the Holy Ghost. Sherline Singleton told me that "it is a proven fact that every shouting doesn't have the Holy Ghost—they just shouting." When I asked her how congregants could shout without the prompting of the Spirit, she answered:

Music. Cause when you were younger and you hear something you like even if you didn't get up and dance, you knew how to move to the music. What are they doing? You know how to dance already— and when you hear drums or hear a good beat on an organ that you can dance to [then you can do it].

When a worshipper is in the midst of what members consider a genuine shout, they are perceived by others to have stopped responding to external stimuli and are acting solely upon the internal stimulus of the Holy Ghost. While in this state others treat the shouter as if she is not in control of her own behavior. However, despite the apparent chaos which sometimes erupts when many people shout at the same time, the conduct of the shouters is highly structured and strictly monitored. Although it may appear to the uninitiated observer that "anything goes," particularly when one sees such behavior as congregants running laps around the church aisles or jumping up and down like a child on a pogo stick, there is actually a tightly defined range of permissible behavior in effect even during these shouting episodes. . . .

"EMOTIONAL" WORSHIP AS COLLECTIVE BEHAVIOR

Ambiguity, Reluctance and the Evocation of Expressive Behavior

So far I have argued that a key difference between an "emotional" and "unemotional" service is simply that response behaviors and shouting are permitted in the former but not the latter. There is more to the story however. In fact, these "emotional" forms of participation are *required* of the congregation, but in a particular way. The norms pertaining to "emotional" response are not imposed in the same way as those which pertain to "nonemotional" activities like singing hymns or responsive liturgical readings. In responsive readings, for example, there is an obligation upon every individual congregant to contribute verbally in a prescribed manner, complete with cues for when to begin and end participation. Thus each person's role is scripted for these segments of the service and there is no ambiguity about what one should be doing from one moment to the next. Things are not so simple in an "emotional" service because expectations of response are diffused throughout the entire congregation and are not assigned to particular individuals. For example, the preacher expects that *somebody*, or a handful of people perhaps, will say "amen" when he or she makes a strong point, yet no person or group of persons is *designated* to respond in this way. According to this structure, the involvement of each congregant is constantly ambiguous in that at each point one may choose to respond or to not respond. There is no set script to follow, although each congregant knows the general story line.

There is another factor at work also. Responses are supposed to become more and more vigorous as the service progresses, culminating in shouting or, sometimes, speaking in tongues. This process was illustrated by the Eastside congregants' reactions to Reverend

Drayton's sermon. At first there was only vocal responses of "amen" and "that's right." Responses progressed to standing, then clapping, then pointing or waving, and then finally into shouting. This process is normative and it is an expectation that is diffused throughout the congregation. That is, no one is designated as the first one to bring congregational responses to the next level. Yet while this process is normative, from the perspective of the individual there is a certain cost to initiating a higher level of response in that the more vigorous responses make one more visible to other congregants, who are in a position to critically evaluate the genuineness of the response. For example, the first person to stand may stand alone for several minutes before someone else joins them, and shouting always makes one highly visible while in the midst of a somewhat embarrassing display of ecstatic behavior. Thus, congregants may be reluctant to initiate the response level to a higher pitch.

These factors of structural ambiguity and resistance to high visibility, both of which operate to inhibit congregational response, must be overcome. It is the task of those in performance roles to evoke congregational participation through the nature and quality of their performances, and in this they draw upon several resources. . . .

From my observations of Eastside Chapel, I noted two rhetorical strategies used for different types of ritual speech. First, there is the use of standard formulas and stock phrases which appear primarily in prayers and testimonies, a phenomenon noted by many other scholars of the African-American church. . . . Such phrases as "I thank the Lord that he woke me up this morning clothed in my right mind. He didn't have to do it but he did," and "He took my feet out of the miry clay and He placed them on a rock to stay" are particular favorites.

Although one might expect that this formulaic repetition would act to dampen congregational response, at Eastside Chapel the use of certain well-worn phrases invariably brought about an enthusiastic, emotional response. In fact, they elicited much more response than a less formulaic statement with the same content would evoke. This was brought home to me in a personal way one morning during the monthly "Men's Prayer Breakfast." When it was my turn to pray, I began to ask for safety on the road for my wife and myself as we were going to be driving a long distance on the following day. In my spontaneous prayer, I framed the request as if I was making ordinary conversation, making it up as I went along. While previous prayers had evoked heartfelt cries of "Yes, Lord" and "amen" from the other men, my prayer did not meet with the same agreement until Lenard Singleton interjected the phrase "We ask for your traveling mercies" over my own words. When this stock phrase was uttered, all of the men responded "Yes, Lord" in unison.

While the use of verbal formulas seem to work during prayers and testimonies, sermons made much more use of metaphor to evoke a strong congregational response. The most effective metaphors were those which were spontaneously generated (or at least appeared that way), involved some sort of word play, and which subverted items of modern life or popular culture into the congregation's spiritual world view. For example, by using the metaphorical strategies recorded in the following short excerpt, Reverend Wright was able to take the congregation into a peak of response and even stimulate about ten minutes of shouting at the very beginning of his sermon. (The congregational responses are indicated in the brackets.)

And I'll tell you what—I'm excited about my Jesus! ["Yeah"]
I'm gettin' more and more excited about him daily
He's my bread you know
That's right, if you come to my house, I got some bread there

That's right, and I didn't get it from the Pig[6] ["That's right"]
But I got it at the foot of the cross ["Well"]
He is my Wonder Bread ["Yeah"]
He is my Roman Meal ["Oh yes"]
Oh yes, when you read Romans 8, I tell you, it will tell you about that Roman meal bread!
[clapping, "Yes Lord!," someone starts shouting—organ starts playing]
He is my Galations bread! ["All right"—more vigorous response]
He is my Revelation bread!
Then, what I like about him—he is not only my bread, but he is meat in the middle of my bread [clapping, shouting, organ]
And you can eat him allllll the day long! [more shouting, organ, drums kick in]
He is good for what ails yah!
Then, I I I I [stutters] can take you to my refrigerator
Then I can take you to my faucet and I can turn it on
And I've got water in my house [drum/organ beat]
I'm not talking about the water that comes out of the ground
But I'm talking about the Living Water that come down from God out of Heaven!
It's good for you if you're thirsty!
It'll quench your thirst!
And give you life on the inside!
My God, my God!

Oh yes! My God! Hallelujah! Oh yes! [Reverend Wright pauses here as many congregants are now shouting]

In fact, many of Rev. Wright's sermons are built around extended metaphors, some of which can be discerned by their titles alone, including "Does the Church Know First Aid?" or "Hostile Takeovers, Friendly Mergers."

Call, Response, and "Circular Reaction"

At Eastside Chapel it is not entirely up to the preacher or choir to move the congregation to higher levels of excitement. A good deal of the responsibility rests upon the congregation itself. In fact, it is impossible for a preacher to fulfill his or her role without the active support and response of the congregation....

When the congregation did not respond with sufficient enthusiasm at Eastside it severely

---

[6]Reference to the Piggly Wiggly supermarket chain.

hampered the ability of the preacher to maintain his or her performance. Because Reverend Wright and other preachers depended so heavily on this response, they made sure that the congregation kept their responses up to a satisfactory level. If the congregation was quiet and unresponsive, the preacher had various ways to signal his or her dissatisfaction and provoke a more vigorous reaction. Such expressions ranged from gentle proddings ("Can I get an 'Amen'?") to somewhat harsher statements; when Eastside Chapel got too quiet, reverend Wright would chide the congregation by saying, "Oh, I wish I had me a church!" and sometimes even pointedly switched roles and made the response himself (*"I'll* say it, *'Amen, preacher!'"*).

By using particular resources, performers are able to evoke a response from the congregation. This response increases the intensity and quality of the performer's actions, which in turn evoke a greater congregational response.... The overall trajectory of this type of behavior is one of oscillating movement toward higher levels of intensity and participation, culminating in widespread and prolonged shouting.

"Emotional" Worship and the Transfer of Control

From the above discussion it is apparent that "emotional" worship services are not simply a matter of an energetic preacher or a particular style of music—the congregational response plays a crucial role facilitating the production of "emotion." In fact, we could say that an "emotional" service is a joint creation, produced cooperatively by both the designated performer, the organist and choir, the "amen" corner, and the rest of the congregation. One necessary precondition of this collective process is that individual congregants allow their actions to be increasingly influenced by the quality of the performance as well as by the actions of other members of the congregation as the levels of participation become more and more intense. The key dynamic here, one which operates in all forms of collective behavior, is the individual's willingness to transfer control over his or her actions to the group. . . .

Darryl Lawson indicated that when congregants had a common desire to worship God unclouded by factional rivalries or resistance toward the preacher, then a higher level of ecstatic behavior would be evident in the service.

If everybody in the church was in one accord—and there have been Sundays that people have been in one accord—God just moves through. But if everybody was on one accord, I mean people—you'd be stepping over people [in the aisle].

Discussion

. . . What are the benefits of a more "emotional" form of worship for the congregation as a whole and for individual participants? In order to answer this, one must first understand what members themselves perceive to be the goal of the worship service. During my year of participant-observation at Eastside, Reverend Wright instituted his own Call to Worship in the Sunday service. The first line of Wright's self-authored liturgy has the minister proclaim: "Effective worship consists of two grand movements," to which the congregation responds, "The people of God must move toward God and God will move toward the people."

The first part of this double movement is represented by the congregation, who "move toward God" by expressing their humility, praise, love, joy, and gratitude in song, prayer, and testimony. By allowing themselves to be caught up in and contribute to the "circular reaction" of performance and energetic response, congregants offer God a "sacrifice of praise," a Biblical phrase which has been incorporated into contemporary African-American sermons and songs. Genuine shouting gives evidence that God has responded to this offering and is moving with power among the people. Thus, intense emotional and expressive participation first *invokes* the presence of God, and the shouting (or, more rarely, speaking in

tongues) then *embodies* this presence within the congregation. This is why it is almost invariably congregants who engage in the most vigorous forms of response behaviors who shout, despite the vast difference in consciousness between the two acts that I discussed earlier. Shouting represents the end point of a process that is begun in such simple acts as saying "amen" or clapping along with a hymn.

It is important to underscore the fact that it is this experience of God's immediate and powerful presence, which Eastside members call a "breakthrough," which is the goal of the worship service. Shouting and other forms of ecstatic display are seen by congregants simply as manifestations of this experience and are not considered to be the goal itself. It is necessary to highlight this because many observers have written as if the whole point of the service was to provoke an emotional release among congregants. . . .

In addition to providing an identity based upon religious fervor, the "emotional" style of worship may also serve to bolster African-American racial and cultural identity. Reverend Wright once remarked that the form of ritual practiced at Eastside Chapel was more true to African worship styles, but that it had been suppressed in the years following emancipation by AME Bishop Daniel Alexander Payne and other highly educated religious leaders. Anthony Scott, one of Eastside's lay ministers, told me that the new type of shout that he had displayed at a recent Sunday morning service was African in origin because he had dreamed of performing the dance within an African tribal village.

In sum, the "emotional" service is a religious ritual guided by collectively recognized norms of emotive and expressive behavior. These norms provide participants the means of attaining a desired end—the experience of God within the worship service—and also serve to bolster congregational and racial identity.

11 Affinity, Identity, and Transcendence: The Experience of Religious Racial Integration in Diverse Congregations

GERARDO MARTI

Although most people in the United States continue to practice their religion in same-race gatherings, not all do. For those in multiracial congregations, Dr. Marti asks an important question: How do members of disparate ethnic and racial heritages come to identify and achieve stable affiliation with their multiracial congregation? It's an important question, because most theory and research tells us why people find it easier and more rewarding to be in same-race gatherings, yet we do have multiracial congregations. See if you can identify his answers.

The study of multiethnic/multiracial congregations is quite new, growing in the last decade, and particularly with the publication of Michael Emerson and Christian Smith's book, *Divided by Faith* (Emerson and Smith 2000). While a notable spurt of scholarship has already occurred (e.g., Becker 1998; Christerson, Emerson, and Edwards 2005, Dougherty 2003; Dougherty and Huyser 2008; Edwards 2008b; Emerson 2006, 2008; Emerson and Kim 2003; Garces-Foley 2007, 2008; [Marti] 2005, 2008b; Stanczak 2006), an understudied dynamic within diverse congregations is the

formation and negotiation of subjective identities among members who join them. How do members of disparate ethnic and racial heritages come to identify and achieve stable affiliation with multiracial congregations?. . .

I set out in this article to more fully examine the subjective process of membership within multiracial congregations. Using ethnographic data from two multiracial congregations and synthesizing the lived religious experiences of members who join them, I suggest a heuristic model for understanding this process. The focus on member experience is what I summarize as "religious racial integration." Religious racial integration is the process by which a person considers the congregation to be *his or her* congregation, considers himself or herself as *belonging* to the congregation, has *committed himself or herself* to the congregation, and see himself or herself as an *extension* of the congregation. Ethnographic study of diverse congregations provides an opportunity to treat "race" and "ethnicity" as analytical concepts that reflect negotiated, subjective identities rather than mere demographic labels. . . .

METHODS

To examine the manner in which participants of multiethnic/multiracial congregations negotiate seemingly disparate ethnic and racial identities in the context of interactions within their congregation, I focus on interviews with attenders and field notes gathered during participant observation in two multiracial churches. These data are part of two larger projects. Between 2001 and 2004, I conducted ethnographic studies of two Los Angeles churches, Mosaic and Oasis, to understand the processes involved in joining and integrating racially and ethnically diverse people into multiracial congregations. Both churches are broadly evangelical. Mosaic is a large Southern Baptist congregation known for creativity and innovation (Marti 2005). At the time of my study, Mosaic had grown from 1,200 to almost 2,000 weekend attenders. Using data from a congregational survey in 2000, 32.8 percent of attenders are white, 30.3 percent Hispanic, 27.8 percent Asian, 4.8 percent Middle Eastern, 1.7 percent African American, 1 percent Native American, and 1.6 percent other. Oasis is a large, nondenominational, and charismatic congregation with strong connections to the Hollywood entertainment industry (Marti 2008b, forthcoming). At the time of my study, Oasis had just completed a four-year growth

spurt, leveling out at around 2,200 weekly attenders. The congregation's racial/ethnic composition is estimated using membership files and systematic observation at weekend services. At 45 percent, African Americans comprise the largest proportion. Whites are the next largest at 40 percent, followed by Hispanics (10 percent), Asians (3 percent), and other including Middle Eastern and nonnative blacks (2 percent).

I spent 12 months of field work in each church sequentially. Rather than impose my understanding of social processes onto leaders, members, and attenders, I tried to attend very closely to the "lived" experience of the participants in both churches and earnestly attempted to uncover the understandings of the attenders and bring conceptual order to what I found (Ammerman 2006; Bender 2003; Orsi 2002). I also attempted to distinguish between "official" pronouncements advocated by church leaders and the everyday happenings of all congregants (leaders and nonleaders) to the actual operations of congregational life. I participated in church events regularly attended by regular members, new guests, and those in the process of joining the church, including both weekend and midweek church functions. As part of being a participant observer, in both churches I went through their "membership process" and also attended various classes and seminars for highly committed volunteer church leaders.

In both churches I reviewed available archival material and conducted personal interviews. Archived sources consisted of selected books published by leaders, sermon and seminar tapes, and pamphlets publicly distributed by the church. In one church, I reviewed membership records in summary form; in another, I randomly sampled individual membership records. Both churches still utilized "oral tradition" to recall their history, so specific historical records were largely absent. Thus, personal interviews were used to reconstruct church history as well as obtain information on member experiences. I interviewed 60 people in the first congregation, and 50 people in the second congregation. Semistructured, face-to-face interviews included leaders (both paid staff and nonpaid volunteers), long-time members, occasional attenders, and first-time guests. I interviewed a wide variety of people currently attending each church. . . .

THREE MOMENTS IN EXPERIENCING RELIGIOUS RACIAL INTEGRATION

My analysis suggests a process of religious racial integration within multiracial congregations. . . . I propose three "moments" that characterize key phases in the lived experience of members in these two churches. These three "moments" represent key phases experienced to some extent in the lived experience of all members in both congregations as they coconstruct common bonds of spiritual kinship.

MOMENT I: AFFINITY WITH THE CONGREGATION

. . . The process of integrating diverse races into a single congregation begins with an individual establishing a form of affinity with the congregation. People in these multiracial churches initially come to the church because they connect with someone or a group within the church on the basis of some form of affinity that highlights something critically important to them as a person. At Oasis, the primary base of affinity is a common striving to "make it" in the Hollywood entertainment industry. A white member said: "Hands down, everybody would seem to agree that if there's one profession, occupation, or area of occupations that people have if they come to Oasis, it appears to be the entertainment industry." Actors, dancers, producers, film editors, and studio musicians find occupational

niches among the social networks of a congregation characterized as "geared toward people in the entertainment industry." They soon broaden their interactions beyond people with similar jobs as involvement in the congregation broadens relational networks to create connections to others in different lines of work. On a broader level, individuals find a concentration of ambitious Christians actively promoting themselves through their various jobs and activities and feeling the frustrations of financial ups and downs while actively branding and marketing themselves in a harsh, competitive economic environment. Damion, an African-American member at Oasis, is like many who said, "I went through a struggling period and stuff. I was on food stamps and all. But, hey, it didn't matter because it was happening." In an urban setting where image matters as much as substance, Oasis provides a safe haven for members of the creative class to find authentic relationships in the midst of anxiety-producing work lives (Marti 2008b, forthcoming). Another African American contrasted the supportive relationships at church as opposed to the false flattery at her work, saying, "I know what genuine warmth is as opposed to the phony stuff."

In both churches, a person initially becomes a part of a congregation because he or she sees it as something that fits with some element of himself or herself. For visitors to Oasis, this is often involvement in the Hollywood entertainment industry; for visitors to Mosaic, it is often contemporary presentation of conservative religious beliefs. Kevin, a white member at Mosaic with experience in several churches, said: "This church is not a Christian church in the typical stereotypical description of it." Not only are sermons integrated with the creative arts, but also the substance of each church service consistently seeks to integrate the historic Christian faith with metaphors and images from the surrounding culture. For example, another committed member speaking about a recent service at Mosaic said: "It was amazing;

it was awesome. Very creative. And it was very solid too because it was the truth that we were celebrating together." However, others find Mosaic "too wild" and "unbiblical," like an Asian frequent attender who was undecided about membership and openly asked: "Where do people learn the Bible?" In order for an affinity to occur, a person must be able to connect some aspect of his or her identity with some aspect of the people and practices of the church; conversely, a person cannot persist in a congregation if aspects of his or her personal identity do not connect at some level of affinity to the people and activities of the congregation.

Multiple opportunities for affinity within a congregation create multiple, overlapping, and interlocking spaces in the activities of the church that not only accept but attract diverse peoples, incorporating them into the ministry activities of the church. Affinity may be theological or denominational; affinity may be based on vocation or career path, like being an artist or an engineer. Affinity may be found through informal or nonformal aspects of the church, and so social groups or arenas of activity may exist either intentionally or unintentionally. People find places of affinity where participants are welcomed, build friendships, and contribute to the ongoing ministries of the church. The affinity may even be in the desire to find a church in which ethnic description based on one's appearance or ethnic performance is not an issue. Kyle is a Japanese American who grew up in Idaho and met and married Margaret, a Caucasian woman of Norwegian ancestry. Both described how their parents were more committed to being Japanese/Norwegian than themselves. Members like Kyle and Margaret ground their interactions less on ethnic or racial differences than on similarity of religious interests as expressed within the congregation. More importantly, what visitors value in a congregation may not match what the leaders of the congregation believe individuals should value; nevertheless, as leaders become aware of what visitors consider attractive about their congregation they become more intentional in maximizing its potential. Points of attraction become absorbed into the public identity of the congregation.

MOMENT II: IDENTITY REORIENTATION

The second moment in the process of integrating individuals from diverse races into a single congregation is identity reorientation. Through affinity-based involvement in the congregation, a person's identity begins to shift away from bases that lie outside of the congregation to one that is rooted directly in the history, values, and beliefs of the congregation. The moment of identity reorientation is when a person moves away from defining himself or herself on the basis of interests, values, and preferences found outside of the congregation but instead defines himself or herself more within a shared identity that is co-constructed within the congregation. And the collective identity achieved is distinctive to the particular context of each congregation.

At Mosaic participants take on the corporate identity of being an *entrepreneurial missionary*. One woman said, "I wasn't missionary minded before, even though I knew that was a Christian's calling to spread the new good news. I knew that in my head, but I was never part of the ministry that actually practiced it. Now, I understand mission is why the church exists." The entrepreneurial missionary engages "nonbelievers" at home, work, school, and church for evangelistic purposes in order to expand the church both locally and globally. Another Mosaic member said:

We are constantly reminded that this is a very big world and that there are many different types of people in this world, many different cultures. We need to understand those cultures, we need to know how to speak out the word into those cultures, and how to love those people. I think we all carry that.

Those who are "dedicated followers of Jesus" at Mosaic are to take their evangelistic fervor beyond church services and programs, creatively introducing people to an evangelistic message based on a biblically driven gospel story. Involvement in the church inspires members to take their faith out into the world. "It's exciting," said one member. "The vision of reaching the world through L.A., that's a grand vision, that's a God size vision. I like it. It's something that I'm willing to die for."

At Oasis, the corporate identity is oriented around being an *empowered worker*. The empowered worker is a "champion of life" who persistently applies his or her talents and gifts to achieve success in places of employment, gain influence in the secular arena, and find opportunities for injecting evangelical moral frameworks in personal relationships, business decisions, and artistic practices. One Latino member said: "The mission of Oasis, our purpose on planet Earth, is to build champions in life [which means] people who are successful in their marriages, successful in their finances, successful in their careers, successful in their social life and in their friendships. People who succeed." Another said: "The core thing is becoming the champion—who you're supposed to be: someone who serves, someone who tithes, someone who's not afraid to make a mistake. Somebody who's able to say they are wrong when they are wrong. Somebody who has good, accountable friends. Someone who keeps striving to be better."

Members at both churches describe and defend their congregation, making distinctive congregational definitions of belief and discipleship the "natural" and "normal" belief of what all Christians are supposed to believe. For example, at Mosaic the zeal for evangelism is emphasized as fundamental to vibrant Christianity. Also, members express a profound belief that Mosaic is not only "ahead of the curve" but also that other churches are destined to reach the same point. An associate pastor boldly stated: "The

future will look more like Mosaic." Members of Oasis see the church as a place to "get priorities right." Establishing right priorities involves members "getting a foundation" and "cleaning up their lives" so they can "then move up and do great things." In talking about the church, an African American stressed, "I really want to make sure I'm lined up right, that in any and everything I do I'm not doing it for any other reason but to glorify God." Such explicit, self-monitoring statements appeared in both churches continually. Christian life as defined by the congregation becomes the normative standard. In the process of participating in the life of the congregation, a person's identity more and more will focus on the dominant metaphors found within each congregation for understanding oneself in the world. For example, embracing the notion of being "on mission" an Asian member at Mosaic said, "I feel I'm joining hands with everyone to impact culture, to impact the world. It's big." An African-American member at Oasis said the church is "an oasis. You can find the rest, the water, whatever it is you need in the desert to help you to get to that place where you know that you can say at the end of the day, 'I'm doing what God wants me to do'."

The process of identity reorientation is officially promoted through sermons, worship music, small groups, Bible classes, practical workshops, books, pamphlets, and an array of other ministry efforts to which an attender is continually exposed. Identity reorientation is also promoted through the informal relationships with people also associated with the congregation either through the intentional involvement of church leaders in the life of an individual or through the more casual involvement of already-committed members who share their testimonies, provide advice, and "nudge" people toward a fuller participation in the church. A person stops saying "them" or "they should" and instead takes on the "my" and "we" kinship language of church life. For example, accommodating their Southern Baptist roots to the streets of

East L.A., Mosaic members come to call each other "Bro" and "Sis" with great affection. And at Oasis, a white member said: "We are family. We can get in each other's business, and we can challenge one another, and we love one another. We are committed to one another. We are family." A Latino member said: "Family is family and it's at a place where I really do forget, 'Oh, you are black and I am not'."

Once identity has been reoriented, the distinction between the way of Christian life in their church and the way of Christian life in other churches is abstracted to be one of being "absolutely right" in contrast with those considered to be "missing it," "off base," or even heretical. A Chinese-American woman said, "I don't go to church, I go to Mosaic." A new orthodoxy is absorbed. The moral pressure to attain and keep with congregational orthodoxy becomes part of what it means to "belong" to the congregation. The corporately constructed identity becomes a corporately enforced identity. Whether as volunteers in various ministry roles or attenders of small group Bible studies, church leaders regularly reinforce the values and objectives that buttress the corporate identity of the church. And leaders regularly spend time in dialogue, alternately teaching and persuading, to guide members and co-leaders toward congregational positions on key issues and appropriate behavior. An Oasis staff member said, "I have to remind them not to get wrapped up in the entertainment industry and not allow whatever they do, dancer, writer, actor, to make that your identity." While attenders are actively encouraged to take on ministry roles, members in both churches are required to do so. Over and over, "serving the church" is equal to "growing spiritually." This is especially true for lay leaders. More than mere voluntarism, service is not merely an appeal to an individual's involvement; it is a strategy for corporate formation.

MOMENT III: ETHNIC TRANSCENDENCE

The third and last moment of integrating people of diverse ethnic and racial heritages into a single religious organization culminates with ethnic transcendence. When a person's shared religious identity overrides potentially divisive aspects of ethnic affiliation in considerations of social interaction, ethnic transcendence has been achieved. At both Mosaic and Oasis, religious identity is consistently more important than ethnic identity. This means that membership in these multiethnic/multiracial churches not only suspends or supersedes ethnic identity but also becomes the basis for a new type of status honor. Within each congregation, different forms of social status occur since every organization allocates social status differently and provides for opportunities of social mobility and social rewards in unanticipated ways. Friendships and status are accrued through relational involvement and intentional exhibition of valued characteristics.

In both churches, ethnic transcendence occurs when individuals claim a new shared identity on the basis of a unique understanding of what it means to be "Christian" within these churches (Marti 2008b, 2005:Ch. 7; see also Garces-Foley 2007:Ch. 4). Potential members must satisfy claims of legitimacy as to the credibility of this particularistic identity and their ability to stake a claim to it. At Mosaic, members are to be "dedicated followers of Jesus" who are "on mission." Within different arenas of organizational involvement at Mosaic, individuals connect to the church not on the basis of racial or ethnic affiliation but rather on the basis of shared affinity to "the mission of Jesus." That mission is expressed by accentuating certain personal characteristics, including the ability to creatively express doctrinal orthodoxy, to show openness and participation to artistry, to encourage and demonstrate an inclination toward innovation, to actively include younger age groups in ministry decisions and activities, and to continually discourage and minimize ethnic enclaves. Through these and other behavioral characteristics, their support of congregational activities is integrated into their understanding of being "dedicated followers of Jesus Christ who are on mission with Him." But after the individual "turns" such that his or her religious identity orients toward an identity continually reconstructed in the congregation, corporate congregational identity supersedes ethnic identity.

In a similar manner, the single guiding image of Christian discipleship of being a "champion of life" at Oasis centers the thought, motivation, and activity of members there. Morality is not tied to a secular vocation but rather in the individual as a tool of God who is connected to God. Members readily connect their own economic lives to their involvement in the congregation as the church is acknowledged as helping them build their career dreams and have the moral strength to pursue those dreams without threatening their Christian practices. Thus, while the image of being a "champion of life" is not deterministic, it is a rich base of commonality that vitalizes both worship within the congregation and work outside of the church. The institutionalized thoughts and practices of this church about what it means to be a member [reorient] and reinforce this identity (see Marti forthcoming).

Practices in the ongoing activity of both congregations stimulate experiences that cultivate a shared identity enacted in the presence of others. Since Mosaic and Oasis are broadly evangelical congregations, the experiences are those often associated with a conservative Christian faith. One such activity is a vocal profession of faith, a visible declaration of allegiance to Jesus Christ. Some members believe the only point of commonality they have to other members of the congregation is their common identity as "Christians." An Asian American said, "I'm excited about

Mosaic because these are all followers of Jesus Christ. I feel at home with God's people. . . . They may speak another language, but they love the same God, they worship the same Jesus, they will live and die for him." Many Protestant congregations provide public occasions for professions of faith whether in a small group or in front of the whole church. Such confession provides a profound basic connection based on religious identity. To the exclusion of any other basic connection, a shared identity as an active believer in Jesus Christ (as understood within each congregation) is indicated as sufficient for feeling spiritual kinship. All respondents in both churches participated in a common confession of being Christians and value the connection this confession formed with other true believers regardless of their ethnic or racial identity. Another common activity within both churches is the rite of water baptism, a ritual that directly and unambiguously affirms an alternative identity. This ritual of dying to the "old self" and being resurrected as a "new self" engages the baptizer, the baptizee, and the witnessing congregation. It affirms religious commitment and asserts that the community of baptized believers are members of the same community.

These different forms of assembly are reorienting experiences that lean people away from ethnic and racial specificity and more toward their religious identity within their congregation. Another common ritual is in the sharing of the Eucharist or the Lord's Supper. By approaching "the Lord's Table" in partaking communion, members participate in a multisensory, common experience of eating and drinking that emphasizes that everyone is part of a common religious community. Yet another opportunity is the public commitment to membership. Membership is a shared ritual process in which a cohort joins together through public ceremony in front of the entire congregation. The ritual of membership is one that involves a public affirmation of commitment by those who want to become members and the public welcoming or receiving of new members by the church community. By the time a person has moved toward committing to membership, he or she has many interethnic friendships within the congregation, has joined a small group or Bible study class with significant diversity, and perhaps is involved in an ongoing ministry team. The commitment to membership is first of all a commitment to God, followed by a commitment to being a person who fulfills particular responsibilities as conservative Christians that guides behavior both inside and outside the church. The membership process itself is a form of acculturation into a shared identity as Christians of a particular congregation, since each congregation has a different slant on what it means to be Christian. Several members described the solidarity that comes from making an explicit commitment to their congregation. The common commitment of membership not only reaffirms the religious identity but also creates connections to other members of the church who reflect their identity back to them. An Asian member said, "I'm excited about Mosaic because these are all followers of Jesus Christ. I feel at home with God's people. And I believe I'm one of them."

In addition to these activities, corporate worship strongly emphasizes believers' shared identity amidst competing identities. The integrative potential of worship has been noted in other studies (Christerson, Emerson, and Edwards 2005; DeYoung et al. 2003; Dougherty and Huyser 2008; Marti 2008b, forthcoming; Yancey 2003). Members of Mosaic and Oasis often emphasize how important the music is to them. For the champions of Oasis, high-quality, energizing, foot-stomping, body-swaying, hand-raising worship at the church encourages spirit-filled believers to accomplish great things in the world as sons and daughters of the King. For example, to be in the worship service at the Oasis is to stand,

clap, sway, and smile as both audience and performers lose themselves in the service. One young white musician said, "I felt God's presence working in my life to get me in the church and to get me working for the kingdom." He concluded: "This is an amazing place and it will change your life." Through participating in a corporate orientation to the sacred, members abandon themselves to worship. Indeed, the key to good worship is to lose self-consciousness and the concern that other people are in the room. An African American said, "I had to learn how to worship, and the way I had to learn how to worship is to just let go, to let go. To let go and let God." An attitude of surrender is implicit to worship. "Any time that you're aware of people around you, then I honestly feel that you're not praising God the way that God wants you to praise him." Timothy Nelson (2004) rightly emphasizes that giving up control is characteristic of emotional worship. Individuals willingly, voluntarily, and with anticipation yield themselves to the elements of worship for the duration of the service in order to experience God and by doing so enhance the performance of those on the platform, increasing their own intensity, which further accentuates the corporate experience in a circular fashion, leaders to worshipers, and worshipers back to leaders.

Neither "dedicated followers of Jesus" nor "champions of life" exist outside of the institutional arrangement of each church. Individuals who take on the identity offered in these settings are taking on a collective identity that is supported and sustained by that collectivity. Understanding the lived experience of member involvement in multiracial congregations reinforces an understanding that modern individuals do not simply exist as free-floating agents but rather negotiate between institutionalized social environments. The self dwells in the collective pattern of self-control. It does not mean that a person must remain in that collectivity at all times in order to remain that person, but by accepting that identity, that is, by identifying oneself as a "dedicated follower of Jesus" at Mosaic or a "champion" as understood by Oasis, that person takes on an institutionalized role that persists even beyond the formal participation in the congregation. Moreover, the strength of attachment to these collective religious identities appears to continue into settings beyond the congregation when individuals take on a variety of different roles in everyday society. In the midst of all competing social roles lies a sacralized self connected to a persistent community seen as working together to fulfill the mission of God.

In short, the distinctive work of multiracial congregations lies in shaping people toward a new identity framed around new interests. In all cases, a person's race-ethnicity is displaced (but never removed) for the purposes of interaction and affiliation. Racial and ethnic distinctives are negotiated by individuals in the face of more commonly shared and corporately promoted distinctives. Church leaders at Mosaic and Oasis provide opportunities for individuals to identify and acculturate themselves religiously as members within their congregations and provide a base for gaining status and rewards on that basis. Indeed, congregationally specific affiliations have the potential to become exclusionary by reinforcing new in/out groups based on religion rather than race. Also, once ethnic transcendence is achieved by a member within one church, it appears that it may be easier to cultivate that same transcendence in another. After the experiential path from affinity through identity reorientation to transcendence has been traversed, connecting with people of different ethnic heritages on the basis of a profound religious commonality becomes familiar. Achieving ethnic transcendence can be so gratifying that believers appreciate the opportunity to relive the process in a different congregational context with a different ethnic and racial constituency (see Garces-Foley 2007).

DISCUSSION AND IMPLICATIONS

Evidence from Mosaic and Oasis suggests that the experience of becoming a member of a multiethnic/multiracial congregation reorients personal identity such that people of various ethnic and racial heritages subdue their ethnoracial distinctions in favor of a common religious identity that forms the basis for affiliation with their congregation and structures these cross-ethnic interactions as nondisruptive. Multiracial churches access a textured, multifaceted identity found among people in highly urbanized contexts, and members discover places within the congregation to express personal values and desires. As individuals become more deeply involved in the congregation, they selectively accentuate and/or obscure their ethnic and racial affiliations. Congregational activities and structures in diverse congregations urge members to take on collective identities, and members of these congregations co-construct a new shared identity, especially through rituals and shared practices. The status system that exists within every congregation contrasts with the varying and competing bases of social status that exist out in the public realm; a particular hierarchy is created and enforced. When integrating, members take on the goals and values of the corporate entity (whether implicit or explicit) to such a degree that they share a common bond to others in the organization regardless of—and even despite—differences in ethnic and racial heritages. The distinctive achievement of multiracial congregations lies in the transcendence of ethnic specificity in favor of a new congregationally based religious identity for cross-ethnic interactions, and the relative persistence of these congregations provides a stable basis for identification and affiliation. . . .

Ethnic transcendence is not to be confused with a type of "color-blind" approach to diversity that intentionally seeks to ignore or erase ethnic differences. Kathleen Garces-Foley (2007), for example, distinguishes between ethnic transcendence and ethnic inclusion in her study, of Evergreen Baptist Church. Yet, while Evergreen acknowledges and celebrates racial and ethnic identities, church leaders place a high priority in creating a shared corporate culture based on a "theology of discomfort." Member connection to the church is based on taking a congregationally specific, shared religious identity, yet they are encouraged to retain a value for their particular ethnicities. Stephen S. Fugita and David J. O'Brien's (1991) study of Japanese Americans also affirms that integration and ethnic identity retention does not need to be a zero-sum relationship (see also Kitano and Daniels 1995). Thus, the integration process observed at Mosaic and Oasis does allow for a high degree of ethnic identification by members; however, the model proposes that individuals connect to diverse congregations on the basis of a shared religious identity rather than their (acknowledged and celebrated) differences in ancestral heritage. Moreover, the occurrence of ethnic transcendence allows significant racial and ethnic issues (e.g., structural racism and institutionalized discrimination) to be discussed or accentuated in the public ministries of the congregation.

Also, because the observations for this article are based on conservative Christian congregations, it may be that only a conservatively Christian, or an evangelical, identity is able to transcened ethnic and racial boundaries. However, I speculate that the process for achieving a congregationally rooted ethnic transcendence among members is present not only in other Christian churches (Roman Catholic, Greek Orthodox) but also in other religious congregations, including Jewish synagogues, Muslim mosques, and Hindu temples. An alternative, yet congregationally specific, identity is co-constructed around what it means to be a properly religious person whether Catholic, Jew, Muslim, Buddhist, etc. . . .

Regardless of the specific mechanisms involved, congregational blending demands the successful negotiation of the multiple bases of identity in a pluralistic society, and the organizational structure of congregations provides a viable, persistent base for constructing a shared corporate identity. To put it in other terms, the potential for "racial reconciliation" (the ability for members of oppressed ethnic and racial groups to share a common congregational life with those of social groups that have historically been defined as the oppressors) exists when members of oppressed and oppressive groups both occupy a subculture in which racial differences are relatively unimportant. To overcome ethnic and racial differences, congregations must either establish or co-opt several subcultures. But since no subculture attracts equal proportions of different racial/ethnic groups, co-opting subcultures will still inevitably exclude individuals on a basis other than race or ethnicity. Complete racial reconciliation may be an impossible goal.

It is important to recognize that not all "races" or "ethnicities" are equally malleable and that the ability of congregations to evoke ethnic fluidity is severely limited by the racialized categories imposed by the dominant society (Edwards 2008a). "Race" continues to be an important analytical category, and the specter of race continues to be relevant as a boundary marker for members of ethnoracial groups who routinely lack identity options and face the imposition of designations that affect life chances for employment, education, health, etc. Neither interpersonal nor congregational dynamics (however intensive or compelling) are sufficient to overthrow the profound ways in which behavior and life circumstances are affected by ethnoracial categories. Structural processes within diverse congregations may lessen the degree of prejudice or discrimination in within-congregation interactions. Yet, to the extent that diverse congregations sidestep ethnic/racial issues of injustice in society, they leave unchallenged the broader structures of institutionalized racism. . . .

REFERENCES

AMMERMAN, Nancy T., ed. 2006. *Everyday religion: Observing modern religious lives.* New York: Oxford University Press.

BARZUN, JACQUES. 1937. *Race: A study in modern superstition.* New York: Harcourt Brace.

BECKER, PENNY EDGELL. 1998. Making inclusive communities: Congregations and the "problem" of race. *Social Problems* 45(4):451–72.

BENDER, COURTNEY. 2003. *Heaven's kitchen: Living religion at God's love we deliver.* Chicago, IL: University of Chicago Press.

CHRISTERSON, BRAD, MICHAEL O. EMERSON, and KORIE L. EDWARDS. 2005. *Against all odds: The struggle of racial integration in religious organizations.* New York: New York University Press.

DEYOUNG, CURTISS PAUL, MICHAEL O. EMERSON, GEORGE YANCEY, and KAREN CHAI. 2003. *United by faith: Multicultural congregations as a response to the problem of race.* New York: Oxford University Press.

DOUGHERTY, KEVIN D. 2003. How monochromatic is church membership? Racial-ethnic diversity in religious community. *Sociology of Religion* 64(1):65–85.

DOUGHERTY, KEVIN D. and KIMBERLY R. HUYSER. 2008. Racially diverse congregations: Organizational identity and the accommodation of differences. *Journal for the Scientific Study of Religion* 47(1):23–43.

EDWARDS, KORIE L. 2008a. Bring race to the center: The importance of race in racially diverse religious organizations. *Journal for the Scientific Study of Religion* 47(1):5–9.

———. 2008b. *The elusive dream: The power of race in interracial churches.* New York: Oxford University Press.

EMERSON, MICHAEL O. 2008. Introduction: Why a forum on racially and ethnically diverse congregations? *Journal for the Scientific Study of Religion* 47(1):1–4.

———. 2006. *People of the dream: Multiracial congregations in the United States.* Princeton, NJ: Princeton University Press.

EMERSON, MICHAEL O. and KAREN CHAI KIM. 2003. Multiracial congregations: An analysis of their development and a typology. *Journal for the Scientific Study of Religion* 42(2):217–27.

EMERSON, MICHAEL O. and CHRISTIAN SMITH. 2000. *Divided by faith: Evangelical religion and the problem of race in America.* New York: Oxford University Press.

FUGITA, STEPHEN S. and DAVID J. O'BRIEN. 1991. *Japanese American ethnicity: The persistence of community.* Seattle, WA: University of Washington Press.

GARCES-FOLEY, KATHLEEN. 2007. *Crossing the ethnic divide: The multiethnic church on a mission.* New York: Oxford University Press.

———. 2008. Comparing Catholic and evangelical integration efforts. *Journal for the Scientific Study of Religion* 47(1):17–22.

KITANO, HARRY H. L. and ROGER DANIELS. 1995. *Asian Americans: Emerging minorities.* Englewood Cliffs, NJ: Prentice-Hall.

MARTI. 2005. *A mosaic of believers: Diversity and innovation in a multiethnic church.* Bloomington, IN: Indiana University Press.

———. 2008b. *Hollywood faith: Holiness, prosperity, and ambition in a Los Angeles church.* New Brunswick, NJ: Rutgers University Press.

———. Forthcoming. Ego-affirming evangelicalism: How a Hollywood church appropriates religion for workers in the creative class. *Sociology of Religion: A Quarterly Review.*

NELSON, TIMOTHY. 2004. *Every time I feel the spirit: Religious experience and ritual in an African American church.* New York: New York University Press.

ORSI, ROBERT A. 2002. *The Madonna of 115th street: Faith and community in Italian Harlem, 1880–1950,* 2nd ed. New Haven, CN: Yale University Press.

STANCZAK, GREGORY C. 2006. Strategic ethnicity: The construction of multi-racial/multi-ethnic religious community. *Ethnic and Racial Studies* 29(5):856–81.

YANCEY, GEORGE. 2003. *One body one spirit: Principles of successful multiracial churches.* Downers Grove, IL: InterVarsity Press.

Reading

12 Gendering Secularization Theory

LINDA WOODHEAD

Woodhead addresses two key issues related to the sociological study of gender and religion. First, shifts in patterns of women's religious affiliation and practice, as well as women's disaffiliation from certain forms of religion, merit more study. Second, these religious changes are related to changes in women's labor force participation, traditional domestic roles, and their efforts to bridge the two. Woodhead highlights how the religious dimensions of men's and women's lives are shaped by the social worlds in which they find themselves.

1. RELIGION AND GENDER

The sociology of religion is not blind to gender, yet its central paradigms remain relatively untouched by an awareness of its significance. This is most obviously true of theories of secularization, which have long constituted the core curriculum of the subject.

Recently, however, there have been signs of change. Callum Brown's *The Death of Christian Britain* (2001) and its sequel *Religion and Society in Twentieth-Century Britain* (2006) remind us of the preponderance of women in the churches throughout the 19th and 20th centuries, and point to evidence that women are now defecting at a higher rate than men. Brown argues that any adequate theory of

secularization must explain women's growing alienation from the churches they once supported. In his account, the death of Christian Britain begins with the sexual revolution of the 1960s which frees women from pious forms of femininity which exalt chastity, modesty, obedience, and responsibility for the moral and spiritual welfare of husband and children. Before the 1960s women are bound by 'conservative moral authorities' and 'ecclesiastical obsession with sex'. From then on they 'revolt against their assigned role of religious and moral guardians of the nation, rejecting church authority in favour of sexual liberalism and feminism' (2006: 16). Thus for Brown, the baby of Christianity goes out with the bathwater of submissive womanhood.

Source: Linda Woodhead, "Gendering Secularization Theory," from *Social Compass*, Volume 55, ©2008 by Social Compass.

I want to propose a related but significantly different account of how existing explanations of secularization can be enhanced by taking account of changing gender relations. If it is to succeed such a theory must be able to do justice to a range of evidence which demands attention, including but exceeding the following evidence, which Brown is able to account for.

1. Not only has religion declined at the mega, meso and micro levels across Europe and, to a lesser extent, in North America, but this decline has accelerated greatly since the 1960s.
2. Women are more religious than men on every index of commitment, outnumbering them by a ratio of around 3:2 in most churches in both Europe and America. The typical churchgoer in Europe is now an older woman (Billiet et al., 2003).
3. For the last decade or so women seem to have been leaving the churches at a faster rate than men, and that this applies both to those who leave in their teenage years and those who leave in middle age (Brierley, 2003: 2.19.4).
4. Women also outnumber men in those forms of 'alternative' spirituality which have burgeoned since the late 1980s, and which include New Age, holistic therapies, and neo-paganism. Research in which I was involved in England between 2000 and 2002 found that women make up 80 per cent of those who were involved in such spirituality, as both clients and practitioners, and there are indications that this level of preponderance may not be untypical (Heelas and Woodhead, 2005).

2. THE RHETORIC OF THE SEXUAL REVOLUTION

In trying to make sense of such evidence I agree with Brown that we must start by taking shifts in gender relations seriously, but I think that he exaggerates the magnitude of the changes that took place in the 1960s. Part of the reason he succumbs to the rhetoric of a sexual 'revolution' is that he dwells on changes in personal attitudes, values, and intimate behaviours to the neglect of what was happening in the public realm of paid and unpaid labour. This, in turn, is related to methodological preference, for Brown follows the fashionable cultural turn in choosing to privilege 'discourse' and what people say over structure and what people do.

My argument is that for all the talk of sexual revolution and a shift to gender equality, studies of male and female patterns of work and employment reveal significant continuities and persistent inequalities. To summarize this situation: prior to the 1960s women carried out the vast bulk of unpaid labour in the home. Subsequent to the 1960s they entered into paid employment in unprecedented numbers, so that today almost as many women as men work in the public sphere for a wage. But women *continue* to carry out traditional duties of unpaid domestic labour and care *as well as* taking on new duties of paid employment (Hochschild, 1990; Wharton, 2005). So Brown is right about the change, but neglects the continuity. As a result, he fails to see that women's assumption of a double burden of work hardly amounts to a straightforward revolution, let alone a liberation.

Women today suffer from the effects of what Arlie Hochschild (1990) calls a 'stalled revolution' which traps them between two incompatible sets of demands. On the one hand they are expected to tend the bodily and emotional needs of others without expectation of pay or reward. They are to be loving mothers and devoted wives who care for those around them, whether at home or in the workplace. This is entirely congruent with a Christian ethic of love and self-sacrifice, as exemplified by the Christ figure, by Mary, and by the saints—an ethic of 'to give, and not to count the cost'. On the other hand, however, women are now entering into the workplace alongside men. Some remain in established roles compatible with women's work of care, such as nursing and other service functions. Others enter into more self-assertive and well-rewarded roles formerly reserved for men—whether as bus drivers, engineers, media professionals, doctors or managers. Those who take the route into traditionally masculine space find themselves having to negotiate a very different form of identity from that conventionally regarded as feminine—an identity which values confidence, assertion, individuality, competitiveness and ambition (all coded masculine) rather than care, compassion and thinking of others before self (all coded feminine).

3. MALE AND FEMALE DISAFFILIATION FROM RELIGION

Before turning to consider how this ambiguous and conflicted state of identity may help explain women's relationships with religion, let me shift the attention briefly to men and male disaffiliation from religion. Many existing theories of secularization single out one or more aspects of modernization as responsible for religious decline, including rationalization, bureaucratization, urbanization, societalization and individualization. Behind them all one discerns a similar narrative, which tells how a rural labourer leaves behind the stable and meaningful world of village life and enters into the modern city where, within the iron cage of factory or office, community gives way to impersonal structures, human meaningfulness is less important than rational efficiency, and the law of competition replaces that of co-operation. In the process the world becomes disenchanted, religion loses its traditional functions, an ethic of duty and self-sacrifice loses its relevance, and our labourer ceases to be a religious believer and belonger. I have no wish to deny the power and plausibility of this way of explaining secularization. But I do want to deny that it does anything more than explain *male* disaffiliation from religion—for the labourer who leaves the shelter of the sacred canopy is a man, not a woman. For women, industrialization is experienced very differently: as exclusion from the public world and confinement to the home and/or low-paid domestic labour and piece-work. Thus women remain urban villagers, carrying tradition into the modern context, feeding not just the survival but the growth of the churches, and easing their men-folk's experience of the iron cage by offering the humanly-meaningful sanctuary of the home.

So existing theories of secularization do a good job of explaining men's religious disaffiliation but a bad job of explaining the situation of the other half of the human race—at least until we come to the 1960s and since, when women enter into paid employment and thus start to feel the same pressures as men. But even then such theories fail to do justice to the complexity of the picture because women do not simply enter the world of paid employment on equal terms with men, but find themselves caught between two forms of labour, two sets of obligation, and two forms of identity. They find their lives poised uncomfortably between the world of work and individualization on the one hand and the world of the home and relational care on the other—or between what Ulrich Beck and Elisabeth Beck-Gernsheim (2002) felicitously refer to as 'living life for others' and 'a bit of a life for myself'.

The consequences for religious commitment are correspondingly complex. Let me simplify by breaking them down into three categories, relating to the three main forms of labour-based identity inhabited by women.

First, women may remain committed to 'traditional' roles of domestic work and care. If they do so it is quite likely that they will shelter under the sacred canopy of religion, since conservative forms of Judaism, Christianity and Islam provide just about the only space in western societies these days in which such identity continues to be affirmed and legitimated rather than stigmatized. Liberal commentators often wonder why such apparently sexist religions attract women. The answer is that it is precisely *because* such religions insist on clear gender differentiation that they appeal to women who want to 'know their place', be honoured for their work of care, find support in female solidarities, and protect themselves from divorce and male flight from family commitment (Brasher, 1998; Griffith, 1997).

Second, women may take the opposite path, and abandon traditional roles in favour of 'having my own career'. To do so they will have to give up having children, or employ a domestic labourer to look after them, or find a good welfare state (probably in Scandinavia). They will also be highly likely to turn their backs on religion. I have always been struck by Andrew Greeley's neglected finding that the *least* well represented group in Catholic churches is college-educated women influenced by feminism whose Catholic mothers were confined to domestic roles during the time their daughters were raised (1990: 230–1). Pre-boomer women are often very well aware of the dynamic. The finding is echoed by an elderly Catholic lady interviewed by one of my MA students who said:

It was the same for everyone ... and you accepted it ... you saw it [domestic work] as a privilege, like you'd been given an 'exulted' role in your own home! [she laughs] ... not that young girls, even my own daughter, would see it like that today! She'd laugh at the idea. They would say we were being duped. Maybe we were.

To a far greater extent than men, women who seek career success are under pressure to abandon domestic commitments in favour of commitments to colleagues, employer and, above all, self, self-development and success in the job. In this complex project of *completely* refashioning identity, traditional forms of religion are more likely to prove a hindrance to women than a help.

So we come to our third, and largest, category of women: those who attempt to 'juggle' two sets of commitment and two types of work. Given the ambiguous nature of their identity, some may find existing forms of

religion congenial, whilst others will find the opposite (or may simply not have any spare time for religious commitment). Where religion *does* attract female commitment it is likely to do so because it manages to assist in one way or another in helping women deal with their double dose of commitments. To take a single example, a middle-aged Anglican whom I interviewed recently explained that:

I'm not looking for community ... I like to go to church for me, it's my personal time ... what religion is for me is my space, my time ... I find the building allows me to focus better ... it's a place I don't have to think about the washing up or the cooking or the gardening or anything else ... And the service can wash over ... it does allow that. I just find some of the incidentals very irritating.

Here, religion succeeds not because it sanctifies domestic labour (even though it does), but because it can be used to provide a brief escape from such labour and a space in which to 'be me'. This is similar to, but far more half-hearted than, the case of alternative spiritualities which seem to be flourishing because they are run largely for women by women, and deal directly with the difficulties of the contemporary feminine condition. My observation in the course of researching such spiritualities is that they make use of a range of body and emotion-focused techniques to assist women in the difficult and novel task of constructing autonomous forms of selfhood. But they do not necessarily serve the construction of a typically masculine mode of independent, self-assertive selfhood. Rather, they fall along a spectrum, depending on whether they emphasize the *self*-in-relation, or the self-in-*relation*. So-called New Age practices tend to lie at the more masculine, individualized end of the spectrum and to offer support in separating the self from dependencies and setting it free for personal success. Holistic and neo-pagan spiritualities are located towards the other end of the spectrum, and tend to be more active in sanctifying distinctly feminine activities (whether miscarrying, birth-giving, childrearing, menstruating, mothering, or magic-making), but on an autonomous basis. Right across this spectrum, alternative spirituality serves as an incubation space for the forging of new forms of identity for those who find the existing options inhospitable.

CONCLUSION

To sum up, my argument is that fresh attention to the significance of gender can help modify and strengthen existing theories of secularization (and sacralization), and make better sense of the otherwise puzzling findings which I outlined at the start. I have suggested that such analysis is most fruitful when it considers how gender relations are shaped in a range of domains, material and institutional as well as symbolic. More generally still, I am advocating an approach to secularization which is attentive to power relations of all kinds—whether in relation to gender, or class, or ethnicity, or sexuality. The broadest message of all is that religion's support for and subversion of unequal distributions of power in society must be taken more seriously if we are to understand its growth, decline and transformation.

REFERENCES

BECK, ULRICH and BCK-GERNSHEIM, ELISABETH (2002) *Individualisation*. London: Sage.

BILLIET, JAAK, DOBBELAERE, KAREL, RIIS, OLE, VILAÇA, HELENA, VOYÉ, LILIANE, WELKENHUYSEN-GYBELS, JERRY (2003) "Church Commitment and some Consequences in Western and Central Europe," *Research in the Social Scientific Study of Religion* 14: 129–60.

BRASHER, BRENDA (1998) *Godly Women: Fundamentalism and Female Power*. New Brunswick, NJ and London: Rutgers University Press.

BRIERLEY, PETER (2003) *Religious Trends 4 2003–2004*. London: Christian Research.

BROWN, CALLUM (2006) *Religion and Society in Twentieth-Century Britain*. London: Longman.

BROWN, CALLUM (2001) *The Death of Christian Britain: Understanding Secularisation, 1800–2000*. London and New York: Routledge.

GREELEY, ANDREW (1990) *The Catholic Myth: The Behavior and Beliefs of American Catholics*. New York: Charles Scribner's Sons.

GRIFFITH, R. MARIE (1997) *God's Daughters: Evangelical Women and the Power of Submission*. Berkeley: University of California Press.

HEELAS, PAUL and WOODHEAD, LINDA (2005) *The Spiritual Revolution: Why Religion is Giving Way to Spirituality*. Oxford: Blackwell.

HOCHSCHILD, ARLIE with MACHUNG, ANNE (1990) *The Second Shift: Working Parents and the Revolution at Home*. Berkeley and London: University of California Press.

WHARTON, AMY. S. (2005) *The Sociology of Gender: An Introduction to Theory and Research*. Oxford: Blackwell.

13 "Islam and Woman: Where Tradition Meets Modernity": History and Interpretations of Islamic Women's Status[1]

JERI ALTNEU SECHZER

Sechzer provides an historical look at the status of women within Islam. While you may be familiar with recent controversies related to the veiling of Muslim women, this essay helps us understand how women's status across the Muslim world has changed as interpretations of Islamic religious teachings, traditions, and laws have changed. While many Muslim countries have increased social restrictions on women, Islamic women have organized to fight for their rights and to improve their status.

HISTORY AND INTERPRETATIONS OF ISLAMIC WOMEN'S STATUS

From 3000 B.C.— A.D. 1100, man's view of himself as superior in all ways to women soon became enshrined in the law and custom of the world's earliest civilizations, those of the Near East. Women became a chattel first of her father, then of her husband, then of her son.
—Reay Tannahill, 1982

The status of Islamic women differs among the various Islamic countries, each with its own view and considerations about women. In addition to the Arab countries all of which follow some form of Islam, there are many non-Arab Muslim countries in which the majority of the population is Muslim. Some include Afghanistan, Indonesia, Iran, Malaysia, Pakistan, and Turkey[3] (Armstrong, 2002; Naipaul, 1998). . . .

It is estimated that there are between 0.7 and 1.2 billion Muslims worldwide, with

---

[1]Part of this paper was adapted from Denmark, Rabinowitz, and Sechzer (2000), with permission of Allyn & Bacon.

. . .
[3]Although 99.8% of the people are Muslim Turkey was established as a secular state and as such does not adhere to Muslim law. Any political group/party that violates the Turkish secular system is declared unconstitutional.

Source: Jeri Altneu Sechzer, "'Islam and Woman: Where Tradition Meets Modernity:' History and Interpretations Islamic Women's Status," from *Sex Roles*, Volume 51, ©2004 by Springer Netherlands.

almost 7 million alone in the United States. Approximately 21% of the world's population are followers of Islam. While Christianity is presently the largest religion and followed by 33% of all people, it has remained stable over many decades; Islam is still growing. If these current trends continue, by mid-twenty-first century, Islam may become the world's most popular religion. As Islam spreads, the different countries and their cultures may interpret Islamic religion and law differently, especially with regard to their attitudes toward women. This has made the picture of the Islamic woman a complex one. These include the basic Islamic rites and laws, different Islamic sects often with different interpretations of how these rites and laws are interpreted and carried out, as well as political structure in each of these countries. Therefore, one must be careful not to either oversimplify or overgeneralize the picture of Islamic women because of changes in how Islam is viewed and the social changes currently taking place in many of these countries. Nevertheless, most Islamic countries have specific beliefs about women and have restrictions concerning them. . . .

EARLY ISLAMIC LAW AND THE STATUS OF WOMEN

Many pagan practices previously observed in pre-Islamic Arabia were no longer mandated, while other practices were embraced by the new religion.

POLYANDRY, POLYGAMY, AND CONTROL OF WOMEN

Both matriarchal and patriarchal systems were evident during Muhammad's pre-Islamic life. Before Islam, most married women retained blood kinship with their tribe. In some cases a woman was even able to find the protection of her own tribe if she was abused or mistreated by her husband. Yet, women were unhappy

about their secondary status, their poverty, and mistreatment. Female infanticide was practiced. Polyandry (the state of having two or more husbands at the same time) was also a pre-Islamic custom. Under the new religion, the matriarchal system was abolished along with polyandry. Female infanticide was prohibited. Women were now controlled by their husbands and by their husbands' families; but in the beginning, this was not rigidly enforced (Ringgren & Strom, 1967). Muhammad had long been concerned about the treatment of women, especially of widows. Muhammad replaced polyandry with polygamy (the practice of having two or more wives); this came about during the time when so many Muslims were killed in the wars against Mecca and their widows were left unprotected. Men were allowed to take up to four wives, provided that they treat each with complete equality. As indicated earlier, Muhammad was familiar with rituals of the Jews and the Christians. He disapproved of the practice of celibacy in Christianity. And although he did not view women's menstruation as unclean nor did he consider menstrual blood as polluting as in Judaism, he did order women not to pray during this time and prevented their attendance at the Mosque. Muslim physicians also questioned whether women should appear at the Mosque at all; most felt that women should not pray in the Mosque, but they were unable to enforce this because Muhammad allowed women to attend the Mosque and pray.

WOMEN AND THEIR RELIGIOUS RESPONSIBILITY UNDER MUHAMMAD

The Qur'an is quite explicit about the religious responsibility of women. Women were required to participate equally with men. In practice, it was not carried out. Some historical data indicate that Muhammad allowed women to pray with him in the Mosque, while others say that women could pray in the Mosque only with the presence and permission of their husbands and standing behind the rows of the men (Doi, 2002). Yet, the Qur'an gave women the rights of inheritance and divorce centuries earlier than such rights were accorded by Western countries. Although divorce under Islam was to the benefit of men, it was not to be taken hastily by husbands. The Qur'an allowed women to keep their dowries and departure of women after divorce was to be conducted with kindness and with no damage to the women's reputation. In pre-Islamic times, women were severely punished if they committed adultery. They were beaten or even stoned to death. This type of punishment was not stated in the Qur'an. The practice originated from the Torah of the Jews. It was however reinstated by the Taliban in Afghanistan in 1994, along with other severe restrictions and punishment of women, and will be discussed in detail in another paper in this issue. Muhammad moderated this practice and strongly encouraged his people to permit the accused to be forgiven because he felt it was better to err in forgiveness than in such severe punishment (Armstrong, 2002; Noss, 1974).

MODESTY

Modesty is the basic principle of dress for both men and women. The Qur'an tells believing men and women to "lower their gaze and guard their modesty" (Qur'an, 24:31–32). Women should not display their *zeenah* (charms, beauty, or ornaments); they should draw their *khimar* (veils) over their bosoms and should display their charms or beauty only to their husbands, fathers, and sons (and other family). Also, women should not strike their feet so as to draw attention to their hidden zeenah (Qur'an, 24:31–32).

The prophet's wives and daughters and believing women are instructed to draw over themselves their *jilbab* (outer garments) when in public so that they are recognized as decent women and not harassed. These are the few verses that address clothing specifically. Their importance is to guard his or her modesty and lower one's gaze to remain pure. This is enhanced by [one's] dress. The purpose of covering oneself is to be recognized as a decent woman and not harassed. The Qur'an is not really explicit about the form of [one's] dress except for women who are instructed to cover their breasts and put on outer garments so as to avoid harassment. The exact rules that have been established are based on interpretation of these verses. Inclusion of a head covering comes from interpretation of the word "khimar." It has been agreed that at the time of Muhammad, this was a loose scarf covering the woman's head, neck, and perhaps her shoulders, leaving the rest of her body exposed. So in the later enforcement of this rule, women had to use a khimar to cover their breasts as well. The interpretation of the khimar explains why Muslims believe that the Qur'an instructs women to cover their hair. This however is not specified in the Qur'an.

In addition to these rules, most Islamic scholars consider a woman's chest, hips, legs, neck, or basically her whole body as zeenah, all of which should be covered. Again, there is no specification in the Qur'an, allowing for different interpretations. The word jilbab, as used earlier, was understood to be loose-fitting clothing, more specifically, a long, loose dress or overcoat worn by many Muslim women today. Conforming to these rules would assure modesty and not draw attention to oneself and avoid enticing the opposite sex. This applies for both men and women. The rules for men are simpler; they must lower their gaze and cover themselves from their [navel] to their knees (Muslim Women's League, 2002).

VEILING (HIJAB)

The Qur'an does have specific instructions for the Prophet's wives. It provides for some degree of segregation and veiling for the Prophet's wives but does *not* require the veiling of all women, nor does it require the seclusion of women in a separate part of their homes (*purdah*) (Armstrong, 2002). The term *hijab* means "curtain" and is not used as an article of clothing. It refers to a screen behind which Muslims were to address the Prophet's wives. When the Prophet's wives went out in public the "screen" was a veil covering their face. At the time of the Prophet Muhammad, veiling was not adopted by other Muslim women, since, it was clearly a special injunction only for the Prophet's wives (Muslim Women's League, 2002). Some time after Muhammad's death these customs were gradually adopted and were extended to *all* women throughout Arab lands. In some communities, the word hijab may also refer to the head covering (Islam for Today, 2002; Muslim Women's League, 2002).

THE STATUS OF WOMEN AFTER MUHAMMAD

Conditions for women began to deteriorate under the rule of Umar, who succeeded Muhammad, and continued over the decades with Umar's subsequent successors.

In addition to the veiling of women, he began to limit women to praying at home, excluding them from the Mosque, even with the opposition from his own family. He essentially succeeded by appointing different imams (teachers) for men and for women. At first, he prevented Muhammad's wives from pilgrimages but later changed his mind. Umar also encouraged and supported the movement to exclude women from partaking in other religious and communal aspects of life. The practice of *exclusion* was a pivotal factor in the deterioration of the status of women in Islam. A second factor was the *seclusion* of women. Smith (1985), who has written extensively about Islam and women, has described seclusion as a process—which began precisely with Muhammad's relegation of *his* wives to a space apart from normal social interaction with men. They remained at home. Muhammad's wives were not allowed to converse directly with men but could only do so with a curtain between them. This type of seclusion (purdah) was subsequently spread to *all* Muslim women. This practice was enforced and led to a rapid withdrawal of women from society, resulting in an essentially male society. Thus, seclusion in this new religion of Islam ensured a diminished role for women Smith has argued, however, that this custom of seclusion would not have been established had the prevailing attitudes of males toward women not been permitted; this custom certainly encouraged such a diminished state for women. The institution of seclusion behind a curtain, which was subsequently declared a divine revelation by Allah, seriously reduced freedom for women, and the limited freedoms that they had became virtually nonexistent.

The custom of *veiling* further diminished the status and role of the Islamic woman in the period of formative Islam. Women not only had to cover parts of their body to prevent enticement for men when they went out, they had to keep their face covered. Many women also felt they had to cover one of their eyes. These customs, after the death of Muhammad, emphasized the obedience of women and worked to assure their chastity, making clear that their main value was procreation. These practices were soon acquired throughout most if not all Muslim lands (Haddad, 1985; Young, 1987).

WITHDRAWAL FROM SOCIETY

Although Muhammad was sympathetic to and supportive of women, at no time during his life or thereafter were women considered qualified to hold powerful positions in the new religion. Very few women were given responsibilities as collectors or for the conveying of the new traditions. Few if any women could be active in public affairs. The enforcement of exclusion and seclusion assured that women would not make gains in these areas. In her extensive writings, Smith (1985) has raised questions about the actual meaning of Islam for women. She felt that there were no truly definitive data to support the fact that the development of Islam and the social revolution that followed did in any way expand the opportunities for women that were not accessible in pre-Islamic Arabia. She strongly suggests that the development of Islam as a religiocultural system profoundly decreased the chances that women could partake of any role in public life. Once the codification of the laws of the Qur'an were taken as a divine revelation to the Prophet the enforcement of these degrading and demeaning practices was crucial in the exclusion of women. These practices, which were administered with little delay after the death of the Muhammad, can been considered as confirmation of the predominant attitude of men, that women were not suited to take an active role in public life or to serve in any way as leaders in their community. That women at the time showed a willingness to submit to these restrictions also signified that they accepted these restrictions as part of the divine revelation to Muhammad.

Yet there are others who are defensive about these criticisms. For example, Armstrong (2002) feels that emancipation of women was a great issue for Muhammad. One criticism is that the Qur'an teaches a double standard with regard to gender. The laws of inheritance show that a woman can only receive, one half of what her brothers receive, because they need to provide for a new family. With regard to being a witness before the law, the role of a woman as a witness is deemed only half as valuable as that of a man. Armstrong reminds us that life in the pre-Islamic period in Arabia included female infanticide as the norm, and where women absolutely had no rights. They were considered an inferior species and treated as slaves. So, when Muhammad established rights for women (not equal to men) the unprecedented idea that a woman could inherit, or even something, or even had a role as a partial witness was astounding. Armstrong compares this with current times when "we are still campaigning for equal rights for women" (Armstrong, 2002, p. 191). Some feel that for women to wear the veil was a symbol of an unacceptable value system that debases women. But other women feel that wearing the veil identifies them as a Muslim, and defines their role in society and their relationship with men—giving them respect and recognition (Walker, 2002).

CURRENT ISSUES AFFECTING THE STATUS OF WOMEN

As noted earlier, Islam spread rapidly throughout Arabia and to the other countries of the Middle and Near East. It has also gained many converts among non-Arab people from Iran, Malaysia, Pakistan, and from Indonesia where in the 1970s only approximately 15% of the people were Muslims and which has now become the most popular Muslim country in the world. Clearly, Islam continues to spread throughout the world and beyond the Middle and Near East.

The family and the woman's role in Muslim societies has been affected by various laws and cultures in different countries in addition to the social, economic, and financial factors including increase in industrial and technological development and urbanization in societies, which until fairly recently were primarily rural and agriculturally based. These changes have been both positive and negative. For example, state health systems lowered infant and maternal mortality and increased life expectancy but as a result, increased population growth and burdens of childbearing, particularly among women in poor and rural communities. Although educational programs have been available to address widespread illiteracy, women have not yet benefitted from this to the same degree as have men. On the other hand, education of women from privileged classes has given these women a wider choice of alternatives and an altered perception of their roles in society and as women.

The issue of exclusion of women and their confinement or seclusion at home (which as noted earlier does not have Qur'anic support) has not proved practical in many poor countries. In most Islamic countries, Muslims cannot afford to confine women who are needed to work and help support the family. Women's detainment in their homes has come to be seen as an elite institution suitable for higher levels of society.

Notwithstanding these practical issues, the Permanent Council for Scientific Research and Legal Opinions (CRLO) was established in Saudi Arabia. It is the official institution entrusted with issuing Islamic legal opinions. Jurists represent all parts of the Islamic world. The Saudi government often adopts the legal opinion of the Council as the law of the land. Some of these deliberations concerned whether wearing a brassiere is permitted in Islamic Law or whether it is permissible for women to wear high heels. Brassieres are permissible for health or medical reasons while "high heels are not permitted by Islamic law because they emphasize a woman's thighs" (El Fadl, 2001, pp. 177–178). It is also unlawful for a woman to travel without a man's permission, leave the house alone, or drive. There are long lists of deliberations by the CRLO affecting women as well as men, and many laws in Islamic countries are based on these deliberations and legal opinions (El Fadl, 2001).

Now that the Taliban has fallen in Afghanistan the issue of women covering themselves completely with a "*burqa*" is not the law and is left to the woman herself or to her husband and family; yet many women are afraid to leave their homes without a veil or burqa.

In other current issues, there has been heightened discussion about the status of women in Islamic countries, which has intensified since September 11, 2001, and women's groups have been involved. Many important factors have brought about this development. Because of the increased ease of communication and transportation, Muslims are able to travel widely, read and watch television, and take advantage of much new information. On the one hand, many Muslims have come to perceive that their own institutions and religious doctrines are inadequate with regard to following the West. This has raised expectations and at the same time increased frustration due to the restricted freedoms in their country. On the other hand, "Muslims feel that they have lost touch with their own Islamic identity and tradition" (An-Naim, 2002) and want to return to more rigid Islamic ideology. A second factor is the change in self-awareness among women in Muslim countries and the demand for women's rights. Pal (2000) has described two simultaneous developments in several Islamic countries: (1) the State making anti-women laws in the name of Sharif (Muslim Law); (2) articulate and powerful women's movements in the respective countries are fighting against such laws. Some of these events are described here.

There are at present only two countries that mandate women to be covered—Saudi Arabia and Iran. Iranian women and men must maintain modest dress in the workplace. Women's hair is considered erotic by Iranians and so covering hair as well as their female form is required. This prevents women from careers in physically active professions in a country where female equality in education is emphasized. For many centuries Iranian women wore the *chador*—a semicircular piece of dark cloth wrapped about the body and head and gathered at the chin. It permits the woman to wear anything she wants underneath but it is restricting because it must be held with one hand. Women have often used their teeth to hold the garment together. Since the Iranian revolution, dress has changed to long dress with long opaque stockings, a long sleeved coat, and head scarf. This again has evolved into a thin shoulder-to-ankle smock or "*manto*" after the French "*manteau*." In Iran, the women look at it as a work uniform and wear jeans or other Western dress underneath. However, Iran has recently tightened controls on the Islamic women's dress code. Robes deemed too revealing are banned. Shops have been stopped from producing and selling "immoral coats" that are body clinging and too short. Women must return to the loose-fitting, ankle-length clothes and cover their hair and neck with scarves. Apparently, Iran has periodic crackdowns after complaints by conservatives that women are flouting the dress code ("Anatomy of [a coverup]," 2003).

In Saudi Arabia where women are completely covered and wear the hijab or veil, women work alongside men. Many are highly educated and have professions in medicine, psychology, or other disciplines. They do not look at this mandatory covering negatively but feel that they achieve what Western women do. They feel that although they do not have as many rights they still deal with the same problems as Western women—juggling careers and families. One recent report regarding the health of veil-wearing Saudi women showed them to be at higher risk for respiratory disease than non-veil-wearing women. This study was carried out with 710 Saudi women at a hospital in Saudi Arabia. The extent of this problem is not yet known but perhaps will have an effect other than having women change their veils more frequently (Ahmad, 2001). Another

aspect of Saudi law is that women are not allowed to drive. But human rights activists have demanded the withdrawal of this law.

In postwar Iraq, new concerns regarding the status of women are alarming. The Shi'a majority has become a powerful political force, calling for Islamic rule in that country. [Iraqi] women are frightened that hard-line Islamic beliefs will be enforced and seriously erode their freedom. Militant clerics have ordered that women be veiled, that the workplace and schools be segregated, and that death-by-stoning be carried out for women who have sex out of wedlock, evoking a Taliban-like situation. Although these conservative groups are a minority, conditions in an unstable Iraq could change very quickly (Susman, 2000).

In other countries still, further events are taking place. The Nigerian State of Zamfara, recently introduced Sharif laws. One provision prevents women and men from traveling together in public transport, causing great problems for families. Shiite groups in that country have criticized this action in that the State does not have the constitutional authority to institute Sharif in a secular and multireligious state like Nigeria. In Kuwait, women are not allowed to vote or hold political office. A 2003 bill to give women this right was narrowly defeated but the fight is continuing. In 2000, Pakistan introduced a progressive law that would protect the human rights of women but was challenged by the federal Sharif court. The court directed the President to amend the law "so as to bring the provisions into conformity with the injunctions of Islam" (Pal, 2000).

A somewhat different state of affairs is taking place in Turkey. In this secular country where Sharif Law is banned, women are fighting for the right to wear a head scarf. Women have been barred from colleges because they refuse to remove their head scarfs; government employees have been fired, demoted, or transferred for the same reason. Women are barred from wearing head scarfs in photographs for [drivers'] licenses (a similar case is ongoing in the United States). The government has taken legal action against writers and journalists who champion the spread of Islam. Thus, in this country, the "modest head scarf has become the object of one of Turkey's most divisive struggles as the country seeks to join the European Union and the globalized economy. The conflict leaves the country straining to balance greater democratic freedom with preserving a secular state in a region of expanding Islamic influence" (Moore, 2000).

Thus the struggle for and against women's rights in Islamic countries continues. As the turmoil in the Middle East goes on amidst terrorism and military action, and with the increasing influence of Islamic fundamentalists versus Western interests, the final status of Islamic women remains to be determined.

REFERENCES

AHMAD, E. F. E. M. (2001). Veil-wearing Saudi women at higher of risk of respiratory disease. *Journal of Asthma, 38*, 423–426.

Anatomy of a coverup. (2003, May 26). *Daily News*, p. 3.

AN-NAIM, A. (2002). The Islamic counter-reformation. *New Perspectives Quarterly, 19*(1), 1–6.

ARMSTRONG, K. (2002). *Islam*. New York: Random House.

DOI, A. R. I. (2002). *Women in Islam*. Retrieved from http://www.usc.edu/dept/MSA/human relations/ women in islam/womeninsociety.html.

EL FADL, K. A. (2001). *Speaking in Gods name; Islamic law, authority, and women*. Oxford: Oneworld.

HADDAD, Y. Y. (1985). Islam women and revolution in twentieth-century Arab thought. In Y. Y. Haddad, & E. B. Findly, (Eds.), *Women, religion and social change* (pp. 275–306). Albany: State University of New York Press.

Islam for Today. (2002) Retrieved *http://www.islamfortoday .com/veil.html*.

MOORE, M. (2000, October 29). The problems of Turkey rest on women's heads. *Washington Post Foreign Service*, p. A32.

Muslim Women's League. (2002). Retrieved http://mwlusa .org/pub_hijab.html.

NAIPAUL, V. S. (1998). *Beyond Belief: [Isamic] Excursions Among the Converted Peoples*. VintageBooks, New York.

PAL, R. M. (2000). [Women's] movement in Islamic countries. *PUCL Bulletin* (December 2000). Drawn from the Lahore based women's organization, Shirkat Gah's News Sheet, Vol. XI, No. 4, and its Special Bulletin, February 2000, entitled Women's Rights in Muslim Family Law in Pakistan: 45 years of Recommendations *vs* the FSC [Judgement].

RINGGREN, H., & STROM, A. V. (1976). *Religions of mankind: Today and yesterday* (p. 44.5). Philadelphia: Fortress Press.

SMITH, J. I. (1985). Women, religion and social change in early Islam. In Y. Y. Haddad and E. B. Findly (Eds.), *Women, religion and social change* (pp. 19–36). Albany: State University of New York Press.

SUSMAN, T. 2000. Women of Iraq Fear the Future. Newsday.

TANNAHILL, R. (1982). *Sex in history*. New York: Stein and Day.

Walker, M. (2002). Impact magazine. Retrieved http://media.is-net.org/offIslam/basics/Women.html.

YOUNG, K. K. (1987). Introduction to women in world religions. In A. Sharma, (Ed.), *Women in world religions* (pp. 1–36). Albany: State University of New York Press.

14 The Embodied Goddess: Feminine Witchcraft and Female Divinity

WENDY GRIFFIN

As Woodhead notes in the opening essay, some women are abandoning traditional forms of organized religion and gravitating to alternative religious traditions which place women's lives and experiences at the center of their spiritual beliefs and practices. Griffin used participant observation and interviews to study feminist witches who belong to the Coven of the Redwood Moon and Womancircle. In examining the rituals and symbols used by each group, Griffin shows how members actively use their religious beliefs and practices to redefine and challenge traditional patriarchal gender relations and power inequalities.

INTRODUCTION

Although individual feminists in this country have long been concerned about the treatment of women in mainstream religions, the first contemporary indications of group challenges to mainstream religious misogyny appeared in the early 1970s. In November of 1971, Mary Daly led "hundreds" on an "Exodus from patriarchal religion" (Daly 1992:7) by walking out at the conclusion of a sermon she delivered in the Harvard Memorial Church. A few months later, in 1972 in Los Angeles, the first coven of feminist witches which practiced "the Craft" as a religion began to

meet under the guidance of Zsuzsanna Budapest. Within a few years, these witches were gathering with several hundred women in the mountains to celebrate their visions of female divinity in religious rituals (see Budapest 1989).

To date, the Goddess Movement, which evolved from these early initiatives, has been studied primarily by theologians and psychologists, but has been relatively ignored by sociologists. As a result, relatively little is known about the way these groups function, who participates and at what level, and how the worldview of the practitioners is developed and shared. In this paper, I use a phenomenological

---

Source: Wendy Griffin, "The Embodied Goddess: Feminist Witchcraft and Female Divinity," from *Sociology of Religion*, Volume 56, ©1995.

approach and descriptive analysis to demonstrate how those who practice feminist witchcraft and/or participate in "goddess rituals" use consciously constructed mythopoeic images in religious ritual to create a framework of meaning which seeks to define a new ethos. This ethos is intended to "revision" power, authority, sexuality, and social relations. As in many other New Religious Movements, the relationship between the spiritual and the material is being redefined, but in the Goddess movement the material is firmly rooted in the female body. In the discussion that follows, I describe this redefined relationship and the significance it has for practitioners by drawing on three mythopoeic images from local rituals and my interviews with feminist witches. . . .

All of the women in both groups identified themselves at one time or another as feminist witches, but there were organizational differences between them. Circle of the Redwood Moon is a radical feminist coven and members are trained through reading assignments and discussions to do a radical feminist analysis of gender and power. Called "Dianics," after the Roman Goddess Diana, they are similar to other neopagan groups in the United States and Britain in that they celebrate "sabbats" or holy days based on seasonal cycles, require an apprenticeship and training in ideology and the practice of magic, value female leadership and divinity, and share the one law of the Craft.[1] They differ from most other neopagans in their feminist analysis, political activism, and in that most of them acknowledge only an autonomous female principal and reject the concept of a male divinity. Men are very rarely invited to participate and are not allowed to become members of Dianic covens. . . .

---

[1]This one Law is sometimes considered two, as it basically says do whatever you want to do as long as it doesn't hurt anyone. If you do hurt someone, be prepared to accept the consequences because whatever is "sent out" will return increased.

Womancircle was much more loosely defined and more typical of the larger Goddess movement. Although some of the women in the movement belong to covens and some have even been trained by or have been Dianics, others prefer less structured groups that demand less commitment and may be less separatist. Still others belong to no group but show up occasionally for public ritual, and some are active members of the Unitarian Universalist church, which has a national educational program on the Goddess and feminist witchcraft. There is no apprenticeship or required training, although workshops are frequently offered on topics that are believed to empower women, such as meditation and visualization techniques or discovering the "Goddess within." As in feminist witchcraft, the spiritual focus is on an autonomous female divinity and the creation of powerful female images, and the group holds rituals to celebrate the seasons. Many women in the Goddess movement practice witchcraft and magic in a manner similar to Dianics and neopagans, although many of them tend not to call themselves witches and to prefer the word "spirituality" to "religion." . . .

Women in both core groups appear to accept uncritically the belief in prehistorical "Goddess Cultures" where women and "women's values" were a major part of the societal ethos. In Womancircle and, to a slightly lesser degree, Redwood Moon, there was a tendency to consider femininity and masculinity as innate characteristics rather than as social constructs. Many of the women have been involved in feminist activities in the community, such as rape crisis centers, family planning centers, and resource centers. Although the witches in Redwood Moon are much more likely to discuss the political ramifications of religion, all the women in both groups consider public ritual to be a political act.

MYTHOS AND SOCIAL RELATIONS

... Mythos, may be partially understood as a cultural vision of the world, one which "links the individual self to the larger morphological structure" of society (Campbell 1988:72). If not reinforced through the regular performance of religious ritual, myths run the danger of being forgotten or reduced to "mere" literature or art (Priest 1970; Campbell 1988). Myths also lose their vitality when they fail to reinforce the link between the self and the experienced world. Sometimes in times of crisis, a new mythos is created that speaks to the devitalized or faded myth.... The new myth and its symbols come into immediate conflict with existing social institutions and authority.

Feminist witchcraft sees women's oppression and environmental abuse, which they argue are intimately linked, as firmly rooted in patriarchal religions. They claim that the mythos of God the Father and Creator of everything is a devitalized one which fails to address the experience of women's lives, and so cannot possibly link them to the larger social structure. In particular, they focus on the differences between the mythic image of a female divinity who creates life alone in an act of parthenogenesis by reaching within her own body in a physical, material act, that of a transcendent, celibate male divinity who created life with a thought or a word and who is above and apart from his creation. They talk about "patriarchal thought-form" based in the latter image and point to how this influences the way we understand the world and human experience in two important ways.

First, feminist witches emphasize the similarities in the hierarchical structures of the world's five major religions, reflected, for example, in angels, saints, jinn, and demigods. Mageara, Redwood Moon's priestess of Ritual Magic who does occasional presentations on witchcraft, says this model trains people to defer their power and responsibility upward. It is reinforced by hierarchical value systems which rank the material, the emotional, the intellectual, and the spiritual in ascending order. Women and femininity are identified with the material and the emotional, the lower half, and men and masculinity are identified with the upper and "superior" half, consisting of the intellectual and the spiritual.

Second, feminist witches point to the linearity of patriarchal myths and intellectual constructs. It is because the material and emotional are devalued in relation to the intellectual and spiritual, they say, that patriarchal religions teach us that "Life is a vale of tears." In order to ascend the hierarchy of values, the material and emotional must be overcome. The body must be disciplined, even mortified, they say, and desire conquered. These religions tend to be salvation-oriented, speaking of a linear life-time with the goal of moving up and beyond to an afterlife, to a sacredness outside of the world. Even when life is understood as a process of reincarnation, the goal is still to move elsewhere, to move beyond the material and break free of the cycle of rebirth. The enlightenment and experience of the divine is one of transcendence. Mageara argues that:

Out of infinite possibilities, this belief system creates social relations that will conform with, reinforce, and maintain itself. This thought-form conceptualizes power as power over, rather than power to do or to be. It turns human activity into forced productivity that leads to the abuse of the earth and women because it compartmentalizes the material, separates it from, and places it beneath the spiritual.

THE MYTHOS OF FEMINIST WITCHCRAFT

Max Weber wrote that the world became "disenchanted" when sacredness was removed from everyday life and moved out into another realm where the divine dwelt....

But the goal of transcendence and the concept of sacredness being separate and external to the self are alien to feminist witches . . . who emphasize the female experience of continuity and connection. Instead of transcendence, the Goddess represents immanence, which they visualize as the flow of energy that connects all things. Through religious ritual and magic, feminist witches and women in the Goddess movement attempt to link what they believe is the divine within them to the divine around them in the natural world. To them, the Goddess is "the normative image of immanence" (Starhawk 1988:9), the mystical experience within of everything that exists without.

Their concept of the trinity, the dynamic cycle of birth, life, death, and rebirth as represented by the Goddess' three aspects of Maiden, Mother, and Crone, reflects and reinforces their belief in connection and immanence. The Triple Goddess is a metaphor that supports cyclical time, like the seasons. As Mageara says:

What comes around goes around and everything is connected. There's no deferring of power or responsibility upward, no linear plane to transcend, no getting off the wheel. Instead of working toward transcendence, the goal is to accept where in the cycle you are and really BE there. You might as well. After all, this is it folks!

Instead of the basic hierarchy of material, emotional, intellectual, and spiritual of patriarchal religions, the symbol used by feminist witches is a circle which contains and balances the intellectual, emotional, material, adds energy as a fourth element, and represents the whole union as spiritual, because the whole is greater than the sum of its parts.

Having rejected "patriarchal thought-forms" as failing to reflect their own experience of reality, these women also reject the core values they grew out of. The four core values emphasized by witches in my interviews were . . . affirmations of female power, body, will, and of women's heritage and bonds. Just as it has been argued that the symbols and mythos in Judeo-Christian tradition have reinforced the interests of men in patriarchy (for examples see: Daly 1973), the women argue that the symbols and mythos of the Goddess shape a new ethos and cultural vision of the world. This mythos uses a definition of power they believe to be free from the dynamics of domination. As Mageara argues, "female power isn't about power over, it is power to do, power to be." It is an articulation of power that, according to recent research on gender differences (Hale and Kelly 1989), is similar to the way that many men and women tend to actually use power in the secular world. Thus their gendered understanding of power and their cultural vision are firmly rooted in the female body and experience, and they believe this presents a serious challenge to patriarchal relations.

FEMINIST MYTHOPOEIC IMAGES

Traditional religious iconography offers one major mythopoeic image for women, that of the Mother. Whether she is portrayed as the young virgin with child or the grieving madonna of the Pieta, she is young, she is beautiful, and she is defined by her relationship to her son. In contrast, the Triple Goddess defines herself and each of her three aspects as a mythic image that is capable of standing alone. This can be illustrated by examining the use of mythopoeic imagery in three public rituals of Womancircle and Circle of the Redwood Moon.

The first was created by Hypatia, Dianic witch and priestess in Redwood Moon. The coven sponsored a weekend of workshops, discussions, and rituals in which I participated along with a group of some sixty women camping in the mountains. My notes describe the scene.

The second night out was a full moon and we waited impatiently for the moon to crest the tall pines so that the ritual could begin. Finally, we saw two flames winding down the mountain path. As they neared, we saw that these were torches, held by priestesses in silver gowns which caught the light from the flames and glittered like pieces of the moon herself. The priestesses paused in the south, and then I noticed the enormous shadow thrown against the hill. It is Diana who comes behind them. Rationally, I know it is Hypatia, but I also "know" it is Diana. A heavy green cape is swept over her shoulders and matches her baggy pants. Her huge breasts are bare, and her chest is crossed with the leather straps that hold her cape and the quiver of arrows on her back. She carries a large bow and her face is hidden behind a mask of fur and dried leaves. Deer horns spring from her head. There is no face, not a human one, anyway. . . . The Goddess pauses between the torches and fits an arrow to the bow. She draws it back and with a "twang" shoots it into the darkness. The sound is a catalyst. We are released like the arrow and begin to cheer (24 August 1991).

Hypatia told me later she neither "became" nor "invoked" Diana, phrases which would suggest that the Goddess was external to her priestess. Rather Hypatia "manifested that part" of her that *was* Diana. But this was no fleet-footed, pony-tailed chaste young goddess of the woods and dells. Hypatia is a powerful-looking, obese woman whose presence in her secular life often intimidates people who do not know her well. As Diana, this sense of power was dramatically enhanced. This was a Diana who looked like she could strangle a boar with her bare hands. But her strength was more than physical; there was a drama in her presence and authority that seemed to stem from within. This is described by a woman in her mid 20s who was a feminist new to Goddess ritual.

Other images of Diana are all sexualized from a male point of view, kind of a scantily clad Playboy bunny in the woods. But when she came walking up and I realized who she was, it was really different. It was really kind of overwhelming and shocking. But after the initial shock, she *was* Diana. This was a female who radiated power with her body and costume. Her unselfconsciousness about her body was powerful and the way she walked was almost majestic. I'll never forget it. *This* was the Diana I want to relate to.

Later in the ritual, Diana asked who was "on her Moon Time" or menstruating. On those women who were, she pinned a sprig of herbs tied with a red ribbon. This same young woman found this wonderful.

Moon Time! What a beautiful concept! If you were menstruating you were special. You had this incredible gift that your body has given to you, something to be proud of! And we got to wear red ribbons so that everyone else would know and be proud of you too!

This was a Goddess who was a virgin in Goldenberg's (1979) sense of being independent of her lovers, not one who was necessarily by nature sexually inactive, a definition popular with feminist witches. With her attire and gift of Moon Ribbons, She celebrated the female body in a uniquely female way. This was a totally different image of Diana than the one with which we are familiar. This was the Goddess of the Moon and the Lady of the Wild Things. With this powerful image, Hypatia manifested the strong, independent Maiden that the witches argue may be found in all women, a natural part of the female self that has been denied and suppressed.

The second mythopoeic image was presented by a priestess from Woman-circle. Almost two hundred people had gathered in a rented church hall to celebrate the Winter Solstice and were seated on blankets and jackets on the floor in a semi-circle around a large round altar decorated in reds and greens and many small goddess figurines. About two-thirds of the people were female, and infants and small children were scattered in the crowd. Light seemed to dance in the air around the altar from the many candles people had brought as offerings. It was well into the ritual when three figures stepped out from the shadows. Like Hypatia's Diana, each figure was a priestess/Goddess. The first was a Black Isis, with a large feathered shawl. The second a Chicana Tonatzin with rattles and beads and feathers. The third was a pale Virgin Mary, draped in white and blue. Each moved slowly around the altar, explaining who she was and why she was there. The image of diversity, the multiple faces of the Goddess, was a striking one, and in itself part of the new mythos. But it was the words and actions of the pale Mary that present the particular challenge to patriarchy explored here.

As she circled the altar, her robes swirling gently around her ankles, Mary smiled and said she too was the Goddess. She told us that we had been taught many things about her. Some of them were true, some of them were lies. She said that being the mother of a child was not all that *any* female was, no matter how important the particular child might be. There was much more to Mary than her chaste visage might suggest. My fieldnotes record what the priestess/Mary said:

"The Church Fathers and their artists always dress me in blue and white. What they never tell you is that under my robes I wear a red petticoat," and she lifted her drape to her knees, revealing a bright red petticoat with flounces! People laughed (22 December 1990).

The laughter was immediate and spontaneous. Several people told me that they had been momentarily startled by the sight, and that was why they laughed. Later, a young woman who had read about the Goddess but was new to ritual told me why she laughed.

It was kind of shocking because it reminded us that the Virgin *had* a body.

And a middle-age women told me she laughed,

... in recognition. It's [the petticoat] a symbol of joy and happiness and sexuality. Life under something else. It's there even if you don't see it. It's like an inside joke. Like lifeblood.

The priestess who had "been" Mary was more specific.

I see many, many connections that can be made between the image of Mary ... and the denigration of women. One of the things that *they* have done to

Mary, they've taken away her sexuality. She was a mother and yet had no sex. She was not a woman, she was just a role. And I see this personified in our relationships with our own earthly mothers. We have this idea of what they should be, but we don't let them be women. So when I said that Mary had a red petticoat underneath, I meant that under the image of serene mother and chaste virgin, whatever, she was a woman with lifeblood, with sexual blood. Kind of reclaiming her sexuality, it was symbolic of that to me.

The small gesture of raising her robe was intended to uncover a new Virgin Mary. Her red petticoat was a metaphor that served to establish a link between the *female* body and the divine, in other words, between the material and the spiritual. Instead of denying the body, this image celebrated it.

The Virgin Mary in this ritual was a Mother Goddess who had a material, female body, who birthed and created life out of her own flesh and blood, who might still be sexually active even after giving birth, and who, in raising her petticoat, metaphorically redefined what it means to be female and to be spiritual. This Virgin Mary did not give the impression she would ever utter the words, "be it unto me according to thy word" (Luke 1:30). Thus "re-visioned," she reclaimed her sexuality, her fertility, her autonomy, and her divinity.

The last image was consciously constructed by several Womancircle priestesses and unaffiliated women in the community. An announcement had gone out to the community that a six-month series of workshops would begin to focus on the Crone aspect of the Goddess. The culmination of these was a ritual in late October, where the women who had attended the workshops publicly "claimed their Cronehood."

Inside the dimly lit rented church, almost all of the one hundred attendees wore black. There were men and children here and there in the crowd that circled two round tables in the very center of the hall. These tables had been placed together and draped in purple velvet, and the effect was a horizontal figure eight, the symbol of infinity. One lone white taper burned on this dark altar; other than that, it was bare. The community of celebrants had been dancing to a small group of drummers, a wild, wide spiral dance that filled the church as people awaited the coming of the Crones. The "handmaiden" who had been sent to invite them into the hall returned, and the dancers stopped in place, forming a large double spiral that led up to the altar. The drums beat slowly as the handmaiden scattered rose petals in the path of the Crones. First came two together, carrying between them a large cauldron symbolizing wisdom, death and rebirth. Behind them, the other Crones glided in one by one. They were dressed entirely in black, their faces partially hidden behind black veils. They carried candles specially made for the occasion, beeswax dipped in black, purple, and red. Some of them carried flowers in their arms, several had small Goddess figures in their hands. The veiled figures circled twice through the human spiral as people spontaneously cried out small encouragements. "Welcome Crones!" "Hail Crone!" "We love you!" "The world needs more Crones!" One of the Crones told me:

It was close, very close. People didn't touch us as we passed through, but we felt emotionally touched. . . . It felt like we entered the body of the Goddess and were birthed as Crones.

The line of Crones reached the altar and encircled it, forming a circle within a circle. Several "called in" their favorite Crone Goddesses—Hecate, Lilith, Medusa—inviting them to join the circle. One by one the women went to the altar candle and used its flame to ignite their own, which they placed around it, along with any flowers and statuettes they carried. When they had all completed this act, they lifted back their veils and turned around to face the community. Singly, each then announced who she was, where she came from, and what she had to offer the community. A typical presentation was:

I am Marilyn, daughter of Dorothy, granddaughter of Judith, great granddaughter of Laura, who was a daughter of Hecate. If you would seek wisdom with a Crone, seek me.

The crowd cheered each crone's declaration. Some of the "gifts" they offered were fairly traditional—wisdom, love, healing. But there were also crones who promised laughter, sexual love, and political power. The last offering evoked a loud, "Grandmothers in '92!"

In claiming their cronehood, announcing their matrilineage, and declaring themselves valuable, these women shattered the stereotypes of aging females, both for themselves and those attending. A 22-year old woman confided:

It was really an exciting, emotional thing. Many of them went back three and four generations. That was amazing. And the power in their voices! In my family the women don't raise their voices and announce who they are. To see such strong women! One said, "if you would seek ecstasy with a Crone, seek me." I've never seen older women in a sexual light before. [It] was really uniting and empowering.

And a 24 year old said:

I felt really connected with the joy and power in these women who were saying, "This is where I am. This is what I want to do, and this is where I'm going." They were like older sisters and what they gave me is what I have to look forward to.

What this ritual represented to her was that she could look forward to an old age in which she could be respected and valued by her community, an old age in which she could be serious, playful, sexual, wise, powerful, political, and humorous, should she so choose. In other words, the image is one of a woman who is old *and* whole. The Crones rejected the limitations imposed by a culture in which female power, such as it is, is tied to youth, beauty, fertility, and male-directed sexuality. They were aging and aged post-menopausal women who symbolically redefined female beauty and worth and so reclaimed their autonomy and power. They clearly believed they had something of value to offer, and their community, in turn, rejoiced.

DISCUSSION

Clearly, each of these examples offers a celebratory vision of female power, female will, the female body, and of women's bonds. Rather than presenting role models for women that are defined and limited by their relationship to divine and secular male authority, as witches claim patriarchal religions do, each seeks to legitimate female power and authority. But instead of being based in dominance or hierarchy, the model of power and authority is rooted in strength and self-knowledge. The Crones said: "This is where I am ... this is where I'm going." Mary "*had* a body" and apparently delighted in it. Diana "radiated power with her body" and provided a source of pride and identification. Each image presented a physical manifestation of the connection between the material and the spiritual and then went on to not only liberate female sexuality from concepts of sin, but actually celebrate the erotic. Taken together as images which contribute to the new mythos, they offer the possibility of what Spretnak calls "an embodied way of knowing and being in the world," which possibility she described as:

... the empowering realization that being is being-in-relation, that we come to know the larger reality of humanity, Earthbody, and cosmos through the body, not by escaping the personal to an abstract system, and that apprehending our dynamic embeddedness in the unitive unfolding brings wisdom and grace to our subjectivity—including our conceptualizing and theorizing (Spretnak 1991:149).

... Of course, whether or not the women involved can sustain these feelings of power and celebration outside the ritual setting in a world that does not share their beliefs is problematic.

But this difficulty is not limited to feminist witchcraft or the Goddess movement, as many individuals experience conflict living up to their religious beliefs in a secular world. In addition, the power of mythopoeic imagery and religious symbolism in post-modern society may be open to debate. Yet regardless of intellectual debate, the women have felt the need to replace one set of mythic images with another, and have created religious images and symbols that have special significance and meaning for them. And as no two rituals are ever exactly alike, they continue to engage in this process of creation each and every time they do ritual.

This is a setting that offers rich material for further study. Do women who experience feelings of personal empowerment in Goddess rituals feel empowered in their daily lives? If so, how are these feelings manifested and do the women attribute them to their religious beliefs and practice? Are they different for women who experience different kinds of oppression, such as women of color or women with physical disabilities? In sum, specifically how do the spiritual beliefs and practices of these women help them to survive in a male-dominated world? What is the relationship between women in the Goddess movement and those who choose to remain in traditional religions but work to incorporate into them the female experience of the divine?

Another area for study involves the differences in the Goddess movement between essentialists, who believe there are universal and specific feminine and masculine qualities rooted in biology, and social constructionists, who argue that gender roles and distinctions are artificial, that they are socially constructed and imposed. How do these frameworks affect the understanding and analyses of patriarchal religious oppression experienced by women and how do they address the issues of race and class in the Goddess movement? Do they affect the religious worldview or how the new cultural vision is articulated? Are there demographic as well as ideological differences between the two groups?

It is clear that the Goddess movement is successful in providing a new framework of meaning for some women who, in growing numbers, are alienated from patriarchal religions. Although it supports other feminist approaches to change, such as in the legal, educational, and political arenas, the Goddess movement is radical in that it argues that the roots of gender oppression are deeper than these changes alone can reach. Religion defines the deepest values of a society, and, as Spretnak points out:

Efforts to radically transform society must fall short if the deepest informing assumptions and core values are not challenged (Spretnak 1991:149).

As these core values are challenged, new questions arise for sociologists. Not the least of these will deal with growing political tensions which are already visible. Feminist witches claim that more and more women are "coming out of the broom closet" and making public demonstrations of their faith. Evidence to support this can be seen in a proliferation of recent mainstream media articles on witches as well as in the list of sponsors and participants for the 1993 Parliament of the World's Religions held in Chicago. Evidence of the tension can be seen in the denouncements of feminist witchcraft and Goddess worship by some leaders of traditional religions, and the tendency of these same leaders to link feminism and all its issues to witchcraft. This public challenge to core values and the resulting potential for conflict is another area in which research may be fruitful.

CONCLUSION

In creating mythopoeic images that are rooted in material manifestations, such as the seasons of the year and the female body, feminist witches and women in the Goddess movement seek to shape a new cultural ethos. In presenting them in public rituals which are highly experiential, they attempt to share the worldview that informs this ethos in the belief that, eventually, this will lead to social change. Whether or not this goal is likely to be realized is beyond the parameters of this paper. What is clear is that these women have rejected the ethos they believe is present in patriarchal religions and, through the conscious construction and enactment of myth, they seek a new cultural understanding and vision that will reconnect and, in the Weberian sense, "reenchant" the world.

REFERENCES

BUDAPEST, Z. E. 1989. *The grandmother of time*. San Francisco: Harper & Row.

CAMPBELL, J. 1988. *The power of myth*. With Bill Moyers. New York: Doubleday.

DALY, M. 1973. *Beyond God the Father: Toward a philosophy of women's liberation*. Boston: Beacon Press.

————. 1992. *Outercourse: The be-dazzling voyage*. San Francisco: HarperSanFrancisco.

GOLDENBERG, N. 1979. *Changing of the gods: Feminism and the end of traditional religions*. Boston: Beacon Press.

HALE, M. M., and R. M. KELLY. 1989. *Gender, bureaucracy and democracy*. Westport, CT: Greenwood Press.

PRIEST, J. 1970. Myth and dream in Hebrew scripture. In *Myths, dreams, and religion*, edited by J. Campbell, 48–68. Dallas: Spring Publications.

SPRETNAK, C. 1991. *States of grace: The recovery of meaning in the postmodern age*. San Francisco: HarperSanFrancisco.

STARHAWK. 1988. *Dreaming the dark*, 2nd. ed. Boston: Beacon Press.

15 The Social Construction of a New Leadership Role: Catholic Women Pastors

RUTH A. WALLACE

Despite much debate following the Second Vatican Council in 1965, the Roman Catholic Church maintains its traditional view that women cannot be priests: as Wallace notes in her essay, women are "laity" no matter what leadership role they hold. As we learn in this essay, however, a shortage of priests in the U.S. has resulted in more women heading congregations as pastors. Wallace examines how women's leadership styles differ from their male counterparts and how their long-term presence in leadership roles affects the attitudes of their parishioners regarding women pastors.

. . .

THE REVISION OF THE CODE OF CANON LAW

Realizing the importance of changes in church law for the implementation of Vatican Council decisions, Pope John XXIII called for the revision of the Code of Canon Law in 1959. The new code, promulgated in 1983, included a change that opened the door for the appointment of laity as parish administrators. In recognition of the priest shortage, this code included a provision for people other than priests to perform some of the duties of the pastor in a parish. The new canon (or rule), number 517.2, reads:

If the diocesan bishop should decide that due to a dearth of priests a participation in the exercise of the pastoral care of a parish is to be entrusted to a deacon or some other person who is not a priest, or to a community of persons, he is to appoint some priest endowed with the power and faculties of a pastor, to supervise the pastoral care.

The phrase "due to the dearth of priests" reveals an important demographic factor as the rationale for this change in church law. In the next section I discuss this and other

Source: Ruth Wallace, "The Social Construction of a New Leadership Role: Catholic Women Pastors." Reprinted with permission, from *Sociology of Religion*, Volume 54, ©1993.

demographic changes that helped to create the opportunity for a greater empowerment of the laity.

DEMOGRAPHIC CHANGES

The increasing shortage of Catholic priests is the key demographic change that must be examined in order to understand why laity are now heading parishes. ... American dioceses will lose an average of 40 percent of their active priest population between 1966 and 2005. A fact that is not well known to the average American parishioner is that at the present time only six of every ten vacant positions throughout the United States are being filled by newly ordained priests.

The priest shortage would be less critical if it were not for the continued growth in Catholic membership. ...

Other demographic factors external to the Catholic Church should be included in this analysis. The contemporary women's movement, which entered a phase of intense mobilization soon after the adjournment of the Vatican Council, had important repercussions for Catholic women. Chief among the external demographics that have affected the internal demographics of the Catholic church are women's greater participation in the labor force, their increased rate of college attendance, and their completion of postgraduate degrees (Kroe 1989:11–13). All of these facilitating factors—Vatican II changes, the revision of church law, and internal and external demographic changes—have expedited women's entrance into new roles in the Catholic Church.

THE SOCIAL CONSTRUCTION OF A NEW LEADERSHIP ROLE

Between June and December, 1989, I visited twenty parishes scattered throughout the United States where women had been appointed by the bishop as administrator of the parish. These parishes were situated in six of the nine census regions of the United States. Because I was interested in comparing nuns and married women as pastors, eleven of the parishes I visited were headed by nuns, eight were headed by married women, and one by a lay woman who was not married. It is important to keep in mind, however, that *all* women in the Catholic Church are laity, including nuns, because ordination to the clerical state is denied to women. The women in my study, therefore, share two characteristics: their gender and their lay state, and as I will show, these shared characteristics have an impact on the way they perceive and perform their duties in their role as pastor.

I stayed for a weekend in each parish, usually living with the woman in her parish house or family home. While there I conducted taped formal interviews with each woman pastor, her sacramental minister (the title for the priest who was assigned as her supervisor or moderator), and two parishioners (one male and one female). This is a qualitative research study, based primarily on formal and informal interviews, and field notes from my own observations. All of the generalizations are based on the clear majority of the subjects, or the dominant pattern. Therefore, when I quote from a particular subject, this represents a common interview theme. Other sources of data were documents such as parish histories, local newspaper articles, diocesan guidelines, church bulletins, contracts, and letters.

Although initially interested in the constraints and resources in the role transition process, I soon realized that these women were not simply following the script of the previous priest pastor. Because they were not ordained, it was impossible for them to perform all of the priestly roles. On the other hand, the lay state that they shared with their parishioners enabled them to break down some of the barriers to communication that had existed under previous pastors. They would not and could not place themselves on a pedestal well above the members of the parish. Instead they were, in conjunction with their parishioners, practicing collaborative leadership, and thus creating a new social reality.

According to Berger and Luckmann (1967), everyday life is socially constructed by the continuous creation, through actions and interactions, of a shared reality that is experienced as objectively factual and subjectively meaningful. Their theory utilizes three key concepts that they describe as moments of a dialectical process: externalization, objectivation, and internalization. Each of these concepts will, in turn, be used in explaining the social construction of a new style of leadership.

The Push for Externalization: The Ethos of the Parishes

In the process of externalization, individuals create their social worlds by their activity with others. It is in the externalization phase that people are seen as creative beings, capable of acting on their environment. The ethos of the parishes upon their arrival was what inspired the women pastors to move toward a new leadership style.

The parishes typically went through a "grieving process" over the loss of their priest pastor. All of these parishes had previously been headed by priests, and the parishioners' identities as Catholics were linked to their priest pastor. In Berger and Luckmann's theory, this change represented a disruption of their previous internalization, a loss of a significant other with whom they strongly identified.

The woman pastor was a "first" for them; many of them had not heard of the legal changes about the appointment of laity to head parishes until shortly before it happened in their parish. Because their new pastor was a layperson, it meant that they would have to depend on a priest to come from another parish, one who was often a stranger to them, to celebrate their Masses and to preside at the

other sacraments. Another constraint was a financial one. In addition to their own pastor's salary, a priestless parish is also expected to pay a stipend to the priest who travels to their parish to perform his sacramental duties.

It is not surprising, then, that there was some initial resistance on the part of parishioners, especially during the first year. When one of the nun pastors arrived at the parish, a male parishioner told her:

I hope you're not sensitive, but it was our turn for a good priest, and we got you. It's not you; you have to know that. No matter how good you are, you are not going to be good enough. People are not going to accept you, and you are going to have a hard time.

The idea of a woman pastor is so incongruous for many Catholics that they can hardly imagine it. It is incompatible with their only image of a Catholic pastor: a priest, an ordained male, the dominant figure in the parish, whose parishioners traditionally both revere and obey him. A woman in charge of a parish does not look like a pastor, does not sound like a pastor, and does not behave like most previous pastors. In short, many Catholics, like the parishioner quoted above, have *reified* the role of pastor, in Berger and Luckmann's terms. They have forgotten that the role of pastor was created by human beings; instead they apprehend the role as a nonhuman fact, incapable of change.

A married woman pastor told of the conflict she had with a very domineering male parishioner who was a member of the parish council. She said "I think the guy had a real problem with women in authority. As long as I would let him have the upper hand, it was okay. One day I didn't do that, and he just blew up."

A belief in patriarchy guarantees a dominant position for males because the primacy of their authority is unquestioned, and the Catholic Church as an institution is the personification of a hierarchical system based on patriarchy. In the Catholic tradition the use of terms like "your eminence" and "your excellency" reserved for cardinals and bishops, all of whom are men, is a case in point. I found that the belief that men should rule was played out in numerous ways in the everyday lives of women pastors. It was particularly evident in the way some of the sacramental ministers (priests) related to them. A nun pastor explained that the priest made it clear to her that he wanted to do things "his way," so she had to be tactful about making any suggestions or recommendations to him. As she described it, "To put it simply, I feel tired if I have to work at being diplomatic with (him), and make a suggestion, and make it sound like he made it in order to make it work out right. Sometimes that wearies me."

Another nun pastor described what ensued when she stood up to a male parishioner at a parish council meeting.

I certainly didn't want to cause a major eruption, but I wasn't going to let this man rule me for the whole time I was there. I tried to be gentle with him, but firm; [to] listen to him, but he was totally disrespectful. It was really a woman issue. . . . And the whole first year had been a real struggle with him.

A female parishioner in another parish said that there was a lot of "hell-raising" when the parishioners heard "that a woman was going to be boss." She quoted one of the women in the parish who told her: "I know these men. They don't want a woman in charge. They think all we are good for is cooking in the kitchen, making love, and having babies."

In Goffman's (1959) view, the women pastors were not able to present the appropriate "personal front." Not only were they the wrong gender, but they also lacked the institutional status of all previous pastors. Not having been ordained, they arrived at the parish sharing an equal status with their parishioners, as laity.

Armed with the Vatican II definition of the church as the people of God, it is no wonder, then, that they soon decided to recruit their parishioners as co-workers. They accomplished this by a combination of strategies: visiting

homes, learning names, including parishioners' concerns in their homilies, and making themselves accessible. On their part, the parishioners were willing accomplices in the creation of this new social reality, partly because they wanted to avoid the alternative, a closing of their parish.

Collaborative Leadership as a Social Fact

One of the most striking differences between the women pastors and their priest predecessors was the leadership style. The dominant pattern of leadership was collaborative. In a collaborative relationship, based on equality rather than hierarchy, all of the persons in an organization work together to achieve a common end. The leader guides, rather than commands, drawing on the talents of others. This is in direct contrast to the priest pastor who typically performs like a "one-man band," rather than a conductor leading the orchestra.

According to Berger and Luckmann, "The common objectivations of everyday life are maintained primarily by linguistic signification." Pastors and parishioners alike spoke of the social reality of participating as co-laborers; one of the women pastors explained her perspective on leadership this way:

Leadership is listening to parishioners' initiatives. A leader listens and then articulates the needs and directions of the community, and finds ways to name it and facilitate it. The most valuable thing I think anybody could have who would find themselves in this position [as pastor] would be to maintain their sense of deep respect for all of the people that you work with and not think that you are in a position of authority over them.

Most of the time parishioners responded positively when the pastor asked them to become involved in the running of the parish. It was only on rare occasions that there was an outright refusal. One of the parishioners explained (Wallace, 1992:78), "It's hard to say no to [her] because people respect her and you want to help her. And she just has a way of asking you that puts you at ease. It's not in a demanding sort of way at all. She always *asks*, never says, 'Do this'."

A priest spoke of the advantages for the married woman pastor in a nearby parish:

One thing that is very highly stressed over there [at her parish] is lay leadership. I can talk about that all day here [at my parish] but it doesn't have the same impact. . . . When [the woman pastor] says, "Well, I'm a mother, too, and I have kids at home, . . . and being the lector is something I enjoy and you would enjoy it, too," they take it in a different way than if it came from me. So in many ways she is better [than I am] with the laity because she is a laywoman.

Parishioners' experience of collaborative leadership is, I would argue, directly related to their changing attitudes and behavior regarding their own women pastors. For example, there was typically not only an increase in the number of parishioners who became actively involved in parish committees, but also an increase in financial contributions in these parishes where parishioners are now making (or contributing to) the parish's financial decisions. One woman pastor said that the finance committee, made up of four parishioners and herself, arrived at the yearly budget by consensus. She explained,

When I meet with them, I give them an update of where we stand, and they see everything. This is something that they have been absolutely flabbergasted with. They never saw the books before. They get an accounting of every last penny. They see everything that comes in, how it is spent, and where we stand.

For their part, many parishioners said that once they responded to their pastor's collaborative leadership by becoming actively engaged in the running of the parish, they became part of the financial solution themselves. A woman pastor described it this way:

Before, [church] services would be over and the people would be gone. Now you see them hanging around, and they really have developed a wonderful sense of community. They are not looking to the

priests any more for their answers. They are really making some decisions in terms of their own parish plans and facilities. Collections have gone way up, and they are making decisions on how to use that.

Internalization of the New Social Reality

When individuals internalize a social reality, they also gain a social identity; and when they conform to the expectations of social institutions, they are simultaneously re-creating them. The creation of a new institution occurs in the moment of externalization; once externalized, it is objectified; and once objectified, it acts back on the individual as an internalized entity (see Berger and Luckmann, 1967).

Having a layperson appointed as their pastor is a "mixed bag" for parishioners. On the one hand, lay identity means that the pastor is "one of them," and leadership that was previously hierarchical is now collaborative. Parishioners in these parishes experience a growing sense of empowerment and of community. On the other hand, the lay state has liturgical and financial costs for the parishioners as well.

Reflecting on the parishioners' internalization, a married woman who had been a member of the parish for several years before her appointment as pastor said,

In all of the years of my gradually doing different things here, being president of the [parish] council, leading prayer services, and all the other things, there was never any time when somebody said, "Wait a minute, [she] can't do that because she's a woman." It's only when you get into the areas of the Sunday Assembly, and the heavy-duty sacramental things, that the issue begins to surface. And it always comes from the top down, from the hierarchy; it isn't a problem for the average people. And those people that do suffer from it and say, "Wait a minute, she's a woman," they didn't learn that themselves. It was taught to them, and they can learn to get past that, just as they can learn to get past judging a person because they are black or Mexican or Oriental.

The issue of "appropriate" behavior for men and women came up in several of the interviews.

For example, the question of whether or not to fire the housecleaner for the parish house was raised. A woman pastor described her response:

[The woman who cleaned the house] came in tears after Father left and said to me, "I suppose now that Father's gone that they won't hire me anymore." She thought that I was going to do the cleaning. I said, "That shouldn't make any difference. I am doing everything Father did. You can be sure as long as I'm here you are going to stay on." Then I heard comments from the people, "Now that Sister is hired she will have more time so she can do her own cleaning." That was all the more reason why I didn't. I said, "I really wasn't trained to do the work of a housecleaner. I know how to do it, but my work is ministry here. And if Father could have somebody, I don't see why I can't." She [the housecleaner] stayed on.

There were several indications that patriarchal beliefs and gender discrimination were being replaced by positive feminist beliefs and gender equality in the parishes I visited. There were a number of occasions when the question of inclusive language emerged. Sometimes it emerged during our conversations, and at other times I observed it in action, usually during the Sunday liturgy. For example, I noticed in one parish that hymns on xeroxed sheets showed words like "his" and other exclusive language had been deleted, and more inclusive language was inserted. In another parish I heard the priest give the last blessing to the congregation at Mass in a more inclusive way. Instead of "In the name of the Father, Son, and Holy Spirit," he said, "In the name of the Creator, Redeemer, and Holy Spirit." On neither occasion did I witness an uprising or even a mild protest from the congregation.

Often I heard my interviewees allude to the sexist stance of the institutional church. A male parishioner said, "I would like to see more liberal views towards women as far as active roles in the church because they are a valuable resource. I think we have done a disservice.... The hierarchy is totally male, so it is hard for them to accept that."

Perhaps the change in attitudes and action that has resulted from a woman pastor's activi-

ties in a parish can best be summed up by a statement from a woman parishioner who was the parish organist and choir director:

I have really come to believe that women can do the job, not as well, but *better*. And believe it or not, when [the woman pastor] first came here, I didn't even change the words in the hymns. That was not an issue at all. So I've grown a lot in the last four years, and realize what women can do for this church. And the position that women are in presently, I don't think it's right.

When it came to the issue of ordination of women, however, the women pastors themselves offered carefully nuanced statements. A typical response was made by one of the nun pastors who said that she "wouldn't want ordination to continue as it's been," adding that to ordain women in the present structure would mean having "a masculine structure with feminine bodies in it." She suggested a new, less hierarchical model of ordination that would reflect the more participatory style of leadership modeled by women pastors.

As is evident in statements from parishioners, they witness the whole gamut of challenges stemming from patriarchal beliefs and practices that their woman pastor meets on a daily basis. And the parishioners, as laity, can identify with her treatment as a second-class citizen. They are beginning to question this inequity. Even those parishioners who described themselves as traditional Catholics told me that they had changed their attitudes and actions regarding women in the church. In fact, the overwhelming majority of the parishioners I interviewed no longer support gender discrimination, and they attribute their change in thinking to their experience with the collaborative leadership of a woman pastor.

CONCLUSION

Given the continued decrease in number of active priests, accompanied by a growing increase in the Catholic population, we can expect that the phenomenon of priestless parishes will not disappear soon in the United States. In addition to Schoenherr's (1990) demographic data, a different type of indicator of this trend can be seen in a recent advertisement in the *National Catholic Reporter* (1992) by a diocese seeking pastoral administrator applicants. The ad states that they are "uncertain of openings now," but that they are in the process of building a file for the future.

Can we expect a continuation of collaborative leadership in these parishes? In order to address this question further research, both quantitative and qualitative, is needed on a number of fronts. For instance, one of the central questions emerging from this study is the extent to which the patterns of behavior and attitudes toward the collaborative leadership exercised in these parishes are due to the lay state or to the gender of the pastor. A comparison of the woman headed parishes with those led by nonordained men (religious brothers and laymen) could help to answer this question. Because most male Catholics who feel called to serve the needs of the church become priests, the number of such parishes in the United States is small; by 1991 there were thirteen pastored by religious brothers. To my knowledge there has been no systematic research on Catholic parishes headed by laymen.

A comparison with Catholic parishes administered by deacons, of which there were forty-seven in 1991, should also be undertaken. Even though deacons are ordained, their clerical ranking is below that of a priest. In contrast to laity, however, deacons have the right to preach, baptize, perform funeral services, and witness marriages. It would increase our understanding of this phenomenon to know the type of leadership practiced by deacons and the behavior and attitudes of parishioners toward them, as compared with parishes headed by laity.

Although some research on Catholic parishes headed by women in South America has been done (Adriance, 1991; Gilfeather, 1977), additional cross-cultural research on other continents could shed some light on cultural differences regarding the use of collaborative leadership. Another line of research could compare Catholic women pastors with female Episcopal priests, holding gender constant while looking at lay/clerical differences in the practice of parish leadership.

Although my study is the first systematic look at an important religious phenomenon, it represents only the tip of the iceberg. The experiences of women pastors and their important role partners—their parishioners, priests, and bishops—have assisted in the process of what Berger and Luckmann (1967:91) would label the dereification of the role of Catholic pastor. I am convinced that their participation in the construction of a new reality of leadership at the parish level will prepare the way for important structural changes in the Catholic Church of the twenty-first century.

REFERENCES

ADRIANCE, MADELEINE. 1991. "Agents of change: the roles of priests, sisters, and lay workers in the grassroots Catholic church in Brazil." *Journal for the Scientific Study of Religion* 30:292–305.

BERGER, PETER L. and THOMAS LUCKMANN. 1967. *The Social Construction of Reality: A Treatise in the Sociology of Knowledge.* Garden City, NY: Doubleday.

GILFEATHER, KATHERINE. 1977. "The changing role of women in the Catholic church in Chile." *Journal for the Scientific Study of Religion* 16:39–54.

GOFFMAN, ERVING. 1959. *The Presentation of Self in Everyday Life.* Garden City, NY: Doubleday.

KROE, ELAINE. 1989. *National Higher Education Statistics: Fall 1989.* Washington, DC: U.S. Department of Education.

National Catholic Reporter. 1992. 28 (April 3):24.

SHOENHERR, RICHARD A. and LAWRENCE A. YOUNG. 1990. *The Catholic Priest in the United States: Demographic Investigations.* Madison, WI: University of Wisconsin-Madison Comparative Religious Organization Studies Publications.

WALLACE, RUTH. 1992. *They call Her Pastor: A New Role for Catholic Women.* Albany, NY: State University of New York Press.

Reading

16 Socioeconomic Inequality in the American Religious System: An Update and Assessment

CHRISTIAN SMITH AND ROBERT FARIS

Smith and Faris's essay sparked renewed interest in studying the links between social class, economic inequality, and religion. After decades of neglect, class analysis has been reunited with studies of religious organizations, their beliefs, and practices. While their study is exploratory, its findings raise important questions about how social class differences are reflected in American religious groups.

American religion has from the beginning of its history been stratified by education, income, and occupational status. Since colonial days, religious differences have played a role in constructing social differentiations that sustained socioeconomic inequalities. As the American religious system grew increasingly pluralistic over time, socioeconomic disparities between different religious communities transformed and persisted.

American sociology has for decades documented and theorized these persistent inequalities between religious communities. Many distinguished works—including H. Richard Niebuhr's *The Social Sources of Denominationalism* (1929), Liston Pope's *Millhands and Preachers* (1942), Gerhard Lenski's *The Religious Factor* (1961), W. Lloyd Warner's *Yankee City* (1963), E. Digby Baltzell's *The Protestant Establishment: Aristocracy and Caste in America* (1964), and N. J. Demerath's *Social Class in American Protestantism* (1965)—have analyzed socioeconomic inequality in American religion. . . .

Socioeconomic inequalities between religious groups have also played an important role in many sociological theories about religion and society. Marx, for example, is famous for theorizing religion's ideological role in legitimating economic inequality and exploitation (Marx 1978a, 1978b [1843, 1845]). Status differences within and between religious groups were important features of Weber's analysis of religion (1978). According to Finke and Stark's

Source: Christian Smith and Robert Faris, "Socioeconomic Inequality in the American Religious System: An Update and Assessment," from *Journal for the Scientific Study of Religion*, Volume 44. Copyright © 2005. Reproduced with permission of Blackwell Publishing Ltd.

(1992) religious economies theory, educational disparities significantly influenced the historical course of religious diffusion in America. Hunter (1983:49–60) theorizes that socioeconomic differences between religious groups explain the persistence of conservative religion in modern society. And Wuthnow (1988) argues that educational mobility was key in the 20th-century restructuring of the American religious system.

Given both the historical stratification of American religion and its significant role in helping to define and sustain economic and political inequality more broadly (Swartz 1996), one would expect scholars to have paid close attention to tracking socioeconomic differences in the American religious system. But we generally have not. In fact, the last, best, systematic empirical analysis of American religious stratification (Roof and McKinney 1987) was published 18 years ago, and was based on General Social Survey data collected between 1972 and 1982, in comparison to data from the 1940s. . . . Although Roof and McKinney's analysis shows striking social class disparities among American religious groups, their larger discussion emphasizes the "fluid and dynamic" changes affecting interreligious inequality during the decades of the mid-20th century (1987: 107–17). They point particularly to the upward mobility of Catholics, Mormons, and evangelical and fundamentalist Protestants, concluding that:

The [social] sources of denominationalism identified by [H. Richard] Niebuhr . . . are still important for understanding the social bases of American religion. The nation's faith communities continue to be divided along lines of social class. . . . We should not, however, minimize the changes that have occurred during [the last fifty years]. The religious map of America is much different today from the time when Niebuhr wrote. . . . The ascriptive bases of the religious communities have declined, creating a more fluid and voluntary religious system. (1987:144–45)

These findings, however, are now decades old.

Much more recently, Thaddeus Coreno (2002) and Jerry Park and Samuel Reimer (2002) have published research on religion and socioeconomic inequality. Coreno (2002) finds that white U.S. Protestant mainliners and fundamentalists represent different class cultures, the two groups are significantly separated by social class and status differences. Park and Reimer (2002) note what they see as a "slow convergence" of different religious groups toward more similar social class positions between 1972 and 1998, noting at the same time, however, the major class differences that remain between different faith communities. We are pleased to see new research published on religion and socioeconomic inequality, but believe further study is warranted. For one thing, both of these articles group religious believers by the major tradition categories of fundamentalist, evangelical, mainline, African-American Protestant, etc.—not by the more specific denominational type we use below. Major religious tradition categories are often very useful analytically but can also obscure dynamics that may occur and be evident with more fine-grained groupings. The consequence of the "slow convergence" Park and Reimer observe may also be rather trivial, in view of the large socioeconomic differences that still separate different religious groups and the fact that nearly any observed change over time would almost inevitably be statistically significant given the very large Ns of their religious categories (e.g., 8,932 evangelical Protestants, 9,502 Catholics). Moreover, neither article reports on changes in the occupational prestige of different religious types over time, which we do below. In sum, we may be seeing early signs of renewed scholarly interest in religion and socioeconomic inequality, but more research is clearly warranted.

This research note is an attempt to update our descriptive knowledge about socioeconomic inequalities among American religious groups. Here we seek to track educational, income, and status stratification in U.S. religion over a 15-year period, from the early 1980s to the late 1990s, in order to assess the extent and structure of social stratification in the American religious system. Our intention is to assess how much, if any, change has taken place, and which religious groups have gained and lost in socioeconomic standing.

DATA AND METHODS

Data for this analysis comes, as they did for Roof and McKinney (1987), from the General Social Survey, a biennial national survey of U.S. noninstitutionalized adults featuring demographic, socioeconomic, and attitudinal data (Davis, Smith, and Marsden 2001). Our approach in the following analysis is to calculate mean values for religious denominations for four socioeconomic indicators: years of education, college degree, job prestige, and household income. For income, we use the GSS-imputed income measure, "REALINC," which is adjusted to 1986 dollars. Job prestige is measured using the Hodge-Siegel-Rossi prestige rating of U.S. Census occupations. Data from the 1980s use the 1970 occupational codes, and data from the 1990s use the codes from the 1980 census. Because some religious denominations are small, to obtain large enough Ns for analysis, we merged the 1983 and 1984 data together and the 1998 and 2000 data together. The correct income variable was unavailable after 1996, so this analysis relies on 1996 data only, rather than 1998 and 2000 data (see http://www.icpsr.umich.edu/GSS/for details).

The reader should note that certain groups in particular years reflect low Ns, and so any interpretation of data on them must be somewhat circumspect, particularly when findings reflect big changes or when they diverge from what other studies show. However, rather than deleting them from analysis, this article includes some lower N cases, with the understanding that readers will use care in interpreting them. In particular, readers should note the Ns for Unitarians (eight in 1983/1984) and some other groups which in some years have Ns in the teens. Fluctuations in Ns across the two time periods may be the result of the geographical-cluster sampling method used by the GSS.

Two comments on religious denominations and groupings. First, the Evangelical Lutheran Church in America (ELCA) was formed officially in 1988 out of a merger of several mainline Lutheran bodies, all of which we group together as "ELCA" for our 1983/1984 analyses. Second, we categorized certain religious groups analyzed here (e.g., conservative Methodist, black Baptist, etc.) by grouping close families of churches and denominations that share a similar religious heritage (e.g., Wesleyan, Free Methodist, etc. churches comprising the group "conservative Methodist").

Mean values for each religious denomination or tradition are presented in Tables 1–4 as percentages, ranked by status in 1998–2000. Tables 1–4 include the Ns for each combined set of years, mean percentages for 1983/1984 and 1998/2000 (except for Table 3, which uses 1996 data), the percent change for the intervening years, and the change in ranking for each religious denomination. Table 5 then compares the average ranking for the four socioeconomic variables, comparing 1983/1984–1998/2000 (and 1996 for Table 3), in order to assess overall ranking change for the intervening time period. Tables 1–5 group the religious denominations and traditions into three clusters, showing the top third, middle third, and bottom third.

RESULTS

Table 1 reveals major disparities between American religious traditions in the percent of adherents who have earned college degrees. At the top, more than 60 percent of Unitarian and Jewish Americans, 46 percent of Episcopalians, and nearly 40 percent of Presbyterian Church in the USA (PCUSA) believers in 1998/2000 hold college degrees. By contrast, seven different religious denominations in 1998/2000 had less than 20 percent of members with earned college degrees. Overall, the highest formal education appears associated with more liberal traditions (Church of Jesus Christ of Latter-Day Saints being one exception), and the lowest with more conservative, sectarian, Pentecostal, and black church groups. Most, but not all, groups increased in percent with college degree, most typically by

4–8 percent when a few low-*N* outliers are excluded. Few groups shifted in ranking by more than a few ranks in the approximately 16 years between 1983/1984 and 1998/2000.

Table 2 presents educational attainment not in percent with college degree, but as average years of education, allowing for the influence of varying distributions to shape the reported number. The rankings in 1998/2000 are very similar to those in Table 1, with the top six and bottom six denominations matching in both. Again, more liberal groups cluster at the top, and more conservative, sectarian, Pentecostal, and black church groups cluster at the bottom. The disparity in total mean years of formal education completed, however, is not as large as with percent college degree. The top denominations in 1998/2000 reflect an average of about 14.5 years; the bottom denominations an average of about 12.5 years. These variations,

TABLE 1   Percent with College Degree, By Denomination, 1983–2000 (Ranked by 1998–2000 Status)

Denomination	N/N (1980s/1990s)	%College 1983–1984	%College 1998–2000	Change in % College	Change in Rank
Unitarian	8/18	75.0	61.1	−13.9	0
Jewish	70/113	55.7	60.2	+4.5	0
Episcopal	65/112	50.8	45.5	−5.2	0
Presbyterian USA	134/151	31.3	39.7	+8.4	0
UCC	14/17	21.4	35.3	+13.9	+4
LDS	66/32	19.7	28.1	+8.4	+4
Nonreligious	224/794	25.9	27.1	+1.2	−2
United Methodist	126/374	23.0	27.0	+4.0	−1
Missouri/Wisconsin Lutheran	32/104	9.4	24.0	+14.7	+8
Conservative Methodist	22/25	22.7	24.0	+1.3	0
ELCA	40/148	25.0	23.6	−1.4	−5
American Baptist	16/41	12.5	22.0	+9.5	+3
Catholic	814/1384	14.3	21.7	+7.5	0
Black Baptist	34/136	14.7	19.9	+5.1	−2
Southern Baptist	107/500	10.3	16.4	+6.1	+1
Nondenominational Conserv. Protestant	22/31	13.6	12.9	−0.7	−2
Adventist	16/25	18.8	12.0	−6.8	−6
Assembly of God	16/29	0.0	10.3	+10.3	+1
Other [Pentecostal]	91/157	3.3	7.0	+3.7	+1
Jehovah's Witness	23/43	0.0	7.0	+7.0	0

Source: General Social Survey (1983, 1984, 1998, 2000).

TABLE 2   Mean Adult Education, By Denomination, 1983–2000 (Ranked By 1998–2000 Status)

Denomination	N/N (1980s/1990s)	Mean Years		Change in Mean Years	Change in Rank
		1983–1984	1998–2000		
Unitarian	8/18	16.38	16.39	+0.01	0
Jewish	70/113	14.80	15.69	+0.89	0
Episcopal	65/112	14.43	14.84	+0.41	0
Presbyterian USA	134/151	13.59	14.59	+1.00	0
UCC	14/17	13.07	13.82	+0.75	+3
United Methodist	126/374	13.23	13.65	+0.42	+1
ELCA	40/148	13.25	13.59	+0.34	−1
Nonreligious	224/794	12.87	13.58	+0.72	+2
LDS	66/32	13.41	13.50	+0.09	−4
Adventist	16/25	12.75	13.44	+0.69	+2
Conservative Methodist	22/25	11.59	13.32	+1.73	+6
American Baptist	16/41	11.69	13.24	+1.56	+2
Catholic	814/1384	12.32	13.15	+0.84	0
Missouri/Wisconsin Lutheran	32/104	12.91	13.10	+0.19	−5
Black Baptist	34/136	11.41	12.59	+1.18	+4
Southern Baptist	107/500	11.65	12.58	+0.93	−1
Nondenominational Conserv. Protestant	22/31	12.82	12.52	−0.30	−6
Jehovah's Witness	23/43	11.48	12.19	+0.71	0
Assembly of God	16/29	10.63	12.17	+1.55	−3
Other [Pentecostal]	91/157	10.20	11.81	+1.62	0

Source: General Social Survey (1983, 1984, 1998, 2000).

however, suggest the difference between at least some college education and a high school diploma as the typical educational experience of adherents. Again, almost all groups enjoyed modest increases in mean years of education. And while a few groups jumped in ranking dramatically, the overall picture in Table 2 is one of stability in educational attainment between 1983/1984 and 1998/2000.

Table 3 presents means and over-time changes in household income for the different religious groups. In the top third for 1996, Jews, Unitarians, Latter-Day Saints, Episcopalians, and members of the PCUSA are joined by non-denominational conservative Protestants (evangelicals), who fared lower in the education tables. Many, but not all, of the same groups who are low in education are, not surprisingly, also low in income. The income variance between the top and the bottom is significant, with top third groups earning nearly twice as

much on average as bottom third groups ($51,871 and $22,153 being the extremes for 1996). Compared to education, we also see greater variance in the change in mean income, ranging from a *decline* of $7,476 for the Evangelical Lutheran Church of America, to an increase of $14,261 for Latter-Day Saints (again, low-N groups should be interpreted with caution here). Except for a few lower-N outliers, the overall ranking of groups between 1983/1984 and 1996 shifted only modestly.

Table 4 examines differences in occupational prestige ranked by 1998/2000 data. The religious groups range from a high of 52.05 for Jews to a low of 39.53 for American (Northern) Baptists. All but these two groups have mean occupational prestige scales in the 1940s, although differences between the groups roughly track differences noted in education and income (notable exceptions being the Assemblies of God and conservative

TABLE 3   Mean Household Income, By Denomination, 1983–1996 (Ranked By 1996 Status)

Denomination	N/N (1980s/1990s)	Mean Income 1983–1984	Mean Income 1996	Change in Mean Income	Change in Rank
Jewish	70/68	50,579	51,871	+1,292	0
Unitarian	8/7	39,842	46,158	+6,317	+2
LDS	66/27	29,254	43,515	+14,261	+6
Episcopal	65/79	48,523	42,953	−5,571	−2
Presbyterian USA	134/63	36,481	40,300	+3,820	+1
Nondenominational Conserv. Protestant	22/20	28,059	38,901	+10,843	+4
Missouri/Wisconsin Lutheran	32/59	26,683	37,686	+11,003	+5
Catholic	814/685	31,122	35,788	+4,666	0
United Methodist	126/190	31,789	33,893	+2,105	−2
UCC	14/8	40,481	32,269	−8,213	−7
Assembly of God	16/23	18,848	30,346	+11,498	+9
Adventist	16/16	25,577	30,094	+4,517	+1
Nonreligious	224/339	27,963	29,086	+1,123	−2
ELCA	40/99	36,520	29,044	−7,476	−9
Southern Baptist	107/273	25,802	28,528	+2,726	−1
Jehovah's Witness	23/17	20,819	27,081	+6,262	+1
Black Baptist	34/69	23,342	23,793	+451	−1
American Baptist	16/28	19,476	23,321	+3,845	+1
Other [Pentecostal]	91/64	19,708	23,174	+3,466	−1
Conservative Methodist	22/15	24,029	22,153	−1,876	−5

Source: General Social Survey (1983, 1984, 1996).

Methodists in the top third on prestige, and the United Church of Christ being in the bottom third). As with the previous tables, with the exception of a few outliers, most groups moved only a few ranking places for occupational prestige between 1983/1984 and 1998/2000.

Finally, Table 5 attempts to summarize the socioeconomic changes observed in Tables 1–4 by calculating the average rank in education, income, and job prestige for each religious group, and comparing between the 1983/1984 and 1998/2000 average ranks to calculate the average rank change for the intervening time period. We see that the majority of religious groups, 16 of the total 20, changed ranks on average no more than two places; 12 of those groups in fact moved less than one ranking place. Overall, Table 5 suggests a picture of over-time stability in overall socioeconomic ranking. As to gainers and losers, to the extent that their somewhat low *N*s do not introduce sampling error here,

the Assemblies of God were the biggest gainers and the Evangelical Lutheran Church in America ([ELCA]), Adventists, and the United Church of Christ Americans were the biggest socioeconomic losers between the early 1980s and late 1990s. The gainers, with a few exceptions, tended to be those at the bottom of the rankings, and thus had more upward room for mobility between the two periods of measurement. Most of those ranked at the top of the scales tended neither to gain nor to lose much in rankings, but simply maintained their high positions.

DISCUSSION

This analysis is a response to the continuing need for an updating and reassessment of our knowledge about socioeconomic inequalities between American religious groups. The findings in the tables above suggest the following general observations.

TABLE 4   Mean Occupational Prestige, By Denomination, 1983–1998 (Ranked By 1996–1998 Status)

Denomination	N/N (1980s/1990s)	Mean Prestige		Change in Mean Prestige	Change in Rank
		1983–1984	1998–2000		
Jewish	70/113	49.50	52.05	+2.5	+1
Unitarian	8/18	51.38	49.44	−1.9	−1
Episcopal	65/112	45.79	49.35	+3.6	+1
Assembly of God	16/29	36.13	48.41	+12.3	+12
Presbyterian USA	134/151	45.53	47.69	+2.2	0
Conservative Methodist	22/25	38.45	47.00	+8.6	+7
United Methodist	126/374	43.02	46.42	+3.4	−1
Adventist	16/25	41.56	46.13	+4.6	0
ELCA	40/148	42.51	46.08	+3.6	−2
Nondenominational Conserv. Protestant	22/31	38.32	44.83	+6.5	+4
LDS	66/32	39.98	44.41	+4.4	0
Nonreligious	224/794	40.58	44.12	+3.5	−3
Catholic	814/1384	39.76	44.02	+4.3	−1
UCC	14/17	47.25	43.29	−4.0	−11
Missouri/Wisconsin Lutheran	32/104	40.23	43.06	+2.8	−5
Southern Baptist	107/500	36.68	42.86	+6.2	−1
Black Baptist	34/136	32.78	42.10	+9.3	+2
Jehovah's Witness	23/43	34.14	41.24	+7.1	0
Other [Pentecostal]	91/157	31.37	40.15	+8.8	+1
American Baptist	16/41	34.27	39.53	+5.3	−3

Source: General Social Survey (1983, 1984, 1998, 2000).

1. *The American religious system at the end of the 20th century reflected major socioeconomic differences between groups within that system.* Certain religious groups—particularly Unitarians, Jews, Episcopalians, and mainline Presbyterians—consistently enjoyed significantly higher levels of education, income, and occupational prestige than most of the groups below them. Likewise, other religious groups—especially members of Jehovah's Witness, black Baptist, Southern Baptist, and other Pentecostal churches—displayed significantly lower levels of socioeconomic status than many other groups. Certain religious groups, on the other hand, reveal noticeable levels of status inconsistencies. Assemblies of God members, for example, appear to have relatively low levels of education, moderate levels of income, and relatively high occupational prestige scores. Nondenominational conservative Protestants, similarly, reflect lower levels of education, higher levels of income, and moderate levels of

job prestige. But on the whole, socioeconomic inequality across measures depicts a great deal of consistency in stratification. The structure of interreligious inequality that Roof and McKinney (1987) mapped of the 1970s and early 1980s continues to hold.

2. *The system of socioeconomic inequality that characterized American religion at the end of the 20th century reflects a high degree of stability in reproducing itself over the years between the early 1980s and the late 1990s.* Although some specific group mobility is evident in the tables above, there is much more continuity than change in the system of inequality. Despite the longest period of economic growth in the nation's history during the 1990s, with few exceptions, the groups that were ranked highest in 1983/1984 were also ranked highest in 1998/2000, and those ranked lowest in the first set of years were also ranked lowest in the second. Since Roof

TABLE 5   Average Change In Ses Ranking, 1983–2000 (Ranked By Average Rank Change)

Denomination	Average Rank (1980s)	Average Rank (1990s)	Average Rank Change (1980–1990)
Assembly of God	17.75	13.00	+4.75
Conservative Methodist	13.75	11.75	+2.00
LDS	6.25	7.25	+1.00
American Baptist	16.25	15.50	+0.75
Black Baptist	16.50	15.75	+0.75
Missouri/Wisconsin Lutheran	12.00	11.25	+0.75
Presbyterian USA	4.75	4.50	+0.25
Jehovah's Witness	18.25	18.00	+0.25
Jewish	1.50	1.50	0.00
Unitarian	1.50	1.50	0.00
Nondenominational Conserv. Protestant	12.25	12.25	0.00
Other [Pentecostal]	19.00	19.25	−0.25
Catholic	11.50	11.75	−0.25
Episcopal	3.00	3.25	−0.25
Southern Baptist	15.00	15.50	−0.50
United Methodist	6.75	7.50	−0.75
Nonreligious	8.75	10.00	−1.25
UCC	5.75	8.50	−2.75
Adventist	11.00	7.50	−3.50
ELCA	6.00	10.25	−4.25

Source: General Social Survey (1983, 1984, 1996, 1998, 2000).

and McKinney's (1987) analysis of 1970s and early 1980s data, then, not a great deal has changed in the overall socioeconomic stratification of American religious groups. And although our comparative time frame is shorter, it may appear that the changes within the system that they observed for the mid-20th century have slowed down to produce a more stable system at the end of that century. . . .

3. *The socioeconomic inequality evident in the American religious system appears to be patterned by theology, race and ethnicity, and liturgical style.* As a generalization, the higher ranked religious groups tend to be more theologically liberal denominations and traditions, while the lowest ranked tend to be more conservative and sectarian. The highest ranked tend toward more hierarchical and federated church polities, whereas the lower ranked tend to represent more "low-church," congregational, or "believer's church" traditions. Socioeconomically higher ranked religious groups also tend to

involve more formal, liturgical, tradition-oriented styles of worship; lower ranked groups tend toward more openly expressive, informal, emotional, and "Spirit-filled" styles of worship. Finally, we know from the racial composition of religious communities that more highly ranked groups tend to have high percentage of whites as members, while lower ranked groups tend to include more racial minorities, particularly black Baptists and Pentecostals and non-Catholic Hispanic Pentecostals. Most of this follows similar observations by Roof and McKinney (1987) about the 1970s and early 1980s.

Explaining exactly how and why socioeconomic inequalities map onto and reproduce themselves within the American religious system will require further research, which cross-sectional survey data such as that analyzed here will not be able to address. Some of the forces at work, such as race, very likely have little directly to do with religion. As African Americans, for example, are socioeconomically disadvantaged in America's racialized society, and African Americans cluster in African-American religious denominations, then African Americans' socioeconomic disadvantage inevitably shows up in their religious denominations. And since both socioeconomic inequality and religious affiliation operate by similar forces of social reproduction and homophily, it is not surprising that the socioeconomic stratification of American religion persists over time.

At the same time, ... we might suppose that religious factors also help to sustain and reproduce some of the socioeconomic inequalities noted above. It may be that different theologies and worship styles are more comfortable for people with different levels of education or different kinds of occupations (Demorath 1965; Fukuyama 1960). Fully entering into an Episcopal liturgical service of worship, for instance, requires a greater appreciation for historical tradition and elegant precision in the English language—both arguably associated with higher education—than most Southern Baptist or Pentecostal services. Religious belief systems and moral orders may also socialize members in ways that directly shape their educational and occupational aspirations. Beyerlein (2004) and Darnell and Sherkat (1997) for example, have argued that Pentecostal and fundamentalist Christianity discourages their adherents from pursuing advanced degrees in higher education. Given what we know about network effects in reproducing business and political elite statuses and in searching for jobs, it is likely that religious congregational involvement plays a significant role in generating advantage and disadvantage. ...

CONCLUSION

American religion has from the beginning been stratified socioeconomically. American sociology has long documented and theorized persistent inequalities between religious communities.

Socioeconomic inequalities between religious groups have also played an important role in many broader sociological theories about religion and society. Since the publication of a collection of important works published in the mid-20th century, however, the social stratification of American religion has been a curiously understudied topic. This research note is an attempt to help update our descriptive knowledge about socioeconomic inequalities between American religious groups. Tracking educational, income, and job status inequality over a 16-year period, from the early 1980s to the late 1990s, we have found that socioeconomic inequality in the American religious system has been persistent and stable—suggesting that the mid-20th century's significant mobility within this system may be declining. Further ethnographic, longitudinal survey, and community-studies research is needed to better understand the causal forces and cultural dynamics of the socioeconomic stratification of American religion, and how inequality between religious groups may interact with and help to sustain the larger system of socioeconomic inequality in the United States.

REFERENCES

BALTZELL, E. D. 1964. *The Protestant establishment: Aristocracy and caste in America.* New York: Random House.

BEYERLEIN, K. 2004. Specifying the impact of conservative Protestantism on educational attainment. *Journal for the Scientific Study of Religion* 43(December):505–18.

CORENO, T. 2002. Fundamentalism as class culture. Sociology of Religion. 63:335–360.

DARNELL, A. and D. E. SHERKATT. 1997. The impact of Protestant fundamentalism on educational attainment. *American Sociological Review* 62: 306–315.

DAVIS, J., T. W. SMITH, and P. MARSDEN. 2001. General Social Surveys, 1972–2000: [CUMULATIVE FILE] [Computer file]. 3rd version. Chicago, IL: National Opinion Research Center [producer]. Storrs, CT: Roper Center for Public Opinion Research, University of Connecticut/Ann Arbor, MI: Inter-university Consortium for Political and Social Research [distributors].

DEMERATH, N. J. 1965. *Social class in American Protestantism*. Chicago: Rand McNally.

FINKE, R. and R. STARK. 1992. *The churching of America*. New Brunswick: Rutgers University Press.

FUKUYAMA, Y. 1960. The major dimensions of church membership. *Review of Religious Research* 2(4):159.

HUNTER, J. D. 1983. *American evangelicalism*. New Brunswick: Rutgers University Press.

LENSKI, G. 1961. *The religious factor*. Garden City: Doubleday.

MARX, K. 1978a |1843|. Contribution to the critique of Hegel's *Philosophy of Right*: Introduction. In *The Marx-Engels reader*, edited by R. Tucker. New York: W.W. Norton.

NIEBUHR, H. R. 1929. *The social sources of denominationalism*. New York: Meridian.

PARK, J. Z. and S. H. REIMER. 2002. Revisiting the sources of American Christianity. *Journal for the Scientific Study of Religion* 41: 733–746.

POPE, L. 1942. *Millhands and preachers*. New Haven: Yale University Press.

ROOF, W. C. and W. McKINNEY. 1987. *American mainline religion*. New Brunswick: Rutgers University Press.

SWARTZ, D. 1996. Bridging the study of culture and religion. *Sociology of Religion* 57(1):77–85.

WARNER, W. L. 1963. *Yankee city*. New Haven: Yale University Press.

WEBER, M. 1978. *Economy and society*. Berkeley: University of California Press.

WUTHNOW, R. 1988. *The restructuring of American religion*. Princeton: Princeton University Press.

17 At Ease With Our Own Kind: Worship Practices and Class Segregation in American Religion

TIMOTHY J. NELSON

As suggested by Smith and Faris, social class differences among religious groups are reinforced by the culture that each group expresses through its language, norms for behavior, and values. Using fifteen classic community studies from the 1930s-1960s, Nelson explores how class differences are reflected in the aesthetics, linguistic styles, and physical expression of American congregations and how this contributes to social class segregation among these congregations.

Theoretically, no obstacle keeps lower-class people out of the Christian Church, but "they wouldn't feel comfortable there."

—James West, *Plainville, U.S.A.* (1964, 160)

[T]he religious segregation of mill workers was not due to the desire of fashionable uptown churches or conservative rural churches to exclude them ... The lives of the mill operatives were different from other people, leading them to desire churches of their own in which they could feel perfectly at ease.

—Liston Pope, *Millhands and Preachers* (1942, 72–3)

For most Protestants, theology plays a minor role in selection of a church. They go where they find their own kind of people.

—W. Lloyd Warner et al., *Democracy in Jonesville* (1964, 166–7)

The relationship between social class and religious behavior is one of the oldest and most well-established areas of inquiry in the field of sociology. Beginning with Marx's comments on religion, alienation, and class ideology, Weber's analyses of religious styles among different social strata, and continuing with eighty years' worth of empirical studies in the United States, it is safe to say that this disciplinary path is a well-trodden one. Although some recent studies have downplayed the role of class in American religion, ... the evidence clearly suggests that class is still a powerful force that continues to shape religious identification and behavior (Smith and Faris 2005; McCloud 2007).

Documenting the correlation between social class and various forms of religious behavior is one thing, however, but explaining them is quite another. In the pages that follow, I briefly summarize the four major empirical findings concerning class and American religion, narrow the focus of this paper to just one of these, and review the most prominent theory that has been offered to explain it. After critiquing this explanation, I then develop an alternative theoretical approach drawn from Pierre Bourdieu's work on class and cultural consumption, focusing on his concept of *habitus*. Dividing the worship service into three dimensions—aesthetic, linguistic and physical—I review a selection of ethnographic studies of American religion to see how they support and illuminate this alternative approach.

SOCIAL CLASS AND AMERICAN RELIGION

Over seventy-five years ago, H. Richard Niebuhr (1929) published his hugely influential work *The Social Sources of Denominationalism*. With the ethical force of an Old Testament prophet, Niebuhr (1929, 25) denounced Protestant denominations in America as "represent[ing] the moral failure of Christianity" by their conformity in reproducing the social order of classes and castes. While never reducing religion to an epiphenomenon of class, he emphasized that the energies, goals and motives of religious movements are channeled by social factors, particularly race and class, into particular forms that reflect their position in

society (Niebuhr 1929, 27). That same year, the Lynds' seminal study of a "typical" American community was published as *Middletown ...* (Lynd and Lynd 1957). Originally intended as a survey of religious life in a "typical" American community, the Lynds took an explicitly anthropological approach to religion by situating it within its broader social context—particularly the two-fold division they found in Muncie, Indiana, between the "business class" and the "working class." In their analysis, the Lynds repeatedly stressed the influence of this class division in shaping the religious behavior, attitudes, and organizations of Muncie....

These two influential works, one historical and one anthropological, set the agenda for the following decades of research on the link between social class and religious expression....

By the beginning of the 1970s the empirical support for the connection between social class and religious behavior in America was fairly well established for the following relationships:

1. Among the general population, higher social status is positively related to both membership in and identification with any organized religious group.

2. Among church members, *higher* status is associated with higher rates of church attendance, with assumption of leadership positions within congregations and higher levels of religious knowledge.

3. Among church members, *lower* status is associated with more concentration of one's friendship network within in the congregation, more personal devotionalism, higher rates of doctrinal orthodoxy and reported rates of religious experience.

4. Among church members, differences in social status are associated with membership in particular kinds of religious organizations (especially for Protestants) and these associations have remained stable for many decades.

In sum, these studies showed that the American population is recruited selectively by social class into any form of religious organization and that possessing a religious identity varies according to social status. Those lower status persons who do belong to or identify religiously participate in quite different ways than do higher status persons, and there is a marked tendency toward segregation by class into different kinds of religious organizations.

It is this last element—the propensity of the church-affiliated public to identify with different religious organizations based, at least in part, upon social class that I want to focus on in this paper. . . .

EXPLAINING THE CONNECTION BETWEEN CLASS AND RELIGIOUS PREFERENCE

To understand the inclination of social classes to separate into different religious organizations, sociologists have taken note of which particular religious groups tend to draw from which social classes. These patterns are not only robust but have also shown remarkable stability since they were first systematically observed. In their examination of pooled data from multiple waves of the General Social Survey, Smith and Faris (2005) conclude that the ranking of American religious groups by the educational attainment, household income and occupational prestige of its members has remained remarkably steady since the 1970s, despite the sustained period of economic growth in the mid-to-late 1990s. The groups at the top of their list—Unitarians, Jews, Episcopalians, and mainline Presbyterians— "consistently enjoyed significantly higher levels of education, income, and occupational prestige than most of the groups below them," and these same religious groups have maintained this position for decades (Smith and Faris 2005, 100). The groups at the other end of this hierarchy—Jehovah's Witnesses, black Baptists, Southern Baptists, and Pentecostals— have also captured the lower portions of the class continuum for a long period of time.

What needs to be accounted for then, is not just the fact of class segregation into different religious groups, but the apparently strong affinity between specific classes and particular religious traditions. However, explaining this connection is complex because religious organizations are multi-faceted and several dimensions could be operative in attracting different classes through their front doors. Is it the congregation's theology, moral code, bureaucratic form, history and tradition, or set of worship practices that are drawing people from one side of the tracks or the other? . . .

The literature on lower class religion tends to be scattered across several disciplines and most published works focus on single historical or ethnographic case studies. Nevertheless, there is an almost ubiquitous mechanism in the explanations for the "fit" between lower class position in society and religious styles of worship. This common mechanism is what I have referred to elsewhere under the label of "psychological functionalism," and which can be characterized as a hybrid approach loosely based upon aspects of both Marxist and Freudian theory (Nelson 1996). The essential argument goes something like this: the unique situation of the lower class (material deprivation, oppression, low self-esteem, alienation, lack of control over life circumstances, etc.) creates a strong impetus for psychic relief from these supposedly unbearable pressures. Particular forms of religion (as well as their functional equivalents such as excessive alcohol consumption, drug use, promiscuous sex, rowdy public behavior and other typically "lower class" behaviors) offer one such avenue of relief—hence their appeal to this class. . . .

The problem with this approach lies in the normative assumptions it makes about both class and religion, assumptions which have the effect of labeling lower-class religious forms as deviant, and then explaining this deviation in terms of the author's own (usually biased) views of the nature of lower class life. I won't take the time here to present extensive evidence for this argument, but support for this assertion can be seen simply in how the practices and beliefs associated with lower-class religion are characterized and how they are contrasted to an implicit norm—those of the middle class. To give one small example, taken from Niebuhr himself: "Religious enthusiasm declined in the later days because Methodist Christianity became more *literate* and *rational* and because, with increasing wealth and culture, other escapes from the monotony and exhaustion of hard labor became available" (Niebuhr 1929, 63, my emphasis).

THE RELIGIOUS HABITUS

Because the alternative approach to class and religious practice I develop here is based on Bourdieu's concept of "habitus," in this section I first define what Bourdieu means by this term, discussing the role it plays in his explanation of class-based cultural patterns and the social processes by which a specific class habitus is formed. Then I extend the discussion to encompass religious practices, particularly as they relate to worship, and offer some predictions and areas for further exploration. . . .

Habitus is a mechanism, internalized within the individual and usually preconscious, which generates both patterns of action and patterns of likes and dislikes for different forms of cultural objects and practices (tastes). These tastes are principles of selection that not only influence one's own actions, but are also judgments on the tastes of others. The habitus thus incorporates both a predisposition for selecting some kinds of cultural objects and practices over others, as well as a scheme for evaluating and ranking one's own preferences relative to all other perceived options.

In addition, Bourdieu argues that the habitus is transposable, that is, the choices one makes in any single field of cultural consumption are not independent but systematically linked to one's choices in all other areas of cultural preference. "Systematicity . . . is found in all the properties—and property—with which individuals and groups surround themselves, houses, furniture, paintings, books, cars, spirits, cigarettes, perfume, clothes, and

in the practices in which they manifest their distinction, sports, games, entertainments, only because it is the synthetic unity of the habitus, the unifying, generative principle of all practices" (Bourdieu 1984, 173).

What gives the habitus such a powerful uniformity in its effects across such diverse areas of cultural consumption? It is the influence of one's cumulative experiences due to social location—particularly class—as well as the recognition of one's place in the status hierarchy. These class-based experiences and perceptions (predominantly those anchored in the formative stages of the life course) profoundly shape one's dispositions regarding cultural choices, even later in life, and even in the face of intragenerational class mobility. For Bourdieu, "experience of the particular class position that characterizes a given location in social space imprints a particular set of dispositions on the individual" (Weininger 2005, 92). Bourdieu's (1984) analysis of French cultural tastes and lifestyles in his work *Distinction* roughly identifies four social types (defined according to the amount of economic and cultural capital they possess) and their corresponding habitus, characterized rather tersely by Swartz (1997, 109) as "ostentatious indulgence and ease within the upper class, aristocratic aestheticism among intellectuals, awkward pretension by middle-class strivers, and anti-pretentious ignorance and conformity within the working class."

These more general orientations are embodied within particular fields of cultural consumption and Bourdieu's analysis of cultural practices places special emphasis on preferences in the realms of art, music and literature because these areas are the most closely tied to the uneven distribution of cultural capital within the social hierarchy. The capacity to fully appreciate "high" cultural objects and practices (e.g. opera, abstract art, or poetry) is typically acquired either through one's family or through the formal educational system. The subordinate classes are relatively excluded, due to family background and poor or truncated schooling, from acquiring the "decoding" tools necessary to appreciate these "high" cultural forms. While not as socially valorized as the fields of music, art and literature, Bourdieu argues that tastes in furniture, clothing, vacation spots, movies, restaurants, and other forms of cultural expression are also structured according to class habitus.

The end result of these processes is that each social class adopts similar sets of tastes and practices across a wide range of cultural fields. This not only predisposes members of the same class to experience feelings of affinity for one another based upon similar lifestyles and preferences, but to feel hostile to, ridicule or reject the cultural choices of those unlike themselves. This "class racism" (Bourdieu's term) is the inevitable result of the clash of styles and preferences held by each class and class fraction and leads, ultimately, to reproduction of the social order.

HABITUS AND WORSHIP PRACTICES

Although Bourdieu's approach to class and culture was inspired by Max Weber's writings on religion, Bourdieu himself spent little time on the topic and never gave it much serious attention (Swartz 1997, 41; Verter 2003). Fortunately, several scholars have begun to take Bourdieu's own approach and apply it to religion, focusing particularly on his concepts of field and cultural capital (Swartz 1996; Verter 2003). The current paper attempts to further this important work by showing the utility of the concept of habitus as it is applied to social class and religious practices. . . .

Following Bourdieu's own analyses and his emphases on particular cultural domains, I suggest the following three broad areas for an initial investigation of worship practices: the aesthetic, the linguistic, and the physical (as far as it involves bodily expression). . . .

The ideal empirical investigation of this approach would be a set of participant-observation studies of the worship practices in one or more class-diverse communities. The community approach is crucial because such a study would have to encompass the whole range of available religious options and capture the sorting processes within a more-or-less self-contained religious ecology. The field observations should first assess the degree to which different social classes are in fact sorted into the area's local congregations, and then determine the patterns of variation within the three dimensions mentioned above. Finally, qualitative interviews with congregants from across the class spectrum would explore whether there is indeed a class-based set of taste preferences operating to sort people into particular congregations.

Unfortunately, to my knowledge, such a study does not exist. But there is a set of data that can give us a sense of whether this theoretical approach may be a useful one. For roughly three decades, from the mid 1920s until the mid 1950s, sociologists and anthropologists conducted over fifteen in-depth studies of various American communities that include the basic social class composition of individual congregations and at least some description of their worship practices (see Table 1). Although imperfect in many ways (including a tendency toward a strong middle-class bias in descriptions of lower-class religion), I use these studies as a kind of data set, and code them for patterns that illuminate the issues under consideration here.

AESTHETICS

I begin with surfaces because, although they are furthest from the core of worship practices, these are the elements first encountered by potential participants and thus are essential to the first impressions sustained. The aesthetic dimension of the worship service includes several diverse elements. First, there is the physical space in which the ritual takes place—its architecture, décor, and physical surroundings, including the neighborhood in which it is

TABLE 1 Community studies, ordered by date of fieldwork with names of communities studied

Study	Dates	Location
1. Lynd and Lynd, *Middletown*	1924–1925	Muncie, IN
2. Warner, *The Social Life of a Modern Community*	1930–1934	Newburyport, MA
3. Powdermaker, *After Freedom*	1932–1934	Indianola, MS
4. Davis, Gardner, and Gardner, *Deep South*	1933–1935	Natchez, MS
5. Dollard, *Caste and Class in a Southern Town*	1935–1936	Indianola, MS
6. Drake and Cayton. *Black Metropolis*	1936–1941	Chicago, IL
7. Pope, *Millhands and Preachers*	1938–1939	Gastonia, NC
8. West, *Plainville, U.S.A.*	1939–1941	Wheatland, MO
9. Hollingshead, *Elmtown's Youth*	1941–1942	Morris, IL
10. Warner, *Democracy in Jonesville*	1940	Morris, IL
11. Rubin, *Plantation County*	1947–1948	Wilcox County, AL
12. Morland, *Millways of Kent*	1948–1949	York, SC
13. Lewis *Blackways of Kent*	1949	York, SC
14. Seeley, Sim, and Loosely, *Crestwood Heights*	1948–1953	Forest Hill Village, Toronto, CAN
15. Vidich and Bensman. *Small Town in Mass Society*	1951–1953	Candor, NY
16. Gallaher, *Plainville Fifteen Years Later*	1954–1955	Wheatland, MO

located. The clothing, hair, and makeup styles of participants are a second element to consider here, and finally, there are the stylistic aspects of the ritual action itself, particularly regarding the music used in the service.

As collective social events, worship services occur in physical space, usually in a building owned by the congregation or the denomination it is affiliated with. Even today's televised religion includes this element, as most are simply broadcasts of services taking place in a specific time and place (and the "PTL" style programs must have a set with furnishings and decorations). Although some worship services are held in rented space or in public areas, there is still ample opportunity for stylistic expression through means other than architecture and décor. As W. Lloyd Warner (1941) and his team discovered decades ago in "Yankee City," the part of town in which a structure is located is also a very important component of social prestige, but one which may be the most difficult for congregations to alter (although the massive relocation of churches and synagogues to the suburbs in the post-World War II era shows that this strategy is far from rare). St. Clair Drake and Horace Cayton (1962, 632), studying the African American scene on Chicago's South Side, note that "[The lower-class African American] religious praise the Lord in vacant stores and in houses, abandoned theaters, remodeled garages, and halls. These small churches tend to be concentrated on run-down, low-rent, business streets and in generally undesirable residential areas."

But what about the buildings themselves? As with residential houses, church buildings tend to reflect the financial resources of the congregation. The Lynds (1957, 336) wrote that in Middletown:

The economic and social considerations which appear to be becoming more potent in marking off one religious group from another are . . . reflected in the houses of worship. Some of these buildings are imposing structures of stone and brick, while others, particularly in the outlying sections inhabited by the poorer workers, are weather-beaten wooden shelters little larger or better built than the poorer sorts of dwellings.

However, according to the approach being developed here, the congregation's level of cultural capital should be almost as important as its economic capital in influencing the architectural style. Unfortunately, none of these community studies compared architectural styles of various church buildings, or interviewed people about their opinions on the matter. There is also a confounding factor: while urban church structures tend to be "recycled" and may have several owners over the years (thus not accurately reflecting the aesthetic preferences of its current occupants), the construction of new churches is mostly confined to the suburban middle class neighborhoods.

Given the greater freedom of innovation—and at far less expense—to individual congregations, class contrasts may appear more strongly in interior decoration than in architectural style or church location. The comparison to residential homes is instructive here as well, and it has been almost a century since social scientists developed an index of social class based upon observations of home furnishings (Lasswell 1965). Working within an explicitly Bourdieuian framework, Douglas Holt interviewed respondents in one community, some with high cultural capital (HCC) and some with low cultural capital (LCC), and uncovered several dimensions of aesthetic cultural preferences (Holt 1997, Holt 1998). Specifically, he found that LCCs evaluate everyday objects like clothing and furniture according to utilitarian properties (durability, ease of care), favored known and unified styles ("Victorian," "Country") in their interior decorating, and aspired to a lifestyle of material abundance and luxury ("having the good things of life"). In contrast, HCCs approached these aesthetic choices from a more eclectic and subjective perspective, valorizing the idiosyncratic over the mass-produced, quality over quantity, and spiritual over material aspects of consumption.

Once again, unfortunately, the community studies do not take the time to describe the interiors of the churches they observed. The one possible exception is Drake and Cayton's summary opinion that in black churches of Chicago's south side, "Upper class church buildings tend to be small, but are very well cared for and artistically decorated," while in contrast, the store front churches are full of "tasteless ornamentation" (Drake and Cayton 1962, 539, 633). Without a more objective description, of course, this doesn't do us much good.

There is more evidence, though, on a matter that gets a little bit closer to the substance of the worship ritual: the style of music used in the service. The most important dimension here is the division between more "classical" styles and "folk" or popular styles. In the time period these community studies were done, the popular jazz form was considered a lower-class musical style and was found more often in the working and lower-class congregations. Morland (1958, 120) observes that in the white churches of York, South Carolina:

There is more of such clapping and tapping of feet at the Church of God than in the Wesleyan Methodist and the hymns are more jazzy.... The music of these hymns, especially in the Church of God, have a definite beat and a fast, swingy rhythm. Most of the songs are "happy" but a few are reminiscent of the blues for example, "If You Ever Leave Me Jesus, I'll Die." Others tell a story in ballad fashion, almost mountain style. The pianist plays all of these hymns in a jazz manner, with numerous off-beats, runs, and trills.

Drake and Cayton (1962, 678) also note that "appeals to middle-class members... take on the form of 'good' music rendered by a well-trained choir singing anthems and other classical religious works." They also describe the strategies used by some larger African American congregations to appeal to all class segments on the South Side of Chicago (Drake and Cayton 1962, 676):

Other features of a Sunday worship service other than the sermon have this dual class appeal. All of Bronzeville's churches have an adult or senior choir, and many have a junior choir. These present ordinary hymns and anthems. Some are highly trained choral groups. But, in addition to these choirs, most Bronzeville churches also have one or two "gospel choruses"— a concession to lower-class tastes. A gospel choir is not highly trained, but it is usually loud and spirited. [...] Chorus members often shout while they sing. In many lower-class churches, there is no choir other than the gospel chorus.

Even more importantly, several of their interviews with South Side residents reveal that musical style is an important factor in sorting classes into different congregations. One middle-class respondent was indignant over the musical styles used in lower-class churches: "I like good music, but I don't like the songs these gospel choirs in the store-fronts sing—these jazz tunes. I think it is hea-then-like to jazz hymns" (Drake and Cayton 1962, 671). From the opposite side, a recent lower-class migrant from the South told why she had decided to leave the larger, more mid-dle-class congregation she had initially affili-ated with to join a small store-front church. After explaining that she sometimes couldn't understand the big words the preacher at her former church used, she added, "I couldn't sing their way. The songs was proud-like. At my little church I enjoy the services" (Drake and Cayton 1962, 634).

LINGUISTIC STYLE

A more central aspect of the worship service is its linguistic component. Prayers, testi-monies and, of course, sermons or homilies come immediately to mind as primary lin-guistic elements in the ritual, but we should not forget the words to hymns and other reli-gious songs, as well as greetings, announce-ments, instructions and other less sacred elements of the service. Bourdieu emphasizes that like art, music, and literature, language is closely tied to success in the formal educa-tional system and a dominant, "correct," way of speaking is often imposed upon the lower orders from above.

Even amidst ordinary social occasions, the bourgeois linguistic style has a tendency toward "abstraction, formalism, intellectualism and euphemistic moderation" in contrast to the "expressiveness or expressionism of working-class language, which manifests itself in the tendency to move from particular case to partic-ular case, from illustration to parable" (Bour-dieu and Passeron 1977, 16, quoted in Swartz 1997, 199). . . . This set of linguistic contrasts—between the abstract and the concrete, the sug-gestive and the emphatic, the intellectually detached and the emotionally heartfelt—should

be apparent in how different class churches express themselves in liturgical language.

The ethnographic evidence on this point is intriguing. Consider the contrast between the middle and upper class emphasis on the ideational or intellectual content of discourse and the working and lower class emphasis on con-crete and graphic depictions, often set in a grip-ping narrative. Hortense Powdermaker (1993, 241), in describing a sermon in a lower-class African American church in Indianola, Missis-sippi, in the early 1930s, wrote that the when the preacher talked about heaven, "he describes [it] graphically in literal Bible terms: the golden streets, the pearly gates, the songs of angels." Lis-ton Pope (1942, 86) compares the songs sung in the high status downtown churches of Gastonia, North Carolina, to the working-class mill churches and finds the latter's music "more con-crete and more rhythmic; it conjures up pictures rather than describes attitudes or ideas." And Morland (1958, 121) also observing a working-class white congregation in South Carolina, was struck that many of the songs "tell a story in bal-lad fashion, almost mountain style." Regarding their observations of African American worship services in Depression-era Chicago, Drake and Cayton (1962, 624) wrote that a sermon in a lower-class church: "is primarily a vivid, picto-rial, and imaginative recounting of Biblical lore. [. . .] A good preacher is a good raconteur of religious tales. His highly embroidered individ-ual variations are accepted as pleasing mod-ifications of an original story with which both the preacher and audience are familiar." John Dollard (1957, 232) who also studied Indianola, Mississippi, in the 1930s, gives the best example of this, recounting over several paragraphs the long, symbol-laden story the preacher gave dur-ing the sermon in a lower-class black church, each detail graphically described.

Lower and working class linguistic style also relies more heavily on stock, repetitive phrases (taking the form of clichés in ordinary conver-sation) rather than on discourse which follows a more expository pattern. . . . This contrast has been remarked upon by many observers, who often seem unable to censor their own point of view as they comment on these church services. Dollard (1957, 242), for example, wrote of one working-class church he observed in Indianola, Mississippi, "the preacher, of course, does not make such a connected discourse as would be expected by a better educated audience. He is allowed to repeat himself without fear of reproach and he utters frequent stereotyped phrases while he is collecting his thoughts." He describes a testimonial service, "various of the members stood up and told how they had been saved, on what day, and how grateful they were. Each went through a little pattern, for the testimony is highly conventional, with many "Amens" and "Thank Gods" from other members" (Dollard 1957, 235) Like others with higher levels of cultural capital, Pope (1942, 87–8) seems to interpret this linguistic style as an indication either of a lack of intellectual curiosity or of prowess:

Mill workers show no interest in theological questions as such; they simply accept notions coming from a wide variety of sources and weld them together without regard for consistency. The following statements, taken from "testimonies" made by them at services and from comments in private conversation, illustrate the ideas and phrases that recur when they attempt to describe their religious beliefs: "Jesus saves, and the way grows sweeter." "I'm so glad my name is written in the Book of Life." . . . "I was a backslider once, but praise God I'm back on the glory road now." [. . .] I'm glad I got the old-time religion and am on my way to glory land."

Interestingly, while Morland observed a similar pattern in his South Carolina churches, he took the opposite evaluative stance, judging the higher status church services from the standpoint of the more lower-class emphasis on emotional resonance and sincerity. Regarding his observations in the most educated congregation, he writes, "the congregation sits apparently unmoved during sermons, which seem to be primarily a juggling of verbal symbols and

an exercise in semantics without visibly touching those listening" (Morland 1958, 115).

The final aspect to touch upon here is the contrast between a working-class "folk" culture based on oral tradition and middle-class "literate" culture based upon formal education. In the worship service this is translated into a working-class emphasis on spontaneous verbal performance (which often relies heavily on memorized stories, phrases, and images) and the middle-class reliance on more authoritative discourse (which often relies on more literary sources). James West (1964, 154–5) who studied the community of Wheatland, Missouri, around 1940, observed (with undisguised bias) that "sermons preached in the [higher status] Christian Church are usually prepared in advance and are coherent, but many revival sermons [in lower-status churches] are utterly incoherent. [. . .] The words vary but are always rhythmic." Drake and Cayton (1962, 624) note this same pattern among African Americans on the South Side of Chicago, but evaluate it somewhat differently, "in "breaking the bread of life' (a phrase referring to preaching), an uneducated minister has a distinct advantage over an educated preacher, for the typical lower-class sermon is an 'unprepared message.'" They note this same spontaneous approach to praying as well (Drake and Cayton 1962, 620):

Lower-class church people look with scorn upon "book prayers," for praying is an art, and a person who can lead his fellows to the throne of grace with originality and eloquence gains high prestige. [. . .] Though each person makes up his own prayer, there is a common stock of striking phrases and images which are combined and recombined throughout the Negro lower-class religious world.

PHYSICAL EXPRESSION

The final dimension I will examine is that of physical expression—the use of the body—in worship practices. This is a topic which certainly sparked the most comment from the authors of these community studies and the strongest feelings from their respondents as well, indicating that this dimension is probably the most potent one in separating the classes into different congregations.

Bourdieu argues that the attitudes and dispositions of the individual toward their own bodies takes on a characteristic element of each class, which he analyzes in the realms of sports, in the selection of food and in the process of eating....

On the whole, we might expect that middle class worship services would first of all de-emphasize the physical in favor of the intellectual, and second, that any demands upon the body during worship will be in keeping with this sense of "high dignity" identified by Bourdieu. We might also expect that working and lower class worshippers would have a more instrumental relationship to their own bodies (as they are instruments of labor) and would use them for "authentic" expression of emotion and commitment with less concern for dignity and restraint.

This is what every community study has found to be the case. I will give just a few examples to illustrate the point. In the extended quote below, Liston Pope (1942, 130–2) gives a "composite and impressionistic" picture of the more active and emotional lower class groups:

The atmosphere is expectant and informal: members of the congregation move about at will, and talk in any tone of voice that suits their fancy. [...] A band, including three stringed instruments and a saxophone, plays occasional music. [...] The stanzas [of a hymn] are punctuated with loud shouts of "Hallelujah," "Thank you, Jesus," "Glory," and the rhythmic clapping of hands and tapping of feet. Almost immediately, various members of the congregation begin to "get the Holy Ghost." One young woman leaves the front row of the choir and jerks about the pulpit, with motions so disconnected as to seem involuntary, weird. A man's head trembles violently from side to side. [...] Then comes a prayer, with everybody kneeling on the floor and praying aloud at the same time, each in his own way. Some mutter with occasional shouts; others chant, with frequent bendings backward and forward; the volume of sound rises and falls, without unified pattern or group consternation. [...] The preacher begins a sermon; more precisely, he enunciates verbal symbols that arouse immediate response from the congregation. [...] Then there is a testimony meeting in which a large number of the more faithful testify to their personal experience and joy in religion, some mutteringly, some loudly, fervidly. [...] The man who had been indulging in the intoxicated laugh defends his right to laugh in church, saying that his religion makes him feel good all over and is not like the stiff coldness of the Methodist church.

Hortense Powdermaker (1993, 244), describing a lower-class rural congregation, writes, "[the preacher] waves his arms, he chants, he shrieks, he tells jokes. His congregation responds with vigor, laughing, continually breaking into 'Amens,' keeping time with their feet." In contrast, the higher status congregations are always characterized by their relative lack of movement and restrained behavior. Morland (1964, 113) also noted that during the service at the higher status Baptist church in York, South Carolina, "the congregation remains seated, no one kneeling or saying 'Amen' during the prayer." Dollard (1957, 246–7) too observed that among the African American churches in Indianola, Mississippi, "The middle-class churches in town are much more reserved and have much more the frozen, restrained characteristics of the white churches. Hylan Lewis (1955, 138) notes that the highest status African American congregation in York, South Carolina, was "the only one of the three churches where the active emotional display known as 'shouting' does not occur. 'Encouragement' for the minister is meager and restrained. The members tend to be proud of their restrained patterns and particular denominational affiliation; with reference to some of the practices of the other churches, members have been heard to say, 'We just don't do things that way.'" Later, Lewis comments on the range of worship practices in this community, and note how closely his words echo those of Bourdieu, "the quality of the expression ranges from the most passive and perfunctory to the highly active and emotional.... The restrained behavior of the more sophisticated is in keeping with their conceptions of themselves and their emotional demands. Similarly, the active, emotional behavior of older, less sophisticated, and marginal persons has meaning in terms of their traditions, statuses, and needs (Lewis 1955, 153).

Like Lewis, most of the authors of these community studies explicitly associate the social status of local congregations to the extent of physical display in their worship services. Powdermaker (1993, 234) notes that in Indianola, "the Methodists and the Baptists look down upon the sanctified, considering their noise and dancing somewhat heathenish." Gallaher, in his mid-1950s restudy of the same community James West had studied a decade and a half earlier, writes that, "the Holiness group, like certain Baptist and Methodist families, ranks low in prestige because of its "emotional" type of worship." Although the behavior exhibited in these services is so distasteful to some middle class members of the community that it "[connotes] mental instability," they can tolerate it as long as they worship in their own congregations. As one man told Gallaher, "you have to have a church for people like that ... that kind don't fit in regular churches" (Gallaher 1961, 215).

Such comments by community members were far from rare. Consider some of the opinions elicited by Drake and Cayton from middle-class African Americans in Chicago. One person stated, "I don't believe in shouting and never did. I like a church that is quiet. I just can't appreciate clowning in church" (Drake and Cayton 1962, 671). Another respondent was even more emphatic, first characterizing store front churches as encouraging "jumping-jack" religion, then declaring, "I think those people are in the first stages of insanity" (Drake and Cayton 1962,

671). Perhaps the most vitriolic statements were collected among African Americans in Natchez, Mississippi, in the early 1930s by Allison Davis and her colleagues (1941, 232), "upon occasion, upper-class [African-Americans] spoke their thoughts about the lower class with equal frankness. [...] Church members who disliked revivalistic ritual spoke of the members of lower-class churches as being 'ignorant as hogs,' 'wallowing in superstition,' 'just like African savages,' or simply 'black and dumb.'"

From the other end of the spectrum, lower-class church members often characterized the worship services of the higher status churches as being "stiff" and "cold." James West reports that in Wheatland, Missouri, "[Holiness people] consider worship in the Christian Church as too 'cold' to properly be called religion. The same criticism of the Christian Church as cold and worldly is offered by Baptists and Methodists, who poke fun, however, with the rest of the community, at the 'ignorant goings-on' of Holiness meetings" (West 1964, 143). Morland (1958, 107) observed this same continuum in York noting that, "The Wesleyans attracted people who desired Holiness doctrine but felt that the Church of God was too undignified, and who, at the same time, did not like the 'coldness' of the Cromwell Baptist Church."

As these quotes make clear, preferences over worship styles were not just matters of opinion but actively worked to sort different classes into separate congregations. The account of one young man interviewed by Drake and Cayton (1962, 538) offers a clear example of this, and is also important for the way it illustrates the variation that can be found across local religious ecologies:

"When I first came to Chicago I was a member of the Baptist Church. But I never joined a church here because I did not like the way people exhibited their emotions. At home, in the church I belonged to, people were very quiet; but here in the Baptist churches I found people rather noisy. For that reason I tried to find a church that was different, and in visiting the various churches I came across the Presbyterian Church, which I joined. I have remained a member ever since."

CONCLUSION

Several decades before Bourdieu developed his theory of social reproduction through class habitus, Art Gallaher summed up his study of the churches in Wheatland, Missouri, this way, "the significance of religion, then, as a criterion for social status, lies mainly in the behavior of the individual in his worshipping" (Gallaher 1961, 215). As we have seen, this observation was overwhelmingly corroborated by every one of the 15 community studies under consideration here. Although the evidence was more abundant about the role of physical expression (particularly the activities of shouting, speaking in tongues and vigorous congregational response) and linguistic patterns in sorting different class groupings into different congregations, there was some support for the role of purely aesthetic considerations as well.

BIBLIOGRAPHY

BOURDIEU, PIERRE. 1984. *Distinction: A social critique of the judgment of taste*. Cambridge: Harvard University Press.

BOURDIEU, PIERRE and JEAN-CLAUDE PASSERON. 1977. *Reproduction in education, society and culture*. London: Sage.

Davis, ALLISON, BURLEIGH B. GARDNER, and MARY R. GARDNER. 1941. *Deep south: A social anthropological study of caste and class*. Chicago: University of Chicago Press.

DOLLARD, JOHN. 1957. *Caste and class in a southern town*. New York: Doubleday Anchor Books.

DRAKE, ST. CLAIR, and HORACE R. CAYTON. 1962. *Black metropolis: A study of negro life in a northern city*. New York: Harper & Row.

GALLAHER, Art Jr. 1961. *Plainville fifteen years later*. New York: Columbia University Books.

HOLLINGSHEAD, AUGUST B. 1965. *Elmtown's youth: The impact of social classes on adolescents*. New York: Wiley & Sons.

HOLT, DOUGLAS B. 1997. "Distinction in America? Recovering Bourdieu's theory of tastes from its critics." *Poetics* 25: 93–120.

———. 1998. "Does cultural capital structure American consumption?" *Journal of Consumer Research* 25: 1–25.

LASSWELL, THOMAS E. 1965. *Class and stratum: An introduction to concepts and research*. New York: Houghton Mifflin Company.

LEWIS, HYLAN. 1955. *Blackways of Kent*. New Haven: College and University Press.

LYND, ROBERT S. and HELEN MERRELL LYND. 1957. *Middletown: A study in modern American culture*. New York: Harvest/HBJ Publishers.

MCCLOUD, SEAN. 2007. *Divine hierarchies: Class in American religion and religious studies*. Chapel Hill: University of North Carolina Press.

MORLAND, JOHN KENNETH. 1958. *Millways of Kent*. New Haven: College and University Press.

NELSON, TIMOTHY J. 1996. "Sacrifice of praise: Emotion and collective participation in an African American worship service." *Sociology of Religion* 57: 379–396.

NIEBUHR, H. RICHARD. 1929. *The social sources of denominationalism*. New York: Holt.

POPE, LISTON. 1942. *Millhands and preachers: A study of Gastonia*. New Haven: Yale University Press.

POWDERMAKER, HORTENSE. 1993. *After freedom: A cultural study in the deep south*. Madison: University of Wisconsin Press.

RUBIN, MORTON. 1963. *Plantation County*. New Haven, CT: College and University Press.

SEELEY, JOHN R., R. ALEXANDER SIM, and ELIZABETH W. LOOSELY. 1956. *Crestwood Heights: A study of the culture of suburban life*. New York: Basic Books.

SMITH, CHRISTIAN and ROBERT FARIS. 2005. "Socioeconomic inequality in the American religious system: An update and assessment." *Journal for the Scientific Study of Religion* 44(1): 95–104.

SWARTZ, DAVID. 1996. "Bridging the study of culture and religion: Pierre Bourdieu's political economy of symbolic power." *Sociology of Religion* 57(1): 71–85.

———. 1997. *Culture and power: The sociology of Pierre Bourdieu*. Chicago: University of Chicago Press.

VERTER, BRADFORD. 2003. "Spiritual capital: Theorizing religion with Bourdieu against Bourdieu." *Sociological Theory* 21(2): 150–174.

VIDICH, ARTHUR J. and JOSEPH BENSMAN. 1958. *Small town in mass society: Class, power and religion in a rural community*. Princeton: Princeton University Press.

WARNER, W. LLOYD. 1941. *The Social Life of the Modern Community*. Madison: University of Wisconsin Press.

WEININGER, ELLIOT B. 2005. "Foundations of Pierre Bourdieu's class analysis." In *Approaches to Class Analysis*, ed. Erik Olin Wright, 82–118. New York: Cambridge University Press.

WEST, JAMES. 1964. *Plainville, U.S.A.* New York: Columbia University Press.

18 Poor Teenagers' Religion

PHILIP SCHWADEL

Much research has focused on how social class affects religious beliefs and practices in adults. But what about teenagers? Drawing on survey data from the National Study of Youth and Religion, Philip Schwadel found numerous differences between poor and non-poor adolescents. Social class is associated—sometimes in surprising ways—with aspects of religion including prayer, reading scriptures, attendance at worship services and emotionally charged religious experiences.

INTRODUCTION

While questions about the relationship between social class and religion are as old as the field of sociology, sociologists have paid little attention to the effects of poverty on American religion in the last few decades. Influential European sociologists, such as Marx, Weber, and Troeltsch, analyzed the effects of social class on religion. Early American sociologists of religion, most notably Niebuhr, continued to focus on the different religious viewpoints of the various social classes. Research on American religion in the 1960s and 1970s empirically examined the relationships between social class and religion hypothesized by Niebuhr, Marx, Weber, and Troeltsch (e.g. Davidson 1977; Demerath 1965; Estus and Overington 1970; Fukuyama 1961; Glock and Stark 1965; Goode 1966; Lenski 1963; Mueller and Johnson 1975; Stark 1972). Recently, however, empirical researchers have largely ignored the relationship between social class and American religion (see Smith and Faris 2005).

The dearth of research on social class and American religion is particularly detrimental to our understanding of adolescent religion since children are considerably more likely than adults to live in poverty in the United States. In 2005, 17.6 percent of Americans under 18 years old lived in homes with incomes below the poverty line, compared to only 11.1 percent of 18 to 64 year olds and 10.1 percent of those 65 years old and older (DeNavas-Walt, et al. 2006). A considerably larger proportion of American children live in homes that fell or will fall below the poverty line at some point during their

Source: Philip Schwadel, "Poor Teenagers' Religion," from *Sociology of Religion*, Volume 69, © 2008.

childhoods (Brooks-Gunn and Duncan 1997). Despite the fairly common role of poverty in the lives of American teenagers, sociologists have failed to address how poverty affects American teenagers' religious activities and beliefs (see Ross 1950 for an exception).

Knowledge about poor adolescents' religion is further limited by the fact that teenagers' religious activities and beliefs do not always follow the same patterns as those of adults. There are sometimes even noteworthy differences between parents and their own children when it comes to religious beliefs, such as differences in their views of God, the Bible, and the importance of prayer (Hoge, et al. 1982; Keeley 1976). As discussed below, factors associated with being poor in the United States suggest that poor adolescents and their parents are particularly likely to differ in their religious outlooks and activities.

Variations between adult and child religiosity and the absence of recent research on poverty and American religion leave us knowing little about the religion of poor, American teenagers. Are poor teenagers active in religious organizations, one of the few contexts where lower class Americans have opportunities to learn and practice valuable civic skills (Verba, et al. 1995)? Do poor teenagers practice devotional activities and emphasize religious faith, which may curb some of the negative social and psychological consequences of adolescent poverty (Sherkat and Ellison 1999)? Addressing the lack of empirical research on social class and adolescent religion, this article examines the effects of poverty on adolescent religion through analysis of recent survey data of teenagers and their parents.

RELIGION AND SOCIAL CLASS

Nineteenth and early twentieth century European sociologists wrote extensively on the topic of social class and religion. Karl Marx's views on the subject are probably the best

known. Religion, according to Marx, is frequently used to pacify the proletariat—religion is sometimes a tool used by the rich and powerful to control the poor (Marx [1844] 1978). In Marx's view, religion becomes destructive to the poor when it shifts their focus to otherworldly concerns, pacifying them against the inequities of this world (see Lefever 1977 for an alternative view). Max Weber's research on the worldviews of the different social classes also informs current views of poverty and religion. Weber ([1922] 1993) proposes a different theodicy of meaning, or religious explanation of chaotic circumstances, for the different social classes. The upper classes, according to Weber, have an immanent conception of the divine and often seek salvation through mystical channels (see Stark 2003 for an alternative viewpoint). Conversely, the poor and lower classes tend to stress a "theodicy of escape," seeking to master the conflicts inherent in this world by retreating into communities of like-minded believers with an otherworldly emphasis. Ernst Troeltsch ([1931] 1992) further describes the upper class tendency towards mysticism and the lower class emphasis on withdrawal from the secular environment. Weber ([1922] 1993) notes that factors associated with stratification other than income, such as status group affiliation, also affect religious worldviews. Speaking specifically of religion in the United States, he points out that that church affiliation is a financial hardship for poor Americans (Weber 1946).

Interest in the effects of social class on religion carried over to American sociologists. H. Richard Niebuhr (1929), influenced by Weber, Troeltsch, and Marx, describes the attributes of the religion of the poor, or what he calls the "churches of the disinherited." Churches of the disinherited promise poor people a reversal of fortunes in the afterlife. The religion of the poor, according to Niebuhr, is an otherworldly religion that emphasizes the next world over this world and places a great importance in personal religious experiences. Following Niebuhr's lead, empirical research on social class and religion in the United States suggests four general characteristics of lower class religion.

First, empirical research on social class and American religion points to the positive effects of income on participation in organized religious activities (Demerath 1965; Fukuyama 1961; Lenski 1963; Stark 1972; see Lipford and Tollison 2003 for an exception). It should be noted that the positive effects of income on religious service attendance are often not very large and may to some degree be a byproduct of the relationship between income and secular organizational activity (Goode 1966; Mueller and Johnson 1975; see Glock and Stark 1965 for an exception). While the effects of income on attending religious services may not be very large and may be partially due to other factors, income has a strong, positive effect on participating in religious activities other than service attendance (Schwadel 2002). Moreover, the lower classes are more likely than the middle and upper classes to not affiliate with organized religion. In other words, lower class Americans are particularly likely to claim no religious preference or to be religious "nones" (Demerath 1965).

The second attribute of lower class, American religion noted by sociologists is the emphasis on conservatism, otherworldly beliefs, emotional religious experiences, and the importance of religion in daily life. Though the strength of the relationship is in question, it is clear that lower class Protestants are more likely than middle and upper class Protestants to affiliate with conservative denominations (Roof and McKinney 1987; Smith and Faris 2005; Wuthnow 1988). Lower class Protestants also tend to hold conservative beliefs and emphasize the importance of religion. In what is probably the most extensive analysis of social class and American religion, N.J. Demerath III (1965) shows that lower class

Americans stress doctrinal orthodoxy, religion having a large influence on everyday life, belief in the afterlife, holding fundamentalist beliefs, and rejecting religious relativism. Stark and Bainbridge (1985) discuss the otherworldly focus of the poor that makes up for poor people's lack of earthly rewards. Stark's (1972) analysis demonstrates that lower class church members are particularly likely to be orthodox, to find meaning and purpose in life in Christianity, and to report having personal religious experiences.

The importance of private devotional activities is the third well-established aspect of lower class, American religion. The lower classes are more likely than the middle and upper classes to pray (Baker 2008; Davidson 1977; Estus and Overington 1970; Fukuyama 1961; Stark 1972) and to read religious scriptures (Demerath 1965). Stark (1972:490) concludes, "Public, organized worship has more appeal for the upper classes, whereas private devotionalism is more predominant among the lower classes."

The fourth characteristic of lower class religion involves lower class Americans' tendency to withdraw from secular society. Poor Americans are considerably less likely than non-poor Americans to participate in secular voluntary organizations (Verba, et al. 1995). While the poor are underrepresented in secular activities, they tend to interact a great deal with people in their religious congregations or with people that hold similar religious beliefs. For instance, Demerath (1965) shows that the lower classes emphasize the communal features of religion, they are especially likely to interact with people in their congregations, and they disapprove of clergy participation in secular affairs. Similarly, Stark (1972) finds that the lower classes are more likely than the middle and upper classes to have three of their five closest friends in their congregations and to have the majority of their organizational memberships in religious organizations.

In general, empirical research on social class and American religion, though somewhat dated, suggests the following relationships between poverty and adult religion: (1) poor people are less active in organized religion than are non-poor people, (2) poor people are likely to emphasize the afterlife, meaningful religious experiences, and the importance of religion in daily life, (3) poor people are likely to perform personal devotional activities, and (4) poor people are less likely than non-poor people to participate in secular voluntary organizations but they are more likely to interact with like-minded believers.

POOR TEENAGERS' RELIGION

Although empirical research, largely from the 1960s and 1970s, explores the effects of social class on the religious attitudes and activities of American adults, adolescents' religion can differ from the religion of adults. For instance, children are generally more likely than adults to attend religious services, particularly adults without school-aged children (Roof and McKinney 1987). Teenagers do not always resemble their own parents when it comes to religious beliefs and activities. Smith and colleagues (2003), for example, show that only two-thirds of teenagers have religious ideas that closely resemble their parents' religious ideas, and one-tenth have religious ideas that are very different from their parents' views. In an analysis of the transmission of religious values from parents to adolescent children, Hoge, et al. (1982:578) found "rather weak relationships." Plenty of other research focuses on the intergenerational transmission of religion in the U.S., and often the surprising lack thereof (Clark, et al. 1988; Dudley and Dudley 1986; Erickson 1992; Keeley 1976; Kieren and Munro 1987). Moreover, parents do not simply pass on their religious attitudes to their children. Children often shape religious discussions in the home, making parent-child religious socialization a reciprocal process (Boyatzis and Janicki 2003). As Regnerus and colleagues (2003:10) conclude in their review of the literature on adolescent religion, "Parent-child transmission of religiosity and religious identity is indeed quite powerful. But it's not inevitable."

Family and contextual factors that affect the intergenerational transmission of religion suggest that the religious outlooks and activities of poor, American teenagers are particularly likely to vary from their parents' religious viewpoints and activities. The quality of the parent-child relationship affects parent-child agreement on religious issues (Hoge, et al. 1982; Myers 1996; Okagaki and Bevis 1999), and poverty has a negative impact on parent-child relationships (Brooks-Gunn and Duncan 1997). The national context also affects intergenerational religious transmission. Parental religiosity has less of an effect on child religiosity in relatively religious nations, such as the United States (Kelley and De Graaf 1997; Nelsen and Rizvi 1984). Thus, it is possible that the religion of poor, American adolescents differs considerably from the religion of poor, American adults.

With notable differences in religious outlook between teenagers and adults and the lack of recent research on poverty and religion, the question remains—how does poverty affect American teenagers' religious viewpoints and activities at the beginning of the twenty-first century?

DATA AND METHODS

The effects of poverty on adolescent religion are examined with survey data from the National Study of Youth and Religion (NSYR). The NSYR is a nationally representative telephone survey of 3,290 U.S. teenagers, ages 13 to 17, and one of each of their parents. The English and Spanish language surveys were administered from July, 2002 to April, 2003 through random digit dialing and in-home randomization methods.[1] To be eligible for the survey, at least one teenager, ages 13 to 17, must live in the household for at least six months of the year. In the case of households identified as containing a teenager but refusing to participate, information about the survey was mailed to the household and then they were called back for possible participation. Diagnostic analyses show that NSYR teenagers are comparable to U.S. teenagers as a whole (see Smith and Denton 2003 for more information on NSYR sampling). A weight variable is applied in all analyses to adjust for the number of teenagers in the household, the number of telephone numbers in the house, and slight variations between NSYR respondents and the national population of adolescents in geographic location and household income distribution.

Primary Independent Variable

The central independent variable is a measure of poverty. The poverty measure follows the U.S. government's 2002 definition of poverty, taking into account the age of the head of the household, the number of children in the house, the number of household members, and the household income (U.S. Census Bureau 2003a). Because the NSYR measure of family income is a categorical variable, the poverty line for each household configuration falls within an income category. Given the low level of income needed to be considered poor, all borderline cases (i.e., those with family incomes in the same income category that the poverty line falls in) are coded as being poor. With this measure of poverty, 18.6 percent of NSYR teens and their parents are coded as being poor. In comparison, in 2002, 16.7 percent of Americans less than 18 years old lived in households with annual incomes below the poverty line and 22.3 percent lived in households that earned below

125 percent of the poverty line (U.S. Census Bureau 2003b; U.S. Census Bureau 2003c).

Dependent Variables

The four sections of the analysis below test the extent to which previous findings on the religion of lower class adults apply to poor teenagers. Table 1 shows the original question wording and operationalization for all dependent variables, divided into the following analytical categories: (1) organized religious participation, (2) otherworldly beliefs, religious experiences, and the importance of religious faith, (3) private devotional activities, and (4) religiously similar friends and secular voluntary activity.[2] First, previous research suggests that poor adults are less likely than non-poor adults to participate in organized religious activities. If this pattern holds true for adolescents, poor teenagers should be less likely than non-poor teenagers to regularly attend religious services,[3] go to Sunday school, and participate in religious

---

[1]About 3.7 percent of respondents completed the Spanish language version of the survey.

[2]Bivariate correlations between dependent variables range from near zero to .50. The following dependent variable combinations are correlated at the .40 level or higher (correlations in parentheses): regular service attendance and Sunday school participation (.49), regular service attendance and youth group participation (.42), youth group participation and Sunday school participation (.50), and importance of faith and prayer (.41).

[3]Religious service attendance is dichotomized at two to three times a month or more versus less than two to three times a month, which is meant to tap regular religious participation. A more stringent measure of regular service attendance, such as weekly or more, might result in religiously active teenagers who have various other life commitments that compete with religious activity, such as sports, clubs, and other social events, being placed in the non-participating category (see Smith 2005 for a discussion of teenagers' various organizational and social commitments that compete with religious activity). Nevertheless, alternative codings of the dichotomous religious participation variable do not seriously affect the results (see notes 5 and 6). Additionally, using the dichotomous measure of service participation rather than the original seven-category variable (never, few times a year, many times a month, once a month, two to three times a month, once a week, and more than once a week) also does not meaningfully change the results (see notes 5 and 6). The dichotomous measure of religious service attendance was chosen over the ordinal measure to keep the analysis consistent with the other binary logistic regression analyses.

TABLE 1   Question Wording and Operationalization of Dependent Variables

Organized Religious Participation
  1. "Regardless of whether you now attend any religious services, do you ever think of yourself as part of a particular religion, denomination, or church?" (no = religious "none" [12%])
  2. "About how often do you usually attend religious services . . . ?" (two to three times a month or more = regular service attendance [53%])
  3. "Are you currently involved in any religious youth group?" (yes = youth group activity [38%])
  4. "In the last year, how often, if at all, have you attended a religious Sunday school?" (a few times a month or more = regular Sunday school participation [47%])

Otherworldly Beliefs, Religious Experiences, and Importance of Religious Faith
  5. "Do you believe that there is life after death" (definitely believe = believe in afterlife [50%])
  6. "Do you believe that there will come a judgment day when God will reward some and punish others, or not?" (yes = believe in a judgment day [73%])
  7. "Have you ever had an experience of spiritual worship that was very moving and powerful?" (yes = had religious experience [52%])
  8. "How important or unimportant is religious faith in shaping how you live your daily life?" (very or extremely important = faith important in daily life [51%])

Private Devotional Activities
  9. "How often, if ever, do you pray by yourself alone?" (a few times a week or more = regular prayer [53%])
 10. "How often, if ever, do you read from [appropriate scriptures] to yourself alone?" (once a week or more = regular scripture reading [26%])

Religiously Similar Friends and Secular Voluntary Activity
 11. After naming their five closest friends, respondents were asked, "which, if any of these people, hold religious beliefs that are similar to yours" (three or more friends with similar religious beliefs = associating with people with similar religious outlooks [67%])
 12. "In the last year, how much, if at all, have you done organized volunteer work or community service?" and "How much, if any, of this volunteer work or community service was organized by a religious organization or congregation?" (any volunteer work not done for a religious organization or congregation = secular voluntary activity [60%])

Note: Percent of teenagers doing or saying concept in brackets. Data weighted to adjust for probability of selection into the sample and potential sampling bias.

youth groups, and more likely to claim no religious preference. Second, if poor teenagers resemble lower class adults, they should be more likely than non-poor teenagers to believe in the afterlife and a judgment day, to report having moving religious experiences, and to say that religious faith is important in their daily lives. Third, the religion of lower class adults disproportionately focuses on private devotional activities, which means poor teenagers should be particularly likely to pray and read religious scriptures. Fourth, research suggests that lower class adults tend to associate primarily with people who have similar religious outlooks and they often shun participation in secular voluntary organizations. Assuming that poor teenagers are similar to poor adults in this respect, poor teenagers should be more likely than non-poor teenagers to report that at least three of their five closest friends hold religious beliefs that are similar to their religious beliefs, and less likely to participate in secular voluntary activities.

Analysis Technique and Control Variables

Binary logistic regression models examine the effects of poverty on teenagers' religious affiliations, practices, and beliefs. Binary logistic

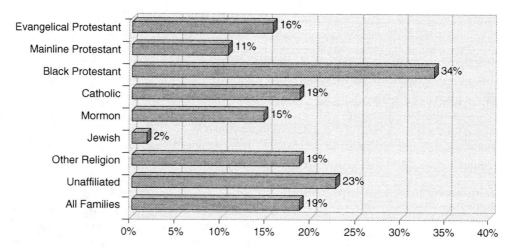

FIGURE 1   Percent of Families Near or Below the Poverty Line within Parents' Religious Tradition

Note: Data weighted to adjust for probability of selection into the sample and potential sampling bias.

Source: National Study of Youth and Religion 2002–2003.

regression models compute the logged odds change in the dichotomous dependent variable for each one unit increase in the independent variables (Menard 1995). Teenagers' demographics, geographic location, and parental/family variables are added to the regression models of the effects of poverty on adolescent religion. Teenagers' ages and a dummy variable for female teens control for age and gender effects, which are both relevant to religious participation and beliefs. Teen religious service attendance, a dummy variable for those who attend at least two to three times a month, is introduced as a control variable in all models following the analysis of the effects of poverty on teens' religious service attendance. Dummy variables for urban and rural teens (with suburban teens being the reference category) and a dummy variable for Southern residence control for geographic variations in religious practice and belief. A dummy variable for teens that live with married parents controls for variations in family stability. Parents' religious activity, which can have a large effect on their children's religiosity, is measured with a dummy variable

for responding parents who attend religious services at least two to three times a month. Finally, but probably most importantly, the religious context of each teenager's home life is accounted for with dummy variables for the responding parent's religious tradition: evangelical Protestant, mainline Protestant, black Protestant, Catholic, Mormon, Jewish, other religions, and unaffiliated.[4] Not only are parents' religious traditions likely to affect their children's religious outlooks, but, as Figure 1 demonstrates, there are large differences in the proportion of families living near or below the poverty line among the different religious traditions. About one-third of teens whose parents are affiliated with black Protestant denominations are growing up in poverty, which is not surprising given the large racial differences in income in the United States. The religiously unaffiliated have the second largest proportion

---

[4]Religious tradition is determined by the responding parent and the variable is constructed by the principle investigator of the NSYR to resemble, as closely as possible, the division of denominations devised by Steensland and colleagues (2000).

of poor families, with 23 percent poor, suggesting that many poor, American teenagers live in homes with little connection to organized religion. Supporting previous research on social class and American religion, evangelical Protestant families (16 percent) are more likely than mainline Protestant families (11 percent) to be poor.

RESULTS

Participation in Organized Religion

As noted, poor teenagers may differ from their parents religiously more than non-poor teenagers differ from their parents. As a quick aside before presenting the logistic regression results, the NSYR data allow for a partial test of this hypothesis. Table 2 shows the correlations between teenagers and their responding parents having no religious preference and regularly attending religious services, for both the poor and the non-poor. The correlation between poor teenagers and their parents having no religious preference is somewhat lower than the correlation between non-poor teenagers and their parents having no religious preference (.34 and .38, respectively). According to

Fisher's *z* Transformation, which transforms the difference in correlations into a normally distributed *z*-score (Cohen, et al. 2003), this difference is not statistically significant. The difference in correlations is far greater when it comes to regular religious service attendance. The correlation between non-poor teens' and their parents' attendance (.50) is much larger than the correlation between poor teens' and their parents' attendance (.30); according to Fisher's *z* Transformation, this difference is highly significant. Alternative codings of religious service attendance result in even greater differences between poor teenagers and their parents compared to non-poor teenagers and their parents.[5] To put this difference in context, 76 percent of non-poor parents who regularly

---

[5]When regular attendance is defined as weekly or more, the correlation between poor teens and their parents is .29 while the correlation between non-poor teens and their parents is .53 (both correlations significant at .001 level). Using the original seven-category measure of religious service attendance, the correlation between poor teens and their parents is .37 while the correlation between non-poor teens and their parents is .60 (both correlations significant at .001 level). According to Fisher's *z* Transformation, the difference in correlations between poor and non-poor teen/parent pairs is statistically significant at the .001 level with both alternate codings of religious service attendance.

TABLE 2   Correlations between Teenagers and Their Parents Having No Religious Preference and Regularly Attending Religious Services, Among the Poor and Non-Poor

	No religious preference	Attends religious services at least 2 to 3 times a month
Poor teen/parent correlation	.34*** (575)	.30*** (574)
Non-poor teen/parent correlation	.38*** (2,511)	.50*** (2,506)
Fisher's *z*[a]	0.82	3.91***

Note: Ns in parentheses. Data weighted to adjust for probability of selection into the sample and potential sampling bias.

[a]Fisher's *z* transforms the difference between poor and non-poor correlations into a normally distributed *z*-score.

*p ≤ .05   **p ≤ .01   ***p ≤ .001 (two-tailed tests)

Source: National Study of Youth and Religion 2002–2003.

attend religious services have adolescent children who also regularly attend religious services while only 58 percent of poor parents who regularly attend religious services have adolescent children who also regularly attend religious services (not shown). In sum, non-poor teenagers and their parents are more religiously similar than are poor teenagers and their parents when it comes to regularly attending religious services, though the same cannot be said of having no religious preference.

Table 3 presents odds ratios from binary logistic regression analyses of teenagers' participation in organized religion. As the first column of Table 3 shows, in the bivariate regression of having no religious preference, poor teens' odds of claiming to be religious "nones" are 55 percent higher than the odds for non-poor teens (the odds ratio is 1.55). In the full model, poor teens' odds of having no religious preference are still 36 percent higher than the odds for non-poor teens, though the statistical significance of the poverty coefficient drops to the .1 level (column 2). The fact that many teens with no religious preference also have parents with no religious preference is evident from the very strong effect of having unaffiliated parents. Nonetheless, teens that live in poor or near poor households are more likely than other teens to be religious "nones," regardless of whether or not their parents are affiliated with a religious tradition.

Religious service attendance is the most common measure of religious participation. As the bivariate regression results in the third column of Table 3 show, poor teens' odds of attending religious services at least two to three times a month are 38 percent less than the odds for non-poor teens $(1 - 0.62 = 0.38)$. The effect of poverty is smaller, but still meaningful, with control variables added to the model. In the full model, poor teens' odds of regular service attendance are 29 percent less than the odds for non-poor teens (column 4). While the statistical significance of the effect of poverty on teenagers' religious

service attendance declines from .001 to .01 when control variables are added to the model, poverty remains a strong and significant predictor of teenagers' religious service attendance. Alternative codings of religious service attendance result in even larger effects of poverty.[6]

The results in Table 3 also show that poor teens are less likely than non-poor teens to regularly participate in Sunday school and belong to religious youth groups. In the bivariate model, the odds of poor teens attending a religious Sunday school at least a few times a month are 30 percent less than the odds for non-poor teens (column 5). With control variables in the model, poor teens' odds of regular Sunday school participation are 21 percent less than the odds for non-poor teens (column 6). The statistical significance of the effect of poverty on teenagers' Sunday school participation declines when control variables are added to the model (from .001 to .1), but remains meaningful.

The difference between poor teens and non-poor teens is even greater when it comes to religious youth group activity. In the bivariate regression, poor teens' odds of religious youth group participation are 46 percent less than the odds for non-poor teens (column 7). In the full model, the odds of youth group participation for poor teens are 37 percent less than the odds for non-poor teens (column 8). In general, the results show that poor teens are less likely than non-poor teens to participate in organized religious activities ranging from simply affiliating with organized religion to religious service and Sunday school attendance to youth group participation.

---

[6]When religious service attendance is dichotomized at weekly or more, the effect of poverty on service participation is stronger than the results presented in Table 3 (odds ratios of 0.57 in the bivariate regression and 0.68 in the full model, both effects significant at the .01 level or higher). Employing OLS regression with the original seven-category ordinal measure of religious service attendance also shows similar results (poverty coefficients of $-.58$ in the bivariate regression and $-.32$ in the full model, both effects significant at the .001 level).

TABLE 3 Odds Ratios from Binary Logistic Regression Models Predicting Participation in Organized Religion, Teenagers Ages 13–17

	No religious preference		Attends religious services at least 2 to 3 times a month		Attends a religious Sunday school a few times a month		Currently in a religious youth group	
POVERTY	1.55 (.13)***	1.36 (.16)+	0.62 (.09)***	0.71 (.12)**	0.70 (.10)***	0.79 (.12)+	0.54 (.10)***	0.63 (.13)***
TEEN VARIABLES								
Age	—	1.07 (.05)	—	0.93 (.03)**	—	0.83 (.03)***	—	0.96 (.03)
Female	—	0.75 (.13)*	—	1.30 (.08)**	—	1.21 (.09)*	—	1.19 (.09)*
Service Attendance	—	—	—	—	—	6.66 (.10)***	—	5.10 (.10)***
LOCATION								
South	—	0.50 (.15)***	—	1.12 (.09)	—	1.22 (.09)*	—	1.42 (.09)***
Urban	—	1.26 (.15)	—	0.86 (.10)	—	0.86 (.11)	—	1.13 (.11)
Rural (Suburban ref.)	—	1.31 (.17)	—	1.39 (.11)**	—	1.11 (.11)	—	1.29 (.11)*
PARENT VARIABLES								
Service Attendance	—	0.15 (.17)***	—	6.48 (.09)***	—	1.97 (.10)***	—	1.95 (.10)***
Married	—	0.92 (.14)	—	1.10 (.10)	—	0.95 (.11)	—	1.02 (.11)
Evangelical Protestant[a]	—	0.61 (.21)*	—	1.45 (.13)*	—	1.64 (.14)***	—	1.16 (.13)
Black Protestant	—	1.10 (.25)	—	0.84 (.16)	—	2.00 (.17)***	—	0.58 (.17)***
Catholic	—	0.68 (.20)+	—	0.86 (.13)	—	0.78 (.14)+	—	0.35 (.14)***
Mormon	—	0.50 (.55)	—	1.82 (.28)*	—	3.96 (.30)**	—	2.70 (.28)***
Jewish	—	0.65 (.48)	—	0.21 (.48)***	—	1.76 (.35)	—	1.07 (.37)
Other Religion	—	2.37 (.31)**	—	0.62 (.26)+	—	0.42 (.31)**	—	0.13 (.39)***
Unaffiliated	—	4.79 (.21)***	—	0.47 (.23)***	—	0.68 (.25)	—	0.41 (.27)***
Constant	−2.09	−2.20	0.03	0.19	−0.06	1.07	−0.40	−1.10
−2 Log Likelihood	2250.18	1732.24	4235.31	3438.64	4223.33	3182.92	4032.77	3153.12
N	3,085	3,085	3,085	3,085	3,073	3,073	3,076	3,076

Note: Standard errors in parentheses. Full models include a dummy variable for parents whose religious affiliation was undeterminable. Data weighted to adjust for probability of selection into the sample and potential sampling bias.

[a]Reference group for all religious affiliation variables is Mainline Protestant

+p ≤ .10   *p ≤ .05   **p ≤ .01   ***p ≤ .001   (two-tailed tests)

Source: National Study of Youth and Religion 2002–2003.

Otherworldly Religious Beliefs, Religious Experiences, and Importance of Religious Faith

Table 4 presents odds ratios from logistic regression analyses of teenagers' otherworldly religious beliefs, their reporting of moving religious experiences, and the importance of religious faith in their lives. Contrary to the common portrayal of lower class religion, poor teenagers are less likely than non-poor teenagers to believe in the afterlife. The bivariate model shows that poor teens' odds of believing in the afterlife are 36 percent less than the odds for non-poor teens (column 1). In the full model, poor teens' odds of believing in life after death are 28 percent less than the odds for non-poor teens (column 2). While adding control variables to the model reduces the significance of the poverty coefficient from .001 to .01, poverty remains a strong predictor of belief in the afterlife.

In contrast to belief in the afterlife, poverty has a strong, positive effect on belief in a judgment day when God will reward some and punish others. In the bivariate regression, poor teenagers' odds of saying they believe in a judgment day are 46 percent higher than the odds for non-poor teenagers (column 3). With control variables in the model, the effect of poverty is even greater. In the full model, poor teens' odds of believing in a judgment day are 72 percent higher than the odds for non-poor teens (column 4). Teenagers' religious service attendance, which is strongly related to belief in a judgment day, appears to act as a suppressor variable (see Cohen, et al. 2003 for more on suppressor variables). Because religious service attendance and belief in a judgment day are strongly and positively related, the introduction of religious service attendance to the model of belief in a judgment day strengthens the effect of poverty by controlling for poor teens' low likelihood of regular service attendance. In other words, considering their low likelihood of regular religious service attendance, poor teenagers are especially likely to believe in a judgment day.

Contrary to research on adult religion that points to lower class adults' emphasis on emotional religious experiences, poor teenagers are not particularly likely to report having had a worship experience that was very moving and powerful. In the bivariate regression, poor teens' odds of reporting moving worship experiences are 40 percent less than the odds for non-poor teens (column 5). This difference is reduced, but still large, with control variables in the model. In the full model, poor teens' odds of reporting moving worship experiences are 27 percent less than the odds for non-poor teens (column 6). The poverty coefficient declines in significance from the bivariate model to the full model (from .001 to .01), but remains highly significant. Even after controlling for the strong correlation between religious service attendance and moving worship experiences, poor teens are still less likely than non-poor teens to report worship experiences that are very moving and powerful.

As research on adult religion suggests, poor teens are considerably more likely than non-poor teens to say that religious faith is very or extremely important in shaping their daily lives. The bivariate regression results in the seventh column of Table 4 show that poor teens' odds of reporting that religious faith is very or extremely important in shaping their daily lives are 24 percent higher than the odds for non-poor teens. The effect of poverty is far greater with the addition of control variables to the model. In the full model, poor teens' odds of saying that religious faith is very or extremely important in shaping their daily lives are 48 percent higher than the odds for non-poor teens (column 8). As with belief in a judgment day, religious service attendance appears to act as a suppressor variable in the relationship between poverty and the importance of faith in daily life.

TABLE 4   Odds Ratios from Binary Logistic Regression Models Predicting Otherworldly Religious Beliefs, Religious Experiences, and the Importance of Religious Faith, Teenagers Ages 13–17

	Believe that there is life after death		Believe in a judgment day		Had moving and powerful experience of spiritual worship		Religious faith important in shaping daily life	
POVERTY	0.64 (.10)***	0.72 (.11)**	1.46 (.11)***	1.72 (.13)***	0.60 (.09)***	0.73 (.11)**	1.24 (.09)*	1.48 (.12)***
TEEN VARIABLES								
Age	—	1.05 (.03)+	—	1.01 (.03)	—	1.10 (.03)***	—	1.01 (.03)
Female	—	0.90 (.08)	—	1.35 (.09)***	—	1.07 (.08)	—	1.30 (.08)***
Service Attendance	—	2.00 (.09)***	—	2.17 (.11)***	—	3.15 (.09)***	—	3.47 (.09)***
LOCATION								
South	—	1.24 (.08)***	—	1.50 (.10)***	—	1.52 (.09)***	—	1.71 (.09)***
Urban	—	1.07 (.09)	—	1.00 (.11)	—	0.98 (.10)	—	0.78 (.10)*
Rural (Suburban ref.)	—	0.74 (.10)**	—	1.26 (.12)+	—	0.68 (.11)***	—	0.99 (.11)
PARENT VARIABLES								
Service Attendance	—	1.56 (.09)***	—	2.10 (.11)***	—	1.70 (.09)***	—	1.97 (.09)***
Married	—	1.06 (.09)	—	1.25 (.11)*	—	1.09 (.10)	—	0.99 (.10)
Evangelical Protestant[a]	—	1.62 (.12)***	—	3.03 (.14)***	—	1.37 (.13)*	—	1.70 (.13)***
Black Protestant	—	1.14 (.15)	—	3.56 (.20)***	—	0.80 (.16)	—	2.53 (.17)***
Catholic	—	0.92 (.12)	—	1.17 (.13)	—	0.39 (.13)***	—	0.87 (.13)
Mormon	—	3.99 (.29)***	—	4.66 (.38)***	—	1.86 (.28)*	—	2.35 (.26)***
Jewish	—	0.64 (.35)	—	0.35 (.37)**	—	1.23 (.32)	—	0.42 (.45)+
Other Religion	—	0.66 (.25)+	—	0.86 (.27)	—	0.48 (.26)**	—	1.21 (.26)
Unaffiliated	—	1.19 (.19)	—	1.12 (.19)	—	0.47 (.21)***	—	0.78 (.22)
Constant	0.08	−1.50	0.95	−0.89	0.17	−2.15	−0.01	−1.77
−2 Log Likelihood	4173.74	3881.58	3430.29	2901.87	4181.66	3543.10	4256.63	3520.70
N	3,034	3,034	2,985	2,985	3,051	3,051	3,080	3,080

Note: Standard errors in parentheses. Full models include a dummy variable for parents whose religious affiliation was undeterminable. Data weighted to adjust for probability of selection into the sample and potential sampling bias.

[a]Reference group for all religious affiliation variables is Mainline Protestant

+ p ≤ .10   * p ≤ .05   ** p ≤ .01   *** p ≤ .001   (two-tailed tests)

Source: National Study of Youth and Religion 2002–2003.

Poor teenagers are highly likely to report that religious faith is important in their daily lives despite the fact that they are not likely to regularly attend religious services, and service attendance is strongly correlated with religious faith being important in daily life. The results in Table 4 demonstrate that poor teenagers' religion resembles the religion of lower class adults in certain respects, such as their emphasis on religious faith and belief in a judgment day. In other ways, however, the religion of poor adolescents differs from the common portrayal of lower class religion, exemplified by poor teenagers' low likelihood of reporting religious experiences and believing in the afterlife.

Private Devotional Activities

Table 5 presents odds ratios from logistic regression models of adolescents' private devotional activities. As the first bivariate regression shows, the odds of poor teens praying alone a few times a week or more are 24 percent higher than the odds for non-poor teens (column 1). With control variables added to the model, the odds of poor teens praying alone at least a few times a week increase to 34 percent higher than the odds for non-poor teens (column 2). Similarly, while the odds of poor teens reading religious scriptures alone at least once a week are 32 percent

TABLE 5   Odds ratios from Binary Logistic Regressions of Private Devotional Activities, Teenagers Ages 13–17

	Pray alone a few times a week or more		Read from scriptures alone once a week or more	
POVERTY	1.24 (.09)*	1.34 (.11)*	1.32 (.10)**	1.45 (.12)**
TEEN VARIABLES				
Age	—	1.05 (.03)	—	0.93 (.03)*
Female	—	1.80 (.08)***	—	1.26 (.09)**
Regular Service Attendance	—	3.07 (.09)***	—	2.99 (.11)***
LOCATION				
South	—	1.40 (.09)***	—	1.16 (.09)
Urban	—	1.34 (.10)**	—	1.22 (.11)+
Rural (Suburban ref.)	—	1.02 (.10)	—	1.08 (.11)
PARENT VARIABLES				
Regular Service Attendance	—	1.60 (.09)***	—	1.46 (.11)***
Married	—	1.08 (.10)	—	0.92 (.11)
Evangelical Protestant[a]	—	1.62 (.13)***	—	1.98 (.14)***
Black Protestant	—	2.01 (.16)***	—	1.90 (.17)***
Catholic	—	1.03 (.13)	—	0.60 (.16)**
Mormon	—	1.95 (.26)**	—	3.68 (.25)***
Jewish	—	0.24 (.49)**	—	1.09 (.47)
Other Religion	—	0.90 (.25)	—	1.68 (.28)+
Unaffiliated	—	0.91 (.20)	—	1.13 (.26)
Constant	0.10	−2.23	−1.11	−1.41
−2 Log Likelihood	4240.16	3674.62	3505.04	3085.06
N	3,075	3,075	3,074	3,074

Note: Standard errors in parentheses. Full models include a dummy variable for parents whose religious affiliation was undeterminable. Data weighted to adjust for probability of selection into the sample and potential sampling bias.

[a]Reference group for all religious affiliation variables is Mainline Protestant

$^+p \leq .10$ $^*p \leq .05$ $^{**}p \leq .01$ $^{***}p \leq .001$ (two-tailed tests)

Source: National Study of Youth and Religion 2002–2003.

higher than the odds for non-poor teens in the bivariate regression (column 3), the odds for poor teens increase to 45 percent higher than the odds for non-poor teens when control variables are added to the model (column 4). Again, religious service attendance appears to act as a suppressor variable. Since devotional activities are positively correlated with service attendance, the positive effect of poverty on prayer and scripture reading is even greater when poor teens' low likelihood of regular service attendance is taken into account. Mirroring research on social class and adult religion, the results in Table 5 demonstrate that poor teenagers are particularly likely to perform private devotional activities.

Religiously Similar Friends and Secular Voluntary Activity

The regression results in the first two columns of Table 6 demonstrate that poor teens are relatively unlikely to perceive their friends as being religiously similar to them. In the bivariate regression, the odds of poor teens saying that at least three of their five closest friends have religious beliefs similar to their religious beliefs are 24 percent less than the odds for non-poor teens (column 1). With control variables in the model, the odds of poor teens saying three of their five closest friends have religious beliefs similar to theirs are 26 percent less than the odds for non-poor teens (column 2).

TABLE 6   Odds ratios from Binary Logistic Regressions of Having Religiously Similar Friends and Secular Voluntary Activity, Teenagers Ages 13–17

	At least 3 of 5 closest friends have similar religious beliefs		Done secular volunteer work in the last year	
POVERTY	0.76 (0.13)*	0.74 (.14)*	0.76 (.09)**	0.89 (.10)
TEEN VARIABLES				
Age	—	0.96 (.03)	—	1.17 (.03)***
Female	—	1.06 (.09)	—	1.24 (.08)**
Regular Service Attendance	—	1.03 (.11)	—	1.35 (.09)***
LOCATION				
South	—	1.34 (.10)**	—	0.89 (.08)
Urban	—	0.90 (.12)	—	1.01 (.09)
Rural (Suburban ref.)	—	0.87 (.12)	—	0.83 (.10)*
PARENT VARIABLES				
Regular Service Attendance	—	1.14 (.11)	—	1.10 (.09)
Married	—	1.05 (.12)	—	1.13 (.09)
Evangelical Protestant[a]	—	1.11 (.15)	—	0.69 (.12)**
Black Protestant	—	1.30 (.19)	—	0.72 (.15)*
Catholic	—	1.05 (.15)	—	0.89 (.12)
Mormon	—	0.92 (.27)	—	0.92 (.25)
Jewish	—	0.19 (.43)***	—	1.55 (.34)
Other Religion	—	0.41 (.33)**	—	0.76 (.24)
Unaffiliated	—	1.06 (.28)	—	1.18 (.18)
Constant	0.72	1.06	0.44	−2.08
−2 Log Likelihood	2685.06	2630.40	4133.86	4044.09
N	2,099	2,099	3,078	3,078

Note: Standard errors in parentheses. Full models include a dummy variable for parents whose religious affiliation was undeterminable. Data weighted to adjust for probability of selection into the sample and potential sampling bias.

[a]Reference group for all religious affiliation variables is Mainline Protestant

*+p ≤ .1   p ≤ .05**   p ≤ .01***   p ≤ .001   (two-tailed tests)

Source: National Study of Youth and Religion 2002–2003.

The results in Table 6 also show that poor teens are somewhat less likely than non-poor teens to participate in secular voluntary activities, but this relationship is not meaningful when control variables are included in the model. In the bivariate regression, the odds of poor teens participating in secular voluntary activities in the last year are 24 percent less than the odds for non-poor teens (column 3). With the addition of control variables, the odds of poor teens participating in secular voluntary activities are only 11 percent less than the odds for non-poor teens, and the effect of poverty is no longer statistically significant (column 4). In contrast to what research on lower class adults suggests, poor teenagers do not appear to be particularly withdrawn from secular society.

DISCUSSION AND CONCLUSIONS

With the lack of recent research on poverty and American religion, the most important conclusion from this analysis of the NSYR data is that social class does matter when examining American teenagers' religious participation and beliefs. Poor and non-poor teenagers differ considerably in their religious outlooks and religious activities. As predicted, poor teenagers are less active in organized religion than are non-poor teenagers. Compared to non-poor teenagers, poor teenagers are more likely to have no religious preference, and less likely to regularly attend religious services, participate in religious Sunday schools, and join religious youth groups. These findings support the notion that social class can impose constraints on religious participation (McCloud 2007; Weber 1946). Religious service, Sunday school, and religious youth group participation cost money, possibly excluding poor teens for monetary reasons (Hollingshead 1949). Poor teens (and their parents) might feel conspicuous because they cannot give to the collection plate or afford nice clothes; they might feel that other attendees will look down on them (Sakalas

1999). Poor teenagers may even have trouble getting to religious activities, as few Americans live within close walking distance of their religious congregations (Chaves 2004). In sum, poor teenagers may not choose to avoid religious activities. Instead, they may not be able to afford to participate.

Building on older deprivation theories of religious affiliation, sociologists recognize that social class can impose constraints on religious activity other than those that are strictly monetary, such as constraints on social networks (e.g. Stark and Bainbridge 1985). Most people interact primarily with those of a similar social class, meaning lower class people tend to interact with other lower class people (McPherson, et al. 2001). These class-influenced social networks are important predictors of the congregations and denominations that Americans affiliate with since people often find their religious institutions through their friends and neighbors (Hoge, et al. 1995; Stark and Bainbridge 1985). Not only are poor teenagers' social networks restricted by the social class homogeneity of most social networks, but, as the above findings show, poor teenagers are particularly likely to view their friends as having religious beliefs that are different from their religious beliefs. This suggests that poor teenagers are disadvantaged in their ability to connect to religious organizations that meet their tastes because they often perceive their friends as religiously dissimilar to them, which may help account for poor teenagers' low likelihood of regularly participating in religious organizations.

The analyses of participation in organized religious activities raise almost as many questions as they answer. Do poor teenagers lack the time and resources needed to regularly participate in organized religious activities? Have religious institutions been co-opted by the middle class and, therefore, no longer appeal to lower class adolescents (see Finke and Stark 1992)? Do poor teenagers have a hard time finding religious organizations and activities that appeal to them due to the social class constraints on their social networks? Perhaps religious institutions focus more on providing material resources to the poor than on supplying them with spiritual and religious resources (Sakalas 1999)? Are churches that operate charities for poor people less inviting to those same poor people when it comes time for Sunday services? These are questions that future research must address.

Poor teenagers are undoubtedly religious, but their religion tends to be private and personal, rather than institutionally-based. The regression models of prayer, scripture reading, belief in a judgment day, and the importance of faith in daily life all show suppressor effects of religious service attendance. Not only are poor teenagers especially likely to pray, read scriptures, believe in a judgment day, and say faith is important in their daily lives, but they are surprisingly likely to do/say these things given their low likelihood of regularly attending religious services.

While poor teenagers' stress the personal and private aspects of religion over the institutionally-based aspects of religion, their personal religious activities are far more conventional than the highly emotional religious experiences that are commonly associated with the lower classes. In contrast to research on adult religion, which suggests that the lower classes are particularly likely to have emotional religious experiences (Stark 1972), poor teenagers are less likely than non-poor teenagers to report meaningful experiences of spiritual worship, even after controlling for religious service attendance. Contrary to the common perception of lower class religion, it appears that poor teenagers' religion is not especially experience-based, but it does have a considerable influence on their lives through prayer, scripture reading, and an emphasis on faith in daily life.

Although it is generally believed that lower class religion focuses on the afterlife, analysis

of the NSYR data reminds us that this is an oversimplification of theories of the relationship between social class and eschatology. While poor teenagers are somewhat less likely than non-poor teenagers to believe in life after death, poor teenagers are far more likely than non-poor teenagers to believe in a judgment day. At first this may seem contradictory and in contrast to the widespread view that poor people usually hold otherworldly beliefs. Nevertheless, poor teenagers' belief in "a judgment day when God will reward some and punish others" is consistent with the idea that lower class religion focuses not just on the afterlife but on the reversal of fortunes in the afterlife (Niebuhr 1929). When addressing the role of the afterlife in poor people's religion, we should not forget that Marx, Niebuhr, and others specified that poor people's religion emphasizes an afterlife *where the misfortunes of this world are corrected*, not just a life after this one. More recently, theories of deprivation and religion point to the implicit exchange promised to poor people, with a deprived this-life being exchanged for of a joyful afterlife (Stark and Bainbridge 1996). The above findings support the view that for poor teenagers an afterlife without mention of divine judgment or the reversal of earthly roles does not have the same promise as a judgment day that will provide the poor with a prosperous eternal existence.

In contrast to poor adults (Demerath 1965; Stark 1972; Verba, et al. 1995), poor teenagers are less likely than non-poor teenagers to interact primarily with teens who have religious beliefs that are similar to their religious beliefs, and poor teens are not much less likely than other teens to participate in secular voluntary activities. In other words, today's poor teenagers do not appear to be particularly withdrawn from secular society. This could be something unique to teenagers since adolescents often lack control over their friendship networks and organizational commitments (Wilson 2000). On the other hand, poor teenagers may continue their relatively high levels of interaction with secular society as they grow older, eventually changing the perception of poor Americans as withdrawn from secular society. In the future, poor adults might be more participatory in secular society than they are now and have been in the past. Further research is needed to assess the long-term implications of poor teenagers' apparently conventional amount of interaction with secular society.

Although this article does not focus on the effects of parental religion on adolescent religion, two conclusions on the subject can be drawn from the above analysis. First, parental religion has a substantial impact on adolescent religion. In all regression models, other than the regressions of withdrawal from secular society (Table 6), both parents' service attendance and parents' religious tradition have strong effects on teenagers' religious outlooks and activities. Second, there appears to be a stronger relationship between parents' religious participation and their adolescent children's religious participation in non-poor families than in poor families—the correlation between parent and child regularly attending religious services is far larger for non-poor families than for poor families. No conclusions can be drawn about the effects of poverty on parent-child agreement on religious beliefs since the parents in the NSYR survey were not asked the same belief questions as the teenagers.

There are various possible reasons for the relatively large differences in regular religious service attendance between poor teenagers and their parents. As noted above, lower class families are disproportionately prone to family conflict (Brooks-Gunn and Duncan 1997). It is possible that the higher level of conflict between teens and parents in poor families is responsible for the large differences in regular religious service attendance between poor parents and their adolescent children. It is also possible that family structure plays a role in this

relationship, with poor families being especially likely to be single-parent families (DeNavas-Walt, et al. 2006). Single parents have other commitments that might conflict with religious service attendance. One parent means there is only one person to take the children where they need to go, to do errands that need to be done, to take care of the home, and to earn the family income. Single parents may simply have less time for religious services. Additionally, it is possible that teens from poor, single-parent households sometimes attend religious services with the non-resident parent, which could lead to large differences in service attendance between teens and their responding parents in these homes. Further research is needed to examine why poor teens and their parents differ in their religious service attendance more than non-poor teens and their parents.

Unfortunately, poverty is a fact of life for a considerable proportion of American children. The physical, social, and psychological consequences of living in poverty are substantial. Increased likelihood of alcohol and substance abuse, high levels of family conflict, early sexual activity, mental health and self-esteem problems, and poor physical health are only a few of the outcomes associated with adolescent poverty (Bianchi 1999). For teenagers, differences in religious outlook and religious activity are another aspect of living in poverty. It is possible that poor teenagers' emphasis on prayer, reading scriptures, and the importance of religious faith can help to mitigate some of the negative effects of living in poverty (Sherkat and Ellison 1999). On the other hand, poor teenagers' lack of regular religious participation is particularly troubling. With poor Americans being underrepresented in most social and political settings, religious organizations are seen as possibly the only context where the lower classes can participate on an equal footing with other Americans (Verba, et al. 1995). Poor teenagers, however, are unlikely to be very active in religious organizations. While it is possible that this will change as these teens age, it is also possible that in the near future poor Americans will be seriously underrepresented in religious organizations, which will further limit the social, cultural, and political resources available to them.

REFERENCES

BAKER, JOSEPH O. 2008. "An Investigation of the Sociological Patterns of Prayer Frequency and Content." *Sociology of Religion* 69:169–85.

BIANCHI, SUZANNE M. 1999. "Feminization and Juvenilization of Poverty: Trends, Relative Risks, Causes, and Consequences." *Annual Review of Sociology* 25:307–33.

BOYATZIS, CHRIS J., and DENISE L. JANICKI. 2003. "Parent-Child Communication about Religion: Survey and Diary Data on Unilateral Transmission and Bi-Directional Reciprocity Styles." *Review of Religious Research* 44:252–70.

BROOKS-GUNN, JEANNE, and GREG J. DUNCAN. 1997. "The Effects of Poverty on Children." *Future of Children* 7:55–71.

CHAVES, MARK. 2004. *Congregations in America*. Cambridge, MA: Harvard University Press.

CLARK, CYNTHIA A., EVERETT L. WORTHINGTON, and DONALD B. DANSER. 1988. "The Transmission of Religious Beliefs and Practices from Parents to Firstborn Early Adolescent Sons." *Journal of Marriage and the Family* 50:463–72.

COHEN, JACOB, PATRICIA COHEN, STEPHEN G. WEST, and LEONA S. AIKEN. 2003. *Applied Multiple Regression/Correlation Analysis for the Behavioral Sciences: Third Edition*. Mahwah, NJ: Lawrence Erlbaum Associates.

DAVIDSON, JAMES D. 1977. "Socio-Economic Status and Ten Dimensions of Religious Commitment." *Sociology and Social Research* 61:462–85.

DEMERATH, N.J. III. 1965. *Social Class in American Protestantism*. Chicago: Rand McNally.

DENAVAS-WALT, CARMEN, BERNADETTE D. PROCTOR, and CHERYL HILL LEE. 2006. "Income, Poverty, and Health Coverage in the United States: 2005." Current Population Report (p60–231), U.S. Census Bureau. Accessed 30 April 2007.(*http://www.census.gov/prod/2006pubs/p60–231.pdf*).

DUDLEY, ROGER L., and MARGARET G. DUDLEY. 1986. "Transmission of Religious Values from Parents to Adolescents." *Review of Religious Research* 28:3–15.

ERICKSON, JOSEPH A. 1992. "Adolescent Religious Development and Commitment: A Structural Equation Model of the Role of Family, Peer Group, and Educational Influences." *Journal for the Scientific Study of Religion* 31:131–52.

ESTUS, CHARLES W., and MICHAEL A. OVERINGTON. 1970. "The Meaning and End of Religiosity." *American Journal of Sociology* 75:760–78.

FINKE, ROGER, and RODNEY STARK. 1992. *The Churching of America, 1776–1990*. New Brunswick, NJ: Rutgers University Press.

FUKUYAMA, YOSHIO. 1961. "The Major Dimensions of Church Membership." *Review of Religious Research* 2:154–61.

GLOCK, CHARLES Y., and RODNEY STARK. 1965. *Religion and Society in Tension*. Chicago: Rand McNally.

GOODE, ERICH. 1966. "Social Class and Church Participation." *American Journal of Sociology*. 72:102–11.

HOGE, DEAN R., BENTON JOHNSON, and DONALD A. LUIDENS. 1995. "Types of Denominational Switching among Protestant Young Adults." *Journal for the Scientific Study of Religion*. 34:253–58.

HOGE, DEAN R., GREGORY H. PETRILLO, and ELLA I. SMITH. 1982. "Transmission of Religious and Social Values from Parents to Teenage Children." *Journal of Marriage and the Family* 44:569–80.

HOLLINGSHEAD, AUGUST DE BELMONT. 1949. *Elmtown's Youth: The Impact of Social Class on Adolescents*. New York, NY: John Wiley.

KEELEY, BENJAMIN J. 1976. "Generations in Tension: Intergenerational Differences and Continuities in Religion and Religion-Related Behavior." *Review of Religious Research* 17:221–31.

KELLEY, JONATHAN, and NAN DIRK DE GRAAF. 1997. "National Context, Parental Socialization, and Religious Beliefs: Results from 15 Nations." *American Sociological Review* 62:639–59.

KIEREN, DIANNE K., and BRENDA MUNRO. 1987. "Following the Leaders: Parents' Influence on Adolescent Religious Activity." *Journal for the Scientific Study of Religion* 26:249–55.

LEFEVER, HARRY G. 1977. "The Religion of the Poor: Escape or Creative Force?" *Journal for the Scientific Study of Religion* 16:225–36.

LENSKI, GERHARD. 1963. *The Religious Factor: A Sociological Study of Religion's Impact on Politics, Economics, and Family Life*. Garden City, NY: Anchor Books.

LIPFORD, JODY W., and ROBERT D. TOLLISON. 2003. "Religious Participation and Income." *Journal of Economic Behavior and Organization* 51:249–60.

MARX, KARL. [1844] 1978. "Contribution to the Critique of Hegel's Philosophy of Right: Introduction." Pp. 53–65 in *The Marx-Engels Reader*, edited by R.C. Tucker. New York, NY: W.W. Norton.

MCCLOUD, SEAN. 2007. "Putting Some Class in American Religion: Resurrecting an Important Concept." *Journal of the American Academy of Religion* 75:840–62.

MCPHERSON, MILLER. LYNN SMITH-LOVIN, and JAMES M COOK. 2001. "Birds of a Feather: Homophily in Social Networks." *Annual Review of Sociology* 27:415–44.

MENARD, SCOTT. 1995. *Applied Logistic Regression Analysis.* Thousand Oaks, CA: Sage.

MUELLER, CHARLES W., and WELDON T. JOHNSON. 1975. "Socioeconomic Status and Religious Participation." *American Sociological Review* 40:785–800.

MYERS, SCOTT M. 1996. "An Interactive Model of Religiosity Inheritance: The Importance of Family Context." *American Sociological Review* 61:858–66.

NELSEN, HART M., and ARSHAD RIZVI. 1984. "Gender and Religious Socialization: Comparisons from Pakistan and the United States." *Journal of Comparative Family Studies* 15:281–90.

NIEBUHR, H. RICHARD. 1929. *The Social Sources of Denominationalism.* Gloucester, MA: Peter Smith.

OKAGAKI, LYNN, and CLAUDIA BEVIS. 1999. "Transmission of Religious Values: Relations between Parents' and Daughters' Beliefs." *The Journal of Genetic Psychology* 160:303–18.

REGNERUS, MARK, CHRISTIAN SMITH, and MELISSA FRITSCH. 2003. "Religion in the Lives of American Adolescents: A Review of the Literature." Chapel Hill, NC: The National Study of Youth and Religion.

ROOF, WADE CLARK, and WILLIAM MCKINNEY. 1987. *American Mainline Religion.* New Brunswick, NJ: Rutgers University Press.

ROSS, MURRAY. 1950. *Religious Beliefs of Youth.* New York, NY: Association Press.

SAKALAS, JOAN. 1999. "Face to Face: Transforming Faith-Based Outreach." Pp. 201–12 in *Welfare Policy: Feminist Critiques*, edited by E.M. Bounds, P.K. Brubaker, and M.E. Hobgood. Cleveland, OH: The Pilgrim Press.

SCHWADEL, PHILIP. 2002. "Testing the Promise of the Churches: Income Inequality in the Opportunity to Learn Civic Skill in Christian Congregations." *Journal for the Scientific Study of Religion* 41:565–75.

SHERKAT, DARREN E., and CHRISTOPHER G. ELLISON. 1999. "Recent Developments and Current Controversies in the Sociology of Religion." *Annual Review of Sociology* 25:363–94.

SMITH, CHRISTIAN. 2005. *Soul Searching: The Religious and Spiritual Lives of American Teenagers* (with Melinda Lundquist Denton). New York, NY: Oxford University Press.

SMITH, CHRISTIAN, and MELINDA LUNDQUIST DENTON. 2003. "Methodological Design and Procedures for the National Study of Youth and Religion (NSYR)." Chapel Hill, N.C.: The National Study of Youth and Religion.

SMITH, CHRISTIAN, and ROBERT FARIS. 2005. "Socioeconomic Inequality in the American Religious System: An Update and Assessment." *Journal for the Scientific Study of Religion* 44:95–104.

Smith, CHRISTIAN, ROBERT FARIS, MELINDA LUNDQUIST DENTON, and MARK REGNERUS. 2003. "Mapping American Adolescent Subjective Religiosity and Attitudes of Alienation Toward Religion: A Research Report." *Sociology of Religion* 64:111–33.

STARK, RODNEY. 1972. "The Economics of Piety: Religious Commitment and Social Class." Pp. 483–503 in *Issues in Social Inequality*, edited by G.W. Thielbar and S.D. Feldman. Boston, MA: Little, Brown.

STARK, RODNEY. 2003. "Upper Class Asceticism: Social Origins of Ascetic Movements and Medieval Saints." *Review of Religious Research* 45:5–19.

STARK, RODNEY, and WILLIAM SIMS BAINBRIDGE. 1985. *The Future of Religion: Secularization, Revival, and Cult Formation.* Berkeley, CA: University of California Press.

———. 1996. *A Theory of Religion.* New Brunswick, NJ: Rutgers University Press.

STEENSLAND, BRIAN, JERRY Z. PARK, MARK D. REGNERUS, LYNN D. ROBINSON, W. BRADFORD WILCOX, and ROBERT D. WOODBERRY. 2000. "The Measure of American Religion: Toward Improving the State of the Art." *Social Forces* 79:291–318.

TROELSTSCH, ERNST. [1931] 1992. *The Social Teaching of the Christian Churches Volume I and Volume II.* Louisville, KY: Westminster/John Knox Press.

U.S. Census Bureau. 2003a. "Poverty Thresholds for 2002 by Size of Family and Number of Related Children Under 18 Years." Accessed 30 April 2007. (*http://www.census.gov/hhes/www/poverty/threshld/thresh02.html*).

———. 2003b. "Age and Sex of All People, Family Members and Unrelated Individuals Iterated by Income-to-Poverty Ratio and Race: 2002 Below 100% of Poverty—All Races." Accessed 30 April 2007. (*http://pubdb3.census.gov/macro/032003/pov/new01_100_01.htm*).

———. 2003c. "Age and Sex of All People, Family Members and Unrelated Individuals Iterated by Income-to-Poverty Ratio and Race: 2002 Below 125% of Poverty—All Races." Accessed 30 April 2007. (*http://pubdb3.census.gov/macro/032003/pov/new01_125_01.htm*).

VERBA, SIDNEY, KAY LEHMAN SCHLOZMAN, and HENRY E. BRADY. 1995. *Voice and Equality: Civic Voluntarism in American Politics.* Cambridge, MA: Harvard University Press.

WEBER, MAX. [1922] 1993. *The Sociology of Religion.* Boston: Beacon Press.

———. 1946. "The Protestant Sects and the Spirit of Capitalism." Pp. 302–22 in *From Max Weber: Essays in Sociology*, edited by H. H. Gerth and C.W. Mills. NY: Oxford University Press.

WILSON, JOHN. 2000. "Volunteering." *Annual Review of Sociology* 26:215–40.

WUTHNOW, ROBERT. 1988. *The Restructuring of American Religion: Society and Faith Since World War II.* Princeton, NJ: Princeton University Press.

19 Upward Wealth Mobility: Exploring the Roman Catholic Advantage

LISA A. KEISTER

Religion can be a force for stability, or a force for change. In this essay, Keister analyzes upward mobility and change within the class structure for white, non-Hispanic Roman Catholics. Prior studies found that Catholics have been economically disadvantaged especially compared to mainline Protestants. Keister's findings, however, suggest that recent generations of Roman Catholics have moved up significantly in their wealth attainment compared to conservative and mainline Protestants.

Wealth is among the most important measures of well-being because it is relatively enduring and related in some way to most other measures of achievement. Wealth—or net worth—is total household assets less total liabilities. For those who own it, wealth can enhance educational attainment, occupational opportunities, political influence and social advantages. It provides a buffer against income interruptions, medical emergencies and other crises such as accidents and natural disasters. Wealth can generate income in the form of interest and dividends, and it can create more wealth when it is reinvested. Wealth can also be passed to future generations to extend these benefits beyond those who initially accumulated it. Wealth ownership is highly concentrated and wealth mobility is rare at least in part because assets can be transferred across generations. In 2001, the top 1 percent of households owned 33 percent of net worth, while 18 percent of households had zero or negative net worth.[1] The distribution of financial wealth is even more unequal. Financial wealth—net worth less net equity in owner occupied housing—is a measure of relatively liquid resources. In 2001, the top 1 percent of households owned 40 percent of financial wealth, and 26 percent of households had zero or negative financial assets. Prior to the 20th century, wealth mobility was extremely unusual, and even today, the majority of people do not change positions in the wealth distribution compared to their parents or over their adult lives (Keister 2005).

Yet whites raised in Roman Catholic families are likely to be an important recent example of an upwardly mobile group (Aizcorbe-Kennickell

Source: Lisa Keister, "Upward Wealth Mobility: Exploring the Roman Catholic Advantage," from *Social Forces*, Volume 85, no. 3. Copyright © 2007 by the University of North Carolina Press. Used by permission of the publisher. www. uncpress.unc.edu.

and Moore 2001: Keister 2005). Less than a generation ago, Roman Catholic families were relatively disadvantaged on a host of measures of well-being, particularly relative to Mainline Protestants (Glenn and Hyland 1967, Lenski 1961; Sherkat and Ellison 1999). In recent years, however, non-Hispanic whites raised in Catholic families have experienced dramatic changes in important demographic behaviors that contribute to wealth ownership including fertility, education and income. Preliminary evidence indicates that whites who were raised in Catholic families are no longer asset-poor and may even be among the wealthiest groups of adults in the United States today (Sherkat and Ellison 1999; Keister 2003, 2005). Although previous research identified Catholics as potentially mobile (Keister 2003, 2005), there has been no systematic investigation of the degree to which their wealth position has changed or, more importantly, of the factors that explain their mobility.

This research takes advantage of the unique opportunity created by changes among Roman Catholics to study wealth mobility. I isolate non-Hispanic whites who were raised in Roman Catholic families and identify the paths they followed during childhood and early adulthood to study the processes that generate mobility.[2] . . . I propose that unique demographic patterns among Catholics including declining fertility, advantageous marriage patterns, rising educational attainment, and a unique set of values regarding work and money contribute to their rising wealth. These ideas are tested using data from the National Longitudinal Survey of Youth 1979 cohort (NLS-Y). My analyses focus on wealth accumulation patterns in early adulthood because saving and accumulation during these years create the base that determines life-long wealth ownership.

CATHOLICS AND WEALTH MOBILITY

Sociologists have debated the material consequences of religious affiliation for most of the 20th century (Darnell and Sherkat 1997; Featherman 1971; Greeley 1969; Lenski 1961). Weber (1930) and later Lenski (1961) asked important questions about how religious orientations shape stratification, and their proposals fueled strong interest in the subject through the 1960s and 1970s (Glenn and Hyland 1967; Roof 1979). Concern with the relationship between religion and material outcomes declined for a time, but it is experiencing a revival recently as improved data and methods allow researchers to isolate and study the relative importance of the many influences on well-being. It is now clear that religious orientation influences education, income, female labor force participation and careers, among a host of other important individual and family outcomes (Sherkat and Ellison 1999). Keister (2003, 2005) showed that religious affiliation and wealth ownership are related, and she demonstrated that Catholics currently have an advantage in wealth ownership that they lacked in earlier decades (Keister 2005, forthcoming). Yet what is missing is a clear account of the wealth position of Catholics compared to affiliates of other religious groups and an exploration of the factors that are responsible for that upward mobility.

There are, indeed, reasons to anticipate that religious affiliation shapes wealth ownership. Adult wealth ownership is a function of behaviors and strategies learned early in life that influence fertility, the timing and ordering of marriage, educational aspirations and attainment, job-related outcomes and attitudes toward saving. Religion affects many of these behaviors and processes, including fertility, marriage and divorce (Alwin 1986; Lehrer 1998, Sherkat and Ellison 1999), and education, female employment rates and earnings (Darnell and Sherkat 1997; Lehrer 1999; Wuthnow and Scott 1997). Religion may also affect saving behavior and portfolio composition directly. Children learn how to save from their families and other acquaintances, and religion can influence the financial lessons they learn. Religion shapes values and priorities and contributes to the set of competencies from which actions such as saving behavior is constructed (Keister 2003a; Swidler 1986). Nearly all churches and related religious organizations offer some guidance for living, often including specific tips for money management such as household budgeting, desirable expenditures and saving strategies. Together, these indirect and direct effects are likely to create a powerful influence of childhood processes on adult wealth ownership.

FERTILITY, FAMILY SIZE AND FINANCES

Family behaviors and outcomes are important predictors of wealth accumulation and mobility, and Catholic fertility patterns have changed in noteworthy ways in recent decades. Religion influences the onset of sexual activity, family formation, age at first birth and family size (Marcum 1981, 1986; Sherkat and Ellison 1999), and the relationship between religion and fertility has been particularly apparent among Catholics in recent decades. In prior generations, Catholics tended to have larger families than Protestants (Alwin 1986; Lenski 1961; Sherkat and Ellison 1999), but Catholics are now similar to Mainline Protestants in their propensity to remain childless and the age at which they have their first child (Lehrer 1996; Pearce forthcoming Sherkat and Ellison 1999). In fact, total fertility for non-Hispanic white Catholics is now lower than for Mainline Protestants (Mosher, Williams and Johnson 1992; Sander 1995; Sherkat and Ellison 1999). . . . These changes, in turn, are likely to increase wealth ownership. Remaining childless is an extremely strong predictor of wealth ownership. Remaining childless is an extremely strong predictor of wealth ownership as children increase expenses that prevent saving. Delayed fertility also increases wealth because it facilitates educational attainment, career development, occupational advancement and

initial saving and investing that can contribute to life-long asset appreciation (Keister 2005). Likewise, there is evidence that saving increases initially with family size as couples save for the added expenses associated with having children, but wealth declines precipitously after approximately two children as expenses increase and saving becomes more difficult (Keister 2005). Thus, *I expect that foregone or delayed fertility and declining family size have contributed to upward mobility in wealth ownership for Catholics.*

MARRIAGE AND MONEY

Marriage behavior is another critical determinant of wealth ownership, and Catholic marriage patterns are likely to facilitate accumulation. It has become clear that religious affiliation affects the likelihood of marriage (Hammond, Cole and Beck 1993; Mosher, Williams and Johnson 1992), the choice of a spouse (Lehrer 1998; Sherkat 2004), marital stability (Lehrer and Chiswick 1993), and the likelihood of divorce (Gall and Heaton 1997; Filsinger and Wilson 1984). Catholics have particularly high marriage rates, high rates of marital stability, low divorce rates and exceptionally high rates of homogamy (Lehrer 1998; Sherkat 2004; Sherkat and Ellison 1999), and these patterns are likely to facilitate wealth accumulation. Marriage increases wealth because two individuals combine their assets when they create a single household. It also creates common goals (e.g., homeownership, retirement objectives) that encourage couples to save. Religious homogamy increases the likelihood that a couple has similar values, priorities and competences regarding finances. When those values favor saving as they do for Catholics, agreement can increase saving and wealth. Homogamy also reduces the likelihood of divorce for Catholics, contributing to even greater wealth (Curtis and Ellison 2002; Lehrer 1998; Sherkat 2004). Divorce tends to reduce wealth because assets are divided, couples maintain two households, and there may be direct costs such as legal fees associated with divorce. For these reasons, *I expect that high marriage rates, marital stability and religious homogamy have contributed to upward mobility in wealth ownership for Catholics.*

EDUCATION

Education is a third important determinant of wealth ownership, and Catholics have been highly upwardly mobile on nearly all education measures in recent decades. Religion affects orientations toward education and educational attainment (Darnell and Sherkat 1997; Lehrer 1999). As a result, religious background can shape both school quality and years of schooling completed. Both men and women raised in Catholic families have achieved levels of education comparable to those of people raised in Mainline Protestant families in recent years, even though Catholics tended to have parents who achieved relatively modest levels of education (Lehrer 1999; Sherkat and Ellison 1999). In addition, there are important advantages resulting from Catholic school attendance. Attending Catholic school is associated with higher test scores (Bryk Lee and Hollan 1993; Hoffer Greeley and Coleman 1985; Sander 1995), higher probabilities of completing high school and attending college (Evans and Schwab 1995; Neal 1997), increased rates of college graduation (Neal 1997), and higher adult salaries and wages (Neal 1997).[3] The success of Catholic school students may result from stricter discipline, increased social capital produced by dense parental networks, and governance structures that allow for more parental choice and consensus than is possible in public schools (Coleman Hoffer and Kilgore 1982a, 1982b). . . .

Upward educational mobility improves occupational outcomes including occupational prestige and income. Highly educated people also tend to experience greater career stability and enjoy greater benefits such as opportunities to save before taxes in instruments such

as 403(b) accounts. Ultimately these patterns are likely to lead to wealth accumulation and upward wealth mobility. For these reasons, *I expect that increasing educational attainment has contributed to upward wealth mobility for Catholics.*

WORK AND MONEY: VALUES AND MOBILITY

Religion can also influence wealth ownership directly by shaping the values that people use to make work and financial decisions (Keister 2003a; Swidler 1986). . . . Religious beliefs attribute value to the act of working, to working for certain organizations, and to working in some occupations. Religious beliefs also attribute value to money, saving, sacrificial giving and other behaviors that directly involve money. The values associated with work and financial behaviors vary dramatically by religious belief, but there is little question that money is meaningful, that values and finances are intimately connected, and that Americans recognize there is a connection (Wuthnow 1994; Zelizer 1978, 1989).

There is evidence that Catholics tend to have unique values related to work and money, and these values are likely to shape their saving behavior and wealth accumulation patterns. Compared to other religious groups, for example, Catholics tend to have an instrumental attitude toward work. That is, there is evidence that Catholics approach work as an activity that produces a result rather than something that is pleasurable in itself (Tropman 1995, 2002). Work is a way to earn money to buy necessary things. Catholics also tend to have a strong orientation toward family, and their motivation to work is extrinsic, usually oriented toward the family (Tropman 2002). . . . Although an instrumental attitude toward work might reduce the incentive to work, the added effect of a strong family orientation has [led] Catholics to work relatively hard (D'Antonio, et al. 2001; Greeley 1979). . . .

Similarly, Catholics have an instrumental attitude toward money. As with work, there is evidence that Catholics tend to see money as a means to acquire necessities (Tropman 1995, 2002). Money is necessary to meet needs, but it is only a tool rather than something with intrinsic value (DeBerri and Hug 2003; Thibodeau, O'Donnell and O'Conner 1997). Again, the strong family orientation is important in speculating about how this value will shape wealth ownership. Catholics tend to save in order to care for their families (Tropman 2002). That is, while an instrumental view of money might reduce saving, having a strong extrinsic motivation will, in contrast, lead Catholics to save and invest in ways that will ensure their families are secure. This suggests that there should be a direct effect of religious affiliation on wealth for Catholics.

In addition, their instrumental attitude toward money suggests that Catholics will save in ways that are relatively low-risk. For example, Catholics are likely to prefer homeownership and stable financial investments (e.g., investments with guaranteed rates of return from banks) to volatile financial investments (e.g., stocks) because they can meet their needs without unnecessarily risking their capital . . . (Steen 1996). For these reasons, *I expect that values related to work and money increase saving, particularly in relatively stable investments, and have contributed to upward wealth mobility for Catholics.*

DATA

I explored these ideas empirically using the 1979–2000 National Longitudinal Survey of Youth (NLS-Y). The Bureau of Labor Statistics administered the first NLS-Y to a nationally-representative sample of 12,686 young adults (ages 14 to 22) in 1979. They conducted follow-up surveys yearly until 1994 and biennially until 2000 when respondents were ages 35 to 43. This study uses data on 4,753 non-Hispanic white non-immigrants from the NLS-Y core

sample.[5] The NLS-Y includes detailed information about family background, transitions to adulthood and adult traits. It also contains detailed religious affiliation data and a comprehensive series of asset and debt questions that were added in 1985 when the youngest respondents were age 20.[6] The NLS-Y wealth modules ask respondents if they own a series of assets and debts and, for those who are owners, the current value. Data from all survey years are used to create independent variables, and data from 12 years are used as dependent variables (1985–1990, 1992, 1993, 1995, 1996, 1998, 2000). These data are ideal for this study because they are longitudinal, include a large representative sample, and contain detailed information about religion and wealth.

MEASURES

Dependent Variables

First, I modeled *family background* traits—father's education, mother's education and inheritances received—to examine arguments that Catholics were relatively disadvantaged in previous generations. Father's and mother's educations were dichotomous indicators that the respondent's biological father or biological mother had ever earned a bachelor's degree or more education.[7] The inheritance measure was a dichotomous variable indicating that the respondent had ever received an inheritance. . . .

Second, I modeled adult wealth using measures of total *net worth*, ownership and value of the *primary residence*, ownership and value of *checking and savings* accounts (i.e., cash accounts), and ownership and value of *stocks*. Each dependent in the respondent's adult family is measured for every survey year from 1985 through 2000, and net worth is quantified as total financial and real assets less total liabilities.[9] The financial assets included stocks and bonds, checking and savings accounts, trust accounts, Individual Retirement Accounts, 401k plans and Certificates of Deposit. The real assets included the primary residence, businesses, farms, investment real estate, vehicles and other possessions.[10] The liabilities included mortgages on the primary residence; debt on businesses, farms and investment real estate; vehicle debt; and other debt such as consumer debt and student loans.[11] ...

Religion Variables

Childhood *religious affiliation* is determined with a series of dichotomous indicators created from 1979 reports of childhood religion.[13] Measures for Catholic, Mainline Protestant, Conservative Protestant, Jewish, other religion and no religion are included. I followed Steensland, et al. (2002) in defining the Protestant groups. Conservative Protestants include members of churches with traditional theological beliefs who accept the Bible as the inerrant Word of God, value personal conversion experiences and emphasize the importance of the Christian faith to social issues (e.g., Assembly of God, Churches of Christ, Pentecostal, Southern Baptist). In contrast, Mainline Protestants are members of churches with more liberal theologies that tend to accept social change more freely (e.g., Lutheran, United Methodist, Presbyterian). ...

Test Variables

Fertility is measured with four variables: a dichotomous indicator that the respondent had any children, and continuous indicators of the respondent's age at first birth, the number of children born and the number of children born squared. ... *Marriage* behavior is measured with a dichotomous indicator that the respondent was ever married, a continuous indicator of the number of marital transitions (i.e., changes in marital status) the respondent experienced prior to the current year and a dichotomous indicator that

the respondent and spouse were both raised in Catholic families.[15] Marital status in the current year is controlled with dichotomous variables indicating whether the respondent was married, separated, divorced or widowed. A series of *education* dummy variables measures whether the respondent had completed high school, some college, a college degree or an advanced degree.[16] I also included a continuous indicator of the total household *income* (logged) and a dichotomous measure indicating whether there were *two income earners* in the household.

Control Variables

I included several family background indicators to control for other characteristics of the family of origin that affect adult wealth ownership. Parents' income in 1978 (logged) is a continuous measure of total household income in the family of origin. ... Two dummy variables give a snapshot of the respondent's family structure at age 14 and a measure of childhood family size. ... The total number of siblings the respondent ever had indicates family size in childhood. Parents' education is measured with a series of dichotomous variables indicating the highest level of education attained by the respondent's biological father and biological mother. Dichotomous variables indicate whether the respondent's parents both worked fulltime (more than 35 hours per week) in 1978 as a gauge of work ethics. I also include measures of parents' immigrant status. I controlled for the receipt of inheritances and the amount inherited where appropriate[17] and recorded gender and age in years.[18]

Geography can also shape asset values, particularly home values and affect net worth. To control for the influence of geography, I used a series of dichotomous indicators of the respondent's *region of residence*. Three dichotomous variables (lagged one year) indicating whether the respondent lived in a north central, a southern or a western state. Northeastern states were omitted because Catholics have tended to be concentrated in those states. I also included a single indicator of *urban* residence in order to capture urban-rural differences in wealth ownership.[19] ...

Table 1 contains means and standard deviations for the control variables. ...

RESULTS: CATHOLICS ARE UPWARDLY MOBILE

The results provide support for each of my arguments. Both descriptive statistics and multivariate analyses provide strong evidence that

TABLE 1   Descriptive Statistics for Exogenous Variables, NLS-Y 2000

	Mean (S.D.)		Mean (S.D.)
Catholic	.32	Parents' income	$15,850.00
	(.46)		($15,900.00)
Mainline Protestant	.29	Stepparent family	.08
	(.45)		(.27)
Conservative Protestant	.30	Single-parent family	.10
	(.31)		(.30)
Jewish	.02	Number of siblings	2.74
	(.13)		(2.02)
Other religion	.03	Father: High school	.35
	(.15)		(.48)
No religion	.04	Some college	.11
	(.20)		(.32)
Have any children	.81	College degree	.11
	(.39)		(.31)
Age at first birth	25.40	Advanced degree	.07
	(5.30)		(.16)
Number of children	1.40	Mother: High school	.49
	(1.20)		(.50)
Ever married	.71	Some college	.11
	(.45)		(.32)
Number of marital changes	1.20	College degree	.08
	(2.00)		(.27)
Both Catholic	.21	Advanced degree	.03
	(.41)		(.16)
Married	.55	Father worked fulltime	.82
	(.50)		(.39)
Separated	.03	Mother worked fulltime	.39
	(.16)		(.49)
Divorced	.12	Father born in the U.S.	.90
	(.33)		(.19)
Widowed	.004	Mother born in the U.S.	.91
	(.06)		(.18)
High school	.43	Ever inherited	.10
	(.48)		(.53)
Some college	.21	Amount inherited	$2,454.00
	(.38)		($21,162.00)
College degree	.16	Residence: Northeast	.16
	(.34)		(.34)
Advanced degree	.12	North central	.23
	(.29)		(.43)
Family income	$65,075.00	South	.41
	($58,530.00)		(.46)
Two earner household	.30	West	.20
	(.44)		(.35)
Male	.49	Urban	.62
	(.50)		(.48)
Age	39.40		
	(2.20)		

Notes: n = 4,753 non-Hispanic white non-immigrants. Parents' income is in current 1978 dollars; converted to 2000 dollars using the CPI: mean = $38,200 (S.D. = $40,100). Education is highest level completed.

TABLE 2   Childhood Religion and Adult Wealth Ownership, NLS-Y 2000

	Father had BA	Mother had BA	Ever inherited	Net worth, mean	Net worth, median
All respondents	11.0%	8.1%	10.2%	$255.6	$65.0
Childhood religion					
Catholic	9.2	7.1	8.0	179.8	82.0
Mainline Protestant	13.7	10.1	12.3	159.2	81.0
Conservative Protestant	5.8	4.3	3.5	107.6	41.6

Notes: n = 4,753 non-Hispanic white non-immigrants. Values are thousands of 2000 dollars.

non-Hispanic whites raised in Catholic families have been upwardly mobile. Table 2 compares respondents' parents' education levels, an important indicator of family socioeconomic status, by religion. The table separates respondents into those who reported being raised in Catholic, Mainline Protestant and Conservative Protestant families.[22] The results show that Catholics' fathers and mothers were less educated than the parents of Mainline Protestants but more educated than the parents of conservative Protestants.[23] Similarly, fewer Catholics than Mainline Protestants ever inherited, but more Catholics than Conservative Protestants ever inherited. Yet Catholic adult wealth is comparable to, or greater than, Mainline Protestant adult wealth, providing initial evidence of upward mobility. Median net worth for Catholics is nearly identical to that of Mainline Protestants, the mean is higher for Catholics reflecting a small number of very wealthy Catholics.

Table 3 includes results of logistic regression models predicting three indicators of family status in childhood: father's education, mother's education and inheritance. For each dependent variable, results are reported with two different omitted categories for Catholics: first Conservative Protestants, then Mainline Protestants Models 1 and 2 show that, controlling for other important predictors, in 1979 Catholics were significantly more likely than Conservative Protestants, but less likely than Mainline Protestants, to have a father who had completed college or an advanced degree. Similarly, Models 3 and

4 show that Catholics were significantly more likely than Conservative Protestants, but less likely than Mainline Protestants, to have a mother who had completed college or more education. Models 5 and 6 show that Catholics were more likely than Conservative Protestants, and less likely than Mainline Protestants, to ever inherit. While parents' education and inheritance are not the only indicators of well-being in childhood, they are essential components of social status that capture much of the variance in overall well-being. Moreover, using other measures of childhood status (e.g., family income, parents' occupational prestige) produced similar results. Taken together, these results provide important evidence that Catholics were raised in relatively disadvantaged families.

Yet Catholics have experienced relatively high levels of intragenerational wealth mobility. That is, non-Hispanic whites raised in Catholic families have moved up in the wealth distribution more rapidly than average. Table 4 compares the percentage of Catholics who were upwardly mobile between 1985 and 2000 to the percentage of the entire NLS-Y cross sectional sample who were upwardly mobile.[24] First shown is the percentage of respondents who moved from the bottom quintile of the distribution of wealth (i.e., net worth, or total assets less total debts) to either of the top two quintiles of the distribution. Of those in the full sample, 22.8 percent were in the bottom quintile of wealth owners in 1985 and in one of the top two quintiles in 2000. For Catholics, the number of upwardly mobile respondents was

TABLE 3   Logistic Models of Family Background Traits, NLS-Y 1979–2000

Education	Father's Education		Mother's Education		Ever Inherited	
Model	1	2	3	4	5	6
Childhood religion						
Catholic	.54***	−.43***	.60***	−.69***	.19***	−.10***
	(.05)	(.04)	(.09)	(.07)	(.03)	(.03)
Mainline Protestant	96**	—	1.29***	—	.28***	—
	(.05)		(.08)		(.03)	
Conservative Protestant	—	−.99***	—	−1.30***	—	−.29***
		(.05)		(.08)		(.03)
Jewish	2.19***	1.22***	1.77***	.48***	1.25***	.96***
	(.08)	(.08)	(.16)	(.15)	(.13)	(.13)
Other religion	1.89***	.92***	2.20***	.91	.46***	.18*
	(.08)	(.08)	(.12)	(.11)	(.08)	(.08)
No religion	.79***	−.17*	1.64***	.35***	.08	−.20***
	(.08)	(.08)	(.12)	(.10)	(.05)	(.05)
Have any children	—	—	—	—	−.04	−.04
					(.03)	(.03)
Marital status						
Married	—	—	—	—	.02	.02
					(.02)	(.02)
Separated	—	—	—	—	−.06	−.06
					(.06)	(.06)
Divorced	—	—	—	—	.09**	.09**
					(.03)	(.03)
Widowed	—	—	—	—	.77***	.77***
					(.16)	(.16)
Education						
High school	—	—	—	—	.47***	.47***
					(.03)	(.03)
Some college	—	—	—	—	.78***	.78***
					(.04)	(.04)
College degree	—	—	—	—	1.14***	1.44***
					(.04)	(.04)
Advanced degree	—	—	—	—	1.48***	1.48***
					(.05)	(.05)
Financial resources						
Family income (log)	—	—	—	—	.02*	.02*
					(.01)	(.01)
Two earner household	—	—	—	—	.01***	.01***
					(.00)	(.00)
Family background						
Parents income (log)	.04***	.04***	−.01	−.01	.01***	.01***
	(.01)	(.01)	(.01)	(.01)	(.00)	(.00)

Continued

TABLE 3   (*Continued*)

Family structure at age 14						
Stepparent family	−.77***	−.77***	−.87***	−.87***	.12**	.12**
	(.08)	(.08)	(.15)	(.15)	(.04)	(.04)
Single-parent family	.08	.08	.79***	.79***	.16***	.16***
	(.06)	(.06)	(.07)	(.07)	(.04)	(.04)
Number of siblings	−.13***	−.13***	−.18***	−.18***	−.03***	−.03***
	(.01)	(.01)	(.02)	(.02)	(.01)	(.01)
Father's education						
High school	—	—	—	—	.23***	.23***
					(.03)	(.03)
Some college	—	—	—	—	.03	.03
					(.04)	(.04)
College degree	—	—	—	—	.44***	.44***
					(.04)	(.04)
Advanced degree	—	—	—	—	.83***	.83***
					(.05)	(.05)
Mother's education						
High school	—	—	—	—	.07**	.07**
					(.03)	(.03)
Some college	—	—	—	—	.33***	.33***
					(.04)	(.04)
College degree	—	—	—	—	.45***	.45***
					(.05)	(.05)
Advanced degree	—	—	—	—	.21**	.21**
					(.08)	(.08)
Father worked fulltime	.60	.60	.07	.07	−.09**	−.09**
	(.05)	(.05)	(.07)	(.07)	(.03)	(.03)
Mother worked fulltime	−.23	−.23	1.04	1.04	.03	.03
	(.03)	(.03)	(.06)	(.06)	(.02)	(.02)
Father born in U.S.	−.08	−.08	−.05	−.05	.32***	.32***
	(.08)	(.08)	(.12)	(.12)	(.06)	(.06)
Mother born in U.S.	−.30	−.30	−.30	−.30	−.18**	−.18**
	(.08)	(.08)	(.12)	(.12)	(.06)	(.06)
Current residence						
North central	—	—	—	—	−.22***	−.22***
					(.03)	(.03)
South	—	—	—	—	−.24***	−.23***
					(.03)	(.03)
West	—	—	—	—	−.06	−.06
					(.04)	(.04)
Urban	—	—	—	—	.24***	.24***
					(.02)	(.02)
x^2	2,018***	2,038***	1,345***	1,343***	5,480***	5,484***

Notes: Standard errors are in parentheses. Sample is 4,753 non-Hispanic white non-immigrants. Also controlled but not displayed are age, gender, and a dichotomous indicator that the respondent did not report childhood family income.
*p<.5 **p<.01 ***p<.001

TABLE 4   Wealth Mobility: Catholics vs. All Respondents, NLS-Y 1985–2000

	All Respondents	*Catholics*
Quintile 1 to Quintile 4 or 5	22.8	32.6***
Quintile 2 to Quintile 4 or 5	27.4	34.4**
Quintile 3 to Quintile 4 or 5	38.0	43.4**

Notes: n = 4,753 non-Hispanic white non-immigrants. Cells indicate the percent of respondents who were in the first quintile in the distribution of net worth in 1985 and in the either of the second quintiles in 2000.
**p < .01   ***p < .001

32.6 percent. Similarly, a significantly larger percentage of Catholics moved from the second quintile (34.4 percent) and third quintile (43.4 percent) to either the fourth or fifth quintiles. The results are comparable if movement in the distribution at comparable ages (e.g., between ages 25 and 35 or between ages 35 and 45 for those with valid data for each year) is compared. As the NLS-Y sample continues to age, their wealth will increase and these differences are likely to become even more pronounced.

Fertility Facilitates Mobility

An important part of the story underlying Catholic wealth mobility is changing fertility patterns. Table 5 presents multivariate models of net worth to examine the role of fertility and other inputs. In all multivariate models, Conservative Protestants is the omitted category and control for being raised Mainline Protestant in order to compare the position of Catholics relative to both groups. The first model in Table 5 shows that Catholics have an important wealth advantage controlling only for individual attributes and other relevant family background factors such as parents' education, family income and family structure. The coefficient estimate for Catholic is positive and significant, and it is larger than the coefficient for Mainline Protestant. Table 3 suggested that Catholics grew up in lower status families compared to Mainline Protestants, but Table 5 provides evidence that Catholics have equal or greater adult wealth than Mainline Protestants. Although the descriptive statistics in Table 2 suggest that average wealth for Catholics

and Mainline Protestants is comparable, the multivariate results in Table 5 suggest that people raised in Catholic families have significantly more wealth than we would expect by chance *given their other background traits*.

Table 5, Model 2 introduces measures of respondent's fertility, marriage behavior and education. The measure for having any children is negative and comparatively quite large, and the effect of age at first birth is positive and significant. Similarly, the coefficient estimate for the number of children ever born is positive, while its square is negative and significant. Each of these patterns is consistent with other research that shows that children reduce wealth (Keister 2005). More important, the effect of a Catholic upbringing on adult wealth is weaker in Model 2 of Table 5 than in the basic model (Model 1)[25] This finding is consistent with other research on the advantages Catholics have in earnings (Lehrer 1996) and provides support for my proposal that fertility patterns contributed to mobility for Catholics. Table 5, Model 3 introduces additional control, including measures of inheritance. Even with this large and comprehensive set of control variables, being raised in a Catholic family is a strong and significant predictor of adult wealth. Notably the effect of being Catholic remains larger than the effect of being raised Mainline Protestant.

The Marriage Advantage

I also proposed that Catholic marriage behavior has contributed to wealth accumulation and mobility. Model 2 of Table 5 introduces family

TABLE 5   General Linear Model Estimates of Net Worth, NLS-Y 1985–2000

	Model 1	Model 2	Model 3
Childhood religion			
Catholic	23.17***	16.86**	14.34*
	(5.41)	(5.97)	(7.01)
Mainline Protestant	15.70*	7.98	4.23
	(6.18)	(6.65)	(9.27)
Jewish	100.94**	102.22**	107.57*
	(41.89)	(46.33)	(70.06)
Other religion	5.39	1.56	−22.66
	(23.30)	(26.50)	(29.47)
No religion	10.36	19.06	25.66
	(16.76)	(17.10)	(24.13)
Fertility			
Have any children	—	−104.71***	−100.34***
		(20.95)	(27.80)
Age at first birth	—	3.66***	3.19***
		(.69)	(.88)
Number of children	—	33.33***	25.90***
		(5.95)	(7.72)
Number of children (square)	—	−4.28***	−2.87***
		(1.29)	(1.56)
Marriage			
Ever married	—	32.04***	22.57***
		(7.43)	(11.56)
Number of marital changes	—	−12.11**	−12.42**
		(5.63)	(8.53)
Both Catholic	—	14.70**	13.24
		(6.74)	(9.39)
Married	—	—	13.06**
			(8.31)
Separated	—	—	−5.27
			(16.60)
Divorced	—	—	−10.77
			(12.41)
Widowed	—	—	43.77
			(34.70)
Education			
High school	—	27.39**	22.99**
		(5.50)	(7.07)
Some college	—	43.30***	35.18***
		(7.67)	(9.67)
College degree	—	61.47***	53.85***
		(9.22)	(11.72)
Advanced degree	—	65.75***	52.23**
		(12.74)	(16.41)
Financial resources			
Family income (log)	—	—	14.86***
			(3.43)
Two earner household	—	—	.41*
			(.16)
Family background			
Parents income (log)	1.99*	1.23	.56
	(.81)	(.94)	(1.30)

Continued

TABLE 5   *(Continued)*

Stepparent family	−9.26	1.03	3.46
	(7.89)	(8.61)	(11.42)
Single-parent family	3.31	6.68	6.64
	(7.57)	(7.42)	(9.71)
Number of siblings	−3.63**	−3.67*	−2.99
	(1.21)	(1.44)	(2.06)
Father's education			
High school	17.09**	10.72	7.43
	(5.88)	(6.40)	(8.72)
Some college	20.36*	11.96	7.34
	(9.72)	(10.26)	(13.87)
College degree	37.31**	23.91	24.39
	(11.33)	(13.36)	(18.02)
Advanced degree	49.56**	30.99	34.03
	(15.58)	(17.01)	(22.85)
Mother's education			
High school	4.74	−4.01	−3.71
	(6.05)	(6.49)	(8.75)
Some college	22.43*	9.52	9.88
	(10.41)	(11.37)	(14.29)
College degree	44.67*	37.48*	48.98*
	(15.36)	(16.88)	(22.56)
Advanced degree	15.02	5.02	12.82
	(17.75)	(19.22)	(26.84)
Father worked fulltime	14.55**	12.90*	16.44
	(6.05)	(6.46)	(8.81)
Mother worked fulltime	−4.54	−6.98	−10.53
	(4.91)	(5.29)	(7.09)
Father born in U.S.	−20.29	−18.45	−18.82
	(13.50)	(14.62)	(16.36)
Mother born in U.S.	−13.51	−17.55	−31.51
	(18.16)	(18.96)	(24.57)
Ever inherited	—	—	19.63**
			(7.26)
Amount inherited	—	—	.01**
			(.00)
Current residence			
North central	—	—	−10.09
			(11.18)
South	—	—	.79
			(13.00)
West	—	—	2.38
			(13.43)
Urban	—	—	−1.79
			(6.62)
x^2	7,573***	7,850***	8,353***

Notes: Standard errors are in parentheses. Models include 4,753 non-Hispanic white non-immigrants or 57,036 (4,753*12 years) observations. Also controlled but not displayed are age, gender, and a dichotomous indicator that the respondent did not report childhood family income.

*p<.05   ** p<.01   *** p<.001

traits and fertility measures to the model of adult net worth. Consistent with this and prior research, the indicator that the respondent was ever married is positive and significant, and the indicator of the number of marital transitions prior to the current year is negative and significant. Likewise, the indicator of marital homogamy is positive and significant. Controlling for all three variables in the same equation enables this study to appropriately model homogamy and transitions for those who have never been married without assigning missing values to those respondents. . . . The introduction of these variables reduces the strength of the effect of the variable indicating that the respondent was raised in a Catholic family[26] Table 5, Model 3 introduces other adult control variables, and the Catholic effect remains strong. Table 5, Model 4 also introduces controls for current marital status. These additional control variables reduce the effect of the other marriage indicators because there is a degree of overlap in the processes that the variables capture. Yet the religion effect remains strong.

Education and Wealth Mobility

The results also provide support for my argument that increasing educational attainment among Catholics has contributed to upward mobility. . . . Table 5, Model 2 introduces measures of respondent's education and demonstrates that education accounts for part of the Catholic advantage in adult wealth ownership.[27] . . . Upward educational mobility improves occupational outcomes including occupational prestige and income. Highly educated people also tend to experience greater career stability and enjoy greater benefits such as opportunities to save before taxes in instruments such as 403(b) accounts. Subsequent models introduce additional adult controls, and . . . the effect of being raised Catholic remains strong even with the most restrictive control variables (e.g., inheritance) in the model.

Work, Money and Mobility

I also argued that Catholics also have distinctive attitudes toward work and money that can lead to unique work behavior and that can affect wealth accumulation directly. In Table 5, Model 3 introduces the dichotomous measure for dual earner households and the continuous measure of household income. Both measures are strong, positive and statistically significant. . . .

In addition, results provide support for my argument that saving and investment behavior contributed to wealth mobility for non-Hispanic whites raised in Catholic families. I proposed that distinctive saving and investment behavior would produce a direct effect of being Catholic on wealth ownership. The final model in Table 5 provides support for that argument. . . .

Finally, I find that Catholics' own a unique combination of assets and have an instrumental attitude toward money that may lead them to save in relatively low-risk ways. Table 6 includes six additional models of the some key components of total wealth that explore this argument. . . . The results show that Catholics are more likely than both Conservative Protestants and Mainline Protestants to own a home and cash accounts (e.g., checking and savings accounts). Both of these assets are considered low risk, while stocks and related financial instruments are higher risk assets. The value of the housing and cash assets that Catholics own is significantly higher than that of Conservative Protestants and Mainline Protestants, suggesting that these assets play a central role in the portfolios of Catholics. . . .

CONCLUSION

Wealth mobility is an important process underlying wealth inequality. However, researchers have paid relatively little attention to wealth mobility, at least in part, because it is so rare. This research took advantage of the unique opportunity created by Roman Catholics in recent decades to focus on the relationship between religion and wealth mobility. . . . I proposed that changing fertility,

TABLE 6   Asset Ownership and Value, NLS-Y 1985–2000

	Home Ownership	Home Value	Cash acct Ownership	Cash acct Value	Stock Ownership	Stock Value
Childhood religion						
Catholic	.13**	14.05***	.33***	3.89**	.22***	1.76
	(.04)	(2.64)	(.05)	(1.40)	(.04)	(2.55)
Mainline Protestant	.09*	4.72	.23***	2.34	.12**	1.49
	(.04)	(2.45)	(.04)	(1.43)	(.04)	(2.46)
Jewish	−.36**	32.68*	−.19	19.64	.30*	15.55***
	(.13)	(15.69)	(.19)	(13.30)	(.12)	(5.20)
Other religion	−.31**	−9.09	−.03	14.95	−.17	−4.98
	(.11)	(7.66)	(.12)	(15.30)	(.12)	(6.61)
No religion	.04	6.91	.09	24.11	.03	8.28
	(.07)	(4.53)	(.07)	(12.93)	(.08)	(5.93)
Fertility						
Have any children	−.36**	−35.27***	−1.45***	−8.03	−1.37***	−19.48*
	(.12)	(6.90)	(.13)	(7.81)	(.14)	(8.22)
Age at first birth	.01**	1.38***	.04***	.37	.05***	.67**
	(.00)	(.25)	(.00)	(.26)	(.00)	(.23)
No. children	.47***	10.87***	.11*	−.08	.19***	5.40
	(.04)	(1.48)	(.04)	(2.27)	(.04)	(3.03)
No. children (square)	−.08***	−1.15**	−.04***	−.16	−.03***	−.50
	(.01)	(.38)	(.01)	(.44)	(.01)	(.77)
Marriage						
Ever married	.25***	8.89**	.08	8.67*	−.06	1.02
	(.06)	(3.25)	(.06)	(4.09)	(.06)	(3.31)
No. marital changes	−.16**	−.82	−.01	−2.52	.02	−2.90
	(.05)	(1.37)	(.06)	(1.81)	(.06)	(1.72)
Both Catholic	.06	11.37***	.11*	−.01	−.05	−3.49
	(.04)	(2.59)	(.04)	(2.92)	(.04)	(2.24)
Married	1.38***	26.34***	.64***	−2.51	.16***	3.61***
	(.04)	(1.45)	(.05)	(3.59)	(.05)	(1.50)
Separated	−.44***	−6.27	−.39***	−5.84*	−.44***	−.43
	(.08)	(5.56)	(.08)	(2.32)	(.11)	(5.38)
Divorced	−.16***	−4.64	−.15**	−4.91	−.09	2.75
	(.04)	(2.58)	(.05)	(3.02)	(.05)	(3.34)
Widowed	.66**	29.33	.26	−2.67	.18	2.18
	(.21)	(16.43)	(.22)	(7.26)	(.25)	(5.62)
Education						
High school	.56***	11.33***	.71***	5.70*	.61***	1.07
	(.06)	(2.37)	(.05)	(2.39)	(.10)	(1.43)
Some college	.58***	16.29***	1.02***	.70	.88***	.36
	(.06)	(3.04)	(.06)	(1.58)	(.11)	(2.33)
College degree	.70***	38.48***	1.62***	6.16**	1.31***	9.70**
	(.07)	(4.02)	(.08)	(2.17)	(.11)	(2.96)
Advanced degree	.44***	34.77***	1.64***	9.34*	1.25***	11.06*
	(.08)	(4.52)	(.09)	(3.70)	(.11)	(5.13)
Financial resources						
Family income (log)	.26***	3.43***	.32***	3.02***	.56***	3.01***
	(.02)	(.35)	(.01)	(.87)	(.02)	(.69)
Two-earner household	.00***	.27***	.01***	−.04	.00***	.03
	(.00)	(.05)	(.00)	(.05)	(.00)	(.04)

Continued

TABLE 6   (*Continued*)

Family background						
Parents' income	.00	1.36***	.01	.02	−.01	−.33
(log)	(.00)	(.29)	(.00)	(.31)	(.00)	(.40)
Stepparent family	−.12*	−1.98	−.02	−5.63*	.07	−4.30**
	(.05)	(3.25)	(.06)	(2.21)	(.06)	(1.40)
Single-parent family	−.16**	−4.31	−.12*	−5.31	−.09	−.41
	(.05)	(3.00)	(.06)	(3.09)	(.06)	(2.76)
No. of siblings	−.03***	−1.24*	−.02*	.06	−.03***	.51
	(.00)	(.50)	(.01)	(.59)	(.01)	(.70)
Father's education						
High school	−.06	5.03*	.05	5.33	.00	−1.07
	(.04)	(2.36)	(.04)	(2.77)	(.04)	(2.07)
Some college	−.22***	.68	.01	6.40	.18**	3.02
	(.05)	(3.53)	(.06)	(3.86)	(.05)	(4.87)
College degree	−.06	12.94**	.18*	6.48	.28***	3.84
	(.06)	(4.55)	(.08)	(3.46)	(.06)	(5.31)
Advanced degree	−.19**	8.57	.18	−.89	.20**	.49
	(.07)	(5.30)	(.10)	(3.49)	(.07)	(6.32)
Mother's education						
High school	.09*	3.41	.14***	−2.29	.27***	.87
	(.04)	(2.27)	(.04)	(2.83)	(.04)	(2.06)
Some college	.23***	9.78*	.10	2.19	.17**	−2.07
	(.06)	(3.92)	(.07)	(4.65)	(.06)	(3.52)
College degree	.06	12.63*	.08	1.92	.39***	16.23*
	(.07)	(5.70)	(.09)	(4.57)	(.07)	(7.81)
Advanced degree	.14	13.15	.02	3.25	.18	13.68
	(.10)	(9.33)	(.14)	(7.77)	(.10)	(10.82)
Father worked	.17***	3.70	.10*	−5.60	.17***	4.80*
fulltime	(.04)	(2.60)	(.04)	(4.41)	(.05)	(2.08)
Mother worked	−.02	−2.00	−.06	1.53	−.07*	−3.29
fulltime	(.03)	(1.98)	(.03)	(2.03)	(.03)	(1.77)
Father born in U.S.	−.09	−12.03*	−.12	1.21	−.23*	−2.87
	(.08)	(5.32)	(.09)	(2.29)	(.09)	(5.62)
Mother born in U.S.	.07	−3.66	.08	.54	.18	−8.42
	(.08)	(5.71)	(.10)	(3.93)	(.09)	(8.03)
Ever inherited	.07*	4.75*	.33***	−.75	.26***	1.88
	(.03)	(1.95)	(.04)	(2.35)	(.03)	(1.75)
Amount inherited	.00**	.00***	.00**	.00	.00**	.00
	(.00)	(.00)	(.00)	(.00)	(.00)	(.00)
Current residence						
North central	.50	−7.44**	−.07	−3.177	.00	−7.17
	(.04)	(2.80)	(.05)	(3.05)	(.04)	(2.94)
South	.43	−6.09*	−.21***	−1.16	−.04	.22
	(.05)	(2.87)	(.06)	(3.40)	(.05)	(3.94)
West	−.01	6.95	−.29***	−3.22	−.19***	−3.36
	(.05)	(3.56)	(.06)	(3.32)	(.05)	(3.82)
Urban	−.24	−2.66*	.07*	4.30*	.04	2.07
	(.03)	(1.35)	(.04)	(1.99)	(.04)	(1.75)
x^2	9,007***	3,288***	5,413***	3,671***	4,432***	3,555***

Notes: Standard errors are in parentheses. Sample is 4,753 non-Hispanic white respondents or 57,036 (4,753* 12 years) observations. Also controlled but not displayed are age, gender, and a dichotomous indicator that the respondent did not report childhood family income.

*p<.05 ** p<.01 *** p<.001

unique marriage patterns, upward mobility and unique values related to work and money combined to propel Catholics upward in the wealth distribution. Results show that non-Hispanic whites raised in Catholic families have accumulated relatively high wealth as adults, despite being raised in comparatively disadvantaged families. I also compared the intragenerational wealth mobility (1985–2000) of Catholics to the sample average and found that Catholics were significantly more likely than the average respondent to move up in the wealth distribution between early and later adulthood. . . .

Although it is rare for an entire group to make such a dramatic move in wealth distribution, the Catholic transformation is consistent with understanding of how this group has assimilated and changed on other important measures of well-being. White Catholics are largely descendents of Irish, Italian, German and Polish immigrants who arrived in the United States starting in the 1840s and initially settled in ethnic communities in medium to large cities in the Northeast. Distance from the immigrant experience may have facilitated the fertility changes and education patterns, yet Catholics are still close enough to their ancestry to retain some of their values. Both male and female Catholic immigrants worked primarily in manufacturing jobs and quickly established themselves as hard working and reliable (Oats 1989). . . . The early participation of women in the workforce set the stage for rather rapid assimilation by increasing household earnings and contributing to occupational opportunities (Kenneally 1989; Oats 1989). There is some evidence that Catholic immigrants also developed a pro-assimilation, pro-education ethic that they actively and consciously passed along to younger Catholics (Oats 1989). . . . It is difficult to determine with certainty whether a pro-assimilation ethic contributed to this transformation, but it is clear that the change has been rather pronounced. The change in wealth ownership is consistent with this history.

What does this pattern suggest for the future trajectory of Catholics? If Catholics do have an instrumental attitude toward work and money (Tropman 2002), it is unlikely that they will continue to move upward in the wealth distribution. Other priorities—such as family—will continue to be more important, and Catholics will simply accumulate enough wealth to have a secure financial cushion. Moreover, if their propensity to invest in relatively low risk assets is an enduring preference rather than a characteristic of an upwardly mobile group, the upward wealth trajectory is unlikely to continue at the rate it has in the past. Rather, it is likely that Catholics will continue to accumulate assets much like Mainline Protestants, making the two groups increasingly similar. Alternatively, if recent Catholic attitudes toward work and money reflect their working class past, it is possible that increasing numbers of Catholics will move into the highest levels of the wealth distribution. If Catholics continue to excel in education, for example, they will continue to gain occupational prestige and to adopt attitudes toward work and money that are similar to Mainline Protestants or Jews who are more likely to have pro-accumulation attitudes. If this happened, Catholics might continue to earn higher income and ultimately to accumulate greater wealth. Of course, these are questions that future research might explore. . . .

NOTES

1. All values are in 2000 dollars. Author's estimates from the Survey of Consumer Finances.

2. I focus on non-Hispanic whites raised as Roman Catholics throughout the paper because minority Catholics did not experience comparable levels of upward mobility. I refer to this group as Catholic to conserve space.

3. While some have raised important objections (Morgan 2001; Morgan and Sorensen 1999), the relationship between attending Catholic school and educational achievement is highly robust.

...

5. Missing data reduced my sample size slightly but I found no significant wealth or religion differences between my sample and the full sample. Experiments with imputing missing data did not change the results. I omitted

58 first-generation immigrants in order to isolate the effect of being raised in an American Catholic family on wealth ownership and to avoid biasing the data with self-selecting, high-status overachievers. Omitting recent immigrants did not change the findings.

6. The survey did not include wealth questions in 1991.

7. Using other indicators such as years of education produced substantively similar results. I opted to model attainment of bachelor's and advanced degrees because, for the generation that included parents of the NLS-Y sample, these are important indicators of high socioeconomic status. Modeling the completion of a bachelor's degree and advanced degrees separately produced comparable results, although very few mothers and relatively few fathers had advanced degrees.

...

9. The results were robust to alternative definitions of wealth such as gross assets (the sum of assets not reduced by debts), total financial assets, total non-financial assets and total liabilities.

10. Excluding other possessions does not change the results significantly.

11. I used the Consumer Price Index (CPI) to adjust all asset and debt values to 2000 dollars.

...

13. The NLS-Y asked about religious affiliation in 1979, 1982 and 2000. I used 1979 reports because they provided the greatest denominational detail, and the three reports are highly consistent with each other. The distribution of respondents across denominations is also consistent with other data sources, including the General Social Survey.

...

15. Age at first marriage was not a significant predictor of wealth.

16. I opted to include the dummy indicators to illustrate the relevance of various discrete education levels to wealth ownership, but substituting a continuous variable produced comparable results.

17. I standardized, logged and converted this variable to 2000 dollars using the CPI. Including those who did not inherit (i.e., those with a zero value) did not appreciably change the results. While it can be difficult to generate accurate estimates of inheritance, the NLS-Y estimates are consistent with measures of inherited wealth in other studies (McNamee and Miller, 1998).

18. I did not control for the square of age because wealth accumulation does not typically follow the standard curvilinear relationship with age that income does. Preliminary investigation confirmed that the squared age term was not a significant predictor of asset ownership in these data.

19. Controlling for residence in New York City, Boston and other locations including northeastern and north central locations that have large Catholic populations did not change the results. While Catholic respondents were more likely than others to be born in the

northeast or north central states, they have relocated throughout the United States. Controlling for regional differences in place of birth, place of residence in each survey year, changes in residence, recent changes in residence, place of residence at significant points in life (e.g., education, first job, subsequent jobs, birth of first child, birth of subsequent children, first marriage, subsequent marriages, etc.) and at significant points in the accumulation trajectory (e.g., first home purchase, most recent home purchase) did not change the results. Controlling for housing price variations, using either median home values or the conventional mortgage home price index, did not improve model fit.

...

22. The proportion of the respondents in each of the religious groups is consistent with estimates from other data sources, including the General Social Survey.

23. Using other measures such as number of years of school completed produces similar patterns.

24. I used 1985 as a starting point because all respondents were at least 20 years old in that year and could be considered adults, and I used 2000 as the end year because it is the most recent year for which data are available. These points capture the sample at early adulthood and when most were in their prime working years and had at least begun to establish their net worth portfolios.

25. Cox tests confirm that differences across models in the effect of the Catholic indicator are statistically significant.

26. Again, Cox tests confirm that this difference is statistically significant.

27. Cox tests confirm that this difference is significant.

REFERENCES

AIZCORBE, ANA M., ARTHUR B. KENNICKELL and KEVIN B. MOORE, 2001. "Recent Changes in U.S. Family Finances: Evidence from the 1998 and 2001 Survey of Consumer Finances." Washington, DC: the Federal Reserve Board.

ALBA, RICHARD D. 1981. "The Twilight of Ethnicity among American Catholics of European Ancestry." *Annals of the American Academy of Political and Social Science* 454:86–97.

ALWIN, DUANE. 1986. "Religion and Parental Childbearing Orientations: Evidence for a Catholic-Protestant Convergence." *American Journal of Sociology* 92:412–20.

BORJAS, GEORGE J. 1999. *Heaven's Door: Immigration Policy and the American Economy.* Princeton University Press.

———. editor. 2000. *Issues in the Economics of Immigration.* University of Chicago Press.

BRYK, ANTHONY S., VALERIE E. LEE and PETER B. HOLLAN. 1993. *Catholic Schools and the Common Good.* Harvard University Press.

CALL, VAUGHN R.A., and TIM B. HEATON. 1997. "Religious Influence on Marital Stability." *Journal for the Scientific Study of Religion* 36:382–92.

CHAVES, MARK, and SHARON L. MILLER, editors. 1999. *Financing American Religion*. AltaMira Press.

COLEMAN, JAMES S., THOMAS HOFFER and SALLY KILGORE. 1982a. "Achievement and Segregation in Secondary Schools: A Further Look at Public and Private School Differences." *Sociology of Education* 55:162–82.

———. 1982b. "Cognitive Outcomes in Public and Private Schools." *Sociology of Education* 55:65–76.

CURTIS, KRISTEN TAYLOR, and CHRISTOPHER G. ELLISON. 2002. "Religious Heterogamy and Marital Conflict: Findings from the National Survey of Families and Households." *Journal of Family Issues* 23:551–76.

D'ANTONIO, WILLIAM V., JAMES D. DAVIDSON, DEAN R. HOGE and KATHERINE MEYER. 2001. *American Catholics: Gender, Generation, and Commitment*. Altamira Press.

DARNELL, ALFRED, and DARREN E. SHERKAT. 1997. "The Impact of Protestant Fundamentalism on Educational Attainment." *American Sociological Review* 62:306–15.

DEBERRI, EDWARD P., and JAMES E. HUG. 2003. *Catholic Social Teaching: Our Best Kept Secret, Fourth Edition*. Orbis Books.

ELLISON, CHRISTOPHER G., and DARREN E. SHERKAT. 1990. "Patterns of Religious Mobility among Black Americans." *Sociological Quarterly* 31:551–68.

EVANS, WILLIAM N., and ROBERT M. SCHWAB. 1995. "Finishing High School and Starting College: Do Catholic Schools Make a Difference?" *The Quarterly Journal of Economics* 110:941–74.

FEATHERMAN, DAVID L. 1971. "The Socioeconomic Achievement of White Religio-Ethnic Subgroups: Social and Psychological Explanations." *American Sociological Review* 36:207–22.

FILSINGER, ERIK E., and MARGARET R. WILSON. 1984. "Religiosity, Socioeconomic Rewards, and Family Development: Predictors of Marital Adjustment." *Journal of Marriage and the Family* 46:663–70.

GLENN, NORVAL D., and RUTH HYLAND. 1967. "Religious Preference and Worldly Success: Some Evidence from National Surveys." *American Sociological Review* 32:73–85.

GREELEY, ANDREW M. 1969. "Continuities in Research on the 'Religious Factor'." *American Journal of Sociology* 75:355–59.

———. 1979. "The Sociology of American Catholics." *Annual Review of Sociology* 79:91–111.

HAMMOND, JUDITH A., BETTIE S. COLE and SCOTT H. BECK. 1993. "Religious Heritage and Teenage Marriage." *Review of Religious Research* 35:117–33.

HOFFER, THOMAS, ANDREW M. GREELEY and JAMES S. COLEMAN. 1985. "Achievement Growth in Public and Catholic Schools." *Sociology of Education* 58:74–97.

KEISTER, LISA A. 2003a. "Religion and Wealth: The Role of Religious Affiliation and Participation in Early Adult Asset Accumulation." *Social Forces* 82:173–205.

———. 2003b. "Sharing the Wealth: Siblings and Adult Wealth Ownership." *Demography* 40:521–42.

———. 2005. *Getting Rich: America's New Rich and How they Got that Way*. Cambridge University Press.

KENNEALLY, JAMES J. 1989. "A Question of Equality." Pp. 125–51. *American Catholic Women: A Historical Exploration*. Karen Kennelly, editor. Macmillan.

LEHRER, EVELYN L. 1996. "Religion as a Determinant of Fertility." *Journal of Population Economics* 9:173–96.

———. 1998. "Religious Intermarriage in the United States: Determinants and Trends." *Social Science Research* 27:245–63.

———. 1999. "Religion as a Determinant of Educational Attainment: An Economic Perspective." *Social Science Research* 28:358–79.

LEHRER, EVELYN L., and CARMEL U. CHISWICK. 1993. "Religion as a Determinant of Marital Stability." *Demography* 30:385–404.

LENSKI, GERHARD. 1961. *The Religious Factor: A Sociological Study of Religion's Impact on Politics, Economics, and Family Life*. Doubleday.

MARCUM, JOHN P. 1981. "Explaining Fertility Differences among U.S. Protestants." *Social Forces* 60:532–43.

———. 1986. "Explaining Protestant Fertility: Belief, Commitment, and Homogamy." *Sociological Quarterly* 27:547–58.

MOSHER, WILLIAM D., LINDA B. WILLIAMS and DAVID P. JOHNSON. 1992. "Religion and Fertility in the United States: New Patterns." *Demography* 29:199–214.

NEAL, DEREK. 1997. "The Effect of Catholic Secondary Schooling on Educational Achievement." *Journal of Labor Economics* 15:98–123.

OATS, MARY J. 1989. "Catholic Laywomen in the Labor Force, 1850–1950." Pp. 81–124. *American Catholic Women*. K. Kennelly, editor. MacMillan.

PEARCE, LISA D. FORTHCOMING. "Religion's Impact on the Timing of First Births in the U.S." *Religion, Families, and Health: New Directions in Population-Based Research*. C.G. Ellison and R.A. Hummer, editors. Rutgers University Press.

ROOF, WADE CLARK. 1979. "Socioeconomic Differences among White Socioreligious Groups in the United States." *Social Forces* 58:280–89.

SANDER, WILLIAM. 1995. *The Catholic Family: Marriage, Children, and Human Capital*. Westview Press.

SHERKAT, DARREN E. 2004. "Religious Intermarriage in the United States: Trends, Patterns, and Predictors." *Social Science Research* 33:606–25.

Reading 20 Culture Wars: The Challenge of Homosexuality

JAMES D. HUNTER

Hunter argues that religious responses to human sexuality generally and homosexuality specifically are rooted in diverse moral understandings of the family as the appropriate context for sexual behavior. Hunter wrote this piece in 1991. Do you think his observations are still relevant today? Consider especially activism by religious groups in favor of and against granting official rights and protections for gays and lesbians through anti-discrimination laws, recognition of same-sex marriages, and ordination to religious leadership positions.

Sexuality, of course, is also at the heart of family life. It is the family more than any other institution that establishes the rules for sexual intimacy—the codes that define the persons with whom, the time when, and the conditions under which sexual intimacy is acceptable. How the family enacts these rules also implies a judgment upon what "nature" will allow or should allow. But what is "natural" in matters of sexuality? The answer goes right to the heart of assumptions about the moral order: what is good, what is right, what is appropriate. Family life, however, is also a "school of virtue," for it bears the responsibility, as no other institution can, for socializing children—raising them as decent and moral people, passing on the

morals of a community to the next generation. How parents view nature in matters of sexuality, therefore, is reflected in the ways they teach children about right and wrong. How the actors in the contemporary culture war view nature in matters of sexuality, in turn, will be reflected in their different ideals of how the moral order of a society will take shape in the future.

Perhaps with the exception of abortion, few issues . . . generate more raw emotion than the issue of homosexuality. The reason is plain: few other issues challenge the traditional assumptions of what nature will allow, the boundaries of the moral order, and finally the ideals of middle-class family life more radically. Homosexuality symbolizes either an

Source: James Davison Hunter, "Culture Wars: The Challenge of Homosexuality," from *Culture Wars: The Struggle to Define America.* Copyright © 1991 by Basic Books, a member of Perseus Books, LLC.

absolute and fundamental perversion of nature, of the social order, and of American family life, or it is simply another way in which nature can evolve and be expressed, another way of ordering society, and an alternative way of conducting family life. . . .

Republican Congressman William Dannemeyer from California, for example, is quoted as saying that the homosexual movement represents "the most vicious attack on traditional family values that our society has seen in the history of our republic." Some in the orthodox alliance have argued that "the family is the fundamental unit of society, for it is the principle of permanence. For most persons it furnishes the primary experience of stability, continuity and fidelity. In this respect, and in many others, it is a school for citizenship. But it can maintain its function over the long run only if we accord it preferential status over alternative sexual arrangements and liaisons." The homosexual movement, therefore, is "destructive of the family and . . . a potent threat to society."

The rejoinder to this orthodox contention is an explicit affirmation of the aim to redefine the family—to proclaim "a new vision of family life." The response of the National Gay and Lesbian Task Force is that "lesbians and gay men are not a threat to families, but are an essential thread in the fabric of American family life." Ours, they contend, "is a vision of diverse family life that is directly opposed to the once-upon-a-time myth promoted by the right wing. Our vision is inclusive, not discriminatory. It is functional, rather than legalistic." Therefore, "threats to the American family do not come from the desire of gay men and lesbians to create loving relationships," but rather "from the right wing's manipulation of ignorance, bigotry and economic injustice. These threats to *our* families must be met with outrage . . . action . . . and resources."

And indeed the gay community has responded in this way within several areas of public policy. Perhaps the most important area over which the issue of the legitimacy of the "gay alternative" is concretely contested is the matter of marriage rights for homosexual couples. Let's be very clear about this: more is at stake here than the emotional rewards of formalizing a shared commitment in a relationship. The practical benefits of marriage are of tangible and often crucial importance to the lives of individuals: marriage partners may take part in the spouse's health plan and pension programs, share the rights of inheritance and community property, make a claim upon a spouse's rent-controlled apartment, and file joint tax returns. These legal and economic advantages were all designed to encourage the economic independence and interdependence of the traditional family unit and indeed, couples in traditional heterosexual marriages have long benefited from them. By the same token, they have been denied to homosexual couples, heterosexual couples living out of wedlock, and living arrangements involving long-term platonic roommates—all of which may involve the same degree of economic and emotional dependence that occurs within a traditional family. . . .

As the contemporary culture war has intensified, the general ambition of gay rights activists has been to push for the legal recognition of homosexual relationships as legitimate marriages or at least as "domestic partners" in order to ultimately secure these economic benefits. This is precisely the conflict we saw between Chuck McIlhenny and Richmond Young in San Francisco at the beginning of the book. While the fifty states have been reluctant to recognize the legality or legal rights of homosexual marriages, a handful of cities such as Los Angeles; New York; Madison, Wisconsin; and Takoma Park, Maryland, do provide bereavement leave for domestic partners who are municipal workers. A few others, such as Berkeley, Santa Cruz, and West Hollywood, offer health benefits for the same. This push has continued in still other cities around the country where laws prohibiting discrimination on the basis of marital status are being examined to see whether they extend to the living arrangements of homosexual couples.

Needless to say, such proposals pose a serious challenge to the traditional conception of marriage and family. . . . Yet even in the gay community there is disagreement about this goal—. . . because the legislation does not go far enough. The campaign for domestic partnership or gay marriage is misdirected, argued one lesbian activist, because it tries to adopt traditional heterosexual institutions for gays rather [than] encourage tolerance for divergent life-styles. "Marriage, as it exists today, is antithetical to my liberation as a lesbian and as a woman, because it mainstreams my life and voice."

The issues of bigotry and discrimination, in the view of homosexuals and of many activists . . . [have] gone beyond disputes over marriage rights or domestic partners to other areas of policy concern. . . .

In . . . policy areas, what is at stake is a tacit recognition on the part of the government that homosexuality is an authentic manner of life, social relationship, family, and community. . . .

Other pivotal institutions in which the legitimacy of homosexuality has been contested are the churches. One might imagine that the deep and longstanding hostility of the Judeo-Christian faiths toward homosexuality would encourage homosexual men and lesbians to leave their faiths altogether. But for those who continue to identify with a particular religious tradition, there appears to be little desire to leave. . . .

The objective is not to be changed by the church but to change the church from the inside. . . .

The key dispute here is over the moral authority of the churches and of religious tradition. The dominant symbolic issue is ordination: can a practicing homosexual be God's representative here on earth? The answer is unequivocally "no" in religious bodies and organizations in the orthodox alliance. Homosexuality is a sin against God, an open violation of His divine and intended order. Mainline and progressive religious bodies and organizations, however, are much more ambivalent about the issue. Only a handful of denominations, such as the Unitarian Universalists, the Swedenborgians, and regional bodies in the United Church of Christ and the Disciples of Christ openly and officially ordain practicing homosexuals. A few Episcopalian and Lutheran bishops have ordained practicing homosexuals against the official teaching of the denominational hierarchy (actions that always raise the ire of lay people and conservative clergy yet frequently generate little more than a call for censure). The Roman Catholic hierarchy has remained staunchly opposed to the ordination of practicing homosexuals and yet estimates of the number of gay priests in parishes range from 10 to 50 percent. On the one hand, then, official ecclesiastical policy in the mainline bodies has been reticent to bestow its ultimate blessing upon homosexuality. There has been, nevertheless, a strong progressive impulse to support the movement from a distance. At least fifteen denominations or official organizations within denominations representing Protestant, Catholic, and Jewish faiths, for example, have formally endorsed the liberal reform of sodomy laws. The pressure upon denominations to do more than this is not likely to fade away since there is at least one (and often two or three) gay and lesbian rights lobby pressing its agenda within virtually every major denomination in America. Still, orthodox-leaning renewal leaders and their followers in the mainline religious bodies (especially in Protestantism) view policy on homosexuality as *the* "watershed issue"—the issue over which they either stay within the mainline or leave. A tremendous amount of money, people, and resources, therefore, would likely disappear if homosexuality were sanctioned any more than it is.

As the strongest institutional bulwarks of traditionalist ideals of gender roles and sexuality, the military establishment and the churches are barometers of how the conflict over homosexuality fares in the larger social order. As the armed forces and the churches go on this issue, so may go the rest of American society. . . .

21 Talking about Homosexuality: The Views of Mainline Protestant Clergy

LAURA R. OLSON AND WENDY CADGE

Many religious leaders are embroiled in debates and controversies surrounding homosexuality. Olson and Cadge explore how sixty-two mainline Protestant clergy from across the United States frame and talk about the issues involved in these debates. Particularly interesting is how many clergy spoke about homosexuality abstractly rather than talking specifically about gay men and lesbians as people in their communities and congregations.

Since they first addressed homosexuality in the early 1970s, mainline Protestant churches have been thinking, talking, and quite often arguing about the subject.[1] These debates have increased in intensity over the past decade as they have been broadcast on the front pages of newspapers across the country: "Protestants Face Schism on Homosexuality," "Issues of Sexuality Split the Presbyterians Again," "At Gay Wedding, Methodists Vow to Take a Stand Against Church Ban" (Kloehn 1999; Niebuhr 1998; Sanchez 1999). The church court trials of Episcopal Bishop Walter Righter for ordaining a gay man and United Methodist minister Jimmy Creech for marrying a lesbian couple have attracted substantial national attention, as have contentious national denominational meet-

ings where votes on ordination and marriage for gay men and lesbians are tallied.

Throughout all of this controversy, mainline Protestant clergy have played important roles in setting the terms of debate about homosexuality. Clergy have participated in denominational conversations about homosexuality by joining national and local interest groups and by ministering to people in their congregations who are concerned about the issue. More than 100 United Methodist clergy recently officiated at a lesbian couple's commitment ceremony—risking their ministerial credentials in the process. On a less visible level, clergy across the United States have the opportunity each week to influence and lead their congregations' opinions about homosexuality. They are discoursemakers with the capability, if they choose to take advantage of it, to affect public opinion in three separate arenas: the congregation, the denomination, and the community at large. How do mainline Protestant clergy understand gay and lesbian issues? On what terms do they feel called to act upon their beliefs?

Mainline Protestant clergy have long been involved and interested in politics. They played nationally visible roles in the civil rights movement, the nuclear freeze movement, and the sanctuary movement for refugees during the Reagan administration (Findlay 1993; Friedland 1998; Hertzke 1988; Smith 1996). Today, many mainline clergy express particular concern about disadvantaged and marginalized members of society (Crawford and Olson 2001; Guth, Green, Smidt, Kellstedt, and Poloma 1997; Olson 2000, 2002). They should be expected to take action on their political concerns because of mainline Protestantism's historic embrace of Niebuhr's (1951) notion of "Christ the transformer of culture"— involvement by the faithful in the broader society is not just tolerated, but encouraged and expected.

Not all mainline clergy, though, find it easy or even possible to involve themselves in politics. Relatively few mainline laity wholeheartedly endorse the liberal political outlook that often accompanies mainline theology—and that clergy learn in seminary.[2] Consequently, since at least the 1960s, dividing lines have been drawn between many mainline clergy and the moderate-to-conservative people in their pews. Homosexuality forms one of the most contentious of these dividing lines. Many clergy hesitate to speak about issues that have the potential to rip their congregations apart because to do so might threaten their job security. Of all contemporary political issues, homosexuality probably has the most potential to divide congregations. As such, even clergy who would like to be vocal advocates for gay and lesbian rights might feel constrained from doing so out of concern for their tenure and

legitimacy in their congregations. And many homosexual clergy do not reveal their own sexual orientation out of fear that they will lose their positions (Comstock 1996). . . .

In this article we portray the many sides of mainline Protestantism's debates about homosexuality through the lens of statements clergy made about the issue in early 2000. In interviews with 62 mainline Protestant clergy across the United States, 40 volunteered their views on the issue of homosexuality without being prompted. We are primarily interested in the frames clergy use to describe their thoughts and feelings about homosexuality. By frames we mean what Goffman (1974) called "schemata of interpretation," or the lenses through which people understand and make sense of events occurring around them. As Benford and Snow (2000) state in their recent review article, "frames help to render events or occurrences meaningful and thereby function to organize experience and guide action." We describe the frames through which clergy understand and articulate issues related to homosexuality in the midst of contentious denominational debate about the subject. We organize our argument around the following key questions: When clergy mention homosexuality, do they speak about conflict within their congregations or within their denominations? Do they refer to homosexuality within the church or in the broader society? What terminology do clergy employ in their discussions of homosexuality— do they speak of homosexuals or gay men and lesbians as people, or of the more nebulous notion of sexuality or homosexuality?

MAINLINE PROTESTANTISM AND CONTEMPORARY DEBATES ABOUT HOMOSEXUALITY

American society at large is expressing increasingly favorable opinions about homosexual people.[3] While 67 percent of those surveyed in 1976 believed sexual relations between people of the same sex were always wrong, only 56 percent in 1996 agreed (Yang 1997). Aside from their opinions about the morality of the sexual behavior of gay men and lesbians, increasing numbers of Americans support the civil rights of homosexual people.[4] Sodomy laws have been repealed in the majority of the 50 states. Many towns and cities have passed laws that forbid discrimination against homosexuals. Increasing numbers of corporations are offering health care and other benefits to the partners of gay and lesbian employees. Vermont recently legalized a form of domestic partnership, called "civil union," between people of the same sex. In the 1990s, homosexual characters appeared on prime time television shows and openly gay candidates were elected to public office.

All of these changes, though, have not automatically translated into favorable treatment of gay men and lesbians by organized religion in the United States. Even though recent data suggest that mainline Protestants are growing more tolerant of homosexuals (Petersen and Donnenwerth 1998), during various historical periods Christianity has been intolerant of homosexuality (Boswell 1980; Greenberg and Bystryn 1982). While mainline Protestantism has taken the rare step of actually debating and discussing homosexuality and related issues, it is not a stretch to say that no issue is more controversial in the churches today.

Homosexuality, after all, means and represents many different things. It is a prism through which all of the denominations' central questions and issues reflect and refract. For these reasons, participants in debates and discussions about homosexuality realize that much is at stake. Homosexuality is about scripture: How is the Bible to be read, interpreted, and understood? It is about creation: How ought the people that God creates behave sexually? Homosexuality is about families and reproduction: Who can be married? Bear children? Adopt children? Raise children? What

lessons should those children be taught about sexual behavior? Homosexuality also raises important questions about who can serve the church and about how those people and the church are to act in the world.

Mainline Protestantism has approached homosexuality primarily through policy debates in denominational bodies and congregations, and through substantial grassroots activity related to the subject on the ground. At both the denominational and congregational levels, the issue has been addressed broadly in terms of homosexuality and more specifically in terms of the rights of gay and lesbian people. Much of the debate about this issue would not have occurred were it not for the efforts of clergy. Clergy helped found the first religiously oriented group designed specifically to address homosexuality, the San Francisco Council on Religion and Homosexuality, in 1964. This organization was designed to work for social justice for homosexuals in San Francisco. After its first event, a New Year's Eve dance for the gay and lesbian community, the Council found itself in the midst of a court battle protesting the arrest of four people at the dance and the use of intimidation tactics by police at the event. D'Emilio (1983) argues that this was a significant moment in gay and lesbian history. The presence of clergy among the Council's defenders, he argues, "Provided a legitimacy to the charges of police harassment that the word of a homosexual lacked."

Clergy also helped to draft many of the first mainline Protestant statements on homosexuality. In 1969, the United Church of Christ (UCC) became the first mainline denomination to make an official proclamation: "The time is long overdue for our churches to be enlisted in the cause of justice and compassion for homosexual persons" (Council for Christian Social Action 1969). Other denominations followed suit, though with less overtly supportive statements about homosexuality. Support groups for gay men and lesbians who belonged to mainline churches also emerged. The UCC's Bill Johnson started a Gay Caucus in his denomination in 1972 to provide support for gay and lesbian UCC members. In 1974, David Baily Sindt founded Presbyterians for Lesbian and Gay Concerns. In 1978, Robert Davidson, a minister at West Park Presbyterian Church in New York City, wrote a statement of conscience that was the first step toward the founding of a grassroots network of congregations that formally welcome gay and lesbian people into their churches. By the 1990s, programs supporting gay men and lesbians existed in all major mainline Protestant denominations. Focus throughout the decade turned instead to the issues of homosexual ordination and marriage, both of which have direct implications on the actions of clergy.

Despite the increase in grassroots activities and public debate during the 1990s, it is important to recognize that the opinions of many mainline clergy and laity on issues related to homosexuality are mixed (Presbyterian Panel 1989, 1996). While some commentators suggest that homosexuality and other social issues are further evidence of the polarization of mainline churches into conservative and liberal factions, recent research in fact suggests that mainline opinion about homosexuality is divided right down to the local level (Ammerman 2000). It is within this local, and often contentious, context that mainline clergy must decide whether, when, and how to express their views on homosexuality.

SOURCES OF DATA

To examine the frames through which clergy understand homosexuality, we rely on data collected from in-depth telephone interviews conducted between January and May 2000 with 62 mainline clergy across the United States. All these pastors are ordained, and all but three were serving congregations at the time of the interview. On average they had been in the ministry for just over 20 years and had been serving their congregations for just over seven years. The interviews ranged in duration from 15 minutes to more than an hour.

These clergy, who represent 35 different states, plus the District of Columbia, serve in the American Baptist Churches; the Episcopal Church; the Evangelical Lutheran Church in America; the Presbyterian Church (USA); the United Methodist Church; and the United Church of Christ. Clergy from all six denominations spoke on homosexuality, but Baptist and Methodist ministers were slightly more likely to mention the issue.

Half the clergy interviewed were chosen on the basis of a national random sample of church ZIP codes, whereas half were specifically identified by their denominations as clergy who are interested in politics.[5] The presence in the sample of so many clergy who are politically aware is valuable because it allows us to assess the attitudes of clergy who are perhaps most likely to become involved in public debates about homosexuality. Exactly half of each of these two subsamples of clergy mentioned homosexuality.

While the interviews were not explicitly designed to assess the clergy's views on homosexuality, 40 of the ministers spoke voluntarily about various homosexuality-related debates occurring in their congregations, denominations, and the broader society.[6] Their comments came in reaction to three questions in particular:

- "What is the biggest problem facing your denomination today?"
- "Is it important for your denomination to stake out clear positions on social and political issues?"
- "What issue or set of political issues concerns you most in this day and age?"

. . . In early 2000 when these interviews were conducted, issues related to homosexuality were simmering in the mainline denominations. Conversations about the subject had been heating up through the 1990s, and by the end of the decade most denominations were debating one or more issues related to homosexuality. The Episcopal Church, for example, was deciding whether to develop marriage or union rites for same-sex couples, and the United Methodists were continuing to think about how to discipline clergy who were performing marriage or union rites for same-sex couples (in clear defiance of denominational policy). The Presbyterian Church (USA) was officially taking a "sabbatical" from the issue, though concerns were clearly still present, and the American Baptist Churches were struggling to decide what to do about some of their churches that had been disfellowshipped from their regional bodies for taking actions that were supportive of gay men and lesbians. Such supportive activities at the grassroots were continuing in Baptist congregations and gay and lesbian interest groups alike. Outside the churches, issues related to homosexuality were also in the public eye. The State of Vermont was considering the issue of homosexual unions, and plans were underway for a nationwide gay and lesbian march on Washington (the "Millennium March" was held in April 2000).

The clergy's comments fall into several different categories, and they use varying language to describe the subject. We begin by presenting three "voices from the field," which are particularly clear representations of the range of views expressed by these clergy. Their voices are presented as examples of how clergy make sense of the multiple issues embedded in the topic of homosexuality. We then describe the range of substantive frames through which the ministers in the sample addressed the issue. Finally, we explore the language clergy use in their discussions of the issue. Do they use the terms "gay," "lesbian," or "homosexual," or do they confine their words mainly to the more diffuse notions of "homosexuality" and "sexuality"?

THREE VOICES FROM THE FIELD

Mainline clergy understand the debate about sexuality and homosexuality in many ways. The case studies that follow illustrate how three clergy feel about the issue and what they think about how the church handles it. One of the ministers openly shares his opposition to gay and lesbian rights and goes on to illustrate the danger the issue poses for his denomination. Another pastor explains that she cannot fathom why gay and lesbian people are ostracized by organized religion. Finally, a third minister portrays the depth of policy struggle over the issue both inside his denomination and in the broader society within which he lives. These three case studies clearly demonstrate the range of opinion among mainline clergy on this issue and how different frames can come together in the comments of individual clergy.

Ethan Thomas,[10] an Episcopal priest in a suburb of a major northeastern city, brought up the subject of homosexuality early in the interview. "There are certain issues, of course, that are tearing at the fabric of who we are. One of those social issues is how we respond to the gay community at this particular time in history." He continues, detailing the substantive and procedural issues that impinge on denominational considerations of homosexuality in great detail. Then, without prompting, he explains his position:

I'm on the conservative side of this issue. I feel that this is an issue that is really going to be a litmus test for many clergy. ... I'm a liberal in every other sense except for this particular issue. I object to it on certain biblical grounds and moral grounds and have a feeling of inclusion for homosexuals, but not an openness to their whole agenda, is the best way of saying it. That's where I'm coming from. But this is really tearing us apart as a denomination. It's probably on the front burner as a social issue in the Episcopal Church [but] it's not my favorite issue.

Thomas clearly thinks sexuality is an important, and even symbolic, issue. As a "litmus test" for clergy it seems to represent more than its face value. He goes on to describe the issue as creating a kind of divisiveness in which conservative and liberal churches will be able to align themselves with the bishops of their choice, moving further and further apart in the process. Thomas makes it clear later in the interview that liberal churches will be the losers in this debate. While there are many liberal churches, not enough of them are liberal about sexuality issues to allow a liberal church so defined to manage financially, he argues. The characterization of liberal churches as open to homosexuals' "whole agenda" further emphasizes the "us versus them" polemic implicit in Thomas' characterization of the debates.

Presbyterian pastor Janet Langenbein, who serves in a suburb of a city in the mid-Atlantic region, is "appalled by the length to which the homosexual debate is dividing the church." She characterizes herself as "open minded about it" and wants "the church to be open and inclusive," but is mostly concerned about the extent to which her denomination's focus on homosexuality is detracting from attention to other issues. She explains: "The church is never going to be able to move on and deal with these other political questions like economic justice and everything if we don't get past this." Furthermore, she expresses concern about the "real fear and paranoia of some factions of the PCUSA" as if the "whole church is going to go to hell" if homosexuals are ordained or married in the church. She believes that due process at national meetings has been disrupted because of the issue, and she worries that concern about the issue has an impact on other church decisions. She cites one example:

I was on the Ecumenical Partnerships Committee and there were people on that committee who didn't want to enter the Churches Uniting in Christ agreement because one of the other churches was UCC, [because] what if a UCC church, which does ordain

gay people,...had a gay pastor and that person came and preached at our church and administered communion?

While the motion to enter this agreement finally did pass, Langenbein is frustrated at how concerns about homosexuality influence denominational business on all levels.

Langenbein is ambivalent about what the Presbyterian Church should do about the "homosexual debate." She does not want the denomination to split, but "there are other times when I'm not sure that the church should stay together because it is so divisive." She continues, "I'm not sure there could ever be an authentic peace, so maybe they should just have a gracious split and [create] two denominations [and] move on." While such a split would make her very sad, she explains, "there are times when we probably all know marriages that shouldn't stay together, where everybody would be better off if they would try it again. Try it in a new way." Such a split, while unfortunate, might be a good way for the church to get on to other more important issues.

Lutheran minister Tim Anderson, who serves a church in southern California, emphasizes just how complicated gay and lesbian issues—and clergy's involvement in the politics surrounding them—can be. He begins to discuss gay and lesbian people in the interview by describing California's Proposition 22, a March 2000 primary ballot initiative that sought to outlaw homosexual marriage (and passed with over 61 percent of the vote, failing only in some Bay Area precincts). As a result, if gay men and lesbians are married in another state and move to California, their marriages are not recognized.

Anderson viewed Proposition 22 as "really a kind of discrimination." He also has "a real problem" with the Evangelical Lutheran Church in America's current stance that gay men and lesbians who are in open covenant relationships cannot be ordained. "That really seems to be contrary to what Christ's message was."

Despite the clarity with which Anderson presents his personal stance, he finds homosexuality a very difficult issue about which to take a position in his congregation. "I have to be careful what I say, because . . . people surprise me." People who are "open about these issues will leave the church over it. It seems to touch some real nerves." Although he feels that the Christian perspective against homosexuality "hurts the whole church" and "even our own personal faith element," he has difficulty deciding when and how to articulate his position to his congregation.

While Anderson does not mention any specific instances when he has discussed homosexuality with his congregation, he does mention speaking about Proposition 22 with two visitors to his church.

I had some people here the other day [who] were from a church and they were surprised when I said I was a Lutheran pastor and I think that proposition is full of hate and I'm going to vote against it. They were kind of surprised. I said, "Well, I don't have all the answers when it comes to this." I'll be the first one to say I've struggled with it and I don't have a clear-cut answer on it explaining everything. But all I know is that when I get to heaven, if anything, I'm going to err on the side of grace.

Anderson explains that the two people to whom he was talking

hadn't thought about it that way before. The older gentleman just kept on. "Well, you're responsible for trying to set other people's lifestyles [that] are wrong right." I said, "Well, that's true in many ways." But again we're judged by the basic question of "Are we loving each other the way Christ loves us?" I think that's the key question to ask. . . . Love, does it mean judge someone or does it really mean being involved and trying to understand someone?

In sharing this example with us, Anderson presents himself as a persuasive spokesperson against Proposition 22. At the same time, though, he reveals a surprising ambivalence about addressing the issue with his congregation because of what its divisiveness could mean to his community.

DISCURSIVE FRAMES ON HOMOSEXUALITY

These case studies suggest several frames through which clergy may present their opinions on homosexuality. Is it a "love" issue as Anderson argues, or is it a question of justice for gay men and lesbians? Are concerns about denominational processes on the forefront of clergy's minds, as is the case for Langenbein, or are these pragmatic concerns secondary to broader ideological positions on the issue? We now examine the content of the 40 clergy's comments more broadly. We consider the ministers' statements on homosexuality through three separate lenses. First, do the ministers confine their remarks to homosexuality's effect on the *church*, or do they speak more generally of its impact on *society in general*? Second, do they speak about the issue as it affects their *congregation*, or the *denomination* more broadly? Finally, we examine the frames that the clergy employ in their commentary on homosexuality.

Despite the visibility of debates about gay and lesbian rights in the broader society, clergy are more focused on the issue *inside* the churches than outside. This fact is reflected by the ministers' propensity to discuss homosexuality's ramifications inside the church instead of its place in more general societal discourse. Of all the comments clergy offered on homosexuality, 72 percent of these statements were directed toward the question of gay and lesbian rights inside the church rather than in the broader society. For the most part, the ministers talked about denominational conflicts, and to a lesser extent, intracongregational squabbles. We discuss both of these themes in further detail below.

Specific policy questions constituted some of the principal themes stressed by the few clergy who discussed the impact of homosexuality on issues external to the church. Two California pastors mentioned Proposition 22, the March 2000 ballot initiative that sought to nullify gay and lesbian marriages. A New England pastor mentioned Vermont's legalization of civil unions. A pastor in the southwest explained that his congregation had been involved in protesting against a violent hate crime against a gay man, and a midwestern pastor outlined his personal involvement in the fight for gay and lesbian rights:

Some of the things I have done would include attempting to offer legislation to repeal sodomy laws that are on the books, . . . testifying before [state] Senate committees, . . . visiting a number of state representatives, speaking publicly at a number of church meetings, writing a number of articles either as letters to the editor of the paper or through interviews that have taken place, developing and presenting in a number of cases biblical and scriptural understandings that would support this particular philosophy that I and many others espouse. (U8)[11]

In a more general vein, an Episcopal priest expressed concern about "the whole political issue that's come up around same-sex unions and rights of coverages, things of that nature. . . . [It's] really discriminatory the way things are being done right now in this country" (E5). Several others decried homophobia among the American public, and some expressed happiness that the gay rights movement has made progress.

Perhaps not surprisingly, clergy were far more likely to speak of homosexuality in their *churches* than in the broader society, and more specifically in their *denominations* than in their congregations. Fully 78 percent of all the ministers' comments occurred within the frame of denominational, rather than congregational, conflict. While the clergy who made these comments share a concern about issues related to homosexuality at the denominational level, they differ in their responses to these concerns.

A northeastern Baptist pastor's comment is quite typical of the majority who focused on denominational conflict: "We've been struggling over issues like homosexuality and sexuality in general. It's very clear within the denomination that there are widely differing opinions" (B2). Another Baptist minister expressed concern that "this last [denominational] convention caused a great deal of trouble because of the homosexual issue in the church, and a lot of homosexual churches pulled out because they were not affirmed by the American Baptists" (B6). As one Presbyterian pastor stated, "the issue is homosexuality. . . . It is really tearing the church apart and we need to find ways that we can agree to disagree and learn to live together" (P8). The same issue surfaces among UCC clergy: "We've lost a lot of churches and a lot of members . . . because the national church has taken a stand in favor of supporting gay and lesbian activity" (U3). The theme of denominational split also surfaced among clergy in other denominations. An Episcopal priest stated, "If you follow the news lately over homosexuality, there is that branch that wants us to make a clear, hard and fast pronouncement that this is right or this is wrong" (E7). "News" here clearly refers to denominational rather than secular developments.

Despite their common concerns about homosexuality at the denominational level, clergy differed markedly in their responses to the debate. Most clergy avoided taking a hard and fast stand on the issue. As one said, "the main mission of the mainline Protestant church is not to . . . convince people one way or another on homosexuality" (M3). Some clergy did try to influence the terms of the debate. One Methodist pastor admitted that she has tried very hard: "I've tried to . . . be a voice in the circles that I walk in and use my own personal influence . . . to ask the church to be broad enough to address sexual orientation issues in how open and inclusive we are" (M8). Others were more sanguine about the debate within their denominations: "I'm happy that the ELCA continues to . . . [take] positions on the social issues . . . they continue to study aggressively the whole matter of homosexuality" (L1). A Presbyterian pastor praised her denomination for being "really ahead of society in struggling right now.... [About the] rights of gays and lesbians" (P1). However, definitive positions on the issue may not be the solution to the debate, as one Methodist minister explained. "I think that on both sides of the issue, some of the extreme opinions have been quick to call names. If you have one opinion, you're automatically a homophobe.... If you have another opinion, you're automatically damned" (M3). A midwestern Lutheran pastor concurred:

There are so many nuances and we're on kind of a curve of discovery or exploration about...this issue of homosexuality. To have one unified position and then not...deviate from that as more information comes along seems to me to be too narrow, and in effect does a disservice because then it shuts down further inquiry. (L7)

Indecision was a common theme among the clergy who focused on gay and lesbian issues in their own congregations. "We haven't joined the Welcoming and Affirming Association, but we've talked about it. That's an issue that we continue to debate actively within our congregation, not in a nasty way, but we hold it up as an issue that we need to be paying attention to" (B8). A handful of ministers explained that their congregations were, in fact, open and affirming of gay and lesbian people. "We have openly gay people ordained here and we send openly gay people to seminary here" (E7). A midwestern Methodist pastor echoed this situation: "We're involved in the gay/lesbian issue. We have a number of gay and lesbian people in the congregation and have taken a leadership role in changing the stance of the church on gay and lesbian issues" (M7). A few clergy also suggested that their congregations were involved in activism surrounding gay and lesbian rights. As one shared, "this congregation has gone so far as to write letters to the College of Bishops, and

to delegates of the General Conference stating the views they hold" (M1).

To provide a broader sense of the types of comments clergy made about homosexuality, we have explored the frames they used to discuss the issue. Some are general; others are specific to particular debates. Some have normative implications, while others are more objective. Some of the frames suggest that debate about homosexuality is healthy, yet others imply that it is divisive and dangerous. The various frames are listed in Table 1.

Denominational struggle of the sort described above, as well as the possibility of denominational split and membership loss, were two of the three most prevalent frames clergy used to discuss homosexuality in the interviews. Also frequently used was the frame of promoting justice, rights, and equality for gay and lesbian people. A typical statement was a UCC pastor's concern about "marginalized people, gay and lesbian people in particular" (U1). As a Lutheran pastor shared, "I think...of the whole issue of gay and lesbian [equality] in terms of just integrity and basic political rights and human rights" (L6). Another Lutheran pastor expressed similar concern about "whether same-sex couples can be legally united and recognized as legal entities in the eyes of the law with respect to property ownership and insurance benefits and tax, IRS code kinds of provisions and so forth" (L7).

TABLE 1   Frames used to Discuss Homosexuality

Denominational struggle	30
Justice, rights, equality	17
Denominational split, member loss	11
Gay marriage	8
My church is open to gay men and lesbians	8
Homosexuality is not important	7
It is good to study this issue	7
This issue is overblown	6
Specific events, policies	5
Comparison with other issues	5
Gay ordination	5
It is hard for me to deal with this issue	3

N = 112 individual mentions.

The next most frequently employed frames were homosexual marriage and the notion that one's congregation is open to and affirming of gay men and lesbians. As one Episcopal priest stated, "There is a tremendous disagreement over . . . whether or not the church ought to offer same-sex blessings to homosexuals" (E4). A Presbyterian pastor went quite a bit further in explaining his view: "It's a little scary to be Presbyterian right now, because . . . of these cases that are coming to the Judicial Commission on same-sex unions" (P9). For those who share this uneasiness about the exclusion of gay and lesbian people, perhaps the best recourse is to open one's congregation to homosexuals in an official capacity. Eight of the clergy interviewed said that their congregations are open and affirming, which as one pastor explained, "means we're working to remove barriers that would inhibit all people from participating" (U5). The decision to become an open and affirming congregation, however, is not always easy. One UCC pastor's story is particularly illustrative:

At [my regional] Conference, they said, "We are inclusive. We welcome gays, lesbians, bisexuals, transsexuals," and the challenge for our churches was to do that, and we've kind of come out of the closet here at [my church] in that arena [by doing] that. I have to say, *I'm* much more out now, that we are a liberal church. It feels good to do that. [Now] I think I know kind of how a gay or lesbian person coming out of the closet might feel. (U11)

Three other frames that emerged in the interviews center around the question of how relevant the debate about homosexuality ought to be for the church. Some argued that the issue is not important. Others said its importance is overblown. Still others, however, made the argument that it is useful and beneficial to study the issue. Among those who complained that homosexuality is either unimportant or overblown, one general sentiment was that focusing on this issue means that other issues get short shrift. As one Baptist pastor argued, "homosexuality right now . . . tends to be at the

forefront of everything else, where everything else is sort of neglected, such as racism. . . . You don't see as much of this enthusiasm over having a viewpoint on racism" (B5). Another view is that clear denominational statements on homosexuality will have no impact on the bigger issue: "It becomes like the old cliché about rearranging the deck chairs on the Titanic. What difference does it make? Who really cares? . . . I'm not convinced that it really matters" (B10). There are also those who would agree with a Presbyterian pastor who confesses: "I honestly for the life of me don't understand why it's the biggest issue in the church" (P9).

Some clergy, however, do not dispute the issue's importance and argue instead that it is a valuable topic for debate. As an African-American Baptist pastor observes, "homosexuality is one [issue] they're going to have to bring to a point like they did slavery" (B6). Debate about the issue can serve the purpose of extending understanding, according to an Episcopal priest in the Southwest: "What is our attitude about sexual orientation? . . . [Asking that question] allows us to learn more, to gain greater awareness" (E8). Successful discourse about homosexuality is also at times a source of pride for clergy, as it is for this northeastern woman: "I thought that the ELCA did a good job. It takes more work for them to do it the way they did it, to do the research" (L10).

Less frequently used frames involve comparison of the issue to other issues, discussion of specific events and policies that touch on homosexuality (such as hate crimes), and homosexual ordination. The African-American pastor mentioned above compared the issue to slavery. Others, such as this Episcopal priest, relate the issue to racism: "I truly believe that all other issues . . . poverty, . . . education, . . . health issues, including AIDS, even . . . sexual orientation, in many respects have their basis in the issue of racism" (E8). Similarly, "There's a lot of homophobia in the culture and that is certainly present in United Methodist churches,...they can be just as prejudiced about it as they have been about racism and sexism" (M10).

Finally, a few pastors admitted that it is difficult for them personally to discuss the issue. In one instance, a minister explained that he feels uncomfortable addressing the issue, even with fellow clergy members: "Just speaking from my own experience here in my conference, it's not even always the case among clergy gatherings [that] it's safe to share your opinion" (M3). He continued by sharing that "both my wife and I have siblings who are gay and lesbian," which makes the issue very personal for him. Stating one's view on homosexuality publicly can be even riskier. As one UCC pastor explains, "[I am] always wrestling with what [I] feel is right in [my] conscience on the whole gay issue...those sticky wickets are the ones [about which] you may or may not be called upon to make a public stand, but you always have to have your opinions" (U4).

In sum, the majority of clergy who discussed homosexuality focused on the issue in their churches instead of in society at large, and in their denominations rather than in their individual congregations. The three case studies presented above notwithstanding, it is important to note that virtually none of the clergy interviewed took hard and fast stands on any homosexuality-related issues. Interestingly, most of the clergy appear to approach the issue in a pragmatic, rather than prophetic, way. Pragmatic concerns about denominational conflict, struggle, split, and membership loss top the list of frames through which clergy present their opinions on homosexuality. While some are concerned with justice, rights, and equality, these prophetic concerns are secondary to more pragmatic matters.

LANGUAGE USED TO DISCUSS HOMOSEXUALITY

In addition to their substantive comments about homosexuality, clergy also frame the issue in terms of the language they use to describe and address the topic. The majority who commented on the issue employed the term "homosexuality." Twenty-three ministers (58 percent) defined the issue specifically in terms of "homosexuality" or the "homosexual" issue. One United Methodist minister offered a typical comment: "A social issue that concerns me most is just how we as a society, as a church, we deal with homosexuality" (M3). In addition to those who framed it in terms of "homosexuality" or the "homosexual" issue, an additional 11 ministers (27 percent) talked about these issues by using the terms "gay" and "lesbian." Thus a full 85 percent of the clergy discussed issues related to sexuality exclusively through the language of "homosexuality," the "homosexual" issue, or the "gay and lesbian" issue.

At various points since debates about homosexuality began in the mainline churches, denominations have tried to steer the conversation into broader considerations of sexuality or human sexuality more generally. The Presbyterian Church (USA), for example, set up a task force to study homosexuality in 1976 and later commissioned studies that considered sexuality more generally (Presbyterian Church (USA) 1980, 1991). The Evangelical Lutheran Church in America responded to debate about homosexuality on the ground (in part) by drafting a social statement in the early 1990s that addressed homosexuality briefly but was framed more generally in terms of "human sexuality" (Evangelical Lutheran Church in America 1996). The Episcopal Church has also responded to questions about homosexuality with efforts to focus on human sexuality more broadly. In 1979, for example, dioceses were asked to develop educational programs about sexuality. When many dioceses did not follow through on this request, the Episcopal Executive Committee called on a denominational committee to develop such materials in 1982. While these materials were designed to address homosexuality, they were to do so in the context of other issues related to sexuality that are also of concern to the Episcopal Church.

In general, efforts to reframe denominational conversations about homosexuality into more general dialogues about sexuality are not evident in the language these clergy use in discussing the issue. Table 2 shows that three clergy (8 percent) in the sample did, however, frame the issue in more general terms. These clergy were disproportionately Episcopalian. While only one minister from a denomination other than the Episcopal Church framed the issue exclusively in terms of "sexuality," one-third of all the Episcopal clergy framed it this way. As the minister of an Episcopal church in the midwest explained, "we are willing to confront difficult issues ... issues of sexuality" (El). Three respondents (8 percent) also framed their comments using both the specific frame of "homosexuality," the "homosexual" issue, or "gays and lesbians" and the more general frame of "sexuality" or "human sexuality."

The dominant focus on "homosexuality" and the "homosexual issue" among mainline clergy has not, however, translated only into detached descriptions of the issue as a distant concept. In fact, one of the main contributions of some mainline churches to the debate has been their ability to personalize the issue. Instead of discussing homosexuality generally, some mainline churches, and especially the 800 gay and lesbian welcoming congregations in the United States, have slanted the discussion toward people who live in the neighborhood or attend the church (Cadge 1997). As Table 3 shows, just over half of mainline clergy who spoke about issues related to sexuality commented specifically on gay and lesbian *people* in their remarks.[12]

A United Methodist minister in Iowa, for example, raised the question of what the "godly approach [is to] people who are gay and lesbian" (M3). Asked to identify the biggest problem facing the Presbyterian Church today, a Presbyterian pastor in the midwest referred to "the rights of gays and lesbians" (P1). She continued,

I think as people become more and more open, people are recognizing more and more that their friends and neighbors who they love are gay and lesbian and recognizing that suddenly this isn't some issue that's facing somebody else, now, it's facing us as a family. (P1)

The extent to which sexuality and homosexuality were defined abstractly rather than specifically (in terms of actual people) was largely dependent on the denominational affiliation of the pastor. Most notably, all but one of the seven United Church of Christ ministers in the sample discussed "gay and lesbian people" (U3), "gay and lesbian folk" (U5), or the "place of gays and lesbians in the community"

TABLE 2   Language used to Discuss Homosexuality

	"Homosexuality"	"Sexuality"	Both	Neither
Baptist	5	1	1	0
Episcopal	3	2	0	1
ELCA	6	0	0	1
Methodist	4	0	1	2
Presbyterian	4	0	1	1
UCC	1	0	0	6
Total	23	3	3	11

N = 40 clergy.

TABLE 3   Discussion of issue in the Abstract or in Terms Of People

	Abstract	People	Both	Neither
Baptist	4	2	1	0
Episcopal	2	1	2	1
ELCA	2	1	3	1
Methodist	3	2	2	0
Presbyterian	3	3	0	0
UCC	1	6	0	0
Total	15	15	8	2

N = 40 clergy.

(U11).[13] The American Baptist clergy, on the other hand, spoke more vaguely and abstractly about "homosexuality" (B5), "homosexual churches" (B6), or the "homosexual issue" (B10). Differences in how United Church of Christ and American Baptist clergy talk about sexuality and homosexuality suggest, tentatively, that clergy in progressive denominations such as the UCC that welcome homosexual people into all aspects of church life (including ordination and marriage) are more likely to talk about homosexual *people* than are clergy in denominations such as the American Baptist Churches, which consider homosexuality incompatible with Christian teachings.

CONCLUSION

Since the early 1970s clergy have been central to mainline Protestantism's national debates about homosexuality. Their opinions have likely influenced how the mainline Protestants in their pews perceive the debates and the issue more generally. The voices of clergy presented here, coupled with the range of frames they employ in their comments, illustrate the richly textured and complicated nature of these debates at present.... Pastors who do speak tend to frame the issue in terms of "homosexuality" or the "homosexual" issue—despite some denominations' attempts to broaden the discussion to a more general focus on sexuality.

Pastors who do speak about homosexuality tend to focus on the issue's impact on the *church* rather than its significance for the broader society. They also focus more on *denominational* debates and division than on discussions or actions within their own congregations. Rather than being played out in terms of what is "loving" or "just," as some denominational debates would suggest, the frames clergy use to discuss homosexuality reveal an overwhelmingly pragmatic approach to the issue. Concerns about denominational struggle, split, and membership loss dominate clergy's comments, and the majority of pastors do not take clear positions on specific issues.

This pragmatic focus on conflict suggests that denominational debate may be breeding more denominational debate, rather than additional denominational debate being sparked primarily by congregational action. The ministers' focus on the denominational level also raises questions about the exact nature of the relationship between local (congregational) and national (denominational) debate. The clergy who spoke about homosexuality with reference to their congregations were *supportive* of efforts to make the church more welcoming to gay men and lesbians. The evident silence of more socially conservative clergy about how homosexuality-related issues affect their congregations may mean that they support the denominational status quo. In short, the debate about homosexuality within and among churches is perhaps a bit more muted than national debates about the subject might suggest. Meanwhile, the debate may now be orienting itself around denominational conflict rather than individual congregational concerns.

The fact that so many clergy spoke about homosexuality without prompting in these interviews clearly indicates that the issue is on mainline pastors' minds today. Clergy have been and will remain central players in debates about homosexuality in mainline churches, so understanding how they frame the issue is central to grasping the complex texture of the debates. Our data do not allow us to connect particular framings of homosexuality to clergy's specific actions around the subject in their congregations, denominations, or communities. We will leave this for scholars to investigate in the future.

NOTES

1. We use the blanket term "homosexuality" throughout this article to refer to denominational debates and clergy's comments about homosexuality, sexuality, homosexual people, and gay and lesbian concerns. We opt to discuss this issue throughout the article primarily in terms of homosexuality because this frame has historically dominated denominational discussions, and it was the primary means by which the clergy we interviewed conceived of and talked about the issue.

2. On the "clergy-laity gap," which posits that mainline Protestant clergy are more liberal than most members of their congregations, see Adams (1970). Hadden (1969), and Koller and Retzer (1980). On the notion that mainline clergy are liberal see Guth et al. (1997) and Wuthnow (1988). On the political lessons inculcated in seminary, see Carroll et al. (1997).

3. The phrases "homosexuals" and "gay men and lesbians" are used interchangeably throughout this article. While we prefer "gay men and lesbians," the denominations have and continue to use both phrases, so both are used here. With the exception of the United Church of Christ, bisexual and transgender people have not been commented on specifically by the mainline clergy, and are therefore not addressed in this article. The UCC presently refers to gay, lesbian, bisexual, and transgender people as one group, and supports them all.

4. In recent surveys 44 percent felt that homosexuality should be considered an acceptable alternative lifestyle while 84 percent believed that gay men and lesbians should enjoy equal employment opportunity (CNN/*USA Today*/Gallup Poll 1996a, 1996b). See Yang (1997) for a detailed discussion of longitudinal data.

5. The names of the politically involved clergy were obtained from denominational offices in Washington, DC, state-level denominational officials, and denominational websites. This sampling technique was employed because

the central aim of the original project was to examine the differences in attitudes that exist between average clergy and those who are networked with their denominational Washington offices (see Olson 2002).

6. Speaking about homosexuality does not automatically translate into support for gay and lesbian people. It is commonly assumed that mainline clergy are more liberal than the members of their congregations. This assumption led us to expect that clergy who spoke about homosexuality would speak in support of gay and lesbian people. Our expectation was bolstered by the fact that some of the questions the clergy were answering when they mentioned homosexuality required them to identify a problem. We assumed that clergy who support gay and lesbian rights would be more likely to think about homosexuality-related matters as problems, because in many religious traditions people who oppose gay and lesbian rights represent the status quo.

. . .

10. Pseudonyms are used to protect the identity of the interviewees.

11. Interviews are coded according to the following system: B = Baptist; E = Episcopal; L = Lutheran; M = Methodist; P = Presbyterian; U = UCC. Numbers greater than or equal to 6 indicate that the pastor has explicit ties with his or her denomination's political leadership; lower numbers indicate that the pastor was from the random sample.

12. None of the clergy interviewed spoke about "ex-gays" (former homosexuals). These are people who previously understood themselves to be homosexual but now understand themselves to be heterosexual.

13. United Church of Christ clergy were also the only clergy to mention "bisexual" or "transgender" people.

REFERENCES

ADAMS, J. L. 1970. *The growing church lobby in Washington.* Grand Rapids, MI: Eerdmans.

AMMERMAN, N. T. 2000. A quick question. <http://hirr.hartsem.edu/research>.

BENFORD, R. and D. SNOW. 2000. Framing processes and social movements: An overview and assessment. *Annual Review of Sociology* 26:611–39.

BOSWELL, J. 1980. *Christianity, social tolerance, and homosexuality.* Chicago, IL: University of Chicago Press.

CADGE, W. 1997. God's rainbow families of faith: Reconciling congregations bridging gay and straight communities. Honors thesis. Swarthmore, PA: Swarthmore College.

CARROLL, J. W., B. G. WHEELER, D. O. ALESHIRE, and P. L. MARLER. 1997. *Being there: Culture and formation in two theological schools.* New York: Oxford University Press.

CNN/*USA Today*/Gallup Poll. 1996a. Homosexuality/gay marriages, March 15–17, 1996. Survey #GO106521.

———. 1996b. Homosexuality/gay rights, November 21–24, 1996. Survey #GO11533.

COMSTOCK, G. D. 1996. *Unrepentant, self affirming, practicing: Lesbian/bisexual/gay people within organized religion.* New York: Continuum.

Council for Christian Social Action. 1969. Resolution on homosexuals and the law. April 12.

CRAWFORD, S. E. S. and L. R. OLSON, 2001. Clergy as political leaders in urban contexts. In *Christian clergy in American politics,* edited S. E. S. Crawford and L. R. Olson. Baltimore, MD: Johns Hopkins University Press.

D'EMILIO, J. 1983. *Sexual politics, sexual communities.* Chicago, IL: University of Chicago Press.

Evangelical Lutheran Church in America. 1996. A message on sexuality: Some common convictions.

FINDLAY, J. F. 1993. *Church people in the struggle: The National Council of Churches and the black freedom movement, 1950–1970.* New York: Oxford University Press.

FRIEDLAND, M. B. 1998. *Lift up your voice like a trumpet: White clergy and the civil rights and antiwar movements, 1954–1973.* Chapel Hill, NC: University of North Carolina Press.

GOFFMAN, E. 1974. *Frame analysis: An essay on the organization of experience.* New York: Harper & Row.

GREENBERG, D. and M. BYSTRYN, 1982. Christian intolerance of homosexuality. *American Journal of Sociology* 88:515–49.

GUTH, J. L., J. C. GREEN, C. E. SMIDT, L. A. KELLSTEDT, and M. M. POLOMA, 1997. *The bully pulpit: The politics of Protestant clergy.* Lawrence, KS: University Press of Kansas.

HADDEN, J. K. 1969. *The gathering storm in the churches.* Garden City, NY: Doubleday.

HERTZKE, A. D. 1988. *Representing God in Washington: The role of religious lobbies in the American polity.* Knoxville, TN: University of Tennessee Press.

KLOEHN, S. 1999. Protestants face schism on homosexuality. *Chicago Tribune* May 3, Section 1.

KOLLER, N. B. and J. D. RETZER. 1980. The sounds of silence revisited. *Sociological Analysis* 41:155–61.

NIEBUHR, G. 1998. Issues of sexuality split the Presbyterians again. *New York Times* March 28, Section B.

NIEBUHR, H. R. 1951. *Christ and culture.* New York: Harper and Row.

OLSON, L. R. 2000. *Filled with spirit and power: Protestant clergy in politics.* Albany, NY: State University of New York Press.

———. 2002. Mainline Protestant Washington offices and the political lives of clergy. In *The quiet hand of God: Faith based activism and the public role of mainline Protestantism,* edited by R. Wuthnow and J. H. Evans. Berkeley, CA: University of California Press.

PETERSEN, L. and G. Donnenwerth. 1998. Religion and declining support for traditional beliefs about gender roles and homosexual rights. *Sociology of Religion* 59:353–71.

———. 1980. The nature and purpose of human sexuality.

Presbyterian Church (USA). 1991. Keeping body and soul together: Sexuality, spirituality, and social justice.

Presbyterian Panel. 1989. Human sexuality. November.

———. 1996. Current issues in PCUSA. February.

SANCHEZ, R. 1999. At gay wedding, Methodists take a vow against church ban. *Washington Post* January 17, Section A.

SMITH, C. 1996. *Resisting Reagan: The U.S.-Central America peace movement.* Chicago, IL: University of Chicago Press.

WUTHNOW, R. 1988. *The restructuring of American religion: Society and faith since World War II.* Princeton, NJ: Princeton University Press.

YANG, A. 1997. Trends: Attitudes toward homosexuality. *Public Opinion Quarterly* 61:477–507.

22 Dare to Differ: Gay and Lesbian Catholics' Assessment of Official Catholic Positions on Sexuality

ANDREW K. T. YIP

Yip's study of Quest, at the time the largest British organization for gay and lesbian Roman Catholics, was one of the earliest sociological studies of religion and sexual identity. Yip found that, despite official Roman Catholic teachings that homosexuality is a disorder and morally wrong, Quest members rejected being labeled as deviants by their Church and more importantly, remained committed to their Catholic identity.

Many consider being gay/lesbian and Christian incompatible because of the seemingly obvious prohibition of homosexuality in the Bible. Identifying oneself as gay or lesbian is therefore a demanding task in a religious environment where religious affirmation and acceptance are scarce. Given such a climate, it is not surprising to observe that, compared to their non-religious counterparts, gay and lesbian Christians generally demonstrate a higher degree of anxiety about the exposure of their sexuality, a greater sense of alienation, as well as a lower degree of self-esteem. . . .

To date, there has been very little empirical research on gay and lesbian Christians. Most of the literature currently available heavily employs a historical-theological-ethical analysis of the issue of homosexuality from a Christian perspective. . . .

On the other hand, empirical research on gay and lesbian Christians is scarce. The majority of research on the gays and lesbians either completely ignores the religious dimension or makes mention of it *en passant*. In general, research that includes the religious dimension focuses on two main themes.

The first theme concerns the salient characteristics of religious gays and lesbians in comparison to their non-religious counterparts. . . .

Source: Andrew Yip, "Daring to Differ: Gay and Lesbian Catholics' Assessment of Official Catholic Positions on Sexuality." Reprinted with permission, from *Sociology of Religion*, Volume 57, © 1998.

The second theme concerns the relationship of religious gays and lesbians and the institutionalized Church. Researchers concluded that religious gays and lesbians have the tendency to reject organized religion and embrace individualized spirituality. . . .

This paper aims to contribute to the little existing empirical research literature on lesbian and gay Christians by examining their assessment of the Roman Catholic Church's official positions on issues directly or indirectly related to homosexuality and their beliefs about how to respond to Church teaching.

THE STUDY

This paper presents data collected through a postal survey from 121 lesbian and gay Roman Catholics associated with Quest, the largest British organization for lesbian and gay Catholics. Established in 1973, Quest's current membership is approximately 350. Its primary aim is to assist lesbians and gays in the face of the lack of acceptance in everyday life. It is also involved in legal reform in association with other non-religious lesbian and gay organizations. . . .

The survey was originally conducted to document the members' views on the ministry of Quest. In addition, it also aimed to collect the members' assessment of the official Catholic positions on, or related to, the issue of sexuality and homosexuality. . . .

THE RESPONDENTS

One hundred and nine of the respondents (90.1 percent) are men, while 11 (9.1 percent) are women. One respondent, however, did not disclose her/his gender. Twelve respondents (10.3 percent, N = 117) had been members of Quest for less than one year. On the other hand, 34 (29.4 percent) had been members for more than 10 years.

The respondents' ages ranged from teenage to above 70. They were quite equally distributed

in age groups between 31 and 60. For instance, there was the same number of respondents (28, 23.2 percent) in the "31–40" and "41–50" age groups. The average age of the respondents was 48.2 years.

The respondents were in general highly educated. Fifty-one (42.1 percent) held a first degree, 25 (20.7 percent) had a Master's degree while 13 (10.7 percent) held a PhD. Also, 50 respondents (41.3 percent) had some form of professional qualifications. . . .

A great majority of respondents (113, 93.4 percent) were Mass-goers. Twelve (10.6 percent) attended Mass daily (some of them are priests). However, the majority (86, 76.1 percent) attended on a weekly basis.

THE ROMAN CATHOLIC CHURCH'S POSITION ON HOMOSEXUALITY

The Roman Catholic Church issued its first official statement on homosexuality in 1975 with the publication of Declaration on Certain Questions Concerning Sexual Ethics (Congregation for the Doctrine of the Faith 1975). Homosexuality and prohibition against it were briefly mentioned alongside other issues such as masturbation, marriage, and sex before marriage.

It is, however, the publication of Letter on the Pastoral Care of Homosexual Persons (Congregation for the Doctrine of the Faith 1986) that proved to be the most widely debated and controversial. The controversy primarily surrounds the terminology used in the statement in the labelling of the homosexual orientation and same-sex genital acts. The homosexual orientation or inclination is labelled as an "objective disorder."

Genital acts between members of the same sex, on the other hand, are labelled "intrinsically disordered" primarily because they are against the perceived prohibition against them in the Old Testament (e.g., Genesis 19: 1–11;

Leviticus 18: 22; 20: 13) and the New Testament (e.g., Corinthians 6: 9; Romans 1: 18–32; I Timothy 1). It is also argued that same-sex genital acts are contradictory to fundamental principles of the Roman Catholic's teachings on sexual ethics. . . .

Because same-sex genital acts are not within the framework of heterosexual marriage and have no possibility for the transmission of new life, they are labeled as "intrinsically disordered." . . .

RESPONDENTS' ASSESSMENT OF QUEST'S POSITIONS ON CURRENT ISSUES

Respondents were asked to rate, on a scale of 1 to 5, their degree of agreement with five statements about Quest's positions on certain current issues. The higher the rating, the higher the degree of agreement. Their responses to these statements are presented in Table 1.

Table 1 indicates that, except for statement (c), the majority of respondents strongly agreed that Quest should be in favor of changes seen as crucial for the well-being of lesbians and gay men. An exceptionally high average rating (4.50) given to statement (d) expresses their deep resentment at being described by the Vatican in quasi-pathological terms suggestive of a sick personality. . . .

Similar objections to the capacity of the moral vocabulary for coping with homosexuality may help to explain the marked discrepancy between responses to statement (b) and those to statement (c). While 41.4 percent strongly agreed that Quest should ask the Church to recognize some heterosexual partnerships outside marriage, a substantial 33.6 percent strongly disagreed. This is the smallest percentage difference in Table 1 between the two extremes. The determining factor may have been the conventional Roman Catholic perception that extra-marital partnerships are a grave threat to the family and marriage as an

institution. Since the respondents did not see any such threat in same-sex partnerships, regarded as nonmatrimonial in any sacramental sense, they were consistently able to agree that Quest should seek church recognition for same-sex partnerships. . . .

Can Catholics Ever Be Practicing Lesbians and Gay Men?

Official teaching, even at the Vatican, does not deny the value of love between members of the same sex, but it forbids any expression of that love through homosexual genital acts, just as all heterosexual activity outside marriage, and much (e.g., contraceptive) activity within marriage, is forbidden. However, what did the respondents themselves think? Out of 116 who responded, 93 (80.2 percent) thought that the full expression of same-sex love within a personal relationship is *entirely* compatible with their Catholic faith.

Three primary reasons were cited in support of this view. The first is that all sexualities are God's gift. The use of this gift within the context of a personal relationship is therefore entirely natural and acceptable. This point is argued in the narratives below.

God created us all and loves us all and when someone loves someone and wants to spend their life with them, sex is part of that relationship. (Respondent 080)

I see sex between loving people as a God-given joy and only by living your life in true conscience as you know it can you have a honest and pure relationship with God. (Respondent 084)

Attributing their sexuality to God's creation is a very powerful argument against the Church's position. To them, their sexuality is created, sustained, and blessed by God. This *ontogeneric argument* unequivocally implies that homosexuality, like heterosexuality, cannot, and most of all, should not be changed and curbed in its expression because it is God's creation. Attributing one's sexuality to God's intended creation is the ultimate justification

TABLE 1   Quest's Positions on Current Issues

Statement	Average Rating	% of Respondents Strongly Agreed	% of Respondents Strongly Disagreed
(a) Quest's dialogue with the Church on the issues of homosexuality is influential for change (N = 116)	3.47	52.6	17.2
(b) Quest should ask the Church to recognize same-sex partnerships (N = 117)	3.85	67.5	16.2
(c) Quest should ask the Church to recognize some heterosexual partnerships outside marriage (n = 116)	3.13	41.4	33.6
(d) Quest should ask the Church to refrain from using the term "intrinsically disordered" in its official teaching on homosexuality (N = 118)	4.50	84.7	6.8
(e) Quest should pay more attention to addressing the issue of HIV/AIDS (N = 118)	3.62	62.7	12.7

for its acceptability and unchangeability. It also invalidates the Church's official position, responsible for the stigmatization that threatens their gay and lesbian identities. This point is argued below.

The expression of love cannot be wrong. Why would God give the desire without allowing fulfilment? I know that I was born gay, so how can the expression of what is my nature be sinful? (Respondent 119)

God created us in his own image—homosexual. He doesn't make mistakes. Our essential Christian vocation is the same as everyone else's—to receive love and to give love. Most human beings are clearly called to a loving, sexual, one-to-one relationship with another. We are, too. It is our *duty* to fulfil our vocation to give love and to receive love in stable relationships. The Church is quite wrong in what it says about this, and doing severe damage to the Body of Christ. (Respondent 121, his emphasis)

The second reason asserts that quality and love are what really count in a relationship, not its sexual form. The respondents thought that same-sex relationships should be affirmed as long as they exemplify conventional Christian values such as commitment and monogamy....

It must be noted that some respondents were particularly adamant that the full expression of same-sex love should only take place within the context of a loving and committed relationship. Casual and anonymous sex is therefore considered unacceptable. Respondent 092 argued, "In a loving relationship between two homosexual Catholics, if one goes cottaging [engaging in anonymous sex in public toilets], he/she is committing adultery in the eyes of God." In the same vein, respondent 102 argued, "If God gave the gifts, as the Church teaches, who are we to abstain, in a committed relationship—but no promiscuity."

The respondents did not speak with one voice in terms of the context(s) within which same-sex love can be expressed fully. This is one of the most debated issues in gay Christian sexual ethics.... Some gay and lesbian Catholics believe that their commitment to the Catholic faith means that same-sex genital acts are prohibited in all contexts. Celibacy is therefore the only option....

On the other hand, some gay and lesbian Catholics uphold the "theology of friendship" which encourages, among others, "inclusiveness." Such inclusiveness might lead to sexual non-exclusivity within a partnership, with consent from the parties involved.

Most gay and lesbian Catholics, represented by most of the respondents in this survey, uphold the "ethic of sexual monogamy" which argues that same-sex genital acts are acceptable within a committed and exclusive partnership, in accordance with the teachings of conventional Christian sexual ethics. . . .

In sum, it can be observed that gay and lesbian Catholics hold a myriad of positions insofar as sexual ethics in relation to homosexuality are concerned. In the search for a behavioral blueprint that the mainstream culture has not provided, gays and lesbians arrive at different positions in this process. This is an outcome of the existence of more than one normative reference framework in the construction of gay and lesbian Christian ethics. Although all have successfully negotiated a new identity that incorporates both their sexuality and religious beliefs, gay and lesbian Christians draw upon different frameworks in constructing the basis of their sexual behavior. . . .

The diversity of these experiences are evidence of the existence of more than one gay and lesbian Christian identity, and of the increasing complexity in the organization of person identity in a constantly shifting moral landscape in postmodern society.

The last primary reason for supporting the full expression of same-sex love is that the Church's official teachings against it are ill-founded and inaccurately formulated. The following narratives represent this argument.

I believe that the official Catholic teachings are based on complete misinterpretations of Old Testament texts and a failure to put St. Paul's Epistles into sociological and historical context. The resulting "tradition" makes the lesbian and gay Catholicism an apparent contradiction in terms. (Respondent 091) . . .

The present state of 'official' teaching is based on discredited Biblical scholarship and equally discredited concepts of natural law. There is room for doubt either way, but in such circumstances one must follow one's own informed conscience. (Respondent 024)

. . . Discrediting the Church in this connection is one of the stigma management strategies many gay and lesbian Christians have developed. In discrediting the Church, they could justifiably dismiss the official position of the Church on the issue of homosexuality. . . .

Absolution for Same-sex Genital Acts

To further explore their values and attitudes in relation to the Catholic faith, the survey asked the respondents to indicate if in their view a Catholic should seek absolution for homosexual acts committed in four significantly different kinds of circumstances. Table 2 presents their views.

Table 2 indicates that an overwhelming majority of the respondents (90.8 percent) thought that gay and lesbian Catholics who committed homosexual acts within a partnership should not seek absolution. This provides further credence for the position of the majority of respondents that the full expression of same-sex love within the context of a partnership is acceptable, despite being at variance with official teaching.

The respondents' views on the second and the third scenarios polarise. No clear majority emerges in either case. Both scenarios place the commission of homosexual acts outside the confines of a partnership, whether it be outside one's own partnership or that of the third party. The polarity of the participants' views reflects the opposing positions in the gay and lesbian Christian community on this issue. I have already mentioned this point.

In the fourth scenario, the majority (67.3 percent) thought no absolution should be sought. However, a substantial minority (32.7

TABLE 2   Seeking Absolution

Scenario	Should Seek Absolution	Should Not Seek Absolution
When she/he commits the acts with her/his partner within a same-sex partnership (N = 109)	10 (9.2%)	99 (90.8%)
When she/he commits the acts with someone outside her/his own partnership (N = 109)	64 (58.7%)	45 (41.3%)
When she/he commits the acts with someone who is herself/himself in a same-sex partnership (N = 109)	56 (51.4%)	53 (48.6%)
When the acts are committed between persons not in a same-sex partnership (N = 110)	36 (32.7%)	74 (67.3%)

percent) indicated otherwise. This further buttresses the point that a minority of respondents take a strict view that the full expression of same-sex love should occur only within the context of a partnership.

Optimism and Pessimism About the Future

Since there is a great discrepancy between what the majority of the respondents believed and the Church's official teachings on the full expression of same-sex love, are they optimistic that the Church would eventually adopt a position consistent with theirs? About two-thirds (65.5 percent) were optimistic that changes in Catholic understanding of homosexuality would bring about a change in official teaching. ...

On the other end of the spectrum, one-third of the respondents (34.5 percent) were not hopeful that the Church will eventually change in this respect. ...

CONCLUSIONS

... Two sociological themes emerge from the analysis of the experiences of these gay and lesbian Catholics. First, despite the social labelling of being "objectively disordered" and "intrinsically disordered" when engaged in same-sex genital activity, the majority of the respondents demonstrated a positive self-image and subsequently rejected this labelling. The narratives presented signify the acceptability of their sexuality by principally attributing it to God's creation and by the counter-labelling of

the Church's position on homosexuality as erroneous.

Their experiences indicate that social actors are not passive agents, falling prey to stigmatizing social labelling without the potential for the development of counter-stigmatization strategies. Socially labelled "deviants" have the ability to transcend their "deviant" circumstances. Associating with a group such as Quest contributes greatly to the development of this positive self identity.

Second, in spite of the lack of religious affirmation and social acceptance within the Church, the respondents have not distanced themselves from the religious institution. Ten and six tenths percent and 76.1 percent of them respectively attend Mass on a daily and weekly basis. This provides evidence that they have arrived at a point of their journey of sexuality where they have successfully developed a re-negotiated identity that incorporates their sexuality and religious beliefs. They appear to construct their identities in opposition to the Church's teachings, the institutional norms. Their experiences illustrate that lesbian and gay identities are indeed "a product of struggles, battle against definition by others, and for self-definition." ...

REFERENCES

Congregation for the Doctrine of the Faith. 1975. *Declaration on certain questions concerning sexual ethics.* London: Catholic Truth Society.

———. 1986. *Letter to the Bishops of the Catholic Church on the Pastoral Care of Homosexual Persons.* London: Catholic Truth Society.

23 "We are God's Children, Y'All:" Race, Gender, and Sexuality in Lesbian- and Gay-Affirming Congregations

KRISTA MCQUEENEY

McQueeney's article examines the complexities of how lesbian and gay Christians are shaped by their other social identities such as race, gender, and class. She studied two congregations, one a black, working-class, lesbian Evangelical Protestant church and the other a white, middle-class, mainly heterosexual, liberal Protestant church. Drawing on participant observation and intensive interviews, McQueeney outlines diverse and complicated strategies for building identities as "good" Christians and as lesbians and gay men.

For most conservative (i.e., fundamentalist and evangelical) Christians, God's will is expressed in a heterosexual family in which male and female are complementary and the primary purpose of sex is procreation (Ellingson, Tebbe, Van Haitsma, and Laumann 2001; Wolkomir 2006). According to a twentieth-century literal interpretation, God created man as protector/leader and woman as nurturer/helper (Ammerman 1987; Bartkowski 2001; Foster 1995). Biblical interpretation of homosexual sex as a sin further consolidates the belief in heterosexual marriage as the only proper context for sexual activity (Roof and McKinney 1987; Thumma 1991). Although evangelicals may redefine male headship in everyday life (Gallagher and Smith 1999; Denton 2004), the gendered, heterosexual family remains at the heart of conservative Christianity (Williams 1974; Wolkomir 2006).

But even as Christianity has been used to justify women's subordination (Daly 1975, Ruether 1974) and to condemn homosexuals (Butler 1990; Moon 2004), its beliefs in the inherent dignity of all people and freedom from oppression represent seeds of liberation (Cone 1975, 1984). For example, nineteenth-century evangelicals read the New Testament as a call to abolish slavery and promote women's suffrage (Hersh 1978; Stewart 1976).

In the twentieth century, Christians developed a liberation theology to challenge class injustice (Smith 1991). Inspired by these Christian beliefs, some Protestant churches have welcomed people who identify as lesbian, gay, and bisexual (Comstock 2001). This article uses participant observation and in-depth interviews in two mainline Protestant, lesbian- and gay-affirming[1] congregations in the South to analyze how lesbian, gay, and straight-but-affirming church members reinterpreted Christian beliefs to include people traditionally stigmatized by their sexuality. One church was predominantly black[2], lesbian, working class[3], and evangelical Protestant, and the other was mostly white, heterosexual, upper middle class, and liberal Protestant.

The lesbian women and gay men I studied—black and white—found themselves caught between dominant Christian culture and gay subcultures. Homosexuality carries a heavy stigma within Christianity, placing lesbians, gays, and bisexuals on lesser ground than their straight counterparts. These black and white lesbian and gay believers sought recognition as Christians and members of the church family,

but they were greeted by traditions that privileged heterosexuality and the twentieth-century evangelical gendered family. Even so, their participation in Christian institutions upset the heterosexual assumption (Foucault 1972; Gramsci 1971). In this article, I challenge binary notions of resistance to or reproduction of inequality by unpacking the complex and contradictory ways that black and white lesbian women and gay men, most raised conservative Christian, resisted notions of homosexual sin[4] *and* reproduced a "politics of respectability" (Warner 1999) among lesbian, gay, bisexual, and transgender (LGBT) people.

Together with their straight-but-affirming allies, lesbian and gay church members engaged in oppositional identity work to challenge homosexual stigma and fashion good Christian identities. Oppositional identity work involves "transform[ing] discrediting identities into crediting ones and redefining those identities so they can be seen as indexes of noble rather than flawed character" (Schwalbe and Mason-Schrock 1996:141). Church members defined homosexuality as normal and moral by mobilizing the "identity formation material" (McRobbie 1994) offered up in their social worlds. As I will show, they mobilized Christian discourse—the very language, beliefs, and institutional arrangements that cast lesbians and gay men as sinful—to "mainstream" (Vaid 1995) or "normalize" (Warner 1999) homosexuality. I will argue that their oppositional identity work emerged as lesbian and gay Christians stood with one foot set to enter a heterosexist institution, and the other poised to kick over the heterosexist beliefs and traditions that deemed them unworthy.

---

[1] I use members' own language to describe sexual identity and the churches' "inclusive" stance. "Lesbian- and gay-affirming" churches welcome lesbians and gay men as full members and clergy. Though members occasionally described their churches as "LGBT" -affirming, non-heterosexuals were usually subsumed under the term "gay." Because participants naturalized sexuality (hetero/homo) as God given, the language of inclusion rarely upset dualistic notions of sexuality (or gender).

[2] Following members' language, I use the term "black" to designate people of African Diaspora living in the United States. For some members, the term African American leaves out black first-generation immigrants and those who do not, for whatever reason, identify as African American.

[3] Though class is always defined in historical, relational, and race- and gender-specific terms (Bettie 2003), I typify the class status of church members based on socioeconomic status (income, occupation, and educational attainment). While this is useful for descriptive purposes, many black Faith Church members (some of whom I categorize as working class) viewed themselves as middle class and upwardly mobile.

[4] Conservative Christians often cite Genesis 19:1–29, Leviticus 18:19–23, Deuteronomy 23:17–8, I Corinthians 6:9–11 and Romans 1:26–27, among other verses, as proof that homosexual sex is an abomination before God. The Bible [refers] to homosexual acts as sinful or unnatural in at least six passages.

How did lesbian, gay, and straight-but-affirming church members construct and perform good Christian identities in the face of this stigma? From a social constructionist perspective, . . . identity does not represent a person's essence; people "do" identities differently across contexts and situations. These church members drew on Christian discourses surrounding sexuality (e.g., monogamy as the moral ideal for sexual relations) that circulate in the culture. But sexuality is never separate from other systems of domination, such as racism and sexism. I will argue that the strategies congregants used to construct and perform lesbian, gay, and straight-but-affirming Christian identities were shaped not only by the institutional and cultural contexts they occupied, but also by their differential locations in systems of race and gender inequality.

As such, this article moves beyond a difference-blind analysis by examining how race, gender, and sexuality—as distinct but intersecting systems that shape knowledge and identity—influenced members' resistance to a stigmatizing Christian ideology. Previous research has offered insight into how white gay men (Thumma 1991; Wolkomir 2006) and white lesbians (Mahaffy 1996) reconcile the conflict between gay/lesbian and Christian identities. Yet these studies have placed sexual-Christian identity negotiation at the analytical center, treating race and gender as secondary. . . . The church members I studied—black, white, lesbian, gay, and straight—all faced a conflict between Christianity and homosexuality. Yet they crafted different strategies to deal with this conflict. These group-specific strategies were rooted in their differential access to resources, power, and meanings. I contend that without examining how sexuality interacts with other social identities—in this case, race and gender—we cannot fully understand the forms and consequences of sexual identity in the contemporary United States. . . .

RESEARCH METHOD

From August 1998 to August 2002, I studied two lesbian- and gay-affirming churches in the Southeast. I observed and participated in worship services, Bible studies, holy unions[5], social events, and regional conferences (I spent over 200 hours in the field). I recorded detailed field notes from memory after fieldwork, and wrote notes-on-notes (Kleinman and Gopp 1993) to develop emerging themes. . . . I conducted 25 semi-structured, open-ended interviews (with 21 parishioners and the 4 pastors), which I tape-recorded and transcribed in full. . . . I also analyzed newsletters, local newspaper articles, listserve messages, and publications disseminated by the churches and their denominations. . . .

SETTINGS

Faith Church

I did participant observation and 11 in-depth interviews[6] with the pastor and lay members of Faith Church from August 1998 to August 2001. Part of the Universal Fellowship of Metropolitan Community Churches (MCC), Faith Church was a 60-member evangelical congregation in a midsize Southern city attended primarily by working class black lesbians. Pastor Paula[7], a

---

[5]Both churches held "holy unions" (same-sex commitment ceremonies). These unions were contentious in the local community; several ministers and congregations had recently been expelled from mainline Protestant denominations for violating church authority on this issue. As a result, the pastors made concerted efforts to "keep the media out of" these ceremonies.

[6]I interviewed 5 black lesbians, [1] black gay man, 5 white lesbians, and the pastor (Pastor Paula) at Faith Church. I used "theoretical sampling" (Glaser and Strauss 1967) to select interviewees using hypotheses that emerged in the field. As a white woman entering a predominantly black church. I hoped to gain enough rapport for participants to share their experiences with me. Therefore, I spent two years in the field before conducting interviews.

[7]All names have been changed to protect the anonymity of study participants.

black lesbian in her mid-30s, founded Faith Church in November of 1997. After serving as a "lay pastor" in a nearby white, gay male sister congregation, Pastor Paula had a vision that God was calling her to create a church home for black LGBT people, who, as she put it, were "marginalized by the white gay community *and* the Black Church."

Church members[8] ranged in age from 14 to 68, but most were in their late 30s and early 40s. The MCC is an ecumenical network that encourages a diversity of beliefs and practices within a Christian-Trinitarian theology. . . .

Given the MCC's loose structure[9] and most members' upbringing in black Baptist churches, their worship style and belief system resembled many contemporary black evangelical Christian churches, with the caveat that all God's children, including homosexuals, possess inherent dignity and worth and are welcome in the church. They were committed to creating an "inclusive" Christian community and to welcoming those who experienced conflict between their sexuality and their faith. The MCC *Mission Statement* reads:

We embody and proclaim Christian salvation and liberation, Christian inclusivity and community, and Christian social action and justice. We serve among those seeking and celebrating the integration of their spirituality and sexuality (UFMCC 2002).

Faith Church positioned itself as on the "vanguard" of Christianity. It vowed to "confront racism, sexism, and poverty through Christian social action" and to create a "new theology of sexuality." At the same time, the MCC distanced itself from a "gay" identity:

While we are often referred to as "The Gay Church," we are also very clear that this is a misnomer. The

phrase "Gay Church" seems to focus on its sexuality. We focus on Jesus Christ. A "Gay Church" would seem to be just for Gay people, we are a church for *all* people (emphasis in original) (UFMCC 2002).

As an MCC church, Faith Church focused on salvation through a personal relationship with Jesus. Faith Church members adapted liberationist language common in black churches to fit gay and lesbian experience. For example, members routinely testified that Jesus "freed" them from the "shackles" of sin and suffering and built a "fence" to protect them from the temptations of Satan and the world.

The leadership at Faith Church viewed the Bible as the inspired Word of God, to be interpreted within its historical context. Consistent with liberation theology, they argued that just as whites used the Bible to deny blacks rights and human dignity, heterosexuals use Scripture to exclude gays and lesbians from God's kingdom. A black lesbian church leader explained:

We live by the Word of God. But black people have always known there was a "Bible within a Bible;" there are stories . . . within the stories . . . it's not . . . the way white people use it. As a people, we have a history of reading the Bible [in a way] that nourishes our journey . . . and brings us closer to Jesus, our Lord and Savior (interview).

By reading the Bible in a way that "nourishe[d] [their] journey" and brought them "closer to Jesus," members claimed full membership in God's kingdom.

Unity Church

I also did participant observation and 14 in-depth interviews[10] with the pastors and gay and lesbian members of Unity Church between July 2001 and August 2002. Unity Church, part of the United Church of Christ (UCC), was a 550-member, predominantly white, middle class, liberal Protestant church in a southeastern university town. Founded in 1910, Unity Church

---

[8]At Faith Church, most members identified as lesbian and a few as gay, bisexual, or transgender. There were also children who attended with their parents. I exclude them from the demographic profile of the congregation.

[9]All congregations follow bylaws, directives, and policies dictated by the denomination, but local congregations have considerable autonomy to create their own style and identity. In the broader denomination, congregations range from evangelical to charismatic to liturgical to New Age.

[10]I interviewed 5 white lesbians, 2 white gay men, and Unity's 3 pastors (Beth, Gary, and Rebecca).

had a history of outreach for peace and justice and legitimacy as a mainline denomination that Faith Church lacked. Members described Unity as an "established," "inclusive," "liberal" alternative to the "exclusive" and "condemning" conservative Christian majority in the South. The UCC's New Testament emphasis encouraged members to model themselves— individually and as a group—after Jesus, who embraced and forgave all believers. Unity became lesbian and gay affirming in 1993 by a nearly unanimous congregational vote, two years after heterosexual parents with adult lesbian/gay children challenged the church to welcome homosexuals as an official church policy.

Unity was a mostly heterosexual, family-oriented congregation. There were three pastors: a white heterosexual couple (Beth and Gary), who were called to ministry in 1979, and a white lesbian associate pastor (Rebecca), who was called in 2000. Rebecca headed the youth ministry, but the heterosexual head pastors and lesbian/gay parishioners also expected her to counsel and befriend the gay/lesbian members since she was a lesbian. . . .

Most of Unity's heterosexual members had relocated to the South from the Northeast or Midwest, where they were raised liberal Protestant (e.g., Episcopal, United Church of Christ, Disciples of Christ). In contrast, most lesbian and gay members—about 10 percent[11] of the congregation—grew up Southern Baptist.[12] Like Faith Church, Unity encouraged parishioners to interpret the Bible in its historical context, an approach the pastors promoted in sermons and small group studies on "Sexuality and the Bible," "Bible Stories Through Different Eyes," and contemporary Christian books. . . . Members centered Unity's identity in inclusivity, often reciting the verse from Galatians 3:28 printed on the weekly bulletin: "In Christ there is neither Jew or Gentile, male or female, slave or free."

THE HOMOSEXUAL/CHRISTIAN CONFLICT

The lesbian, gay, and straight-but-affirming[13] Christians at Faith and Unity churches came to resist heteronormative conceptions of sexuality, gender, and the family because of the perceived identity conflict that they, their children, or their fellow church members faced. Raised as conservative Christians, most of the lesbian and gay members based their sense of themselves as good people on a set of beliefs that now condemned them as abominations before God. Some had been cast out of their home churches and birth families. Even those who were not still experienced feelings of guilt and shame. Emily, a 36-year-old white lesbian raised Southern Baptist, recalled:

Feeling like I was gay was against everything I knew about homosexuality in the Bible growing up, that gays and lesbians were not good people, and I had always considered myself a good person . . . I accepted Jesus Christ as my personal savior [at] 13 . . . so I struggled for years with . . . am I good, or am I not (interview)?

For Emily and others, being a Christian was a "moral identity" (Katz 1975; Kleinman 1996)— it signaled her worth as a person. Identifying as

---

[11]Unity's pastors and church members reported that 10 percent of the congregation was gay/lesbian, based on profiles in the church directory.

[12]Several gay and lesbian Unity members said in interviews that they would prefer to attend a church more like the conservative Christian churches of their upbringing, but that did not condemn homosexuals. Because such churches did not exist in the area, lesbian and gay members settled for a more "liberal" church. Unity members often noted that lesbian and gay members knew more about the Bible, and embraced a more literal biblical interpretation, than their heterosexual counterparts.

[13]While I interviewed Unity's heterosexual co-pastors. I did not interview heterosexual church members. However, I talked to everyone I could (while trying not to assume members' sexual identification) before and after church, at Bible studies, and at social events. The quotes I provide from heterosexual members come from their public avowals or informal conversation.

"gay" violated a biblical interpretation that, in no uncertain terms, marked her as not "a good person." This conflict was not easy to resolve. Most of these lesbians and gay men had relied on their Christian identity since childhood as evidence that they were good people; few could simply reject the Christian identity. But nor did they feel they could suppress their same-sex desires. "In retrospect," Emily continued, "I wish I'd known of a stable resource like the church I go to now, where I could have said, 'OK, I can be gay and be a quote unquote normal person.' These churches gave lesbian women and gay men a space to redefine their stigmatized sexuality by constructing and performing identities as lesbian/gay *and* Christian. In doing so, many lesbian and gay parishioners aligned their moral identity with their sexual identity and reclaimed a sense of dignity and worth.

Meanwhile, straight-but-affirming Christians did not face a sexual stigma directly. But they, too, had a reason to do oppositional identity work. The Unity members who challenged their church to become lesbian and gay affirming were parents of lesbian or gay children, and confronted a "courtesy stigma" (Goffman 1963) by virtue of that association. Thus, their identity as good middle class parents was threatened by an ideology that blames parents for their children's successes and failures (Berger 1981, Fields 2001). Additionally, all members—regardless of sexual identity—risked their Christian legitimacy by being part of a church that declared a lesbian- and gay-affirming mission. In short, identifying as a straight-but-affirming Christian in the Southern Bible Belt—where churches were expelled and pastors defrocked for accepting gays and lesbians—cast all members, as one put it, as "heretics or radicals" in the Christian eye. Thus, *all* members did oppositional identity work to disassociate from the heretic (religious) and radical (political) categories.

MINIMIZING, NORMALIZING, AND MORALIZING SEXUALITY

Drawing from the "cultural toolkits" of gay/lesbian culture and Christianity, lesbian, gay, and straight-but-affirming members used three group-specific strategies to construct and perform good Christian identities. While I treat these strategies as analytically distinct, members often drew on more than one in practice. First, some black lesbians *minimized* homosexuality by treating it as secondary to the Christian identity. Second, most lesbians and gay men—black and white—*normalized* their sexuality by enacting monogamy, manhood, or motherhood (this was the most common strategy). Third, some lesbian, gay, and straight-but-affirming members *moralized* the sexual-Christian identity: they defined themselves as more generous and moral than "condemning" Christians who excluded homosexuals. . . .

Minimizing

Members of mostly black, working class Faith Church were keenly aware of the image of homosexuality as abnormal and sinful. They believed that many heterosexuals in their communities, and even many black lesbians and gay men, dismissed "gay churches" as illegitimate. As Pastor Paula noted, to foreground sexuality was particularly discrediting in the black church, where talking about sex was taboo:

only once a month will the word "gay" come out of my mouth . . . When people come to church and hear something other than sex, sex, sex, they realize this is a real church, and gay people aren't all about sex. Especially in our community, the black community, sex is not something you talk about in church. [In other black churches] you know the pastor's got up with half the sisters in the front row, but it's understood: you just don't talk about it (interview).

Pastor Paula strove to present a good Christian image not only to her congregation, but also to black Christians who may disapprove of talk of sex or homosexuality. Pastor Paula routinely invoked the silence around sex and sexuality, common in black churches, to legitimize Faith Church and its members. She defined sexuality as separate from, and subordinate to, the core Christian self. An excerpt from one of her sermons typifies this message:

In my house, we worship the Lord. So if there's anyone who still thinks their sexuality gets in the way of having a relationship with Jesus, you need to talk to me. Despite all the garbage people tell us, y'all, we're Christians first and foremost . . . God loves us for who God made us to be, and our sexuality has nothing to do with that (field notes).

Members typically spoke of being lesbian or gay as how God made them to be, but here Pastor Paula uncoupled sexuality from the Christian identity. Why? By focusing on a relationship with Jesus—key to an evangelical Christian identity—she positioned Faith Church as a "real" church, and its members as "real" Christians. She deemed sexuality irrelevant, urging members to emphasize their faith in Jesus over all other identities.

A few black lesbian members minimized their lesbian identity by arguing that sexuality, like race, is irrelevant to one's character. When I asked Michelle, a 36-year-old black lesbian, if any Christian morals were important to her as a lesbian Christian, she said:

No, because . . . I like to keep the two separated. It's the same thing when people find out what church I go to. I'd like to see a point where people don't see it as a gay church, but just any other church. You know, if someone says, "I go to Baptist Rock," they don't think in terms of, that's a black church or a white church, or a gay church or a straight church, it's just a church (interview).

Michelle used color-blindness, as a parallel to sexuality-blindness, to ask that she be judged not by her race or sexuality, but by the content of her character (she added, "God loves me for being a Christian."). She moved sexuality and race to the background, defining herself as a Christian first. Fragmenting her race and sexuality from her core Christian identity enabled Michelle to deflect the stigma she faced as a black lesbian.

Though some black lesbians (e.g., Michelle and Pastor Paula) downplayed their race and sexuality, when I asked black lesbians in interviews which identity was most important to them, all but one considered race second to their Christian identity. As Joy, a 42-year-old black lesbian Faith Church member, testified in worship:

The first lessons I learned from my parents were, number one, I was black, and never to be ashamed of being black. Number two, people are gonna mistreat me because I'm black . . . I had to be strong . . . Being black was how I saw myself . . . sexuality came later, it wasn't as important (field notes).

Like many black women (King 1988), these black lesbians privileged race over other identities (e.g., gender and sexuality). Privileging the Christian identity lent them authenticity as black, while conferring them with the dignity and worth culturally associated with being a Christian. Insofar as many blacks regard black gays and lesbians as "selling out" to white gay culture (Cohen 1996; Greene 2000) and shaming "the race" (Giddings 1996; Griffin 2001), minimizing sexuality allowed black lesbians to construct and perform identities as both Christian and black. In a racially segregated context in which racism undermines the shared interests of black and white women, it is not surprising for black lesbians to seek solidarity not with other lesbian women, but with the black community. . . .

While these members minimized their sexual identities, they found comfort in the black lesbian community at Faith Church. They appreciated the cultural solidarity they found there, and the freedom to be open with their friends and lovers. It seemed that these members wanted to participate in a lesbian- and gay-affirming church, but rejected explicit talk about sex and sexuality, given the immoral meanings that homosexuality carried (recall Pastor Paula's assertion that "gay people aren't all about sex"). In addition to attending Faith Church, several black lesbians worshiped in traditional black Baptist or Pentecostal churches[14] where they were not "out" about their sexuality. This "double dipping," as one member dubbed it, helped them achieve dual goals: staying connected to the black community by attending a mainline church in the morning *and* "being who they were" by attending Faith Church in the afternoon. Seen in this way, these black lesbians resisted the imposition of a single sexual status, insisting on a complicated identity.

By minimizing homosexuality, black lesbians claimed dignity and worth as Christians. It is important to note, however, that this strategy defined lesbians as good Christians only within church walls. In the world outside, minimizing sexuality upheld a heterosexual assumption. Given deep-seated biblical prohibitions against same-sex activity, church members would presumably have to remain celibate or hide their sexuality to be seen as Christians. Minimizing allowed black lesbians to accommodate to heteronormativity, the view that "heterosexuality constitutes the standard for legitimate and proscriptive social sexual arrangements" (Ingraham 1996:169). But it left the belief in homosexual sin unchallenged. Just as Patricia Hill Collins (2005 argues that women experience sexism differently by virtue of their race, black and white lesbians suffer the costs of heterosexism differently. These costs—which stemmed from their positions in systems of race, gender, and sexual inequality—help explain the divergent identity work of white and black lesbian church members. Specifically, white lesbians' "whiteness" or

belonging in a "white community" was not threatened by explicit talk of their sexuality. For at least some black lesbians, however, the cost of being ostracized from the black community seemed too high to challenge the institutional structures (e.g., heterosexual marriage) and cultural ideologies (e.g., homosexuality as sinful) that privilege heterosexuality in the culture.

Normalizing

Most lesbian and gay members—black and white—*normalized* their sexual identities as part of who they were as Christians. This strategy was encapsulated on a t-shirt church members wore to an MCC conference: "Just your average Christian." The majority of lesbian and gay members in both churches performed normal ("average") Christian identities by invoking and enacting three biblical discourses: manhood (Faith Church), motherhood (Faith and Unity Churches), and monogamy (Faith and Unity Churches). Lesbian and gay members used this strategy to claim that they were "normal" in spite of their sexuality. . . .

Monogamous Relationships. Both churches affirmed same-sex couples through holy union ceremonies, couples' retreats, communion[15] and prayer blessings. By constructing and performing monogamy, same-sex couples—with the support of their straight allies—both accommodated to *and* challenged a heterosexual definition of marriage.

Several white lesbians and gay men I interviewed at Unity Church viewed secular lesbian and gay communities as immoral. Attending a mostly straight-but-affirming church allowed them to be "who God made them to be" (as they put it) and live by Christian morals. For example, when I noted that some gays and lesbians reject

---

[14]Service was held on Sunday afternoon, and several black lesbian/gay parishioners also attended morning services at mainstream black Baptist or Pentecostal churches. I did not meet any white lesbian or gay Christians who attended mainstream white churches in addition to Faith or Unity Church.

[15]At Faith Church, members could receive communion as a "family" with their partners and/or children (rather than strictly as individuals). Partnered members typically received communion and a prayer blessing as a couple.

Christianity because it condemns them, Patty, a 35-year-old-white lesbian Unity member, said:

Well, maybe they feel guilty, because it's just like being heterosexual. If you're gay, and you sleep around all the time, yeah, I have a problem with that, you know, in the community ... A lot of lesbians do that, I have friends who do that, and I'm like, okay?! ... I'm not a follower, I never have been (interview).

Patty interpreted my comment as a question of sexual behavior, not sexual orientation. She distanced herself from a promiscuous lesbian community and its sexual norms ("I'm not a follower, I never have been"), claiming a Christian identity by invoking her ten-year relationship with her female partner. In doing so, she challenged a definition of good Christian relationships as exclusively heterosexual, even as her claim to a normal Christian identity relied on an image of lesbians as "sleep[ing] around all the time." Patty thus reinforced an image of promiscuous lesbians in order to construct a Christian identity inclusive of long-term same-sex couples.

Unity lesbians also did oppositional identity work by differentiating themselves from church members they saw as confirming the promiscuous stereotype. In an interview, I asked Grace, a 63-year-old white lesbian, if most Unity members were single or coupled. She said Unity was a "family church" and that most were "married." She added:

But there is one [lesbian] woman who is always getting in different relationships with several different folks ... I think people are concerned about her spiritual growth and would like to see her settle down with somebody ... [I: What do pastors Beth and Gary think?] Well, they try not to be judgmental ... we all do, but I think they'd like to see her take relationships more seriously (interview).

While I posed the question in sexuality-neutral terms, Grace pointed to a single lesbian instead of the many single heterosexuals she could have invoked. She symbolically resisted the definition of "marriage" as one-man-one-woman, which was the standard even within the church. Though she couched her disapproval in nonjudgmental language, she cast this single lesbian as lacking in spiritual maturity. It was not simply that this woman was nonmonogamous ("always getting in different relationships with several different folks") but also that she was not mature in her relationship with Christ ("people are concerned about her spiritual growth and would like to see her settle down with somebody"). Like Patty (above), Grace challenged a heterosexual definition of marriage, normalizing monogamous lesbians and gay men by setting them off from those who have yet to "settle down" and become spiritually mature.

Images of lesbians in popular culture also offered foils against which white lesbians defined themselves as normal. In one group study of "Sexuality and the Bible," Unity's white lesbian associate pastor Rebecca gave an example of a lesbian couple who had come to her for pastoral counseling. During the counseling, one of the women disclosed that she was married to a man. Rebecca continued:

This happens more in same-sex couples than you'd think! I told them: "Your relationship is not an abomination because you are two women, but it *is* an abomination because you're breaking the covenant one of you made before God!" Just like, I see a lot of people in serial relationships, hopping from one bed to the next, without concern for the person [someone in back shouts: "Anne (Heche) and Ellen (Degeneres)!" *Rebecca laughs*] Exactly! It's not about same-sex or opposite-sex, it's about treating your partner with love and respect (field notes).

... By distinguishing lesbians in long-term relationships from lesbian bed-hoppers, Rebecca offered members a model for constructing and performing a lesbian Christian identity.

The white lesbians' normalizing strategy emphasized their similarity to straight Christians and distanced them from the perceived promiscuity of the lesbian world. They accommodated to heteronormative notions of monogamy and marriage, while refusing to assimilate (e.g., through abstinence, heterosexuality, or "aversion therapy").... They expanded of Christian community to include lesbian and gay Christians in monogamous, long-term relationships.

Black lesbians at Faith Church also valued monogamy, but performed it differently. When a group of black lesbian church leaders began to hold holy union ceremonies in 2001. I noted that the masculine-identified partner in these butch-fem couples was often congratulated for "turning in [their] player's card." At Faith Church, members referred to a group of six butch lesbians as the "mack daddies."[16] This group shrank during my fieldwork: by 2001, only one mack daddy remained because all the others had held union ceremonies with their partners.[17] The mack daddies held honorary status at Faith Church because they embodied redemption. They served as testaments to how God, and the church, changes lives. For example, when I asked why she attended Faith Church, Stacy, a black lesbian church leader, said:

One way I know this church is so powerful is hearing how people have changed . . . when people talk about how God has moved in their life. You see that. Look at J.R. now. She's in a loving relationship with Barbara, she has a good woman who really loves her. You never would've thought it could happen—ten years ago she had so many women she could man a basketball team . . . She had a woman for every role on the team . . . she was out there mackin' and playin' people. But God put Barbara in her life. God has a way of doing that for people (interview).

With the support of their peers, the Faith Church mack daddies used gender bending to atone for "sinful" behaviors like "mackin' and playin' people." They invoked a masculine trope with great currency in mainstream black culture—i.e., being saved from a "player's life" by a "good woman"—to perform identities as good black Christians who were committed to the church and family (Boyd 1997; [Kelley] 1996). The mack daddy image normalized black lesbians as good Christians, in part, because it rooted their identities in black culture. It mapped their spiritual growth from a life of "running the streets" and "using people," as J. R. put it in a testimony, to being "at peace." . . . The transformation from mack daddy to monogamous Christian was a way to claim a real *black* self, a self that was respectable and upwardly mobile according to common understandings of upward mobility in the culture.

By performing butch-fem monogamy, black lesbians creatively subverted a biblical gender order based on male-female complementarity. By modeling their relationships on a masculine leader/provider and a feminine nurturer/helper, they defined themselves as monogamous and normally gendered. At the same time, the mack daddies—not their "good woman" partners—were singled out and celebrated for being monogamous. Black lesbians who "did" a feminine or androgynous style could not draw on the mack daddy trope as readily. Members viewed the mack daddies' fem-performing partners as "good"—loving, nurturing—women whose duty it was to reign in and redeem the butches. By performing identities as "honorary men," then, the mack daddies challenged a *biological* view of male headship as natural. But they reinforced femininity as subordinate: the value of a good woman depended on her relationship with an (honorary) man (Wilkins 2007). The "reformed player" narrative thus cemented masculine privilege: only the masculine-performing butches got extra points for doing monogamy and settling down. The fem "good women" were only doing what was expected of them. . . .

Given Faith Church members' belief that men are God's chosen leaders of the church

---

[16]The mack daddy icon arose in 1970s "blackploitation" films and persists as a common metaphor in hip-hop culture. The mack daddy is a pimp-like figure (typically a man) who has many women at his disposal. Similarly, a "player" is a charming, hypermasculine man who engages in sex with many women.

[17]The last remaining mack daddy said in an interview that members often passed her notes during service to ask when she and her partner of six months were getting married. She saw this as flattering, but didn't feel "ready" to have a holy union.

and family (discussed later), gender bending both challenged heteronormativity and reinforced a two-gender system that devalues the feminine. Also, while gender bending legitimated butch lesbians as leaders and providers inside the church, it may not have helped them appear normal outside church walls.

Faith Church's Pastor Paula also drew on cultural meanings and symbols associated with masculinity to accommodate (but not assimilate) her lesbian relationship to a male-female, pastor-pastor's wife model. Like the mack daddies, this butch-fem performance legitimated her as a lesbian pastor: she was the leader of her family, and her church, with a good woman as her "backbone." Church members referred to her partner, Wendy, as "the pastor's wife" or the "first spouse." They often recognized Wendy as a "good woman" who was willing to sacrifice her interests for the pastor's career. Wendy sang in the choir, but told a local newspaper reporter that she chose not to serve in leadership, though she was able, because she was the "pastor's wife." Pastor Paula wore pants suits or robes when she preached[18]. Wendy always wore dresses or skirts to church (but rarely outside it), accentuating her femininity. Arranging their "expressive equipment" (Goffman 1959) in conventionally gendered ways helped Pastor Paula to "do" a symbolically masculine pastoral identity because she had a good woman as her helper.

In private, I often heard Wendy voice frustration with the burdens of being a pastor's wife.[19] In public, however, she upheld an image as an upright Christian woman who put her own interests and needs second to those of the pastor. Associate Pastor Rebecca at Unity did not (in interviews or church services) perform masculinity, nor did her partner act as a feminine "pastor's wife" (though Rebecca and her partner frequently cited the fact that they had held a holy union). Considering the emphasis on supporting women clergy and combating sexism in the UCC, a masculine performance would likely have seemed out of place for Associate Pastor Rebecca. Nor did the white lesbians at Unity *need* to play up their masculinity, because their whiteness gave them a respect and "normal" status that is denied to black lesbians in a racist society. For Pastor Paula, a masculine clergy identity seemed to confer legitimacy as a normally gendered (i.e., masculine) pastor in the black (heterosexual) Christian world. Masculinity conferred respect, bringing her closer to being a "real" pastor even though she was female.

Monogamy lent same-sex couples normal and moral status, but threatened Faith Church's "inclusive" identity and reinstated hierarchies among sexual minorities as a group. This came to light when Se'von, a butch black lesbian, attended church in April 2001 with two fem-performing black women dressed in black, who were ostensibly her lovers. Wearing leather collars etched with the moniker "love slave," they accompanied her arm in arm. Se'von had been an active member during Faith Church's early years (1997 through 1999), when she served as the sound system manager and held a union ceremony at the church with a previous partner. . . .

Se'von's appearance constituted a . . . test of the group's inclusive identity. Pastor Paula welcomed Se'von as the threesome entered the church foyer. Some members shot each other confused or disapproving looks as they spotted her "love slaves;" others acknowledged her with nods or handshakes. The respect vanished when Se'von and her partners stepped into the

---

[18]In part because the Unity pastors dressed in pastoral robes, clothing was not a resource they used to perform gender identities (though pastoral robes clearly signified a clergy identity).

[19]At house parties, regional conferences, and Pride events, I often traveled in members private worlds. When Wendy attended these events alone, she always expressed relief from the pressure to "represent" herself as the pastor's wife, even though she affirmed her love for Pastor Paula.

communion line toward the end of service. It was customary for the Pastor to bless couples and families (in addition to individuals) in communion at Faith Church. But when Se'von approached the altar with her lovers, members shifted uncomfortably in their seats and looked at one another with raised eyebrows. Pastor Paula offered them communion and a distinctly rushed prayer.

The three then moved to the left to receive a prayer blessing from a lay leader; she turned her head to avoid them. Seeing this, Se'von shuffled her lovers over to the next lay leader in line. That lay leader paused, looking to Pastor Paula for direction. She gave them a short blessing, avoiding physical contact. At the end of service, Se'von and her partners exited quickly; rudely (in Faith's church culture), she hurried her lovers out the door without lining up to greet Pastor Paula. As I sat with members at the potluck, there seemed to be an awkward silence. Finally, a black lesbian at the table said, "I guess they're right, we just gonna do whatever: homosexuality, polygamy, bestiality!" A black lesbian church leader responded: "You talkin' bout the love slaves? That is *not* who we are. *That* was just some drama." The use of a "slave" image in a black church was likely part of the reason members took offense. Still, the importance of monogamy to members' collective identity as normal and moral was striking. Faith Church celebrated its "inclusive" identity, but multiple partners (especially "love slaves") were not acceptable. Se'von's identity performance seemed to stain the normal and morally respectable image Faith Church members strove to uphold.

Same-sex couples received support in these churches that the heterosexual world lacks (Weston 1991). By recognizing same-sex relationships, church members redefined heterosexual monogamy—and made a symbolic claim for marriage—to include same-sex couples. However, using monogamy to be normal and moral meant being only selectively inclusive.

Particularly in the Southern Bible Belt, for lesbian and gay Christians to be inclusive of sexual practices such as sado-masochism (SM) and polyamory clearly violated the boundary of a good Christian.

Manhood. Some working class black gay men at Faith Church normalized their homosexuality by "doing" Christian manhood; and for their part, many black lesbians encouraged their performance. In contrast, the white upper middle class gay men at Unity never claimed male headship. This reflected both the institutional context (the UCC rejects male headship as unbiblical) and members' social locations. Whereas working class black gay men are denied many of the privileges of masculinity by their class, race, and sexuality (Anderson 1999; Majors and Billson 1992), the white middle class gay men at Unity came closer to (hetero)normal because of the moral and cultural currency their high-paying jobs, monogamous relationships, and whiteness offered.

In 1999, Pastor Paula often asked Leonard, a black gay man ordained in the Holiness Church, to preach. After the Columbine shootings, he gave the following sermon:

Everywhere you look—even here at Faith Church, y'all—men are not taking up the battle, we're not being soldiers of the Lord. The Bible tells us men have to be the providers, no matter whether we're gay or bisexual or heterosexual, we're supposed to be the leaders of the family and the church . . . Men aren't doing their part, and our families are falling apart. When I was coming up, it never would've crossed my mind to shoot someone, or even touch that gun, because my daddy was 6 foot 6 inches tall and he would of killed me . . . he would of brought me back and shot me again, just to teach me a lesson (field notes).

Invoking biblical literalism, Leonard asserted a normal Christian identity as a gay man. He included gay and bisexual men within a biblical notion of male headship, normalizing gay and bisexual black men as heads of household and leaders of the church. It is important to note that this sermon was situated in the wider cultural discourse of the "crisis of the black male" (Anderson 1999) and black family "pathology" (Moynihan 1965). Seen in this way, Leonard strove to redeem black men, regardless of sexuality, as good Christians and real men. He distanced himself from stereotypes of black (heterosexual) men as lazy and irresponsible *and* black gay and bisexual men as traitors of the black family and community (Hutchinson 2001; Cohen 1996). . . .

The dominant masculinity that Leonard valorized left little room for black lesbians to craft a positive identity. Black women and lesbians are not only excluded from leadership in many white circles, but their leadership in black communities and black churches has been constrained by the belief that black men are the natural leaders and representative of the race (Collins 2000; [Hooks] 1992). . . . This may help us to unpack black lesbians' seemingly ironic support for a belief in "natural" male headship. In response to Leonard's sermon, many of the black lesbians in attendance called out "Amen," and "Preach, brother!" They gave Leonard a standing ovation. When I asked Yvette, a 42-year-old black lesbian church leader, what she thought of the sermon, she said:

I support any brother who's called to preach in this church. I think a lot of brothers are intimidated by all these women. [What do you think of him saying men are supposed to be the leaders and providers?] Well, the Bible does say that. There's no gettin' around it (field notes).

While church members challenged a literal interpretation of homosexuality as sinful, Leonard, Yvette, and others left a biblical reading of men as heads of household and church intact. Their gendered and raced performance of "normal" Christian identity emerged in a social context where many black communities seek to restore the "absent" black man in the church and family (Lincoln 1965; Staples 1999). Privileging black men showed that black lesbians

were not man-haters (Pharr 1988), but normal black women who, as members proclaimed in worship, "love their brothers." The assumption seemed to be that supporting black men would uplift the entire black community, including black women.

The changing demographics of Faith Church—which was about 30 percent male and 90 percent black in 1998, and almost 100 percent female and 30 percent white by 2001—likely contributed to this response. When Leonard delivered this sermon, Faith Church had lost most of its male members. Many of the black gay men who attended early on in the church's history now attended a largely white gay male church nearby (where Pastor Paula had formerly served as a lay pastor). Only one black gay man remained from Faith Church's founding, and less than five men attended service weekly. As in some black student organizations (Kolb 2007), the flight of black men threatened the church's legitimacy in the eyes of outsiders and members alike. Pastor Paula said, "We serve the whole community . . . without men, people don't see us as a real church." As a result, members often discussed how to attract more (black gay) men. When I asked black men why they preferred the mostly gay male church, some mentioned dating prospects; others said going to a church where they could see images of themselves felt "right." In contrast, several black lesbians I interviewed blamed women who "had issues with men" or were "not welcoming" for driving black gay men out of church. One member exclaimed in an interview, "some people don't like men, and if they don't, they can just get out!"

I never heard the white lesbians at Unity blame one another for man-hating or dividing the community. Again, this was consistent with Unity Church's support for gender equality *and* members' social identities. Unlike Faith Church, which was mostly black lesbian and losing men rapidly, Unity Church was about 40 percent white heterosexual male. The few black gay men who still attended Faith Church were working class and gay identified. They confronted symbolic and material barriers that white heterosexual and white gay men at Unity did not: as working class gay black men, they were seen as needing support to take responsibility as leaders of the church and the race. For many at Faith Church, being "normal" Christians meant defending black manhood *and* the racial authenticity of black gays and lesbians. It seemed that white Unity Church lesbians had more freedom to challenge male authority because they didn't have to defend their (white) brothers. . . .

Motherhood. White lesbians mobilized "family values," a discourse with considerable moral currency in Southern religion and politics (and the culture at large), to normalize their sexuality. Invoking and enacting "good mother" identities allowed them to accommodate to the "Christian family" while resisting its heterosexual exclusivity (Lewin 1993). Although the few gay men in the churches did not make claims to fatherhood, they supported white lesbians' "good mother" performances.

In U.S. culture, as in Christianity, "mother" is a moral identity; it confers moral worth on those who enact it (McMahon 1995). But not all women have the resources to achieve this. As a result, white middle class heterosexual married women are more likely than others to be seen as worthy (McMahon 1995; Solinger 2000). Black single mothers, on the other hand, are often blamed for the decline of the black community (Kaplan 1997). Further, the ideology of "intensive mothering"—which urges mothers to devote "large quantities of money . . . professional-level skills and copious amounts of physical, moral, mental, and emotional energy" (Hays 1996:4) to child rearing—sets up an ideal that only middle and upper class mothers can afford. It was in this context that white middle class lesbian couples—whose race and class privileges brought them closest to this cultural ideal of the "good mother"—invoked motherhood. Working class black lesbians, many of whom were single and had children from previous heterosexual relationships, *never* invoked motherhood to define themselves as normal Christians.

White lesbians drew on their unmarked (Phelan 1993) identities as white and middle class to define themselves as "good mothers" despite being lesbian. When I asked how she thought church members viewed her, Peggy, a 42-year-old white lesbian at Unity, said:

We have a great family, our family is kind of different than everybody else's, but we have the same struggles, the same trials, and the same joys any other family with a four-year-old has. And I think that's how we're seen in the church, as just another family with a young child. It doesn't matter that we have two moms, which I think is great (interview). . . .

White gay men and lesbians at Unity noted repeatedly in interviews how "impressive" and "wonderful" it was that lesbian mothers were accepted by heterosexuals in the church. The performance of motherhood thus normalized white lesbians as good Christian women, while signaling that gays and lesbians, as a group, moved in the mainstream of church life.

Like the white lesbians at Unity, white lesbians at predominantly black Faith Church normalized their lesbian identities by invoking their status as mothers, or soon-to-be-mothers. In August 2002, members invited a white lesbian couple to church to celebrate their son's baptism. Pastor Paula spoke of the trials this couple had faced in adopting the child from Guatemala:

We know this child is blessed. He had prayer warriors to get him here. They believed in the power of prayer, y'all! They put their hearts and souls on the line to ask God to send him. His mothers, and people in this church, prayed 24/7, without fail, to get him here safe and sound. His mothers loved God so much, and God blessed them (field notes).

These white lesbians had never attended Faith Church, and did not attend any other church. Yet their status as white middle class monogamous mothers seemed to give them immediate normal and moral legitimacy....

In my three years of fieldwork—after such claims had become scripted in the church discourse—black lesbians *never* invoked motherhood as a moral identity. This was all the more striking in light of the value and recognition accorded to mothers in many black communities (Collins 2000). Even on Mother's Day, black lesbians testified about the strength and sacrifices of their own mothers (not themselves). Perhaps their status as black single mothers, which can signify a moral failure of the black community, explains their distancing from the identity of "mother" (Kaplan 1997). Lacking the resources to accomplish a good mother identity, they sought other ways to signify their worth.

The only time a black lesbian referenced her identity as a mother during my fieldwork was when confessing to feeling like a "bad" mother. Vera, a single black lesbian in her late 30s, testified about the hardships she faced as a single mother:

They say love makes a family, and that's really nice, but money holds a family together. With my boys, I never felt I could raise 'em right... they needed a man in their lives... Anyone who knows me will tell you I love my kids more than life itself, but I couldn't shake the feeling that I was a bad mother. I was a single mother, working at Wal-Mart, doing what I could to support them... I did things I'll always regret. I gave my kids up 'cause I thought [other family members] could take care of 'em better than I could... But God worked it out, thank you Jesus (field notes)!

Vera's testimony makes sense in a culture that paints single black mothers as unworthy. She claimed victory in regaining custody of her kids, but her narrative highlights the material and cultural barriers that many women—especially poor, black, single, and/or lesbian—face to being seen as good mothers. Normalizing white middle class lesbian couples as good mothers masked the social, financial, and legal structures and norms that deny many same-sex parents (especially those without money) recognition as worthy parents—and in some cases exclude them from parenting at all. In addition, it relied on a traditional notion of femininity that bases women's worth on domesticity, nurturing, and reproduction (Hays 1996; Hochschild 1989).

Moralizing

A few black lesbians and gay men at Faith Church, and white straight-but-affirming members at Unity, *moralized* their sexuality. They claimed that their sexuality—lesbian, gay, or straight—gave them a special calling as Christians. Much like some gay men living with HIV/AIDS redefine their disease from a "curse" to a "blessing" by becoming HIV/AIDS educators and activists (Sandstrom 1990), some black lesbians and gay men at Faith Church saw in their stigmatized sexuality a mission to save lesbian/gay souls. Being a straight "ally" also lent moral authority for white heterosexuals at Unity: like heterosexual parents who "ennoble" themselves as especially generous and loving advocates for their gay or lesbian children (Fields 2001), Unity's heterosexual co-pastors and some straight-but-affirming members claimed a special calling, as straight allies, to make Christianity more inclusive.

A small number of black lesbians and gay men at Faith Church believed they were "called" to fight homophobia within Christianity. In a 1999 sermon, Rev. Howard Edgarton, a black gay Baptist minister who guest-preached at Faith Church five times during my fieldwork, announced his "crusade" to end prejudice against gay men living with HIV/AIDS. He prefaced his sermon by saying:

Even though I'm not a member of Faith Church, I'm a member in spirit. It's so wonderful to be in a church where I don't have to leave my sexuality at the door. That's what this church is all about... Because society has oppressed us . . . for so long, we finally had enough and started a place of our own . . . where nobody can tell us we're not God's children . . . we are God's children, y'all, and I venture to say that we might even be God's chosen ones (field notes). . . .

Church members responded to this message with far less enthusiasm than they had to Rev. Howard's previous sermons. At the post-service potluck, a black lesbian said, "Is that dude on a mission or what? I'm gay and I'm proud!" Another black lesbian replied: "I like to hear him preach, but tone it down a few notches, brother!" Pastor Paula, too, saw Rev. Howard (her longtime friend and colleague), as "too gay."[20] When I asked in an interview what she thought of his sermon, she said, "when people get up there and preach about gay, gay, gay, it takes away from [our focus, which is to] worship God." Though I observed Rev. Howard at church twice after this sermon, he was never invited to preach again. . . .

Erika, a black lesbian in her late 20s, also did oppositional identity work by moralizing her sexuality. She claimed a moral identity by ennobling her integrated lesbian-Christian identity. In August of 1998, she testified that God had called her to leave her home in the Deep South to embark on a faith journey. From my field notes:

I was stifled in my hometown . . . God told me I couldn't find my calling [there] . . . I was like David, an outcast of the community. God told me to go out on faith. I had to find a place where I could do what He was calling me to do . . . everything happens for a reason. I knew right away, y'all, this [church] was where God was calling me to go—I had to get away from the prejudice and the drama so I could find my calling as a preacher [and] let people know that being gay is a blessing.

Erika claimed a moral identity by teaching other lesbian and gay Christians that being gay

is not an abomination, but a "blessing." She suggested that Faith Church was more authentically Christian than her intolerant home community, and that her identity as a lesbian Christian gave her a mission to promote acceptance and save other lesbian/gay Christians from outcast status.

Erika, Rev. Edgarton, and two other members I interviewed defined their sexual marginalization as grounds for a special moral identity. . . . But most members, especially the pastor and church leaders, rejected the moralizing strategy. . . . Pastor Paula kept Erika at an arm's length, at least in part, because her attempts to highlight homosexuality might jeopardize their acceptance in the black heterosexual world. While moralizing constituted an identity work strategy for a few Faith Church members, it was more important because it exposed the collective boundary of a normal Christian that members took for granted. Like church members' disapproval of Se'von and her love slaves, their rejection of the homosexual moralizers showed the limits of their "inclusive" ideal. . . .

Back at Unity Church, the white straight-but-affirming members faced a "courtesy stigma" (Goffman 1963) through their association with the "sinful" identity and behavior of gay and lesbian members. Members believed that the homosexual stigma had led to the dissolution of the (mostly white heterosexual) choir's alliance with a nearby black (heterosexual) UCC church. Before Unity Church's decision to become lesbian and gay affirming, white members had traveled with the black choir members to perform in the United States and abroad. . . .

Members of the black church still sang at Unity's services, but left immediately after the opening hymns. And members no longer performed together outside of service. When I asked a white heterosexual choir member what happened, she said: "They've pretty much disowned us. They thought we were fringe before,

---

[20]The resistance of Pastor Paula and church members to Rev. Edgarton's sermon may have also been related to his more (religiously) charismatic and "feminine" style than the traditionally "masculine" image that Pastor Paula favored.

but the [lesbian- and gay-affirming decision] really put us out there, like we were heretics or radicals."

The leadership at Unity, especially the head co-pastors, countered the perception that they were "heretics or radicals" by defining lesbian and gay inclusion as an act of Christian love, true to Jesus's example, not a rejection of Christian tradition or a political position. They depoliticized lesbian and gay inclusion by highlighting Unity members' special calling to include those who were "different." In framing inclusion as a moral (not a political) act, they urged straight members to include gays and lesbians as an act of Christian charity. Head co-pastor Gary routinely used language that situated white middle class English-speaking heterosexuals as the normative group. By implication, it was the white heterosexual majority who received bonus points for including the marginalized, . . .

Similarly, some straight-but-affirming members came forward to publicly affirm gays and lesbians. For example, after lesbian associate pastor Rebecca testified during Lent about her struggle to accept her calling as a lesbian pastor, a heterosexual white woman stood up to say:

I give thanks and praise for this church, because I've been a member of exclusive churches, Baptist churches, holier-than-thou churches, my whole life. Thank you God . . . for leading me to a church that accepts everyone. I give all the thanks and praise to you, Jesus, for helping me and my husband become living examples of your love and grace.

Attaching a moral calling to heterosexual inclusion both challenged and reinforced heteronormativity. These Unity members took brave and progressive steps to combat homophobia in the church. But because members of dominant groups in our society (e.g., heterosexuals, whites) are not taught to recognize their privileges, or to see their ability to "include" others as a product of this privilege, church members failed to see that only privileged groups earned bonus points for being

inclusive. Claiming a moral mission to include the "other" is less workable for groups already defined as other in our society (e.g., lesbian and gay Unity and Faith Church members). . . .

CONCLUSION

These lesbian, gay, and straight-but-affirming Christians struggled to alter deep-seated beliefs and practices that defined heterosexuality as the index of a good Christian man or woman. In these churches, many lesbians and gay men found new families that accepted them, bringing them back into God's universal family. With this belonging they felt healed of the suffering and rejection that had burdened them. Thus, these church members created new possibilities for a Christian way of life in which homosexuality was seen as natural, normal, and potentially moral.

Both churches were committed to including all persons in community and challenging racism, sexism, poverty, and homophobia. But being inclusive, as a group ideal, was difficult if not impossible to achieve because church members' construction and performance of good Christian identities was enmeshed in race, class, gender, and sexual meanings and hierarchies in the church and society. For example, by essentializing sexuality and defining its expression as proper only in two forms—hetero- or homosexual monogamy—members made the churches less inclusive to bisexuals, transgender people, and gender and sexual nonconformists who seek freedom from sexual roles and hierarchies. As well, family values discourses are encoded with race and class assumptions that may not be fully inclusive of lesbians and gay men who, by virtue of their race and/or class identities, can accommodate less easily to a white middle class ideal of parenting and family (Collins 2000). . . .

These findings . . . call "inclusivity" itself into question on two levels. First, discourses around inclusivity characteristically imply that one group (the socially privileged) should accept another group (the others). This reinscribes the subordination of the others by framing them as in need of help and approval and gives credit for the act of inclusion to the privileged group. . . . Second, church members' inclusive ideal created an expectation that they would include and affirm all people in community. This was perhaps impossible to do in practice. Most churches, including these, promote morals and standards about what is acceptable—they do not welcome everyone or affirm all behaviors. The inclusive ideal made it difficult for church leaders to enforce the Christian morals and standards they valued without being seen as hypocritical (i.e., not "inclusive"). Church members were sincere in their desire to include all and to create safe spaces of freedom, equality, and acceptance. But when inclusivity appeared to threaten core traditions, morals, or beliefs, inclusivity took a back seat to church authority. And perhaps rightly so. Christian communities rely on the creation and maintenance of boundaries; churches are not a place where anything goes.

Faith-based constructions of homosexuality and LGBT rights are gaining popularity as a way to reclaim "moral values" from the conservative right. For example, advocates for marriage equality argue that the legalization of same-sex marriage will expand family values to include all regardless of sexual orientation, thereby integrating lesbians and gay men in mainstream culture (e.g. Sullivan 1995). Likewise, many lesbian, gay, and straight-but-affirming members of these churches implicitly or explicitly mobilized a discourse of family values to argue for lesbian and gay inclusion in Christianity. But the normalizing strategy they favored relied on conventionally gendered discourses and practices grounded in white middle class respectability: monogamy, manhood, and motherhood. These findings indicate that normalizing lesbian/gay identity through a moral discourse of "family values"

may not liberate all lesbians and gay men equally. Instead, it seems to benefit those already closest to the mainstream (Cohen 1997). This matters not only for understanding how faith shapes the construction of homosexuality as a social problem, but also for political strategizing in the struggle for LGBT rights. Lesbian and gay liberation can never be achieved without challenging racism, sexism, and class inequalities.

To fully understand sexual-religious identity negotiation, we must analyze the other identities that shape people's lives. Considering race, gender, religion, and sexuality together reveals the necessity of putting intersectional frameworks into practice empirically. As . . . scholars have shown, when groups challenge one boundary (e.g., sexuality) they may reinforce others (e.g., gender and race) (e.g., Wilkins 2007). . . .

REFERENCES

AMMERMAN, NANCY. 1987. *Bible Believers: Fundamentalists in the Modern World.* New Brunswick, NJ: Rutgers University Press.

ANDERSON, ELIJAH. 1999. *Code of the Street: Decency, Violence, and the Moral Life of the Inner City.* New York: W.W. Norton & Company, Inc.

BARTKOWSKI, JOHN. 2001. *Remaking the Godly Marriage: Gender Negotiation in Evangelical Families.* New Brunswick, NJ: Rutgers University Press.

BERGER, BENNETT. 1981. *The Survival of a Counterculture: Ideological Work and Everyday Life among Rural Communards.* Berkeley: University of California Press.

BETTIE, JULIE. 2003. *Women without Class: Girls, Race, and Identity.* Berkeley: University of California Press.

BOYD, TODD. 1997. *Am I Black Enough For You?* Bloomington: Indiana University Press.

BURKLO, JIM. 2000. *Open Christianity: Home by Another Road.* Los Altos, CA: Rising Star Press.

BUTLER, JUDITH. 1990. *Gender Trouble: Feminism and the Subversion of Identity.* New York: Routledge.

COHEN, CATHY. 1996. "Contested Membership: Black Gay Identities and the Politics of AIDS." Pp. 362–59 in *Queer Theory/Sociology,* edited by Steven Seidman. Cambridge, MA: Blackwell.

———. 1997. "Punks, Bulldaggers, and Welfare Queens: The Radical Potential of Queer Politics?" *GLQ: A Journal of Gay and Lesbian Studies* 3(4):437–65.

COLLINS, PATRICIA HILL. 2000. *Black Feminist Thought: Knowledge, Consciousness, and the Politics of Empowerment.* [2nd] ed. New York: Routledge.

———. 2005. *Black Sexual Politics.* New York: Routledge.

COMSTOCK, GARY DAVID. 1996. *Unrepentant, Self-Affirming Practicing: Lesbian/Gay/Bisexual People within Organized Religion.* New York: Continuum.

———. 2001. *A Whosoever Church: Welcoming Lesbians and Gay Men into African American Congregations.* Louisville, KY: Presbyterian Publishing Corporation.

CONE, JAMES. 1975. *God of the Oppressed.* San Francisco: Seabury Press.

———. 1984. *For My People: Black Theology and the Black Church.* Maryknoll, NY: Orbis Books.

DALY, MARY. 1975. *The Church and the Second Sex.* New York: Harper & Row.

DENTON, MELINDA. 2004. "Gender and Marital Decision Making: Negotiating Religious Identity and Practice." *Social Forces* 82(3): 1151–80.

ELLINGSON, STEPHEN, NELSON TEBBE, MARTHA VAN HAITSMA, and EDWARD LAUMANN. 2001. "Religion and the Politics of Sexuality." *Journal of Contemporary Ethnography* 30(1):3–55.

FIELDS, JESSICA. 2001. "Normal Queers: Heterosexual Parents Respond to Their Children's Coming Out." *Symbolic Interaction* 24(4):165–87.

FOSTER, DAVID KYLE. 1995. *Sexual Healing.* Nashville, TN: Mastering Life Ministries.

FOUCAULT, MICHEL. 1972. *The Archaeology of Knowledge.* New York: Pantheon.

GALLAGHER, SALLY and CHRISTIAN SMITH. 1999. "Symbolic Traditionalism and Pragmatic Egalitarianism: Contemporary Evangelicals, Family, and Gender." *Gender & Society* 13(2):211–33.

GIDDINGS, PAULA. 1996. *On When and Where I Enter: The Impact of Black Women on Race and Sex in America.* New York: Quill/W. Morrow.

GLASER, BARNEY and ANSELM STRAUSS. 1967. *The Discovery of Grounded Theory.* Chicago: Aldine de Gruyter.

GOFFMAN, ERVING. 1959. *Presentation of Self in Everyday Life.* Garden City, NY: Anchor Doubleday.

———. 1963. *Stigma: Notes on the Management of a Spoiled Identity.* Englewood Cliffs, NJ: Prentice Hall.

GRAMSCI, ANTONIO. 1971. *Selections from the Prison Notebooks.* New York: International Publishers.

GREENE, BEVERLY. 2000. "African American Lesbian and Bisexual Women." *Journal of Social Issues* 56(2):239–49.

GRIFFIN, HORACE. 2001. "Their Own Received Them Not: African-American Lesbians and Gays in Black Churches." Pp. 110–25 in *The Greatest Taboo: Homosexuality in Black Communities,* edited by Delroy Constantine-Simms. Los Angeles: Alyson Publications.

HAYS, SHARON. 1996. *The Cultural Contradictions of Motherhood.* New Haven, CT: Yale University Press.

HERSH, BLANCHE Glassman. 1978. *The Slavery of Sex: Feminist-Abolitionists in America.* Urbana: University of Illinois.

HOCHSCHILD, ARLIE. 1989. *The Second Shift.* New York: Penguin Books.

[HOOKS, BELL.] 1992. *Black Looks: Race and Representation.* Boston: South End Press.

HUTCHINSON, EARL OFARI. 2001. "My Gay Problem, Your Black Problem." Pp. 2–7 in *The Greatest Taboo: Homosexuality in Black Communities,* edited by Delroy Constantine-Simms. New York: Alyson Books.

INGRAHAM, CHRYS. 1996. "The Heterosexual Imaginary: Feminist Sociology and Theories of Gender." Pp. 168–94 in *Queer Theory/Sociology,* edited by Steven Seidman. Cambridge, MA: Blackwell.

KAPLAN, ELAINE BELL. 1997. *Not our Kind of Girl: Unraveling the Myths of Teenage Motherhood.* Berkeley: University of California Press.

KATZ, JACK. 1975. 'Essences as Moral Identities: Verifiability and responsibility in Imputations of Deviance and Charisma." *American Journal of Sociology* 80(6): 1369–90.

[KELLEY, ROBIN.] 1996. "Kickin' Reality, Kickin' Ballistics: Gangsta Rap and Postindustrial Los Angeles." Pp. 117–58 in *Droppin' Science,* edited by W. E. Perkins. Philadelphia: Temple University Press.

KLEINMAN, SHERRYL. 1996. *Opposing ambitions: Gender and Identity in Alternative Health Organizations.* Chicago: University of Chicago Press.

KING, DEBORAH. 1988. "Multiple Jeopardy, Multiple Consciousness: The Context of a Black Feminist Ideology." *Signs* 14(1):42–72.

KLEINMAN, SHERRYL and MARTHA COPP. 1983. *Emotions and Fieldwork.* Thousand Oaks, CA: Sage.

KOLB, KENNETH. 2007. "Supporting Our Black Men: Reproducing Male Privilege in a Black Student Organization." *Sociological Spectrum* 27(3):257–74.

LEWIN, ELLEN. 1993. *Lesbian Mothers: Accounts of Gender in American Culture.* Ithaca, NY: Cornell University Press.

LINCOLN, C. ERIC. 1965. "The Absent Father Haunts the Negro Family." *New York Times Magazine,* Nov. 28, pp. SM60–SM65.

MAHAFFY, KIMBERLY. 1996. "Cognitive Dissonance and its Resolution: A Study of Lesbian Christians." *Journal for the Scientific Study of Religion* 35(4):392–402.

MAJORS, RICHARD and JANET BILLSON. 1992. *Cool Pose: The Dilemmas of Black Manhood in America.* Lexington, MA: Lexington Books.

MCMAHON, MARTHA. 1995. *Engendering Motherhood: Identity and Self-transformation in Women's Lives.* New York: Guilford Press.

MCROBBIE, ANGELA. 1994. *Postmodernism and Popular Culture.* London, UK: Routledge.

MELTON, J. GORDON. 1991. *The Church Speaks on: Homosexuality*. Detroit, MI: Gale Research.

MOON, DAWNE. 2004. *God, Sex, and Politics: Homosexuality and Everyday Theologies*. Chicago: University of Chicago Press.

MOYNIHAN, DANIEL. 1965. *The Negro Family: The Case for National Action*. Washington, DC: U.S. Government Printing Office.

PHARR, SUZANNE. 1988. *Homophobia, a Weapon of Sexism*. Inverness, CA: Chardon Press.

PHELAN, PEGGY. 1993. *Unmarked: The Politics of Performance*. New York: Routledge.

ROOF, WADE CLARK and WILLIAM McKINNEY. 1987. *American Mainline Religion: Its Changing Shape and Future*. New Brunswick, NJ: Rutgers University Press.

RUETHER, ROSEMARY RADFORD. 1974. *Religion and Sexism*. New York: New Press.

SANDSTROM, KENT. 1990. "Confronting Deadly Disease: The Drama of Identity Construction among Gay Men with AIDS." *Journal of Contemporary Ethnography* 19:271–94.

SCHWALBE, MICHAEL and DOUG MASON-SCHROCK. 1996. "Identity Work as Group Process." *Advances in Group Process* 13:113–47.

SMITH, CHRISTIAN. 1991. *The Emergence of Liberation Theology: Radical Religion and Social Movement Theory*. Chicago: University of Chicago Press.

SOLINGER, RICKIE. 2000. *Wake Up Little Susie: Single Pregnancy and Race Before Roe vs. Wade*. New York: Routledge.

STAPLES, ROBERT. 1999. *The Black Family: Essays and Studies*. Belmont, CA: Wadsworth.

STEWART, JAMES. 1976. *Holy Warriors: The Abolitionists and American Slavery*. New York: Hill and Wang.

SULLIVAN, ANDREW. 1995. *Virtually Normal: An Argument about Homosexuality*. New York: ALFRED A. KNOPF.

SWIDLER, ANN. 1986. "Culture in Action: Symbols and Strategies." *American Sociological Review* 51(2): 273–86.

THUMMA, SCOTT. 1991. "Negotiating a Religious Identity: The Case of the Gay Evangelical." *Sociological Analysis* 52(4):333–47.

United Fellowship of Metropolitan Community Churches (UFMCC). 2002. "Mission Statement of UFMCC." Retrieved September 1, 2003 (*http://www.mcchurch.org/missionstatement.htm*).

VAID, URVASHI. 1995. *Virtual Equality: The Mainstreaming of Gay and Lesbian Liberation*. New York: Anchor Books.

WARNER, MICHAEL. 1999. *The Trouble with Normal: Sex, Politics and the Ethics of Queer Life*. New York: Free Press.

WESTON, KATH. 1991. *Families We Choose: Lesbians, Gays, Kinship*. New York: Columbia University Press.

WILKINS, AMY. 2007. *Wannabes, Goths, and Christians: The Boundaries of Sex, Style, and Status*. Chicago: University of Chicago Press.

WILLIAMS, MELVIN. 1974. *Community in a Black Pentecostal Church: An Anthropological Study*. Pittsburgh, PA: University of Pittsburgh Press.

WOLKOMIR, MICHELLE. 2006. *Be Not Deceived: The Sacred and Sexual Struggles of Gay and Ex-Gay Christian Men*. New Brunswick, NJ: Rutgers University Press.

Reading 24 Secularization and
Its Discontents

BRYAN WILSON

Dr. Wilson is one of the world's leading secularization theorists, and this reading presents some of his work. The world, he says, has been secularizing and religion is shrinking. He presents reasons why this has been and will continue to be so. Be sure you understand his arguments.

THE THESIS OUTLINED

Secularization is a word which, for sociologists, is as much a concept as a mere descriptive term. The phrase, *the secularization thesis,* denotes a set of propositions, often loosely stated, which amount almost to a body of theory concerning processes of social change that occur over an unspecified period of historical time.... My concern is fundamentally with the recent past of advanced western society, but the thesis itself implies that there are processes of society 'becoming more secular' which extend backward in time over the long course of human history, and which have occurred intermittently, and with varying incidence and rapidity. It is, perhaps, today scarcely necessary to say that, in describing such a process, the

sociologist is not endorsing, much less advocating or encouraging, secularization. To put forward the secularization thesis as an explanation of what happens in society is not to be a secularist, nor to applaud secularity; it is only to document and to illustrate social change, and to organize that documentation into a general pattern which provides some explanatory apparatus for each individual instance.

Secularization is not only a change occurring *in* society, it is also a change *of* society in its basic organization. It is one of several concomitant processes of fundamental social change, even though it occurs in diverse ways and contexts. Some secularizing changes have been deliberate and conscious, as in the divestment of the power of religious agencies, or in the

---

Source: "Secularization and Its Discontents" in *Religion in Sociological Perspective*, by Bryan Wilson. pp. 148–157, 159–162, 174–177. By permission of Oxford University Press.

laicization of church properties—to describe which the term was originally used. Others, such as the gradual diminution of references to the supernatural in everyday life, have occurred with very little conscious stimulation. . . .

Secularization relates to the diminution in the social significance of religion. Its application covers such things as the sequestration by political powers of the property and facilities of religious agencies; the shift from religious to secular control of various of the erstwhile activities and functions of religion; the decline in the proportion of their time, energy, and resources which men devote to super-empirical concerns; the decay of religious institutions; the supplanting, in matters of behaviour, of religious precepts by demands that accord with strictly technical criteria; and the gradual replacement of a specifically religious consciousness (which might range from dependence on charms, rites, spells, or prayers, to a broadly spiritually-inspired ethical concern) by an empirical, rational, instrumental orientation; the abandonment of mythical, poetic, and artistic interpretations of nature and society in favour of matter-of-fact description and, with it, the rigorous separation of evaluative and emotive dispositions from cognitive and positivistic orientations.

These phenomena are likely to be causally linked, and yet they occur in varying order, and with different degrees of rapidity. In what measure, or in what priority they occur, is an empirical question for each specific case, and cannot be settled, *a priori*. . . . If I may, for purposes of clarity, resort to a definition of secularization that I first used some years ago, and which I have found no reason to modify, let me say that, by the term *secularization*, I mean that process by which religious institutions, actions, and consciousness, lose their social significance. What such a definition does *not* imply is that all men have acquired a secularized consciousness. It does not even suggest that most individuals have relinquished all their interest in religion, even though that may be the case. It maintains no

more than that religion ceases to be significant in the working of the social system. Clearly, that that should be so, may release many individuals from religious obligations and involvements that they might otherwise have found it necessary to sustain: religion's loss of social significance may cause men to gain psychological or individual independence of it, but that is a matter to be investigated, since there may be other nonreligious constraints which operate to hold men to religious institutions or to persuade them to go through the motions of religious rituals. The definition that I have used is intended to cover any or all of the various applications of the concept that I have indicated above. We may see them as related phenomena, even if we cannot always state the terms of that relationship.

It is sometimes objected that the process implicit in the concept of secularization concedes at once the idea of an earlier condition of social life that was not secular, or that was at least much less secular than that of our own times. We can readily make that concession, even though it must be clear that by no means all men, even in the great ages of faith, were devoutly religious, and that, at the time of its most effective organization, the church in Europe, for example, was bedevilled by internal heresy and external heathenism, and by laxness, lassitude, and corruption. None the less, by most criteria, the social significance of religion for the conduct of human life was greater than it is now. If we go back to earlier times, the evidence becomes even more overwhelming. Simpler cultures, traditional societies, and past communities, as revealed by their archaeological remains, appear to have been profoundly preoccupied with the supernatural (even though they may not have distinguished it by that name). Simpler peoples appear to have taken cognizance of themselves, of their origins, social arrangements, and destiny, by reference to a projected sphere of the supernatural. Their ultimate concerns, expressed perhaps most cogently with regard to death, were super-empirical, and such ideas, beings, objects, or conditions, commanded solemn attention and perhaps dedication. Everyday life was deeply influenced, and sometimes completely organized, with respect to a realm of transcendental suppositions.

In traditional societies, too, we may observe that the largest buildings are those devoted to religious activities, or raised in the consciousness of transcendent realities; the code by which life is lived is largely given from a supposed supernatural source (or perhaps from several); the symbols and the badges of identity that people employ are at least augmented, where they are not totally supplied, by religious authorities; and the ultimate goals of a people are set forth in other-worldly terms that relate to spheres beyond the empirical experience or the total comprehension of anyone. The remnants of such phenomena are still about us of course, even in the most advanced nations, still summoning recognition and even regard, although they are no longer the commanding heights of the polity, the economy, or any other realm of social organization.

Secularization, then, is a long-term process occurring in human society. The actual patterns in which it is manifested are culturally and historically specific to each context and in accordance with the particular character of the conceptions of the supernatural that were previously entertained, and of the institutions in which they were enshrined. Let me, to bring us to consideration of contemporary western society, instance the variation that occurs which respect to institutional associations. In Sweden, where the church is virtually a department of state, and where it is supported by taxation, the church remains financially strong, even though attendance at services is phenomenally low. In Britain, where the association with the state persists in a somewhat more attenuated form, and where the church receives no public funding, attendances are not so low, but voluntary donations are very small. In the United States, where church and state

are firmly separated, attendances are high, and giving is generous. What three such cases show is that the meaning that is attached to church-going and church-giving differs in different societies. A straight comparison of the appropriate statistics tells us nothing about secularization, unless we can interpret those statistics in the context of culture and history. Thus, in the United States, with its high immigrant and highly mobile population, churches have functioned as much more basic foci of community identity than has been their role in settled societies. Or, to take a different consideration into account, few observers doubt that the actual content of what goes on in the major churches in Britain is very much more 'religious' than what occurs in American churches; in America secularizing processes appear to have occurred *within* the church, so that although religious institutions persist, their specifically religious character has become steadily attenuated. What this implies, then, is that the indicators of secularization may be specific to particular cultures. . . .

THE CONTEXT OF SECULARIZATION

Secularization occurs in association with the process in which social organization itself changes from one that is communally based to a societally based system. Unfortunately for the clarity of discussion, the term 'society' has been used, not only by laymen, but also by sociologists, to refer to any permanent, bounded, and internally co-ordinated collectivity of human beings, whether it be the two hundred members of the Dobu tribe or the two hundred million members of the United States of America. A keystone of sociological analysis has long been the distinction between *Gemeinschaft* and *Gesellschaft*, between local community and impersonal association. If we take the community to be the persisting local, face-to-face group, as typically represented by the clan or the village, we may contrast it with the extensive, impersonal, politically co-ordinated state society. Western history, and perhaps history everywhere, documents the process by which local communities are fused into a wider system of relationships, the texture of which is not predominantly that of bonds between total persons, but that of bonds between role performers. Initially, the societal system may have been no more than the extension of uncertain political power, which affected local life only intermittently and in very limited respects. Increasingly, it has become the total coordination of local life into an extensive network, extending to every aspect of political, economic, judicial, educational and recreational activity. Local crafts, local products, local customs, local dialects have all shown a rapid diminution in our own times. . . .

Religion may be said to have its source in, and to draw its strength from, the community, the local, persisting relationships of the relatively stable group. It is clear that religion may, in certain circumstances, be provided with a framework of a large-scale organization of relationships that transcend the local, regional, or national level, as no one concerned with the history of Christianity could forget. Yet such a structure is only the political apparatus acquired—in the case of Christianity, borrowed or inherited—from the secular sphere. In essentials, religion functions for individuals and communities, at its worst for a client, and at its best for a fellowship. Its votaries are served as total persons, not as role performers, and in the same spirit, the service demanded of them by their faith is that of earnest personal commitment.

The course of social development that has come, in recent times, to make the society, and not the community, the primary locus of the individual's life has shorn religion of its erstwhile function in the maintenance of social order and as a source of social knowledge. Of course, religion does not disappear: institutions survive, consciousness lingers, religious

individuals and groups persist. New movements emerge, and often by presenting religion in a more demotic and rationalized form, attach large followings. Yet, whereas religion once entered into the very texture of community life, in modern society it operates only in interstitial places in the system. The assumptions on which modern social organization proceeds are secular assumptions. The processes of production and consumption; the coordination of activities; the agencies of control; the methods of transmission of knowledge, and its substance—all things that were once powerfully conditioned by religion—are in modern society all organized on practical, empirical, and rational prescriptions. Social organization demands the mobilization of intellectual faculties; it contrasts with the desiderata of communal order, which depends, instead, on the mobilization and manipulation of affective dispositions. One might, then, juxtapose the two phenomena: the religious community and the secular society.

The salient differences between life in the community and life in the society may be set over against each other in terms that, if not themselves religious, carry with them connotations of religious commitment. Communal relations among total persons entail trust, loyalty, respect for seniority, and clear patterns of authority that build on biological determinants. Persons matter more than role, and goodwill more than performance. The society is based on impersonal role relationships, the coordination of skills, and essentially formal and contractual patterns of behaviour, in which personal virtue, as distinguished from role obligation, is of small consequence. Whereas, in the community, the individual's duties were underwritten by conceptions of a morality which was ultimately derived from supernatural sources, or which had reference to supernatural goals, in the society, duties and role performances are ultimately justified by the demands of a rational structure, in which skills are trained and competences certificated; roles are assigned and co-ordinated; rewards are computed; and times are measured and allocated.

Societal organization is itself the result of processes of rationalization, and clearly it takes time for a predominantly rational societal system to supersede the patterns of communal order. The system becomes more effectively rationalized as new techniques and planned procedures are adopted and institutionalized. Technology, indeed, encapsulates rationality. The machine and the electronic device are supremely rational; every superfluous element of structure and function is eliminated. Means are precisely related, as efficiently as possible, to properly specified, empirically testable, ends. The thrust is towards the eradication of the incidental, the whimsical, the wayward, the poetic, and the traditional. As a passing illustration, consider how our social equipment has become increasingly purely functional, increasingly cost effective. Until less than a century ago, all manner of utilitarian objects—from spades to houses and from boats to factories—were artistically embellished, often at considerable cost in time and effort. Aesthetic effort had social implications, and the ornamentation itself was often suffused with cultural and religious meaning. Controlled emotion—and it was often controlled by the invocation of directly religious concepts and symbols—was welded, sewn, painted or hewn into even the simplest, or even the most costly, of man's instruments and equipment. Man invested his emotion, his uncertainties, and his *joie de vivre* in the works of his hands, even when his products were primarily and essentially functional. His rational acts were shot through with what, from a strictly rational perspective, were entirely gratuitous accretions—customs and conventions, traditions and celebrations, artistry and invocations. The cult of functionalism in architecture and design has not become the vogue of modern society merely incidentally, as a random and transient artistic style.

Rather, its dominance pays tribute to the logic of the rational, economic, and technological order, which increasingly presses its imperative demands on the form, content, style, and ethos of every branch of human activity. In rational artefacts, art becomes excrescence; traditions become waste of time; customs become anachronisms; rituals (divested of their emotional content) become routines; and, except in well-encapsulated areas, even creativity may be perceived as a potential threat to the regulated order on which the system depends, unless it can be tailored to rational need.

Rational precepts affect not only the economic system, and through it, the cultural sphere; they have powerfully affected the political organization of social life. The rationally constituted economy has been followed by the rationally constituted society, and this has increasingly become the conscious goal of modern states. Social functions are increasingly systematized. The consistent application of the criteria of cost efficiency would alone ensure the steady rationalization of administrative procedures throughout a state system. With ignorance or disregard of the often powerful latent functions which they fulfil, for such matters as a sense of identity or social cohesion, non-rational elements, no matter what their antiquity, are not to be justified in the terms by which the system increasingly operates. Anything which impedes the thrust towards total rationalization induces pressure for its own elimination or diminution. Such pressure comes not from sinister, hard-faced, politically acute men who are in any way either *personally* animated or even intellectually well-formed, but from the imperatives of the system itself. Of course, a state system may be said to serve certain, necessarily arbitrary, ends, and these may be expressed in the form of political slogans—freedom, democracy, equality, and so on. In practice, the political tendency follows the economic in the compulsive and progressive further rationalization of the various departments of social life. . . .

THE COLLAPSE OF COMMUNITY AND CUSTOM

Religion, by which I mean the invocation of the supernatural, was the ideology of community. In every context of traditional life, we may see religious symbolism and religious performances used to celebrate and legitimate local life. There were religious procedures to protect the local settlement; there were supernatural agents to whom the family or the clan and its members could relate; by reference to religion men were reassured of their power, secured in their status, justified in their wealth, or consoled for their poverty. Religion could give the best guarantees of fertility for mankind and the abundance of the means of sustenance. It provided the means for according public recognition and identification to the young; for healing the sick; for inducing respect for the elderly; and for coping with bereavement. Its points of reference were to things local (some of which were, of course, also things universal). It built on the biological basis of relationship, and its language was often the language of the emotions, conspicuously so in Christianity, with its symbolism of father, brethren, mother, and child. In its higher forms at least, religion intimated an ethic for social comportment, provided the basis for shared moral expectations and moralizing exhortation.

All of these one-time functions of religion have declined in significance as human involvements have ceased to be primarily local, and as human associations have ceased to be communal. Industrial society needs no local gods, or local saints; not local nostrums, remedies, or points of reference. The means of sustenance are not local. Personal gain is the common sense of modern life, needing no further legitimation, whilst material provision, not spiritual solace, is what society now offers to the poor. Fertility is no longer a positive virtue; it is to be thwarted rather than facilitated. Public recognition and identification

are impossible for the vast majority, and men even enjoy their anonymity: in our large [conurbations], people do not always know, and even more often do not care, in which borough they live, and have no notion of where its bounds might be beaten. Local life now needs no celebration: what is there to celebrate when the community that sleeps together is not the community that works together or plays together? Diurnal mobility and life in localities which demand demographic imbalance now become normal. Even the surrogate communities that are based on functioning groups such as the professional guilds, which do not take locality as their organizing principle, no longer seek religious legitimation for their distinctiveness. A pope may appoint a patron saint for, shall we say, bank managers or car dealers, but those occupations scarcely operate to any particular saintly maxims. As for the family, it is protected by insurances of a different kind from those laid up in heaven, and power, status, and wealth are no longer justified in the terms of the Christian conception of natural law. The idea that God ordered men's estates died perhaps not so long after Archdeacon Paley, and today men do not accept, but rather are encouraged to dispute, their claims to 'estates' (something that we now refer to as 'differentials'). So much the worse, then, for what, in the halcyon days, sociologists used to call 'value consensus'. Sickness today is only very marginally a matter for religious action, and, for them that mourn, funeral services today often appear less a source of comfort than an occasion for [discomfiture].

If the stable community declines because of the common pattern of diurnal mobility in the world of commuters; because of annual migrations, and tourism; because of the frequency with which careers demand that families move house; because of the separation of school from home, indeed the separation of everything which people now call 'life' from work; then what need is there for a child to be publicly received and initiated? What indeed, would he be initiated into, and what would be the effective way of doing it? When community is not a reality, initiation must be either a sentimental recollection or a travesty. If divorce becomes increasingly the recognized way to terminate a marriage, as abortion terminates a pregnancy, then the symbolism of baby, mother and father cease to have that resonance of ultimate verities that, in settled communities, they may once have had. We have learned to use different categories with which to interpret social life, and these categories are not emotionally resonant, particularistic symbols, but conceptualized abstractions, the purported generality and objectivity of which are often backed by statistical indicators: such categories are class, role, age-cohort, labour-unit. We develop these new concepts to grasp the impersonal and rational order which the old intimate symbolism could never comprehend.

The large-scale societal system does not rely, or seeks not to rely, on a moral order, but rather, wherever possible, on technical order. In this sort of social arrangement, much less importance is attached to personal dispositions, to conformity with a code of custom, to the education of the emotions, to the processes of socializing the young into responsible humane personal attitudes. After all, if, by time-and-motion studies, data retrieval systems, credit-ratings, conveyor-belts, and electronic eyes, we can regulate men's activities, and in particular their vital economic functions, then why burden ourselves with the harrowing, arduous, time-consuming weariness of eliciting moral behaviour? Since the socialization of children is so delicate a task, demanding all the balanced arts of persuasion, sensitivity, refinement, courage, patience, and high moral standards in the teachers themselves, why not, now that we have such effective quasi-coercive techniques of social control, cut short the

process and rely on them? We go further. We assume that if there are residual moral problems with which technology and instrumental techniques cannot cope, then we can legislate about them—as in codes on racial or sexual discrimination. Where morality must persist, then it can be politicized, and subject to the direct coercive force of the state. As for purely personal morality, that quaint concept, so vital to communities in the past, modern man might ask whether it had not become redundant. In modern language, to be moral is to be 'uptight'; to express moral attitudes is to inhibit people when they want—as modern men say that they have a right to want—'to do their own thing'. To canvass the maintenance of public morality, except in areas where morality can be politicized, is, apparently, to favour censorship, constraint, or, in the opinion of some sociologists, to reveal that what one is really afraid of is of losing one's own precarious social status. To espouse such a cause would be to set oneself in opposition to all the diverse forces of contemporary 'liberation'.

The balance of the communal order was struck in a personalized world that was part of a moral universe. The individual was involved in a society in which moral judgements were the basis of decisions, or purported so to be. To say this is not to say that those judgements were right, but only to indicate that this was the style of decision-making. The world was suffused with values, and the values often occluded the facts. In a societal system, such judgements cease to have relevance; custom, which was the code in which many such values were enshrined and given partial expression, falls into decay. It no longer services as a buffer zone, protecting men from the abrasiveness of the operation of the law; no longer operates to communicate a sense of rectitude and to state the terms in which men may enjoy the goodwill (or the ill-will) of their fellows. The society is underwritten by no such values, but by empirical facts and their rational co-ordination: what good is custom when we have discovered a faster, cheaper, quicker, way to go about things?

The traditional patterns of order were sustained by what, at their best, were shared intimations and apprehensions of the supernatural. The moral order was, ultimately, order derived from intimations (of whatever specific kind) of a superempirical sphere. In the advanced societal system, the supernatural plays no part in the perceived, experienced, and instituted order. The environment is hostile to the superempirical: it relies on rational, humanly conceived, planned procedures, in the operation of which there is no room for extraempirical propositions, or random inspirational intuitions.

THE SOURCES OF OUR DISCONTENTS

The modern social system leaves no space for a conception of ultimate salvation, any more than modern scientific anatomy leaves space for the individual soul. In so far as modern men might seek proximate salvation, their recourse must increasingly be to rational procedures institutionalized in the social system. Today, religious perceptions share an uneasy and shrinking frontier with rational precepts. To survive, the great religions have made many concessions to the demands of rationality, particularly in matters of organization. Within the ranks of traditional religion there are those who actively canvass, as the only prospect for success, the need to grasp modernity, to rationalize their own procedures, to reorganize and rebuild on the pattern of some secular institution, of which the army is a favourite model. These radicals seek to divest faith of the time-honoured custom which had become the foil of its timeless truths. Much more vigorously, the new religions, themselves less trammelled by tradition, have conjoined, in the dissemination of their message, modern and rational procedures with the substantive,

arbitrary values of their specific religious message. Yet, even here, the latent tensions between faith and reason are not entirely obviated in the consciousness of individual believers. As everyday life in modern society demands ever extending commitment to rational procedures, so the personal, religiously-inspired caveats of the truly religious man are likely to become increasingly vestigial, and he the more likely to acquire a sense of his own marginality. Even the votary of a new religion, which conforms in so many external particulars to the demands of rational organization, may find himself attacked because somewhere at the core of his faith there are [arbitrary] elements which, by the standards implicit in the social system, people readily declare to be obscurantist, irrational, emotional, or even magical. . . .

The expectation that commitment to religion should be a total commitment is well exemplified in the case of the religious functionary—for instance, in the Christian priest or minister. His calling is presented as far more than a job or even a profession: it implies total loyalty to an ethic, an unending obligation to a way of life and to the values of faith. His work transcends all contractual commitments; it belongs to an ancient order, to relationships rooted in community. The criteria that apply to the religious calling are not those of efficiency, cost, speed, or co-ordination; they are not the concerns for the most cost-effective means to specified ends. They are diffuse, and coterminous with all that is human. Thus, the implications of this calling could not be further removed from the considerations that dominate almost all other departments of modern life. For the minister of religion, men in themselves are ultimate ends, just as religious activity is an end in itself. Yet, in modern society, men are not ends-in-themselves: as role-performers, they become adjuncts to the machine, units of input in a system which matters more than they do. Their personal attributes, their sensitivity, their native dispositions, and their purely personal needs become irrelevant in their role-performance; men, in such a system, are merely the means. The antithesis between the religious conception of humankind and its responsibilities, and that of any modern social system (capitalist or communist) could not diverge more sharply.

The advanced technological society is, then, an inhospitable context for the religious *Weltanschauung*. Religious institutions compete on increasingly unfavourable terms with other agencies which seek to mobilize and manipulate men's resources of time, energy, and wealth. Those other agencies can employ, much more effectively than traditional religion, all the techniques of modern science and organization;

they are unhindered by the types of impediment to the adoption of rational systematization that are found even in the new religions. Religious perceptions and goals, religiously induced sensitivities, religiously inspired morality, and religious socialization appear to be of no immediate relevance to the operation of the modern social system. For every social problem, whether of economy, polity, law, education, family relations, or recreation, the solutions proposed are not only non-religious, but solutions that depend on technical expertise and bureaucratic organization. Planning, not revelation; rational order, not inspiration; systematic routine, not charismatic or traditional action, are the imperatives in ever-widening arenas of public life....

25 An Unsecular America

ROGER FINKE

Dr. Finke and his colleagues have taken a very different position on religion in society compared to secularization theorists. In this reading, he argues that as modernization advances, religion does not decline and disappear, as is often thought to be the case in secularization theories. As you read this work look at how secularization is defined (even if only implicitly defined) and the evidence used to make the argument for the continued strength of American religions.

Since the founding of the discipline, sociologists have used the secularization model to explain the inevitable decay of religion. Harboured within the broad theoretical framework of modernization, the traditional model has long proposed that as industrialization, urbanization, and rationalization come to dominate a society, religion will recede. Yet support for this model is far from uniform and, in recent years, debate over the secularization model has come to the fore. . . .

In this essay I propose to test the secularization model against the empirical evidence on religion in the USA. Does the evidence reveal a decay of religion since the advent of modernization? And what is the relationship between religious change and the major social changes

of the past two centuries? Since the secularization model describes an historical process that occurs in conjunction with modernization, I will first use historical data to follow the long-term trends in religion. Then I will select several time periods to test the relationship between religion and the various measures of modernization. Here I will attempt to test the specific predictions the model offers on the relationship between religion and the various aspects of modernization. For example, is religion inversely related with urbanization, industrialization, and rationalization? Finally, I will suggest that the deregulation of religion in America helps to explain why the religious changes there have not paralleled those of western Europe.

Source: "An Unsecular America," Roger Finke, from *Religion and Modernization* (1992) edited by S. Bruce. By permission of Oxford University Press.

But, first, let me clarify how the concept of secularization will be defined and measured.

THE TRADITIONAL MODEL

When Hadden summarized the model of secularization proposed by early sociologists, he offered the following three-sentence translation of secularization theory:

Once the world was filled with the sacred—in thought, practice, and institutional form. After the Reformation and the Renaissance, the forces of modernization swept across the globe and secularization, a corollary historical process, loosened the dominance of the sacred. In due course, the sacred shall disappear altogether except, possibly, in the private realm. (Hadden, 1987)

Although this model has undergone revisions and challenges, the core continues to guide the research and theory of sociologists. The dominance of the sacred is in decline.

In contemporary work, Bryan Wilson is probably the most widely cited and well-respected proponent of the traditional model. He has written extensively on how the traditional model applies to contemporary societies and has helped to clarify both the definitions and the relationships between the concepts used in the traditional model of secularization. He explains that secularization relates to the decrease in the 'social significance of religion' and goes on to outline how this can be applied to contemporary societies. . . .

The applications, or indicators, proposed by Wilson fall into three broad areas. The first area addresses Church[-]State relations and the functions performed by each, the second touches on the vitality of religious institutions, and the third covers the behaviours, thoughts, and beliefs of individuals.

I will *not* attempt to test the first area since the principles for separating Church and State are given in the First Amendment, and are supported by numerous court cases. Indeed, if the separation of Church and State is used as an indicator of secularization in the USA, the process of secularization preceded the advent of modernization and the USA is currently far more secularized than western Europe. . . .

The next two areas—institutional vitality and individual behaviour, thoughts, and beliefs—will receive extensive attention in this essay. Have religious institutions followed a trend of 'decay'? Did the 'time, energy, and resources which men [and women] devote to super-empirical concerns' decline? For each of these areas there are historical data to document the long-term trends of institutional resources and individual commitment. Using a variety of indicators, I will look at the vitality of religious institutions and the willingness of individuals to commit time, energy, and resources to super-empirical concerns.

The most difficult challenge will be to measure historical trends in individual thoughts and beliefs. Documenting longterm trends in 'religious consciousness' or 'artistic interpretations of nature' would be nearly impossible even if we had the benefit of eighteenth and nineteenth-century surveys. None the less, I will report evidence that indirectly addresses these issues. Which churches continue to retain a popular appeal to the people? In order to attract members have they been forced to make their teachings more rational, more positivistic and less mythical? I begin by looking at American religion over the past two hundred years. Do the trends support the traditional model of secularization?

FROM COLONIAL TO CONTEMPORARY RELIGION

The vibrancy and growth of American religious institutions presents the most open defiance of the secularization model. Historians have long noted the low level of religious involvement in colonial America, as compared to modern levels of involvement; but in recent work Rodney Stark and I have provided more accurate estimates on church membership during the late-eighteenth and mid-nineteenth century (Finke & Stark, 1986; Stark & Finke, 1988). The church adherence rate more than doubles from 1776 to 1860 (17 percent to 37 percent), declines slightly following the immense dislocations of the Civil War, and continues on a steady increase from 1870 to 1926. Since 1926 the rate has hovered around 60 percent. If we were able to conduct a closer year-by-year inspection, the trend line would probably show a slight decline in the 1930s (Handy 1978), a small increase in the 1950s, another slight decline in the late 1960s and early 1970s, and a small increase in the 1980s; but the dominant trend since 1926 is that of stability. Rather than declining, the proportion churched showed rapid growth from 1776 to 1890 and has shown exceptional stability from 1926 to the present. Rather [then] decaying, religious institutions have shown a remarkable capacity for mobilizing people into the pew.

However, critics might rightfully suggest that church membership requires little individual commitment and provides no guarantee of institutional health. What happens after people join churches? Are they willing to sacrifice valuable personal resources for the survival of their church? In other words, will they give of their money and time?

. . . Contributions per member . . . when standardized to 1967 dollars . . . more than doubled between 1950 and 1986. . . . The value of church property per adherent, as reported by the census, more than doubled between 1850 and 1906 (when controlling for inflation). And, since the rate of church adherence was increasing rapidly at the end of the nineteenth century, the value of church property per person in the population more than tripled (again, controlling for inflation). Whether it is the nineteenth or twentieth century, people are not simply joining churches, they are making large financial sacrifices to support their church, and the sacrifice per member is increasing rather than declining. . . .

But perhaps the most convincing evidence of the people's willingness to still give time, energy, and resources to religion is the rapid growth of the most demanding religions. In 1972 Dean Kelley's book, entitled *Why Conservative Churches are Growing*, documented the growth of strict and demanding churches. The trend has not changed since 1972. Table 1 shows the remarkably close correspondence between a denomination's membership growth and the commitment of their membership from 1972 to 1984. In fact, the Pearson r between membership growth and denominational commitment is a huge .79, and the correlation between membership growth and percent attending church regularly is an identical .79. The growing churches are making strong demands on their members' time, energy and resources (Iannaccone, 1989).

Moreover, this trend is not confined to recent decades (Finke & Stark, 1989). In the early nineteenth century, Methodist members were expected to attend class meetings, Sunday services, and camp meetings, as well as conform to the strict demands of the *Discipline*. The demands were no less stringent for the clergy, indeed, the local clergy received little or no pay, and of the first 700 Methodist circuit-riders, nearly half of them died before age 30 due to the extreme hardships of traveling the circuits: 199 of them within the first five years of service (Clark 1952). Yet the Methodists went from 3 percent of all adherents in 1776 to more than 33 percent of all adherents in 1850. Once again, the demanding organizations showed the most rapid increase in membership.

Besides making greater demands of their members' resources, these growing churches also place greater demands on what their members believe. Rather than accommodating to the accepted beliefs of the dominant culture or de-emphasizing the mythical beliefs of religion, these churches have rigid beliefs on what God demands of the faithful, and members offer

TABLE 1   Membership Growth, Denominational Commitment, and Regular Church Attendance by Denomination, 1972–84

	1972–1984 % Change in Members	*% High Denominational Commitment*	*% Attend Church Regularly*
Assemblies of God	85.2	70	73
Mormons	64.8	59	64
Jehovah's Witnesses	61.8	58	77
Church of God	52.6	59	57
Adventists	42.2	59	63
Nazarenes	27.5	59	63
Southern Baptists	18.9	48	52
Catholics	7.9	42	55
Lutherans	−4.6	41	45
Reformed	−8.3	59	64
Presbyterians	−9.3	32	40
Episcopalians	−9.4	32	33
United Church of Christ	−10.5	39	44
Methodists	−10.6	32	38
Disciples of Christ	−16.3	50	51

Note: The first column is based on denominational membership reports given in the *Yearbook of American and Canadian Churches* and the final two columns are based on General Social Surveys given between 1972–84 (taken from Roof and McKinney, *American Mainline Religion*). Since the GSS data are based on the respondent's self-reported denominational affiliation and refer to general denominational families, the measure on membership change is based on the largest denominations (over 200,000 members) within the denominational family. A few of the categories reported by Roof and McKinney were omitted since they did not correspond closely to specific denominations, or data on membership were not available.

frequent testimonial on how God intervenes in their lives. One of the most consistent demands of sectarian churches in this century is that their members should hold a firm belief in the words of their sacred text. As shown in Table 2, members of the growing denominations are much more likely to believe that 'the Bible is the actual word of God and is to be taken literally, word for word'. Indeed, the correlation between denominational growth and the proportion of members believing the Bible is the literal word of God is .76. The denominations accommodating to modern thought are the very churches that are rapidly losing their membership, while the denominations that have resisted this process are showing rapid growth curves.

A final point should be noted from Table 2. The growing churches are not merely small denominations. The Assemblies of God is now larger than the United Church of Christ; the Church of God in Christ is larger than the United Presbyterians and the Episcopal Church; and the Southern Baptists are far ahead of the United Methodists. The growing churches, which are placing strict demands on the behaviour and beliefs of members, are rapidly outnumbering the so called mainline denominations.

Regardless of the indicators used, the long-term trends do not show religion in a state of decay. On the contrary, the *long-term* trends have shown patterns of increasing vitality for religious organizations and increased commitment on the individual level. And the *short-term* trends, which I consider to be those of the last 50 years or so, show remarkable stability. The secularization model's prediction of religious decay is simply not supported by the historical trends in the USA. Modernization was not accompanied by the long-forecasted process of secularization.

But why not? Why did the process of modernization not lead to the anticipated decline of religion in the USA? Here we need to look at

TABLE 2   Membership Growth and Literal Interpretation of the Bible*

| | Members per 1,000 US Population | | | % Literal Interpretation |
	1960	1983	% Change	
Church of God in Christ	2.2	15.9	623	90
Assemblies of God	2.8	8.5	204	76
United Pentecostals	1.0	2.0	100	81
Jehovah's Witnesses	1.4	2.8	100	61
Seventh-Day Adventists	1.8	2.7	50	62
Church of the Nazarene	1.7	2.2	29	47
Southern Baptists	54.3	60.7	12	60
Roman Catholics	234.7	223.4	−4	23
Ev. Lutheran Ch. in Am.	29.2	22.6	−23	34
United Methodists	55.1	40.3	−27	33
Episcopal Church	19.2	12.0	−38	15
United Presbyterians	23.2	14.0	−40	28
United Church of Christ	12.5	7.3	−42	15

Note: * Adapted from Stark, *Sociology*.

the measures of modernization and understand their relationship to religion.

URBANIZATION AND INDUSTRIALIZATION

Too often empirical tests of the traditional model of secularization have focused only on the rise or fall of religion. If religious activity is up and religious institutions are strong, then the model is questioned (or at least revised); if religion is down then the model must be right. Yet the model goes beyond this simple prediction. The model also explains the source of this anticipated change.

At the heart of the secularization model are the widely accepted propositions that urbanization and industrialization lead to secularization. Indeed, in the beginning pages of *A General Theory of Secularization*, Martin comments that 'certain broad tendencies towards secularization in industrial society have already been fairly well established'. The first three tendencies he listed are as follows:

that religious institutions are adversely affected to the extent that an area is dominated by heavy industry;

that they are the more adversely affected if the area concerned is homogeneously proletarian; and

that religious practice declines proportionately with the size of an urban concentration.

Based on existing research of industrialization and urbanization in Europe, especially in England, these 'tendencies' would seem [to] be supported. But are these trends supported in the USA?

Once again, the evidence fails to support the predictions of the traditional model. As shown in Table 3, the results are quite the opposite of what it predicts. For each of the time periods tested, the rate of adherence for urban areas never falls below that of rural areas; and in three of the four time periods the rate of adherence is five to seven percentage points higher in urban areas than in the surrounding hinterland. Moreover, the correlation between size of city and rate of adherence is never significant in either direction for any of the time periods tested. Whether you were in the city or the countryside made a difference, the size of city did not. Contrary to the prediction of the traditional model, the process of urbanization did not undermine the

TABLE 3   Church Adherence Rates for Urban Areas, Rural Areas, and the Nation: 1890, 1906, 1926, and 1980*

	Urban Areas	Rural Areas	Nation
1890	.49	.44	.45
1906	.56	.50	.51
1926	.63	.56	.58
1980*	.55	.55	.55

Notes: In 1890, 1906, and 1926, urban areas are defined as cities with a population of greater than 25,000. For 1980 all counties with a population of over 100,000 are defined as urban. Rural areas included all areas not defined as urban.
* The 1980 data are not corrected for the numerous small religious bodies omitted from data set used in Quinn *et al., Churches.*

individual's involvement in religion or the vitality of the religious institution.

Indeed, the only time period where urban adherence rates do not exceed those of rural areas is in 1980. I would suggest that this change is the result of two factors. The first is the major improvement in transportation between 1926 and 1980. Whereas the urban resident has always had a church within a relatively short walking-distance, rural residents are often miles from the nearest church. This does not present a problem with modern roads and cars, but it was a major obstacle at the turn of the century. This improvement in transportation has also given the rural resident a greater number of choices. Rather than being confined to a nearby country church, rural residents now have the option of attending a variety of churches in the nearest community. For the rural residents of 1980, attending church is much easier and their choice of churches is much greater than the ruralites at the turn of the century.

A second factor involves the data used to compute the rates. Since the 1980 data do not include numerous denominations and small sectarian groups, the rates reported are lower than the true rates; the national rate is 0.55, instead of the more accurate 0.62 (Stark, 1987). Even though I have made corrections for the missing black denominations and

Orthodox Jews, I could not make the necessary corrections for the other missing religious groups. Omitting these denominations would not be of major concern if they resided in equal proportions in the rural and urban areas; however, as Fischer has shown, small religious groups, like ethnic groups, tend to congregate in cities where they can attain a critical mass (Fischer, 1982).

I would suggest that with improved data, urban areas would still have slightly higher adherence rates than the countryside. The difference is not as great due to improved transportation, but a small difference probably still remains.

If urban areas have higher rates of adherence than the countryside, this also raises questions about the effects of industrialization. Why do cities have higher church adherence rates when they are the home of industries?

To test this proposition I looked at the relationship between the percentage of the labour force in manufacturing and the rate of adherence. The correlations are reported in Table 4. Regardless of whether states or urban areas are used as the unit of analysis, or whether it is the turn of the century or the last decade, the adherence rate increases in areas where a higher percentage of the labour force is employed in manufacturing. Based on these zero-order correlations it would be premature

TABLE 4 Correlations Between Percent of Labour Force in Manufacturing and Church Adherence Rates, 1906 and 1980 (Using Urban Areas and States)

States	Correlation
1906 (N = 48)	.39**
1980 (N = 50)	.31*
Urban Areas 1906 (N = 150)	.17*
1980 (N = 393)	.27**

*$p < 0.05$
**$p < 0.01$

to suggest that manufacturing increases religious involvement. Yet it is clear that the results fail to support the traditional model. Churches were effectively mobilizing members even in areas with industry.

Why? One explanation concerns the presence of sectarian movements. Whether the sectarian movements were Baptist, Assembly of God, Church of the Nazarene, or Roman Catholic, they made an effective appeal to the industrial working class.

Even in the late eighteenth century the established churches recognized that the sectarian groups had a unique appeal to the less privileged. In a tract entitled *Impartial Inquiries Concerning the Progress of the Baptist Denomination*, the Congregational minister Noah Worcester acknowledged the rapid growth of the Baptists, but noted that 'they reached only the most shallow, ignorant, and uneducated classes' (McLoughlin, 1971). This appeal to the 'uneducated' continued into the nineteenth century and it soon became clear that the sectarian groups, and their revivalistic style of religion, could appeal to workers in the industrial areas. Using Hammond's data on revivalism in upstate New York from 1825 to 1835, Richard Rogers found that revivalism flourished in manufacturing and commercial centres. Rogers concluded: 'Strong support has been found for the argument that the evangelical movement drew its strength from cites

and towns specializing in manufacturing and commerce (Rogers, 1987). By the beginning of the twentieth century, the Roman Catholic church (a sect when first arriving in America) had proved successful at appealing to the immigrant labourer and a close tie between Roman Catholics and the labour movement was becoming evident (Dolan, 1985). And in the 1970s, when Earle, Knudsen, and Shriver repeated Liston Pope's study of the industrial community of Gastonia, they concluded that 'mill churches, regardless of denomination, were frequently sectarian in character, and sect-type groups have continued to emerge especially amongst the poor and socially marginal of the city' (Earle, Knudsen, & Shriver, 1976). For each of the time periods, the ever-emerging sectarian groups proved attractive to the working class.

A final component of the process of modernization, which is closely tied to the process of urbanization and the constantly emerging sectarian movements, is that of religious pluralism. As forcefully argued by Berger, modernity has led to pluralism, and pluralism undermines 'the authority of all religious traditions' (Berger, 1967, 1979).

Yet this prediction has faced increased opposition and revision in the past decade (Iannaccone, 1991; Caplow, Bahr, & Chadwick, 1983; Fischer, 1983). In recent work Rodney Stark and I computed an index to measure the religious diversity of American cities in 1906 (Scherer, 1970; Lieberson, 1964; Greenberg, 1956). The consequences of religious diversity are shown in Table 5. When we control for the proportion of Catholics in the population, the diversity index has a positive effect on the rate of church adherence. Unfortunately contemporary data are not well suited for testing this hypothesis but I have replicated this result for cities in 1890 and 1926 (Finke & Stark, 1989). The results are consistent. Religious diversity and the percentage of the population Catholic have positive effects on religious adherence

TABLE 5   Regression Coefficients for Religious Diversity, Percentage Catholic, and Population Growth, With Rate of Church Adherents as the Dependent Variable: 1890, 1906, and 1926

	1890		1906		1926	
	B	β	B	β	B	β
Religious diversity	.26	.24*	.79	.72**	.29	.33**
Percent Catholic	.62	.62**	1.35	1.19**	.73	.69**
Population growth	−.33	−.03**	−.12	−.04*	−.23	−.03**
$R^2 =$	.39		.62		.38	

*$p < 0.05$
**$p < 0.01$

rates and the rate of population growth has a negative effect. The diversity of religions in urban areas stimulated the growth of traditional religious institutions rather than stifling such growth.

However, the powerful impact of religious competition is not limited to large cities or to church membership. In the early 1920s the Institute of Social and Religious Research conducted a survey of 140 farming villages across the nation ranging in size from 250 to 2,500 residents. The principal investigator, Edmund des Brunner, was adamantly opposed to small communities supporting a diversity of churches (especially small emotional sects) but he conceded that competition increased the involvement of the people. In the fifth and final volume published from this massive study, Brunner reports:

[an] increase in the relative number of churches was found to be associated with a progressive increase in the proportion of the population enrolled in the membership of local churches, in the proportion enrolled in the Sunday schools, in the number of resident ministers per 1,000 inhabitants, in the ratio of average attendance at church to the population, and in local expenditures by the churches per inhabitant (des Bruner, 1927).

Thus, as Table 6 shows, when villages have a variety of churches, the people are more likely to join and more likely to become active in the church. In villages, towns and cities, diversity has stimulated institutional

growth rather than decline (Land, Deane, & Blau, 1991).

But two points should be clarified on the relationship between diversity and religious involvement. First, like commercial markets, religious markets are sometimes effectively dominated by one firm. For example, Catholics have effectively dominated many urban areas since the late nineteenth century and Mormons currently dominate all urban areas within Utah. This is why I controlled for the proportion of Catholics in the reported equations. The question is: how could the Roman Catholic church mobilize such a large portion of the population in the midst of a diversity of religious options?

A part of the answer is obvious: they were united by their minority status and their Catholic backgrounds. But this is not the whole story. They were also successful because they tolerated diversity within their organization. Because the parishes were homogeneous by ethnicity and class, there was a wide range of variation across parishes. According to the 1916 Census of Religious Bodies, twenty-nine languages were being used for religious services in Catholic parishes, and approximately one half (49 percent) of all parishes held services in a language other than English. This diversity of languages also translated into a diversity of patron saints, style of worship, and choice of rituals. The Church Protestants viewed as a Roman monolith was, in fact, a mosaic of

TABLE 6   Pluralism and Religious Involvement in Rural Communities*

	Number of Churches per 1,000 Population			
	One	Two	Three	Four or more
Percent who belong to a church	27.4	36.0	34.8	43.4
Percent enrolled in Sunday schools	15.8	22.3	25.2	37.4
Percent of population attending church*	24.1	29.9	36.5	65.9

Note: * These figures are based on the average attendance at the 'principal service'. Though Brunner does not explicitly state whether children are included in the membership and attendance counts, it appears that most denominations include only adult members, whereas adults and children are counted in the attendance figures.
Source: Adapted from Brunner, *Village Communities.*

regional, ethnic, and national parishes. The local parish appealed to a specific immigrant group or social class, and the diversity of parishes appealed to a broad spectrum of the population.

A second issue that needs clarification is the relationship between denominational regionalism and diversity. Although several authors have identified the predominance of Catholics in the Northeast, Lutherans in the Midwest, and Baptists in the South, these broad generalizations should not distract from the diversity within these regions (Hill, 1985; Newman & Halvorson, 1980; Shortridge, 1977; Zelinsky, 1961). While the South might be dominated by an evangelical style of religion, it is not dominated by only one denomination. Not only are there a variety of Baptists (the *Yearbook of American and Canadian Churches* reported twenty denominations with the word 'Baptist' in their name), there is also a variety of evangelical and pentecostal sectarian groups with an affinity for the South, not to mention the long-established Presbyterian, Methodist, and Episcopal churches. In the Midwest the Lutherans have pared down from the twenty-one different denominational groupings reported in the 1926 census, but their share of the population has also been reduced. In 1980 the four largest Lutheran denominations represented only 13.7 per cent of the population in the West North Central and 6.5 per cent in the East North Central. The

caricature of denominational regionalism is only partially accurate. There is a large number of Lutherans in the Midwest and Baptists in the South, but neither area is lacking for denominational diversity.

Urbanization, industrialization, and pluralism have all been cited as sources for the anticipated long-term process of secularization. Yet, in the USA, urban areas have held higher rates of involvement, the percentage of the labour force in manufacturing is positively associated with adherence rates, and pluralism has stimulated growth and involvement rather than decline. The sources for secularization, proposed by the traditional model of secularization, have all been associated with higher levels of religious involvement, rather than decline. But the trends I have reported on religion in the USA stand in sharp contrast with those found in Europe. In the final section, I turn my attention to explaining this variation.

REGULATION OF RELIGION AND RELIGIOUS CHANGE

As part of an evolutionary model of modernization, the traditional model of secularization was designed to explain decline, not variation. More specifically, it was designed to explain the decline of religion in western Europe. Yet religious change in Europe is not representative of all nations facing modernity and the USA is not the only case that fails to fit the model

(Swatos, 1989). Explanations of religious change must recognize variations by countries and must be able to explain revivalism as well as secularization.

When explaining the growth of organized religion in the USA, one of the key variables of interest must be the regulation of religion. Whereas European countries have traditionally had a close tie between Church and State, and continue to regulate religion, the USA has attempted to separate Church and State, and minimize regulation. The result: low start-up costs for new religions.

Splitting from a church with ties to the State can be costly due to a loss of subsidies or a perceived increase in persecution; when there are no regulations to favour existing churches, the new movement must only garner the support of the people to survive. Hence, whether the religious organization is an upstart sect, or a venerable church, the life of the organization relies upon the support of the people, not the State.

The lack of regulation in the USA leads to a proliferation of new sectarian movements each trying to meet the needs of some segment of the population. And though only a handful of the numerous movements ever become sizable denominations, their presence forces all denominations to compete for adherents. Moreover, the lack of regulation allows sects to serve as a testing ground for religious innovation. Most will fail, but a few succeed.

Finally, a proliferation of new religious movements mobilizes segments of the population often alienated by the more 'respectable' churches. Since sectarian movements often flourish in the working classes, it is the working-class churches that benefit the most from the lack of religious regulation. Rather than joining a church that is led by educated clergy and politically aligned with their employer, the workers can support a church that addresses their needs and concerns.

In sharp contrast, when there is religious regulation, the start-up costs are higher and sectarian movements strive harder to reduce the tension with their environment—leading to more rapid secularization. A poignant example is offered in the divergent histories of American and English Methodism. Whereas camp-meeting revivalism played a key role in the success of American Methodism, the Methodists of England feared the camp meetings because they threatened the 'fragile nature of religious toleration' (Hatch 1989). When Lorenzo Dow first came to England to introduce the American camp meeting, he reports that 'they warned the Methodists against me, to starve me out . . . they offered to pay my passage home, if I would quit the country, and promise never to return, which in conscience I could not do' (Dow, 1849). The camp meetings generated support from the laity, but the Methodist Conference quickly ruled against such meetings: 'It is our judgment, that even supposing such meetings to be allowable in America, they are highly improper in England, and likely to be productive of considerable mischief: and we disclaim all connections with them.'

Regardless of the popularity of camp meetings, Methodist authorities in England did not want to risk the consequences of this uncontrolled evangelical fervour. Approximately a decade before Dow's arrival, a 'gentleman of rank' had called the 'constitutional loyalty of provincial Methodists' into question. Just a few years later, in 1811, Lord Sidmouth attempted to control the activity of itinerant preachers by proposing a bill that would limit preaching certificates to ministers attached to a specific congregation. The bill was defeated, but the fear of regulation evoked responses of loyalty from Methodist leaders and led to a self-regulation of the evangelical itinerants.

The traditional model has often ignored these dramatic differences in religious regulation.

Instead, secularization is treated as an inseparable companion of modernization and the trend of secularization in Europe is forecast as the inevitable trend for all. But not all countries have followed the trend of Europe and modernity has not been the only, or even the primary, cause of religious change.

CONCLUSION

The historical evidence on religion in the USA does not support the traditional model of secularization. Based on the evidence reviewed in this essay, modernization did not usher in a new era of secularization in America.

Instead, the evidence displays the vitality of religious organizations and the continuing commitment of individuals. Rather than declining, church adherence rates have shown a rapid increase in the nineteenth century and remarkable stability throughout the twentieth. Contributions have shown a steady increase, even when controlling for inflation. And though it is difficult to measure the thoughts and beliefs of individuals, it is clear that the growing denominations do not shy away from God-talk or religious experiences. Indeed, the most rapidly growing denominations hold a firm belief in the literal interpretation of the Bible and place strict demands on their members. The long forecasted decay of religion is not supported by the evidence.

The explanation offered for the anticipated decline is not supported by the evidence either. Whereas the model predicts that secularization will be closely tied to the process of modernization, the indicators of modernization reviewed in this essay show no support for the model. In fact, the results were contrary to the predictions. Adherence rates were higher in urban areas and positively correlated to the percentage of the population in manufacturing. Moreover, diversity has a positive impact on adherence rates, when a control is entered for the percent of the population

Catholic. In the case of the USA, the advent of modernization has *not* been a source of religious decay.

Yet the traditional model offers no explanation of why modernization would have less impact on one society than another. If we are going to explain variations in religious change, we must look beyond modernization for the answer.

In this essay I have highlighted the importance of religious regulation in explaining the 'exceptionalism' of the USA. Without fear of penalty or the loss of privileges from the State, sectarian movements have formed quickly on the American religious landscape. These movements have served as a testing ground for religious innovation, have mobilized large segments of the population, and have held a special appeal to the working classes. Thus, the lack of religious regulation has had a major impact on the expression and organization of religion in the USA.

BIBLIOGRAPHY

BERGER, P.L. 1967. *The Sacred Canopy*. New York: Doubleday and Co.

BERGER, P.L. 1979. *The Heretical Imperative: Contemporary Possibilities of Religion Affirmation*. New York.

CAPLOW, T., H.M. BAHR, & B. CHADWICK. 1983. *All Faithful People: Change and Continuity in Middletown's Religion*. Minneapolis.

CLARK, E.T. 1952. *An Album of Methodist History*. Nashville.

DES BRUNER, E. 1927. *Village Communities*. New York.

DOLAN, J.P. 1985. *The American Catholic Experience*. New York.

DOW, L. 1849. *Lorenzo Dow's Journal*, 6th edition. New York: pg. 256.

EARLE, J.R., D.D. KNUDSEN, & D.W. SHRIVER, Jr. 1976. *Spindles and Spires: A Restudy of Religion and Social Change in Gastonia*. Atlanta, pg. 115.

FINKE, R. & R. STARK. 1989. "How the upstart sects won America: 1776–1850." *Journal for the Scientific Study of Religion* 28:27–44.

FINKE, R. & R. STARK 1989. "Evaluating the evidence: Religious economies and sacred canopies." *American Sociological Review* 54: 1054–1056.

FISCHER, C.S. 1982. *To Dwell Among Friends*. Chicago.

HADDEN, J.K. 1987. "Toward desacralizing secularization theory." *Social Forces* 65: 598.

HANDY, R. T. 1978. "The American religious depression, 1925–1935." In J.M. Mulder & J.F. Wilson (eds.), *Religion in American History*. Englewood Cliffs, NJ.

HATCH, N. 1989. *The Democratization of American Christianity*. New Haven.

HEMPTON, D. 1984. *Methodism and Politics in British Society, 1750–1850*. Stanford.

HILL, S.S. 1985. "Religion and region in America." In W.C. Roof (ed.), *The Annals: Religion in America Today*. Beverly Hills, CA.

IANNACCONE, L.R. 1991. "The consequences of religious market regulation," *Rationality and Society* 3:156–177.

LAND, K.C., G. DEANE, & J.R. BLAU. 1991. "Religious pluralism and church membership: A spatial diffusion model." *American Sociological Review* 56:237–249.

LIEBERSON, S. 1964. "An extension of Greenberg's linguistic diversity measures." *Language* 40:526–31.

MARTIN, DAVID. 1978. *A General Theory of Secularization*. New York: Harper and Row.

McLOUGHLIN, W.G. 1971. *New England Dissent, 1630–1833*. Cambridge. Pg. 700.

NEWMAN, W.M. & P.L. HALVORSON 1980. *Patterns in Pluralism: A Portrait of American Religion*. Washington, DC.

R. FINKE & R. STARK 1986. "Turning pews into people: Estimating 19th-century church membership." *Journal for the Scientific Study of Religion* 25:180–192.

ROGERS, R. 1987. "Revivalism and manufacturing in Upper State New York." Paper presented at the annual meeting of the American Sociological Association, New York.

SCHERER, F.M. 1970. *Industrial Market Structure and Economic Performance*. Chicago.

SHORTRIDGE, J. 1977. "A new regionalism in American Religion." *Journal for the Scientific Study of Religion* 16:143–153.

STARK, R. 1987. Correcting Church Membership Rates: 1971 and 1980. *Review of Religious Research* 29: 66–77.

STARK, R. & R. FINKE 1988. "American religion in 1776: A statistical portrait." *Sociological Analysis* 49: 39–51.

SWATOS, W.H. 1989. "Losing faith in the 'religion' of secularization: Worldwide religious resurgence and the definition of religion." In W.H. Swatos, Jr. (ed.), *Religious Politics in Global and Comparative Perspective*. Greenwood Press.

ZELINKSY, W. 1961. "An approach to religious geography of the United States: Patterns of membership in 1952." *Annals of the American Association of Geographers* 51: 139–93.

26 Secularization as Declining Religious Authority

MARK CHAVES

Whether the world is secularizing has been debated for hundreds of years. As we saw in the first two readings of this section, some say yes and have good evidence. Others say no and have good evidence. Dr. Chaves attempts to advance the debate by clearly defining what we mean by secularization. What do you think about his definition? Do you agree this is the way we ought to understand secularization?

A longstanding consensus around classical versions of secularization theory has broken down in recent decades. Religion's stubborn refusal to disappear has prompted major reevaluation of inherited models of secularization. The "facts" are not much disputed: New religious movements continue to arise; older movements like Pentecostalism and Mormonism are expanding; religious fundamentalisms thrive throughout the world; and, at least in the U.S., substantial segments of the population continue to say they believe in God and continue to participate in orthodox organized religion. However, the significance of these facts is very much disputed. Does the persistence of religion falsify secularization theory? Or does the form of religion's persistence render its persistence

irrelevant to, or even supportive of, secularization theory? The current secularization debate may be understood as a Kuhnian paradigm clash, where theoretical perspectives compete, not over the truth or falsity of facts, but over their relevance.

At such a time it is worth the effort to reassess the "inherited model" of secularization (Wilson 1985) with an eye towards discerning what is valuable and what must be abandoned. This is an especially urgent task for those who believe, as do I, that currently fashionable claims suggesting that secularization theory has been decisively falsified (Hadden 1987; Hout & Greeley 1987; Stark & Iannaccone 1992) throw the baby out with the bathwater. This article takes up the challenge

Source: Mark Chaves, "Secularization as Declining Religious Authority," from *Social Forces*, Volume 72, no. 3. Copyright © 1994 by the University of North Carolina Press. Used by permission of the publisher. www.uncpress.unc.edu.

of rethinking secularization in light of the valid criticisms that have been directed against it. It offers a reformulation of secularization rather than a defense of the classical view (cf. Lechner 1991).

If secularization theory is always about, in one way or another, religion's decline, then how religion is understood determines secularization theory's direction (Shiner 1967). Durkheimians, on the one hand, to whom religion refers to a set of collective representations providing moral unity to a society, either rule secularization out by definition or dread it as social disintegration. Weberians, on the other hand, to whom religion is more substantively conceptualized as bodies of beliefs and practices concerning salvation, see secularization in social change that renders these religious meanings less and less plausible. As these well-known examples illustrate, how we understand secularization's object — religion — has a dramatic effect on how we understand secularization. This article takes advantage of this fact in that it attempts to reconceptualize secularization by reconceptualizing its object.

My central claim can be stated simply: Secularization is best understood not as the decline of religion, but as the declining scope of religious authority. More provocatively, I propose that we abandon religion as an analytical category when studying secularization. This proposed focus on religious authority (1) is more consistent with recent developments in social theory than is a preoccupation with "religion"; (2) draws on and develops what is best in the secularization literature; (3) reclaims a neglected Weberian insight concerning the sociological analysis of religion; and (4) suggests new and promising directions for empirical investigations of religion in industrial societies. Ironically, shifting the focus in this way does indeed spell the end of secularization theory as a distinct body of theory, but in a different way than previous critics have appreciated. Hence, understanding secularization as declining religious authority

avoids the theoretical cul-de-sacs about which Turner warns us, and within which too much contemporary sociology of religion flounders.

THEORETICAL CONTEXT

New Differentiation Theory

My starting point is the same as that of virtually every other analyst of religion in "modern" societies: the social fact that various institutional spheres are more or less differentiated from religion (Tschannen 1991). Religion, in this situation, has been understood ambiguously. It has at once referred both to the differentiated sphere of religious roles and institutions and to vague sets of values and beliefs believed by some to provide the social glue necessary to counteract the centrifugal forces of differentiation. But this ambiguity is not a necessary part of a sociological approach to religion; nor is it a virtue. . . . One development, which I call "new differentiation theory," is particularly useful for resituating secularization.

New differentiation theory is an attempt to reevaluate and rethink processes of institutional differentiation that were central to Parsons's vision of the social system. The theoretical task is largely one of separating out what was unsustainable and problematic in Parsons's influential formulation of differentiation as "a paradigm of evolutionary change" (Parsons 1966:21). This evolving perspective can be characterized by four key elements: (1) the assumption of a master trend towards differentiation in all spheres is dropped (Alexander 1990; Tilly 1984:48); (2) the "functionalist fallacy" — by which we infer that extant institutions meet some legitimate societal need merely because they exist — is avoided (Alexander 1990:xiii; Coleman 1990:336); (3) the requirement for value integration is dropped, replaced by the idea that societal integration is achieved via institutional arrangements whereby functional spheres refrain from "producing insoluble problems" for other spheres (Dobbelaere 1985:383; Luhmann 1982, 1990); and (4) rather than identifying the ends of one or another societal sphere, say the state or the economy, with the ends of the society as a whole, new differentiation theory understands no single sector as necessarily primary in the sense of gathering within itself the essential goals of the entire society (Luhmann 1990).

This broad shift in perspective appropriately highlights the political, conflictual, and contingent nature of relations among societal institutions in general and between religion and other spheres in particular. Here, society is understood as "an interinstitutional system" rather than as a moral community (Friedland & Alford 1991:232). In such an interinstitutional system religion is understood primarily as another mundane institutional sphere or organizational sector; it can no longer claim any necessary functional primacy. The religious sphere may, in a given time and place, have its "domain of possibilities" circumscribed to some extent by the state or by science or by the market (Luhmann 1982:225). At other times and places, or in other ways at the same time and place, religion may circumscribe the domains of possibility for other spheres. There is no presumed master trend, no contentious notion that religion provides a moral integration that is assumed to be functionally necessary, and no a priori scaling of some institutions as more "primary" or "dominant" than others. Religion enjoys no theoretically privileged position, but neither does it languish in a theoretically disprivileged position. It is one relativized sphere among other relativized spheres, whose elites jockey to increase or at least maintain their control over human actions, organizational resources, and other societal spheres.

At a stroke, a new world of sociological investigation opens up in which the subject is the multitudinous relations involving the religious sphere. Instead of that which integrates, religion represents one profane institutional sphere among others, with its own concerns and interests. Perhaps it is declining in power and influence, perhaps not. Unlike classical versions of the secularization hypothesis, in which other societal spheres (e.g., the state, science) are theorized to increasingly dominate social life at the expense of religion, new differentiation theory leaves this open to investigation. This theory opens the door to a new approach to secularization: one that situates religion and religious change in a concrete historical and institutional context. Secularization occurs, or not, as the result of social and political conflicts between those social actors who would enhance or maintain religion's social significance and those who would reduce it. Secularization, as Dobbelaere (1981) has pointed out, is carried by some social actors and resisted by others. The social significance of the religious sphere at a given time and place is the outcome of previous conflicts of this nature.[1] Understanding and explaining secularization thus requires attending to these conflicts.

New differentiation theory provides the context for what is to follow. Given differentiation, how is religion to be conceptualized so that its place in contemporary societies is adequately grasped and empirically accessible? I will suggest that, in a differentiated society, an adequate sociological approach to secularization requires redirecting attention away from the decline (or resurgence) of religion as such and towards the decreasing (or increasing) scope of religious authority. . . .

SECULARIZATION AS THE DECLINING SCOPE OF RELIGIOUS AUTHORITY

My suggestion is fairly radical. I advocate nothing less than abandoning religion as secularization's object, replacing it with religious authority. In this section of the article I present a concept of religious authority that develops a basic Weberian insight. Then, I draw heavily on the work of Dobbelaere to reconceptualize secularization as the declining scope of religious authority on three different dimensions. . . .

The Concept of Religious Authority

It is well known that Weber ([1968] 1978) began his sociology of religion by notoriously refusing to define religion. Less famous, but significant here, is the fact that Weber did define religious organization, and he did so by reference to religious authority:

A "hierocratic organization" is an organization which enforces its order through psychic coercion by distributing or denying religious benefits. . . . A compulsory hierocratic organization will be called a "church" insofar as its administrative staff claims a monopoly of the legitimate use of hierocratic coercion. (54)

Clearly, Weber conceived religious organization by analogy with political organization. Indeed, the above passage comes immediately after Weber's famous definitions of political organization and the state, which also are defined by reference to the nature of the authority contained therein. Since "there is no conceivable end which *some* political association has not at some time pursued," political authority must be defined "only in terms of the *means* peculiar to it" (Weber [1968] 1978:55, emphases in original). For political authority, of course, the characteristic feature of those means is the actual or threatened use of force.

Weber extended that emphasis on means, rather than on ends, to religious authority. Just as the multiplicity of possible political purposes implies that political organization cannot adequately be defined by reference to ends, the multiplicity of possible religious ends led him to a similar conclusion. For both political and religious authority, the decisive distinguishing criterion has to do with the means used to gain compliance rather than with the ends pursued by elites within a structure. Just as political authority rests on the threatened use of physical coercion, religious authority rests, for Weber, on the threatened use of "psychic coercion." What follows builds on this basic Weberian insight: Adequately characterizing religious authority requires attending to the nature of that authority rather than to the nature of the ends pursued.

Weber's characterization of religious authority, however, needs modification, mainly because the direct analogy Weber drew with political authority cannot be sustained. Political authority relies at least in part on its potential to use actual physical violence. Authority that did not have this component would not be political authority. Some other types of authority, similarly, may be delineated by reference to the nature of the power that could be called upon. The authority of managers, for example, is authority backed by the threat of dismissal; the authority of teachers is backed by the threat of low grades; and so on. But there is no distinct type of reserve power that would delineate religious authority in a comparable fashion.

Weber's "psychic coercion" will not do. Unlike physical coercion or dismissal from a job, the efficacy of psychic coercion itself requires explanation. Once we say that political authority rests on the threat of physical violence, we need not say more by way of definition. That the ability to inflict physical violence could back claims to authority does not need further explanation, and it is perfectly intelligible to demarcate a type of authority structure on these grounds. But psychic coercion does not provide a satisfying basis for authority in the same way. To say that religious authority is authority that rests on its ability to coerce psychically is to beg other questions: Why does the psychic coercion work? What is its basis? The threat of psychic coercion does not fully characterize the nature of religious authority in the same way that the threat of physical coercion characterizes the nature of political authority.

Religious authority, therefore, cannot be adequately demarcated either by reference to the ends it pursues or by reference to the means it may or may not use to coerce compliance. It can, however, be characterized by the manner in which it legitimates its demands for compliance. Whatever ends it pursues and whatever actual power does or does not underlie it, religious authority can be distinguished by a particular kind of legitimation. Its defining characteristic is in its means of legitimation rather than in the means used to back authority in times of crisis.

Following this line of argument, then, I will define a religious authority structure as a social structure that attempts to enforce its order and reach its ends by controlling the access of individuals to some desired goods, where the legitimation of that control includes some supernatural components, however weak.

Religious authority, like other forms of authority, has a staff capable of withholding access to something individuals want. When that withholding is legitimated by reference to the supernatural, authority is religious. It is worth pointing out that this concept sidesteps the old and sterile debate between functional and substantive definitions of religion because it partakes of both. It is functional in that it demarcates an object of study — structures of religious authority — by focusing on what those structures do: attempt to maintain themselves by using the supernatural to control access to something individuals want. This notion of religious authority structure shares with functional definitions in general the virtue that it prevents us from treating the culturally or historically specific content of some particular religion as if it were the defining characteristic of religion as such. It partakes of this virtue by placing no limit on *what* religious authority controls access to. At the same time, this concept avoids being all-inclusive and thereby empty by specifying a limit on how religious authority legitimates itself.

The distinguishing feature of religious authority is that its authority is legitimated by calling on some supernatural referent. The supernatural referent need not be activist in the sense that gods and spirits with personalities inhabit another, unseen, realm. An authority structure is religious as long as its claims on obedience are legitimated by some reference to the supernatural, even if the supernatural is impersonal and remote (cf. Stark & Bainbridge 1985). To say this another way, religious authority structures are distinguished by the fact that their claims are legitimated at least by a language of the supernatural. In contemporary U.S. society, that means that religious authority structures at least use "god-talk."[4]

The desired goods to which religious authority might control access will have different content from one religious authority structure to another. The substance in the definition is in the means that elites use to legitimate their control of access to valued goods, not in the nature of the goods themselves. The "goods" to which a religious authority structure controls access might be deliverance from sickness, meaninglessness, poverty, desire, sin, or other undesirable conditions. Or, religious authority might offer a positive good such as eternal life, nirvana, utopian community, perfect health, great wealth, or other valued states. The manner in which these goods are obtained might vary from membership in a certain community, to withdrawal from the world, to the profession of certain beliefs, to following a set of dietary laws or ritual obligations, and so on. The point here is that "religious goods" can be otherworldly or this-worldly, general or specific, psychic or material, collective or individual. Religious authority structures cannot be demarcated by reference to the content of the goods to which they control access because no good is inherently a religious good. Goods become religious goods by virtue of being embedded in a particular kind of social structure, a social structure that legitimates its control of those goods by reference to the supernatural.

Secularization as declining religious authority, then, will refer to the declining influence of social structures whose legitimation rests on reference to the supernatural.

SECULARIZATION AND RELIGIOUS AUTHORITY IN THREE DIMENSIONS

There is a fair degree of consensus that secularization, however else we think of it, must be multidimensional. The most well-developed and increasingly influential statement of secularization's multidimensionality is found in the work of Dobbelaere (1981, 1985, 1987). He identifies three dimensions of secularization, dimensions that I will label: laicization, internal secularization, and religious disinvolvement.[5]

Laicization refers to the process of differentiation whereby political, educational, scientific, and other institutions gain autonomy from the religious institutions of a society. The result of this process is that religion becomes just one institutional sphere among others, enjoying no necessary primary status. The second dimension, internal secularization, is the process by which religious organizations undergo internal development towards conformity with the secular world. Religious disinvolvement is Dobbelaere's third dimension of secularization and refers to the decline of religious beliefs and practices among individuals. These dimensions also may be understood as operating at three different levels of analysis. Laicization refers to a societal process; religious change to transformations at the level of the religious organization; and religious disinvolvement to shifts among individual persons.

These dimensions may be reconceptualized in terms of religious authority's declining scope. At each level it is possible to ask a similar question: what is the scope of control exercised by religious authority? Secularization at the societal level may be understood as the declining capacity of religious elites to exercise authority over other institutional spheres.

Secularization at the organizational level may be understood as religious authority's declining control over the organizational resources within the religious sphere. And secularization at the individual level may be understood as the decrease in the extent to which individual actions are subject to religious control. The unifying theme is that secularization refers to declining religious authority at all three levels of analysis.[6] . . .

Theoretical Promise of Secularization as Declining Religious Authority

Any conceptual innovation brings new features of the social world from the background into the foreground as some features are rendered theoretically irrelevant in favor of others that take on new significance. The test of such an innovation is whether or not focusing on the newly prominent features redirects empirical research in ways that promise greater understanding of the social world. Reformulating secularization as declining religious authority holds such promise: It prompts more fruitful theorizing about secularization both as an independent variable and as a dependent variable, making secularization more accessible both as *explanans* and as *explanandum*. Moreover, it does this by building bridges — or, more precisely, illuminating bridges that already exist but are underused — between the sociology of religion and other subdisciplines of sociology, a consequence that presumably is desirable, ceteris paribus.

Secularization as Explanans. Students of social movements have long been intrigued by the complex relationships between religion and social movements. Religion figured prominently in Hobsbawm's (1959) explorations of "primitive rebels." Smelser's (1962) classic work is replete with examples of religious movements. More recently, the prominent presence of religious organizations, leaders, or themes in major social movements (see, e.g., Beckford 1989; McAdam 1982; Morris 1984), as well as resurgent fundamentalisms, both in the U.S. and elsewhere (Marty & Appleby 1991), have alerted analysts of social movements to the fact that religion retains a certain political efficacy in a variety of circumstances. To date, however, there has been little systematic effort devoted to theorizing variation in the relationship between religion and social movements. Refocusing on religious authority rather than on religion offers a way to fill this gap.

I have the space only to sketch the insights prompted by focusing on religious authority, but hopefully the sketch will make clear the theoretical promise. The relation between religion and social movements, we might hypothesize, will vary depending on religious authority's scope in a given time and place. Figure 1 presents the possibilities in two dimensions: secularization at the societal level and secularization at the individual level.[10] Societies with low levels of societal-level secularization (i.e., a wide scope of religious authority at the societal level) are those in which institutions like education, science, and the state are rather directly influenced by reli-

gious authority, either because religious authority never has been historically differentiated from other spheres (as in some traditional societies) or because a differentiated religious authority has managed to exert (or reexert) control over other spheres (as in medieval Europe or contemporary Iran). Societies with high levels of societal secularization are those of the contemporary industrialized world, where religious authority exerts minimal and sporadic influence over the goings-on within the state, the economy, the arts, science, and so on.[11]

In societies with low levels of individual-level secularization, religious authority significantly regulates or influences individuals' actions. The extent of individual secularization will vary within societies as well as across societies. Within the contemporary U.S., for example, individual-level secularization has been considerably lower among blacks and continues to be lower among white Protestant fundamentalists than among other segments of the society. Individual-level secularization may also vary across geographical regions. Thus, the extent to which individual actions are subject to or respond to religious authority varies across communities. The U.S. is an

		Societal-level Secularization	
		High	Low
Individual-level secularization	High	Most areas of contemporary industrial societies 1	Medieval Europe Colonial U.S. 2
	Low	African American Communities U.S. Protestant Fundamentalism 3	Some traditional societies Contemporary Iran 4

FIGURE 1   Secularization in Two Dimensions: Social Settings

example of a society in which rather uniformly high societal-level secularization coexists with substantial internal variation on individual-level secularization.

This is not simply a sterile classification game. The theoretical pay-off is that this two-dimensional space predicts something of considerable interest: the nature of the relationship between religion and social movements. Figure 2 contains the predicted relationships. In cell 1, where there is substantial societal and individual secularization, religion, to the extent that it is relevant at all, will serve as a cultural resource for social movements. That is, in such a setting a social movement may draw on religious symbolism and ideas in efforts to motivate and mobilize its constituency. It may draw on religion as a cultural resource because that is all it can expect from religion in a setting that is highly secularized on both of these dimensions. To say this another way, religious ideas and symbols may be salient in social movement rhetoric, but religious organizations and elites will not be significant players. This is how Beckford (1989, 1990), for example, understands the religious themes that occur in some "new social movements."

. . .

Returning to Figure 2, the fourth cell contains settings in which secularization is low at both societal and individual levels. Here, we would predict the occurrence of full-fledged religious/political movements in which it is impossible to distinguish between religious action and political action. Traditional societies with undifferentiated religious and political/social authority would fit here. In this kind of setting, religious rebellion is political rebellion and vice versa. This kind of movement is where, for example, speaking in tongues is cause for police action and baptism is politically radical because it undermines the authority of local religious and social elites (see Fields 1985). We would also expect this kind of movement in theocratic settings such as contemporary Iran.

In cell 3 are settings where religious authority is narrow with respect to other societal spheres (i.e., high societal secularization) but wide with respect to individuals (i.e., low individual secularization), as in some African American communities, especially in rural areas, and among Protestant fundamentalists in this country. Here (unlike in cell 1) religious organizations and religious elites will be more significant players in social movements because they are able to effectively mobilize certain

Societal-level Secularization

		High	Low
Individual-level secularization	High	Religion as cultural resource 1	Anticlerical movements 2
	Low	Religion as organizational base 3	Religio-political movements 4

FIGURE 2   Secularization in Two Dimensions: Hypothesized Relationships between Religion and Social Movements

individuals. Hence, black churches provided significant human and organizational resources in the civil rights movement (Morris 1984), and contemporary Protestant fundamentalism has been able to mount a significant political movement (Liebman & Wuthnow 1983). This situation also describes prerevolutionary Iran; hence the hugely significant role of Muslim elites and organizations in that revolution is not surprising. The key feature of the relationship between religion and social movement in settings like this is that religion will be able to serve as an organizational base for mobilizing a variety of human and material resources.

Finally, in cell 2, are settings where religious authority has significant influence over other societal institutions (i.e., low societal secularization) but minimal control or influence over individuals' actions. The classic case is that of the Roman Church in medieval Europe, which Turner (1991) describes as follows:

> If religion was "dominant," then it played an important role in the economic and political organizations of the land-owning class, but it cannot be suggested that the peasantry was significantly controlled by Christian belief and institutions. (153)

To give just one example, although the Lateran Council of 1215 made regular confession obligatory for laity, there "is certainly clear historical evidence that there was considerable lay opposition to the coercive nature of confession and priests experienced difficulties in bringing their flock to the confessional" (Turner 1991:152). Recent historical work on colonial America, most notably that of Butler (1990), suggests that this was another setting that would fit in cell 3.

In such settings — societally powerful religious authority with a weak hold on individuals — we would expect social movements that are explicitly anticlerical or anti-religious-authority. This is because the social/political authority of religious elites makes them likely targets for movements of discontent, and the absence of legitimate authority over individuals makes

them more vulnerable targets. Hence, anticlerical movements like the Protestant Reformation and the democratic anticlerical movements of the seventeenth- and early eighteenth-century America (described by Hatch 1989) are, unsurprisingly, observed at such times and places.

All of this, of course, could be elaborated further, and the hypothesized connections between secularization and the relationship between religion and social movements should be subjected to more systematic empirical tests. In the present context, however, the point is this: A multidimensional focus on the scope of religious authority has transformed a notoriously vague pair of ideas (religion and secularization) into a relatively straightforward conceptual scheme, a scheme that appears likely to bear immediate theoretical fruit in at least this one area of sociological inquiry.

Secularization as Explanandum. More traditionally, sociologists have been concerned with secularization as a dependent variable. Here, too, shifting the focus to religious authority suggests new ways to think about, investigate, and attempt to explain the varying scope of religious authority across time and space. I have the space only to briefly indicate the productive directions at each analytical level.

Societies. Here, the key task is to describe and explain variations in religious authority's capacity to significantly influence the functioning of other institutional spheres. Previous approaches to this task (e.g., Wilson's and, to some extent, Dobbelaere's) have tended to see functional differentiation as identical to religion's capacity to influence other institutional spheres. Consequently, these approaches have tended to lump extensively differentiated societies together into a homogeneous "secularized" mass. The current approach, however, promotes research into the variable societal influence of religion even among societies with extensive functional differentiation.

Today, the most significant source of variation in this regard is the relative societal power of various religious fundamentalist movements. The Iranian Revolution provides the most obvious example of religious authority that has won control over other institutions in the society, and Beyer's (1993) analysis of that revolution, which highlights the role of religious authority, provides an instance of productive analysis and explanation of religious authority's changing societal scope.

Three features of Beyer's analysis bear emphasizing. First, he places the increased "public influence" of the Muslim religious authorities (i.e., the mullahs) at the center of attention, and attempts to explain how such an expanded scope of societal-level religious authority came to be. His dependent variable, in other words, is precisely variation in the scope of religious authority at the societal level.

Second, he provides a historically and sociologically grounded explanation of the successful revolution, highlighting (in addition to the usual variables of urban migration and exclusion of the masses from political participation) such variables as the prerevolutionary autonomy of *ulama* (religious scholars) from political authority, conflict between religious and secular authority over control of the courts and education, and the organizational network of Iran's mosques. Beyer's explanation of the "theocratic triumph" is thus an explanation of a successful social movement that expanded the scope of religious authority over other societal spheres. It is, of course, a matter for further research whether this analysis is of more general value in explaining success vs. failure of fundamentalist movements. Here, the point is that focusing on variations in the scope of religious authority promotes exactly this kind of grounded empirical work.

Third, Beyer's analysis incorporates secularization as an independent variable as well. That is, despite the stated goals of Khomeini and other leading clerics to establish total religious authority over all other spheres, the successful revolution almost immediately encountered

pressures that continue to cause conflicts precisely around the issue of the appropriate scope of religious authority. The pressures are manifest as conflicts between religious authorities and other elites over issues such as the manner and degree of state intervention in the economy, or the proper relationship between parliament and the Council of Guardians, a religious authority. To oversimplify, there seem to be structural limits to religious authority's capacity to impose itself in a society that participates at all in a global institutional environment that is highly secularized.

Thus, this analysis both identifies societal secularization as a key feature of the modern global system *and* offers an explanation for local variation in that secularization. Two questions require additional investigation: (1) What explains success or failure of fundamentalist movements? (2) What constraints does a wider, secularized environment place on even the most successful religious fundamentalist movements? The second question emerges directly from the focus on religious authority. While the first question does not require reconceptualizing secularization to either ask or answer it, it is nevertheless significant that this reformulated notion of secularization, by emphasizing organized conflicts among proponents and opponents of religious authority, so easily connects to the sociology of social movements.

Organizations.   On the organizational level, the focus on religious authority's scope provides an intellectual handle for investigating what has been perhaps the most slippery of concepts within the secularization literature: internal secularization. The notion of internal secularization solved a theoretical problem for earlier versions of secularization theory: High levels of involvement in institutional religion were not as embarrassing to classical secularization theory if the institutions themselves could be rendered somehow less religious. But these early approaches to internal secularization (e.g., in Berger 1969 and Luckmann 1967) have been justifiably criticized. First, they relied on vague assertions about the "accommodation" or "adaptation" of religious organizations to the secular world; about the "lack of depth" underlying much religious activity; about the "replacement" of sacred values by secular values; about the "attenuated religious character of churches." But how, exactly, does one tell the difference between a sacred and a secular value? Between a religious and a secular activity? By what criteria are the current practices of religious organizations more secular than past practices? The early accounts of internal secularization sidestepped these questions by failing to specify exactly what would and would not count as internal secularization. Second, these early accounts did not recognize variation in internal transformations among religious organizations. They proceeded as if all U.S. religious institutions were equally subject to secularization pressures and all homogeneously followed the same developmental path towards internal secularization. This assumption prompted more hand-wringing than empirical investigation.

The focus on religious authority, however, suggests any number of concrete indicators of religious authority's scope within organizations. Dobbelaere (1988), for example, has examined internal secularization within Belgian Catholic schools using such variables as the number of liturgical services performed and the number of lay relative to religious professionals on teaching staffs. To take another example, I have elsewhere examined internal secularization within American Protestant denominations by examining the shifting career backgrounds of those who become denominational CEOs (Chaves 1993). The idea here is that selecting a leader reflects intraorganizational politics in denominations, just as in secular organizations (Fligstein 1987). Hence, a trend away from choosing denominational CEOs from within the religious authority structure (i.e., away from choosing bishops and active clergy and towards choosing professional administrators) indicates internal secularization. Focusing on religious authority inside religious organizations

suggests indicators like these that promise to open new windows to internal secularization.

As important as providing new ways to describe religious authority's scope within organizations, however, is the fact that this approach opens new ways to explain variations in that scope. Most obviously, the entire body of developing organizational theory can be brought to bear. But there is another theoretical bridge whose relevance becomes clear when we remember that variations in religious authority's scope result from social and political conflicts between those who would extend religious authority and those who would limit it. Concretely, as Schoenherr (1987) has argued, this will mean emphasizing the position of religious elites, most prominently clergy. This focus on clergy, in turn, makes it possible to draw on sociological theory concerning competition and conflict among competing professional groups for control of organizations and other social resources.

Abbott's (1988) theory of professional systems may be particularly relevant here because of its explicit focus on jurisdictional battles among professionals. Theorists of internal secularization, who would be most interested in jurisdictional battles involving clergy, could put Abbott's variables to work in analyses of variation in the jurisdictional power of clergy within (and without) religious organizations. Several variables seem particularly promising: the extent to which professionals are able to hide from public view the assimilation of professional knowledge by others in the workplace; the prestige accorded the profession's academic knowledge (i.e., theology) as opposed to its practical knowledge (i.e., preaching, running a church, counseling, etc.); the extent of professional organization; the extent to which a profession is positioned to control the new work created by technological or organizational changes, and so on. For each of these variables, contemporary U.S. clergy would be coded in a way that would lead us to predict that they are increasingly disadvantaged in jurisdictional disputes with other professionals. But clergy in other times and places would have different characteristics. Far from a positing a "master trend," this framework provides a way to investigate historical and cross-sectional variation in the scope of religious authority. The dual point here is that the focus on religious authority renders internal secularization more empirically available, and it builds bridges over which sociological theories like Abbott's can travel en route to new explanations of observed variations in religious authority's scope.

Not incidentally, the concrete focus on religious authorities (i.e., clergy) as professionals competing for jurisdictional control over various activities has the potential to enable theoretical linkages between the organizational and the societal level. Abbott's "system of professions," after all, is a theory about societal power. The power of clergy within religious organizations will, of course, affect and be affected by their power in society. Some of the same variables that may help to explain waxing and waning religious authority inside religious organizations, then, may help to explain variations in religious authority's scope over other institutions and organizations as well.

Individuals. This approach apprehends microlevel social life in a way more consonant with the nature of individual identity in complex societies. Individuals in such societies, with very few exceptions, live their lives within a number of overlapping spheres, with some of their actions regulated by the authority of bosses at work, some by the demands of legal systems, some by family obligations, some by the rules of religions, etc. In such a society, the relevant individual-level questions for secularization are not questions about belief (how many people say they believe in God?) or mere organizational affiliation (how many people are members of religious organizations?). In such a society, the relevant questions about the scope of religious authority over individuals are questions about the extent to which actions are regulated by religious authority.

Thus, at the individual level, religious authority redirects attention away from religious ideas, sentiments, and affiliations and towards religious control/influence over actions of individuals. Hence, data about religious intermarriage, religious authority's attempted control over reproductive behavior, diets, voting, etc. are much more relevant to debates about secularization than are data about belief in God or church membership. Importantly, shifting our attention in this way gives a much different picture of the extent of individual-level secularization in the U.S.

Any investigation of individual-level secularization will be constrained by the availability of relevant trend data. While we might think of many indicators of religious authority's scope over individual action, trend data will be available for very few. Fortunately, religious intermarriage is one indicator for which such data are available. Even in the absence of religious proscription of intermarriage, this is a particularly good measure of religious authority's scope. Since strong religious authority will, by definition, affect some behaviors (e.g., diet, dress, weekend behavior), the more salient it is to individuals, the higher religious endogamy will be, if only because of a general tendency toward behavioral and cultural homogamy in marriage. Higher rates of religious intermarriage, therefore, bespeak weaker religious authority. To say this another way, if religious differences are increasingly irrelevant for marriage decisions, then religious authority's scope surely is narrowing.

Kalmijn (1991) has provided the most extensive analysis of intermarriage trends for Protestants and Catholics in the U.S. His "central finding" is that "intermarriage between people from Protestant and Catholic backgrounds increased dramatically between the 1920s and the 1980s" (797). At the same time educational homogamy has increased, indicating a general trend away from ascriptive and towards achieved statuses as most salient for marriage.

In the U.S., only Catholics are a large enough group to investigate the scope of a specific religious authority with survey data. The evidence clearly shows a substantially narrowing scope for Catholic religious authority over Catholic individuals. The percentage of Catholics who agreed that it is "certainly true that Jesus handed over leadership of his church to Peter and the popes" dropped from 70% in 1963 to 42% in 1973. By 1990, only 12% of U.S. Catholics accepted the Church's ban on artificial contraception (Christiano 1992). Research reviewed by Kalmijn (1991) finds largely nonexistent differences between Protestants and Catholics with respect to family-size preferences, marital fertility, and birth control practices. As Christiano (1992) put it, there is "loyalty, but not obedience" (1535) among U.S. Catholics. To rephrase, there is religion, but there is little effective religious authority.

Thus, although mere religious activity (as indicated by belief in God, church membership, and church attendance) apparently has been quite stable in the twentieth-century U.S. (but see Hadaway, Marler & Chaves 1993), religious authority's capacity to regulate actions of individuals has indeed declined. It is this kind of important shift in descriptive understanding that results when secularization is seen as declining religious authority rather than as declining religion. Moreover, individual level secularization becomes more amenable to grounded sociological explanation, as in connecting declining religious endogamy to the increasing salience of education for marriage choice.

CONCLUSION

Secularization has been reformulated within the context of new differentiation theory. When the social fact of institutional differentiation is de-Parsonsified, and when religion is construed as one institutional sphere among others, the study of secularization becomes the study of a concrete, differentiated social structure. The notion of religious authority structure delineates the social structures of interest, and the study of secularization becomes the study of religious authority's variable scope on three dimensions. This reformulation yields a number of descriptive and theoretical pay-offs by making it possible to clearly conceptualize and use secularization as both independent and dependent variable in a variety of sociological analyses. . . .

I am attempting a . . . shift in emphasis by advocating religious authority as the object of secularization rather than religion itself. Religion as the content of individual consciousness is like strain theory's diffuse discontent. When studying social movements, a fascinating and primary question is how and why diffuse discontent occasionally is mobilized into movements and organizations. Analogous questions may be asked of religion. The religious beliefs, sentiments, etc. in the minds of individuals are socially efficacious only when they become mobilized and institutionalized as structures of authority. Secularization as the declining power of these religious authority structures represents secularization as a truly sociological phenomenon.

Let me be clear here that this argument to replace religion with religious authority applies only with respect to secularization. I do not wish to limit the entire sociology of religion to the study of religious authority. My point is not that investigations of religious culture, religious markets, religious meanings, etc. are inherently unsociological. My point is merely that they have nothing to do with secularization.

The second concluding point is that, as the examples in the previous section indicate, there is very little reason to believe that explaining the variable scope of religious authority across and within societies will require a separate and distinct body of secularization theory. If religious authority is one among several authority structures in contemporary societies, then what is needed is general theory explaining why this authority structure at this time and place seems to be dominant while that one at that time and place seems dominant. Explanations of resurgent (and sometimes successful) fundamentalist movements, for example, would be subsumed under theories of social movements and political revolutions. Explanations of new religious authority structures based on new configurations of religious ideas, sentiments, and practices, will be subsumed under more general theories of cultural innovation and its institutionalization. Explanations about variable degrees of religious authority within religious organizations — internal secularization — will be subsumed under general theories of organizational change.

As I argued above, since the relevant actors within religious authority structures are the religious professionals who people those structures, and since a focus on the scope of religious authority means, concretely, a focus on the reach of these individuals within a society, theories of variations in this reach may be subsumed under more general theories of professionalization. Abbott's (1988) theory of professional systems may be particularly relevant in that its explicit focus is on the jurisdictional battles among professionals. Variation in the scope of religious authority may very well turn out to be best understood as a special case of variation in professional jurisdiction over actions, work, and organizational resources.

Thus, reformulating secularization as a concept that enhances our ability to grasp the variable place of religious authority in contemporary societies may very well spell the end of secularization theory, but not in the way imagined by previous critics.

NOTES

1. Fenn (1978) also develops this point, paying particular attention to ways in which "civil religion" is a contested construction rather than a unifying cultural center.

...

4. God-talk itself, however, is not enough to constitute a religious authority structure. The motto on our currency, "In God We Trust," or the phrase, "one nation under God," in the Pledge of Allegiance do not automatically make the U.S. government a religious authority structure. Religious authority is demarcated by the use of such language to

legitimate controlled access to something individuals want. Fenn (1982) has explored more deeply the difference between religious language that is truly legitimating and religious language that is subordinate to some other authority. His intriguing analysis of religious language in contemporary U.S. courts of law shows that the mere presence of religious language in oaths and testimony does not bespeak the recognition of religious authority by those same courts. In these settings, religious authority clearly is subordinate to legal authority. Similar analyses of religious language in political settings would surely yield similar conclusions.

5. Dobbelaere's labels are laicization, religious change, and religious involvement. I find the "religious change" label for the middle dimensions too vague. After all, religious change occurs in one way or another on all three levels. I change the valence on the third dimension to match that of the other two dimensions.

6. As Dobbeleare (1989) put it, secularization is about religion's impact "on the rules governing the different institutional domains . . . on the micromotives of the citizens . . . [and] on the enactment and application of laws, on court decisions, and on the preservation of traditional mores" (38).

...

10. Compare Fenn (1978:67).

11. An additional complexity is that a given society might be very secularized with respect to one sphere (e.g., science) while at the same time quite unsecularized with respect to another institutional sphere (e.g., education).

REFERENCES

ABBOTT, ANDREW. 1988. *The System of Professions*. University of Chicago Press.

ALEXANDER, JEFFREY C. 1990. "Differentiation Theory: Problems and Prospects." Pp. 1–15 in *Differentiation Theory and Social Change: Comparative and Historical Perspectives*, edited by Jeffrey C. Alexander and Paul Colomy. Columbia University Press.

BECKFORD, JAMES A. 1989. *Religion and Advanced Industrial Society*. Unwin Hyman.

———. 1990. "The Sociology of Religion and Social Problems." *Sociological Analysis* 51:1–14.

BELL, DANIEL. 1980. "The Return of the Sacred?" Pp. 324–54 in *The Winding Passage*. Basic Books.

BERGER, PETER L. 1969. *The Sacred Canopy*. Anchor Books.

BEYER, PETER. 1993. *Religion and Globalization*. Sage.

BUTLER, JON. 1990. *Awash in a Sea of Faith: The Christianization of the American People, 1550–1865*. Harvard University Press.

CHAVES, MARK. 1993. "Intraorganizational Power and Internal Secularization in Protestant Denominations." *American Journal of Sociology* 99:1–48.

CHRISTIANO, KEVIN. 1992. "Contemporary Developments in American Religion." Pp. 1526–55 in *Handbooks to the Modern World: The United States*. Vol. 3, edited by Godfrey Hodgson. New York: Facts on File.

COLEMAN, JAMES S. 1990. "Commentary: Social Institutions and Social Theory." *American Sociological Review* 55:333–39.

DOBBELAERE, KAREL. 1981 "Secularization: A Multi-Dimensional Concept." *Current Sociology* 29:1–216.

————. 1985. "Secularization Theories and Sociological Paradigms: A Reformulation of the Private-Public Dichotomy and the Problem of Societal Integration." *Sociological Analysis* 46:377–87.

————. 1987. "Some Trends in European Sociology of Religion: The Secularization Debate." *Sociological Analysis* 48:107–37.

————. 1988. "Secularization, Pillarization, Religious Involvement, and Religious Change in the Low Countries." Pp. 80–115 in *World Catholicism in Transition*, edited by Thomas M. Gannon. Macmillan.

————. 1989. "The Secularization of Society? Some Methodological Suggestions." In *Secularization and Fundamentalism Reconsidered*, edited by Jeffrey K. Hadden and Anson Shupe, pp. 27–43, Paragon House.

FENN, RICHARD K. 1978. *Toward a Theory of Secularization*. Society for the Scientific Study of Religion, Monograph Series, no. 1.

————. 1982. Liturgies and Trials. *The Secularization of Religious Language*. Pilgrim Press.

FIELDS, KAREN E. 1985. *Revival and Rebellion in Colonial Central Africa*. Princeton University Press.

FLIGSTEIN, NEIL. 1987. "The Intraorganizational Power Struggle: Rise of Finance Personnel to Top Leadership in Large Corporations, 1919–1979." *American Sociological Review* 52:44–58.

FRIEDLAND, ROGER, and ROBERT R. ALFORD. 1991. "Bringing Society Back In: Symbols, Practices, and Institutional Contradictions." Pp. 232–63 in *The New Institutionalism in Organizational Analysis*, edited by Walter W. Powell and Paul J. Dimaggio. University of Chicago Press.

HADAWAY, C. KIRK, PENNY MARLER, and MARK CHAVES. 1993. "What the Polls Don't Show: A Closer Look at U.S. Church Attendance." *American Sociological Review* 58:741–52.

HADDEN, JEFFREY K. 1987. "Toward Desacralizing Secularization Theory." *Social Forces* 65:587–611.

HATCH, NATHAN O. 1989. *The Democratization of American Christianity*. Yale University Press.

HOBSBAWM, E.J. 1959. *Primitive Rebels: Studies in Archaic Forms of Social Movements in the Nineteenth and Twentieth Centuries*. W.W. Norton.

HOUT, MICHAEL, and ANDREW M. GREELEY. 1987. "The Center Doesn't Hold: Church Attendance in the United States, 1940–1984." *American Sociological Review* 52:325–45.

KALMIJN, MATTHIJS. 1991. "Shifting Boundaries: Trends in Religious and Educational Homogamy." *American Sociological Review* 56:786–800.

LECHNER, FRANK J. 1991. "The Case Against Secularization: A Rebuttal." *Social Forces*. 69:1103–19.

LIEBMAN, ROBERT C., and ROBERT WUTHNOW (eds.). 1983. *The New Christian Right: Mobilization and Legitimation*. Aldine.

LUCKMANN, THOMAS. 1967. *The Invisible Religion*. Macmillan.

LUHMANN, NIKLAS. 1982. *The Differentiation of Society*. Columbia University Press.

————. 1990. "The Paradox of System Differentiation and the Evolution of Society." Pp. 409–40 in *Differentiation Theory and Social Change*, edited by Jeffrey Alexander and Paul Colomy. Columbia University Press.

MCADAM, DOUG. 1982. *Political Process and the Development of Black Insurgency, 1930–1970*. University of Chicago Press.

MARTY, MARTIN E., and R. SCOTT APPLEBY (eds.). 1991. *Fundamentalisms Observed*. University of Chicago Press.

MORRIS, ALDON D. 1984. *The Origins of the Civil Rights Movement*. Free Press.

PARSONS, TALCOTT. 1966. *Societies: Evolutionary and Comparative Perspectives*. Prentice-Hall.

SCHOENHERR, RICHARD A. 1987. "Power and Authority in Organized Religion: Disaggregating the Phenomenological Core." *Sociological Analysis* 47:S52–S71.

SHINER, LARRY. 1967. "The Meanings of Secularization." *International Yearbook for the Sociology of Religion* 3:51–62.

SMELSER, NEIL J. 1962. *Theory of Collective Behavior*. Free Press.

STARK, RODNEY, and WILLIAM SIMS BAINBRIDGE. 1985. *The Future of Religion*. The University of California Press.

STARK, RODNEY, and LAURENCE R. IANNACCONE. 1992. "Sociology of Religion." Pp. 2029–37 in *The Encyclopedia of Sociology*. Vol. 4, edited by EDGAR F. BORGATTA and Marie Borgatta. Macmillan.

TILLY, CHARLES. 1984. *Big Structures, Large Processes, Huge Comparisons*. Russell Sage Foundation.

TSCHANNEN, OLIVIER. 1991. "The Secularization Paradigm: A Systematization." *Journal for the Scientific Study of Religion* 30:395–415.

TURNER, BRYAN S. 1991. *Religion and Social Theory*. [2nd.] ed. Sage Publications.

WEBER, MAX. [1968] 1978. *Economy and Society*, edited by Guenther Roth and Claus Wittich. University of California Press.

WILSON, BRYAN. 1985. "Secularization: The Inherited Model." Pp. 9–20 in *The Sacred in a Secular Age*, edited by PHILLIP E. HAMMOND. University of California Press.

27 Secularization and Sacralization Deconstructed and Reconstructed

N. J. DEMERATH III

Dr. Demerath is well aware of the secularization debates. In this article, he attempts to provide a fuller way to look at the issue, essentially showing why it is possible to have secularization and what he calls sacralization at the same time. That is, from his perspective, religion can both be on the rise and on the decline at the same moment.

Until some thirty years ago, increasing faith-lessness was an article of faith among scholars and elites throughout the West, if not world-wide. The notion that religion might give way to non-religion and perhaps irreligion was not only taken for granted by sinners outside the sacred ranks but was actually depended upon by saints within the fold. Philosophers and kings begrudged the influence of organized religion and welcomed the decline of what they perceived to be institutionalized superstition. At the same time, religion everywhere played off the dangers of secularity. Cautionary tales of the slippery slope away from the sacred have long constituted a master religious narrative.

In recent years, much of this has changed. Today anyone who takes 'secularization' seri-ously and says so runs the risk of being labeled antediluvian, anti-church, or anti-social. At least in some circles, a concept that was once an unquestioned staple of scholarly work has been shunted to the unmucked stables of scholarship past. In the eyes of its critics, secu-larization is a hypothesis that has been proven false and a term that should be expunged from proper usage. The very fact that religion per-sists and often thrives is ample rebuttal to the 'secularization thesis' and a signal to abandon both its explicit assumptions and its implicit agenda.

Secularization has taken on different mean-ings for different camps. It matters whether the reference is to religion's displacement, decline, or change; to the sacred at the level of the indi-vidual, the institution, the community, or the culture; and to a pattern that is long-term, linear

Source: N. J. Demerath III and James A. Beckford (eds.), "Secularization and Sacralization Deconstructed and Recon-structed," from *The Sage Handbook of the Sociology of Religion*, © Sage Publications, 2007. Reproduced by permission of SAGE Publications, London, Los Angeles, New Delhi and Singapore.

and inevitable or short-term, cyclical, and contingent. Clearly, it is possible to construct versions of secularization that are either outrageous or reasonable. It matters greatly how the concept is deployed. For some, it is a prophecy of religious demise – whether a tragic jeremiad or a triumphant anticipation. For others, it is a set of historically and sociologically specified processes that move less linearly and with less certainty through time. For still others, secularization converges with sacralization to form a stream of constantly shifting conceptions and locations of the sacred. Whichever option is at issue, the stakes are far from idle.

Debate here has become deeper and more raucous than is common in the academy, perhaps because the issues concern not just scholarship but all of the potentially personal overtones of religion, not to mention the livelihood of every student of religion. In fact, one of this chapter's objectives is to recapture the argument for social science and rid secularization of connotations that mistakenly threaten both religion and the religious. . . .

FROM CLASSICAL TO CONTEMPORARY CONCEPTIONS OF SECULARIZATION

Both the process and the thesis of secularization have precursors in the mist of early history, but it is the Western Enlightenment that provides their first codification – at least for Western consumers. The term itself dates from France in the mid-seventeenth century. The first high priest of this anti-church was the French bourgeois intellectual, Francois-Marie Arouet Voltaire (1694–1778). A professed 'deist' whose belief in impersonal forces stood in sharp contrast to 'theistic' conceptions of a personal God, his writings railed against the Church's sanctimonious superstitions and ecclesiastical trappings (cf. Voltaire, 1756). But Voltaire was not the most materialist figure of his day, and he was distinguished more by the

expression of his views than their substance, including his sense that the end of religion was near – quite possibly in his lifetime. The main thrust of his views was shared by many Europeans and Americans, including Benjamin Franklin and Thomas Jefferson.

And the prophets of secularization multiplied. By the second half of the nineteenth century, they included the sometimes infamous father – or at least namer – of 'sociology,' the French positivist, Auguste Comte (1852). Comte was a prophet of rationalism who conceived of a future controlled more by social science than by religion. His view was shared by contemporaries such as England's Herbert Spencer (1874), whose non-fiction sales rivaled those of Dickens' novels, and by the German, Karl Marx, whose political migrations had by then taken him through France and Belgium to his final residence in England. Marx's conception of religion as an opiate is well-known, though it is often lifted out of its more compassionate – indeed more spiritual – context as follows:

Religious distress is at the same time the expression of real distress. Religion is the sigh of the oppressed creature, the heart of a heartless world, just as it is the spirit of an unspiritual situation. It is the opium of the people.

Of course, Marx and Engels envisioned a de-narcotized future once the masses learned the real secret of their misery, substituted class consciousness for false consciousness, and exchanged this-worldly action for other-worldly hopes.

Max Weber and Emile Durkheim continued the tradition into the first two decades of the twentieth century. Their positions concerning religion were suffused with irony. Although both came from upstanding religious homes – Lutheran for Weber and Jewish for Durkheim, who came from a long line of rabbis – Weber's self-description as 'religiously unmusical' was apt for Durkheim as well. Still, both provided classic statements concerning the importance of religion – whether Weber's 'Protestant ethic' as a pre-condition of capitalism or Durkheim's conception of religion as the latent worship of society itself. At the same time, each became sensitive to secularization without using the term, though they differed somewhat in their assessments of it.

For Weber (1904), secularization was an implication of the 'rationalization' that was so uniquely characteristic of the West. He was ambivalent about the results. On the one hand, he appreciated its cultural underpinnings of everything from capitalism and bureaucracy to developments in architecture and music. On the other hand, Weber wrote within the legacy of German historiography and a concern for the '*Geist*' or spirit of every age. He lamented a dark side of rationality that would lead to a hollow disenchantment. Towards the very end of his famous *Protestant Ethic and the Spirit of Capitalism*, he summarizes the new capitalists pessimistically as follows:

Today, the spirit of religious asceticism . . . whether finally, who knows? Has escaped from the cage . . . and the idea of duty in one's calling prowls about in our lives like the ghost of dead religious belief. No one knows who will live in this cage in the future, or whether at the end of this tremendous development entirely new prophets will arise, or there will be a great rebirth of old ideas and ideals, or, if neither, mechanized petrification, embellished with a kind of convulsive self-importance. For of the last stage of this cultural development, it might well be truly said: 'Specialists without spirit, sensualists without heart; this nullity imagines that it has attained a level of civilization never before achieved' (Weber, 1904 (1995): 182).

Durkheim was more positive about secularization, in part because he was more positivistic, working selectively within the tradition of Comte and French positivism. Durkheim (1961) was optimistic about a secular morality and an autonomous ethic for society. But while he envisioned religious beliefs being displaced by science, he reasoned that the sense of society as a sacred collectivity would remain, and

he envisioned a waxing and waning of sacred commitments as part of the natural rhythm of social change. In a passage that might well serve as the text for this sermon, he describes France on the eve of World War I and then looks to the future:

If we find a little difficulty today in imagining what (the) feasts and ceremonies of the future could consist in, it is because we are going through a stage of transition and moral mediocrity. The great things of the past which filled our fathers with enthusiasm do not excite the same ardor in us, either because they have come into common usage to such an extent that we are unconscious of them, . . . or else because they no longer answer to our actual aspirations; but as yet there is nothing to replace them. In a word, the old gods are growing old or already dead, and others are not yet born. . . . It is life itself, and not a dead past which can produce a living cult. But this state of incertitude and confused agitation cannot last forever. A day will come when our societies will know again those hours of creative effervescence, in the course of which new ideas arise and new formulae are found which serve for a while as a guide to humanity. . . .

By the mid-twentieth century, secularization had become one of the master motifs of the social sciences. By then, however, sociology had begun to develop more nuanced versions of secularization. Perhaps not surprisingly, the 1960s produced a bumper crop as a possible response to a decade in which changes of all sorts seemed at hand. In 1960, Talcott Parsons was among the first to develop the notion of societal differentiation as it applied to American religion. As society becomes more complex, all of its institutions become more differentiated from each other and enjoy more autonomy but less overall influence. However, the process does not occur equally, and traditional institutions such as religion are more affected by the changes. And yet Parsons distinguished between religious change and religious decline, arguing that, if anything, religion's new place in the differentiated scheme of things offered it protection against some of the more corrosive secularization:

. . . a process of differentiation similar to that which has affected the family has been going on in the case of religion and has reached a particularly advanced stage in the United States. . . . Through this process of differentiation religion already has become a more specialized agency than it had been in most other societies. But since the Renaissance and the Reformation (this) process has been going on . . . (Parsons 1960: 304).

Two works developed this theme in different ways in the late 1960s, though both Peter Berger's *The Sacred Canopy* (1967) and Bryan Wilson's *Religion in Secular Society* (1966) restored the connotation of religious diminishment. Berger dealt with both the rise and decline of religion. Having described religion's importance as a source of meaning for a cosmos that is often inchoate, he went on to note factors involved in religion's erosion. These included privatization, pluralism, and a new religious marketplace, all contributing to a secularization which he defined as '. . . the process by which sectors of society and culture are removed from the domination of religious institutions and symbols' (1967: 107). The definition has a somewhat backwards quality, as if religion remains and remains unchanged, but society leaves by the backdoor. But clearly religion itself was changing, and Berger assigned some of the blame to influences within the churches rather than laying all the blame on external factors in the secular context. He argued that liberal clergy and theologians were often out ahead of the process in diluting religion to avoid conflicts with a lapsing laity.

If Berger's conception of secularization suggests society pulling away from a still religious core, Bryan Wilson conveyed the opposite scenario by which religion itself recedes to the margins and suffers a diminution of influence. For him, secularization is 'the process whereby religious institutions, actions, and consciousness lose their social significance' (Wilson 1966: xiv). But Wilson was aware of a profound difference between the declining influence of the established churches and the often surging growth of sectarian movements (cf. Wilson, 1990).

Both Berger and Wilson were part of a growing choir singing the anthem of societal differentiation. . . . The Belgian sociologist, Karel Dobbelaere (1981) draws a parallel between secularization and the French term 'laicization,' which Durkheim and others used to denote a loss of priestly control with a resulting decanonization of religion. While developing the concept for European settings, Dobbelaere draws two important distinctions, one between the processes of differentiation, decline, and change (1981) and the other between religion's role at the quite different levels of the individual, the organization, and the society (1985). We will return to these distinctions later.

Meanwhile, by this time, secularization had become a major priority on the agenda of social scientists examining religion. Returning to the U.S., Richard Fenn (1979) stressed that secularization involves a blurring rather than a sharpening of the boundaries between the sacred and the secular; still more recently, Fenn refers felicitously to secularization as the 'domestication of charisma' (1993). Certainly secularization is at least a sub-theme of Robert Bellah *et al.* in *Habits of the Heart* (1985), a work that depicts the community's losing struggle with individualism – perhaps the ultimate form of differentiation at the personal level. Wade Clark Roof and William McKinney (1987) describe a similar pattern as a 'new voluntarism' that has displaced old denominational loyalties. And Robert Wuthnow (1988) notes still other forces of differentiation at work to shift religious action away from the denominations and congregations in the direction of 'special purpose groups' whose single-issue agendas are often more a reflection of political morality than religious doctrine or theology. Wuthnow also describes a differentiation between America's liberal and conservative 'civil religions.'

Mark Chaves (1993) distinguishes between declining religion and declining religious authority, noting that the two do not always go hand-in-hand in secularization. Chaves documents the emergence of differentiated 'dual structures' within denominations. He argues that secularization involves a split between declining 'religious' authority, on the one hand, and increasing secular 'agency' authority, on the other. This is consistent with other traditions of organizational analysis within religion, including the classic distinction between 'sects' and 'churches,' and the common process by which the purity of the former's religious authority ultimately gives way to the latter's agency authority.

Still another strand of secularization theory has stressed the shift in location and content of traditional religion. A notion first predicted by Weber's colleague Ernst Troeltsch in the 1920s under the possibly mis-translated term, 'mysticism,' involves the individuation or 'privatization' of religion as subsequently developed by Thomas Luckmann along with his sense of a 'shrinking transcendence' (Luckmann, 1967, 1990). Recently Roof has noted similar developments in his survey of 'baby boomer' religiosity and their turn away from traditional religious forms towards spirituality and New Age pursuits (Roof 2001).

Finally, a very recent addition to the reach and contingencies of secularization comes from Pippa Norris and Ronald Inglehart (2004). Their globally comparative study uses a wide variety of data – especially the series of Euro-Barometer and World Values surveys – to test the theories of others and buttress a theory of their own. Essentially they argue that secularization is a function of 'existential security' or confidence in basic life subsistence and life conditions; this explains why it is a clear trend in the West by almost any measure. At the same time, countries experiencing existential *in*-security in Latin America, the Middle East and South Asia show the opposite trend of increasing religious involvement, including extremist religious movements and behavior. In a sense, this returns us to a very old conception of the relationship between social class and religiosity: because the 'poor are always with us' so is religion as a theodicy of needed other-worldly escape and compensation.

So much, then, for a rapid review of some of the high points of the rise of secularization theory in sociology. But even the most ardent supporters of the theory would concede that the review has been one-sided. It is high time to introduce the theory's critics and criticisms.

THE MYTH OF THE MYTH OF SECULARIZATION?

Today it is common to hear that secularization has been categorically 'disproven'. After all – the critics contend – just a quick glance at home or abroad indicates that religion is booming everywhere for weal and for woe. There is no question that this argument has a certain face validity. But the secularization debate runs deeper and is not so easily decided.

In its most recent incarnation, the late Jeffrey Hadden (1987) was among the first to lay down the gauntlet with a stinging attack on secularization theory and theorists, arguing that the latter had neglected research and analysis in their zeal to convert secularization into a 'taken-for-granted ideology.' Over the next ten years, the rumblings and grumblings grew louder. When Peter Berger partially recanted his earlier secularizationist views in 1997 and later elaborated the point by pointing to a global religious efflorescence (Berger, 1997, 1999), this certainly drew blood. But when the emerging leader of the anti-secular opposition, Rodney Stark, administered secularization's last rites, 'requiescat in pace,' in 1999, he was premature. As so often happens in such debates, the disagreement involves a number of different arguments passing each other in a starless night. In fact, the debate can be dis-aggregated into five debates over five quite different issues.

1. First, there is the question of *degree*; i.e. whether secularization should be considered as a massive

all-or-nothing transformation between conditions where religion is all dominant to conditions in which religion has disappeared altogether OR secularization may also be found in smaller, more nuanced shifts well within the former continuum rather than at its poles.

The British anthropologist, Mary Douglas (1982) was among the first to chastise secularization proponents for imagining a mythical past against which the present will inevitably come up short. In her case, the past involved those simple, undifferentiated societies studied by anthropologists but stereotyped by others as convenient foils. Thus, even here religious piety and participation are not always either deep or universal. If these are the beginnings of the neo-evolutionary process of modernization, their religion bears inconvenient similarities with the religion of complex societies toward the end of the process.

Rodney Stark (1999) picked up the point and elaborated it for early Western societies. To the extent that a secularizing trend depends upon a contrast with a pious ancient and medieval Europe, Stark cites evidence suggesting that this is mythical. Once one looks beyond the public displays of ecclesiastical officialdoms, the masses appear to be at the very least anti-church, if not anti-religious. Attitudes towards organized faith were conspicuous for their alienation, their corruption, and their sheer raucousness. The religion of many 'Christian' nations founded in these early years was only inches deep as a pious surface covering an often impious base.

In its earliest formulations by such foregoing Enlightenment sages as Voltaire (1756), Marx (1844), Comte (1852), and Spencer (1874), there is little question that secularization involved a linear and inexorable decline of religion to the point of its disappearance. Put in this extreme form, it is once again not hard to reject the 'secularization thesis,' as this version of it has come to be known. Both of its extreme poles buckle beneath the weight of evidence. The critics are no doubt correct that the very notion of a totally religious society is a mythical construct unsustained by either historical or anthropological evidence. Whether reaching back to ancient societies or reaching out to isolated tribes, one may find religion as a potent force but never omnipotent. Competing interests, rival claims, status jostling within and without the priesthood – all of these have taken their toll on religious domination. Nor is secularity itself unknown in such settings; people

on the margins often become alienated from or indifferent to religion. And at the other extreme, where is the society with no traces of religion? Certainly not the U.S. or anywhere else in the West. Nor for that matter in the several countries around the globe who have mounted official campaigns against religion – the People's Republic of China or the former U.S.S.R. True, religion is sometimes a minority phenomenon in these and other countries, but in no instance can it be described as fully dormant, much less dead.

Surely this should be the death knell of secularization. But once again, not so fast. There is a sense in which the anti-secularization critics have inflated the secularization argument to a point that makes it especially vulnerable to pricking. Using an all-versus-nothing criterion is a very stringent test indeed, and it ignores the important dynamics and variations that may occur in between these extremes. Such prophecy has been virtually non-existent among more measured twentieth-century analyses. Recent critics have preferred to concentrate their fire on the earlier and more extreme versions of the argument and then generalize the results to secularization of any sort and form. Even if secularization is seen as a straight-line, linear process from high to – low and most would argue that this is rarely the case – one can surely imagine a society whose religion is powerful but not all powerful from which there is religious change without decline, and decline that does not reach demise. To deny conceptual standing to lesser changes along the continuum because they do not involve a shift from the extreme maximum to the extreme minimum is akin to denying scientific standing to all sorts of fluctuations from temperature gradients to demographics. The critical dynamics in virtually all matters of change occur within the mid-range of the distributions rather than at the ideal-typical poles.

Virtually all of the major sociological work on behalf of secularization over the past seventy-five years has occurred in this more closely grounded and finely raked terrain. Social scientists have described various aspects of religious decline in the complex societies of the West, but none has made so bold as to claim or predict religion's omnipotent universality or its disappearance especially with the proliferation of sects and cults – or 'new religious movements' as the latter are now called euphemistically. Nowadays religion's mere persistence masks a host of questions concerning religion's changing terms and circumstances. The 'secularization thesis' of mythical proportions with a mythical beginning and a mythical end is indeed in error, but as I have argued elsewhere, it is a largely non-instructive error somewhat akin to disproving Newton, or denying the hypothesis of global warming because we have not yet been burned to a crisp and the nights do, after all, still get cooler (Demerath 1998, 2000c).

2. Meanwhile, even within a less extravagant range of secularization, there are debates. A second major issue concerns *levels*, i.e. does secularization occur at the macro-level of whole societal cultures and structures, the meso-level of religious institutions and organizations, the micro-level of individual forms of religious belief and participation, or all or none of the above?

Surprisingly, once the focus shifts to these less extreme versions of secularization, the disagreement narrows considerably. Consider the following remark regarding the macro- and meso-levels from the arch-critic of secularization, Rodney Stark:

This refers to a decline in the social power of once-dominant religious institutions whereby other social institutions, especially political and educational institutions have escaped from prior religious domination. If this were all that secularization means, there would be nothing to argue about. Everyone must agree that, in contemporary Europe, for example, Catholic bishops have less political power than they once possessed, and the same is true of Lutheran and Anglican bishops. . . . Nor are primary aspects of public life any longer suffused with religious symbols, rhetoric, or ritual (Stark, 1999: 4–5).

This greatly reduces the gap between secularization's advocates and at least one key antagonist. For many of his opponents, Stark's acceptance of 'macro' as opposed to 'meso' and 'micro' secularization suggests a battlefield conversion – though, in fact, it is not a new position for him (cf. Stark and Bainbridge 1985). Nor is it a trivial concession. Many of the twentieth-century theories of secularization reviewed in the previous section pivot around this point, especially Parsons, Berger and Wilson. But if there is at least some agreement at this one level of secularization, debate continues at the other two levels of institutional and individual religion.

It is here that Stark has concentrated his relentless fire against secularization. His book with Roger Finke, *The Churching of America* (1992), uses actual and reconstructed church membership data to argue that individual religiousness has increased rather than decreased over the last two centuries, and that the real 'winners' have been conservative churches, while the real 'losers' have been the more liberal (and more secular) churches. Critics note that the work is not without problems – for example, spectacular growth rates are less likely among already large denominations and more likely among successful start-ups that have nowhere to go but up, and the thesis refers to rates of growth and decline rather than absolute size where the liberals continue to lead. Moreover, the study assumes that membership is a constantly reliable measure of general religiosity over time when, for example, in the early years it was more a measure of elite community standing than individual piety. Finally, as James Hunter (1987), Philip Jenkins (2002) and others have pointed out, even today's radically conservative churches experience secularization over time and may become tomorrow's modernists.

Many scholars have also noted the continued vitality of religion in America. Stephen Warner's 'new paradigm' (1993) provides a systematic statement of how the American case may differ from the European scene that spawned secularization theory in the first place. But recently Stark has taken his methods and his 'market' model of religion abroad. He and economist Laurence Iannaccone (1994) have argued that even the secularization of European religion was greatly exaggerated – an argument that has had both supporters (Davie 1994; Swatos and Gissurarson 1997) and detractors (cf. Bruce 1995; Dobbelaere 1993; Wilson 1998). Stark and his compatriots use a 'supply-side' interpretation of the religious marketplace, in which they argue that individual demand is less important than the religious organizations' supply. The supply may involve a religious monopoly or religious competition in any given society or region, and their disputed findings indicate that competition is more favorable to religion because it allows the consumer to exercise more 'rational choice' in seeking out the religious benefits.

3. Meanwhile, a third source of contention involves the question of just how should one measure secularization? There are a variety of barometers ranging from the standard counts of church membership, church attendance, and religious media consumption to legislative and judicial decisions, and the uneven compliance with both. However, all of these indices are suspect in one

way or another. Grace Davie (1994) has argued, for example, that a common current syndrome in Britain involves 'believing without belonging.' By contrast, a steady stream of research in the U.S. has long indicated that one can be a church member – even a church attender – without being a believer in the traditional sense. American church membership totals generally exceed church attendance rates by 50%, and recent work by Haddaway *et al.* (1993) has shown that claimed church attendance routinely exaggerates actual church attendance by 50% or more. On the other hand, Robert Woodberry (1998) has shown inflated attendance reports are due largely to religion's continued high standing in the culture and the bias that results from the normative desirability of attendance.

...

Judicial decisions concerning religion may be subject to the reverse misinterpretation. When the U.S. Supreme Court ruled against prayer in the public schools in 1963, this was by no means a reflection of dominant public sentiment. Like most decisions in the area of religion over the past half-century, these reflected the court's protection against the first clause of the Constitution's First Amendment guarding against a religious establishment. In most such cases, the originating plaintiffs were aberrant non-religious types with thick wallets and thicker skins who were resisting local practices. Indeed, many such practices – including school prayer – that have been ruled unconstitutional have been continued below the national radar. It is speculated that even today some 25% of the nation's public classrooms begin with some form of spoken or silent prayer the Supreme Court notwithstanding.

Meanwhile, the dispute over secularization is not confined to the West. In fact, the Western version of the debate is comparatively innocuous because it is largely confined to scholars removed from the political ramparts and because the politics of religion has generally been laid to rest save in a few cases such as the tragically contested Northern Ireland and the recent anti-climactic decision of Sweden to sever state ties with the Lutheran Church as of 2000. But once one leaves the West to visit countries elsewhere (cf. Demerath 2000a, 2001), it is hard not to be struck by one area after another where assessments of secularization and secularity have become volatile public issues exacerbated by the ideological conflict between forthright pro- and anti-secularists. From Poland

and Eastern Europe through the remains of the U.S.S.R. to Afghanistan; from the Balkans through Turkey and into Iran; from Algeria through Egypt to Israel; from Pakistan through India to Sri Lanka; from Indonesia through China to Japan – these are just a few countries whose national identities now hang in the balance of a prolonged conflict over secularization (cf. Juergensmeyer 1993). I shall have more to say about these non-Western cases later. But the struggles may involve both one religious group versus another and religion generally versus a secular culture.

4. These cases cue still a fourth issue that fuels the larger debate over secularization. Just as we can reject an all-to-nothing temporal trajectory for secularization, it seems clear that we must reject all-or-nothing generalizations that apply to all individuals, all churches, all regions, all social classes, all communities, all religions, or all societies, much less to the world as a whole. Although there has been a persistent tendency towards such overdrawn characterizations, this moves us out of sociology and the world *as it is* into more philosophical and theological treatments of the world *as it ought to be* – as if there were consensuses here.

Since so much of the empirical literature in sociology makes this point, it is hard to know where to begin or end in citing references. But the aforementioned Norris and Inglehart (2004) volume might suffice for traversing the widest array of such differences in its global survey of secularization. As they make clear, secularization is not a global phenomenon, given major differences between East and West, North and South. Nor are these immune to further macro-, meso-, and micro- variation. World faith traditions differ between themselves (e.g. the more secular Buddhists vs. the less secular Hindus).

But there are also differences within Faith traditions (e.g. within the Abrahamic tree, the more secular wings of Liberal Protestants and Reform Jews versus the generally less secular branches of Islam). Within each of these general groupings, churches, temples and mosques vary, as do the members in or around them. The well-known distinction between churches, sects, and cults reeks of secularization, and certainly some of each are more secular than others. Even among evangelical, fundamentalist or Pentecostal groups, some have moved further down the road to secularization than others, partly as a result of the search for organizational stability and membership growth. Finally, the sociology of religion is replete with demonstrations that individuals within even quite specific religious groups will differ. As sociologists of religion have long demonstrated, individuals differ by parental background, age, gender and ethnicity and social class – to name only a few variables that bear upon the extent of secularization and the degree of secularity.

All of these findings have a self-reflexive impact upon the very scholars researching them. One reason why the secularization paradigm went so long without being challenged is that so many of the scholars supporting it came from cultures, sub-cultures, and organizations that were part of it. In the West, this meant scholars who were themselves largely secular or from the more secular religious backgrounds of Liberal Protestantism and Catholicism or Reform Judaism, as opposed to newer and more conservative movements. As the saying goes, what you see depends upon where you are seated. But to the extent that secularization becomes a more variegated phenomenon as opposed to a single massive depiction of the world, it is in a better position to draw upon scholars from different backgrounds who will not feel they have personal axes to grind or personal identities at stake.

5. Finally, the fifth and last principal topic for debate concerns the relationship between secularization as religious decline or religious change. Here too Rodney Stark has helped to bring the issue to the fore:

   Of course, religion changes. Of course, there is more religious participation and even greater belief in the supernatural at some times and places than in others, just as religious organizations have more secular power in some times and places than in others. Of course, doctrines change – Aquinas was not Augusteine, and both would find heresy in the work of Avery Dulles. But change does not equate with decline (Stark 1999: 29).

Once again, Stark appears to concede a great deal before snatching it away with his last sentence remark that . . . 'change does not equate with decline.' He is certainly correct that the two are not identical. Moreover, only one equates with secularization, and that is change rather than decline. Of course, there is little question that secularization has come to connote decline, whether in its long-range or short-term form. But as I shall argue momentarily, change may involve secularization without decline; indeed, secularization can be part of a process that is necessary to maintain or even increase religiosity.

DEFINING SECULARIZATION AND INTRODUCING SACRALIZATION

At this point, we are now sufficiently acquainted with the key issues surrounding secularization to consider a definition that is a bit more formal and considerably broader than those mentioned earlier. Of course, there are almost as many definitions as there are broad treatments of the topic, and there is certainly no paucity of the latter, since any serious sociological treatment of religion requires a treatment of secularization (e.g. Beckford 2003). Still, here is my definition:

Secularization is a process of change by which the sacred gives way to the secular, whether in matters of personal faith, institutional practice, or societal power. It involves a transition in which things once revered become ordinary, the sanctified becomes mundane, and things other-worldly may lose their prefix. Whereas 'secularity' refers to a condition of sacredlessness, and 'secularism' is the ideology devoted to such a state, secularization is a historical dynamic that may occur gradually or suddenly and is sometimes temporary and occasionally reversible.

Several aspects of the definition are worth emphasizing. *First*, it refers to a process of religious change, but not necessarily to religious decline, let alone demise. After all, if religion involves notions of transcendence that are ritually reinforced and collectively supported, this is not immutable; it may take varying forms, and it is not always the oldest or most traditional versions that are the most compelling. Indeed, I will argue momentarily that effective religion often depends upon change – and secularized change at that.

Second, the definition carries no sense of linearity or inevitability. It may – or may not – occur among individuals as an accretion or an epiphany, among institutions such as cults, sects, churches, denominations, and whole faith traditions, and among communities and societies where a particular form of the sacred suffers a diminution of influence.

And *third*, note the emphasis on 'a particular form of the sacred.' Secularization is not a process that sweeps everything sacred before it. As some sacred beliefs, rituals, or influences undergo change, others within the same firmament may remain constant or even experience recrudescence or enhancement.

In fact, this is the cue for the entrance of *sacralization* as the dialectically opposing process which is crucial in understanding the larger context in which secularization often operates. Turning the above definition of secularization on its head, *sacralization is the process by which the secular becomes sacred or other new forms of the sacred emerge, whether in matters of personal faith, institutional practice or political power. And sacralization may also 'occur gradually or suddenly, and may be sometimes temporary and occasionally reversible.'*

Sacralization may take a number of forms. Even established religions generate new sacred commitments over time: witness Catholicism's relatively recent devotion to Mariolatry, beginning in the nineteenth century; Islam's increasingly sacred enmities between Sunnis and Shia where power hangs in the balance, and radical Hinduism's effort to sacralize India as an officially Hindu state. Within American religion, sacralization is apparent in both the tendency of religious 'sects' to revive or revitalize older religious beliefs and practices and the tendency of 'cults' to develop new religious forms, whether through the innovation of a prophetic and virtuosic leader within the society or by importing a religion from outside the society that is effectively new within it. Virtually every Protestant denomination began as either a sectarian effort to recapture a lost religious truth or a theological and organizational innovation. Groups like the Christian Scientists, Mormons, Adventists, the Jehovah's Witnesses, and Waco's Branch Davidians continue to bear strong traces of their original efflorescence. Imported movements such as the

Unification Church (South Korea), the Hare Krishna (India) and the Soka Gakkai (Japan) have also had deeply sacralizing effects for their American members.

Sacralization is also apparent at certain points in the history of U.S. 'civil religion,' i.e. *any nation's sense of its shared sacred heritage and commitments.* It is not unusual for a country's civil religious sensibility to wane and wax over time. It would be too simple to argue that its shared Judeo-Christian legacy tends to secularize during relatively uneventful periods of collective complacency, only to sacralize during times of national crisis. But a sense of common religious dedication does tend to surge during and immediately after major external crises, e.g. a true world war or the events of 9/11 when church attendance experienced a temporary spike. However, contrary to the old axioms, there are atheists in both foxholes and deathbeds, and some types of internal societal crises may reduce religion's credibility, as happened in the U.S. during the progressive movements of the 1960s.

The important point is that neither secularization nor sacralization alone is adequate to describe the U.S. or any other nation in holistic and linear terms. While both short- and long-term trends in one direction or another are common, the two tendencies often oscillate and even play off one another as partners in a dialectic. And while these apparent adversaries sometimes respond to each other's pulls in the opposite direction, the next section will point out that they can also be allies. Secularization often serves as a form of adaptation to historical change, and it can prepare the way for a sacralization that is more attuned to contemporary circumstances once the detritus of tradition is cleared away.

Certainly I don't mean to advocate some law-like proposition by which secularization and sacralization are always linked to insure some constant level of sacredness in an individual or social unit. Nor do I mean to suggest a rigid model of religious crop rotation by which secularization always clears the ground for a new sacred planting, since new forms of the sacred may precede and influence the secularization of older forms. The major argument is that tendencies in each direction generally check each other to ward off all-or-nothing extremes of either sort. In fact, this is not a new perspective. As pointed out by Goldstein (2006), virtually every one of the classic and contemporary sociological proponents of secularization – not to mention their critic, Rodney Stark himself (e.g. Stark and Bainbridge, 1985) have made reference to some form of oscillating cycles of more and less religion. Still, exceptions do occur, and there is at least a loose sense in which sacralization without secularization is the equivalent of 'pre-modernity;' secularization without sacralization is not a bad definition of 'post-modernity,' while the two in tandem are central to much of what 'modernity' itself entails. As this suggests, pre-modernity, modernity, and post-modernity are far more defensible as iterative cyclical moments rather than static phases of a single linear trend.

PARADOXES OF SECULARIZATION AND SACRALIZATION

At just the time when one might expect work on secularization to yield a consensually validated paradigm (cf. Tschannen 1991), it is far closer to producing a new set of contentiously divisive paradoxes. Much of this pivots around the very terms at issue. Both 'secular' and 'sacred' are mutually referential in that each makes a statement about the other. To be secular is to be non-sacred; to be sacred is to transcend and transform the secular. Much the same is true when we shift from semantics to social processes. Just as an object must have been sacred for it to be subsequently secularized, so must it have been secular for it to be subsequently 'sacralized.' And just as secularization marks a decline of the sacred, so does sacralization denote an increase in the sacred in one form or another and at one level or another.

But linking the processes of secularization and sacralization can have paradoxical results. Consider the following eight propositions as examples:

1. *Religious 'awakenings' require previous religious 'naps.'* American religious history has been commonly charted in terms of its eighteenth, nineteenth and possibly twentieth century awakenings (cf. McLoughlin 1978). But later revivals imply earlier slumbers which have equal merit as historical focii (e.g. May 1949; Erikson 1966; Turner 1985). It is the combination of the two that establishes the most basic rhythm of a country's religious history. If this is true at the macro-level, it has a micro-parallel. There is a similar relationship between individuals' religious conversions and their earlier religious indifference. Newspaper headlines and scholarly accounts that stress the former but neglect the latter fail to capture the critical interaction between sacred and secular.

2. *Modernization may lead to both secularization and sacralization.* The grand narrative of the 'secularization thesis' holds that religion beats a steady and linear retreat in the face of mounting modernization. There is some truth to this, but also some halftruth. In fact, this is what Peter Berger referred to in recently recanting some of his earlier writing on secularization (Berger 1997, 1999). To unpack the mystery, modernization does often lead to forms of secularization, but these in turn often spark a sacralizing response – one that ironically uses the means of modernity to protest the ends of modernity. Gorski (2000) makes a similar point in discussing the effects of the Protestant reformation in modernizing Europe: it was *both* secularizing and sacralizing. This duality also characterizes the putative 'fundamentalisms' everywhere, whether in the original Christian version in the U.S., or in the Islamic and Hindu variants around the global girdle of religious extremism. As noted earlier, India is one of many countries offering scarred testimony to religion's continuing presence. On the other hand, these countries also bear witness to the incursions of secularity as a perceived threat to religious interests. If either religion or secularity were fully dominant in these settings, the conflicts would be obviated (Beteille 1994).

3. *The rise of a vital 'religious marketplace' is also evidence of both secularization and sacralization.* As noted earlier, Stark and his colleagues (1999, 2000) and the early Berger (1967) invoke the

'religious marketplace' as a telling metaphor, but each draws out different implications. For Berger, such a marketplace involved an increase in competition that was staged in increasingly secular terms and reflected the crumbling of religion's prior structural monopolies and/or cultural hegemonies. For Stark *et al.*, on the other hand, religious competition led to a rational-choice process by which choosers seek out the most satisfying religious options according to religious criteria. And yet the new consumer's mentality may involve more stained-glass window-shopping than long-term buying, i.e. actually joining a church. The aforementioned debate over changing patterns of religiosity turns on this point, as does a current dispute over the significance of religious 'switching' in the U.S. (cf. Demerath and Yang 1998).

4. Because movements running against the societal grain often create more friction and more headlines than trends running with it, one must be careful not to mistake the sacred exceptions for the secular rule. It is sometimes tempting to interpret the high heat of a small religious movement as more important than the smoking embers of a larger and more secularized tradition. In the same spirit, one must be wary of confusing growth rates with size. Both have their place, but even those small, conservative religious movements with high growth rates may still be marginal to the larger population and culture. Many of Finke and Stark's (1992) 'winning' conservative denominations with high recent growth rates are still small compared to most of the 'losing' denominations that remain far larger despite recent attrition.

5. *Sacred manifestations may reflect secular forces, and vice versa.* The relationship between any form of behavior and the motivations behind it is problematic. As we have seen, standard indicators of religiosity such as civil religious loyalty, church membership, church attendance, and religious belief are all subject to myriad interpretations, not all of which are unambiguously sacred (cf. Demerath 1998; Haddaway *et al.* 1993). It may be more that the civil is religious than that the religious is civil; church membership and attendance reflect a variety of sacred and secular meanings that vary across a population and across time; affirming a religious belief may be less a matter of cognitive conviction than of cultural affiliation and continuity. Even the various 'fundamentalist' movements around the world may not be as uniformly or fanatically 'religious' as they are often portrayed. Many

of their members have a predominantly secular agenda that is aided by religious legitimation, hence religion may serve in some instances as a means rather than an end in its own right (Demerath 2001). At the same time, a withdrawal from conventional religious frameworks may coexist with a more privatized faith, namely the 'little voice' of the pseudonymous 'Sheila Larson' in Bellah *et al.* (1985: 221). And surely there are any number of conventionally secular commitments that take on sacred valences for their devotees, as noted earlier.

6. *Moderate secularization can be a prophylactic against ultimate secularization.* Changing social conditions require changing forms of the sacred if they are to be relevant. Hence, some degree of secularization may serve as a form of sacred adaptation. As one early example, the British historian R. H. Tawney (1962) amended Weber's heavily theological account of the development of Calvinist pre-destinationism, whereby success in this life ultimately became a clue to salvation in the next life. Tawney showed that this was due to a series of takes-and-gives between Geneva's rising middle-class parishioners and a clergy willing to make secularized compromises to keep their pews filled. The same dynamic has been a tactic in the trajectory of Liberal Protestantism over the past century, as pastors and theologians have made comparable concessions to their secularizing adherents (cf. Berger 1967; Demerath 1992). The tactic has been challenged by advocates of strict doctrine and strict churches (Kelley 1972; Iannaccone 1994). But the possibility remains that cleaving to strictness might have cost the churches far more defections than did adapting to the secular.

7. *Secularization may be more common in conservative than liberal religious communities.* Because secularization involves change, the question is where the greatest change is likely to occur. Since liberal religious organizations have already undergone considerable secularization, many now face a stained glass floor as a constraint against further change. On the other hand, conservative religious groups are closer to the traditional ceiling and have further room to change in a more secular direction. While it is clear that evangelical, fundamentalist and Pentecostal churches are less secular than more mainstream churches, it is by no means clear that they have recently experienced less secularization. The point is well-made by the classic sect-to-church dynamic whereby newer, smaller, and often more precarious religious movements make secular adaptations in the quest for

organizational stability. A number of recent studies have described the kind of sacred-secular tensions that often result within conservative religions churches – for example over issues of gender (viz. Bartkowski 2001; Gallagher 2003), and still others have discredited the stereotype of conservative churches as static and homogeneous (e.g. Hunter 1987, and Greeley and Hout 2006).

8. *Focusing on the fate of old forms of religion may deflect attention from new forms of the sacred.* Obsessing over secularization of the past may preclude analysis of sacralization in the present and future. Just as conventional religion may not necessarily be sacred, so are new sources of the sacred not necessarily religious. Today one hears a good deal of talk – some of it glib – about a growing distinction between religion and spirituality and about profound sacred commitments in everything from socialism to sex. Just because they have attained cliché status does not mean they should be jettisoned as possibilities for deeper investigation (cf. Demerath 2000a).

. . .

SHIFTING FROM RELIGION TO CULTURE AT LARGE

To some readers, my earlier definitions of secularization and sacralization may suffer from a glaring omission: they contain no specific mention of religion *per se*. This is not an oversight. I want to stress the broader category of the sacred, noting that religion is only one of many sources of the sacred, and not all of religion qualifies as sacred. In emphasizing the relation between secularity and the 'sacred,' I want to push beyond religion to consider a sociologically richer vein of the sacred; namely, culture.

Of course, secularization is no stranger to cultural analysis. Virtually every major cultural theorist and cultural historian has taken religious secularization into account as either an effect or a cause of historical change, as we have already seen with Marx, Weber, and especially Durkheim who noted the civic

origin of ceremonies that, by their object, by their results, and by the techniques used, are not different in kind from ceremonies that are specifically reli-

gious. What basic difference is there between Christians' celebrating the principal dates of Christ's life . . . and a citizen's meeting commemorating the advent of a new charter or some other great event of national life? (Durkheim 1912: 429).

This seminal passage was later re-born in Robert Bellah's (1967) famous account of 'civil religion' with specific reference to the U.S. national polity. However, it is worth remarking that Bellah gave the concept a far more narrowly religious thrust than had Durkheim – or for that matter, Durkheim's own predecessor in these matters, the eighteenth-century social philosopher, Jean Jacques Rousseau (1960).

As this suggests, France has been a special source of secularization accounts. The eighteenth-century decline of the French monarchy and the ensuing French Revolution involved a fundamental 'de-sacralization' of the link between church and crown that has been widely analyzed by historians (cf. Merrick 1990; Darnton 1995; Gordon 1998). This in turn is linked to France's role as a seedbed for Enlightenment thought, which provided such critical intellectual second-guessing of religion from Voltaire forward. One strand of this tradition took the form of French positivism. As represented by the mid-nineteenth-century visionary, Auguste Comte, positivism – like Marxism – both sought and prophesied the replacement of religion by social science.

Subsuming religion within a larger category of the sacred has a more extensive pedigree. The great comparativist, Mircea Eliade (1959), was consistently at pains to talk of 'hierophanies' that afforded contact with the 'sacred', rather than concentrate on religion itself. For him conventional religion by no means exhausted sacred possibilities. If religion was explicitly sacred, other forms qualified implicitly. In fact, Edward Bailey (1998) has made explicit the notion of 'implicit religion' that is itself implicit in the work of Eliade and others. As Rousseau, Durkheim, and Weber would also have agreed, sacred meanings may emanate from the political, the familial, and the quotidian. The quality of sacredness is not inherent in a thing or idea; rather, sacredness is imputed from within a social context.

Meanwhile, if religion is only one form of the sacred, the sacred in turn is one important dimension of something broader still; namely, culture. The relation between religion and culture can be so close as to be confusing. Consider the two definitions below from the anthropologist, Clifford Geertz, and see if it is immediately obvious which refers to religion and which to culture:

a) _____ is 1) a system of symbols which acts to 2) establish powerful, pervasive, and long-lasting moods and motivations in men by 3) formulating conceptions of a general order of existence and 4) clothing these conceptions with such an aura of factuality that 5) the moods and motivations seem uniquely realistic (Geertz, 1973: 190).
b) _____ is . . . the framework of beliefs, expressive symbols and values in terms of which individuals define their world, express their feelings, and make their judgements. (It) is the fabric of meaning in terms of which human beings interpret their experience and guide their action (Geertz 1973: 144–5).

Both definitions have that perverse element of abstraction that qualifies them as social scientific; both share an emphasis on the kind of 'control system' that Geertz found essential. The first refers to religion and the second to culture, but in the often arbitrary world of conceptual definitions one could do far worse than reverse them.

And yet Geertz' emphasis on cognitive control neglects another element that both phenomena have in common. It is true that both religion and culture are symbol systems that perform powerful directive functions. But one of the reasons for their power is precisely a shared quality of sacredness. The point scarcely needs elaboration for religion. But arguing that culture carries a sacred dimension may be more controversial.

Take the very word 'culture.' In strict etymological terms, it traces back to the notion of 'horticulture' and the spreading of manure – something many critics of culture's conceptual

softness will have no difficulty crediting. But if one adds a historically indefensible but conceptually strategic hyphen to produce the term 'cult-ure,' this cues a more instructive story. 'Cult' in its older, non-pejorative, Durkheimian sense refers to that behavioral core of religious beliefs and practices that constitute the center of any religion and perhaps any cultural system as well (Demerath 2003).

Can a culture operate effectively without having a cultic or sacred component? In responding no, I am using the term sacred in its broader connotation rather than as a synonym for the conventionally religious. Taken in this way, any cultural system of symbols, beliefs, and values is a sacred system in that its components must be accorded a reverential status that allows for the leap of faith required in converting what are often relative and arbitrary judgements into absolute normative standards. Culture's credibility depends less upon the objective, empirical, or rational standing of its tenets than upon a subjective, non-empirical, and a-rational belief in its guidance. This requires a special status that involves the quality of sacredness in at least a latent, if not always manifest, sense. So much for a bridge to our concluding section.

A TYPOLOGY OF SECULARIZATION SCENARIOS

If secularization is alive and well within religion, and if religion is only part of the wider sphere of the sacred which is in turn a crucial component of culture, then it follows that secularization should be an active dynamic within culture itself. The insight is surely not an original revelation. However, it is little acknowledged in the various discussions of cultural change that have occurred in the social science literature. While older theories of history and the more recent but now largely recessed literature on 'modernization' refer to secularization, both refer almost exclusively to the secularization of religion *per se* (e.g. Germani 1981). Secularization of culture as distinct from religion is commonly neglected.

Virtually any form of cultural change both reveals and depends upon the opposite but often symbiotic processes of secularization and sacralization. Take any episode of transition, and it is not hard to find the waning of older 'sacred' beliefs and values, along with the frequent waxing of new ones. This applies to every type of symbol – whether political, economic, scientific, or indeed religious. As indicated above, all cultural components require a sacred quality, and generally this quality must erode before the components may decline and possibly give way to new commitments.

Cultural secularization may involve various syndromes which have rarely been disentangled. As noted previously, even within the narrow sphere of religion, secularization is generally discussed in all or nothing terms. When gradations are admitted, they are gradations of degree not of kind. But in what follows, I want to delineate four basic kinds of secularization that are framed by the intersection of two fundamental distinctions. The two distinctions involve *internal* versus *external* sources and *directed* versus *non-directed* scenarios. The former distinction refers to the difference between secularization that emerges from within the social context of the cultural system at issue versus secularization that is imported or imposed from outside. (See Table 1.)

The latter distinction refers to secularization that stems downward from authorities in control versus secularization that seeps upwards from within the cultural system itself. Putting the two distinctions together produces four combinations or types of secularization: 'emergent,' 'coercive,' 'diffused,' and 'imperialist.' In describing each, I shall draw on a wide array of examples, including some drawn from a recently completed fourteen-nation comparative study of religion and politics around the globe (Demerath 2001). This applies the types to whole societies, but they could also be relevant to the secularization of

TABLE 1   A typology of secularization scenarios

	Internal	External
Non-directed	Emergent	Diffuse
Directed	Coercive	Imperialist

sub-cultures, communities, institutions, or even social movements within a society.

1. **Emergent Secularization:** This form of internally evolved and non-directed secularization is the classic model for religion. Here secularization is seen as a kind of drift to the left - the unintentional product of increasing education, industrialization, modernization, and differentiation in the social context. This is the secularization described in a stanza of Matthew Arnold's 'Dover Beach:'

   The sea of faith
   Was once, too, at the full, and round earth's shore
   Lay like the folds of a bright girdle furl'd
   But now I only hear
   Its melancholy, long, withdrawing roar,
   Retreating to the breath
   Of the night-wind down the vast edges drear
   And naked shingles of the world.

   Arnold wrote in England in the mid-nineteenth century when a number of Western intellectuals had begun to sense that perhaps the Enlightenment had gone too far and produced saddening changes on the part of the many, not just the few. . . .

   The historian, James Turner (1985), dates the legitimation of unbelief among American intellectuals at the end of the Civil War. But the Enlightenment altered more than religion; it affected a whole conception of human self-consciousness that included what Arthur Lovejoy (1936) called 'the great chain of being' and what Owen Chadwick (1975) termed 'The Secularization of the European Mind.' Moreover, the Enlightenment was not just an assault upon faith, but a substitution of one faith for another. The notion of progress through thought became a sacred cult in its own right – albeit one that has been subject to secularization since. Meanwhile, there is little question that the rise of Newtonian and Darwinian science as well as the advent of major universities set apart from religious seminaries represented a major cultural change (cf. Koyre 1957; Foucault 1966). There was no single event, let alone decree, that produced the shift. Certainly this was not the result of any authoritative edict. Rather, it depended on cultural forces that were themselves dependent upon forms of non-religious secularization. Weber was right to point to the rise of the Protestant Ethic as a historical watershed, but most historians now agree that he overestimated the effects of religion and theology themselves. Insofar as Protestantism broke the spell of Catholic dominance over a tightly undifferentiated world, it released a series of developments in the newly differentiated and autonomous spheres of society. Gradually, politics, the economy, and the world of science and education began to march to their own cultural drummers, but not before drumming out some of the older sacred tenets that had conserved the past and inhibited change. In each case, new sacred commitments depended upon the secularization of older cultural faiths.

In politics, democracy took various structural forms, but its cultural core arose only after 'desacralization' was well under way for the French monarchy and other absolutist regimes in the West. It is true that part of the legitimating code of the 'ancien regime' involved its ties with the church. But it also involved a conception of top-down civil authority that went far beyond religion.

The rise of capitalism – and most especially its Weberian 'spirit' depended upon the secularization of a prior economic stage with its attendant economic rituals. Here structural changes influenced the cultural shift, and one might paraphrase Karl Marx to stress the importance of changing modes of economic production in de-sacralizing old social practices. . . .

But all is not lost, and somehow enchantment has persisted (cf. Schneider 1993). The historian, Daniel Gordon, offers a telling rebuttal to the Weberian despair:

But when Weber spoke of an 'iron cage,' he meant an absence of meaning, an economy that had no moral ground at all. . . . Yet, had Weber known more about the Enlightenment and its sacralization of capitalism, he would not have created such a radical antithesis between the Reformation and modernity (Gordon, 1998: 151).

Here then is the cultural cycle of secularization and sacralization enacted within the economic sphere itself. The spirit or culture of capitalism had achieved autonomous standing but it had become sacralized in its own terms and for its own sake. While Weber and others might quarrel with the quality of meaning involved, there is little question of its quantity.

The rise of science and education, of democracy and capitalism – these are among the great cultural transformations in Western history. Each depends upon a succession of secularization and sacralization, even though none is conventionally religious. All of this illustrates an internal, non-directed, 'emergent' form of secularization that is more glacial than explosive. It is a cultural dynamic that nevertheless moves mountains.

2. **Coercive Secularization:** Here is another form of internal secularization but one that is purposely directed by some type of effective authority. There are many types of direction, and the term 'coercion' is meant to suggest a top-down exercise of power – legitimate or not. There are many *loci* and levels of coercion, but for simplicity's sake, I shall focus here mainly on the societal.

Surprisingly, there are those who would place the U.S. in this category. Although no political leader would dare exert public influence on behalf of secularization, this is at least one interpretation of the first part of the First Amendment to the Constitution: 'Congress shall make no laws respecting an establishment of religion. . . .' Of course, the clause goes on to support the 'free exercise of religion.' But the establishment ban and the judicial decisions in its wake concerning prayer in the public schools, Christmas celebrations on public property, etc. have often been construed as governmental coercion on behalf of 'secular humanism.' This is not the place to debate the greater wisdom of the establishment clause, especially since I have elsewhere defended it as the often neglected but unique mark of genius within the First Amendment (Demerath 2000b . . .). However, it is clear that both clauses of the First Amendment have had both secularizing and sacralizing impacts.

Meanwhile, there are other instances of coercive secularization in the U.S. On the one hand, consider the federal government's role in restricting Native Americans, both territorially and culturally, with secularizing consequences. On the other hand, the federal government has also played a secularizing role in reining in racism and racial segregation. There is little question that racism has long been a part of American culture, especially following the Civil War when emancipation of the slaves required new doctrines of racial inferiority to justify continued discrimination. But how does one change racism? Put more familiarly, how can one secularize the values, norms, and rituals that it entailed? When the government stepped in to produce and implement civil rights legislation that integrated schools, public accommodations, and voting practices, the required changes in behavior ultimately brought about corresponding changes in both social psychology and culture. This is a clearer instance of coerced secularization paving the way to change, though some might argue that the coercion was more external than internal because it came from Washington and the federal government rather than the South.

Insofar as laws and political regimes can influence change, and insofar as virtually every social change requires some secularizing of an older culture to make way for or accommodate the new, virtually every country offers examples of coercive secularization. . . .

3. **Imperialist secularization:** This is another form of directed secularization, but one that emanates externally, that is, from forces outside the society at issue. . . .

. . . There are ample instances of imperialist secularization. . . . India has been a reluctant host to outside powers for almost a millennium. The Muslim Mogul emperors began their succession in the early sixteenth century, only to be followed by the British 'raj.' Both empires exerted secularizing influence over Hinduism, though Hinduism has certainly survived. Both also had secularizing impacts on other aspects of the subcontinent's culture. For weal and for woe, the British altered the area's entire political, economic, and educational infrastructure with wrenching cultural changes. Imposed modernity has had a major secularizing impact on India's traditional culture – including job and educational 'reservations' as a counter to untouchability and the prohibition of practices such as 'sati' when a wife is expected to throw herself on her husband's funeral pyre.

There have been few more imperialistic forces in world history than the converting armies of Christianity. These mobilizations on behalf of new sacred systems have been perhaps more effective in secularizing older ones, sometimes leaving a confused void as a result. In addition to their obvious effects on indigenous religions, they have had important consequences for non-religious cultural elements. For example, Lamin Sanneh (1991) notes that missionary activities in Africa were not all negative from the standpoint of African political development. Because they offered educational programs with a new common language, they tended to break down (secularize) older

tribal cultures and divisions, thus clearing the way for new nationalistic bonds.

4. **Diffused Secularization:** The typology's final scenario of secularization involves external forces that spread more by diffusion than direction. These are often the unintended consequences of culture contacts. They result from transmitted cultural innovations that become hegemonic in new locales, and in the process serve to displace old practices, rituals, and beliefs – whether formally or informally sacred.

Imagine the reactions of the New Guinea fishing villagers who, sometime in 1943, awoke to see for the first time a substantial fleet of the U.S. Navy anchored offshore and establishing beach installations with jeeps, guns, and communications equipment, which the villagers were seeing for the first time as the wondrous bounty of a divine providence. It was incidents like these that led to the famous 'cargo cults' of Oceania. These cults worshiped new gods of Western materialism and waited – largely in vain – for their own cargo to materialize. Of course, any new religion comes at the expense of the old. In this instance, sacralization preceded secularization.

Today's 'globalization' offers parallels to the cargo cults, except that here the materialism does materialize. Accounts are legion of television sets aglow in dark slum dwellings in Calcutta, cosmetic sales on the upper Amazon in Brazil, internet communication between stay-at-home families in China and their migrating children, and surgical miracles being performed in African villages. . . .

I have used the term 'diffused secularization' for this syndrome in several senses. Obviously it refers to the consequences of the diffuse spread of cultures around the world. But it also needs pointing out that host cultures tend to diffuse and give their own local twists to foreign cultures that reach them, hence the now fashionable but awkward amalgam, 'glocalization.' Finally, local cultures themselves experience some diffusion and dilution as a result. We have certainly witnessed aggressive assertions of traditional faiths and identities as sacralizing responses to this general secularizing trend. 'Fundamentalist' Islamic and Hindu movements as well as more direct political opponents of Western culture have become major players on the world stage.

CONCLUSION

. . .

After a historical review of classical and contemporary conceptions of secularization, I introduced its critics and showed how the great secularization debate has been poured into five teapots. I shifted discussion away from ultimate prophecies of decline and demise to proximate fluctuations in secularization and its dialectically linked concept of 'sacralization.' More nuanced analysis revealed a series of some eight paradoxes that serve to check simplistic and hyperbolic interpretations either for or against secularization.

But if part of the chapter's objective was to reduce the issue of secularization, another goal was to broaden it. The chapter has sought to alter the emphasis from religion to the sacred, and then go one step further by expanding the reach of secularization from religion and the sacred writ small to culture writ large. Here I presented a typology of secularization scenarios, ranging from the emergent, the coercive, and the diffused to the imperialist. Indeed, I argued that secularization and its companion sacralization are critical to understanding the historical dynamics of all culture, whether at the micro-level or the macro-level.

In one sense, then, I have tried to domesticate secularization by removing its fangs. In another sense, I have tried to enliven and enrich the discussion by widening its scope and raising the stakes. Secularization is by no means a process restricted to religion in its conventional sense. And given our experience with religion as a primary case of the sacred and a major facet of culture, sociologists have an expertise to share. To paraphrase two early prophets of secularization,

we have a world to win and nothing to lose but our brain.

REFERENCES

BAILEY, EDWARD 1998. *Implicit Religion: An Introduction.* London: Middlesex University Press.

BARTKOWSKI, JOHN P. 2001. *Remaking the Godly Marriage: Gender Negotiations in Evangelical Families.* New Brunswick: Rutgers University Press.

BECKFORD, JAMES A. 2003. *Social Theory and Religion.* Cambridge: Cambridge University Press.

BELLAH, ROBERT N. 1967. 'Civil Religion in America,' *Daedalus* 96: 1–21.

BELLAH, ROBERT N., RICHARD MADSEN, WILLIAM M. SULLIVAN, ANN SWIDLER, and STEVEN M. TIPTON 1985. *Habits of the Heart.* Berkeley: University of California Press.

BERGER, PETER L. 1967. *The Sacred Canopy.* Garden City, NY: Doubleday.

BERGER, PETER L. 1997. 'Epistemological Modesty: An Interview with Peter Berger,' *Christian Century* 114: 972–78.

BERGER, PETER L. 1999. *The De-Secularization of the World.* Washington, DC: Ethics and Public Policy Center.

BETEILLE, ANDRÀE 1994. 'Secularism and the Intellectuals,' *Economic and Political Weekly* 29 (10): 559–66.

BRUCE, STEVE 1995. 'The Truth About Religion in Britain,' *Journal of the Scientific Study of Religion* 34: 417–30.

BRUCE, STEVE 2002. *God is Dead: Secularization in the West.* Oxford: Blackwell's.

CHADWICK, OWEN 1975. *The Secularization of the European Mind in the Nineteenth Century.* Cambridge: Cambridge University Press.

CHAVES, MARK 1993. 'Denominations as Dual Structures: An Organizational Analysis,' *Sociology of Religion* 54: 147–69.

COMTE, AUGUSTE 1852 (1891). *The Catechism of Positive Religion* (3rd edn). London: Routledge.

DAVIE, GRACE 1994. *Religion in Britain Since 1945: Believing Without Behaving.* Oxford: Blackwell's.

DAVIE, GRACE 2002. *Europe: The Exceptional Case.* London: Darton, Longman and Todd, Ltd.

DARNTON, ROBERT 1995. *The Forbidden Best-Sellers of Pre-Revolutionary France.* New York: W.W. Norton.

DEMERATH, N. J. III 1992. 'Snatching Defeat From Victory in the Decline of Liberal Protestantism: Culture Versus Structure in Institutional Analysis.' In N. J. Demerath, P.D. HALL, T. Schmitt, and R.H. Williams (eds), *Sacred Companies.* New York: Oxford.

DEMERATH, N. J. III 1998. 'Secularization Disproved or Displaced.' In Rudy LAERMANS, BRYAN Wilson, and Jaak Billiet (eds), *Secularization and Social Integration,*

Essays Honour of Karel Dobbelaene. Leuven: Belgium: Leuven University Press, pp. 7–11.

DEMERATH, N. J. III 2000a. 'The Varieties of Sacred Experience:' Finding the Sacred in a Secular Grove,' *Journal of the Scientific Study of Religion* 39:1–11.

DEMERATH, N. J. III 2000b. 'Secularization.' In *Encyclopedia of Sociology* (2nd edn), edited by Edgar F. Borgatta. New York: Macmillan, pp. 2482–91.

DEMERATH, N. J. III 2000c. 'Secularization Extended: From Religious Myth to Cultural Commonplace.' In *Companion to the Sociology of Religion*, edited by Richard Fenn, Oxford: Blackwell's.

DEMERATH, N. J. III 2001. *Crossing the Gods: World Religions and Worldly Politics.* New York: Rutgers University Press.

DEMERATH, N. J. III 2003. 'Cults, Culture and Manure: Why the Root of the Second should be the First rather than the Third.' In J. A. Beckford and J. T. Richardson (eds), *Challenging Religion: Essays in Honor of Eileen Barker.* New York: Taylor and Francis.

DEMERATH, N. J. III 2006. 'Criss-Crossing the Gods: Globalization and American Religion.' In Bruce Mazlish and Nayan Chanda (eds), *The United States in a Global History Perspective.* Palo Alto: Stanford University Press.

DEMERATH, N. J. III and YONGHE YANG 1998. 'Switching in American Religion: Denominations, Markets, Paradigms?' In Madeleine Cousineau (ed.), *Religion in a Changing World.* Westport: Praeger.

DOBBELAERE, KAREL 1981. 'Secularization: A Multi-Dimensional Concept,' *Current Sociology* 20: 1–216.

DOBBELAERE, KAREL 1985. 'Secularization Theories and Sociological Paradigms.' *Sociological Analysis* 46 (4): 377–87.

DOBBELAERE, KAREL 1993. 'Church Involvement and Secularization: Making Sense of the European Case.' In Eileen Barker, James A. Beckford, and Karel Dobbelaere (eds), *Secularization, Rationalism, and Sectarianism* Oxford: Clarendon Press.

DOUGLAS, MARY 1982. 'The Effects of Modernization on Religious Change.' In Douglas and Steven M. Tipton (eds), *Religion in America: Spirituality in a Secular Age.* Boston: Beacon.

DURKHEIM, EMILE 1912 (1995). *The Elementary Forms of the Religious Life*, trans. by Karen Fields. New York: Free Press.

DURKHEIM, EMILE 1961. *Moral Education.* New York: Free Press.

ELIADE, MIRCEA 1959. *The Sacred and the Profane.* London: Harcourt, Brace, Jovanovich.

ERIKSON, KAI 1966. *Wayward Puritans.* New York: John Wiley and Sons.

FENN, RICHARD 1979. *Toward a Theory of Secularization.* Society for the Scientific Study of Religion Monograph.

FENN, RICHARD. 1993. Crowds, time, and the essence of society. In *Secularization, Rationalism and Sectarianism, op. cit.*, edited by Eileen Barker, James A. Beckford,

and Karel Dobbelaere. pp. 287–304. Society for the Scientific Study of Religion Monograph.

FINKE, ROGER and RODNEY STARK 1992. *The Churching of America, 1776–1990: Winners and Losers in Our Religious Economy.* New Brunswick, NJ: Rutgers University Press.

FOUCAULT, MICHEL 1966. *The Order of Things.* New York: Vintage Books.

GALLAGHER, SALLY K. 2003 *Evangelical Identity and Gendered Family Life.* New Brunswick, NJ: Rutgers University Press.

GEERTZ, CLIFFORD 1973. *The Interpretation of Culture.* New York: Basic Books.

GERMANI, GINO 1981. *The Sociology of Modernization* New Brunswick, NJ: Transaction.

GOLDSTEIN, WARREN S. (ed.) 2006. *Marx, Critical Theory, and Religion: A Critique of Rational Choice.* Leiden: Brill Academic Publishers.

GORDON, DANIEL 1998. 'The Great Enlightenment Massacre.' In HAYDN T. MASON (ed.), *The Darton Debate.* Oxford: Voltaire Foundation.

GORSKI, PHILIP 2000. 'Historicizing the Secularization Debate: Church, State, and Society in Late Medieval and Early Modern Europe, ca. 1300–1700.' *American Sociological Review* 65: 138–67.

GREELEY, ANDREW M. and Michael Hout 2006. *The Truth About Conservative Christians.* Chicago: University of Chicago Press.

HADDAWAY, C. KIRK, PENNY LONG MARLER, and MARK CHAVES. 1993. 'What the Polls Don't Show: A Closer Look at U.S. Church Attendance.' *American Sociological Review* 58: 741–52.

HADDEN, JEFFREY 1987. 'Toward Desacralizing Secularization Theory.' *Social Forces* 65: 3 (March) 587–611.

HUNTER, JAMES Davidson 1987. *Evangelicalism: The Coming Generation.* Chicago: University of Chicago Press.

IANNACCONE, LAURENCE R. 1994. 'Why Strict Churches are Strong.' *American Journal of Sociology* 99: 1180–1211.

JENKINS, PHILIP 2002. *The Next Generation: The Coming of Global Christianity.* Oxford: Oxford University Press.

JUERGENSMEYER, MARK 1993. *The New Cold War: Religious Nationalism Confronts the Secular State.* Berkeley: University of California Press.

KELLEY, DEAN 1972. *Why Conservative Churches Are Growing.* Macon, GA: Mercer University Press.

KOYRE, ALEXANDRE 1957. *From the Closed World to the Infinite Universe.* Baltimore: Johns Hopkins University Press.

LOVEJOY, ARTHUR O. 1936. *The Great Chain of Being.* Cambridge: Harvard University Press.

LUCKMANN, THOMAS 1967. *The Invisible Religion.* New York: Macmillan Co.

LUCKMANN, THOMAS 1990. 'Shrinking Transcendence, Expanding Religion.' *Sociology of Religion* 50 (2): 127–38.

MADAN, T. N. 1998. *Modern Myths, Locked Minds.* Delhi: Oxford University Press.

MARTIN, DAVID 1969. *The Religious and the Secular.* New York: Schocken Books.

MARX, KARL 1844 (1963). 'Contribution to the Critique of Hegel's Philosophy of the Right.' In THOMAS B. BOTTOMORE (ed.), *Early Writings.* New York: McGraw-Hill.

MAY, HENRY F. 1949. *Protestant Churches in Industrial America.* New York: Harper and Bros.

McLOUGHLIN, W. G. 1978. *Revivals, Awakenings, and Religious Change.* Chicago: University of Chicago Press.

MERRICK, JEFFREY W. 1990. *The De-Sacralization of the French Monarchy in the 18th Century.* Baton Rouge: Louisiana State University Press.

NANDY, ASHISH 1990. 'The Politics of Secularism and the Recovery of Religious Tolerance.' In Veena Das (ed.), *Mirrors of Violence.* Delhi: Oxford University Press.

NORRIS, PIPPA and RONALD INGLEHART 2004. *Sacred and Secular: Religion and Politics Worldwide.* New York: Cambridge University Press.

PARSONS, TALCOTT 1960. *Structure and Process in Modern Societies.* Glencoe, IL: The Free Press.

ROOF, WADE CLARK 2001. *The Spiritual Marketplace: Baby Boomers and the Remaking of American Religion.* Princeton: Princeton University Press.

ROOF, WADE Clark and WILLIAM McKINNEY 1987. *American Mainline Religion.* New Brunswick, NJ: Rutgers University Press.

ROUSSEAU, JEAN JACQUES 1960. 'Of Civil Religion.' In Ernest Barker (ed.), *Social Contract.* London: Oxford University Press.

SANNEH, LAMIN 1991. 'The Yogi and the Commissar: Christian Missions and the New World Order in Africa.' In W. C. Roof (ed.), *World Order and Religion.* Albany: SUNY Press.

SCHNEIDER, MARK 1993. *Culture and Enchantment.* Chicago: University of Chicago Press.

SPENCER, HERBERT 1874. *Essays Moral, Political and Aesthetic.* New and Enlarged Edition. New York: D. Appleton and Co.

SPENCER, HERBERT 1915. *Essays Scientific, Political, Speculative* (3 vols). New York: Appleton.

STARK, RODNEY 1992. 'Sociology of Religion.' *Encyclopedia of Sociology.* New York: Macmillan, pp. 2029–37.

STARK, RODNEY 1999. 'Secularization R.I.P.' *Sociology of Religion* 60: 249–273.

STARK, RODNEY and LAURENCE R. IANNACCONE 1994. 'A Supply-side Reinterpretation of the "Secularization"

of Europe.' *Journal for the Scientific Study of Religion* 33: 230–52.

STARK, RODNEY and BAINBRIDGE, W.S. 1985. *The Future of Religion.* Berkeley, California: University of California Press.

STARK, RODNEY and ROGER FINKE 2000. *Acts of Faith: Explaining the Human Side of Religion.* Berkeley: University of California Press.

SWATOS, WILLIAM H. JR 1985. *The Future of Religion.* Berkeley: University of California Press.

SWATOS, WILLIAM H. JR and LOFTUR Reimar Gissurarson 1997. *Icelandic Spiritualism: Mediumship and Modernity.* New Brunswick, NJ: Transaction Books.

TAWNEY, R. H. 1962. *Religion and the Rise of Capitalism.* Gloucester, MA.: P. Smith.

THAPAR, ROMILA 1989. 'Imagined and Religious Communities: Ancient History and the Modern Search for a Hindu Identity.' *Modern Asian Studies* 23: 209–31.

TOENNIES, FERDINAND 1887 (1957). *Community and Society,* trans. and ed. by Charles Loomis. East Lansing: Michigan State University Press.

TSCHANNEN, OLIVER 1991. 'The Secularization Paradigm: A Systematization.' *Journal of the Scientific Study of Religion* 30: 395–415.

TURNER, JAMES 1985. *Without God, Without Creed.* Baltimore: Johns Hopkins Press.

VOLTAIRE, FRANÇOIS-MARIE AROUET 1756 (1963). *Essai sur les Moers et l'Esprit des Nations* (2 vols). Paris: Garnier.

WARNER, STEVEN 1993. 'Work in Progress Toward a New Paradigm for the Sociological Study of Religion in the U.S.' *American Journal of Sociology* 98: 1044–93.

WEBER, MAX 1904 (1995). *The Protestant Ethic and the Spirit of Capitalism.* trans. by Talcott Parsons, Intro. by Randall Collins. New York: Roxbury Press.

WILSON, BRYAN 1966. *Religion in Secular Society.* London: Penguin.

WILSON, BRYAN 1990. *The Social Dimensions of Sectarianism.* Oxford: Oxford University Press.

WILSON, BRYAN 1998. 'The Secularization Thesis: Criticisms and Rebuttals.' In R. LAERMANS, B. Wilson, and J. Billiet (eds), *Secularization and Social Integration, op.cit. Essays Honour of Karel Dobbelaere.*

WOODBERRY, ROBERT D. 1998. 'When Surveys Lie and People Tell the Truth: How Surveys Over-Sample Church Attenders.' *American Sociological Review* 63: 119–22.

WUTHNOW, ROBERT 1988. *The Restructuring of American Religion.* Princeton: Princeton U. Press.

WUTHNOW, ROBERT 1998. *After Heaven: Spirituality in America Since the 1950s.* Berkeley: University of California Press.

Reading 28 Selections from *Sociological Writings*

MAX WEBER

Weber writes about three sources of legitimate power, or "authority." His classical theoretical statement on why and how people cede authority to leaders applies well to religious organizations. In the US, authority in religious organizations is often vested in bureaucratic structures, though traditional and charismatic leaders also persist.

Authority is the probability that specific commands (or all commands) will be obeyed by a given group of people. Thus not every means for exercising power and influence over other people is involved here. Authority, in this sense, can be based in each individual case on the most varied motives for compliance: from dull habit to purely rational calculation. A certain minimal willingness to obey; that is, an interest (external or internalized) in obeying is essential in every real model of domination. . . .

[E]very system of authority exercising power over a number of people normally requires a staff of individuals (administrative staff); that is, certain reliable, obedient individuals who normally can be trusted to order their conduct so as to execute general instruction as well as specific commands. This administrative staff may base

obedience to their superiors simply on custom, on pure affection, on material interests, or value-rational motives. The type of motive largely determines the mode of authority. . . .

Obedience ideally signifies that the conduct of the obeyer proceed as if he has made the content of the command a maxim for his own activity and for its own sake. Without concern for his own valuation of the command as such, his activity ideally occurs exclusively for the sake of the formal obligation. . . .

There are three pure types of legitimate authority. The basis for their claim to legitimacy may be primarily one of:

1. *Rational* character—resting on the common belief in the legality of rules and the right of those empowered to exercise authority (i.e., legal authority); or

Source: Excerpt from *Sociological Writings: Max Weber*, edited by Wolf Heydebrand, © 1994. Reprinted by permission of the Continuum International Publishing Group.

2. *Traditional* character—resting on the common belief in the sanctity of existing traditions and the legitimacy of that authority thereby empowered (i.e., traditional authority); or

3. *Charismatic* character—resting on an uncommon devotion to the sanctity, heroism or otherwise impressive character of an individual and to the dispositions openly enacted by that person (i.e., charismatic authority).

In the case of statutory authority, obedience is accorded the legally prescribed technically impersonal order. This obedience is further accorded specific persons in whom authority is vested on the basis of the formal legitimacy of this legally prescribed order, its dispositions and its scope. In the case of traditional authority, obedience is accorded that individual empowered by the tradition who is (within its domain) bound to that tradition. Obedience is accorded on the basis of loyalty to the leader within the scope of custom. In the case of charismatic authority, it is the charismatically qualified leader to whom obedience is accorded and on the basis of a personal trust in the leader's revelation, his heroism or his exemplary character within the parameters of the individual's willingness to believe in this charisma. . . .

Charismatic authority, due to its extraordinary character, stands opposed to rational forms of authority (bureaucratic forms in particular), as well as to traditional forms (especially those characterized by a patriarchal, patrimonial or estate structure). Both of these primary types are specific everyday forms of authority; the genuine charismatic form is specifically the opposite. Bureaucratic authority is specifically rational in the sense of its debt to intellectually analyzable rules; charismatic authority in contrast, is specifically irrational in the sense of its inherent freedom from rules. Traditional authority is bound to the precedents of the past, and as such, is likewise associated with rules. Within its sphere of influence, charismatic authority subverts the past, and in this sense is specifically revolutionary. Whether it be on the part of the leader or socially privileged status

groups, no authority of this type recognizes the appropriation of power on the basis of the possession of property. On the contrary, authority is only legitimate to the extent and for the duration that the leader is able to sustain his personal charisma; that is, as long as it is accorded recognition and as long as loyal subjects, disciples and other followers are charismatically useful over time. . . .

Charismatic authority, in its genuine form, is of a character specifically foreign to everyday routine. Social relationships subject to it are of a strictly personal nature and play an important role in the validity of charismatic personal qualities and their confirmation. If these, however, are not to remain purely ephemeral, but demonstrate a quality of permanence, such as community of fellow worshipers, warriors, disciples, a party organization, or any type of political or hierocratic group, it is necessary that the character of the charismatic authority be fundamentally altered. . . .

With the routinization process, the charismatic authority is essentially transformed into one of the everyday authorities—the patrimonial form, especially in its estate or bureaucratic variant. . . .

Routinization does not occur, as a rule, without a struggle. Initially, personal claims on the charisma of the leader are not forgotten, and the struggle between office-based or hereditary, charisma and personal charisma is a typical historical process. . . .

In all cases, [one] primary motive for the routinization of charisma is, naturally, a striving for [security]. This entails the legitimization, on the one hand, of the social prestige of positions of authority and, on the other, the economic opportunities for the followers and supporters of the leader. An additional motive develops, however, out of the objective necessity of adapting the orders and the administrative staff to the average everyday exigencies and the conditions of an administration. Connected to this is the particular need for guiding principles to establish an administrative and jurisdictional tradition, a need equally necessary to both the administrative staff and those subject to its authority. Furthermore, there is a need for the ranking of positions held by members of the administrative staff. Finally, and of greatest important, it is necessary that all administrative regulations be adapted to the everyday economic terms. . . . It is not feasible to fund a permanent, everyday administration in a fashion similar to that of a warring or prophetic charismatic authority; that is,

via booty, contributions, gifts, hospitality, and the like. . . .

The problems of the routinization process, therefore, are not confined to the problem of succession and, in fact, involve much more than just this. The primary problem involves the transition from charismatic administrative staffs and corresponding administrative principles to a routinized system. But the problem of succession is crucial because it concerns the routinization of the charismatic core—the leader himself and his claim to legitimacy.

29 Transformations in New Immigrant Religions and Their Global Implications

FENGGANG YANG AND HELEN ROSE EBAUGH

Yang and Ebaugh explore how new immigrants are adopting a quintessentially American form of religious organization: "congregationalism."

. . .

Historically, religious institutions were among the most important resources that immigrant groups used to reproduce their ethno-religious identity in new surroundings and to help them adjust to the challenges of surviving in a demanding and often threatening environment (Alexander 1987; Bodnar 1985; Dolan 1975, 1985; Herberg 1960; Park and Miller 1921; Pozzetta 1991; Smith 1978; Thomas and Znaniecki 1918–1920; Wind and Lewis 1994). Whereas the role of religion and religious institutions in the lives of earlier immigrants is well documented, little scholarly attention has been given to religious factors among recent migrants.[1] . . .

However, compared with earlier immigrants, who came mostly from Judeo-Christian Europe, many of the new immigrants from Asia have brought Islam, Hinduism, Buddhism, and other religions, and immigrants from South and Central America and some Asian countries have imported distinctive forms and styles of Catholicism and Protestantism. Amid the debate regard-

[1]There are several reasons why religion has been neglected in studies of contemporary migration (Kivisto 1992; Warner 1998). First, immigration researchers, by and large, use survey data collected by government agencies such as the Bureau of the Census, the Immigration and Naturalization Service, and the Bureau of Labor Statistics—such agencies are not allowed to ask questions about religion. Other national surveys (e.g., the General Social Survey of the National Opinion Research Center) fail to include sufficient numbers of small religious populations, such as Vietnamese Buddhists or Argentine evangelicals, to make analysis possible. Second, it is often insiders who study their own religious and/or ethnic group and we do not yet have a crucial mass of immigrant social scientists interested in a variety of religions. Third, there is often an antireligious bias among Asian, Hispanic, and African scholars in ethnic studies departments who associate religion with the Christian missionaries who joined with politicians and businessmen to colonize Third World countries (Yoo 1996).

Source: Fenggang Yang and Helen Rose Ebaugh, from "Transformation in New Immigrant Religions and Their Global Implications." *American Sociological Review*, Vol. 66, No. 2 (Apr., 2001), pp. 269–288.

ing how "new" this new immigration is compared with the "old," the limited but growing literature on religion and the new immigrants shows that religion, both Judeo-Christian and other traditions, continues to play the dual role of facilitating assimilation of its members and preserving ethnicity (Kim and Hurh 1993; Min 1992; Numrich 1996; Warner and Wittner 1998; Williams 1988; F. Yang 1999a). In the study of the new immigration, religion, and social changes, an important question is yet to be answered: What institutional changes do new immigrant religious communities undergo?

The issue of religious transformations raises important theoretical questions in the study of new immigration.... The religiosity of many of the new immigrants is one factor contributing to the current robustness of religion in America (Ebaugh and Chafetz 2000a; Warner and Wittner 1998), a trend that is reminiscent of the religious vitality that existed in this country during the earlier waves of European migration. Moreover, our data show that internal and external pluralism, instead of leading to the decline of religion, in fact promotes institutional and theological transformations that energize and revitalize the religions.

In the course of immigration and settlement, immigrants commonly transplant their traditional religious institutions in their new land. Rather than simply recreating religious structures as they existed in their home countries, however, both "old" and "new" immigrants adapt their religions to social conditions of the host country....

METHODS

We focus on the rapidly increasing number of religious institutions in the United States whose membership is wholly or predominantly composed of "new immigrants," that is, those who arrived since the mid-1960s. In addition to thousands of informal places of worship including house churches, scriptural study groups, parali-

turgical groups, domestic altars, and neighborhood festivals, immigrants have established many of their own formal places for worship and have changed the demographics of existing Anglo congregations that they have joined. According to the best available estimates, there are over 3,500 Catholic parishes where Mass is celebrated in Spanish, and 7,000 Hispanic/Latino Protestant congregations, most of them Pentecostal or Evangelical churches, and many of them nondenominational (Warner 1998). In 1988, the last count available, there were 2,018 Korean-American churches in the United States, and in 1994 there were approximately 700 Chinese-American Protestant churches. In the early 1990s, there were between 1,000 and 1,200 mosques and Islamic centers, 1,500 to 2,000 Buddhist temples and meditation centers, and over 400 Hindu temples (Warner 1998).[3] Unlike previous eras in American history, in many neighborhoods today, Islamic mosques, Hindu and Buddhist temples, Sikh [gurudwaras], and various ethnic shrines and storefront churches exist alongside church steeples.

Despite the growing presence in American society of non-Christian religious institutions, the vast majority of new immigrants are Christian. While we have no exact data on the religious affiliations of immigrants, given what we do know about the national origins of immigrants, religion in their home countries, and statistical data on the growth and changing demographics of church membership in the United States, it is clear that the new immigrant and ethnic groups are overwhelmingly Christian. Many come from Latin American origins that are predominantly Christian, such as Mexico, Puerto Rico, the Dominican Republic, Cuba, Haiti, El Salvador, and Guatemala. Filipinos (the second largest Asian-origin immigrant group) are predominantly Christian

---

...

[3]For a discussion of the difficulties associated with enumerating the number of members as well as the religious institutions of new immigrants, see Numrich (2000).

as well. While Christianity is a minority religion in Korea, Vietnam, and India, there has been selective immigration by Christians from those countries (Chai 1998; Hurh and Kim 1990; Warner 2000). Rather than immigrants "de-Christianizing" religion in America, they have, in fact, "de-Europeanized" American Christianity (Busto 1996; Maffy-Kipp 1997; Warner 1998; F. Yang 1999a). Moreover, as Maffy-Kipp (1997) argues, "The rapidity with which Asians have become Christian and Latinos have become Protestant forces us to reconsider our notions of Christianity as a 'Western' tradition that has encountered the mysterious East and triumphed over it" (p. 127). In the past 30 years, therefore, the immigrants have not only introduced "new and strange" varieties of religion into the United States, they have also changed the face of American Christianity.

Most of the data we report here were collected as part of the Religion, Ethnicity, and New Immigrants Research (RENIR) project in Houston, Texas. Ethnographic case studies of 13 immigrant religious institutions in the Houston metropolitan area were conducted by a team of researchers between Spring 1997 and Summer 1998. Common observation protocols and interview schedules were used at each site to ensure comparable data (available from the authors on request).[4] Interviews were conducted with clerical and lay leaders, new immigrants, and established residents and youth. Samples were representative of members' ages, length of residency in the United States, length of membership in the congregation, gender, social class, and degree of participation in the services and activities of the congregation. The 13 congregations we studied include one Greek Orthodox church; one Hindu temple; one Zoroastrian center (most of whose members come from Pakistan); two Buddhist temples

(one Vietnamese and the other Chinese); a Muslim mosque (mostly Indo-Pakistani in membership); two Roman Catholic churches (one overwhelmingly Mexican and the other composed of seven formally organized nationality groups); and five Protestant churches (one composed of 49 nationalities, one dominated by Argentines, one mostly Mexican, one totally Korean, and one almost totally Chinese). The senior author also spent several years studying Chinese Christian churches in the Washington, D.C. area and has been a participant observer in Chinese Buddhist temples and Christian churches in other metropolitan areas. In addition to these data sources, we draw on findings from published works by other scholars on immigrant religions in other parts of the country and of the world.

. . .

ADOPTING THE CONGREGATIONAL FORM

Contemporary immigrant religions are adopting the congregational form in two ways: in organizational structure, and in ritual formality. Each of these processes characterizes the structure of American Protestantism and, given that approximately 60 percent of Americans identify as Protestant (Kosmin and Lachman 1993; Roof and McKinney 1987), adapting to the Protestant model is one form of organizational assimilation or Americanization.

Congregational Structure

In contrast to religious institutions in their home countries, as immigrants establish places of worship in the United States they tend to structure them along the model of U.S. Protestant congregations. Warner (1994:54) calls this "de facto congregationalism," a structure modeled on the reformed Protestant tradition of the congregation as a community that gathers voluntarily. Warner (1994:73) argues that "the congregational mentality has great practical

---

[4]For a complete description of the methodology, see Ebaugh and Chafetz (2000a). Members of the research team (including the authors) conducted the interviews, most of which were tape recorded.

force as an unofficial norm in American religious life." Congregationalism is especially foreign to many non-Judeo-Christian religions. However, not only are immigrant Christian churches developing de facto congregationalism, but so are many non-Christian religious communities (Bankston and Zhou 2000; Beyer 1998; Numrich 1996; Wind and Lewis 1994). In contrast to denominational hierarchies, congregationalism focuses on the local community as a congregation, which includes the increased voluntary participation of members in religious functions, a lay-centered community, and multiple functions of the religious community (Ebaugh and Chafetz 2000c; Warner 1994).

Voluntary Membership. In home countries from which the new immigrants migrated, people tend to be born into a religion that has been the tradition for generations for the nation or ethnic group. In contrast, there is less social pressure in America to adhere to a particular religion, or any religion at all—alternatives to one's traditional religion are many and easily accessible. Consequently, joining (or leaving) a religious group is more likely a conscious, personal act of choosing and is part of the "new voluntarism" that characterizes contemporary American religion (Roof and McKinney 1987). For example, Buddhism is a major traditional religion in China and Vietnam and has long had vast influence in these cultures. Buddhism is diffused within other institutions and is something "in the air" (C. Yang [1961] 1967). Therefore, responding to poll or survey questions, many Chinese and Vietnamese immigrants choose Buddhism as their religious preference (Dart 1997). In the United States, however, Buddhism remains an obscure minority religion, a "new religious movement" or "cult" (Numrich 1996; Prebish and Tanaka 1999). Those immigrants who want to experience Buddhism have to make efforts to attend a Buddhist temple or join a Buddhist group (Huynh 2000; F. Yang 2000). Muslim and Hindu immigrants react in

the same way (Badr 2000; Jacob and Thakur 2000). One Muslim immigrant explained,

Due to city ordinances, the Adhan, or call to prayer, is not broadcast via loudspeaker to the surrounding neighborhood here, but you can hear it everywhere on the streets in Muslim countries. When you walk on the street and hear the call for prayer, you are constantly reminded of prayer. However, over here, you have to find the time yourself, do everything yourself.[5]

Many immigrants whom we interviewed expressed this feeling—in the workplace or the neighborhood community, they have to be with many other kinds of people. But the mosque or temple is a secluded place where they can be comfortable with each other and do their own thing. Therefore, they make efforts to attend the temple or mosque.

Organizationally, the religious community "cannot assume the loyal adherence of its members as if they were all part of the same tribe; it must actively recruit them" (Warner 1994:63). Immigrant religious organizations—Buddhist, Hindu, Muslim, and Zoroastrian as well as Christian—all have developed various programs and activities to attract immigrant adherents. For this reason, the Chinese Buddhist Hsi Nan Temple[6] in Houston abandoned its original secluded site and built a new temple in the center of the Chinese immigrant community in southwest Houston. The temple also widely advertises its regular and special activities through local Chinese newspapers and on the Internet. While the temple is open to all people who want to come, monks and lay leaders actively recruit people to join, and design programs to increase their participation and commitment. They make these adaptations in order to compete for followers with other religions as well as other Buddhist groups in the pluralist social environment.

[5]Several quotations from members of religious communities appear in the text of this article. These quotations come from RENIR interviews and site reports.
[6]Pseudonyms are used for the immigrant religious groups surveyed in the RENIR project.

The growing Protestantization of Latin America (Levine 1995; Martin 1990; C. Smith 1994; Stoll 1990) is also reflected in the United States in the competition between Catholic and Protestant (especially evangelical) churches for Hispanic immigrants. In the Argentine Protestant evangelical church that we studied there were many members who converted from Catholicism upon their arrival in Houston. The conversion was partly because of the large community of Argentine members of that Protestant church as well as the absence of a specifically Argentine Catholic church in the city. Likewise, priests in the Mexican immigrant Catholic church in our study, located in the oldest barrio in Houston, constantly bemoan the threat posed by the Protestant evangelical churches that are rapidly expanding in the neighborhood. While some parishioners defect and join these other churches, many others attend both churches—a behavior that is threatening to the Catholic clerics who fear the continued loss of Hispanic Catholics to Protestantism. In this barrio, competition for members has become a major issue in the religious market (Finke and Stark 1992; Iannacone 1991). Immigrant religious leaders from Christian and non-Christian congregations alike are aware of the need to reach out to new immigrants, rather than waiting for them to come to the temple or church; many leaders fear they are losing the immigrants, especially young people, to other religions.

Lay Leadership. In many Buddhist, Hindu, and Muslim societies, lay believers usually are not leaders in their temples and mosques. Traditionally, Buddhism in some Asian countries (e.g., Korea and China) is a monastery-centered religion where monks and nuns live in temples, often monasteries in secluded mountains, whereas lay believers are pilgrims or spiritual clients. In many countries, lay Buddhists do not become members of a particular temple, but patronize more than one temple. In the United States, however, many immigrant Buddhist groups have started a membership system with annual dues. For example, the Chinese Buddhist Hsi Nan Temple started with a structure much like traditional Chinese Buddhism. In 1979, a monk came to Houston, purchased a house outside the city, and began to gather Chinese Buddhist believers. However, in order to register with the government as a nonprofit religious organization, a board of trustees was formed that included the monk and all his initial eight followers. Three years later, the temple started a membership system in which an individual or family paid $10 a year to be listed as a member. After it built a new temple in 1990 in the center of the Chinese immigrant community, the temple's membership grew to several hundred members. By the mid-1990s, the temple further strengthened its organizational structure by selecting core members to be "Dharma Guardians" (*hu fa weiyuan*) who are certified as regular, dues-paying members who have the right to vote and to be nominated as candidates for trustees. While three monks are permanent trustees, 18 lay trustees are elected by and among the core members. The board of trustees is the decision-making body for temple affairs, and because the monks are permanent trustees, the power structure of the temple remains monk-centered. However, lay participation in administration and decision-making is established and has increased over time. The division of labor and functions of each administrative department are defined in writing; legalistic procedures are followed with a written constitution and bylaws. In effect, the ownership of the temple is shifting from the monks to the laity.

Similarly, many immigrant Hindu temples, Islamic mosques, and other religious communities are gradually developing some type of membership system, and lay participation in decision-making is increasing. In fact, many immigrant religious institutions are initiated and established by lay believers. Because of immigration regulations, religious immigrants (priests, ministers, monks, nuns, etc.) often come to the United States as employees of an established immigrant congregation. These changes toward a lay-centered community are in part adjustments to federal or local government regulations, and in part are adaptations to the social and cultural norms of American society. Some immigrants, especially clergy, try to resist these changes because of theology or religious tradition. However, American laws and democratic norms appear to be overriding forces favoring the changes toward a lay-centered religious community.

Christian immigrant churches in the United States also tend to be more lay-led than they are in home countries (Alexander 1987; Buczek 1991). For example, the Greek Orthodox church in Houston, whose membership is 95 percent Greeks and Greek-Americans, is governed by a priest and parish council cooperatively, along with a board committee consisting of elected members who are in good standing in the church. In contrast, in Greece the priest usually has supreme legislative authority.

Expansion of Services.   Another characteristic of adopting a congregational structure is the expansion of types of services provided to members. Immigrant congregations are no longer just sites for religious worship; they are assuming multiple functions, including both religious and secular classes, provision of social services, recreational centers, and social spaces for civic functions such as voting and citizenship classes. The Argentine church in Houston recently built a new building, constructed by immigrants themselves in a heavily immigrant neighborhood. Its large community center complex includes classrooms, a swimming pool, basketball and soccer courts, and a park with barbecue grills for the typical Argentine asada. In fact, the congregation changed its name from Evangelical Christian Church to the Center for Family Ministries, a name change indicative of the church's new mission to provide numerous social programs as well as a place for worship and religious services.

In many religions, traditionally, the central religious site is designated for religious purposes only. For example, the Muslim mosque is traditionally for collective prayer and a Hindu shrine is for personal devotions. In the United States, however, the function of these religious centers is diversifying. Like U.S. Christian churches, Buddhist and Hindu temples, Islamic mosques, and Zoroastrian centers are changing from prayer and ritual centers to community centers where immigrants celebrate weddings, conduct funerals, counsel families, provide social services to the needy, hold cultural activities, and so on (Ebaugh and Chafetz 2000c). In Vietnam and China, Buddhists commonly have weddings at home or in restaurants, but never at a temple, which is perceived as a place to honor the dead and to teach people to rid themselves of worldly pleasures. In the United States, however, Buddhism gives worldly life more positive affirmation. The senior author observed a "Buddhist wedding" at a temple in Chicago at which a monk presided, consecrated, and blessed the marriage. Temple records show that the Hsi Nan Temple in Houston has also held Buddhist weddings and recorded them as innovative practices. Some families even have the abbot come to their homes to bless newborn babies. Many of our Buddhist respondents remarked that these "Americanized" practices are unthinkable in their traditional home societies.

While Christian churches have a long tradition of social service involvement, leaders in Buddhist and Hindu temples, Muslim mosques, and Zoroastrian centers are learning to run charity and welfare programs, and are establishing parochial schools. Immigrant congregations are also incorporating Christian ways of imparting religious education by offering Sunday school classes for children and adults. For example, some Buddhists hold sutra study classes for the youth as well as adults; the Zoroastrians have Gatha classes, modeled on Protestant Bible study groups.

Organizational Networks. While adopting de facto or de jure congregationalism in local organization, some immigrant congregations are also developing regional, national, and international networks and organizations—structures that resemble Protestant denominations. Denominationalism is often seen as an American form of religious organization in which local congregations that share traditions and doctrine are part of a large-scale organization that controls or coordinates member congregations (Niebuhr 1929). Among the immigrant religious communities, the Fo Kuang Shan (Buddha Light Mountain) from Taiwan is a Buddhist monastery order or denomination that was founded in 1967 by the charismatic monk Hsing Yun. The banner of this denomination is *ren jian fojiao* (Buddhism in the world, or humanistic Buddhism), which emphasizes building the Buddhist ideal Pure Land in this world (*ren jian jingtu*). It has many branch temples or centers throughout North America, with headquarters at the famous Hsi Lai Temple near Los Angeles. The True Buddha Sect, a Vajrayana or esoteric Buddhism founded in Seattle in the 1980s by an immigrant from Taiwan, has established branch temples in most metropolitan areas of the United States and Canada. Some Vietnamese temples in North America have formed the World Vietnamese Buddhist Order. An independent Korean Presbyterian Church denomination in the United States has been present for many years. There is also an established Taiwanese-speaking Evangelical Formosan Church, which has about 30 churches throughout North America and has expanded to Central America, Australia, and New Zealand. Zoroastrians have had a World Zoroastrian Organization (WZO) that operated in London. However, the WZO membership includes both individuals and associations, which makes it hard to function as a worldwide body. In the 1970s, consciously following the Christian denominational model,

a Federation of Zoroastrian Associations in North America (FZANA) was formed. FZANA accepts only association members. Now the FZANA model is expanding to other parts of the world, and the Houston Zoroastrians have organized a World Zoroastrian Congress (WZC), which was held for the first time in 2000 in Houston. The WZC, based on the FZANA model, is competing and probably replacing the WZO as the highest worldwide organization of Zoroastrians. Muslim and Hindu immigrants have also formed their own regional, national, and international associations. Similarly, ethnic nondenominational Christian churches, such as the independent Chinese Christian churches, are uniting in regional and national associations.

Congregational Ritual

In addition to organizing their religious institutions along a congregational model, many immigrant religions are also taking up ritual formalities commonly found in Protestant churches, the second aspect of adopting a congregational form. This includes changes in times, places, and procedures of gatherings, roles of the clergy, forms of religious education, and replacing a sacred language with a vernacular one.

Times for Worship. In most religious groups, times of worship and sacred holidays follow time cycles. In Christianity, the cycles are weekly worship and annual liturgical seasons, cycles based on scriptures, doctrine, and traditions. In the United States and many other countries, the weekly cycle has become the societal norm and rules the rhythms of work as well as public and private lives. Christmas and Easter are national holidays with social and cultural celebrations. Non-Christian religions traditionally do not follow these Christian cycles, but immigrants in America frequently adapt to these societal rhythms. Therefore, Buddhists, Hindus, Muslims, and Zoroastrians increasingly gather on Sundays rather than on their traditional day of worship. Some Buddhists continue to hold chanting rituals on the first and fifteenth days of the month of the lunar calendar, but Sunday religious gatherings have become more frequent, partly because of members' work schedules. Even the celebration of the Buddha's birthday is adjusted to a weekend day closest to it, as are many birthdays of important Hindu gods. While immigrant Muslims in Houston continue to gather for the traditional Friday prayer, some mosques also regularly hold Sunday gatherings and Sunday school classes. Similarly, Zoroastrians in Houston have had a Sunday school offering religious education for children and youth since the early 1980s.

Ways to Worship. Likewise, customs relating to ways of worship have also changed in immigrant congregations. In traditional Chinese and Vietnamese Buddhism, when people gather in the temple for collective chanting, they often sit cross-legged on cushions on the floor. Today, Hsi Nan Temple has installed long pews in two columns, just like those commonly seen in Christian churches. During the Sunday service, instead of the traditional fan-bei (bhasa) music that aims at calming the mind, a choir often sings hymns with praising themes, some with traditional Protestant melodies. While the leading monk sits on a special cushion in front of the congregation, he leads the collective chanting and rituals, and also presents expositions of a sutra, reminiscent of preaching in Christian churches. Preaching has increasingly become the central act of the religious gathering in Muslim mosques, and in Hindu and Zoroastrian temples as well. Moreover, some non-Christian congregations are consciously modeling their services after Christian ones. For example, shortly after some visits to Christian churches, a monk of Hsi Nan suggested that the temple adopt procedures to allow people to stand and sit during the Sunday service, and to have ritual responsorial exchanges between the monk and the congregation. Hindu and Zoroastrian temples used to be places for individual prayers and devotion; today, many temples have begun collective chanting and praying.

Roles of the Clergy. In the United States, the roles of religious clergy in immigrant communities are also changing. In traditional society, the clergy are usually experts in religious rituals and scriptures. In the United States, however, immigrant believers seek out the clergy for various kinds of help, including counseling on marriage and family life, visiting the sick, and receiving traveling members and guests. These are normally defined as pastoral work in Christian churches, but are nontraditional roles for most Buddhist, Hindu, and Islamic clergy. As the religious community becomes a congregation, the clergy are obligated to provide these pastoral services to their members.

Language of Worship. Many immigrant religious communities face a language problem when trying to pass on their traditional religion to the younger generations. Whereas the immigrant generation wishes to pass on the traditional language, which they regarded as integral to their ethnicity, American-born and American-raised children often have English as their first or only language. Mullins (1987) develops a three-stage model that immigrant-ethnic churches often follow. The first stage of a monolingual immigrant church evolves into the second stage, characterized by a bilingual minister who conducts services in English as well as in the ethnic language as an accommodation to the needs of both immigrant and later generations. The third and final stage is a monolingual (English), often multi-ethnic church. A major dilemma present in each of the immigrant congregations we studied was that of encouraging the participation of young people (many of whom are pressing for English services) while maintaining the ethnic/cultural character of the congregation. In many instances, second-generation members are establishing their own worship services in English while maintaining the strong ethnic and religious character of the immigrant church (Chai 1998; F. Yang 1999b). While many new immigrant religions are committed to the use of their holy language in parts of their formal worship rites (e.g., Arabic, Sanskrit, Pali, Avestan, classic Chinese), increasingly they are translating their holy scriptures into English, preaching in English (or in the ethnic language with consecutive English interpretation), praying in English, and teaching the religion to the young people in English.

In addition to challenges posed by an English-speaking second generation, in some Chinese, Indian, and Muslim communities, immigrants come from diverse home states and themselves speak very different dialects or languages. For them, English is often their only shared language. Therefore, because of the pragmatic need to communicate, English is becoming increasingly prominent in such immigrant religious communities (Ebaugh and Chafetz 2000b). Historically, adopting the vernacular language was one of the fundamental changes Protestants made when they broke from the Roman Catholic Church. Today, various immigrant religions in America are following suit.

. . .

REFERENCES

ALEXANDER, JUNE GANATIR. 1987. *The Immigrant Church and Community: Pittsburgh's Slovak Catholics and Lutherans, 1880–1915*. Pittsburgh, PA: University of Pittsburgh Press.

BADR, HODA. 2000. "Al-Noor Mosque: Strength through Unity." Pp. 193–227 in *Religion and the New Immigrants: Continuities and Adaptations in Immigrant Congregations*, edited by H. R. Ebaugh and J. S. Chafetz. Walnut Creek, CA: AltaMira.

BANKSTON, CARL L., III and MIN ZHOU. 2000. "De Facto Congregationalism and Socioeconomic Mobility in Laotian and Vietnamese Immigrant Communities: A Study of Religious Institutions and Economic Change." *Review of Religious Research* 41:453–70.

———. 1998. "The Modern Emergence of Religions and a Global Social System for Religion." *International Sociology* 13:151–72.

BODNAR, JOHN E. 1985. *The Transplanted: A History of Immigrants in Urban America*. Bloomington, IN: Indiana University Press.

BUCZEK, DANIEL S. 1991. "Polish-Americans and the Roman Catholic Church." Pp. 39–61 in *Immigrant Religious Experience*, edited by GEORGE E. POZZETA. New York: Garland.

BUSTO, RUDY V. 1996. "Response: Asian American Religious Identities: Building Spiritual Homes on Gold Mountain." *Amerasian Journal* 22:187–90, 195.

CHAI, KAREN. 1998. "Competing for the Second Generation: English-Language Ministry in a Korean Protestant Church." Pp. 295–331 in *Gatherings in Diaspora: Religious Communities and the New Immigration*, edited by R. S. Warner and J. G. Wittner. Philadelphia, PA: Temple University Press.

DART, JOHN. 1997. "Poll Studies Chinese Americans, Religion." *Los Angeles Times*, July 5, p. B5.

DOLAN, JAY P. 1975. *The Immigrant Church: New York's Irish and German Catholics, 1815–1865*. Baltimore, MD and London, England: Johns Hopkins University Press.

DOLAN, JAY P. 1985. *The American Catholic Experience: A History from Colonial Times to the Present*. Garden City, NY: Doubleday.

EBAUGH, HELEN ROSE and JANET SALTZMAN CHAFETZ. 2000a. *Religion and the New Immigrants: Continuities and Adaptations in Immigrant Congregations*. Walnut Creek, CA: AltaMira.

———. 2000b. "Dilemmas of Language in Immigrant Congregations: The Tie That Binds or the Tower of Babel?" *Review of Religious Research* 41:432–52.

———. 2000c. "Structural Adaptations in Immigrant Congregations." *Sociology of Religion* 61:135–54.

FINKE, ROGER and RODNEY STARK. 1992. *The Churching of America, 1776–1990: Winners and Losers in Our Religious Economy*. New Brunswick, NJ: Rutgers University Press.

HERBERG, WILL. 1960. *Protestant-Catholic-Jew: An Essay in American Religious Sociology*. Garden City, NY: Doubleday.

HURH, WON MOO and KWANG CHUNG KIM. 1990. "Religious Participation of Korean Immigrants in the United States." *Journal for the Scientific Study of Religion* 29:19–34.

HUYNH, THUAN. 2000. "Center for Vietnamese Buddhism: Recreating Home." Pp. 45–66 in *Religion and the New Immigrants: Continuities and Adaptations in Immigrant Congregations*, edited by H. R. Ebaugh and J. S. Chafetz. Walnut Creek, CA: AltaMira.

IANNACONE, LAURENCE. 1991. "The Consequences of Religious Market Structure." *Rationality and Society* 3:156–77.

JACOB, SIMON and PALLAVI THAKUR. 2000. "Jyothi Hindu Temple: One Religion, Many Practices." Pp. 229–42 in *Religion and the New Immigrants: Continuities and Adaptations in Immigrant Congregations*, edited by H. R. Ebaugh and J. S. Chafetz. Walnut Creek, CA: Alta Mira.

KIM, KWANG CHUNG and WON MOO HURH. 1993. "Beyond Assimilation and Pluralism: Syncretic Sociocultural Adaptation of Korean Immigrants in the US." *Ethnic and Racial Studies* 16:696–713.

KIVISTO, PETER A. 1992. "Religion and the New Immigrants." Pp 92–107 in *A Future for Religion? New Paradigms for Social Analysis*, edited by W. H. Swatos, Jr. Newbury Park, CA: Sage.

KOSMIN, BARRY A. and SEYMOUR P. LACHMAN. 1993. *One Nation Under God: Religion in Contemporary American Society*. New York: Harmony.

LEVINE, DANIEL. 1995. "Protestants and Catholics in Latin America: A Family Portrait." Pp. 155–78 in *Fundamentalisms Comprehended*, edited by M. Marty and S. Appleby. Chicago, IL: University of Chicago Press.

MAFFY-KIPP, L. F. 1997. "Eastward Ho! American Religion from the Perspective of the Pacific Rim." Pp. 127–48 in *Retelling U. S. Religious History*, edited by T. Z. Tweed. Berkeley and Los Angeles, CA: University of California Press.

MARTIN, DAVID. 1990. *Tongues of Fire: The Explosion of Protestantism in Latin America*. Cambridge, MA: Blackwell.

MIN, PYONG GAP. 1992. "The Structure and Social Functions of Korean Immigrant Churches in the United States." *International Migration Review* 26:1370–94.

MULLINS, MARK R. 1987. "The Life-Cycle of Ethnic Churches in Sociological Perspective." *Japanese Journal of Religious Studies* 14:321–34.

NIEBUHR, H. RICHARD. 1929. *The Social Sources of Denominationalism*. New York: Henry Holt.

NUMRICH, PAUL DAVID. 1996. *Old Wisdom in the New World: Americanization in Two Immigrant Theravada Buddhist Temples*. Knoxville, IN: University of Tennessee Press.

NUMRICH, PAUL DAVID. 2000. *Old Wisdom in the New World: Americanization in Two Immigrant Theravada Buddhist Temples*. Knoxville, IN: University of Tennessee Press.

PARK, ROBERT E. and HERBERT A. MILLER. 1921. *Old World Traits Transplanted*. New York: Harper and Brothers.

POZZETTA, GEORGE E., ed. 1991. *American Immigration and Ethnicity: A 20 Volume Series of Distinguished Essays*. Vol. 19, *The Immigrant Religious Experience*. New York: Garland.

PREBISH, CHARLES S. and KENNETH K. TANAKA, eds. 1999. *The Faces of Buddhism in America*. Berkeley, CA: University of California Press.

ROOF, WADE CLARK and WILLIAM MCKINNEY. 1987. *American Mainline Religion*. New Brunswick, NJ and London, England: Rutgers University Press.

SMITH, CHRISTIAN. 1994. "The Spirit and Democracy: Base Communities, Protestantism and Democratization in Latin America." *Sociology of Religion* 55:119–43.

SMITH, TIMOTHY L. 1978. "Religion and Ethnicity in America." *American Historical Review* 83:1155–85.

STOLL, DAVID. 1990. *Is Latin America Turning Protestant?* Berkeley, CA: University of California Press.

THOMAS, WILLIAM I. and FLORIAN ZNANIECKI. 1918–1920. *The Polish Peasant in Europe and America*. Urbana and Chicago, IL: University of Illinois Press.

———. 1994. "The Place of the Congregation in the American Religious Configuration." Pp. 54–99 in *American Congregations*, vol. 2, edited by J. P. Wind and J. W. Lewis. Chicago, IL: University of Chicago Press.

———. 1998. "Approaching Religious Diversity: Barriers, Byways, and Beginnings." *Sociology of Religion* 59:193–215.

———. 2000. "Religion and New (Post-1965) Immigrants: Some Principles Drawn from Field Research." *American Studies* 41:267–86.

WARNER, R. STEPHEN and JUDITH G. WITTNER, eds. 1998. *Gatherings in Diaspora: Religious Communities and the New Immigration*. Philadelphia, PA: Temple University Press.

WILLIAMS, RAYMOND BRADY. 1988. *Religions of Immigrants from India and Pakistan: New Threads in the American Tapestry*. New York: Cambridge University Press.

WIND, JAMES P. and JAMES W. LEWIS, eds. 1994. *American Congregations*. 2 vols. Chicago, IL: University of Chicago Press.

YANG, C. K. [1961] 1967. *Religion in Chinese Society: A Study of Contemporary Social Functions of Religion and Some of Their Historical Factors*. Reprint, Berkeley and Los Angeles, CA: University of California Press.

YANG, FENGGANG. 1999a. *Chinese Christians in America: Conversion, Assimilation, and Adhesive Identities*. University Park, PA: Pennsylvania State University Press.

———. 1999b. "ABC and XYZ: Religious, Ethnic and Racial Identities of the New Second Generation Chinese in Christian Churches." *Amerasia Journal* 25:89–114.

———. 2000. "The Hsi-Nan Chinese Buddhist Temple: Seeking to Americanize." Pp. 67–87 in *Religion and the New Immigrants: Continuities and Adaptations in Immigrant Congregations*, edited by H. R. Ebaugh and J. S. Chafetz. Walnut Creek, CA: AltaMira.

YOO, DAVID. 1996. "For Those Who Have Eyes to See: Religious Sightings in Asian America." *Amerasia Journal* 22:xiii–xxii.

30 All Creatures Great and Small: Megachurches in Context

MARK CHAVES

Megachurches fascinate religion's observers, leading many to wonder what draws people to such large and complex churches. Chaves takes a different approach to this question, however, by thinking through the underlying processes leading to a signifi-cant shift in how religion is organized in the US: specifically, that more and more believers are concentrated in the largest churches in a wide range of Protestant denominations.

Megachurches—by which I mean very large Protestant churches—are increasingly difficult to ignore. By the latest count there are approximately 1,200 Protestant churches in the country with weekly attendance of at least 2,000 people (Thumma 2005), and by every account these very large churches have proliferated in recent decades. Journalists and scholars have by now paid a lot of attention to these churches, and as a result we know a lot about them. Case studies have taught us about their worship and organizational practices, surveys of members have been informative about the demographic characteristics of people involved with them, and Scott Thumma's ongoing work identifying and surveying the churches themselves has alerted us to the scale of the phenomenon, the

geography of it, and the variations of style and emphasis that exist among these very largest churches.

There are many questions one might ask about the megachurch phenomenon. Why do some churches, and not others, grow very large? What kinds of people are attracted to megachurches? How do these churches operate internally? How variable or similar are they to each other in content and style? How influential are they on American religious culture? How politically active and influential are they?

These are all interesting and important questions, but I'm not going to address any of them. Instead, I want to tackle the question of why these churches have become an increasingly visible part of the religious landscape in recent

Source: Mark Chaves, "All Creatures Great and Small: Megachurches in Context," from *Review of Religious Research*, Vol. 46. © Religious Research Association, Inc. 2006. All rights reserved.

decades. Others have addressed this question, but I'm going to approach it from a different perspective. I want to start by recognizing that the very largest churches are the tail end of a size distribution that includes all churches, and I want to try to gain leverage on the question of megachurch proliferation by shifting our attention from megachurches themselves to the overall size distribution of American Protestant churches. I'm going to ask how the size distribution of American Protestant churches has changed over time, and I'm going to ask why it has changed in the way that it has.

FROM MEGACHURCHES TO SIZE DISTRIBUTIONS

The basic idea behind this conceptual shift from megachurches themselves to the size distributions in which they are embedded is that a size distribution is a visible trace left by a process that underlies and produces that distribution. Different institutional, ecological, economic, mechanical, biological, physical, and social

processes all yield size distributions of varying shapes, but these processes often are less empirically accessible to us than the size distribution itself. So we study size distributions in the hope of learning something about the underlying processes generating those distributions.

Here is a simple example in which different size distributions clearly reflect different processes. Figure 1 shows the size distribution of Southern Baptist churches in 2002. There is nothing in this picture that ought to surprise anyone. Most Southern Baptist churches are small—the peak of the distribution is under 100 members—and the distribution is highly skewed, with a very long, slowly decaying, tail that has a peak at the high end only because I have truncated the distribution at 3,000 members or larger. Almost all religious denominations in the United States have size distributions that are highly skewed in this way.

Almost all, but not literally all. Figure 2 shows the size distribution (on the same scale as Figure 1) of Mormon wards in 2003. Note that

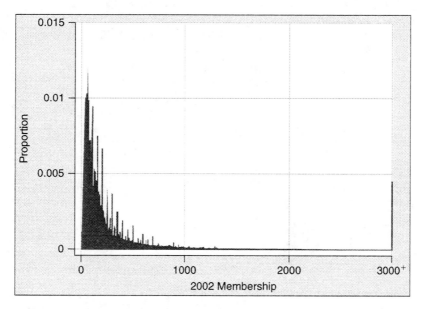

FIGURE 1   Church Size Distribution, Southern Baptist Convention, 2002

the Latter-day Saint distribution has a center in a way the Southern Baptist distribution does not.[1] More directly relevant to our purposes, though, the Mormon distribution is hardly skewed at all. Even more significant for our purposes is change over time in the tails of these two distributions. The number of Southern Baptist churches with more than 2,000 members has dramatically increased in recent decades. Not so for Mormons.

We know why the Mormon distribution is not skewed, and why it has not become more skewed in recent decades: the LDS Church splits wards when they get to 600 people or so, and this administrative action makes for a less skewed size distribution in cross-section, and it prevents the tail from stretching over time. This example illustrates how a size distribution reflects an underlying process. In the case of the Mormon Church, we know what that process is, so it is easy to see it reflected in the size distribution. There are no Mormon megachurches, and we know why.

... I am trying to understand the underlying process that has produced a change in church size distributions that manifests itself in part as the proliferation of very large churches. This is difficult, and it is made more difficult by the fact that different processes can produce similar distributions.

...

HOW HAS THE CHURCH SIZE DISTRIBUTION CHANGED?

...

We know a lot about *today's* church size distribution. Denominations always have gathered data about their churches' size, and many now keep those data in an electronic from that makes it easy to generate and examine the distribution, as I did above for the Southern Baptists and the Mormons. We also have the 1998 National Congregations Study (NCS), which enables us to examine at a national level the church size distribution across all denominations and religious groups.

From both denominational sources and the NCS it is by now well appreciated by informed observers that today's church size distribution is highly skewed, as we saw in the Southern Baptist distribution I showed you earlier. This skewness can be summarized succinctly: most

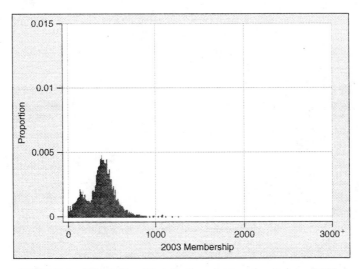

FIGURE 2   Ward Size Distribution, Latter-day Saints, 2003

churches are small, but most people are in large churches. Among all Protestant churches, for example, the biggest one percent of churches have approximately 15 percent of all the people, money, and full-time staff. The biggest 20 percent of churches have between 60 and 65 percent of all the people, money, and full-time staff.... People and resources are heavily concentrated in the biggest churches.[2]

Methods

. . .

The seven denominations for which we have data over a longer time period are Presbyterians (1900, 1930, 1960, and 1983-2002), Episcopalians (1930, 1940, 1960, and 1990-2002), Missouri Synod Lutherans (1900, 1930, 1960, and 1967-2003), Church of the Nazarene (years ending in eight beginning in 1908, 1974, 1980, 1985, 1990, and 1995-2003), Christian Reformed Church (years ending in zero between 1900 and 1990, and 1992-2004); Church of the Brethren (1940, 1970, 1980, and 1999); and Reformed Church in America (every year beginning in 1900, thanks to the labors of Don Luidens and Roger Nemeth [Luidens and Nemeth 2004]).

. . .

Results

So what did we find? I will emphasize three patterns. First, across the Protestant spectrum, there are more very big churches. There were 145 Southern Baptist churches with more than 2,000 members in 1972; in 2002 there were 458. The number of Assemblies of God churches of this size increased from 60 in 1981 to 149 in 2003. This increase might not be surprising for these two denominations, since they have grown in membership over this period, but the same trend is evident in denominations that have declined in membership over this period. The number of Episcopalian churches of this size increased from 65 in 1990 to 82 in 2002.

The number of Evangelical Lutheran Church in America churches of this size went from 199 in 1987 to 230 in 2002. The number of United Methodist churches of this size went from 245 in 1974 to 287 in 2002. The bottom line is that the number of very large Protestant churches has increased in almost every denomination on which we have data, and it does not matter whether the denomination is big or small, liberal or conservative, growing or declining.

The rate of increase in the number of very large churches seems to pick up after 1970, but the trend towards more very big churches did not begin in the 1970s. It is a longer-term trend. The number of Presbyterian churches with more than 2,000 members, for example, increased from 5 in 1900 to 74 in 1983. The number of Episcopalian churches of that size increased from 7 in 1930 to 33 in 1960; for Missouri Synod Lutherans the number goes from 2 in 1900 to 23 in 1967. Conventional wisdom on this subject says that the number of very large churches has increased *recently*, and the results bear that out, but conventional wisdom does not recognize that this is not entirely a post-1970 trend.

The long-term nature of this trend suggests that simple population growth and increased population density are partly responsible for megachurch proliferation. If you need a town or city or suburb of a certain size in order to support a 2,000-person church, then the more communities of that size there are, the more 2,000-person churches there will be. So simple population growth probably is part of the story of the increasing number of very large churches.

A second pattern I want to emphasize is that the very biggest churches are getting bigger. . . .

A long-term trend of this sort could occur by a demographic process of growth proportional to size. If churches simply keep growing by natural increase, for example, or by a process in which new people are pulled into churches of all sizes via social ties to current members, then the biggest churches would constantly get bigger. This simple demographic explanation breaks down, however, because it implies that yesterday's biggest churches would be the same as today's biggest churches. The biggest churches would be bigger than they were before, but the same churches still would be at the tip of the size distribution's tail. But this is not the case. Yesterday's very biggest churches are not today's very biggest churches. . . . If you look at the 20 biggest churches at time 1, only half of them are still on that list 20 years later, only one quarter are still on the list 40 years later, and only 2 are still on the list 60 years later. It is not that these very large churches peak and then shrink dramatically, although some do. Rather, the biggest churches of the moment are overtaken by a new cohort of churches that have caught that decade's cultural wave and ridden it to the top, and then those churches are overtaken by the next wave, and on and on.

. . .

To me, the most interesting development is a third trend: *people are increasingly concentrated in the very largest churches*. Figure 3 shows the percent of people in the largest 1 percent of churches in 12 denominations, seven of which from early in the 20th century to the present. This, to me, is an extraordinarily interesting, even astonishing, picture because *every* denomination shows the same pattern of steadily, in some cases rapidly, increasing concentration from 1970 to the present, with no end in sight to this trend. Denominations vary in how concentrated their people are in the very largest churches, but all of them show the same trend towards increasing concentration since about 1970.[5]

Let me be explicit about something that has been implicit to this point. I am not focusing here only on true megachurches. In some denominations, the largest 1 percent of churches includes churches with 1,000 or so members, which means churches with only 500 or so attenders on an average weekend. This is much smaller than the megachurch of popular parlance, but the important point here, and throughout this article, is that we should understand megachurches as

one manifestation of a broader phenomenon by which churchgoers are increasingly concentrated in the very largest churches.

 . . . *In every denomination on which we have data, people are becoming increasingly concentrated in the very largest churches, and this is true for small and large denominations, for conservative and liberal denominations, for growing and declining denominations*. I find it remarkable that the same trend appears so uniformly across the board. . . .

This increased concentration may be changing American religion's social and political significance. For one thing, increased concentration makes religion more visible, since one 2,000-person church is more visible, if only because of the size of its building, than ten 200-person churches. Increased concentration also probably increases religion's potential for social and political influence, since one 2,000-person church is easier to mobilize for social or political action than ten 200-person churches, a politician is more likely to address one 2,000-person church than ten 200-person churches, and the pastor of one 2,000-person church probably gets an appointment with the mayor more easily than the pastors of ten 200-person churches. Increasing concentration seems likely also to have repercussions for intra-denominational politics and the development and diffusion of worship practices. And increased concentration also can fool observers into thinking that there is a religious revival occurring when really there is a change in the social organization of religion. These consequences of increasing religious concentration make trying to understand what is behind it a worthy agenda.

WHY THE INCREASING CONCENTRATION?

 . . .

It sometimes is said that the secret to megachurch success is that they have figured out how to attract the unchurched, and they thereby bring

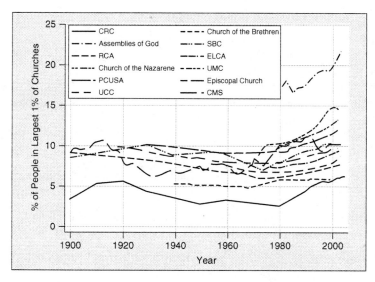

FIGURE 3 Percent of People in Largest 1% of Churches in Twelve Denominations

people into churches who were not previously involved. Willow Creek is famous, for example, for their profile of "Unchurched Harry" as their ideal-typical target recruit. If new church-goers were going disproportionately to the very largest churches, this would indeed increase religious concentration.

One problem with this explanation, however, is that church attendance overall is not increasing. . . . So the increasing concentration of people in the very largest churches is *not* a consequence of megachurches tapping into a previously uninvolved population. Increased concentration is occurring mainly because people are shifting from smaller to larger churches, not because people are shifting from uninvolvement to involvement in big churches.

Neither can we explain this trend by reference to some constant advantage of size. It surely is true that there are Durkheimian, collective effervescence, attractions to worshiping as part of a big group. It also surely is true that big groups enjoy a kind of status advantage that comes from being perceived as where the action is, or where something interesting is happening. . . .

But these cannot explain the concentration trend we have observed. Constant advantages of bigness imply a trend towards concentration that should have begun long ago with the appearance of the first big churches, not just in 1970. And constant advantages of bigness also imply that the biggest churches at some early point in the process are the ones that constantly get bigger and stay at the top. But we already have seen that neither of these is true. . . .

A third, and somewhat more subtle explanation, invokes suburbanization, the proliferation of automobiles and, more generally, decreasing travel costs, perhaps in interaction with the eternal advantages of bigness. Maybe people always did prefer big churches . . . but perhaps they could not act on those preferences because it was too difficult to get to a big church. Perhaps increases in population density outside of central cities made it easier for religious entrepreneurs to build very large buildings on affordable tracts of land at the edge of the developed zone. And once these big churches are built and everyone has a car and access to paved roads on which to drive quickly and cheaply to the very big church at the outer edge of the suburbs just like we drive to the mall, perhaps only then were people able to easily attend the big churches they always would have preferred.

... The problem with the suburbanization and travel cost explanation of increasing concentration is that the trend lines do not line up properly. ...

The suburbanization and travel-cost explanation implies that religious concentration should have started to increase decades sooner than it actually did. Megachurches often are compared with shopping malls, but the cars and suburbanization story works much better for malls than it does for churches. Large regional shopping malls start to proliferate immediately after World War II, directly on the heels of rapidly increasing suburbanization (Hanchett 1996, Jackson 1996). Religious concentration and the fast increase in very large churches starts 25 or 30 years later.

. . .

A fourth possible explanation is that megachurches are a new, innovative organizational form designed by religious entrepreneurs, perhaps those associated with the church growth movement, who were particularly attuned to post-1970 society and culture. Several early megachurches—both Willow Creek and Saddleback, for example—began only after a religious entrepreneur walked neighborhoods and surveyed people about what kind of church they would want to attend, and only then designing the model that proved to be wildly successful and therefore mimicked by churches across the country. This kind of explanation rests on the creative action of these innovators in developing a new type of church.

The main problem with this sort of explanation is that, in key ways, today's megachurches are *not* a new organizational form. Consider these two paraphrased descriptions of large churches from H. Paul Douglass's *1000 City Churches*, published in 1926:[7]

An African American church in a northern city experienced dramatic growth during the pastoral leadership of a "remarkable man." It is known as a "young people's church," with a very strong Sunday School and much teen participation. Its membership is divided into eighteen small groups, called "Circles of Service." It is known for its excellent music, and its building is used daily for such things as cooking classes, art classes, boys' clubs, and an employment bureau.

A Disciples of Christ church in Missouri built a "plain but commodious church building designed to house numerous activities." The building included a full-size gymnasium and "unusually well-designed provision for general social life and meetings of small groups." Sunday evening services were on "sensational" topics such as "William J. Bryan says universities are hot beds of infidelity and irreligion. Is he right?" There were "three to seven meetings of subsidiary groups per day ... an average of 147 per month." In addition to several choirs, small group activities included drama, sewing, orchestra rehearsal, athletics, and movie watching.

Note that characteristics typical of today's megachurches—rapid growth under a gifted leader, high quality music, multi-function buildings, many and varied small groups and activities—are evident in these descriptions from the 1920s.

. . .

Perhaps, however—and this is a fifth potential explanation for the increasing concentration of people in the very largest churches—recent cultural change has given a new advantage to an organizational form that has existed for a long time. Perhaps people today are *more* comfortable with bigness, *more* attracted to spectacle, or *more* drawn to a church in which they can choose to be anonymous, or in which they can choose between anonymity in a big crowd and intimacy in a small group. ... It is not good enough to point to attitudes or [preferences] that have changed steadily over the long term; we need instead evidence of attitudes or preferences that change abruptly circa 1970 and stay changed after that.

Observers often posit the Baby Boom generation as the carriers of the post-1970 cultural change that is responsible for the proliferation of megachurches. The timing works here, but again there is a missing link in the argument. We need evidence that baby boomers and succeeding cohorts are systematically different from previous cohorts in ways that are relevant to megachurches. . . .

I think there is indeed a cultural affinity between what megachurches offer and what contemporary churchgoers want, and I think this affinity helps explain which churches grow and which ones do not grow. But I do not think that cultural change since the 1970s gives us the complete story behind the concentration trend that we have observed.

A sixth potential type of explanation might seek to connect increased concentration in religion to increased concentration in other spheres. Comparing concentration trends in religion with concentration trends in other organizational populations may well be fruitful, but two initial observations suggest that such comparisons will not immediately yield a compelling explanation of religious concentration. First, it is not the case that concentration has increased across all sectors of the economy (White 2002), so religious concentration is not simply part of a society- or economy-wide general trend. Second, although concentration has increased in retail, and at first glance megachurches seem similar to "big box" stores such as Walmart, Home Depot, Best Buy, and so on, there is a significant dissimilarity between the social organization of retail concentration and the social organization of religious concentration. Increased retail concentration seems to be produced mainly by significant economies of scale realized at the *firm* level rather than at the *establishment* level (Vias 2004). It is telling that all the major big box stores are chains. The situation is very different for churches. Approximately one third of very large churches are independent, and even when very large churches are affiliated with a denomination, it is difficult to see how that affiliation might create

advantages analogous to those enjoyed by retail chains. It seems more likely that increased concentration in religion, though similar on the surface to increased concentration in retail, has different sources.

. . .

A NEW HYPOTHESIS ABOUT INCREASING CONCENTRATION IN RELIGION: RISING COSTS

. . . I'm going to propose that the increased concentration of people in the very largest churches is caused in part by rising costs that make it more and more difficult to run a church at a customary level of programming and quality. . . .

Churches suffer, I think, from "Baumol's Cost Disease." This is a phenomenon identified in the mid-1960s by the economists William J. Baumol and William G. Bowen in their analysis of performing arts organizations (Baumol and Bowen 1966). The basic idea is simple. If there is increasing productivity—increases in efficiency—somewhere in the economy, and if wages increase in those sectors, then wages also will increase in other sectors of the economy, or else talent will move to the sectors in which wages are increasing.

Crucially, however, some kinds of activities cannot be made much more efficient. It probably takes about as much preparation and effort now to produce Hamlet, or perform a Beethoven symphony, as it did centuries ago. Activities that have at their core human effort, training, practice, attention, and presence cannot be made much more efficient. . . .

Congregational religion also has very few ways to become more efficient, so churches also will be subject to Baumol's cost disease. Like schools, universities, theater companies, and symphony orchestras, churches too will have ever rising real costs with no significant opportunities to reduce those costs by becoming more efficient. The only options in such a situation are to increase revenue or reduce quality.

Rising real costs are not a problem for an enterprise, not even one for which efficiencies are not available, so long as revenue keeps increasing at the same rate as costs increase. For churches, this was true for a long time. Americans are famously generous to their churches, and it is well known that real donations to religion have increased over the long term in both total and per capita amounts. This is an often celebrated fact about American religion. But increases in donations are not often compared to the rate at which the costs of running a church have increased, and I want to suggest that circa 1970 the rate at which donations increased stopped keeping pace with the rate at which the costs of running a church increased.

. . . The qualitative picture is that, from 1940 to 1960 real increases in revenue for the average congregation far outpaced real increases in clergy salaries, and *that gap narrows* considerably from 1960 to 1980, with the lines even crossing between 1990 and 2000, indicating that real median clergy salary increased at a higher rate than real donations between 1990 and 2000. Again, I do not want to put too much weight on these preliminary results, but they do suggest that churches faced a qualitatively different, more stressful, revenue-cost situation after 1960 or 1970 than they faced before 1960.

When cost increases outpace revenue increases, churches will cut corners and reduce quality by deferring maintenance, declining to replace the youth minister who graduated from seminary and moved on, replacing the recently retired full-time minister with a half-time person, and so on. In short, churches will find it difficult to maintain the same level of programming and quality they had before. And this will be true even if the church loses no members. If costs rise faster than revenues, a 200-person church will be unable to produce the same level of programming and quality it produced before *even if it stays a 200-person church*. Moreover, the minimum size at which a church can be economically viable

will increase. The result is that, when cost increases outpace revenue increases, people will be pushed out of smaller churches that no longer meet their minimum standards and into larger churches that still do.[10]

. . .

Larger churches also are affected by the cost disease, and they also are affected by the increased difficulty of keeping pace with these rising costs that came into play after about 1970, but the key point is that, in a situation of rising costs, people will have to go to larger and larger churches in order to achieve the same level of programming and quality.

. . .

I am not claiming that the cost-disease mechanism is the only thing driving increased concentration in religion. Cultural change, or shifts in economic and urban geography, may well be part of the story. Technological advances in audio-visual equipment, telecommunications, and computers also may have helped mitigate some of the ways in which very large size might otherwise lead to reduced quality in church services, pastoral care, and programming. A complete explanation of increasing religious concentration surely will not be monocausal.

CONCLUSION

Among other things, I have called attention to forces that are pushing people out of smaller churches as well as pulling them into bigger churches. Scholars and journalists who have written about megachurches have focused almost exclusively on the pull factors, but shifting attention from megachurches themselves to the size distribution as a whole leads us to pay attention to the underlying system operating here, and that means attending to push factors as well as pull factors.

Even if the cost-disease explanation leaves you cold, I hope you are as amazed as I am at the discovery that, in every Protestant denomination on which we have data—large or small, liberal or conservative, growing or declining—people are increasingly concentrated in the very largest churches. This increasing concentration is, I think, a significant change in the social organization of American religion. We do not yet fully grasp its causes and consequences, but I hope you will help me try to understand it better.

ACKNOWLEDGEMENTS

This work was made possible by a grant from the Louisville Institute, by the generosity of denominational researchers who shared their data with us, and by the skill and dedication of a team of graduate students, led by Shawna Anderson and including Jessica Hamar, Michael Jacobs, and Lorien Lake. Warren Bird, Art Farnsley, Nancy Martin, James Montgomery, Scott Thumma, and Rhys Williams commented helpfully on an earlier version. This article is adapted from the H. Paul Douglass lecture delivered at the RRA meetings in Rochester, New York in November, 2005. That talk included color graphs and photographs that are not reproducible in the journal.

NOTES

1. The LDS distribution is bimodal; the reasons for this are not clear.

2. People and resources are not as concentrated in churches, however, as they are in places of employment. According to the 1991 National Organizations Study, the biggest 10 percent of establishments employ approximately 75 percent of full-time employees (Kalleberg et al. 1996:49).

. . .

5. It is difficult to discern which lines in this figure correspond to which denomination. A color version of this figure is available from the author. Fortunately, the key point is how similarly shaped all the lines are, which is why I include this black and white version here despite its visual limitations.

. . .

7. The first is Case XXII, pp. 185-186; the second is Case XIX, pp. 166-168.

. . .

10. Comparing American Judaism with American Protestantism might be instructive about the plausibility of this proposed mechanism. We have data from Conservative Jewish synagogues between 1992 and 2005, and we have data from Reform Jewish synagogues between 1977 and 2004. Interestingly, neither Conservative nor Reform Judaism has become more concentrated over this period. Has American Judaism avoided the increasing concentration trend evident within Protestantism because the membership dues system used by synagogues is more effective than a pledge-plus-free-will-offering system at keeping revenue increases in line with cost increases?

REFERENCES

BARIBA'SI, ALBERT-LA'SZLO'. 2003. *Linked: How Everything Is Connected To Everything Else and What It Means For Business, Science and Everyday Life.* New York: Penguin.

BAUMOL, WILLIAM J. and WILLIAM G. BOWEN 1966. *Performing Arts: The Economic Dilemma.* Cambridge: MIT Press.

DOUGLASS, H. PAUL. 1926. *1000 City Churches: Phases of Adaptation to Urban Environment.* New York: George H. Doran Company.

HANCHETT, THOMAS W. 1996. "U.S. Tax Policy and the Shopping-Center Boom of the 1950s and 1960s." *American Historical Review* 101:1082–1110.

JACKSON, KENNETH T. 1996. "All the World's a Mall: Reflections on the Social and Economic Consequences of the American Shopping Center." *American Historical Review* 101:1111–1121.

KALLEBERG, ARNE L., DAVID KNOKE, PETER V. MARSDEN and JOE L. SPAETH. 1996. *Organizations in America: Analyzing their Structures and Human Resource Practices.* Thousand Oaks, CA Sage Publications.

LUIDENS, DON and ROGER NEMETH. 2004. "RCA Congregational Data: 1817-2000." Machine readable data file. Holland. MI: Department of Sociology, Hope College.

THUMMA, SCOTT. 2005. "United States Has More Megachurches Than Previously Thought." Web Report. Hartford: Hartford Seminary. Downloaded from www.hartsem.edu/events/news_mega.htm. 2001. "Megachurches Today: Summary of Data from the Faith Communities Today Project." Web Report. Hartford: Hartford Seminary. Downloaded *from /hirr.hartsem .edu/org/faith_megachurches_FACTsummary.html.*

VIAS, ALEXANDER C. 2004. "Bigger Stores, More Stores, or No Stores: Paths of Retail Restructuring in Rural America." *Journal of Rural Studies* 20:303–318.

WHITE, LAWRENCE J. 2002. "Trends in Aggregate Concentration in the United States." *Journal of Economic Perspectives* 16:137–160.

Reading **31** The Public Perception of "Cults" and "New Religious Movements"

PAUL J. OLSON

Language matters. Olson finds that people have more negative perceptions of "cults" than of "new religious movements."

For the better part of two decades, Barker (1986, 1989), Richardson (1993), and several other sociologists of religion, as well as religious studies scholars such as Miller (1996) and Wessinger (2000), have argued that the term "cult" has become laden with negative connotations among the general public and media and have advocated dropping its use in academia. They contend that the term has become a pejorative label given to religious groups the user does not like or understand, and that merely using the word to describe a group elicits negative, stereotypical images about what the group is like before any factual information has been obtained. James R. Lewis argues that "minority religions lose their chance at a fair hearing as soon as the label 'cult' is successfully applied to them" (Lewis 2003:206). Wessinger maintains that "[t]he word *cult* dehumanizes the religion's members and their children. It strongly implies that these people are deviants; they are seen as

crazy, brainwashed, [and] duped by their leader" (Wessinger 2000:4, italics in original). Furthermore, scholars who have examined the 1993 Branch Davidian standoff have almost routinely argued that the ability of the government, media, and former members to define the Davidians as a "cult" and David Koresh as a "cult leader" played a significant role in bringing about the horrific conclusion of the siege (Lewis 1995; Richardson 1995; Tabor and Gallagher 1995; Wessinger 2000; Wright 1995). Taking this research into account and because the term cult is "virtually never used by a contemporary religious group in regards to itself," Christiano, Swatos, and Kivisto (2002:11) take the position that use of the term cult in academic literature is an "ethical breach" for modern social scientists.

In order to still be able to discuss the groups that are commonly referred to as cults, while avoiding that term, scholars have offered several alternatives. Miller (1996) prefers "alternative religious movements" to describe groups the popular media refer to as cults. Ellwood (1983, 1986) suggests "emergent religions." Harper and Le Beau (1993) find "marginal religious movements" the best option. Beckford (1985), Barker (1989), and numerous others use the term "new religious movements" (NRMs), which has gained a strong foothold in the sociology of religion. The assumption behind all of these suggestions is that by changing the term used to describe a cult, readers will not be affected by the negative connotations the term carries and will be less judgmental of a religious movement. Questions remain, however: Will simply changing the terminology used to describe cults alter people's perceptions of such groups? Will the general public be less tolerant and accepting of "cult members" than of the members of NRMs?

The goal of this article is to answer these questions. To this end, 814 randomly selected Nebraskans were asked about their feelings toward cults, another 831 were asked about their feelings toward NRMs, and 769 were asked about "new Christian churches." If Miller, Barker, Richardson, and Wessinger, among others, are correct, Nebraskans will respond much more negatively to questions about cults than they will to questions about either NRMs or new Christian churches.

. . .

THE STUDY

The data were collected as part of the 2003 Nebraska Annual Social Indicators Survey (NASIS) conducted by the Bureau of Sociological Research at the University of Nebraska–Lincoln. A telephone survey was completed by 2,426 noninstitutionalized Nebraskans between the ages of 19 and 72 from December 2003 to May 2004 who were selected using random digit dialing. Of the likely households selected, 44.4 percent completed interviews, 42.6 percent refused, and 13 percent went unresolved. . . .

. . . The respondents were essentially divided into three subsamples and asked two questions about either cults, NRMs, or new Christian churches with the terminology of each question determined at random. Approximately one-third of the respondents ($N = 814$) were asked the following two questions about cults:

1. Researchers at the university are interested in the growing diversity of religious groups in the United States. How comfortable would you be if your neighbor joined a cult?
2. Do you agree with the following statement? The government should have the right to regulate the activities and practices of cults.

For the first question, respondents were given the options of "very comfortable," "somewhat comfortable," "somewhat uncomfortable," "very uncomfortable," or "don't know" as potential answers. In response to the second question, participants could either "strongly agree," "somewhat agree," "somewhat disagree," or "strongly disagree" with the statement (they were also given the "don't know" option).

The wording of the questions for the other respondents was exactly the same as for the first one-third of the respondents with one notable exception: the term cult was replaced by either NRM ($N = 831$) or new Christian church ($N = 769$). The term NRM was selected as an alternative to cult because it is widely used in the sociological literature. New Christian church was selected in an effort to determine if simply including "Christian" and "church" would be enough to make the respondents more accepting of their neighbors and opposed to governmental regulation. The new Christian church could easily require the drinking of poison, handling of deadly snakes, and complete obedience to the group's charismatic leader, but no information about the nature of the group was given. It was up to the respondent to fill in the blanks about what the groups were like.

TABLE 1   Responses to the Question: How Comfortable Would You Be If Your Neighbor Joined A . . .

Response	Cult	New Religious Movement	New Christian Church
Very comfortable	43 (5.2%)	236 (28.4%)	460 (59.9%)
Somewhat comfortable	84 (10.3%)	294 (35.4%)	221 (28.8%)
Somewhat uncomfortable	314 (38.6%)	187 (22.5%)	36 (4.7%)
Very uncomfortable	348 (42.8%)	55 (6.6%)	11 (1.4%)
Don't know	23 (2.8%)	53 (6.4%)	36 (4.7%)
Refused	2 (0.2%)	6 (0.7%)	4 (0.5%)
Total	814	831	768

$\pm 3.5\% (p = 0.05)$.

RESULTS

The survey results reveal that Nebraskans have an overwhelmingly negative view of cults but hold a much more positive view of NRMs and new Christian churches. As Table 1 shows, nearly 43 percent of the Nebraskans surveyed stated that they would feel *very* uncomfortable if their neighbor joined a cult and an additional 38.6 percent would feel somewhat uncomfortable. Only 29.1 percent said they would feel either very or somewhat uncomfortable if their neighbor joined an NRM, and when the group was overtly placed within the context of Christianity, a scant 6.1 percent said that they would be at all uncomfortable if their neighbor joined a new Christian church.

Nebraskans responded less strongly to the idea of government regulation of all religious movements, but a bias against cults was still evident. As Table 2 reveals, approximately 56 percent of the Nebraskans surveyed agreed with the statement that the government should be able to regulate the activities of cults (30.6 percent agreed, 25.6 percent strongly agreed). Just over 25 percent agreed that the government should be able to regulate the activities of NRMs, and 12.4 percent agreed that the government should be able to regulate new Christian churches' activities. Nebraskans strongly opposed government regulation of the activities of NRMs and new Christian churches, but only 35.8 percent of the respondents were willing to extend the courtesy to cults.

. . .

DISCUSSION

The results of the 2003 NASIS . . . reveal that Nebraskans have an overwhelmingly negative

TABLE 2   Responses to the Question: How Much do you Agree with the Following Statement? The Government Should Have the Right to Regulate the Activities and Practices of . . .

Response	Cults	New Religious Movements	New Christian Churches
Strongly agree	208 (25.6%)	47 (5.7%)	16 (2.1%)
Agree	249 (30.6%)	165 (19.9%)	79 (10.3%)
Disagree	194 (23.9%)	314 (37.8%)	302 (39.3%)
Strongly disagree	97 (11.9%)	259 (31.2%)	333 (43.3%)
Don't know	65 (8.0%)	39 (4.7%)	30 (3.9%)
Refused	1 (0.1%)	7 (0.8%)	9 (1.2%)
Total	814	831	769

$\pm 3.5\% (p = 0.05)$.

attitude toward cults, but do not hold such a negative view of NRMs even when they know nothing else about the group. Simply changing the terminology used to describe a religious group does, in fact, make a very large difference. This supports the position of scholars such as Barker, Miller, and Wessinger who argue that the term cult has become laden with pejorative connotations that skew people's abilities to judge a religious group on its own merits. Additionally, although no questions were asked about where the respondents had acquired information about cults, NRMs, or new Christian churches, I believe the results can be seen as supporting Pfeifer's (1992) conclusion that members of the general public have negative schematic representations of cults that are most likely created and reinforced by exposure to negative representations in the media. Because the term NRMs is used almost exclusively in academic literature and not in the mainstream media where the general public would encounter it on a regular basis and associate it with Jonestown, the Branch Davidians, or Heaven's Gate, people simply do not have a negative schematic representation of NRMs. Furthermore, in a state like Nebraska where a large majority of the population is Christian, "religion" and religious movements could simply be associated with Christianity for many people and, thus, be seen as relatively harmless.

Not surprisingly, when the term new Christian church was used to describe a movement, Nebraskans were very opposed to government regulation of its activities and felt comfortable having a neighbor join the group. When the unnamed group was placed within a Christian context and [referred] to as a church rather than a movement, Nebraskans had few qualms over it. Because some NRMs that are often labeled cults by the ACM are within the Christian tradition, using a term that links them to that tradition may be beneficial when discussing the movement in nonacademic arenas.

CONCLUSION

The results of this survey demonstrate that an NRM (despite the problems several scholars have with that term) is viewed much more positively by Nebraskans than a cult is, but perhaps an alternative religious movement, emergent religion, or marginal religious movement would have been equally well received. Certainly, a replication of the study using any of these alternative terms, and a national sample, could be done to give us an even better picture of the general public's attitudes toward cults and NRMs.

Beyond giving us a better understanding of the general public's view of cults, this study has implications for scholars studying such groups. Using technical jargon in academic journals and books published by scholarly presses for an academic audience is fine; all of the sciences, social or otherwise, have their own languages. These languages are understood by professors and graduate students, but for people not trained in the field or only being introduced to it, this may not be the case. Thus, when college freshman read textbooks in "Introduction to Sociology" that discuss cults, what images do they have in their minds? When sociologists of religion or religious studies scholars discuss cults in the popular media, can we assume that the audience knows that we use cult in a neutral, technical manner, and not the same way that people in the ACM use it? Do judges and juries understand and use the technical definition of a cult in child custody cases or trials? The results of the 2003 NASIS reveal that, at least in Nebraska, the general public certainly does not view cults in a neutral way. Because the use of the term has such potentially severe consequences, we must be extremely careful with it and, I believe, that it is time that we become "cult-phobic" (Richardson 1993:355) and do our research with more neutral terminology.

ACKNOWLEDGEMENTS

The author would like to thank the Bureau of Sociological Research at the University of Nebraska–Lincoln, especially Dan Hoyt and Stacia Halada, for all of their help in the data collection portion of this research project. The author would also like to thank Hugh Whitt, Helen Berger, and the anonymous *JSSR* reviewers for their comments on earlier drafts of this article.

REFERENCES

BARKER, E. 1986. Religious movements: Cult and anticult since Jonestown. *Annual Review of Sociology* 12:329–46.

————. 1989. *New religious movements: A practical introduction.* London: Her Majesty's Stationery Office.

BECKFORD, J. 1985. *Cult controversies: The societal response to the new religious movements.* London and New York: Tavistock.

CHRISTIANO, K. J., W. H. SWATOS, Jr., and P. KIVISTO. 2002. *Sociology of religion: Contemporary developments.* Walnut Creek, CA: AltaMira Press.

ELLWOOD, R. 1983. *Introducing religion: From the inside and outside,* 2nd ed. Englewood Cliffs: Prentice.

————. 1986. The several meanings of cult. *Thought* LXI(241):212–24.

HARPER, C. L. and B. F. LE BEAU. 1993. The social adaptation of marginal religious movements in America. *Sociology of Religion* 54:171–92.

LEWIS, J. R. 1995. Self-fulfilling prophecies, the anticult movement, and the Waco confrontation. In *Armageddon in Waco: Critical perspectives on the Branch Davidian conflict,* edited by S. A. Wright, pp. 95–110. Chicago: University of Chicago Press.

————. 2003. *Legitimating new religions.* New Brunswick, NJ: Rutgers University Press.

MILLER, T., ed. 1996. *America's alternative religions.* Albany, NY: State University of New York Press.

PFEIFER, J. E. 1992. The psychological framing of cults: Schematic representations and cult evaluations. *Journal of Applied Social Psychology* 22(7):531–44.

RICHARDSON, J.T. 1993. "Definitions of cult: From sociological-technical to popular-negative."*Review of Religious Research* 39(2):116–36.

————. 1993. Definitions of cult: From sociological-technical to popular-negative. *Review of Religious Research* 34(4):348–56.

————. 1995. Manufacturing consent about Koresh: A structural analysis of the role of media in the Waco tragedy. In *Armageddon in Waco: Critical perspectives on the Branch Davidian conflict,* edited by S. A. Wright, pp. 153–76. Chicago: University of Chicago Press.

TABOR, J. D. and E. V. GALLAGHER. 1995. *Why Waco? Cults and the battle for religious freedom in America.* Berkeley and Los Angeles, CA: University of California Press.

WESSINGER, C. 2000. *How the millennium comes violently: From Jonestown to Heaven's Gate.* New York: Seven Bridges Press.

WRIGHT, S. A. 1995. Construction and escalation of a cult threat: Dissecting moral panic and official reaction to the Branch Davidians. In *Armageddon in Waco: Critical perspectives on the Branch Davidian conflict,* edited by S. A. Wright, pp. 75–94. Chicago: University of Chicago Press.

32 Apocalypse at Waco

JAMES D. TABOR

Some alternative religions have conflicted with legal authorities. Tabor recounts his efforts to better understand the worldview of the Branch Davidians and communicate it to the FBI.

The government doesn't understand, I said to myself as I watched the drama of the Branch Davidians at Waco, Texas, unfold on CNN day after day. Was there anything I could do to help, I wondered. As my frustration mounted, I decided to offer my services to the FBI, which by this time had taken over the Bureau of Alcohol, Tobacco and Firearms. It was clear to me that the drama at Mt. Carmel, as David Koresh called his Branch Davidian compound, was being played out as a fulfillment of the New Testament Book of Revelation—and the authorities were dangerously ignorant of the apocalyptic world in which David Koresh was living.

I first called my friend Philip Arnold, director of Reunion Institute in Houston, Texas, who was physically closer to the scene than I. I told him that I thought we could be of help. Like me, Phil has a Ph.D. in New Testament and has specialized in both ancient and modern apocalypticism.

He shared my assessment of the situation and we agreed to present ourselves to the FBI as a team—experts in the Bible, apocalypticism, and especially the Book of Revelation.

The FBI welcomed our assistance. It was obvious that, whatever their expertise in siege warfare, they knew little about the Bible.

7:25 Sunday evening, February 28, 1993. CNN anchorman David French is conducting a live interview on a phone hookup. I rush to the TV set. It is David Koresh, his voice edged with an appealing intensity. A photo of the young man with glasses and long wavy hair, which was later to become familiar around the world, is on the screen against a backdrop of a map of Texas with a place marked as "Mt. Carmel," near Waco. (Earlier that day, at 9:55 in the morning to be exact, the Bureau of Alcohol, Tobacco and Firearms had raided Mt. Carmel, resulting in a two-hour gun battle with the

Source: James D. Tabor, "Apocalypse at Waco," from *Bible Review IX(5).* © 1993.

Branch Davidians that left four ATF agents dead and 16 more wounded.) A steady stream of biblical quotations is issuing from the voice at Waco. Koresh is talking about the Seven Seals from the Book of Revelation. French, on the other hand, keeps trying to get Koresh to talk about the morning raid—how many cult members had been killed or wounded and whether he planned to surrender. Koresh admits that he is badly wounded, that his two-year-old daughter was killed and that others from his group were killed and wounded. It is clear that Koresh wants mainly to quote Scripture, mostly the Book of Revelation. He was the Lamb, he said, chosen to open the Seven Seals.

The phone conversation over CNN went on for about 45 minutes. I was utterly mesmerized. If this was the world Koresh was living in, neither his own death nor that of his followers would hold any dread for him. It was then that I decided the authorities might need some help.

"Koresh," the name that David had legally adopted for himself, is Hebrew for Cyrus, the name of the ancient Persian king who destroyed the Babylonian empire in 539 B.C.E. Almost 50 years earlier (in 686 B.C.E.), the Babylonians had destroyed Jerusalem and God's house, the Temple built by King Solomon. Cyrus, or Koresh, was an Israelite hero: He not only defeated the mighty Babylonian empire, but soon thereafter permitted the Jews to return from Exile and rebuild their Temple.

As I listened to Koresh quoting from Revelation, I was almost dizzied by the incongruity of it all: Here we were in 1993 and this young Cyrus, would-be challenger of modern Babylon, was actually delving into the details of the Book of Revelation on prime time over a worldwide television network. I pulled out a Bible and turned to Isaiah 45, where the ancient Persian king Cyrus was addressed by God himself:

"Thus says the Lord to Cyrus (*Koresh*) his *anointed* whose right hand I have grasped to subdue nations before him and strip kings of their robes." (Isaiah 45:1)

Here Cyrus is actually called "messiah." The Hebrew word is *mashiach*, which simply means one who is anointed. In biblical times both the high priests and the kings of Israel were anointed in a ceremony in which oil was poured over the head and beard (see Psalm 133). The Greek translation of the Hebrew *mashiach* is "Christos," from which we get our term "Christ." In this sense, one could accurately say that this ancient Persian king was called Christ. But in this general sense of the term, the Bible speaks of many christs or messiahs, not just one. Indeed, the word came to refer to anyone who was especially selected by God for a mission, as was the Persian king Cyrus. David Koresh was claiming to be such a christ.

This biblical terminology led to endless confusion and miscommunication between the secular media and the FBI on the one hand, and the followers of Koresh, who lived and breathed these ancient texts, on the other. It was widely but incorrectly reported, even by the most responsible media, that David Koresh claimed to be Jesus Christ, or even God himself. But he was in fact claiming to be a messiah, or christ, in the same sense that his namesake Koresh (Cyrus) was messiah or christ-one chosen by God for a special mission. If his words were interpreted in terms of the apocalyptic world he inhabited, he never believed, or claimed, that he was Jesus Christ.

Koresh believed that he was the one chosen to open the Seven Seals of the Book of Revelation and thereby bring about the downfall of "Babylon." The opening of the mysterious Seven Seals in the last book of the New Testament led, in an apocalyptic sequence, to the Day of Judgment and the end of the world.

The Greek word *apocalypsis* means "to uncover, to reveal." The Book of Revelation is called the Apocalypse. An apocalyptic group believes that the end of history is near and that the signs and secrets of the final scenario have been revealed to them. The followers of Jesus were an apocalyptic movement within ancient

Judaism. So were the people who produced the Dead Sea Scrolls. Since the third century B.C.E., many such groups, first Jewish and later Christian, proclaimed the imminent "end of the world" on the basis of their understanding of prophetic texts in the Bible. Phil Arnold and I were convinced that any chance for a peaceful resolution of the crisis at Waco would require an understanding of the apocalyptic world in which David Koresh and his dedicated followers were living. They were clearly willing to die for what they believed, and they would not surrender under threat of force.

In our initial contact, the FBI admitted to being hopelessly confused by Koresh's lengthy expositions of Scripture, which were occurring regularly in their daily telephone negotiations. One FBI agent told us how he and his colleagues had been frantically reading through the Book of Revelation in the Gideon Bibles in their hotel rooms. The image struck me as almost comical, but at the same time frightening. The agent also told us they found the Book of Revelation and David Koresh's extended biblical monologues wholly incomprehensible. "What is this about the Seven Seals?" they wanted to know. One agent thought the seals were amphibious animals with whiskers; after all, there were a lot of other animals—lions, oxen, eagles, horses, wild beasts, even monsters—in the book. Why not seals?

In the next few weeks, Phil and I spent hours talking with Livingston Fagan, an articulate member of the Branch Davidians whom Koresh had allowed out of the compound as a spokesperson. Fagan was being held in jail. From these conversations, in which the three of us examined the biblical texts quite closely and often technically, Phil and I slowly began to understand how Koresh was interpreting them: The Branch Davidian group understood itself to be living through the opening of the Seven Seals, leading to the Day of Judgment and the end of time and the world. The Seven Seals are on a scroll held by the one who is seated on the heavenly throne. Each of the seals, stamped in wax, can be opened only by a figure variously referred to as the Lamb, the anointed one (in other words, messiah or christ) or the Branch of David. David Koresh claimed to be this person.

In Jewish tradition, the Messiah will be a descendant of David, literally the branch of David. That is why in Matthew and Luke, containing the genealogies of Jesus, he is descended from King David. That is also why David Koresh's group is called the Branch Davidians. And that is why Vernon Howell from Houston, Texas, chose the first name David when he changed his name to David Koresh and traced his own ancestry to King David. Koresh saw himself as he who was sent to the world before the end of the age, empowered to remove the seals and open the scroll.

Psalm 45, which Koresh understood to refer to himself, speaks of a mighty king, anointed by Yahweh (in this sense the *mashiach*, or messiah), who rides victoriously, marries princesses and fathers many sons who will rule the earth (Psalm 45:4–7, 10–16). This psalm is the source of Koresh's sexual exploits. He had sexual intercourse with the wives of his male followers, forbidding the husbands from doing likewise to ensure that the seed was his. According to his interpretation of Psalm 45, these sons would be "princes in all the earth" (Psalm 45:16). In his mind, Koresh was the Branch of David who was to build up a dynasty that would someday rule the world (Jeremiah 23:3–5).

David Koresh believed that he had already opened the first four seals of the Seven Seals described in the Book of Revelation and that the Branch Davidians were now in the fifth seal.

The Book of Revelation is written as a vision of John, who describes what he saw in the first person. Here is how he describes the opening of the fifth seal:

"When he [the Lamb] opened the fifth seal, I saw under the altar the souls of those who had been slaughtered for the word of God and for the witness they had borne; they cried out with a loud voice, 'O, Sovereign Lord, holy and true, how long before you will judge and avenge our blood on those who dwell on earth?' Then they were each given a white robe and told to wait *a little longer*, until the number would be complete of their fellow servants and of their brothers and sisters who sere *soon to be killed* as they themselves had been killed" (Revelation 6:9–11).

We discussed the chilling implications of these verses with the FBI. For Koresh and his group, the Book of Revelation was like a script, setting forth in vivid detail that would transpire in instructing them what they should do. They refused to come out of their compound because God was telling them in these verses to wait "a little longer." But the verse goes on to predict that they, like the others who had been killed in the AFT raid on February 28, would also be killed. They were thus doomed to die—unless they could be persuaded that they were misinterpreting these passages.

Speaking of the February 28 raid, Koresh later told an AFT agent: "I knew you were coming before you knew you were coming."

On the morning of that raid Koresh told an undercover AFT agent who was spying on the group and whom David suspected was a federal agent, "What thou doest, do quickly" (John 13:27). It was as if the entire situation in Waco was locked into a predetermined pattern, set forth in a book written around 96 C.E., during the reign of the Roman emperor Domitian.

If Koresh were living "in the fifth seal," did that make it inevitable that the remaining men, women and children in the Mt. Carmel compound must also die? Would they provoke a violent end simply because they felt it was the predetermined will of God, moving things along to the sixth seal, which was the great Judgment Day of God?

Koresh insisted to the FBI that God had told him to "wait" an unspecified time. The FBI, impatient and frustrated, pushed him, asking "how long?" The entire drama was being played out according to a biblical script.

The Book of Revelation presented—and presents—two major difficulties. First, it is written in veiled, symbolic language, lending itself to countless interpretations, often wild and uncontrolled by the normal tenets of biblical exegesis. Second, it contains unequivocal statements about the impending end of the age that were never literally fulfilled and thus demand constantly revised interpretation. Ironically, these two problems probably led the book's inclusion in the canon, as well as its preservation and popularity. The imprecise symbolic language allowed for continuous revisions of interpretations and ingenious reapplications to subsequent periods and situations. In short, the Book of Revelation became a timeless script of the end-time scenario, ever flexible and mobile through time and place. It has provided countless movements and groups with interpretations of their own situations and has fueled the hopes, dreams and schemes of a perpetually revised apocalyptic agenda.

Gradually, Phil Arnold and I had fleshed out the apocalyptic scenario or script that David Koresh and his followers were expecting. We were absolutely convinced that Koresh would never surrender to pressure or harassment—which was what the FBI was doing, cutting off the compound's water and electricity, blaring painfully loud noise and beaming high-intensity floodlights at the members day and night to prevent sleep, threatening them, doing anything to make their lives miserable. Given Koresh's understanding of himself as the messenger or anointed one, who had been appointed to open the Seven Seals, he would act only as he felt God was leading him. And the text of the Book of Revelation was his primary guide.

Slowly Phil and I formulated a plan to approach Koresh with an alternative scenario, seeking to meet him within his own interpretive world. We had to convince him that within the context of his apocalyptic, properly interpreting his apocalyptic texts, especially Revelation, there was an alternative path, something else he should be doing. We would try to convince him that he was not "in the fifth seal"—which would mandate the death of the group. We would argue that "a little longer" (or "little season") in Revelation 6:11, after which they would be killed, could be interpreted as a very extended period. In short, death was not necessarily imminent. For this, we would rely on Revelation 7:1–3, which, if read literally, implies a considerable delay: "Four angels standing at the four corners of the earth [hold] back the four winds of the earth … [and] another angel … with the seal of the living God … [says] to the four angels that had been given the power to harm, … 'Do not harm … till we have sealed the servants of our God upon their foreheads.'"

We would also rely on Revelation 10: An angel has "a little scroll"; the angel swears there will be no more delay. A voice tells the author to take the scroll. He does so, but the angel with the scroll tells him to eat it, that it will be bitter in his stomach and sweet in his mouth. He eats, and it is as the angel had said. Then he is commanded to prophesy, presumably based on the content of the scroll, to "many peoples and nations and tongues and kings." We would try to convince Koresh that he must first write this scroll and transmit it to the people.

The next question was how best to engage him in a discussion of Revelation and its proper interpretation. One suggestion was that we send in a tape addressed to Koresh. Another involved a local radio talk show, hosted by Ron Engleman. Koresh and his followers tuned in to this show each morning on their battery-operated transistor radios. Koresh liked Engleman, who had been very critical of the ATF for the way it had handled the raid of February 28 in which Koresh's two-year-old daughter and five other Branch Davidians as well as four federal agents, had been killed. Indeed, Koresh has a banner hung from the compound saying "We want Ron." We decided this would be the better way to reach Koresh, at least initially:

Phil and I would talk about the text of Revelation and its interpretation on Ron Engleman's talk show. Engleman agreed to give us full use of air time, and Dick DeGuerin, Koresh's attorney, who had been meeting with Koresh regularly, assured us that Koresh and his followers would listen to our discussion.

On April 1, 1993, in give-and-take-dialogue form, we went live on the air and presented a rather technical discussion of an alternative interpretation of the Book of Revelation that we thought David Koresh might accept. Our approach was hypothetical: Given Koresh's general worldview and the interpretation he was following of the Seven Seals, was there a reasonable alternative understanding? The show went well, we thought. Just to make sure he heard it, we sent a tape of the discussion into the compound with Koresh's lawyer DeGuerin, so Koresh and his followers could study it if they wished. April 1 was a Thursday.

The following Wednesday, after his Passover celebration, Koresh dictated a letter to DeGurerin. It wasn't clear just how much of our interpretation he had bought, but it was clear that he was now going to write up the decoded message of the Seven Seals and that he would then "come out."

"I am presently being permitted [by God] to document in structured form the decoded messages of the Seven Seals. Upon the completion of this task, I will be freed of my waiting period. I hope to finish this as soon as possible and stand before man and answer any and all questions regarding my activities … [The writing of these seals will cause the winds of God's wrath to be held back a little longer. … I have been shown that as soon as I am given over to the hands of man, I will be made a spectacle of and people will not be concerned about the truth of God, but just the bizarrity of me in the flesh.... I am working night and day to complete my final work of writing out these seals. I thank my father. He has finally granted me this chance to do this.... As soon as I can see that people like Jim Tabor and Phil Arnold have a copy, I will come out and then you can do your thing with this beast.... We are standing on the threshold of great events. The Seven Seals in written form are the most sacred information ever."

Phil and I were of course elated.

Unfortunately, the FBI's reaction was different. The FBI simply stepped up its pressure tactics, demanding once and for all that Koresh and his people surrender. They thought Koresh was simply stalling, as they claimed he had done in the past. Passover, an eight-day Jewish holiday celebrating the freeing of the Israelite slaves from Egyptian bondage, had just ended. Earlier Koresh had said that after Passover he would announce his plan for surrender. Koresh had unintentionally irritated the FBI because each day of the holiday, he announced that it was Passover. Some FBI agents thought Passover was a one-day holiday, the date of which Koresh was changing every day. In their daily press briefings, the FBI belittled Koresh as a grade-school dropout who would hardly be capable of writing a book. They characterized him as a manipulating madman who thought he was God and who interpreted the Bible through the barrel of a gun.

Nevertheless, the FBI allowed writing supplies, including typewriter ribbons, to be delivered to the Mt. Carmel compound. They did this as late as Sunday evening, April 18, the very evening before the final assault. At 5:50 Monday morning, they called the compound and informed the group that if they did not surrender the place would be gassed. Steve Schneider, Koresh's spokesman, was so upset by this sudden shift in plans that he ripped the compound's phone from the wall and threw it out the window. A few minutes after six, an armored combat engineer vehicle with a steel nose began to nudge the corner of the compound. A second soon joined in, buckling the walls. A tank crashed through the front door. Tear gas enveloped the buildings. Rounds of bullets rained down on the attackers. Shortly after noon, explosions rocked the compound as ammunition stores blew up. Fire soon mingled with the tear gas as 30-mile-per-hour winds turned the scene into an inferno. By evening, 86 people, including David Koresh and two dozen children, were dead. The 51-day siege had ended. Like Jesus, David Koresh was 33 years old when he died, and, again like Jesus, he died at about Passover time.

One of the few survivors told me the last time he saw David Koresh was about 5 a.m. that morning. David had come down from his room and looked very tired. He said he had been working most of the night on his manuscript on the Seven Seals.

We can only speculate what Koresh must have thought when the attack came, as the buildings shook and the walls were punched with holes and tear gas injected. My own view is that, given his mindset, he can only have concluded he was in the fifth seal after all, and that the remaining Davidians must now die like all the others. The FBI's attack must have forced David to revise his most recent apocalyptic understanding. Given this recent turn of events, there was absolutely no chance that he or his followers would "come out and surrender to proper authority," as the FBI loudspeakers demanded that morning. To Koresh and his followers, the only proper authority was God, not the forces of the wicked Babylonians. In their minds, based on Revelation 6:11, they saw their deaths as a necessary martyrdom, a self-sacrifice that would lead to the final collapse of the enemy and the coming of Jesus Christ.

I have not the slightest doubt that David Koresh would have surrendered peacefully had he been allowed to finish his manuscript. Shortly after fire consumed the compound, some federal agents said they doubted that Koresh was even working on a manuscript. They took what Koresh had said about God's allowing him to write the interpretation of the Seven Seals as a ploy to delay matters still further. We now know this was not the case. Ruth Riddle, one of the few survivors, had a computer disk in the right pocket of her jacket when she escaped. She had been typing David's handwritten manuscript the day before the attack. On the disk was his exposition of the first seal. The disk is now in the possession of the federal authorities.

33 Discourses of Authenticity within a Pagan Community: The Emergence of the "Fluffy Bunny" Sanction

ANGELA COCO AND IAN WOODWARD

Coco and Woodward explore the tensions between paganism and consumerist capitalism. Within pagan groups, "authenticity" is defined in contrast to "fluffy bunnies:" those whose belief is superficial or tainted by commercialism.

. . .

I first heard the expression "fluffy bunny" one evening at a Pagans in the Pub (PITPub) gathering early in 2001. Pagans in the Pub is an event that migrated from the UK through the United States to Australia. Pagans select a central location where they meet on a regular basis once or twice a month. Over time I observed that most individuals seldom consumed more than one alcoholic drink during these sessions (if any). On the evening in question, about twelve people had gathered, a mixture of males and females seated in a warm, dimly lit, far corner of the hotel lounge with tables pushed together to facilitate discussion. Patrick, a young University student, was responding to a question from one of those present. He ended his comment by saying " . . . and not all the fluffy bunny stuff."

This expression drew comment from the gathering who wanted him to clarify what he meant. He said, "Oh you know, people who watch *Charmed* and *Buffy* and . . . ."

Comments that followed suggested that images and symbols presented in witchcraft-type television programs were sentimental and skimmed the surface of "real" magic, signaled by Danny's quip that "there's more to it than waving a wand around." People felt the craft was trivialized, for example, the talking black cat in *Charmed*. Privately, two of the women confided to me that they were *Buffy* fans; they thought she was "OK." Other public figures came under attack for the same reasons. Notably Lorna Horne and Deborah Gray, who were also the focus of Ezzy's reflections on the commodification of witchcraft (2001), were named as promoting and selling warm fuzzy

Source: Angela Coco and Ian Woodward, "Discourses of Authenticity Within a Pagan Community: The Emergence of the 'Fluffy Bunny' Sanction," from *Journal of Contemporary Ethnography* 36(5): pp. 479-504, copyright © 2007. Reprinted by Permission of Sage Publications.

ideas about the craft through their many publications and Web pages. PITPub participants felt that misrepresentations of the craft and surface meanings they generated were exacerbated by the commercial availability of products like spell kits and fairy wands that were perceived to promote those interpretations. It surprised me when those present named two young females who lived in the southwest Summerland region (the area where this study was undertaken) as exemplary offenders. These women conducted magic workshops and sometimes posted to e-lists. The exchanges between individual pagans at the pub revealed a questioning of the authenticity of media representations of the craft and of some pagans' extensive use of advertising, late capitalism's primary vehicle for promoting consumerism, as a means of promoting their pagan beliefs and practices (and making a living).

The fluffy bunny discussion revealed people's concern with how consumer culture impacted on the formation and negotiation of pagan identity; effects well documented by Foltz (2005). There were suggestions that the craft was made an object of entertainment, trivialized, rendered superficial, fetishized, sentimentalized, and devalued through commodification of tools and practices of spiritual meaning and worth. This was a group boundary defining exercise based on moral judgments of the type theorized by Lamont (1992). It explored pagan ethics associated with the deployment of pagan artifacts and spiritual understandings. Implicit in the discussion was a sense of a "them" who were seduced by media images and popular practices, or implicated in producing them, and a (serious, authentic) "us" who presumably distanced ourselves from such things.

Members of new social movements including environmentalists (Shepherd 2002), lesbians and gays (Kates and Belk 2001), and witches (Neitz 1994) often struggle to reconcile movement ideals with meaningful lifestyle practices. In regard to neopaganism, tensions

have been noted between spiritual ideals and pragmatic (including economic) concerns, between the idea of serious practitioners and "dabblers" in the craft, and between those who would want to mainstream the religion and those who feel that paganism's strength lies in its subcultural "cutting edge," its esotericism (Berger, Leach, and Shaffer 2003; Pearson 1998; Neitz 1994). These tensions were evident in the present study. What we offer here is a reflection on how similar concerns emerged in everyday pagan discourse when issues of profit making and charging for pagan services were discussed. . . .

IDENTITY, COMMODITY, AND COMMUNITY

Neitz (1994) characterizes paganism as quasireligion because members negotiate cultural meanings via loosely structured networks rather than through the traditional organizational and denominational means characteristic of other religions. She adopts Gusfield's (1981) notion of "carriers" of a movement's practices and symbols to describe how pagans "carry over" symbols from one social context to another and "carry on" practices in their initiatory rites in small groups. Structure per se is provided by the broader culture via the provision of material resources and cultural norms. While Neitz investigated in-group perpetuation of the craft, we suggest that symbolic icons and practices are not necessarily carried over "intact" but are modified and evaluated in a dialogical way with images in mainstream consumer culture. We examine the interplay between values in the broader social structures of consumerism, the media and capitalism, and pagan ideals. Our interpretation takes Neitz's project a small step further to investigate how pagans debate these cultural strains.

. . .

While pagans may be ambivalent about the relationships between spiritual ideals and capitalist values they nevertheless seem to be comfortable in moving between religious activity and consumer capitalism, consumption and mediated representations of pagan spirituality (Foltz 2005). Drawing on ethnographic data we identify the ways consumer values and media representations of witchcraft are used as foils for the discursive construction of an authentic pagan identity. We explore pagans' reflections on ethics and aesthetics and their negotiations of truths, values, and the good in their everyday discourse. A range of tensions emerges which we argue indicates the ways pagans in late-capitalist (or postmodern) society reflexively create meaning-structures around the production and consumption of goods and services that have become popularized as "pagan." The nuanced features of these tensions reveal the conceptual distinctions and symbolic boundaries pagans create in establishing an "authentic" pagan identity.

OBSERVING THE NEOPAGAN SCENE IN SOUTHWEST SUMMERLAND

My seven-year experience in a Dianic Wiccan group afforded some legitimacy for wanting to participate in and study neopagan culture and I entered the field by seeking conversations with and support from key informants. I described my research as the Circle Pagan Study and the informants extended valuable information about how to enter and respect the community ethos in both online and offline environments. Wiccans and neopagans as grouped by Neitz (2000) form the major part of the community under study. One prominent pagan posted information about the study on his Web site, which acts as a portal for several pagan organizations and sites in Australia. I included an invitation to people to contact me through this page if they were willing to participate in an interview. Pagans were also informed and regularly reminded of my presence on the e-mail discussion lists where I used my

own first name and university e-mail address. Once or twice a year, notices were posted to inform any new people on the lists that I was still researching the community. My methods included observation, almost daily, and irregular participation on pagan e-mail lists for a two-year period. This involved perusing between ten and seventy-five online messages in one day. As discussion themes emerged the dates and posting number of sample messages were noted in small diaries that were used for keeping ethnographic records of e-mail discussions.

. . .

To illustrate how pagans think about consumerism and connect commercial practices with pagan ethics and aesthetics we present . . . online and offline excerpts that illustrate the breadth and depth of their reflexive negotiation of individual and collective pagan identity.

. . .

OFFLINE

Magical Fair, 2001—A Public Forum

The Magical Fair ran for three days in spring at a central cultural venue in Circle. On entering the large hall, I was greeted by an explosion of bright colors both in people's dress and in the decoration of stalls, though black predominated. Pagans dressed in a variety of clothing styles, in Medieval-type costumes, jeans and shirts, short skirts and adornments emblematic of their pagan craft. There was a feeling of calm enjoyment, with a pagan band playing in the background. On moving through the crowds I discovered the stage at the far end of the room with an open floor space in front. A huge dark blue banner covering almost the entire wall behind the stage featured a gold pentacle with a silver crescent moon on either side of it. Vendors engaged in conversation with potential buyers, taking time and often explaining and discussing the possible uses for the commodity, particularly if they learned that the customer was not a pagan. Pagan entrepreneurialism evidences a qualitatively different vendor-purchaser relationship than that found in the mass-marketing of witchcraft in mainstream society (Foltz 2005). Through large windows one could see outside. Along a walkway outside the windows and overlooking the river, Tarot readers had lined up their round tables, covered with colorful cloths falling to the ground. Each reader was concentrating with customers on the divination at hand. I spoke to the person at the first table as I exited through a door onto the walkway. She informed me that she was responsible for taking the Tarot reading bookings. Prices were advertised for half- and one-hour sessions.

During the afternoon of the third day two well-known members of the community organized a public forum in the stage and dancing space. They invited four pagans with different craft backgrounds—none of whom are represented in the e-list excerpts quoted earlier—to participate on a panel that would field questions from the floor. I was approached to act as a panel member—a request I immediately experienced (perhaps overreactively) as a challenge to prove the veracity of my pagan identity claim. My participation impressed some pagans present. Julie, a woman in her mid-forties who had been a pagan since her teenage years, commented, "A lot of people are still afraid to stand up and be counted." The audience was composed largely of about twenty recognized pagans as most of the more general public attendance was thinning out at this stage. Some people moved around the edges, dropping in and out of the discussions, as they moved between stalls purveying crystals, clothing, aura imaging, healing massages, jewelry, and craft tools, as well as astrological, craft, and self-help literature.

One woman asked the panel, "What do you think about the popularization of paganism?" I asked for clarification as to what she meant by "popularization." George, a long-standing

pagan who had trained with Jason and joined his coven, said in dismissive tones, "You know things like the spell kits for teenagers, you can buy them in the newsagents." Discussion focused around the proliferation of spell kits, now widely available in Australia, which usually include a candle, some incense and a slip of paper with instructions to do a spell, for example, to make your boyfriend love you. The indirect reference to young women (young gay men were not usually referenced in this manner) resonates with elements of the "fluffy bunny" discussion held at PITPub noted earlier. In this pagan community there is strong evidence similar to that recognized by Neitz in her study of Dragonfest (2000) that even though neo-pagan imagery and practice open up new possibilities for performing sexuality, heterosexuality continues to define gender relations. The commercialization of craft magic was particularly anathema to pagans attending the forum. They said that you needed more than the tools to affect change. Magic needed to be conducted in the appropriate context with "right intent" and energy supported and evaluated by a community of others. Craft tools, sold as commodities in the absence of a context of practice was seen to promote "dabbling" in the craft, not a serious engagement with its general principles and philosophy. These exchanges illustrate Miller's theory that commodities act as symbolic goods around which meanings and morality are negotiated.

In the forum exchanges, a distinction was being made between naïve and experienced members of the craft, where the naïve believe that using a few commodities that have become popular signs of the craft will affect a life change in the direction they wish. There is a strain between surface and deeper meanings of craft symbolism and between the subjective use of tools invested with personal meaning and the objectification of them as commodities. These communally derived meanings about the appropriate attitudes to, and understanding and deployment of craft tools act as generalized mechanisms of exclusion of "inauthentic pagans." Some pagans hypothesized … a trajectory of meaning-making and identity formation via consumption practices. They suggested that commodities may enable initial attraction to the craft. If seekers delved further into pagan literature and understandings about the tools they purchased or discussed them with pagans, it could lead them to a spiritual community. They pointed out that seekers cannot start in the craft already adept or experienced in ritual. An example of conversation from the Pagan Fair serves to illustrate how pagans think about the value of entertainment and marketing to promote their religion.

Pagan Fair, 2002—Personal Conversations

The Pagan Fair was held in a prominent open-air public space in the center of Circle. It was a hot spring day with clear blue skies. There were many retail outlets lined in parallel around the perimeter of the space purveying pagan type commodities such as drums, attire, ritual tools, herbs, crystals, and literature. Laura set up her stall of pagan artifacts there, and Julie, accompanied by close friends, had erected a tent that advertised the features of her new coven. Throughout the day public rituals and stage events were performed on the large lawn space left between stalls and formal talks were scheduled in rooms in a nearby public building. As part of the formal talks, I gave a presentation titled "Studying Pagans: My Experience." …

Public rituals at the Pagan Fair were managed by practicing pagans who set up the accoutrements for ritual and who knew the routines and meanings of symbolic gestures. Newcomers followed instructions given by the leaders (high priest and priestess in this case).

I found that public rituals were always surrounded by a large crowd of onlookers as well. For Jason, and pagans I spoke to during this and other public rituals, these events were staged as a way of giving the nonpagans an aesthetic experience that might attract them to pursue the pagan worldview further. From the point of view of some pagan adepts then, the event, both the markets and public rituals, are designed to be an entrée into pagan culture for the casual inquirer or even for just the Sunday consumer. In public performances, those pagans who wish to mainstream the religion demonstrate the appropriate use of commodities, for example, athame (ritual knife), bowls and crystals, and connect them with authentic meanings and practices of the craft. However, a person who came up to me after my talk had quite a different view. From diary notes:

> One woman came up the aisle towards me from the back looking quite agitated. I could see she was probably quite serious about her pagan identity. She was dressed comfortably in a "folky" kind of dark coloured dress, wearing some talismans and recognisable goddess symbols like a pentacle. She explained to me that she had been away from the pagan community for several years and had come back to have another look. She said she was "disgusted", "nothing's changed", the whole show was just "commercialization."
>
> At the Pagan Fair in 2003, I was sitting on a concrete garden wall getting some rest in the shade when another pagan, who had driven three hours to attend, voiced similar kinds of emotions unsolicited. "I came all the way from [the south] today, just for this! It doesn't matter ripping off the public ('to rip someone off' means to charge unnecessarily and/or excessively for goods), but when you rip off your own—I won't be doing this again."

On the one hand some pagans see commercialization as manifested in events like the Pagan Fair as an outright betrayal of the craft, while others see it as a mechanism for raising public awareness. In the pagan festival we can see a reconfiguration of the relations of production and consumption. As both producers and consumers of culture, pagans share knowledge and information with public others who purchase their commodities or services. However, pagan markets not only sell commodities, but in the same space provide rituals, and free talks and entertainments that serve to link symbolic meanings to commodities sold in stalls. Nevertheless, both Jason and the women who were disgusted, felt that "real" paganism was something quite different from what could be garnered from a public festival and its commercial tone. Again the tension is over the values of commerce and the values of pagan spirituality. "Real" pagans distance themselves from commercial interests and popular representations of the craft.

. . .

COMMERCIALIZATION, CAPITALISM, AND PAGAN IDENTITY

. . . A discourse has emerged in which the "authentic" pagan is being constructed through ongoing conversations around a series of distinctions. Issues of pagan identity, commercialization of the craft, and capitalist enterprise revealed many semiotic tensions regarding:

1. practical issues and religious ideals
2. capitalist values and spiritual values
3. naïve and experienced practitioners of the craft
4. "modern" pagans and traditionalists
5. expansionism and esotericism
6. surface and deeper meanings of the craft
7. practices that were judged to be peripheral or central to community identity (for example the peripheral, pagan-type Harry Potter movie)
8. playful and serious engagement with the craft
9. media representations of witchcraft and pagan reality.

It should be stressed at this point that whether there is such a being as an authentic pagan or not is not the issue. Through the production and consumption of craft artifacts and services pagans engage in what Lamont (1992) describes as aesthetic and moral projects of the

self, by weighing their values and judgments against those of others, perhaps renegotiating them, and developing shared values as members of a community that calls itself pagan. It is pagans' reflexive engagement in these discussions both online and offline that gives them a sense of belonging and identity and a way of marking boundaries between themselves and others. E-mail lists provide the continuity for this negotiation keeping it alive and available to hundreds of others on a day-to-day basis (Berger 1999). Most cogently though, we find that pagans are conscious of and practically engage in discussions about constructions of pagan identity and commodification of the craft which is exemplified in the notion of the "fluffy bunny."

A long discussion thread took place on L2 during 2002 in which participants debated what it meant to be a "fluffy bunny." Analysis of the various contributions revealed that a "fluffy bunny" would exhibit the kinds of characteristics illustrated by the first terms in the nine tensions listed above, pragmatic, profiteering, dabbling, modern, superficial, peripheral to community, playful, and using multimedia to further practical and capitalist values. Some voices (a minority) argued that being a fluffy bunny was as legitimate a position as any other as not all people come to the craft with experience, for example. The first example links the "fluffy bunny" to those people who gain a surface grasp of pagan practices but fail to incorporate pagan beliefs into their day-to-day life practices.

Posted—2002

What about weekend pagans? What about people who only ever read 1 book and are [*]happy[*] with that? What about if they do fairy rituals (and yes, I've been to one!) and find some sense of inner peace in that? If that satisfies their yearning for a spiritual experience? (*sic*) If that is all the spiritual development they're capable of? Or what if they never finished high school and reading any decent research is like trying to comprehend German?

So perhaps my definition of a fluffy is someone who views their religion as an adjunct—not as a lifes (*sic*) work—and it (*sic*) so, great. It gains nothing to be elitist and ask them to push further if they have stopped at the beginning of their path and started building a two-storey brick house. Or perhaps their path is just a wee bit shorter *shrugs.*

In the following posts the "fluffy bunny" is linked to the person who is uninformed, immature, and lacking in their understanding of the forces of nature and consequently dangerous because they may misuse magic.

Posted—Three Days After Above Post
Ummmmmm a fluffy
For me a fluffy is a person who doesn't know what they are talking about, or as was said not steadfast in there (*sic*) beliefs. I am sure that we have all met the 12 year old who is a high priestess and the leader of huge demonic armies and has alliances with the elves!!!!
Posted—Same Day as "Ummmmm a Fluffy" Above
What do I see as a 'fluffy'. To me these *are* people who see things in terms of sparkles and rainbows. Not. Like (*sic*) (Leanne's) friend, in a conscious effort to improve the world—a difficult path that I respect—but out of a refusal to accept or acknowledge unpleasant aspects of reality, and more importantly in themselves. It is one think (*sic*) to be aware of human frailty, or the shades of dark and light in life, and to strive ever to make it better and happier place, and quite another to bury one's head in the sand, preach love and light, but take no responsibility for their own actions and impulses (conscious or unconscious) by simply refusing to see them . . . perhaps what bugs me most about these type (*sic*) is not so much the superficiality (which the 'fashion-witch' has in spades) but the hypocrisy (*sic*) which often enables them to do harm whilst preaching love and light, and never once recognizing the results of their own actions.

These discussions identify what are perceived as the superficial engagement with the craft, something one does on weekends, in their leisure time, not as a moral and spiritual code that informs their modes of being in the world. They refer to the superficial practitioner's tendency to focus only on the light, happy side of life without balancing it with the dark and difficult aspects of experience. Such unbalanced views, if promoted to unenlightened others,

may have detrimental consequences for their welfare. Superficial practitioners, offering rituals and spells with only these elements, are likely to be unaware of how such imbalances can lead to harm for others.

During the fluffy bunny online discussions it became clear that the expression "fluffy bunny" was one that most people felt/hoped did not apply to them, though some people argued the finer points of the "dark" and "light" experiences and why the idea of a "fluffy bunny" engaged people's attention at all. One person's mail in a semiotic play of meaning humorously exemplified this concern. After someone else had mentioned that they "pretend" to be a fluffy bunny in contexts where people would find a "real" pagan too threatening, they posted:

Oh this is good, it's hard enough keeping up with the Fluffy Bunny discussion, are we now going to have one on TRAINEE?/FAKE FLUFFIES? Fake fluffies? Is that like the difference between fake fur and real fur, how am I going to know the difference between a real fluffy and a pretender to the throne? Has anyone got any ideas on this? I can't believe it's not a Fluffy! When is a Fluffy not a Fluffy? A new breed of Fluffy? Do you mean like a Hybrid? or (*sic*) is a Fake Fluffy some type of genetically engineered being that has been created in a lab (or read circle if you prefer)? Just when I thought I could safely recognise a Fluffy, now I read that there are Fake ones out there, oh I think I need a BEX! (medication for headaches) This whole Fluffy discussion is a riot, keep it up..........regards.

The expression "fluffy bunny" has come to be used as a shorthand way of signaling people's inauthentic engagement with witchcraft. At the 2003 PSG, the woman who acted as high priestess for the Summer Rite warned the gathering that the event was not about "fluffy bunny" paganism. The expression "fluffy bunny" is used at all levels of pagan social interaction from interpersonal conversations to discussions at national gatherings and beyond. There are now many Web pages dedicated to the discussion (just search the net with terms—"fluffy bunny pagan"). It is often shortened to "fluffy" and was used in this manner when the organizer of Pagan Pride Day was interviewed for *Witch-Craft* magazine. In describing her encounters with the media, she said, "I did however get an easy introduction to radio interviewing . . . , fielding some light and *fluffy* questions from a nice, happy DJ about being a Witch and my broom being superseded by a vacuum cleaner" (my emphasis, Porter 2003, 21).

CONCLUSION

. . . The establishment of an "authentic" pagan identity is formed partly by one's ability to discern the proper limits of commodification and consumerism in the pursuit of religious practice. These limits are debated by and with others who may or may not be known to them. Others are "present" communicatively in online fora (if not in offline places) and it is the negotiation of the proper relation between production, consumption, and spiritual quest that makes possible constructions of authentic personal lifestyles. It is this aspect of pagan communications that reveals one way that postmodern citizens in consumer culture construct identities around the production and consumption of commodities.

REFERENCES

BERGER, H. 1999. *A community of witches: Contemporary neo-paganism and witchcraft in the United States.* Columbia: University of South Carolina Press.

BERGER, H. A. LEACH, E. A., and SHAFFER, L. S. 2003. *Voices from the pagan census,* Columbia: University of South Carolina Press.

EZZY, D. 2001. The commodification of witchcraft. *Australian Religion Studies Review,* 14(1):31–44.

FOLTZ, T. G. 2005. The commodification of witchcraft. In *Witchcraft and magic,* edited by H. A. Berger, Philadelphia, University of Pennsylvania Press.

GUSFIELD, J. 1981. Social movements and social change: Perspectives of linearity and fluidity. In *Social movements, conflict and change.* vol. 4, edited by L. Kreisberg, 317–339. Greenwich, CT: JAI Press.

HEELAS, P. 1994. The limits of consumption and the post modern religion of the New Age. In *The authority of the consumer,* edited by R. Keat, N. Whitely, and N. Abercrombie, 102–115, London: Routledge.

KATES, S. M. and R. W. BELK. 2001. The meanings of Lesbian and Gay Pride Day. *Journal of Contemporary Ethnography* 30(4):392–429.

LAMONT, M. 1992. *Money, morals, and manners. The culture of the French and American upper-middle class.* Chicago: The University of Chicago Press.

NEITZ, M. J. 1994. Quasi-religions and cultural movements: Contemporary witchcraft as a churchless religion. *Religion and the Social Order,* 4:127–149.

NEITZ, M. J. 2000. Queering the Dragonfest: Changing sexualities in a post-patriarchal religion. *Sociology of Religion,* 61(4):369.

PEARSON, J. E. 1998. Assumed affinities: Wicca and the New Age. In *Nature religion today: Paganism in the modern world,* edited by R. H. Roberts and G. Samuel, 45–56. Edinburgh, Edinburgh University Press.

PORTER, A. 2003. Interview with Pagan Pride coordinator, Angelique Porter, *WitchCraft,* December/January: 20–21.

SHEPHERD, N. 2002. Anarcho-environmentalists: ascetics of late-modernity. *Journal of Contemporary Ethnography,* 31(2): 135–157.

34 "They Must Be Crazy:" Some of the Difficulties in Researching "Cults"

MARYBETH AYELLA

Reviewing reports from a number of ethnographers of new religious movements, Ayella explores the complexities and difficulties inherent in studying "cults."

This article examines some of the methodological difficulties encountered in researching "cults." The last 10 years have seen an enormous amount of research and writing on groups known variously as "cults," "new religious movements," "charismatic groups," or "world-rejecting groups," to name some of the most commonly used terms.[1]

In this article, I use the term "cult." What I am interested in exploring is how one does research on groups popularly labeled "cults." This labeling of a group as a cult makes this a sensitive topic to study, for given the public's predominantly negative assessment of cults,[2] one is researching a group considered by many to be deviant.

I will discuss some of the methodological problems which I think are particularly vexing in the study of cults, and I will point to some solutions suggested by researchers. My exami-nation will be limited to one kind of research done by sociologists: field research.[3] I focus on this type of research because it seems to have been stimulated by cults. Robbins (1988) pointed to a virtual explosion of anthropological-like studies by sociologists of religion. Field research seems to be an attempt to get behind the strangeness and controversial aspects of cults. This method provides the closest look at cult groups, and it thus has the potential to provide in-depth understanding of the group examined, as well as the group's self-understanding. This research has as its strong point debunking overly psychiatric or psychological "brainwashing" perspectives, in showing the interactional aspect of becoming and remaining a cult member. This humanizes cult members–they are portrayed as more than crackpots, psychological basket cases, or brainwashed robots.

Source: Marybeth Ayella, "'They Must Be Crazy:' Some of the Difficulties in Researching 'Cults,' from *American Behavioral Scientist* 33(5): pp. 562-577, copyright © 1990. Reprinted by Permission of Sage Publications.

GAINING ACCESS

Contingencies of Research

Mitchell, Mitchell, and Ofshe (1980, chap. 9), Wallis (1977a, 1977b), Bromley and Shupe (1979, Shupe & Bromley, 1980), and Barker's (1984, chap. 1) discussions of their research on Synanon, Scientology, and the Unification Church highlight the contingencies of research, which are those aspects of research over which the researcher has little or no control. One very important contingency is the group's present social reputation.

Richard Ofshe's research on Synanon began in the summer of 1972 with a chance visit to Synanon's Tomales Bay facilities. Ofshe's neighbor, a marine biologist, was asked by Synanon for help in setting up a lab for a sewage-treatment system. Ofshe accompanied him on a visit, and was given a trail-bike tour of the ranching facility. After the visit, Ofshe asked the ranch director if he could come back to do research. During the next year, Ofshe paid over 50 visits, during which he did participant observation, to the ranch and Synanon facilities in Oakland, San Francisco, and Santa Monica. In addition, five of his students did research on Synanon over a three-month period, joining the Oakland "game club" and participating in games and in Synanon community life to varying degrees.

Ofshe's and students' professional interests and intentions to observe and analyze were made known to management and community members from the initial contact. Ofshe's entry was welcomed. Two aspects of Synanon's history seem important in explaining his welcome: (a) in 1972, Synanon considered itself a social movement and an alternative society, and it welcomed middle-class professionals, hoping to recruit them as members; and (b) Ofshe followed three researchers who had visited Synanon and written books favorable to the organization. Synanon's openness seemed based on its changing self-conception and its good reputation, which grew largely out of its claims of unprecedentedly effective drug rehabilitation.

Roy Wallis offers a contrasting example. He presented himself at an introductory "Communications Course" in Scientology as an interested newcomer. He wanted "to learn how 'anyman' coming in off the street would be received, not how a visiting sociologist doing a thesis on Scientology would be treated" (Wallis, 1977b, p. 155). He arranged to stay in a Scientology "boarding house" during this course. Wallis left after two days because he found it too difficult to continue. He felt he would have been able to stay only if he were in agreement with what he was officially learning. Not feeling this agreement, Wallis felt it would have been dishonest to indicate agreement. When Wallis later officially requested help from the movement's leaders, this earlier abrupt exit, as well as the movement's knowledge that Wallis had surveyed (with a questionnaire) present and ex-members, needed to be explained. Scientologist David Gaiman commented in an appendix to Wallis' article that he "could not understand at that time, and still do not understand, the ethics of his failing to declare this to me in his initial approach" (Wallis, 1977b, p. 168).

Wallis had initially thought to do covert participant observation, because he anticipated a hostile reaction to an open request from a sociologist, given previous, critical investigations by the Food and Drug Administration (FDA) in the United States and by government bodies in Australia and New Zealand, and because he thought "that approaching the leaders and officials of such a public-relations-conscious social movement directly, for assistance with my research, was simply to invite public relations" (Wallis, 1977b, p. 152).

David Bromley and Anson Shupe's simultaneous participant observation of the Unification Church (UC) and the "anti-cult" movement seemingly originated in two chance events. While writing a conference paper on the enormous negative media coverage of the

Unification Church, they requested information from the headquarters for the National Ad Hoc Committee – Citizens Engaged in Freeing Minds (CEFM) – and discovered that it was based in a nearby metropolitan area. At the same time, two high-ranking and 50 rank-and-file members of the Unification Church arrived in the area, seeking to recruit university students. One of the researchers was acting chair of his university's sociology department and he agreed, "on civil libertarian principles," to be faculty sponsor for a UC campus student organization. In exchange, Bromley and Shupe were permitted to conduct in-depth interviews and were allowed to observe the group.

Eileen Barker's research on the Unification Church is unique in that, after two years of negotiating with the Church to do research on her terms (e.g., receiving a list of all members, so that she might draw a random sample to interview), she seemed to have been granted relatively free access to the group. However, she did not search out the Unification Church; rather, she was in the favorable position of being sought out by the Church to do research on it. Being sought out may have put her in a more powerful position to negotiate for a favorable research "bargain".

The UC apparently sought her out as an established sociologist of religion. She participated in one conference which the UC sponsored, and in a "series of three residential weekend 'Roundtables on Science and Religion'" (Barker, 1984, p. 13) held at the UC's national headquarters in London, before she was asked if she would like to write about the Church. A Moonie she knew sought her out because he was worried about a sociologist of religion doing research on the group, based on negative reports. Barker replied that it was "hardly surprising that he had to rely on negative reports, as it was well-nigh impossible to get any other kind of information" (p. 14). She later found out that the UC agreed to let her do her research because she "had been prepared

to listen to their side of the argument, and they could not believe that anyone who did that could write anything worse than what was already being published by people who had not come to find out for themselves" (p. 15). They felt she was open-minded enough to present a fair picture of them. This seeking her out, and her negotiating for certain conditions of research, allowed her free and long-term access to the group.

There are several points worth noting from these brief descriptions of extant research on cults. Most important, the researcher should be critical of access, asking the question of why the group has allowed the researcher in, looking to the recent history of the group and its present self-understanding in answering this question. One should question the kind of access one is being given, ever conscious of the possibility of sanitization or impression management. The researcher should not simply assume that the group he or she is studying understands and agrees with the unfettered pursuit of scientific inquiry. The researcher should learn as much as he or she can about the group – through newspaper/media accounts, public relations materials, or efforts such as open houses, and through interviews with ex-members or present members – before undertaking field research. These actions, however, may have unforeseen consequences.

Researcher As Person

Downes and Rock (1982, p. 30), in discussing research on deviance, made the point that "one will not be at ease everywhere. There are always likely to be certain social groups who defy research by certain sociologists. . . . Many of the barriers which divide people form one another in everyday life also keep the sociologist at bay." Field research highlights the researcher. Some researchers, like informants, are simply better able to establish rapport and to feel at ease in a new, let alone strange, setting. Wallis (1977b, p. 155) said of himself in his brief participant observation on Scientology: "Good participant observation required a particular personality or discipline which I did not possess. Outside a 'mass' context I felt uncomfortable in my role. It felt like spying and a little dishonest. In general, I tried to shift the situation to an 'open' interaction context as quickly as possible."

Among the problems relating to the researcher are: culture shock, handling emotional responses to the group (the chief difficulty here is that overrapport may hinder objectivity), handling conversion attempts of the group, and the stigma of investigating a group considered by many to be deviant.

Balch (1985, p. 24) emphasized that the authoritarian social worlds of cults may rub against the grain of researchers' views of reality, since researchers tend to be humanists. In addition, there is the question of dealing with bizarre behaviors. Balch stated his first reaction to the UFO cult which he and Taylor studied: "My gut reaction to this message was something like: 'They look normal to me, so how can they possibly believe this nonsense?'" (p. 24). Continued interaction with the group overcame these responses, in a way similar to anthropologists' dealing with culture shock.

Whose Perspective? Sampling Members

In researching any group, the question arises immediately as to who and what to sample. The problem of sampling interacts with that of brief field research. That is, if one is going to observe a group for a very short time, the question of who one interviews becomes more important. With longer time in the group, one can make efforts to gain a sampling of members to represent the various viewpoints that are present in the group.

Drawing a representative, random sample of a cult or of ex-cult members (of one group or of all groups) is very difficult. If the group presents a sample of members to a researcher, how does the researcher know if these members are representative? Perhaps they are more intelligent, more likely to be "true believers," or those thought more likely to present the group in a good light than other members. How does the researcher determine how they were selected? Given the high turnover in most cults, longitudinal analysis of a sample of members is also difficult, and such longitudinal analyses of conversion are few (Balch, 1985).

Different understandings within a group are a fact of life. These differences of perspective are the result of one's role and status in the group, one's length of time in the group, and analytical abilities, among other things. In studying any group, the researcher needs to get a sampling of views from all factions to come up with a complete picture of the "reality" of the group. One problem in identifying these factions is that cults often are precisely those organizations which brook no public dissent, so that the only view expressed is the official view. That is, the group presents the appearance of unanimous agreement to outsiders and insiders. Factions do not emerge as organized entities with a recognized different point of view. Individuals remain in a state of pluralistic ignorance of discontent and doubt or criticism of the group. They do not know that others share doubts; they feel only they have doubts (Ayella, 1985; Bainbridge & Stark, 1980).

An additional aspect of sampling remains. New religious movements (NRM) researchers have often described leavers of cult groups as "apostates," and they discount their accounts (of their entry, life, and exit from the group) as being valid sources of data on the group, as being biased – as being not more than "atrocity tales" cultivated in deprogramming sessions. On the other hand, they often accept accounts from current members as being acceptable sources of information on the group. Beckford (1985) is one NRM researcher who has criticized this approach to ex-members' accounts, asserting the desirability of taking ex-members' testimony as seriously as that of current members, and rejecting "the idea that ex-members' accounts can all be subsumed under the heading of 'atrocity tales'" (p. 146). Having made this statement, Beckford felt compelled to defend himself from the assumption that he is an anti-cultist (pp. 146-147).

. . .

If one sees only ex-members, one's sample is likely to be of people who were unhappy enough with the group to leave on their own, or people who were deprogrammed. The methodological question is how one interprets these ex-members' versions of the group and its effect on them. One way is to recognize the contextual construction of individual accounts of participation and leave-taking – that is, the fact that such accounts are strongly shaped by individuals' present reference groups. Thus a present member's account is shaped by other members' views, including the desirability of presenting the appearance of complete commitment.

. . .

MAINTAINING ACCESS

Easy Access, Difficult Maintenance

Conversion-oriented groups provide a paradoxical research setting, where access may be easy, but continued presence or interaction is more difficult. This is the result of their expectation that one should accept the group's perspective – and convert – within some specified time period. This carries with it the expectation that one's behavior should change to reflect this conversion or commitment (e.g., living with the group, and giving up previous ties or jobs).

John Lofland, in his now-classic (and disguised) study of the early Unification Church, "assumed the standard seeker's posture, namely, interested and sympathetic but undecided" after he and two fellow graduate students decided in 1962 to study the group (Lofland, 1966, pp. 270–271). The group pressured the three to

commit themselves to serious study of the Divine Principle (the group's theology) and to move in with the group. Lofland then expressed interest in doing a sociological study of the group and met with enthusiastic approval from the group's leader. For 11 months, he did participant observation on the group: From February through October of 1962, he spent about 15 hours a week with the group; and from November 1962 through January 1963, he lived in the center four days a week. During this time, Lofland thought there was a shared understanding of his interest in the group, that "I was personally sympathetic to, and accepting of, them and desired to understand their endeavors, but I was not likely to be a convert" (p. 274). In January 1963, the leader told Lofland "that she was tired of playing the 'studying the movement' game" (p. 274). Given his apparent unlikeliness to convert, the leader saw no further reason for his presence, and Lofland left the group. However, a sociology undergraduate student who feigned conversion and joined the group provided information to Lofland until June 1963.

Lofland's experience highlights the problem of adopting a long-term, participant-observer stance to a conversion-oriented group. What happens if one does not convert after what the group considers a reasonable time? Robbins, Anthony and Curtis (1973) also illustrated an unsuccessful resolution of this dilemma in Anthony's participant observation study of a Jesus Freaks group. When confronted by questions as to his religious beliefs, Anthony refused to discuss them, feeling that the religious beliefs he held would alienate group members and end his observation. This response brought strenuous pressure by the group on him to convert. Anthony responded to the pressure by gradual withdrawal.

Richardson, Stewart, and Simmonds (1978) suggested that this outcome of ejection from the group may be averted by the expression of honest difference of opinion, admitting (in their case, that of a fundamentalist commune) that one is aware of the necessity to be "saved," but that one rejects it. This strategy apparently was successful, for they had maintained a relationship with the group for almost seven years at the time of publication of this article. Gordon (1987), too, found this strategy to be successful in his research on two fundamentalist Jesus groups. He suggested that researchers in these groups cultivate distance in the interaction. Two methods of doing this are to be forthright about one's own, differing beliefs, and to emphasize one's research role. Doing so did not alienate members of the group he studied; paradoxically, he felt a sense of greater rapport. Gordon theorized that this open discussion and emphasized researcher role kept the group from feeling that their persuasion efforts had failed.

Shupe and Bromley's (1980; Bromley & Shupe, 1979) articles describing their research on both the Unification Church and the anticult movement also illustrated initially easy access and difficulty as interaction continued. Their role as sociologists was important in two ways in reducing the barriers between themselves and the groups: The role itself "carried a certain degree of legitimacy," and "each group was seeking some type of legitimation to which it was perceived we might contribute" (1980, p. 8). Underpinning both groups' welcome of the researchers was the understanding that "to 'really know' their respective positions was to come to believe in them" (1980, p. 12). The difficulties arose when this did not occur in each group with greater knowledge.

Each group knew that Bromley and Shupe were investigating both groups, and this presented one of the difficulties they faced. Neither group could understand why the researchers needed information from the other group, and Bromley and Shupe were continually forced to explain each dealing with the other group. When time passed and it was clear the researchers were no longer ignorant of the group, members of each group pressured them to take a public stand in support of

their respective group, advocating for the group in the media and to other interest groups. Their delicate solution to this persistent dilemma was to "avoid interviews that seemed superficial, highly partisan, or exploitative" (1980, p. 13), and to present each group in its complexity when doing an interview or giving a public talk.

As their research proceeded, Bromley and Shupe sought more extensive and more sensitive information. In attempting to visit the UC's seminary, they became involved in a lengthy negotiation process. They feared this access would not be granted because "the authors' published work was perceived as not sufficiently 'objective' and sensitive to the uses to which the information might be put by others" (1980, p. 9). The UC scrutinized their written work, requested a list of the questions they wanted to ask, and a seminary faculty member visited their campus to "test fully our good will, honesty, and neutrality" (1980, p. 14). Part of the UC's concern stemmed from the fact that they were unable to locate Bromley and Shupe on a supporter/opponent continuum, and they felt they had been harmed by previous researchers to whom they had granted access.

How can researchers cope with the pressures to adopt the group's perspective, to become a committed participant instead of a researcher concerned with objectivity? Richardson, et al. (1978) emphasized the importance of maintaining a base camp at the research site to daily reinforce, through conversation with co-workers, one's alternative (to the group) reality. This may facilitate the handling of culture shock and prevent researcher conversion, but it also helps the researcher in other ways. Two (or more) researchers can share the moral dilemmas encountered during the research; they can correct each other's biases (Stone, 1978); and they can alleviate the loneliness of the "professional stranger" role. Barker (1984, pp. 21-22) described her reaction to a BBC producer who spent some time with me doing "joint participant observation" in preparation for the filming. Each time we ended a visit I would thrust a tape recorder into her hands and beg her to pour out whatever occurred to her. The fact that her impressions largely coincided with my own did not, of course, prove that we were right and everyone else wrong, but it was enormously reassuring to learn that I was not totally idiosyncratic.

The Researcher's Role in the Group

Groups vary in the kind of access they allow; "potential convert" may be the only way they conceptualize outsiders, in spite of the researcher's identification of self as researcher. In my three-week participant observation of the Unification Church (Ayella, 1977), I identified myself as a researcher from the start. I was told I could observe the group, but I was treated throughout more as a "potential convert" than as a researcher. When attempting to get background information on members or newcomers, I was repeatedly interrupted and asked to do something else. One night, when I chose to skip a lecture (I had learned that that week's set of lectures was virtually identical to the set of lectures given the previous week) to read and take notes, I was confronted with repeated requests from other members to attend. Finally, I decided to do so, thinking that the members would simply stay with me and request until the lecture was over. When I returned to the trailer in which I was staying, the article I had been reading (on Synanon) was gone, as were some notes. No one remembered seeing the article when I questioned members; neither article nor notes ever turned up. This incident was one of the events that destroyed my trust – I doubted the group really meant for me to do research. The consequence was that I stopped taking notes to the degree that I had previously.

In contrast, Rochford (1985) mentioned that at the time of his research on the Hare Krishnas, the movement was changing from an exclusionist group to more of an inclusionist group. As an exclusionist group, one was either an insider or an outsider. At the time of Rochford's research, the movement was developing a role for less committed individuals: that of movement sympathizer. This allowed him to continue participant observation beyond the stage allowed for in the "potential convert" role. This also illustrates some of the contingencies of research. That is, Rochford was in the right place at the right time to do long-term participant observation.

Rochford's reflections (1985, chap. 2) on his research on the Hare Krishna group also highlight the difficulties of long-term participant observation. The Hare Krishnas demanded high commitment and belief from members, so one problem was how much to participate in the group's activities. As Rochford stated, "Because of strong pressures to participate in the activities of the group, it often becomes difficult to work out a role that is acceptable both to the researcher and to those under study" (1985, p. 22). Rochford's role in the group evolved over the seven years of his research. After the first year, he became a "fringe" member of the group, and he was able to maintain this "fringe" devotee role in the group's Los Angeles community for the next several years. This status enabled him to research ISKCON (International Society for Krishna Consciousness) communities in other parts of the country: "I sent each of these communities a letter from a well-known and respected devotee, who showed his support for my research and pointed out my general sympathies toward Krishna Consciousness and ISKCON" (1985, p. 29). In his own letter of request, Rochford emphasized his five years' involvement, his interest both sociologically and spiritually, and his involvement in the community school and the "bhakta" program for newcomers. He gained stronger support for his research in the form of a higher rate of questionnaire completion from the other communities. However, in his own (Los Angeles) community, Rochford's fringe devotee status resulted in the lowest rate of questionnaire completion.

Rochford pointed out other instances in which his being a fringe member made research personally difficult; for example, at times he was shown to be an "incompetent" member of the group by his repeated ignorance of Sanskrit. Reflecting on this, he realized that learning the language was of lesser importance to him than were other research occupations. In addition, he had "little or no access to the dynamics of recruitment," and he avoided asking questions when he was not sure of something, because he was "very sensitive not to appear ignorant in the eyes of devotees" (1985, p. 31).

LEAVING THE FIELD

After successfully gaining access to a group and studying it in-depth, several important questions confront the researcher: To what, if anything, can one generalize from one's research? How representative of the group are one's observations? How representative of cults is this group? While field research may substantially increase our understanding of a particular group, it certainly complicates generalization.

The longer one is with the group, the more confident one may be that one has (a) pierced the public front of the group; (b) gained the trust of members, which often precedes the researcher's entry to back regions of a group; and (c) seen the difference between attitude and behavior. Cults, as social movements, change continually in response to both internal (e.g., in response to a charismatic leader's desires) and external events (e.g., a spate of negative media publicity); thus "snapshots" of the group may soon be outdated. Knowledge of the long-term development of the group may help to establish how representative a snapshot of the group is, but the difficulty is that one does not know at times whether one is at the beginning, the middle, or the end of the group's history. Lofland's (1966) *Doomsday Cult* portrayal of the early Unification Church

would not have led one to predict its evolution into a larger and more successful group.

Very few researchers are going to be able to do many in-depth studies – for example, Barker had been studying the Moonies for six years before she published *The Making of a Moonie* (1984). At the time of publication of "Researching a Fundamentalist Commune" (1978), Richardson et al. had been doing research for almost seven years on this group. Rochford had studied the Hare Krishnas for about eight years before his *Hare Krishna in America* was published in 1985. Compounding the difficulty, Balch (1985, p. 24) argued that one cannot compare groups using other people's research, for "any secondary analysis of the current research is apt to get bogged down by ambiguous terms, incomplete data, and idiosyncratic research methods."

In addition to the question of what the researcher can generalize to after doing field research, there is the difficulty of getting published. Cults may attempt to prevent critical research from being published, or may respond to published critical research by litigation. Both Beckford (1983) and Horowitz (1981) pointed to the Unification Church's efforts to prevent their research from being published and distributed. Wallis's (1977b) account of his difficulty in getting his research on Scientology published is daunting. Synanon responded to the publication of Mitchell, et al.'s (1980) book, *The Light on Synanon*, with libel suits, necessitating countersuits by the defendants which dragged on for years.

CONCLUSION

If politics are present at the level of the individual researcher and cult, they are also present at the level of scientific community and society. Jonestown seems to have been a watershed event in terms of public awareness and evaluation of cults. This event was widely publicized, and in its wake, greater credibility was given to those critical of cults, stimulating government investigations and legislation to regulate cult practices (Barker, 1986). As Barker (1986, p. 332) saw it:

After Jonestown they tended to be all lumped together under the now highly derogatory label "cult." Despite pleas from the movements themselves ..., all the new religions were contaminated by association, the worst (most "sinister" and "bizarre") features of each belonging, by implication, to them all.

Applying Schur's (1980) concept of "deviantizing," cults are engaged in "stigma contests," or battles over the right to define what shall be termed deviant. The outcome of deviantization is the loss of moral standing in the eyes of other members of society. A negative assessment of a group by a researcher may be used in this stigma contest and may change public opinion significantly, making it more difficult for the group to mobilize resources of people and money to accomplish its goals. Conversely, a positive assessment may assist the cult in countering accusations of deviance (e.g., being labeled as an "unauthentic" religion). In Schur's analysis of the politics of deviance, the more powerful group usually has the edge in stigma contests. In this instance, the more powerful cults have the resources to use the courts to assert their rights. Robbins (1988, p. 181) described cults' reaction to the "anticult" movement: "However, the latter, buoyed by their initial 'institutionalized freedom' and insulation from routinized controls, stridently affirms their 'rights,' which are interpreted as granting to 'churches' freedom from all interference."

If the group studied is powerful, it can use its resources to hinder critical evaluations from being published. Scientology's wealth enabled it to successfully insist on changes in Wallis's manuscript, using the threat of an expensive libel suit, which neither Wallis nor his publisher wanted. Synanon is another group which used its considerable resources – the unpaid labor of its many lawyer members – to discourage journalists and other observers from making critical public comment. The group's use of lawsuits charging libel and seeking multi-million-dollar damages so deterred large newspapers and news magazines that the small newspaper, the *Point Reyes Light*, was the only one willing to publish the negative reports of Synanon (Mitchell et al., 1980).

Co-optation of the researcher can be a major problem for the unwary researcher, because he or she can become, without intent, a "counter" in the ongoing stigma contest between cult and anticult. Openness to social scientists (with their relativizing, "debunking" perspective) can be used as evidence to counter accusations of extreme authoritarianism or totalism of belief and practice. The researchers' participation in cult-sponsored conferences and publication in cult-printed publications can lend the prestige of social science to the group, fostering social respectability. Perhaps the most note-worthy example of this is the Unification Church's sponsorship of conferences and publication of the conference proceedings. The journal *Sociological Analysis* devoted a 1983 issue to discussion of a conference on the propriety of participation in such proceedings. Beckford (1983) emphasized that individual participation may have long-term "transindividual" negative consequences for social scientists specializing in the study of new religious movements. In this instance, Beckford worried that UC sponsorship of conferences and publications will restrict publication to those approved by the UC, and divide the academic specialist community.

The point here is that research has consequences: to generate favorable or unfavorable publicity; an increase or a loss of social prestige; funding or financial support or its loss; or an increase or loss of moral standing (in the case of people considered to be "cultists," they are not just regarded as less prestigious people, but as different kinds of people – as "nuts" or "crackpots"). The fact that many of the groups referred to as cults are social movements, which need an ongoing relationship with the society outside their doors to survive and to grow, means that they are particularly sensitive to public opinion. In the wake of Jonestown, however, I am arguing that "stigma contests" increased, making cults even more sensitive to public opinion.

Stigma contests over what is acceptable behavior continue to be fought by cults. It is inevitable that researchers will be caught up in these contests, because concerns with respectability and social power are ever-present concerns of cults, given the widespread perception of them as deviant. This fact of stigma contests can influence researchers' gaining and maintaining of access, their analysis of research, and their perceived credibility. The important point to emphasize here is that the researcher should not let his or her research agenda be set by the movement. Maintaining one's own agenda will undoubtedly cause various problems, not all of which can be determined in advance.

NOTES

1. It is impossible to explore here the range of theoretical and methodological issues involved in this research. Whichever term we use, these groups have been very controversial, and this is also true of the research done on the groups. The two predominant theoretical positions are those of the "new religious movements" and the "destructive cult" researchers. For the [uninformed] reader, I recommend Robbins's *Cults, Converts, and Charisma* (1988) for the most comprehensive and well-balanced analysis of the research. Beckford's *Cult Controversies* (1985) provides a compelling analysis of the controversiality of cults. Both of these are from the perspective of "new religious movements" researchers. For a statement of the issues from "destructive cult" researchers, I suggest Clark, Langone, Schecter, and Daly's *Destructive Cult Conversion: Theory, Research, and Treatment* (1981).

2. Barker (1984, p. 2) illustrated widespread public awareness and negative assessment of these groups and events by referring to a late 1970s survey in which

a thousand Americans born between 1940 and 1952 were given a list of 155 names and asked how they felt about each of them. Only 3 per cent of the

respondents had not heard of the Reverend Moon. Only 1 per cent admitted to admiring him. The owner of no other name on the list elicited less admiration, and the only person whom a higher percentage of respondents did not admire was the ritual killer Charles Manson.

Elsewhere, Barker (1986, p. 330) referred to a December 1978 Gallup Poll which found that "98% of the US public had heard or read about the People's Temple and the Guyana massacre – a level of awareness matched in the pollsters' experience only by the attack on Pearl Harbor and the explosion of the atom bomb."

3. I suggest the collection of papers edited by Brock K. Kilbourne, *Scientific Research and New Religions: Divergent Perspectives* (1985), as the best source of information on this research. Both "new religious movements" and "destructive cult" researchers are represented, so that one obtains a sampling of both perspectives as they influence analyses of research.

REFERENCES

AYELLA, M. (1977). *An analysis of current conversion practices of followers of Reverend Sun Myung Moon.* Unpublished manuscript.

AYELLA, M. (1985). *Insane therapy: Case study of the social organization of a psychotherapy cult.* Unpublished doctoral dissertation, University of California at Berkeley.

BAINBRIDGE, W.S., & STARK, R. (1980). Scientology: To be perfectly clear. *Sociological Analysis, 41,* 128–136.

BALCH, R. W. (1985). What's wrong with the study of new religions and what we can do about it. In B. K. Kilbourne (Ed.), *Scientific research and new religions: Divergent perspectives* (pp. 24–39). San Francisco: American Association for the Advancement of Science.

BARKER, E. (1984). *The Making of a Moonie.* New York: Blackwell.

BARKER, E. (1986). Religious movements: Cult and anticult since Jonestown. *Annual Review of Sociology, 12,* 329–346.

BECKFORD, J. A. (1983). Some questions about the relationship between scholars and the new religious movements. *Sociological Analysis, 44,* 189–196.

BECKFORD, J. A. (1985). *Cult controversies.* New York: Tavistock.

BROMLEY, D. G., & SHUPE, A. D. (1979). Evolving foci in participant observation: Research as an emergent process. In W. Shaffir, A. Turowitz, & R. Stebbins (Eds.), *Fieldwork experience: Qualitative approaches to social research* (pp. 191-203). New York: St. Martin's.

CLARK, J. G., Jr., LANGONE, M. D., SCHECTER, R. E., & DALY, R.C.B. (1981). *Destructive cult conversion: Theory, research, and treatment.* Weston, MA: American Family Foundation.

DOWNES, D. & ROCK, P. (1982). *Understanding deviance.* New York: Oxford University Press.

GORDON, D. (1987, August). *Getting close by staying distant: Field work on conversion-oriented groups.* Paper presented at the annual meeting of the American Sociological Association, New York City.

HOROWITZ, I. (1981). The politics of new cults. In T. Robbins & D. Anthony (Eds.), *In gods we trust* (pp. 161–170). New Brunswick, NJ: Transaction Books.

KILBOURNE, B. K. (Ed.). (1985). *Scientific research and new religions: Divergent perspectives.* San Francisco: American Association for the Advancement of Science, Pacific Division.

LOFLAND, J. (1966). *Doomsday cult.* Englewood Cliffs, NJ: Prentice-Hall.

MITCHELL, D., MITCHELL, C., & OFSHE, R. (1980). *The light on Synanon.* New York: Seaview Books.

RICHARDSON, J. T., STEWART, M. W., & SIMMONDS, R. B. (1978). Researching a fundamentalist commune. In J. Needteman & G. Baker (Eds.), *Understanding the new religions* (pp. 235–251). New York: Seabury.

ROBBINS T. (1988). *Cults, converts, and charisma.* Newbury Park, CA: Sage.

ROBBINS, T., ANTHONY, D., & CURTIS, T. (1973). The limits of symbolic realism: Problems of empathetic field observation in a sectarian context. *Journal for the Scientific Study of Religion, 12,* 259–272.

ROCHFORD, E. B. (1985). *Hare Krishna in America.* New Brunswick, NJ: Rutgers University Press.

SCHUR, E. M. (1980). *The politics of deviance.* Englewood Cliffs, NJ: Prentice-Hall.

SHUPE, A. D., Jr., & BROMLEY, D. G. (1980). Walking a tightrope: Dilemmas of participant observation of groups in conflict. *Qualitative Sociology, 2,* 3–21.

STONE, D. (1978). On knowing how we know about the new religions. In J. Needleman & G. Baker (Eds.), *Understanding the new religions* (pp. 141–152). New York: Seabury Press.

WALLIS, R. (1977a). *The road to total freedom.* New York: Columbia University Press.

WALLIS, R. (1977b). The moral career of a research project. In C. Bell & H. Newby (Eds.), *Doing sociological research* (pp. 149–169). London: Allen & Unwin.

Reading  ## 35 Correcting a Curious Neglect, or Bringing Religion Back In

CHRISTIAN SMITH

Religion can be seen as a "toolbox" of cultural resources that social change move-ments draw upon to achieve political goals. Smith's essay remains one of the only exhaustive attempts to categorize the resources available to movements from reli-gious beliefs, practices, and structures. As you will see, religion has the potential to provide the beliefs and ideological support necessary to motivate people to act while also supplying the practical organizational resources that allow a movement to go forward.

Disruptive religion? For many, the phrase is an oxymoron. Integrating religion? Sure. Consoling religion? Okay. Legitimating religion? Right. But disruptive religion? Since when is religion in the business of social disorder, collective con-frontation, or political protest? When was the last time anyone saw a nun rioting, or heard of a Sunday school teacher plotting to subvert a gov-ernment, or knew of a rabbi arrested for civil dis-obedience? Religion is too busy conducting funerals, expounding theology, collecting tithes, burning incense, and offering opening prayers at local Kiwanis luncheons to be mobilizing protests, boycotts, and insurrections. Right?

Partly right. Religion typically *is* in the business of supplying meaningful world-views and moral systems that help to integrate and harmonize societies; of providing comforting theodicies to those distressed and suffering; of rendering ideologies that legitimate the often-times unjust status quo. There certainly are plenty of military chaplains who sanctify the work of war, theologies that proffer health-and-wealth and pie-in-the-sky by-and-by, pas-tors who preach patient submission to injustice and indignity, and parishioners whose faith rouses them to little more than regular church attendance and charity.

But there is another face to the sacred-social phenomena we call religion. For the world-views, moral systems, theodicies, and organiza-tions of religion can serve not only to legitimate and preserve, but also to challenge and overturn social, political, and economic systems. Religion *can* help to keep everything in its place. But it can *also* turn the world upside down. . . .

RELIGIOUS ASSETS FOR ACTIVISM

If and when religious believers or organizations initiate or become caught up in a collective mobilization for disruptive activism, what attributes or assets do they embody or possess that can help to constitute and facilitate that action? . . .

Transcendent Motivation

All social movements confront the problem of motivating their participants to make and maintain a commitment to the collective cause, especially when the activism is costly for participants. Religion offers some important and sometimes unique solutions to this problem of motivation.

Legitimation for Protest Rooted in the Ultimate or Sacred. Perhaps the most potent motivational leverage that a social-movement can enjoy is the alignment of its cause with the ultimacy and sacredness associated with God's will, eternal truth, and the absolute moral structure of the universe. People can compromise, in the end, on wage increases and job security; they can pragmatically negotiate their best political advantage on many publicpolicy issues. But God's will is something apart—it is not up for grabs or negotiable. What is sacred is sacred. What is absolute is absolute. What is eternal is eternal—at least that is how reality can be constructed under some conditions. The social activism of religious "true believers," therefore, often reflects an uncompromising and tenacious certainty and commitment that sustains activism in the face of great adversity. . . .

Divine imperative does not merely raise the stakes of the game; it can, under some conditions, infuse the struggle with non-negotiability, and relativize what might otherwise seem insurmountable. Human preference and choice can be supplanted by divine compulsion. Such a motivational wellspring can be a tremendous asset for many social movements.

Moral Imperatives for Love, Justice, Peace, Freedom, Equity. Social movements emerge, in part, when people come to define their situations as needlessly unjust and susceptible to change. Scholars have labeled this situation-redefining process variously as adopting an "injustice frame" (Gamson et. al. 1982), "cognitive liberation" (McAdam 1982), and the development of "insurgent consciousness" (Smith 1991). However labeled, the essential idea is that people determine that something about their world so egregiously violates their moral standards—of what is right, just, fair—that they must engage in collective action to correct it (Smith 1996). Determining this, of course, requires possessing a set of fundamental moral standards against which the status quo can be judged. In most societies, religion has served as a major source of those kinds of moral standards.

Religion not only attempts to tell us what ultimately *is*—Yaweh reigns sovereignly over the universe, there is no god but Allah and Mohammed is his prophet, reality is an endless succession of birth, death, and rebirth. Religion also aspires to tell us what, therefore, *should be*, how people *must* live, how the world *ought to* operate—thou shalt not murder, love your neighbor as yourself, honor the spirits of the dead, and so on. The meaning and direction for life that religion provides is inextricably tied to the ethical systems it advocates. In religion, the *is* and the *ought*, the true and the necessary assume and reinforce each other. . . .

By possessing rich storehouses of moral standards by which social realities can be weighed in the scales and found wanting, religion can, has, and does serve as a principal source of a key element that generates the insurgent consciousness driving many social movements.

Powerfully Motivating Icons, Rituals, Songs, Testimonies, Oratory. Religion not only can help to generate and define the grievances that breed disruptive collective activism, it can also supply the symbolic and emotional resources needed to sustain that activism over time. . . .

Social movements need symbols, rituals, narratives, icons, and songs. They use these to construct their collective identities, to nurture solidarity, to express their grievances, and to draw inspiration and strength in difficult times. Religion, as a major creator and custodian of powerful symbols, rituals, icons, narratives, songs, testimonies, and oratory, is well-positioned to lend these sacred, expressive practices to the cause of political activism. The solidarity, inspiration, articulation, and education that these sacred expressions generate can then become channeled into political mobilization. The songs and sermons of black churches across the American South, for example, are renowned for the energy and hope they generated for civil rights activists in the 1950s and 60s (McAdam 1982). Likewise, the sermons, prayers, and marches of many mideastern Islamic militant groups—such as Lebanon and Palestine's Islamic Jihad and Hamas—help to sustain their commitment and sacrifice in the face of tremendous opposition and uncertain prospects for success. . . .

Ideologies Demanding Self-Discipline, Sacrifice, Altruism. One major practical and analytical problem for social movements and those who study them concerns how and why individuals can be motivated to sacrifice their own personal well-being for a collective good. Why *has* Aunt Helen devoted her entire life to the elimination of nuclear weapons? A world in which individuals only act to secure divisible rewards for themselves would be one devoid of

social movements. For sustainable social movements require that some, perhaps many people, take risks, set examples, and pay prices on the movement's behalf, the personal costs of which are rarely fully repaid, even if the social-movement succeeds. This is especially true in early phases of movement mobilization. Movements need people who will sacrifice a great deal of time, money, energy, security, emotional resources, alternative opportunities, and sometimes even their lives in order to build the momentum and organization necessary to mount significant political challenges. Where does that kind of self-sacrifice come from? It can come from many places, of course, but an important source of such a self-sacrificial orientation is religion. . . .

Faith-based self-sacrifice can help to generate a critical mass of participants early on, even when the cause is idealistic, unrewarding, and unpromising. It can encourage individual self-expenditure for what is believed to be a higher good— whether that be world peace, a better way of life for one's grandchildren, or the repeal of widespread, burdensome taxes.

Legitimation of Organizational and Strategic-Tactical Flexibility. Strong social movements need to manage organizational, strategic, and tactical flexibility; they need to be able to devise organizations, strategies, and tactics that are appropriate for the peculiar political and cultural environments they face; and they need to be able to adjust their organizations, strategies, and tactics as the struggles within which they are engaged develop, particularly as the strategies and tactics of their antagonists evolve (McAdam 1983). In many cases, to the extent that religion becomes a motivating factor in social-movement activism, it may aid in that organizational and strategic-tactical flexibility.

The sacred texts of all major religions are sufficiently ambiguous that they may be interpreted in disparate directions (see Hart

1992: 124). It is possible, therefore, for faith-based activists to find in their sacred texts—perhaps especially when important political interests are at stake—legitimations for a variety of political, organizational, and tactical approaches that may satisfy their movement's needs. A movement for whom violence commends itself as a useful element in its tactical repertoire, for example, can find legitimation for such violence, if it so desires, in the New Testament, the Torah and Prophets, the Koran, the Mahabharata, the Shu Ching, and so on (Lewy 1974: 11–54). Jesus said, "I have not come to bring peace, but a sword" (Matthew 10: 34). However, a movement dependent on a strategy of non-violent resistance can likewise find legitimating support for that strategy in the very same sacred texts. For Jesus also said, "Put your sword back in its place; for all who draw the sword will die by the sword" (Matthew 26: 52). . . .

Organizational Resources

Social movements require more than compelling motivations, moral judgement, symbols, self-discipline, and flexibility to generate political disruption. Movements also need a variety of organizational resources by which to mobilize and through which to channel their energy. Organized religion is well-equipped to provide, when it so desires, these key resources to social movements.

Trained and Experienced Leadership Resources. . . . All established religions—by definition collective phenomena—take on some kind of organizational form that, like social movements, necessitates the operation of active leadership. Well before any social-movement in need of resources appears, religious organizations have already established functioning systems of leadership. In many cases, the religious leaders are specialists, formally or informally educated, trained, and experienced in interpersonal communications, group dynamics, and collective-identity construction. Typically, these religious leaders also enjoy influence among their followers, linkages with their colleagues, relative autonomy and flexibility in their daily schedules, and extensive contacts in their broader communities. All of these are invaluable potential assets for a burgeoning social movement. Thus, when a social-movement in need of resources *does* appear, if the religion is sympathetic to its cause, it stands capable of lending its already-functioning leadership resources to the movement. . . .

Financial Resources. Two decades of resource-mobilization theory have clearly established the importance of the flow of financial resources in the fate of social movements. Money may not determine the outcome of collective action, but it certainly shapes it. It takes money to pay organizers, rent office space, print flyers, make telephone calls, send direct-mail appeals, construct banners and placards, transport protesters to protests, bail demonstrators out of jail, attract the attention of the media, consult lawyers, and offset the costs of boycotts, strikes, and sanctions. All other things being equal, for movements, more money buys more power.

Organized religion often possesses extraordinary financial resources that it can—if it so chooses—funnel, directly and indirectly, into social-movement activism. In the United States, for example, Protestant and Catholic churches each year collect from their adherents more than $39 billion in tithes and other contributions (Statistical Abstract 1994: 72). Furthermore, multiple para-church and other religious organizations raise additional hundreds of millions of dollars annually. If and when a religious organization judges that a political-activist cause falls within the bounds of its legitimate religious mission, it often possesses significant financial resources that it can contribute to the cause. Instances of movements obtaining funding from religious organizations—as diverse as Pat Robertson's Christian Coalition, the Unitarian Universalist Service Committee, and the Reverend Moon's Unification Church—abound.

Congregated Participants and Solidarity Incentives.

Besides leaders and money, of course, social movements need deployable rank-and-file activists to implement their strategies. Grassroots participants are needed to strike, boycott, collect signatures, write letters, stuff envelopes, recruit new members, lobby, contribute money, protest at demonstrations, and fill the jails. The larger the numbers of participants, the better, for larger numbers of grassroots activists helps to spread work out, reduce the expected costs of high-risk activism, and boost activists' perceptions of political efficacy.

Organized religion is well-equipped to expand the ranks of grassroots activists by providing ready-made opportunities for network- and bloc-recruitment of new members into movements. Movements rarely recruit new members individually, straight "off the streets." Rather, movements typically recruit new participants through existing relational and organizational networks. . . . Religious organizations—which comprise in the United States, for example, the largest share of all types of non-profit, voluntary organizations— can represent a veritable "field ripe for the harvest" for movement recruiters whose issues resonate with religious actors. Viewed in reverse, religious leaders committed to mobilizing disruptive activism have at their disposal readymade, extensive recruitment networks and organizations. So, for example, in the Sanctuary, civil rights, and pro-life movements, and in the Nicaraguan, Salvadoran, and Iranian revolutions, entire congregations of churches and mosques were drawn *en mass* into disruptive activism, helping to rapidly expand the growth of these movements. . . .

Pre-Existing Communication Channels.

Social movements require not simply an abundance of warm bodies; they also need the ability to coordinate the actions of participants, to get them thinking and acting in unity. Movements require the capacity to deploy their forces with strategic coordination, to get participants meeting, lobbying, and protesting together. The fundamental issue here is the problem of communication. . . .

Just as organized religion is well-positioned to loan its leadership, financial, and personnel resources to social movements, so, too, it can lend its pre-existent communications systems. In effect, the religion's established communications infrastructures—its newsletters, bulletins, weekly announcements, telephone directories, magazines, television and radio programs, address lists, journals, synods, presbyteries, and councils—that normally transmit information related to the religion's spiritual mission, become employed or are coopted to transmit information related to political activism. The synagogue telephone-tree is used to announce a rally; the worship service bulletin includes a notice about an organization's need for volunteers and donations; the denominational newsletter publishes an article about a social injustice and organizations working to respond; the Imam announces details of a planned protest at the end of Friday prayers. In each case, by piggybacking on the pre-existent communication structure, rather than creating its own structure *ex nihilo*, the social-movement is able to spend energy and resources it otherwise would have devoted to organizational self-maintenance, on direct political engagement instead. . . .

Enterprise Tools.

The organizational work of social movements is greatly aided by the availability of equipment and facilities that expedite information communication and storage. These basic but important "enterprise tools" (Smith 1991: 61) include typewriters, telephone lines, office space, desks, photocopy and mimeograph machines, computers and software, internet access, fax machines, e-mail accounts, bookshelves, office supplies, file cabinets, secretarial help, and legal advice. Especially in movements' formative stages, quick and easy access to these tools can make a critical difference in the speed and extent of mobilization. Organized religion typically possesses many of these enterprise tools, and can greatly aid the mobilization of political activism by making them readily available to budding social movements. . . .

Shared Identity

. . . Social movements must . . . construct and maintain collective identities that signify to themselves and the world who they are, what they stand for, and what kind of society they hope to create. Movements lacking coherent shared identities are likely to be culturally and politically ineffectual. Constructing and maintaining collective identities entails a significant amount of "identity work," whereby groups, through a process of lived experience, draw on available cultural codes, ideologies, worldviews, values, symbols, and traditions to develop and sustain a meaningful sense of their own character and purpose vis-a-vis their social environments . . . .

Common Identification Among Gathered Strangers.

At the micro level, religion can provide a basis upon which strangers can work together with relative ease in common purpose. Learning that others one meets for the first time—at a street march, an organizer's meeting, or in jail—are, like oneself, also Catholics, Muslims, or Jews, can immediately foster a sense of ease, trust, and loyalty that greatly facilitates group communication and solidarity. . . . [Religious] actors know what assumptions to make about the others, what rhetorical style to employ, which values and symbols will resonate, and so on. They know

which songs to sing, which authorities to cite, what moral commitments they ought to uphold. . . .

Religion can provide the basis for common identification and mutual cooperation between otherwise quite different groups of people. Most religions are national and transnational by nature, and therefore create common bonds between people of differing national and global regions, races, and classes, which can transcend and defy more proximate loyalties. So, for example, one critical factor helping to generate the 1980s United States Central America peace movement against President Reagan's policy in El Salvador and Nicaragua was the common religious bond felt between North American Christians and their counterparts in Central America. This mutual identification engendered a sense of moral responsibility among the North American believers to stop the United States-sponsored wars in Central America. Without the influence of this pre-existent transnational religious identity, that movement would certainly have been much smaller and less politically significant (Smith 1996). . . .

Privileged Legitimacy

In many societies, organized religion enjoys a certain authority, legitimacy, and protection not enjoyed by other social institutions and organizations. This is because religion deals with the sacred and the supernatural; and perhaps, because in some situations, it may have a history or current status as a socially powerful institution. This authority, legitimacy, and protection can be put to good use for the cause of social-movement activism.

Political Legitimacy in Public Opinion.

In many societies, and under certain circumstances, public opinion accords relatively greater authority to the voice of religion than to other voices. When a bishop, rabbi, ayatollah or other religious leader or teacher denounces an injustice, lodges a complaint against the government, or calls people to support a cause, it is often taken at least somewhat more seriously than the same declaration would be if spoken by a politician, business person, or secular activists. In the United States, the American public may view the voice of religion—especially grassroots religion and religion viewed as normally nonpartisan—as politically naive, perhaps, but also generally as sincere and honorable. Therefore, when religious voices speak on behalf of social movements, they can lend a valuable extra force or earnestness to the movements' causes.

When, for example, the Reverend Billy Graham speaks against nuclear arms, San Salvador's Archbishop Oscar Romero denounces military repression, Tibet's [Dalai] Lama criticizes Chinese imperialism, Iran's Ayatollah Khomeni calls for uprisings in the streets, South Africa's Desmond Tutu condemns the apartheid regime, and Manila's Cardinal Sin demands the end of the Marcos dictatorship, people listen. At another level, when a local minister denounces violence against women, members of a religious congregation become visibly involved in a recycling campaign, or a group of rabbis march on behalf of racial equality, the public also takes notice. This is partly a product of abiding or latent public respect for religion; and partly a product of the media's desire to cover the novel and dramatic. In any case, religion can often capitalize on these factors to draw attention and lend credibility to activist causes, or undermine potential state or counter-movement charges that a social-movement represents marginal or extremist elements. . . .

Institutional Self-Interest

Finally, in some cases, religion can aid the cause of a social movement, not so much through its privileged legitimacy, per se, but rather as a result of the purposeful defense of its institutional self-interest. The resulting positive effects for the social-movement may be felt directly or indirectly.

Institutional Resistance to State Encroachment. Sometimes, an established religion will begin to feel the State encroaching on domain it believes it "owns." For example, the State may take over a social function previously controlled by religion, such as education; it may ban religious symbols from public places and discourse; or it may actually attempt to eliminate the presence of religion altogether. In response, religious leaders will often begin to mobilize forces to defend and possibly win back pieces of "their territory." In the process, the religion will often develop a language and rituals of resistance, devote institutional resources to defiance of the State, and establish formal or informal alliances with other, nonreligious regime opponents. When this happens, the religious institution can itself become a center of anti-regime activism. And nonreligious movements also opposing the State can benefit from the religion's attitude, resistant rhetoric and rituals, institutional resources, and political alliances.

This process can develop in totalitarian situations. In East Germany, for example, the state increasingly impinged upon the affairs of the church. In defense of its own institutional autonomy and values, the churches and religious base communities became the center of resistance and mobilization. . . . But this process of institutional resistance can also develop in more democratic situations. In the United States, for example, in recent decades, many conservative religious groups believe that the State has encroached on education by forbidding school prayer, denying meeting space to student religious groups, and by teaching "secular humanism" or "new age religion" in public schools. Others believe the State has overstepped its rightful boundaries by outlawing manger scenes on public property or by imposing equal-opportunity laws for homosexuals as employees in religious schools or churches. In many cases, religious leaders, sensing a threat to their own religious freedoms, have organized movements to counter what is perceived as illegitimate state infringement. . . .

REFERENCES

GAMSON, W., BRUCE FIREMAN, and STEVEN RYTINA. 1982. *Encounters with Unjust Authority.* Chicago: Dorsey Press.

HART, S. 1992. *What Does the Lord Require?* New York: Oxford University Press.

LEWY, G. 1974. *Religion and Revolution.* New York: Oxford University Press.

MCADAM. D. 1982. *Political Process and the Generation of Black Insurgency:* Chicago: University of Chicago Press.

————. 1983. "Tactical Innovation and the Pace of Insurgency." *American Sociological Review.* 48 (December): 735–754.

SMITH, C. 1996. *Resisting Reagan: the U.S. Central America Peace Movement.* Chicago: University of Chicago Press.

————. 1991. *The Emergence of Liberation Theology: Radical Religion and Social-movement Activism.* University of Chicago Press.

Statistical Abstract. 1994. *Statistical Abstract of the United States: 1994.* Bureau of Census.

WEIGEL, G. 1992. *The Final Revolution: The Resistance Church and the Collapse of Communism.* New York: Oxford University Press.

36 Church Culture as a Strategy of Action in the Black Community

MARY PATTILLO-MCCOY

Patillo-McCoy documents how African American religion provides a toolbox for mobilizing community political activism. This essay represents a practical application of Smith's theoretical outline of religious resources used by movements trying to achieve social and political change. Here we see the black church as a gate-keeping institution that can channel religious beliefs, meeting space, finances, and other cultural resources to movements whose political efforts in turn, shape church members and the broader African American community.

According to domestic and transnational polls on religious beliefs and commitment, "American blacks are, by some measures, the most religious people in the world" (Gallup and Castelli 1989: 122). This intense religiosity refers to the great importance of God and religion in African Americans' lives, the high frequency of church attendance and church membership, and the prevalence of prayer in daily life (Gallup 1996; Ploch and Hastings 1994; Roof and McKinney 1987). Even among blacks who claim no religious affiliation and have not attended church since age 18, 40 percent report praying *every day* (Taylor 1988). Black Christianity extends outside church walls: "It has proved itself to be

a source of power, not locked behind stained-glass windows, but used wherever Black people seek God's will and respond to His way" (Carter 1976:116). Using ethnographic data from Groveland, an African American neighborhood in Chicago, I illustrate the power of church rituals as cultural tools for facilitating local organizing and activism among African Americans. . . .

FUNCTIONS OF THE BLACK CHURCH

The black church is the anchoring institution in the African American community (DuBois 1899; Lincoln and Mamiya 1990; Myrdal 1944). The church acts simultaneously as a

Source: Mary Pattillo-McCoy, "Church Culture as a Strategy for Action in the Black Community." *American Sociological Review, Vol. 63, No. 6 (Dec. 1998), pp. 767–784.*

school, a bank, a benevolent society, a political organization, a party hall, and a spiritual base. As one of the few institutions owned and operated by African Americans, the church is often the center of activity in black communities.

Black Christian spirituality is based on themes of deliverance and freedom.... The freedom aspired to and attainable through religion differs from the EuroAmerican notion of freedom as the individual's free choice, or the individual's freedom *from* the actions or beliefs of others. In the black Christian view, freedom is an explicitly collective endeavor signifying both spiritual deliverance into God's kingdom and worldly deliverance from the material realities of racial oppression. Using the call-and-response style, the preacher and the congregation, in musical and verbal cooperation, make the journey toward freedom as one body (Hamilton 1972; Levine 1977). The result is the "dynamic process of communion" (Marable 1989:326), ultimately "rejuvenating a community gripped by psychic and economic depression" (Washington 1985:92).

The collective orientation of black Christian rhetoric and ritual is the key to understanding why these are appropriate tools for conducting social action in the black community. The organizational goals voiced by Groveland residents—taking ownership of all neighborhood youths or unifying against drug houses—are "socially realized" (Gubrium and Holstein 1997:50) in the practices of black church culture. Practices such as holding hands during prayer, participating through antiphonal calls of agreement or dissent, and singing, clapping, and swaying to music all enact the collective goals expressed in the content of social action. Repeating biblical excerpts that illustrate God's concrete interventions on behalf of the faithful and singing together the refrain "Jesus on the main line, tell him what you want," serve similar purposes in mustering activist fervor and optimistic determination. . . .

Churches provide social and economic support by meeting emergency needs, providing a network of friends for emotional and physical well-being, and attending to families' special needs (Caldwell, Green, and Billingsley 1992; Taylor and Chatters 1988). Black churches are significantly more likely than white congregations to participate in civil rights activities and to sponsor programs that benefit needy residents of their local communities (Chaves and Higgins 1992). In a national survey of 2,150 black congregations, Lincoln and Mamiya (1990) find that black churches are committed to projects of social justice. Over 90 percent of the clergy approved of their clerical peers' taking part in protest marches on civil rights issues, and believed that churches should express their views on political and social matters. . . .

The social agenda of the black church is most apparent in the activities of the civil rights movement, which exemplified simultaneous attention to religious, political, economic, and social concerns. Studies of the civil rights movement emphasize the preexisting church-based organizational networks, as well as the financial and physical base that black churches provided (McAdam 1982; Morris 1984). Black churches were the sites of civil rights meetings and centers of information and activity; ordained and lay religious ministers led the struggle for racial justice; news about marches and sit-ins or killings and jailings was passed on among fellow churchgoers. Less fully analyzed, however, is the fact that church hymns were transformed into songs of freedom, and that sermons doubled as political addresses. Such happenings are the cultural components of social movements.

The mass movement for civil rights has passed; yet the civic activism of black churches and church members persists at the local level and provides an opportunity to investigate these groups' daily organization-building activities. . . .

Organizational culture is practiced and performed at the small-group level. Thus, the qualitative data in this paper focus on both the politico-religious leaders and the rank-and-file community activists who use specific cultural tools to get things done. Black church culture—which expresses in both language and affect the communal nature of activism, and God's direct involvement in human affairs—is the unnoticed *how* of social action in Groveland.

SETTING AND METHODS

Groveland is a predominantly (99 percent) black neighborhood in Chicago with a population of more than 11,000 (Chicago Fact Book Consortium 1995). African Americans first moved to Groveland in the 1960s as the traditional Black Belt in Chicago expanded southward, displacing middle-class whites who were being pushed and pulled to the suburbs. Groveland has been predominantly African American since 1970; this fact of racial segregation in American residential and social life fosters culturally distinct forms of behavior and interaction. . . .

Despite considerable economic heterogeneity, Groveland residents generally refer to their neighborhood as middle-class. It is largely residential, and single-family homes predominate. Over 70 percent of the residents own their homes, and the neighborhood contains no public housing. The neighborhood's median family income is above the Chicago median, and most workers are employed in white-collar occupations. Eleven churches in Groveland represent 10 Christian denominations. The local congregations that belong to predominantly white denominations—Roman Catholic, United Methodist, Lutheran, United Church of Christ—are as large and as active as the neighborhood's mainline black churches. A denomination's liberal or conservative reputation does not seem to influence its level of community involvement (with the possible exception of the local Church of Christ, which is conspicuously uninvolved in local activities); the size of the local congregation matters more than its national political persuasion. Six of the 11 neighborhood churches belong to the Groveland Clergy Association, which hosts an annual interdenominational revival, a commemorative Dr. Martin Luther King Jr. celebration, and an Image Awards ceremony.

I collected the data for this study over a 3-year period in the mid-1990s. The research began as a part of a comparative ethnography of four Chicago neighborhoods: one white, one Mexican American, one changing from white to Mexican American, and one African American (Groveland). During the first phase I conducted an extensive participant observation study of various neighborhood institutions and organizations, including the Catholic church and school (especially the youth group, the choirs, and the community outreach team); the Groveland Clergy Association; the Chamber of Commerce; the Chicago Alternative Policing Strategy (CAPS) program; Groveland Park (the summer day camp, weekly volleyball, and a youth sports program); and the local Democratic political organization. I interviewed key leaders of these institutions.

In the second research phase I moved into Groveland, continued the participant observation study, and conducted 31 taped, open-ended interviews with residents. I collected newspaper clippings, demographic information, and neighborhood flyers and announcements throughout the research period. The participant-observation field notes from Groveland are the primary data used in this article. . . .

"THERE IS POWER IN PRAYER"

The community activist groups in Groveland include block clubs, church-based community outreach committees, Chicago Alternative Policing Strategy beat associations, school councils, and the neighborhood's political organization. These groups' efforts to close down a drug house, secure the neighborhood park, or prevent youths from loitering follow a call-and-response form, and are infused with Christian prayer and imagery. Many public meetings are held in one or another of the neighborhood's Christian churches, a fact that facilitates and validates the use of church styles. Yet even organizations such as the Groveland Chamber of Commerce, which meets in a restaurant, exhibit similar cultural forms. . . .

All the churches involved in the Groveland Clergy Association sponsor a variety of outreach ministries ranging from summer day camps and food pantries to trips to jails and shelters. Two of the larger congregations include committees that function expressly to solicit neighborhood residents' involvement in addressing problems of gangs and drugs. The open meetings of these community outreach committees are generally businesslike in format, and are conducted with a sophistication that reflects the neighborhood's middle-class status. Residents' comments and complaints are restricted to a specified time limit, and must be relevant to the meeting's theme. Often an official timekeeper is present to ensure compliance with the schedule. This regimen, however, makes generous allowances for spiritual improvisation by speakers and attendees.

The Outreach Committee of the Groveland United Church of Christ provides an example. This group's first community meeting in June of 1995 was attended by nearly 100 residents who decided that closing down three identified drug houses in the neighborhood was a priority. The Outreach Committee reported the illegal activities to the police and demanded that the police dismantle these drug operations. Throughout the summer, the Outreach Committee met with police officials on the status of this project.

Three months after the first meeting, the Outreach Committee invited Sgt. Trey Bishop,

the neighborhood relations officer for the Chicago Police Department, to speak on the progress made in closing down the three drug houses. Dressed in his uniform, badge gleaming and gun at his hip, Sgt. Bishop began his remarks: "It's always a pleasure to be in the house of the Lord." The residents agreed with him with drawled responses of "Amen." Departing from the printed agenda, the sergeant then told the following parable about a rich man who was a member of a poor rural congregation:

Every Sunday the collection plate would be passed to this man, and he would peel off a one-dollar bill from the wad of money he kept in his pocket. One Sunday, as the collection plate came to the rich man, a chunk of plaster fell from the ceiling of the shabby church and hit the rich man on his head, knocking the entire wad of money into the collection plate. When the pastor received the collection plate and realized what had happened, the pastor called out, "Hit him again, Lord."

This parable had a clear moral: God's people, who were assembled for the present meeting, should not wait for the Lord to hit them on the head before they give to their community.

Sgt. Bishop's lesson was received with laughter, applause, and approving "Amens." The parable signified to his audience that he was like them. He was schooled in the same black church traditions, and could use traditional tools from his repertoire when he needed to affiliate with his audience. Moreover, Sgt. Bishop employed black church styles in an otherwise secular event to convey a central message of black Christianity—that God is actively involved in human lives. His strategy was well received, and he sat down to more applause.

The shortcomings in the *content* of Sgt. Bishop's official remarks are illuminating, however. He reported somewhat vaguely that at two of the identified drug houses "arrests [had] been made in and about the location," while no progress had been made at the third. At the previous meeting, the group had demanded that operations at all three houses be shut down completely. Yet Sgt. Bishop's partial failure as a representative of the police department was forgiven because of his cultural savvy. He was able to use black church cues to identify himself as a member of the community, aware of the collective imperatives of black Christianity, and committed to helping the neighborhood. . . .

POLITICS AS USUAL?

The party-based political organization in Groveland is a public, secular organization. As a microcomponent of the larger system of city, state, and federal governance, it should be the most responsive to matters of church-state separation. Yet the repeated use of church styles by partisan political actors and organizers in Groveland indicates how closely activist culture corresponds to religious culture. Various appearances made by the alderman, as well as her campaign organizational meetings, illustrate the constant enactment of black church culture among leaders and participants.

The Ward Regular Democratic Organization (WRDO) is the political home of Groveland's Alderman Ramsey. . . .

Organizational meetings for Alderman Ramsey's 1995 reelection campaign similarly illustrate the importance of church styles. Unlike other community events, the alderman's campaign meetings were held not in a church, but at the WRDO headquarters. Situated in a strip of greeting-cards shops, tax offices, and small furniture stores, the WRDO office serves the basic functions of handling residents' concerns (at the front counter) and hosting community meetings (at the cafeteria-style tables). There is nothing sacred about the space itself. In addition, the WRDO is a hierarchical organization with duties clearly assigned to well-defined positions and officers. The weekly meetings held during the aldermanic campaign were conducted according to *Robert's Rules of Order*, followed

a strict schedule, and included a controlled "open forum" at the end. Embedded within this formal structure, however, were elements of black church culture. . . .

One of the major public events of the aldermanic campaign was the gospel rally held at the Groveland United Church of Christ. Alderman Ramsey's challenger, Charles Thompson, had hosted his own rally at Groveland Church two weeks earlier. At a planning meeting, one campaign worker informed WRDO members that Thompson's rally had been poorly attended, and declared, "So we wanna show him, and have standing room only." Ramsey's campaign chairman also encouraged the members to spread the word, because an impressive turnout would show "Blankety Blank [the opponent] that he ain't have no business even running." Although the gospel rally—part musical concert, part Ramsey hurrah—was religiously grounded, the WRDO's goals also were fiercely competitive. . . .

Inside the church, away from the political tension sustained by biting winds, the mood was decidedly more serene. Groveland Church, built at the end of the nineteenth century, is a medium-sized building seating approximately 250 persons. The high wooden ceiling and the intricate stained-glass windows inspire reverence. The Christian decorations— a depiction of Jesus in a stain-glass window, passages from scripture etched into plaques and murals around the church, the Bible placed at the front of the sanctuary, and the hymn books in each pew—conspicuously welcomed the participants in the gospel rally. The physical space itself made it difficult for participants to separate the secular political rally from its Christian environment.

In accordance with custom, the program began with a welcome and a prayer by the pastor of the Groveland United Church of Christ. Then Millie Simpkins introduced the master of ceremonies, Reverend Glenda Corliss from Hillside United Methodist Church. . . .

Reverend Corliss was an eloquent speaker whose formal training in dance added vitality to her sermons. She was dressed in full African-inspired regalia in exuberant colors, even to her apple-red fingernails. Declaring, "In the beginning," in her preacher's voice, she took the audience from the beginnings of civilization in Africa (another commonsense assertion) to the candidacy of Alderman Ramsey, who descended from those mighty African civilizations. Reverend Corliss's opening remarks set the mood for the gospel rally: highly energetic, highly emotional, and explicitly sanctified.

St. Mary's choir began the program with three selections, including an updated arrangement of the black national anthem. Their final selection featured a fast-paced piano solo by a teenage musician. People stood in the pews, clapping, singing along, and raising their hands in praise, prompting Reverend Corliss to joke, "Y'all didn't know Catholics could jam like that, did you?"

The 30-voice choir from Savior's Rock Baptist Church followed St. Mary's choir. After their first song, the audience pleaded for more with applause and shouts of "Hallelujah." The choir's director, explaining that she was trying to stay within the planned schedule, announced, "The program said we were supposed to do *a selection*, and I believe in being obedient." Even so, she could not ignore the energy that filled the rally. She thought quickly, looked at Alderman Ramsey, and said, "I know that she knows that she could not have come this far if it wasn't for God." After this remark, the choir performed a spontaneously tailored rendition of a song titled "All of My Help." The soloist sang to Alderman Ramsey:

When you don't know what to do;
When you're tired and just can't seem to lead no more;
When you can't seem to find the answer;
Just remember, all of your help comes from Him.
Hallelujah. From the Lord. Just call on Him.

. . . The next soloist's soprano voice quieted the mood of the gathering, but reinforced the explicitly Christian tenor of the gospel rally, and reiterated the belief that God was on Alderman Ramsey's side. The soloist sang "His Eye Is on the Sparrow," whose words exemplify Christian faith.

Why should I feel discouraged?
Why should the shadows come?
Why should my heart feel lonely?
And long for my heavenly home?
King Jesus is my portion.
A constant friend is He.
His eye is on the sparrow.
And I know He watches me.

The religious power of this song moved several people in the congregation to tears.

As the organizers had planned, the excitement of the rally built with each song, each speech, and each time someone in the audience stood in prayerful thanks-giving. The choirs were responsible for calling up the attendees' positive energies. Between songs, Ramsey's colleagues spoke about the pressing neighborhood problems that Ramsey would work hard to solve. The choirs and the speakers both used the cultural tools of the black church—preaching and singing as well as politicking—to raise people to their feet in praise. Whether the praise was addressed to God or to Alderman Ramsey and the WRDO was precisely the ambiguity that such tools were meant to produce. With ingredients from the black church, the goal of encouraging support was achieved. . . .

As a consummate politician, Ramsey graciously thanked all of those responsible for the gospel rally: the choirs, the ministers, and her colleagues. As a *black* politician, she launched into her own rendition of "In the beginning," which she had borrowed extemporaneously from Reverend Corliss's introduction. Intertwining biblical, Afro-centric, and political themes, Ramsey arrived at her campaign theme: dedication, commitment, and devotion.

She spoke about the areas of greatest concern in the neighborhood: "We have to hold on to our gangs and make sure that our neighborhood isn't blighted like some other areas, and on the decline," she declared, expressing the ideas of collective responsibility (the *whats*) that the church rituals underscored (the *hows*).

Ramsey maintained the audience's excitement by using important "vernacular resources" (Ibarra and Kitsuse 1993:32–33). Even though she was a less masterful preacher than Glenda Corliss, the political sermon is not a solo act. The assembly knew what to do: when to say "Amen," when to raise a hand in agreement, when to say "Yes," and when to clap. Energized by the music and the preaching, and encouraged by her supporters' confidence that she would receive 90 percent of the vote, candidate Ramsey stayed in step with the religious imagery and the biblical phrasing that had dominated the day. She rejoiced,

I know if God is with me, who can be against me? And if His eye is on the sparrow, then I know He's watching me. If He has eighty percent in store for me, then I know I'll get it.

When someone in the audience called out "Ninety percent," Alderman Ramsey changed he statement accordingly and continued:

If not, sure I'll be sad for a while, but I'll know that He must have even bigger and better doors to open for me. I really do think that it was His divine plan to place me in the alderman's seat. Together, we can work to make our community whatever we want it to be. When I am victorious, I'll bring back the spoils to you. On February twenty-first, punch thirty-five!

...The alderman's gospel rally was so much like church that it was difficult to distinguish the political figures who spoke in support of the candidate from the ministers who delivered the blessings. The crowd reacted with equal enthusiasm regardless of the speaker's official capacity. There was nothing disingenuous about the WRDO's complex integration of church form and political content. As an organization containing many African American Christians versed in the style of the black church, the WRDO planned a program that was relevant to its members. Members of the organization shared institutional affiliations and cultural tools with the voting public. The importance of the black church lies not only in its organizational ability to supply the foot soldiers for a social movement or to garner political support for a candidate or a cause, but also in its cultural strength as a common language that leaders and followers, workers and supporters can share to coordinate action.

CONCLUSION

The black church is a more encompassing institution than are white religious bodies because of blacks' inability to participate fully in the economic, social, and political life of the majority society, and because it has been the only institution controlled completely by blacks (Morris [1984]). For this reason, studies of the black church are needed to clarify various aspects of social and organizational life in black communities. The role of the church in predominantly black social movements, such as the civil rights movement, has received considerable attention, but observers often have emphasized the networks and resources possessed by the black church. In this article I have extended the research on the black church to include its cultural importance for everyday organizing activities in black communities....

REFERENCES

CALDWELL, CLEOPATRA, ANGELA GREEN, and ANDREW BILLINGSLEY. 1992. "The Black Church as a Family Support System." *National Journal of Sociology* 6:21–40.

CARTER, HAROLD. 1976. *The Prayer Tradition of Black People.* Valley Forge, PA: Judson.

CHAVES, MARK and LYNN HIGGINS. 1992. "Comparing the Community Involvement of Black and White

Congregations." *Journal for the Scientific Study of Religion* 31:425–40.

Chicago Fact Book Consortium, eds. 1995. *Local Community Fact Book, Chicago Metropolitan Area, 1990*. Chicago, IL: University of Illinois Press.

DuBois, W. E. B. 1899. *The Philadelphia Negro: A Social Study*. Philadelphia, PA: University of Pennsylvania Press.

Gallup, George, Jr. 1996. *Religion in America 1996*. Princeton, NJ: Princeton Religion Research Center.

Gallup, George, Jr. and Jim Castelli. 1989. *The People's Religion: American Faith in the 90's*. New York: MacMillan.

Gubrium, Jaber F. and James A. Holstein, 1997. *The New Language of Qualitative Method*. New York: Oxford University Press.

Hamilton, Charles V. 1972. *The Black Preacher in America*. New York: William Morrow and Company.

Ibarra, Peter R. and John I. Kitsuse. 1993. "Vernacular Constituents of Moral Discourse: An Interactionist Proposal for the Study of Social Problems." Pp. 25–58 in *Reconsidering Social Constructionism: Debates in Social Problems Theory*, edited by J. Holstein and G. Miller. New York: Aldine de Gruyter.

Levine, Lawrence. 1977. *Black Culture and Black Consciousness: Afro-American Folk Thought from Slavery to Freedom*. Oxford, England: Oxford University Press.

Lincoln, C. Eric and Lawrence Mamiya. 1990. *The Black Church in the African American Experience*. Durham, NC: Duke University Press.

Marable, Manning. 1989. "Religion and Black Protest Thought in African American History." Pp. 318–39 in *African American Religious Studies: An Interdisciplinary Anthology*, edited by G. Wilmore. Durham, NC: Duke University Press.

McAdam, Doug. 1982. *Political Process and the Development of Black Insurgency*. Chicago, IL: University of Chicago Press.

Morris, Aldon. 1984. *The Origins of the Civil Rights Movement: Black Communities Organizing for Change*. New York: Free Press.

Myrdal, Gunnar. 1944. *An American Dilemma: The Negro Problem and Modern Democracy*. New York: Harper and Row.

Ploch, Donald and Donald Hastings. 1994. "Graphic Presentations of Church Attendance Using General Social Survey Data." *Journal for the Scientific Study of Religion* 33:16–33.

Roof, Wade Clark and William McKinney. 1987. *American Mainline Religion: Its Changing Shape and Future*. New Brunswick, NJ: Rutgers University Press.

Taylor, Robert Joseph. 1988. "Correlates of Religious Non-Involvement among Black Americans." *Review of Religious Research* 30: 126–39.

Taylor, Robert Joseph and Linda Chatters. 1988. "Church Members as a Source of Informal Support." *Review of Religious Research* 30:193–203.

Washington, James Melvin. 1985. "Jesse Jackson and the Symbolic Politics of Black Christendom." *Annals of the American Academy of Political and Social Sciences* 480:89–105.

37 Public Opinion on Church-State Issues in a Changing Environment

CLYDE WILCOX AND RACHEL GOLDBERG

Studying individual attitudes regarding the separation of church and state has been a common focus in exploring the links between religion and politics in the United States. Using survey data collected in the Washington D.C. area in 1993 and 2000, Wilcox and Goldberg examine changes to and continuities of these attitudes in the face of increasing religious diversity.

Over the past 20 years, debates over church-state issues have been a prominent feature of American politics. The First Amendment pronouncement that "Congress shall make no law respecting an establishment of religion or prohibiting the free exercise thereof" has inspired heated debates in law journals, political campaigns, and in the public square. But as the United States has become more diverse religiously, these debates have taken on a new character.

The first clause of the First Amendment, commonly referred to as the "establishment clause," is most relevant to questions of governmental endorsement of majority religious sentiments and practices.[1] Thus the Supreme Court has dealt with issues such as whether cities can display nativity scenes on public land (Swanson 1992), public prayers at high school graduation ceremonies and football games, and displays of religious symbols and texts in courthouses and other public places. State legislatures have sought to mandate the display of the 10 commandments in schools and the teaching of creationism, and have adopted state mottoes that seem to endorse Christianity.

Religious diversity intrudes into these debates because it changes the nature of one of the most common tactics of those who advocate accommodation between church and state—the attempt to include non-Christian elements in religious displays, thereby demonstrating that the display is neutral among religions. The most common example of this tactic has been to include the Menorah in Christmas displays, or to invite Jewish rabbis to deliver the graduation prayer at high school events. Yet when communities begin to include significant numbers of Muslims, Hindu, Sikhs, and Buddhists, public support for inclusion is likely to erode, and it is unlikely that Texas football fans would sit quietly for a Buddhist chant before the kickoff.

The second clause of the First Amendment is commonly called the "free-exercise clause," and is generally relevant to laws that might limit the practice of minority religions. Thus courts have dealt with issues such as the use of peyote in Native American religious ceremonies, animal sacrifice in Santerian services, and the wearing of special Jewish orthodox head coverings in the armed services (Jelen 2000). State and local governments deal with issues of special religious clothing in public schools and special religious holidays from public employment.

Religious diversity has changed the nature of these issues as well, although here it is more a question of degree rather than kind. Especially in large urban areas near both coasts, governments increasingly confront larger numbers of non-Christian minorities, and with growing numbers these communities have become more confident in requesting freedom to pursue their own religious vision.

Although the nuance in positions on church-state issues is infinite, it is helpful to think of both establishment and free-exercise issues as being debated by two opposing sets of protagonists. On establishment issues, accomodationists argue that the Constitution mandates that the government be neutral among competing religions, but not between religion and the lack of religion. Accomodationists would therefore generally oppose particularistic religious symbols of single Christian denominations, but not the display of more general Christian symbols such as the nativity scene on public property. Accomodationists believe that religion provides an underpinning to social and political life, and that the Judeo-Christian tradition serves to unify the United States (e.g., Reichley 1985). In contrast, separationists believe that the government should be neutral between religion and irreligion. Religion is seen as a potentially divisive force, and government entanglement in religion is seen as a potential threat to religion's power to critique the state (Jelen and Segers 2000).

On free-exercise issues, communitarians argue that certain religious traditions lie outside the moral consensus of society and that their rituals and practices may be accorded somewhat less protection than those of the majority. Elected officials might limit certain religious practices so long as they do not prohibit worship. In contrast, libertarians argue that religious practice is constitutionally protected no matter how unpopular, and that the government should limit religious freedom only in exceptional circumstances (see Reichley 1985 Jelen and Wilcox 1995).

PUBLIC ATTITUDES ON CHURCH-STATE ISSUES IN A TIME OF RELIGIOUS DIVERSITY

In the first major study of public opinion on church-state issues, Jelen and Wilcox (1995) reported that the general public and elites alike support separation of church and state in the abstract but not in the concrete. Majorities simultaneously supported a "high wall" of separation of church and state, but most also supported extensive government endorsement of and support for majority religions. Similarly, there was a consensus that minority religions have a right to their rituals and practices, but there was also widespread support for limiting even the most symbolic public expression of minority religions.

Jelen and Wilcox included in their study a survey of residents of the Washington, D.C. metro area in 1993. Since that time, the religious diversity of the Washington area has grown remarkably. The diversity of religious life in the Washington area is seen in a 10-mile stretch along New Hampshire Avenue in Montgomery County, a suburb of Washington, D.C. Included in this small area are a synagogue, a mosque, a Cambodian Buddhist temple, a Hindu temple, a Unitarian church, and 29 Christian churches, including three Catholic (one of which is Ukrainian), one Ukrainian Orthodox, two Seventh Day Adventist, two Jehovah's Witness Kingdom Halls, and 21 Protestant churches. The Protestants range from Presbyterian, United Methodist, and Lutheran to a large and growing nondenominational Bible church. Some of the Protestant and Catholic churches serve particular immigrant communities, including the Choong-Moo Evangelical Church of Washington, the Sung Hwa Presbyterian Church, and the Our Lady of Vietnam Roman Catholic Church. Although the many religious citizens and residents worship different gods in different languages, they have joined together to lobby government about zoning and to remove graffiti from a mosque (Levine 1997).

Yet the area's religious diversity is significantly undercounted by a census of churches. One small Presbyterian church in Wheaton, Maryland (another Washington suburb) is home to four different congregations, speaking three different languages. After a worship service by a relatively sedate, older congregation of largely white Presbyterians, an affluent congregation of Taiwanese Presbyterians meet and worship in Chinese. Still later the New Baptist Creation Church, an African-American congregation headed by a forceful woman pastor, meets for a lively service. In the late afternoon, the Iglesio Pentecostal Christo Rey (Christ the King Pentecostal Church) holds a Spanish-language service that attracts immigrants from El

Salvador, Nicaragua, and Guatemala and that often lasts more than four hours (Ruane 1999).

In the seven years since Jelen and Wilcox's survey, this religious diversity has increased significantly. Across the region, residents encounter Muslims and Hindus and Sikhs and Buddhists in PTA meetings and at public parks. They listen to recordings of the Koran in taxicabs and hairdresser shops. Many D.C.-area residents have over the past few years had a dramatic increase in their exposure to non-Christian faiths.

How might growing religious diversity affect the substance of church-state attitudes? At the most basic level, the addition of increasing numbers of non-Christians to the population is likely to lead to decreased support for establishment of Christian symbols and practices. A more interesting question, however, is how members of various Christian groups might change their attitudes in response to increased exposure to non-Christian groups.

A religious conflict model might suggest that when the hegemony of majority religious groups is threatened by the rapid influx of those with sharply different beliefs and traditions, religious conflict might result. Orthodox Christians may see growing diversity as threatening their religious hegemony and as undermining the nation's status as a "Christian nation." Within the context of evangelical doctrine, a growing non-Christian minority might be seen as threatening the nation's status as specially blessed by God.

On establishment issues, this might show itself as renewed support for more public displays of majority religious symbols, for example, school prayer and nativity displays. On free-exercise issues, it might manifest itself as support for increased limitations on the displays of nonmajority religious symbols and practices.

A religious exposure model might suggest that interactions with those of other faiths might lessen religious prejudice and increase support for free exercise. This might lead to increased support for displays of nonmajority religious symbols on establishment issues, and less support for limits on free exercise. When Christian mothers trust their children to Muslim daycare providers in northern Virginia, it may become more difficult for either group to harbor narrow prejudices of the other. When Maryland residents ride in cabs driven by Sikhs with special religious attire, it may lessen objections to such attire in public schools. As D.C. residents come to know their Buddhist neighbors, they may be less willing to support school prayers that might isolate and stigmatize their neighbor's children.

Jelen and Wilcox (1995) reported that respondents in focus groups sometimes changed their positions on establishment issues as they confronted the true diversity of their communities. On school prayer, for example, some evangelical Protestants began with the position that all children should listen to a spoken prayer—one that might rotate among the religious traditions present in the classroom. They became less confident of this view when the religious rights of Catholics were included in the religious mix, and abandoned the position if Buddhists were included. These participants objected to having Christian children listen to a Buddhist prayer and many simply abandoned support for spoken prayers in school rather than allow spoken prayers from non-Christian religions.

In this article, we update Jelen and Wilcox's results with data from a similar survey conducted in 2000. This latter survey used identical questions to the 1993 survey and resulted in 349 usable surveys.[2] These data provide a glimpse into the stability and change of church-state issues in a geographic area of growing religious diversity.

CONTINUITY AND CHANGE IN CHURCH-STATE ATTITUDES

A comparison of the two samples supports the notion that religious diversity in the D.C. area has increased. Those who identified with a Christian denomination—mainline or evangelical Protestant or Catholic—decreased from 72 percent in 1993 to 62 percent in 2000. There was an increase in those who identified as Jews, seculars, and eclectically religious, and those outside the Judeo-Christian tradition (Muslims, Hindu, Buddhists, etc) almost doubled. The small sample size in the 2000 survey makes comparisons among smaller religious groups problematic, but the decline in the number of Christians between the two surveys is statistically significant.

Table 1 shows the portion of metro-area residents who took accomodationist positions on establishment issues in 1993 and 2000. Table 2 shows the percentage of respondents who took libertarian positions on free-exercise issues. We begin our discussion with the substance of attitudes in 2000, and then focus on changes over time.

In 2000, minorities of metro-area residents opposed a high wall of separation or supported government efforts to protect a Judeo-Christian heritage or to help religion. But majorities also supported nativity scenes and Menorahs on public property, and both Buddhist and Christian funded chaplains in the military. A substantial majority favored allowing religious student groups to meet on school property after hours, and a narrower minority would allow a moment of silence, both issues that also involve free exercise of religion.

Minorities would require that schools teach Judeo-Christian values, teach creationism as an alternative to evolution, or allow public prayer at high school sporting events. A majority also opposed various provisions to provide public funding for religious education, either through tax deductions, exemptions, or direct government vouchers.[3] These new items suggest at least initial resistance to school choice plans that would channel tax funds into religious schools.

Nearly all respondents in 2000 agreed that people have the right to practice their religion

TABLE 1   Establishment Attitudes in D.C.-Metro Area, 1993–2000 (% Accomodationist)

	1993	*2000*
High wall of separation	19%	23%
Government protect Judeo-Christian heritage	54%	34%**
Government not help religion	24%	24%
Tax deductions for religious school tuition	na	44%
Parents of children in religious schools should subtract cost of tuition from tax bill	na	36%
If children go to religious schools, shouldn't pay taxes to support public schools	na	21%
Government reimburse for costs of religious schools	na	14%
Nativity scene on government property	71%	55%*
Menorah on government property	58%	54%
Christian chaplains for military funded by government	78%	83%
Buddhist chaplains for military funded by government	60%	69%
Require that schools teach Judeo-Christian values	36%	25%*
Teach creationism as an alternative to evolution	47%	34%*
Public prayer at high school sports events	48%	36%*
Moment of silence in schools	64%	56%*
Allow religious groups to hold meetings on school property	64%	70%

no matter how weird it may seem to others, but clearly many D.C.-metro area residents have an impoverished conception of weirdness. Among those who indicated that they believed people had the right to practice strange religions, 6 percent would appear to be willing to ban a turban for a Sikh boy in public school, 30 percent would ban peyote use by Native Americans in their ceremonies, and more than half would apparently ban the sacrifice of a goat by Santerians.

Yet, overall, D.C. metro residents are libertarian. Overwhelming majorities would allow religious headgear for public school children, allow Jews to be excused from work on religious holidays, permit religious leaders to picket pornographic shops, allow fundamentalist preachers to proselytize on college campuses, and oppose infiltration of Moslem groups by the FBI. Majorities would allow conscientious objectors to avoid military conflict, Hare Krishnas to solicit in public airports, and Native Americans to take peyote in their ceremonies.

Large minorities would allow children to be exempt from the Pledge of Allegiance if their religion forbade it and would allow Satan worship. Sizable majorities would ban animal sacrifice, cults from converting teens, and would

allow the state to provide medical care for children of Christian Scientists.

Between 1993 and 2000, aggregate attitudes on abstract and concrete issues were remarkably stable, despite changing political and religious contexts. This suggests that church-state attitudes are anchored in important orientations and values, primarily religion and support for civil liberties. Yet there was some attitude change in this period, and in each case where that change was statistically significant attitudes changed in the same direction: toward more separatism on establishment issues, and more libertarian positions on free exercise.

Metro-area citizens in 2000 were significantly less likely to believe that the government should protect a Judeo-Christian heritage, or compel public schools to teach those values, than were residents in 1993. Support also declined sharply for public displays of nativity scenes, for public prayers at high school sporting events, and for a moment of silence in public schools.

It seems logical that these changes might be related to the changing composition of the metroarea population, especially the decline in the proportion of Christians. Yet when we compared the attitudes of Christians in the two surveys, the results were essentially identical, indeed, support for public prayers at high school sporting events declined more rapidly among Christians than among the overall population. On only one item, the teaching of Judeo-Christian values in public schools, did the increase among Christians narrowly miss statistical significance.

The data in Table 2 show that support for free exercise of religious minorities also increased. Metro residents in 2000 were significantly more supportive of religious headgear by school students, of allowing religious leaders to picket pornographic shops, of Satan worship, animal sacrifice, and Hare Krishna soliciting in airports. Changing cultural contexts probably explain some of this change: in 1993 there were a spate of news stories about Satan worship among high school students that were not repeated in 2000. Moreover, in 1993 many residents recalled the seemingly unavoidable blandishments of Hare Krishnas in public airports, but by 2000 these were at best a distant memory.[4] Once again, these changes are not due to the changing religious composition of the population, for the changes are evident also in the attitudes of Christians.

Taken together, these data provide some support for the notion that increased exposure to citizens with different religious faiths may foster greater tolerance for religious practices and a concomitant decrease in support for public displays of majority religious symbols.

CHANGING STRUCTURE OF CHURCH-STATE ATTITUDES

In their original study, Jelen and Wilcox reported that church-state attitudes were structured along substantive lines. Factor analysis of the 1993 data revealed that Washington metro-area residents distinguished among concrete establishment issues that involved public funds, public schools, and public displays of religion. In 2000, residents drew similar distinctions. The data show that attitudes on public funds for religious schools are distinct from attitudes on teaching Judeo-Christian values and creationism. Attitudes on public funds for military chaplains (Buddhist or Christian) are distinct from those on public displays of religious symbols (the crèche or Menorah). Attitudes on public prayer at high school sporting events are distinct from any of the other attitudes.

TABLE 2   Free Exercise Attitudes, 1993–2000 (% Libertarian)

	1993	*2000*
People have right to practice strange religion	96%	93%
Obey law even if it limits religious freedom	21%	27%
Immigrants should convert to Christianity	89%	85%
Permit religious headgear in schools	82%	90%*
Allow Jews to not work on High Holy days	81%	84%
Allow religious leaders to picket porn shops	65%	75%*
Forbid fundamentalist preachers from evangelizing on college campuses	59%	58%
Allow conscientious objectors in wartime	55%	53%
Require Pledge of Allegiance of all children	44%	45%
FBI infiltrate Moslem groups	81%	86%
Allow Native Americans to take peyote in religious ceremonies	58%	57%
Ban Satan worship	35%	46%*
Ban Hare Krishna solicitations in airports	40%	52%*
Allow animal sacrifice	28%	36%*
Ban unusual cults from converting teens	31%	34%
Christian Scientists can keep kids from medical care	15%	20%

It is in concrete attitudes on free-exercise issues that the 2000 results diverge from those in 1993. In 1993, free-exercise attitudes were structured along a dimension that reflected perceived danger from the nonmajority religious groups. Respondents appeared to distinguish between religions that might convert their children (cults, fundamentalist preachers), and those that might pose a danger to society (Muslims, Satan worshipers, Hare Krishnas soliciting at airports),[5] less dangerous activity (religious headgear in classrooms, Jews missing work on High Holy days, and Native Americans taking peyote in their ceremonies). In addition, a much less important dimension, focused on religion and immigration—the FBI infiltrating Muslim groups and immigrants being encouraged to convert to Christianity.

In 2000, this final, smaller dimension had become paramount, including a large number of items. The principle dimension in concrete church-state attitudes was one of majority versus minority religions. This dimension was defined by the belief that immigrants should convert to Christianity, and by opposition to the view that everyone had a right to freely practice their religion even if it is strange to most Americans. Concrete issues that loaded on this factor included attitudes toward the FBI infiltrating Muslim groups, Jews taking off High Holy days, children wearing religious headgear to schools, forcing students to pledge to the flag, and allowing religious leaders to picket pornographic shops. A second dimension identified dangerous religious groups—in this case Satan worshipers, cults that tried to convert teens, and Hare Krishna solicitors in airports.

We should not read too much into these exploratory factor analyses, but the data do hint that at the same time that attitudes among some metro-area residents are becoming more accommodating of religious minorities, a cultural conflict is brewing between orthodox Christian respondents and religious minorities.

One of the most interesting results from the factor analysis was the shift in loadings for the item about Jews missing work on High Holy days. In 1993, this item loaded with a factor that identified minority religious practices thought to be largely benign (peyote among Native Americans, religious headgear in classrooms). In 2000, peyote remained as a separate item that did not load on either factor, whereas Jewish religious holidays loaded with a factor that might be thought of as a "nativist" religious response. Indeed, the correlation between the question that suggested that immigrants should convert to Christianity and the question on Jewish holy days was 0.11 in 1993 and 0.39 in 2000. Closer analysis suggested that support for allowing Jews to not work on holy days declined among African-Americans.

The other interesting shift was on the "dangerous religion" dimension. In 2000, both Muslims and fundamentalist campus evangelists were no longer part of this dimension. This probably reflects the absence in the news of Islamic terrorist activity in the United States, and the decline in visibility of campuswide evangelists, who used to be a common rite of spring on American colleges and universities.

Of course, the attacks on the World Trade Center and the Pentagon in September 2001 are likely to have greatly increased public support for FBI infiltration of Muslim groups in the United States. In addition, it seems likely that Muslims will be perceived by the public as a dangerous group—far more dangerous than Moonies or fundamentalist preachers on college campuses. Indeed, it may well be that Muslims would anchor a distinctive dimension on church-state attitudes in surveys conducted early in the 21st century.

DISCUSSION

Overall, D.C.-metro areas are less supportive of the public displays of Christian symbols, and more supportive of free exercise by minority religious groups. Moreover, these results hold when comparing only Christians in the two surveys. These data suggest that contact with non-Christians may lead some D.C.-area residents to be more tolerant of religious diversity.

Yet the changing structure of free-exercise attitudes also suggests that many residents are beginning to think of church-state issues as Christians versus non-Christians. Instead of drawing distinctions between groups they consider dangerous, some respondents are now primarily distinguishing between "us and them." This might hint of a future religious conflict.

Further research is needed to help determine the impact of religious diversity on attitudes. Such studies could benefit from questions that ask respondents how often they see residents of different religious faiths, if they know personally someone of another faith, and, perhaps, their knowledge about the worship styles and beliefs of other religions. In addition, contextual analysis could show whether those citizens who live in the most rapidly diversifying parts of the metro area are responding differently from those who live in homogenous neighborhoods and see diversity only in shopping malls or other public places.

NOTES

1. Of course, the First Amendment would equally apply to issues relating to minority religions, but religious minorities seldom have the political power to establish displays of their practices or symbols.

2. The survey was conducted by Georgetown University students, who were trained in the same manner as those who administered the earlier survey. Telephone exchanges were selected to represent the metro area, random digit dialing within those exchanges was used to reach unlisted numbers. The data in both years have been weighted to adjust for a bias toward higher-educated residents. The demographic profile of the sample closely resembles information from Census data.

3. It is interesting that vouchers are much less popular than direct tax rebates. Under a rebate plan, only those who paid sufficient taxes to qualify for the rebate would have government support for tuition; under a voucher plan the poor could also use government money to pay for religious education. It is unclear whether this distinction was understood by respondents.

4. It might also be that the context of pornography changed with greater access to the Internet, which freed those who might wish to consume such materials from the annoyance of picketing preachers.

5. The inclusion of the Hare Krishnas on this factor might suggest a different interpretation—that these religions are seen as simply very different from Christianity. However, anyone who was ever accosted by Krishnas in the 1970s can attest that the danger of violence (by those solicited) was always present.

REFERENCES

JELEN, T. G. 2000. *To serve God and mammon: Church-state relations in American politics.* Boulder, CO: Westview.

JELEN, T. G. and C. WILCOX. 1995. *Public attitudes toward church and state.* Armonk, NY: ME Sharpe.

LEVINE, S. 1997. A place for those who pray; Along Montgomery's "highway to heaven," diverse acts of faith. *Washington Post* August 3:B1.

REICHLEY, A. J. 1985. *Religion in American public life.* Washington, DC: Brookings.

RUANE, M. 1999. A church with four faces. *Washington Post* February 21:A1.

SEGERS, M. C. and T. G. JELEN, 1998. *A wall of separation? Debating the public role of religion.* Lanham, MD: Rowman-Littlefield.

SWANSON, W. 1992. *The Christ child goes to court.* Philadelphia, PA: Temple University Press.

38 Evangelicals in the Power Elite: Elite Cohesion Advancing a Movement

D. MICHAEL LINDSAY

Lindsay contributes to our understanding of religious dimensions of politics and policy-making in this study of 360 evangelical elites. In looking behind the scenes at an elite social group we know little about, we see how powerful evangelicals across many sectors of U.S. society use their shared religious identity, social networks, and evangelical groups and initiatives to build cohesion among themselves. It is important to also note the individual and structural challenges facing elite evangelicals who try to use their power and position to achieve desired cultural changes.

Much of the literature on elite power suggests that those who occupy "commanding positions" in society have deep connections with one another. Typically, these connections develop from shared decision-making (Hunter 1953, Mills 1956), shared backgrounds and experiences (Baltzell 1958, 1964), shared institutional positions (Useem 1984), or a shared social milieu (Bourdieu 1984; Domhoff 1975).... Missing from ... every other analysis of elite power conducted to date—is the important role played by evangelicals who have joined the nation's elite....

The rise of evangelicals to influential positions illustrates a wider point often overlooked in the social movements literature—namely, the role of leaders in a movement's advance. Their role is almost entirely subsumed under the category of resource provision, beyond which the focus then turns to grassroots mobilization....

Not nearly enough attention, however, has been paid to the place of salient religious identity for movement leaders and its implication for existing power structures. I am particularly interested in the ways that evangelicalism has created novel forms of cohesion among public leaders—leaders who head significant institutions within American public life. As others have suggested (Andrews 2001, Minkoff 1997), sympathetic, resource-rich elites can fund organizations and

Source: D. Michael Lindsay, "Evangelicals in the Power Elite: Elite Cohesion Advancing a Movement." *American Sociological Review, Vol. 73, No. 1 (February, 2008), pp. 60–82.*

create politically-advantageous environments for particular movements and, indeed, a range of movement organizations. As Gieryn (1983) argues, leaders can create niches for institutions seeking to differentiate themselves from other entities, and elites can play particularly important roles in setting and maintaining boundaries for movements seeking to advance into new social territory. I use the term "advance" to discuss the evangelical movement's forward momentum. This entails both an extension into different sectors of society—politics and the world of business, for example—as well as the introduction of evangelicalism into society's upper strata.[1]

... Evangelicals were largely ignored in empirical studies of elites conducted in the 1950s through the early 1980s (Baltzell 1964; Domhoff 1975; Keller 1963; Mills 1956). However, evangelicals persisted. Leaders such as Ockenga, Carl F. H. Henry, and Billy Graham—with financial support from business tycoons like J. Howard Pew of Sun Oil Company—established journals such as *Christianity Today* and founded Fuller Theological Seminary, an institution they likened to a "Cal Tech of the evangelical world."[2]

Graham remained popular in the 1960s, but it was an era of widespread social change. Evangelicals were relatively minor players among the cast of powerful social actors of the 1960s and early 1970s. ... In 1976, dubbed "the year of the evangelical," both *Time* and *Newsweek* ran cover stories about the resurgence of conservative Christianity in American public life as Jimmy Carter became the first self-described "born-again"

evangelical in modern history to be elected to the White House. Since then, others have noted the place of evangelical rhetoric and priorities in political discourse (Smith 2006), intellectual debates (Schmalzbauer 2003), and corporate life (Miller 2006).

Scholars have paid more attention to evangelicals in recent years (Balmer 2004, Marsden 2006; Smith 2000; Smith et al. 1998), yet we know practically nothing about adherents who serve in elite positions of public life. In this article, I address this gap and attend to the role of religious identity, social networks, and strategies for influence that have engaged evangelical elites over the last 30 years. Empirical studies often explore the extent to which leaders are united by social backgrounds and worldviews (Baltzell 1958; Domhoff 2006; Dye 2002; Mills 1956) or fragmented and specialized (Keller 1963; Mannheim 1940). My analyses highlight whether or not a segment of the nation's elite are united by a brotherhood of shared evangelical conviction[3] in any meaningful way and, if so, the mechanisms that sustain such unity. ... The analyses offered in this article elucidate the mechanisms that evangelicals have sought to use in realigning the informal power structures among the nation's elite. In this regard, I highlight specifically the efforts, strategies, and overarching goals of evangelical elites, while also considering barriers and limitations that have emerged in their attempt to exercise greater cultural influence. I propose "convening power" as the decisive structural advantage that elites enjoy. And, it is the salience of religious

---

[1]American evangelicalism has evolved as a movement, and this transformation has facilitated its advance. By the term "advance," though, I do not mean to imply that there is a normative ideal for evangelicalism, one that it has somehow reached in its most recent transformation. In this regard, I view the various stages of American evangelicalism discussed in this article as categorically, not ordinally, different. In this article, I treat American evangelicalism as a social movement, following the lead of Young (2006), Smith (1996), and others.

[2]Both California Institute of Technology and Fuller Theological Seminary are located in Pasadena, California.

[3]Nash's study (1994) confirms the general impression that evangelical public leaders are almost entirely white males. Hence, "brotherhood" is an appropriate term. By evangelical "convictions," I mean norms, reasoning, and ideology—matters of belief. I define "evangelical" as a branch of conservative Christianity that affirms (1) the Bible as the ultimate religious authority for faith and daily life; (2) the importance of a personal relationship with God through Jesus Christ (which typically entails a "born again" experience); and (3) an activist approach to faith whereby religious convictions shape how an adherent interacts with others.

identity to evangelical elites that makes their convening power especially noteworthy. . . .

DATA AND METHODS

I conducted and analyzed semistructured interviews with 360 elite informants in six arenas of influence: (1) government/politics, (2) arts/entertainment/media, (3) religion, (4) the nonprofit/social sector, (5) higher education, and (6) business/corporate life. Because I was particularly interested in the role of the evangelical movement among America's leadership cohort, practically all of the religious leaders I interviewed were evangelical. . . .

Informants include two former presidents of the United States; 48 Cabinet secretaries and senior White House staffers; 101 CEOs or senior executives at large firms (both public and private); three dozen accomplished Hollywood professionals; more than 10 leaders from the world of professional athletics; and approximately 200 leaders from the artistic, nonprofit, educational, and philanthropic arenas. . . . Table 1 details the professional background of study informants, including a list of representative titles held by informants, organizations they lead, and cultural goods they produce. . . .

Elite education remains an important determinant to elite power. Among those who attended highly selective institutions,[7] a plurality earned a degree from Harvard (11 percent). With regard to the racial and ethnic profile of study participants, . . . this study's informants are almost entirely white (95 percent). The few people of color in this study (African American, Asian American, and Hispanic) attend mostly white congregations and affiliate with evangelical groups and initiatives that serve a largely white constituency. . . . In this study,

10 percent of the public leaders are women, although there may be a slight bias in that number; I intentionally oversampled women. . . .

RESULTS

This study confirms the general impression that evangelicals have become more prominent within the power elite over the last 30 years, even though the number of self-identified evangelicals in the United States has not changed dramatically since the late 1970s (Hackett and Lindsay 2004). Demographic change explains part of this development. A segment of the evangelical movement today is wealthier than ever before (Nash 1994), more prominent in national politics (Martin 1996), and has made remarkable gains in higher education (Riley 2005). All of this is associated with elite status, and indeed, many evangelicals in this study come from elite backgrounds. With a net worth exceeding $8 billion, Philip Anschutz is one of the world's wealthiest evangelicals. Along the same lines, one knowledgeable informant told me he visited with 20 evangelical families over the course of a single year, each of whom had a net worth in excess of $1 billion. Beyond wealth, evangelicals have attained levels of elite education that is on par with other elites. . . .

Religious Identity

The religious profile of these public leaders looks different from the general evangelical population. Over half (56 percent) made a significant spiritual decision about their evangelical faith after age 17, and nearly one-third (29 percent) do not come from families that attended church—a figure double the general population (14 percent according to 1992 to 1998 aggregated Gallup Poll data). Across sectors, I found scores of public leaders who embraced the evangelical faith while occupying the corridors of power. This happened across social sectors—in both business and Hollywood—and across political divides. In fact,

---

[7]The following institutions are coded "highly selective": the eight Ivy League campuses (Brown, Columbia, Cornell, Dartmouth, Harvard, University of Pennsylvania, Princeton, and Yale) as well as the University of Chicago, Duke University, Oxford University, and Stanford University.

TABLE 1   Professional Descriptive Statistics of Informants, PLATINUM Study, Phase 1, 2003 to 2006

Industry and Sector Details	*Frequency*	
Government		*Select Positions among Informants*[a]
Carter White House	2	President of the United States
		Deputy White House Chief of Staff
Reagan White House	7	Attorney General
		Secretary of the Treasury
		Secretary of the Interior
		Secretary of Energy
		Surgeon General
		Counselor to the President
		National Security Advisor
Bush (41) White House	10	President of the United States
		White House Chief of Staff
		Secretary of State
		Secretary of Health and Human Services
		Solicitor General
		Chairman, Federal Communications Commission
Clinton White House	7	Deputy Secretary of Defense
		Secretary of the Navy
		Administrator, USAID
		Ambassador-at-Large for International Religious Freedom
Bush (43) White House	22	Secretary of Commerce
		Chair, White House Council of Economic Advisors
		Assistant to the President
		Senior Advisor to the President
		Director, Office of Personnel Management
Business		*Select Companies among Informants*[c]
Mining/Oil and Gas	8	Texaco, ConocoPhillips, Halliburton
Utilities	5	AES, The Southern Company
Manufacturing	12	Herman Miller, Boeing, Interstate Batteries, Raytheon
Wholesale Trade	2	Hughes Supply Company
Retail Trade	11	Wal-Mart, Target, Helzberg's Diamonds, Anne Klein II,
		Kay-Bee Toys, Laura Ashley, Lenox, Macy's, JC Penny
Transportation	4	Continental Airlines, Alaska Air Group, Burlington Northern Santa Fe
Information	11	Intel, Apple, Cisco Systems, Borders
Finance and Insurance	17	State Street Investment Corporation, Keiner Perkins Caufield &
		Byers, Colonial Penn Life Insurance, Prudential Financial Services
Real Estate	10	CB Richard Ellis, Fieldstone Communities, Trammell Crow
Professional, Scientific, and Technical Services	11	ServiceMaster, Oxford Analytica
Healthcare and Social Assistance	3	Sunrise Assisted Living
Arts, Entertainment, and Recreation	2	Electronic Arts, The Walt Disney Company
Accommodation and Food Services	9	Chick-fil-A, Ritz-Carlton, Tyson Foods, PepsiCo
Religion		*Select Institutions among Informants*
Denominational Bodies	7	North American Mission Board, National Association of Evangelicals, Willow Creek Association, Cooperative Baptist Fellowship
Parachurch Organizations	12	Alpha, Billy Graham Evangelistic Association, Purpose Driven
Church Leadership	12	Willow Creek Community Church, Menlo Park Presbyterian Church, Redeemer Presbyterian Church
Higher Education		*Select Institutions among Informants*
Professors	8	Notre Dame, Harvard
Administrators	16	The Julliard School, Harvard Business School, Wheaton College, Wake Forest
Ancillary Organizations	14	Council for Christian College and Universities

Continued

TABLE 1   *(continued)*

Nonprofit Sector		*Select Institutions among Informants*
Philanthropy and Fundraising	19	Fieldstead and Company, The John Templeton Foundation, The Gathering, Stewardship Foundation
Social Service	4	World Vision, International Justice Mission
Education	11	The Renaissance Institute, Institute for Global Engagement
The Arts	6	International Arts Movement
Advocacy	3	Families Northwest
Think Tanks	4	Ethics & Public Policy Center, Center for Public Justice
Leadership	18	CEO Forum, Young Presidents' Organization
Culture		*Selected Cultural Goods Produced or Directed by Informants*
Television/Film Executive	18	*Star Wars, The Passion of the Christ, Home Improvement, Raiders of the Lost Ark, That 70s Show, Happy Days, Mission Impossible, Charlie's Angels, Hawaii Five-O, Sesame Street, The Question of God, The Chronicles of Narnia, Because of Winn Dixie, JAG, Touched by an Angel, Planet of the Apes, X Men*
Actor/Entertainer	8	*Matlock, Live with Regis and Kathie Lee, Kids Say the Darndest Things, St. Elsewhere*
Writer/Publishing	9	*Batman Forever, Books & Culture, Elf, Image*
Media/Journalism	14	*ABC World News Tonight, Fortune, Newsweek, The Dallas Morning News,* The Gallup Poll, *Time*
Artist	5	National Council on the Arts
Professional Athletics	19	Miami Dolphins, Professional Golfers Association, Arizona Diamondbacks, San Antonio Spurs, Cincinnati Reds, Phoenix Suns, Arizona Cardinals, Seattle Seahawks, World Professional Figure Skating, U.S. Professional Tennis Association

[a] Because of space constraints, listed positions are not exhaustive; they are simply a representative selection of roles held by informants.

. . .

[c] Informants serve or have served in executive positions at these companies, most often as president, chairman, or chief executive officer.

Robert "Bud" McFarlane, who served as National Security Advisor during the Reagan administration, recounted his spiritual pilgrimage in ways that resonated with that of Alonzo McDonald, one of President Carter's chief advisors. When I noted this, McFarlane responded:

I think it is a process of maturing that everybody goes through. There's nothing unique about me. At the time it led to me asking, "Well, if you believe passionately as I do in the salvation that I have experienced through the love of Jesus Christ and his sacrifice, then you must ask, 'What is the highest and best use of me?'" . . . [I determined that I] could be just as effective [as a Christian witness] if not more . . . in the military [as opposed to the ministry because there] are a lot more folks that you could reach in the foxhole than in the narthex.

This sense of embracing an evangelical faith and then using it in one's leadership motivated nearly all (91 percent) of the leaders I interviewed. For many, faith motivated them to action and provided a sense of meaningful vocation for their work (55 percent).

. . . Table 2 enumerates the frequency of various religious variables among the 203 public leaders interviewed.

There are a number of common elements to the spiritual lives of these informants. Beyond the prevalence of faith in the exercise of their public leadership and the ways in which Christianity provides a meaningful framework for their sense of professional vocation, most of these leaders (67 percent) report regularly talking with their professional colleagues about their faith. In most contexts, this involved alluding to one's faith when talking with a colleague about a personal concern (such as the

TABLE 2   Frequency of Religious Identity Variables among Evangelical Public Leaders (PLATINUM Study Phase 1, 2003 to 2006)

	Percent	*N*
Made a significant spiritual decision after age 17	56	113
Invokes personal faith in public leadership	91	185
Faith provides a sense of "calling" or meaningful vocation for public leadership	55	111
Faith became more important after occupying elite position	66	133
Hesitant to describe self as "evangelical"	23	47
Family did not attend church while growing up	29	58
Low denominational loyalty	59	120
Talk to colleagues about faith on a regular basis	67	136
Actively involved in a faith-based small group	57	116
Report "ambition" is a personal struggle with one's faith and public leadership	34	69
Have served on an evangelical parachurch board	72	146
Has a family foundation for personal philanthropy	24	48
Is pessimistic about America's declining moral state	22	44

Note: N = 203

illness or death of a loved one) or an invitation to attend a Bible study or church event. Rarely did this involve an explicitly evangelistic conversation, and practically none of the informants reported tension with colleagues over the invocation of personal faith at work.

Informants are far more loyal to faith-based small groups than to particular congregations or denominations. In fact, denominational loyalty is relatively low among these leaders; nearly three in five (59 percent) switched denominations at least once since turning 18. Fifty-seven percent of these leaders are currently involved in a small fellowship group. ... These small groups and involvement as a board member of an evangelical parachurch organization are two of the most important contexts where these leaders regularly engage their faith among peers.

Although the content of informants' evangelical faith was relatively uniform—expressing traditional evangelical beliefs about the Bible, Jesus, and personal spiritual journeys—there were noticeable differences on what the term "evangelical" means. In fact, 23 percent of informants affirmed the characteristics most scholars use to define evangelicals (Bebbington 1989; Hackett and Lindsay 2004; Martin 1996; Smith et al. 1998) but did not like to describe themselves as evangelical. Some of the most common

phrases informants used to describe what "evangelical" means include "orthodox Christian faith," "a biblical faith" that is "personally appropriated," "born again," and "theologically conservative." Not a single informant associated their evangelical faith with the Religious Right, ... As an aside, only 43 percent of informants said they were Republicans.

Despite these differences, personal religious identity is strikingly salient for the evangelical public leaders I interviewed. Evangelicalism is a faith a believer "owns" himself; most evangelical churches require adherents to make a personal profession of faith, as opposed to simply inheriting the faith from one's parents. It also seems to be a faith that compels leaders to action, and the wider evangelical movement has spurred the ascent and sustained spiritual cohesion among many of them. Between 1976 and 2006, more than 100 evangelical groups and initiatives were launched to support the spread of evangelicalism into higher circles. These included programs in every center of elite cultural production—such as Washington and Los Angeles—as well as efforts aimed at multiple domains. I found four arenas of particular activity: politics, arts/entertainment/media, higher education, and business. Groups such as Impact XXI, The Trinity Forum, and a Washington-based group called the Fellowship reach leaders from government, business, entertainment, and the nonprofit world. They sponsor Bible studies (often conducted via conference call), conferences, retreats, and regular support groups. In total, I identified 142 groups and initiatives directed to various elite constituencies within the broader evangelical movement.

. . .

Among the various evangelical initiatives—which include publications, parachurch organizations, small group ministries, regular events, and training programs—cohesion is formed across sectors through interpersonal friendships. In this way, shared religious faith provides a framework for ongoing interaction and the development of personal ties. The informality and occasional nature of some of these interactions create many different kinds of relations—deep friendships for some and casual acquaintances for others. While these friendships and the shared spiritual identity that facilitates their formation are mutually reinforcing, without the religious component these ties would be far less salient.

Some programs are more explicitly focused on elite constituents in particular domains. For example, the White House Christian Fellowship, while it invites speakers from other sectors (most often the arts and entertainment world), is a gathering of Christians in a single sector within a single institution. Analogous ventures can be found in business, higher education, and entertainment. . . .

Against the backdrop of the numerous affiliations these leaders have (in their professional and personal lives), the salience of these ministries and fellowship groups is significant because these are *the* most important groups with which many are regularly involved. They are not simply affiliations; they involve bonds of loyalty cemented through spiritual cohesion. Across this study, informants related stories of incredible commitment to others within these circles of spiritual friendship. For example, CEO Tom Morgan spoke about the support he felt from Douglas Holladay, a fellow evangelical business leader, when his company imploded and his personal fortune (including a beloved family farm) was at great risk. When I interviewed Morgan in his Orlando office, he related the following incident:

> Doug called me one day and said, "I just want you to know I'm praying for you through this thing, and I know how hard it is. . . . I know you're concerned about your farm and [that] you may lose it all. . . . I want you to know that's not going to happen. I'll buy it if I have to."

This example points to the empathetic support that many of these evangelical public leaders provide one another.

Thirty-two informants related similar experiences. Informants reported assistance with job-related and financial crises, family troubles, challenges within their organizations, and personal health issues. These relational ties were developed through various evangelical groups, and the groups provided powerful reinforcements for those involved. Two interesting trends appeared: First, the stories of loyal friendship occurred most often among leaders in politics, rather than leaders in business. Only one Hollywood informant related a story along these lines. Second, not a single woman talked about this kind of friendship. . . .

Networks: the "Fulcrum" of Evangelical Cohesion

. . . I found that the evangelical parachurch sector provided a critical institutional environment for generating cross-domain cohesion among evangelical public leaders. In particular, . . . service on the boards of these large nonprofit organizations provided social networks among elites from different sectors and facilitated the establishment of loose, informal alliances among evangelicals in powerful places.

Looking at the boards of 10 leading evangelical organizations, I found that most had representatives drawn from several elite sectors. Some, like Christianity Today International and Fuller Theological Seminary, draw

TABLE 3   Sector Representation among Directors at 10 Leading Evangelical Organizations[a]

Organization	Headquarters and Year Founded	Government & Politics	Business & Corporate Life	Arts, Entertainment, & Media	Religion[b]	Nonprofit Sector[c]	Higher Education
Billy Graham Evangelistic Association	Charlotte, NC (1950)	2	7	1	4	5	1
Christianity Today International	Carol Stream, IL (1956)	1	3	1	1	3	3
Evangelical Council for Financial Accountability	Washington, DC (1979)	—	3	1	—	9	1
Focus on the Family	Colorado Springs, CO (1977)	3	5	—	—	4	—
Fuller Theological Seminary	Pasadena, CA (1947)	1	18	1	5	4	3
InterVarsity Christian Fellowship	Madison, WI (1941)	—	9	—	2	2	5
Prison Fellowship Ministries	Washington, DC (1976)	1	9	—	1	4	3
Wheaton College	Wheaton, IL (1860)	1	9	1	1	4	4
World Vision	Seattle, WA (1950)	2	3	1	4	7	3
Young Life	Colorado Springs, CO (1941)	—	18	—	1	3	2

[a] Directors are classified according to the category that helped them secure a board seat if they are eligible for multiple categories or are retired. Classifications are based on data gathered through interviews with organizational executives and fellow board members, board archives, and observation at board meetings.

[b] Category includes church leaders and denominational executives.

[c] Category includes the CEO of the evangelical organization profiled (unless it is an institution of higher education) as well as directors whose primary role involves relations with the major donor community.

representatives from government, business, entertainment, religion, the nonprofit sector, and higher education whereas others do not have quite as wide a spread. Informants suggested that board meetings for these organizations are some of the most sustained dialogue they regularly have with leaders from other sectors. Although they claim not to discuss "business matters" at board meetings, nearly all acknowledge that regular interactions afforded by their joint involvement in these established relationships of trust and mutual understanding "came in handy" when they need expert advice or a personal introduction to someone in a field different from their own. As Table 3 shows, the largest representation of directors' seats (84) comes from the business and corporate sector. Arts, entertainment, and media have the smallest representation with only six directors' seats. Within evangelical parachurch governance, the most common form of network overlap involved public leaders from business and the nonprofit sector.

WORLD VISION: A CASE OF STRUCTURAL COINCIDENCE.   When I observed the board meeting of World Vision—one of evangelicalism's largest organizations[8]—I was struck by the number of representatives from different institutional sectors: government, business, the media, and religion. Board documents show that the presence of these diverse representatives is intentional. At every board meeting, there is a spreadsheet detailing the social, religious, and professional profiles of current members. Internal board documents state that World Vision's board *must* have representation from four sectors critical to the organization: individuals who have experience (1) with the poor, (2) with financial management, (3) with the major donor community in the United

[8]In 2005, World Vision had annual revenues of $905 million, contributed from more than 5 million donors and volunteers. As a Christian relief and development organization, World Vision's programs reached more than 100 million people in nearly 100 countries in 2005.

States, and (4) with the church and ministry world. Other sectors are also included: relief and development, law, education, medicine, human resources, the media, fundraising, governmental affairs, and senior corporate leadership. World Vision board meetings provide opportunities for evangelical public leaders to interact, develop friendship ties, and collaborate on projects. For several years, World Vision has been the site of leadership personnel overlap for the evangelical community, the corporate world, USAID, and the Department of State. The State Department's first ambassador-at-large for International Religious Freedom, Robert Seiple, assumed the post after stepping down as CEO of World Vision in 1998. His successor, Richard Stearns, came to World Vision after stints as CEO of Parker Brothers Games and Lenox, the fine china firm. Brady Anderson, the USAID administrator under Clinton, currently sits on the World Vision board, and the USAID administrator during President George W. Bush's first term, Andrew Natsios, once served as a vice president at World Vision. This overlap of individuals and institutional sectors can also be found among other parachurch boards of directors; examples include Prison Fellowship Ministries, Christianity Today International, and Fuller Theological Seminary.

The Evangelical Advance And Countervailing Forces

Evangelicals have acquired and deployed resources to create a social environment that is amenable to network formation.... Social settings like boarding schools and debutante societies provided the contexts that facilitated close relationships among the nation's leaders. While these elements of the social elite can still be found today, the thrust of new social movements has facilitated the formation of additional modes of social organization. As new networks and elite organizations have formed within the evangelical movement, they have fulfilled a similar function, enabling public leaders who share religious commitments to develop personal and professional networks.

Network formation is critical to the advance of a new idea or a social agenda advancements come through well-connected leaders. I found multiple examples of overlapping networks of public leaders: evangelicals in the White House knew evangelicals in Hollywood, and vice versa. Moreover, these were not simply acquaintance networks; many times they were collaborators. For example, several years ago a group of Washington evangelicals established a group called "Faith and Law." Most of the participants are senior Congressional or White House staffers. At one Faith and Law gathering, a woman talked about her interest in the world of fashion and entertainment; even though she was serving in government, she was interested in "making a difference" through the entertainment world. After that meeting, she and some of her Faith and Law colleagues decided to see what difference they could make as a group. They arranged a breakfast meeting among several high-ranking government officials with Philip Anschutz, a fellow evangelical who is an incredibly successful business executive.[9] After the breakfast meeting, Anschutz agreed to convene a group of business leaders and media "gatekeepers," including then-chairman of AOL Steve Case, who is also part of the larger evangelical world. Out of that meeting, two initiatives were started, one of which commissioned a Harvard study to monitor the media's effect on children....

In the face of these opportunities and possibilities, however, I found a number of countervailing forces. Larger-than-life egos inhibited cooperation among elite evangelicals, and one-third of informants (34 percent) reported struggling with their personal ambitions and their faith. Business leaders, college presidents, and politicians also talked about the bureaucratic challenges they face when they attempt to infuse more religion into public institutions that serve a pluralistic constituency. For instance, George Bennett, an evangelical in Boston, served as Harvard's treasurer for several years and was a member of the powerful Harvard Corporation—the seven-member board that runs the university. He very much wanted to resurrect the Christian ethos that characterized Harvard's past, but in the end, Bennett concludes he did not have much of a spiritual impact on the campus. ...

Beyond institutional inertia, evangelical ambitions have been chastened by philosophical differences among the faithful. ... These differences of opinion can be powerful barriers to achieving particular goals. ... Currently, disagreement abounds on whether the movement ought to champion environmental concerns or maintain its traditional focus on abortion and homosexuality.

DISCUSSION

Convening Power

What difference do these networks make in actual policy deliberations or elite cultural production? ...

Convening power falls within a more efficacious perspective that regards power as a transaction between social actors. Convening power involves the ability to bring disparate

groups together, for example, by introducing a congressional staffer to a senior media executive. It is the ability to set agendas and to coordinate activity, but it is more than simply establishing a legislative agenda. It entails interaction and coordinated effort where elites are able to bridge network disjunctures for mutual advantage. Elites in a variety of spheres are able to draw on their convening power to bring other elite actors together. Kerbo (1993) argues that elite power is the power over social networks; convening power specifies the content of that structural advantage. It enables elites to marshal resources, share information, and deflect criticism. Through these networks, elites are brought together; they then introduce and recruit other elites to join their causes.

...

Convening power, however, is not enough to accomplish particular goals: that is a function of decision-making power. Obviously, bringing parties together is fundamental to decision-making, but overlapping networks, in and of themselves, can't produce specific outcomes. A leader can bring people together to discuss an issue, but she can't make them act. Convening power leads to cohesion, but not necessarily collusion. I found little support for the hypothesis that evangelicals are colluding to take over America, as some have suggested (Kaplan 2004; Phillips 2006). Cultural influence has certainly been evangelicalism's goal, but dozens of informants talked about the difficulties they face when trying to steer large bureaucracies or powerful institutions toward their evangelical aims. ... This inertia, coupled with the range of opinions on particular politics and strategies of action, has diminished the consensus required for a collusive takeover. Cohesion has, of course, emerged from the shared religious identity of evangelical elites. But to determine if these overlapping networks actually result in the achievement of particular outcomes, one must analyze the mechanisms of decision-making

---

[9]It is important to say that the "difference" advocated by these evangelical leaders was not a sectarian aim; as they related the story, it largely involved concern over the effect of mainstream media on children. Mores on what was deemed "appropriate" content for the media was, of course, born of evangelical conviction. This was not a religious aim per se, but the moral conviction that something ought to be done and the drawing of boundaries between "acceptable" and "unacceptable" content were certainly shaped by evangelical norms. Further, my sense is that these leaders had deeper levels of conviction on the matter because of their evangelical faith.

that operate in a specific setting, in all its particularity. . . .

Modeling Elite Agency: How Evangelicals Could Bring Social Change

How do the contributions of individual, motivated leaders result in cultural change? The rising prominence of American evangelicalism since 1976 provides a good example of how a movement once relegated to the "disadvantaged ranks of the stratification system" (Wuthnow 1995) might attempt to move into the corridors of power through restructuring elite networks. . . .

Within American evangelicalism, I found two important mechanisms that have generated robust networks and alliances among elite actors: parachurch boards (which intentionally draw leaders together from different sectors) and specialized initiatives targeting public leaders, hundreds of which have been launched or expanded over the last 30 years. These reinforce a shared identity that provides a binding element among public leaders. . . .

The convening power of evangelicals has been so potent because their religious identity is so salient, even as they have risen in education and socioeconomic status (Smith and Sikkink 2003). Shared spiritual identity builds cohesion among leaders who are separated geographically and institutionally. Evangelicalism provides a moral framework through which these public leaders make sense of their lives and endow their work with special meaning. Of course, evangelical identity is but one of many salient identities these leaders must manage in their lives. As Cadge and Davidman (2006) show, religious adherents blend different parts of their lives together creatively in their own spiritual narratives. The competing logics of action that exist within the different realms of religion and the professions require ongoing negotiation for individuals who exist in both worlds. This is especially important for leaders whose actions influence not only their own lives, but the lives

of many others as well. I found that the demands of that negotiation process are what brought many of these leaders into spiritual fellowship with one another. Most of their small groups center around the challenges of being a faithful evangelical, a successful professional, an engaged family member, and a virtuous person—all at the same time. The spiritual friendships formed in these small groups cement deep ties of loyalty, and while practically on one I interviewed would acknowledge that these ties directly influence business decisions or political dealings, it is inconceivable that such factors have not been at work.

Despite the number of high-ranking evangelicals I found, one must not overstate the movement's influence. Even within the current Bush administration—the most evangelical in modern history—evangelicals still represent a minority among the senior staff. Jews and secularists are just as prevalent. Moreover, in Hollywood, only one evangelical, Philip Anschutz, has the power and resources to "green light" a movie project. Among film directors with active careers between 2000 and 2005, no more than 5 percent could be considered conservative Christians, and among those, many would not necessarily be considered "evangelical." Among successful actors, the number of evangelicals is even lower (Lindsay 2007). The reason evangelicals have received so much attention in recent years is because they represent a prominent, new group entering elite ranks. . . .

Evangelical institutions have facilitated the rise of networks that bring leaders from different parts of society together. This cross-domain cohesion, which accompanied the evangelical movement's advance, is difficult to achieve, and in our highly differentiated, segmented society, its emergence is noteworthy. Evangelicalism's rise points to various forms of social organization that facilitate the rise of any movement—cohesive networks, strategic resource allocation, and cultural production, among others. . . .

Evangelicalism, as a movement grounded in religious conviction, has been particularly effective in generating cohesion among elite actors. Moreover, its flexible institutional structure enabled it to spawn initiatives and organizational forms that have brought the movement into the corridors of elite power.

REFERENCES

ANDREWS, KENNETH T. 2001. "Social Movements and Policy Implementation: The Mississippi Civil Rights Movement and the War on Poverty, 1965 to 1971." *American Sociological Review* 66:71–95.

BALMER, RANDALL. 2004. *Encyclopedia of Evangelicalism*. Waco, TX: Baylor University Press.

BALTZELL, E. Digby. 1958. *Philadelphia Gentlemen: The Making of a National Upper Class*. New York: Free Press.

———. 1964. *The Protestant Establishment: Aristocracy and Caste in America*. New York: Random House.

BEBBINGTON, DAVID. 1989. *Evangelicalism in Modern Britain: A History from the 1730s to the 1980s*. London, UK: Unwin Hyman.

BOURDIEU, PIERRE. 1984. *Distinction: A Social Critique of the Judgment of Taste*. Translated by R. Nice. Cambridge, MA: Harvard University Press.

CADGE, WENDY and LYNN DAVIDMAN. 2006. "Ascription, Choice, and the Construction of Religious Identities in the Contemporary United States." *Journal for the Scientific Study of Religion* 45:23–38.

DOMHOFF, G. WILLIAM. 1975. *The Bohemian Grove and Other Retreats: A Study in Ruling-Class Cohesiveness*. New York: Harper Torchbooks.

———. 2006. *Who Rules America? Power, Politics, and Social Change*. 5th ed. New York: McGraw-Hill.

DYE, THOMAS R. 2002. *Who Is Running America: The Bush Restoration?* 7th ed. Upper Saddle River, NJ: Prentice Hall.

GIERYN, THOMAS F. 1983. "Boundary-Work and the Demarcation of Science from Non-Science: Strains and Interests in Professional Ideologies of Scientists." *American Sociological Review* 48:781–95.

HACKETT, CONRAD and D. MICHAEL LINDSAY. 2004. "Measuring Evangelicalism: Consequences of Different Operationalization Strategies." Presented at the Annual Meeting of the Society for the Scientific Study of Religion, October 21–24, Kansas City, MO.

HUNTER, FLOYD. 1953. *Community Power Structure: A Study of Decision Makers*. Chapel Hill, NC: University of North Carolina Press.

KAPLAN, ESTHER. 2004. *With God on Their Side*. New York: The New Press.

KELLER, SUZANNE. 1963. *Beyond the Ruling Class: Strategic Elites in Modern Society*. New York: Random House.

KERBO, HAROLD R. 1993. "Upper Class Power." Pp. 223–37 in *Power in Modern Societies*, edited by M. E. OLSEN and M. N. MARGER. Boulder, CO: Westview Press.

LINDSAY, D. Michael. 2007. *Faith in the Halls of Power: How Evangelicals Joined the American Elite*. New York: Oxford University Press.

MANNHEIM, KARL. 1940. *Man and Society in an Age of Reconstruction: Studies in Modern Social Structure*. New York: Harcourt, Brace, and World.

MARSDEN, GEORGE. 2006. *Fundamentalism and American Culture*. 2nd ed. New York: Oxford University Press.

MARTIN, WILLIAM C. 1996. *With God on Our Side: The Rise of the Religious Right in America*. New York: Broadway Books.

MILLER, DAVID. 2006. *God At Work*. New York: Oxford University Press.

MILLS, C. WRIGHT. 1956. *The Power Elite*. New York: Oxford University Press.

MINKOFF, DEBRA C. 1997. "The Sequencing of Social Movements." *American Sociological Review* 62:779–99.

NASH, LAURA L. 1994. *Believers in Business*. Nashville, TN: Thomas Nelson.

PHILLIPS, KEVIN. 2006. *American Theocracy: The Peril and Politics of Radical Religion, Oil, and Borrowed Money in the 21st Century*. New York: Viking.

RILEY, NAOMI SCHAEFER. 2005. *God on the Quad: How Religious Colleges and the Missionary Generation are Changing America*. New York: St. Martin's Press.

SCHMALZBAUER, JOHN. 2003. *People of Faith: Religious Conviction in American Journalism and Higher Education*. Ithaca, NY: Cornell University Press.

SMITH, CHRISTIAN. 1996. *Disruptive Religion: the Force of Faith in Social Movement Activism*. New York: Routledge.

———. 2000. *Christian America? What Evangelicals Really Want*. Berkeley, CA: University of California Press.

SMITH, CHRISTIAN, with MICHAEL EMERSON, SALLY GALLAGHER, PAUL KENNEDY, and DAVID SIKKINK. 1998. *American Evangelicalism: Embattled and Thriving*. Chicago, IL: University of Chicago Press.

SMITH, CHRISTIAN and DAVID SIKKINK. 2003. "Social Predictors of Retention in and Switching from the Religious Faith of Family of Origin: Another Look using Religious Tradition Self-Identification." *Review of Religious Research* 45:188–206.

SMITH, GARY SCOTT. 2006. *Faith and the Presidency: From George Washington to GEORGE W. BUSH*. New York: Oxford University Press.

USEEM, MICHAEL. 1984. *The Inner Circle: Large Corporations and the Rise of Business Political Activity in the U.S. and the U.K.* New York: Oxford University Press.

WUTHNOW, ROBERT. 1989. *Communities of Discourse*. Cambridge, MA: Harvard University Press.

———. 1995. *Christianity in the Twenty-First Century: Reflections on the Challenges Ahead*. New York: Oxford University Press.

Young, Michael P. 2006. *Bearing Witness against Sin: The Evangelical Birth of the American Social Movement*. Chicago: University of Chicago Press.

Reading 39   The Role of Religion in International Terrorism

THOMAS J. BADEY

As the title tells us, Badey asks what role religion plays in international terrorism. His answer? Its role has been greatly exaggerated; other factors are the primary cause of terrorism, not religion itself. Be sure to understand his argument. What evidence is used? And ultimately, do you agree?

Over the past decade, the topic of religion has played an increasingly prominent role in discussions about international terrorism. Fears concerning the resurgence of what some have called fundamentalist Islam have spawned visions of inevitable clashes of civilizations (Huntington 1996). Even before the events of September 11, 2001, the term religious terrorism had become a staple in the vocabulary of many policy-makers. In light of recent events, vital questions concerning the ideologies of violence and the role of religion in international terrorism must be answered. Does so-called religious terrorism really exist? What is the function of religion in international terrorism? Is religion the cause of terrorist violence, or is it simply a convenient way of polarizing populations? In this paper, I argue that religion is not the cause of contemporary international terrorism. Instead, it is an ideology, which like communism and nationalism, is used to mobilize populations toward political violence.

THE PROBLEM OF DEFINING RELIGIOUS TERRORISM

One fundamental problem in the study and analysis of contemporary international terrorism is the lack of an accepted definition of the problem. Despite decades of academic literature on the subject of terrorism, no commonly accepted definition has been found. Rather than restating previous arguments concerning the ongoing definitional dilemma, international terrorism is defined here as "the repeated use of politically motivated violence with coercive intent, by non-state actors affecting more than one state" (Badey 1998, p. 92).

. . .Operational definitions of religious terrorism, particularly those that can be used to distinguish it from other types of terrorism, are rare. Barry Rubin has made one of the more interesting contributions to this discussion. Rather than focusing on terrorism, Rubin attempts to define radical (Islamic) fundamentalism and in doing so provides what he describes as a three-part definition of the movement's key premises:

1. Islam is the answer to the problems of their society, country and region.
2. Implementing Islam and resolving the huge problems of the peoples and states require the seizure and holding of power by radical Islamic groups. . . .
3. The only proper interpretation of Islam is the one offered by a specific political group and its leaders (Rubin 1998, p. 2).

It is interesting to note that if one were to substitute the term "Islam" in each of the key premises with "communism" or "nationalism" and apply them to various groups engaged in international terrorism, the basic premises would still be true.

Because there seems to be no effective way to distinguish between the majority of incidents generally described as political terrorism and religious terrorism, two possible conclusions can be reached. Either our study and understanding of the religious dynamic in contemporary international terrorism is inadequate, or there are no characteristic features that distinguish the two.

IDEOLOGIES AND INTERNATIONAL TERRORISM

Some argue that religion, particularly a specific brand of Islamic fundamentalist extremism, has become a major ideological force in contemporary international terrorism. Ideologies are systems of beliefs that justify behavior. They serve three primary functions: (1)

They polarize and mobilize populations toward specific objectives; (2) They create a sense of security by establishing systems of norms and values in the pursuit of common objectives; and (3) They provide a basis for the justification and rationalization of human behavior. While some may argue that ideologies provide the very basis for the political, economic, social, and security institutions of a society, it is the perceived failure of the existing institutions and ideologies for particular groups, which drives the desire for change. In Weberian terms, during periods of heightened uncertainty, people seek stability by subscribing to new norms, values, and ideologies advocated by charismatic leaders. The norms and values advocated are assumed to provide solutions to existing problems. If successful, this process results in the codification of new norms and values and a shift in the ideological foundations on which a society is based.

Three major types of ideologies have influenced and shaped the evolution of contemporary international terrorism since the late 1960s. Communism and left-wing revolutionary philosophies espoused by organizations such as the Red Army Faction of Germany, the Red Brigades of Italy, and the Popular Front for the Liberation of Palestine dominated the early development of contemporary international terrorism in the 1970s. Nationalism and reactionary ideals represented in organizations such as the Provisional Irish Republican Army (PIRA), the Basque Nation and Liberty Movement (ETA) of Spain, and the Tamil Tigers in Sri Lanka took the forefront in the 1980s. Some argue that religious ideologies subscribed to by groups such as the Islamic Resistance Movement of Palestine (HAMAS), the Armed Islamic Group of Algeria (GIA), and the Islamic Group of Egypt (Al-Gama'a al–Islamiyya) have emerged to play a critical role in international terrorism in the 1990s and may dominate the next decade (Laquer 1999). Ideologies, however, do not cause violence. They simply provide an effective means of polarizing populations.

Causes of Violence

The use of political violence is a form of communication. Violence becomes a primary form of communication when other forms of communication fail. This basic axiom holds true at all levels of analysis, from suicide to domestic violence, from gang warfare to political terrorism, from interstate conflicts to world wars.

Political violence, more specifically international terrorism, does not occur in a vacuum. Terrorism is a response to real or perceived conditions. These conditions are generally referred to as causes of violence and may be the result of either internal or external factors (Kegley 1990). While some authors tend to confuse the issue by failing to distinguish between causes of violence and their justifications (Combs 2000), most would agree that the causes of international terrorism can be divided into four basic categories: political, economic, social, and security.

Real or perceived political isolation or oppression, economic disparity and poverty, social and ethnic cleavages and discrimination, and threats to security such as fear of persecution or attack, caused by internal or external factors, are the underlying causes of most contemporary international terrorism. Often, the lack of a ventilation mechanism such as communication channels to perceived oppressors and the inability independently to change the existing conditions increase frustration and anger in the affected populations. Violence often becomes the primary means of communication when such other forms of communication fail.

Religion and Terrorism

As ideologies, religions do not cause violence. They are systems of belief that mobilize populations toward common objectives and justify their behavior in the pursuit of these objectives. Unlike the religious terrorism of previous centuries, like the *Thugs* in India, who killed to sacrifice the blood of their victims to the Goddess Kali (Rapoport 1990), most of today's Islamic terrorists see religion as a means of achieving political, economic, social, and security objectives, rather than as an end in itself. In most cases, religious ideologies have taken over after other ideologies failed to achieve desired objectives.

David Rapoport (2001) notes, "It's rather striking that many of the Islamic fundamentalists were originally Marxists. Then they shifted their view of the world.... Their most active groups are groups that are not fixed at all times. All they are fixed in is their hatred of the status quo. The way they organize their hatred varies from period to period depending upon political events" (p. 1). The primary focus of many terrorist groups is the resolution of perceived inequities. Religious ideologies, such as fundamentalist Islam, provide a voice for their dissatisfaction with the status quo and become a way of organizing their hatred.

Oppressive political regimes and the systematic persecution of political opposition by authoritarian leaders in many countries have undermined the development of a legitimate democratic opposition. In many cases, Magnus Ranstrop (1996, p. 53) argues, political violence perpetrated by religious factions becomes the lone alternative for those facing corrupt and oppressive regimes. In some cases, religion is seen as the only legitimate vehicle of political opposition. The relationship between causes, ideology, and violent action is diagrammed in Figure 1.

CONCLUSIONS

The role of religion in international terrorism has been exaggerated. While groups with religious affiliation engage in violence, factors other than religion appear to be the cause of this violence. Rather than serving as a catalyst for violence, religion is a means of polarizing

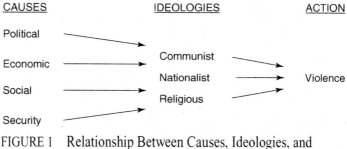

FIGURE 1   Relationship Between Causes, Ideologies, and Action

Causes of terrorism derived, with modifications, from Kegley (1990).

populations, often taking the place of other ideologies that have failed. Perceived political, economic, social, and security inequities or threats and the lack of an effective ventilation mechanism, rather than ideologies, create conditions that lead to international political violence. Preconceptions of U.S. policymakers who have adopted the term religious terrorism as a euphemism for violence committed by Muslim extremists further obscure this issue. As John Esposito notes (1992), "The challenge today is to appreciate the diversity of Islamic actors and movements, to ascertain the reasons behind confrontations and conflicts, and thus to react to specific events and situations with informed, reasoned responses rather than predetermined presumptions and reactions" (p. 168). To do so, one must realize that religion is not a precipitant of contemporary international terrorism but rather a polarizing mechanism exploited by some who choose to engage in political violence.

REFERENCES

Badey, Thomas J. 1998. "Defining Terrorism: A Pragmatic Approach." *Terrorism and Political Violence* 10:90–107.

Combs, Cindy C. 2000. *Terrorism in the Twenty-First Century*. 2nd ed. New Jersey: Prentice Hall.

Do Ce'u Pinto, Maria. 1999. "Some Concerns Regarding Islamist and Middle Eastern Terrorism." *Terrorism and Political Violence* 11:72–96.

Esposito, John L. 1992. *The Islamic Threat: Myth or Reality?* New York: Oxford University Press.

Huntington, Samuel P. 1996. *Clash of Civilizations and the Remaking of the World Order*. New York: Simon & Schuster

Kegley, Charles W. Jr. 1990. *International Terrorism: Characteristics, Causes and Controls*. New York: St. Martins Press.

Laquer, Walter. 1999. *The New Terrorism*. Oxford, England: Oxford University Press.

Merari, Ariel. 2000. Testimony. "Hearings on Threats to U.S. Interests in the Middle East." *CIS Congressional Universe*. 13 July 2000. (http://congcomp/doc...AA&_md5=28408da84d2a94551d132dd03b6127c).

Ranstrop, Magnus. 1996. "Terrorism in the Name of Religion." *Journal of International Affairs* 50:41–62.

Rapoport, David C. 1990. "Religion and Terror: Thugs, Assassins and Zealots." Pp. 146–157 in *International Terrorism: Characteristics, Causes and Controls*, edited by Charles W. Kegley Jr. New York: St. Martins Press.

———. 2001. "Terrorism a Case Study: Present." *Global Terrorism Decoded*. (http://globalterrorism.com/secure/interviews/drap2.html).

Rubin, Barry. 1998. "Islamic Radicalism in the Middle East: A Survey & Balance Sheet." Middle East Review of International Affairs 2:1–8. (http://www.biu.ac.il/SOC/besa/meria/journal/1998/issue2/jvol2no2in.htm).

40 Contrasting Secular and Religious Terrorism

JONATHAN FINE

*In stark opposition to the first article in this section, Dr. Fine believes it is danger-
ous to underestimate the role of religion in terrorism. He examines the motivations
behind both secular and religious terrorism and concludes that religion matters,
perhaps even more that the average person on the street might think. Compare the
arguments in this reading and the first reading in this section. Does either convince
you more? Why?*

Since Iran's 1979 Islamic revolution, there has
been a steady rise in Islamist terrorism. Too
many analysts underestimate the ideological
basis of terrorism and argue instead that ratio-
nal-strategic rather than ideological principles
motivate Islamist terror groups. Comparison
between terrorist groups with secular and religious agendas, however, suggests that ideology matters for both and that downplaying
religious inspiration for terrorism in an effort
to emphasize tactical motivations is both inac-
curate and dangerous.

   Some researchers suggest that to understand terrorism it is more important to study
what terrorists do rather than what they say.[1]
University of Chicago political scientist
Robert Pape argues, for example, that Islam

has little to do with suicide bombing. Rather,
he suggests, that suicide bombers, wherever
they are in the world, are motivated much more
by tactical goals. He juxtaposes the suicide terrorism of the (non-Islamic) Liberation Tigers
of Tamil Eelam (LTTE) with Islamist suicide
bombing to demonstrate that a desire to end
occupation is the common factor rather than
religion. Therefore, he suggests focus upon
religion is a distraction and that policymakers
seeking to stop the scourge of suicide attacks
should work instead to address root causes,
which he sees as the presence of troops or
interests in disputed or occupied lands.[2]

   Despite the revisionism advanced by Pape
and others, the fact remains that most suicide
bombings since 1980 in the world in general

Source: Jonathan Fine, "Contrasting Secular and Religious Terrorism." Originally published in the Winter 2008 *Middle
East Quarterly*, pp. 59–69. Reproduced with permission.

and in the Middle East in particular are sponsored by Islamist and not secular terrorist groups. Pape avoids this conclusion by gerrymandering his data so that he does not need to include the significant numbers of suicide bombings conducted by Sunnis against Shi'a in Iraq.[3]

Middle East expert Martin Kramer suggests that Pape's theses may be comforting to Western readers who want to believe that if only the United States were to pull its military forces from the Persian Gulf and if only all occupation in the Middle East would end, that there would be no more suicide bombings. Western thinking admires empirics, metrics, and pie charts. The secular emphasis of Pape's theories also comforts. But comfort does not correlate with reality. Islamism is an ideology, and that it does not fit neatly into existing political theory should be beside the point.[4]

IDEOLOGICAL UNDERPINNINGS OF TERRORISM

Inattention to the ideological upbringing of terrorists is counterproductive. Although the empirical tools of political science are ill-equipped to assess culture, ideology, and motivation, difficulty in quantifying these factors does not mean they do not exist. Rather than filter evidence to fit the model, responsible political scientists should adjust their models to accommodate the evidence. Important differences exist between those terrorist groups striving to implement secular revolutionary principles based on the thinking of Vladimir Lenin, Mao Zedong, or Ernesto "Che" Guevara[5] and the groups motivated by the religious revolutionary theories of Muslim Brotherhood theoretician Sayyid Qutb, Iranian [Ayatollah] Ruhollah Khomeini, or Palestinian theologian Abdullah Yusuf 'Azzam, whose concept of defense of Muslim lands as every Muslim's personal obligation had major influence on Al-Qaeda founder Osama bin Laden.[6]

The writings of leading terrorist theoreticians offer insight into their political objectives. Whether secular or religious, most terrorist and guerrilla organizations hold sacred a few influential works. Among canonical works secular revolutionaries may embrace are Mao[7] and Guevara's[8] books on guerilla warfare; General Võ Nguyên Giap's Peoples Army—Peoples War,[9] Carlos Marighela's Handbook of Urban Guerrilla Warfare,[10] or Abraham Guillién's Teoria de la Violencia (The theory of violence).[11]

Islamists have supplanted these with a new canon including Egyptian Muslim Brotherhood founder Hasan al-Banna's essays,[12] the writings of the Muslim Brotherhood's main theoretician Sayyid Qutb,[13] essays on Islamic governance by Ayatollah Ruhollah Khomeini,[14] Abdullah Yusuf 'Azzam's Join the Caravan,[15] and bin Laden deputy Ayman al-Zawahiri's Knights under the Prophet's Banner.[16] After analyzing the religious foundations of suicide bombing, David Bukay, a lecturer in political science at the University of Haifa, explains, "Suicide bombing in the Muslim world cannot be separated from religion. . . . The ideological basis of such an interpretation has deep roots in Islamic theology, but it came to prominence with the twentieth-century rise of Muslim Brotherhood theorists such as Banna and Qutb and was further developed by their successors."[17]

SECULAR AGENDA TERRORISM

There is nothing new about terrorism inspired by secular agendas. Although Plato, Aristotle, and leading Christian theologians such as Thomas of Aquinas, John of Salisbury, and George Buchanan discuss political violence, most terrorism experts mark Maximilian Robespierre's "Reign of Terror" during the French Revolution as the beginning of modern, political, systematic terrorism.[18] Beginning in the early nineteenth century, German and Italian radicals embraced terrorism and, in the 1880s, Narodnaya Volya (People's will), which conducted a violent campaign of assassination to fight autocracy in Russia,[19] became a role model for similar groups established by Armenians, Macedonians, Bosnians, and Serbs prior to World War I.[20]

Between 1914 and 1939, there was a visible decline in terrorism perpetrated by independent political groups although Fascist governments and the Soviet Union sometimes sponsored terror against their own populations for internal political objectives. During World War I, British operative T.E. Lawrence's assistance to the Arab revolt in the Hijaz laid the foundation for modem guerrilla warfare, a subject later developed by Chinese revolutionary Mao Zedong.

Between 1945 and 1979, there were three principle types of terrorist entities: organizations struggling for independence from colonial occupiers such as the Front de Libération nationale (FLN) in Algeria or the Mau Mau in Kenya; separatist groups such as the Irish Republican Army (IRA) in Northern Ireland and the Basque Euzkadi Ta-Askatasuna (ETA) in Spain; and socioeconomic revolutionaries such as the Montoneros in Argentina, the Sandinistas in Nicaragua, the Baader Meinhof Gang in West Germany, and the Red Brigades in Italy.[21] A commonality among all groups, though, would be an attempt to justify their actions in economic or social theory. In most if not all cases, the definition of the opponent by secular agenda guerrillas and terrorist groups was confined to a socioeconomic concept such as "Yankee" capitalism or resisting the imperialism of countries such as Great Britain or France.[22] Even the Palestine Liberation Organization (PLO) infused its national liberation agenda with Marxist rhetoric.[23]

Among anti-colonial movements, a terrorist group's victory did not seek to shatter the nation-state system or eradicate the defeated side. Although many left-wing radicals sincerely believed in universal change with respect to the individual and his role in society, their actual policies were oriented more toward local rather than global interests. Guevara's attempt to export the Cuban revolution to Congo and Bolivia floundered,[24] and all attempts by Latin American guerillas to unite failed. Nor did Mao Zedong and Ho Chi Minh seek global export of their ideology or practice[25] although neither of them was averse to utilizing instruments of state power to aid proxy groups in neighboring states. Further, in almost every case, if a terrorist group seized a government or defeated a colonial power, it, nevertheless, found it in its interest to restore diplomatic and economic relations quickly. In Algeria, for example, the FLN reestablished close ties with France upon winning Algerian independence. In 1963, the year, after Algeria won its independence, Paris provided it with 1.3 billion francs (US$260 million) in loans.[26] In no instance did the enemy associate with a particular civilization or culture, as now occurs with pan-Islamist terrorism.

While it was popular to talk about the internationalization of terrorism in the 1970s, incentives for terrorist groups to cooperate had more to do with tactical concerns than with ideological motivation. For example, when George Habash, leader of the Palestinian Front for the Liberation of Palestine (PFLP), assembled representatives in May 1972 from the Irish Republican Army, the Baader Meinhof Gang, and the Japanese Red Army for a meeting in northern Lebanon's Badawl refugee camp, he sought to trade PLO and Libyan offers of training bases for European and Asian terrorist groups in exchange for facilitation by European groups of PLO operations in Europe.[27] The PFLP's participation in a January 31, 1974 Japanese Red Army attack on a Shell oil refinery at Pulau Bukom, off the coast of Singapore, was motivated less by PFLP ideology than by an agreement to pay the Japanese Red Army for its May 30, 1972 attack on the Lod (later renamed Ben Gurion) Airport outside of Tel Aviv.[28]

SECULAR TERROR TACTICS

Terrorist goals shape tactics. Groups immersed in the rhetoric of liberation, for example, target governing officials and foreign residents. The Viet Minh initially targeted only the French and those they deemed to collaborate with the French before expanding their campaign to drive out all foreigners.[29] The Mau Mau and FLN pursued similar patterns of attacks.[30]

Among terrorist groups seeking autonomy or separation, favorite tactics included the kidnapping and murder of government and military officials. The IRA targeted British policemen, soldiers, and the British intelligence apparatus while the Basque ETA concentrated its attacks on local politicians and judges. Warnings prior to attacks that might harm the general population show that these groups sought more to make a political statement and less to cause a blood bath.

Social and economic revolutionaries targeted businessmen and bankers. In 1975, for example, the Ejército Revolucionario del Pueblo (People's Revolutionary Army) kidnapped wealthy Argentine heirs for a $60 million ransom. The Italian Red Brigades seized and, on March 16:1978, executed Aldo Moro, a former Italian prime minister. Baader Meinhof did similarly with Hanns-Martin Schleyer, a West German businessman.

Controlling time is a unifying characteristic of secular agenda terror. Hostage taking and voicing demands against a deadline leads many governments to negotiate, and some, such as the West German government, to capitulate, as Bonn did when it freed three Black September terrorists who remained alive after the September 1972 Munich massacre of Israeli Olympians.[31] Hostage-taking also amplifies media coverage into what Gabi

Weiman, a Haifa University professor of communication, calls "the theater of terror."[32] British prime minister Margaret Thatcher recognized the same phenomenon when she declared after a terror attack in 1985, "We must find ways to starve the terrorists and hijacker of the oxygen and publicity on which they depend."[33]

The most common secular agenda terrorist demand, at least historically, is for the release of prisoners. Between 1972 and 1980, most European negotiations with PLO terrorists involved the PLO's demands to free imprisoned terrorists. Moro's Red Brigade kidnappers and the Black September terrorists, who on March 1, 1973, seized the U.S. embassy in Khartoum, also demanded prisoner releases.[34]

Suicide bombing was never and still is not as frequent a tactic for secular agenda terrorists as it is for Islamist groups. While a few secular agenda terrorists starved themselves to death in prison in Germany or Ireland,[35] their suicides were not part of operations but came only after capture. However, there have been three secular terrorist campaigns that have embraced suicide terrorism: pro-Syrian secular groups in Lebanon in the early 1980s, the Tamil Tigers in Sri Lanka, and the Kurdistan Workers Party (Partiya Karkerên Kuridstan, PKK) in Turkey.

Between 1983 and 1986, the Syrian Social Nationalist Party was responsible for ten suicide bombings; Syrian Baath Party members conducted seven, and the Socialist Nasserite party executed two suicide bombings.[36] Although the LTTE was founded in 1972, it did not launch its first suicide attack until 1987, four years after Hezbollah pioneered such tactics in Lebanon. The change in Tamil strategy came when the Sri Lankan army forced their collective backs against the wall, arresting most of the LTTE leadership in 1981 and making significant military inroads. While the Tigers initially provided their fighters with a poison capsule in order to enable them to avoid interrogation, between 1981 and 1987, they began to attack targets with explosive-laden trucks, the driver exiting the vehicle moments before the explosion. Such attacks were imprecise and so, between 1987 and 2000, some 200 Tamil terrorists, 30 percent of whom were women, conducted 168 suicide bomb missions.[37]

The PKK only began using suicide-bombing tactics in 1995, targeting government and military installations rather than populated areas. Suicide bombing was never a major component of its terrorist operations; it launched only fifteen suicide attacks between 1995 and 1999, some of which were particularly deadly;[38] gunfire, land mines, and delayed fuse bomb attacks account for the majority of its operations, which have killed thousands since 1984. Again, suicide attacks have been the exception rather than the [rule]. Too little is known about the motivation of the attackers, here. Some may have been terminally ill or promised significant financial reward to support their families; others may have believed they could escape alive.[39] PKK suicides are few and far between.

ISLAMIST AGENDA TERRORISM

Paris-based sociologist Farhad Khosrokhavar's *Suicide Bombers: Allah's New Martyrs*[40] has been at the forefront of efforts to emphasize the tension between religious motivation and more rational and temporal strategic considerations. Khosrokhavar, perhaps because of his greater familiarity with Islamic tenets, is correct to see it as a function of jihad. There has been an evolving and, perhaps, dominant strand of modem Islamist thought which finds Western culture to be inimical to Islam and, therefore, a legitimate target for jihad.[41] One of the biggest ideological differences between religious and secular terrorists is their definition of the enemy: While secular terrorists see their opponents as representatives of a certain

socioeconomic order or regime, Islamist terrorists espouse a broader definition. Qutb, for example, revived the Qur'anic term jahiliya, the pre-Islamic age of ignorance in which paganism flourished, to describe the state of any society not by his definition Islamic.[42] Abdullah Yusuf 'Azzam's understanding of dhimmi (subjugated religious minority) status also inserted into modem political discourse the early Islamic bifurcation of the world into the dar al-Islam (abode of Islam) and dar al-Harb (abode of War). In the former, where Muslims ruled, Jews and Christians could convert or accept second class status while Muslims conducted violent jihad to bring minorities under their control. While traditional theologians might argue that Muslims had a duty to protect dhimmis so long as they continued to pay inflated taxes and adhere to special codes, 'Azzam, bin Laden, and their fellow travelers have argued that Jews and Christians have gone astray from their "original religions," and are agents of the modern West, undeserving of any protection.[43]

Arab Sunnis returning from fighting the Soviet occupation in Afghanistan as well as various Palestinian groups such as Hamas and Palestinian Islamic Jihad inaugurated a new phase in religion-inspired terrorism.[44] 'Azzam spun a mystique of invincibility around the Muslim warrior following the Soviet Union's defeat in Afghanistan. One of his most famous slogans during the Afghan war was, "Jihad and the rifle alone. No negotiations, no conferences, no dialogue"[45] On March 6, 1995, Hamas spiritual leader Sheikh Ahmad Yasin declared that any suicide bomber who had received the blessing of a certified Muslim cleric should be considered a shahid (martyr) who had fallen in the service of jihad rather than one who had committed suicide by personal intent,[46] something forbidden in Islam. Sheikh Yusuf al-Qaradawi, an influential Sunni cleric based in Qatar, affirmed Yasin's approach the following year.[47] Then, on February 23,

1998, bin Laden announced the establishment of the International Islamic Front for Jihad against the Crusaders and the Jews and declared it legitimate to kill any American, whether military or not.[48]

While Qutb provided the theoretical basis for modem Sunni Islamism, Khomeini provided the exegesis to legitimize Shi'l theocracy in his 1970 essay, "Hukumat-i Islami" (Islamic government). Permeating Khomeini's writing is a perception of the West as an opponent to Islam, the concept of martyrdom, and the self-identification of Shi'a as oppressed people.[49] He saw the superpowers as responsible for all the world's wrongs and suggested that it was the obligation of all Muslims to mobilize the oppressed to remove the superpowers from the global arena.[50]

Khomeini's linkage between asceticism and suicide is crucial to understand the rise of suicide bombing into the principal tactic by Islamic terrorist organizations.[51] He believed humanity can only crush its selfish desires by spiritual devotion to the umma or community, which is being threatened by the West.[52] The only way to cope with the human obsession with materialism is total denial. Khomeini, in fact, goes to the extreme of justifying the deliberate giving of one's life for the Islamic cause insofar as death is the ultimate denial of one's material self. While martyrdom has long been a theme of Shi'ism, Khomeini's teachings and charisma led many Shi'a to rationalize the justification of suicide on religious grounds.

ISLAMIST TERROR TACTICS

The major Islamist terror tactic has, since the early 1980s, been the suicide bomber. In contrast to secular terrorists, Islamist suicide terrorists need not escape; their planning focuses instead on how to deliver the perpetrator to the target area. Suicide bombers are walking smart bombs, able to position themselves among crowds or in restaurants to achieve maximum carnage. During the 2001-02 terror wave in Israel, Hamas and Islamic Jihad bombers, for example, made last minute target selections in order to bolster the number of civilians they could kill.[53] Islamist terrorists also need not use time to augment their demands. While the Marxist groups of the 1970s might have threatened hostages against concrete demands, Islamists seek to kill first and lecture later. Islamists do take hostages but, in such cases, their goal is as likely to be to draw out terror in a 24-hour news cycle than to win concessions.[54]

The 9–11 hijackers, for example, resisted U.S. air traffic control attempts to communicate because their goal was not a wish to transmit demands but rather the desire to kill as many people as possible. Al-Qaeda's decision to launch the attacks cannot be disengaged from ideology and the dream of renewing a lost caliphate. One of bin Laden's most important objectives was to accelerate recruitment of new volunteers for global jihad and Islam. Bin Laden said that the "war in Afghanistan has exposed America's weakness. Despite the clear technological advantages of its war machine, it cannot defeat the Muslim mujahideen.... The number of people who embraced the Islamic faith after the campaign was greater than the number who had grasped Islam in the past eleven years."[55] Hijacker Muhammad Atta's last will and testament, found in the trunk of his car, suggests very different considerations than a secular agenda terrorist event.[56]

SELF-SACRIFICE OR SUICIDE?

There remains much controversy, at least in the United States and Europe, about the origin and motivation of religiously justified terrorism. Pape and University of Georgia political scientist Mia Bloom, author of Dying to Kill: The Allure of Suicide Terror,[57] are among the most influential revisionists. But, despite the popularity of their theses in a field which seeks to mitigate if not exculpate the influence of religion, their arguments fall short.

Pape makes two major assumptions about suicide bombing: first, that it is motivated primarily by resistance to foreign occupation and, second, that religious ideology has only a minor role in suicide attacks perpetrated by Muslims.[58] Bloom also argues that suicide bombers kill themselves only as a means to an end, using suicide only "to outbid rival militias through the use of shocking tactics" and, in the Palestinian case, to "compete for leadership."[59] According to Pape and Bloom, strategy and political objectives rather than religion are the primary incentive for suicide attacks. But religion, rationalism, and strategic planning are not incompatible. The Tamil Tigers may have embraced suicide bombing in their separatist fight against the Sri Lankan army, but suicide bombers in Casablanca and London were not motivated by occupation but rather by jihadist ideology. While Western scholars may have internalized the separation of church and state legislated in the United States and practiced in Europe, for Khomeini, Hezbollah's Hasan Nasrallah, bin Laden, and Qaradawl, no such separation exists. They are rational but see the world differently.

Unlike Pape and Bloom, Khosrokhavar looks for the deeper, individual rather than organizational motivations behind suicide bombing. With comparative analysis of martyrdom in Christianity and Sikhism, Khosrokhavar argues that it is particularly Islamic to sanction sacred death for the sake of the community (umma).[60] Perhaps this is why Khosrokhavar warns that political science arid economics are not sufficient to understanding the human factor in religion-inspired terror. Both individuals and terrorist organizations see suicide bombing as a rational and integral aspect of ideology, strategy, and tactics. Israel counterterrorism expert Boaz Ganor elaborates on this self-image of the suicide bomber

and his supporters. Ganor explains, "The term suicide attack is misleading. In the eyes of the attacker and his community this phenomenon has nothing to do with committing suicide.... Committing suicide is forbidden in Islam but instead, he is seen as a shahid—a martyr who fell in the process of fulfilling the religious commandment of jihad."[61]

Khomeini's influence on Islamist terror suggests that suicide bombing has a wider ideological and strategic foundation than just opposition to occupation. Rather, the basis for suicide bombing is threefold: First, suicide for jihad cleanses the perpetrator of the world's evils. Second, suicide for the community purifies the umma. Third, suicide bombing serves the goal of opposing Islam's enemies.

Pape's interpretation of cause and effect is questionable. He claims that terrorism forced Israel to withdraw twice from Palestinian areas during the 1990s: in April 1994, when Israel withdrew from parts of Gaza, and between October 1994 and August 1995, when Israel pulled back from portions of the West Bank. He also credits terrorism with Jerusalem's decision to release Hamas spiritual leader Ahmed Yasin from prison in October 1997.[62] His assumption is faulty, though. Pape neglects to mention that Israeli leaders agreed upon this withdrawal policy in the Oslo accords' "Declaration of Principles."[63] The Israeli public persuaded its leadership to seek peace with the Palestinians, not because of terror—Israeli forces had contained if not defeated the first intifada—but rather because they thought the Oslo adventure might achieve a reasonable political solution.

By focusing only on occupation and national liberation,[64] though, Pape overlooks a complicated web of incentives and motivations that undercuts his argument.

Marc Sageman, a former CIA case officer, psychiatrist, and University of Pennsylvania political scientist, pursues a different thesis in his book Understanding Terror Networks.

Sageman seeks to refute the regular notions regarding causes for terror, such as poverty and brainwashing, and emphasizes instead social bonds and networks. He argues that the best way both to understand and to counter global jihadism is by mapping and analyzing the Islamists' social structure. Although Sageman argues that social bonds among terrorist networks play a stronger role then ideologies, he avoids Pape's mistake of seeking to claim exclusivity for his theory, and so encourages counterterrorist intelligence communities to train case officers versed in Muslim cultures and language and acknowledges the individual dedication of the 9-11 terrorists, which, as their "martyrdom" videos and Muhammad Atta's last will and testament show, was rooted in religion.[65]

Supporters of Pape's revisionism blur the difference between self-sacrifice and suicide to downplay the dissimilarity between secular terrorism and Islam-inspired suicide bombing, that is, to downplay the distinction between readiness to sacrifice oneself for a cause as opposed to a conscious decision to carry out a suicide attack. Every soldier who enlists to a combat unit knows that he or she could be killed in action; many young men and women are willing to take that risk, not because of a desire to die but rather because of the conviction that under certain circumstances it may be necessary to lose one's life in the line of duty. Secular terrorists also acknowledge risk without expressing the desire to kill themselves. Guevara writes, for example, "The guerrilla combatant ought to risk his life whenever necessary and be ready to die without the least sign of doubt, but at the same time, he ought to be cautious and never expose himself unnecessarily. All possible precautions ought to be taken to avoid defeat or annihilation."[66]

Jamal al-Gashay, one of the three Black September terrorists captured by West German police after the Munich massacre and later released in exchange for the return of hostages on a hijacked Lufthansa jet, gave a television interview subsequent to his release. "We knew that achieving our objective might cost lives," he said, "but since the day we joined up, we had been aware that there was a possibility of martyrdom at any time in the name of Palestine."[67]

Motivation and readiness for sacrifice is not the same as willingness to embrace certain death. There is a huge difference between the Latin American battle cry, Viva la Muerte! (Hail Death!) and the declaration suicide bombers make on video prior to their mission, Ana ash-shahid al-hayy, "I the living martyr." For the suicide bomber, such words are not a mere slogan but rather the expression of deep religious values.

Ganor defines a suicide attack as "an operational method in which the very act of the attack is dependent upon the death of the perpetrator.... This is a unique situation in which the terrorist is fully aware that if he does not kill himself, the planned attack will not be carried out."[68] While in the 1970s, terrorists devoted much effort to establishing escape routes or to releasing their fellow terrorists from prison, for the suicide bomber such efforts are unnecessary.

Although Pape and Bloom argue that religion-inspired terrorists do not kill as an end in itself, Al-Qaeda strikes suggest otherwise. Regardless, the difference in modus operandi between religious and secular terrorists differs enough that they should be considered distinct groups which do not necessarily share the same temporal motives.

CONCLUSIONS

Analyzing the differences between secular agenda terrorists and their religious counterparts is crucial to understanding the special nature of contemporary terror. Unlike the activities of secular guerrillas and terrorists between 1945 and 1979, the war against the enemies of Islam is not limited by time, territory, or a specific socioeconomic agenda, and it is being waged against an entire culture and civilization. Therefore, "resisting occupation," as Pape suggests, is only one limited stage in a much larger scheme for a new world order. This is evident in Khomeini's vision of a wide Shi'l crescent extending from Iran through Iraq and linking up with Lebanon, or in Al-Qaeda's dream, of a new Islamic caliphate stretching from Spain in the west to Iraq in the east and eventually including Southeast Asia and Europe as well. Far from being empty slogans, these objectives reflect deep ideological commitment to a new world order.

In order to better understand the political mindset of Islamist terrorist organizations, the formative texts of the Sunni and Shi'l leaders should receive as much if not more attention than the strategies and tactics they apply.[69] Giap, the mastermind of North Vietnamese guerrilla operations, once said, "Political activities are more important than military operations, and fighting is less important than propaganda."[70] In confronting Islamist terror, ideology is perhaps even more crucial.

FOOTNOTES

[1]*Alex P. Schmid and Albert Youngman, "Typologies of Terrorism," Political Terrorism: A New Guide to Actors. Authors, Concepts. Data Bases, Theories and Literature (New Brunswick and London: Transaction Publishers, 2006), pp. 40–9.*

[2]*Robert Pape, Dying to Win: The Strategic Logic of Suicide Terrorism (New York: Random House, 2005), pp. 83–8.*

[3]*Ibid., pp. 3, 275–80.*

[4]*Martin Kramer, "Suicide Terrorism: Origins and Responses," Sandbox, Nov. 8, 2005.*

[5]*For a good overview of Marxism and guerrilla warfare, see William J. Pomeroy, Guerrilla Warfare and Marxism (New York: International Publishers, 1984).*

[6]*See David Bukay, "The Religious Foundations of Suicide Bombings," Middle East Quarterly, Fall 2006, pp. 27–36.*

[7]*Mao Tse-Tong, On Guerrilla Warfare (Urbana and Chicago: University of Illinois Press, 2000).*

[8]*Ernesto Guevara, Guerrilla Warfare (Lincoln: University of Nebraska Press, 1998).*

[9]*New York and London: Frederick. A. Praeger, 1962.*

[10]*Trans. John Butt and Rosemary Sheed (London: Penguin, 1971).*

[11]*Buenos Aires: Editorial Jamcana, 1965.*

[12]*See, for example, Hasan al-Banna, Five Tracts of Hasan al-Banna, (1906-1949), Charles Wendell, trans. (Berkeley: University of California Press, 1978).*

[13]*Sayyid Qutb, Ma'alim fi al-Tariq [Milestones] (Beirut: Dar ash-Shuruq, 1968).*

[14]*Ruhollah Khomeini, Islam and Revolution, Hamid Algar, ed. and trans. (Berkeley: Mizan Press, 1981).*

[15]*London: Azzam Publications, 2001.*

[16]*Casablanca: Dar an-Najah al-Jadida, 2001.*

[17]*Bukay, "The Religious Foundations of Suicide Bombings."*

[18]*Bruce Hoffman, Inside Terrorism (New York: Columbia University Press, 2006), p. 3.*

[19]*Ibid., pp. 5-6.*

[20]*Walter Laqueur, The Age of Terrorism (Boston and Toronto: Little, Brown & Company, 1987), p. 16.*

[21]*Yehoshafat Harkaby, Milchama ve Estrategia (Tel Aviv: Israel Ministry of Defense, 1994), pp. 191-3; Schmid and Youngman, Political Terrorism, pp. 45-9.*

[22]*Guevara, Guerrilla Warfare, p. 11.*

[23]*Moshe Maoz, "Manhigut Palastinit Ba Gada Ha Maaravit: 1948-1978," in Moshe Maoz and B'Z Keidar, eds., Ha Tnua Ha Leumit Ha Falastinit: Me Imut Le Hashioma? (Tel-Aviv: MOD, 1997), p. 226; Moshe Shemesh, "ASHAF: 1964-1993: Mi Maavak Mezuyan Le Chisul Medinat Yisrael, Le Hesken Shalom Ita," in Maoz and B'Z Keidar, Ha Tnua Ha Leumit Ha Falastinit, pp. 302-3; Hadj Ali Bashir, "Lessons of the Algerian Liberation Struggle," in William J. Pomedrov, ed., Guerrilla Warfare and Marxism (New York: International Publishers, 1970), pp. 254–61.*

[24]*Jon Lee Anderson, Che Guevara: A Revolutionary Life (New York: Grove Press, 1997), pp. 610–23.*

[25]*Ibid., p. 601.*

[26]*Alistair Home, A Savage War for Peace: Algeria, 1954-1962 (New York: The Viking Press, 1978), p. 540; idem, Milchama Pirit Le Shalom (Tel-Aviv: Ministry of Defense, 1989), p. 566.*

[27]*Edgar O'Ballance, The Language of Violence: The Blood Politics of Terrorism (San Rafael, Calif.: Presidio Press, 1979), pp., 150-1; Claire Sterling, The Terror Network (New York: Berkley Books, 1983), p. 243.*

[28]*Sterling, The Terror Network, p. 23; O'Ballance, The Language of Violence, p. 145.*

[29]*Yehoshafat Harkaby, Al Ha-Guerrilla (Tel Aviv: Ministry of Defense, 1971), p. 28.*

[30]*Frank Furedi, "Introduction," Mau Mau War in Perspective (Athens: Ohio University Press, 1989), pp. 1–14; Walter Laqueur, Guerrilla: A Historical and Critical Study (Boston: Little, Brown and Company, 1976), p. 271; Douglas Pike, Viet Cong: The Organization and Techniques of the National Liberation Front of South Vietnam (Cambridge: MIT Press, 1966), pp. 154–65.*

[31]*Simon Reeve, One Day in September (New York: Arcade, 2006), pp. 155–7.*

[32]*Gabi Weiman, "The Theater of Terror: Effects of Press Coverage," Journal of Communication, Winter 1983, pp. 38–45.*

[33]*Financial Times (London), July 16, 1985.*

[34]*O'Ballance, The Language of Violence, pp. 190-3.*

[35]*Ariel Merari, "The Readiness to Kill and Die: Suicide Terrorism in the Middle East," in Walter Reich, ed., Origins of Terrorism: Psychologies, Ideologies, Theologies. States of Mind (Washington D.C.: Woodrow Wilson Center Press, 1998), p. 196.*

[36]*Merari, "The Readiness to Kill and Die," pp. 31, 204.*

[37]*Shaul Shay, The Shahids: Islam and Suicide Attacks (London: Transaction Publishers, 2004), pp. 139–40.*

[38]*Ibid., pp. 102–3.*

[39]*Daniel Pipes, "The Scourge of Suicide Terrorism," National Interest, Summer 1986.*

[40]*London: Pluto Press, 2005.*

[41]*Bukay, "The Religious Foundations of Suicide Bombings"; Uriya Shavit, "Al-Qaeda's Saudi Origins," Middle East Quarterly, Fall 2007, pp. 13–21.*

[42]*Qutb, Ma'alim fi al-Tariq, pp. 88–92; Emmanuel Sivan, Kanaei Ha Islam (Tel Aviv: Am Oved, 1994), pp. 94–5.*

[43]*Abdullah Azzam, Al-Qaeda Wa Athraha fi Binai Algil (Beirut: Dar Ibn Chazm, 1990), pp. 37-8; idem, "Hasabna Allah wa Naam Alukil," Al-Jihad (published by 'Azzam and bin Laden in Afghanistan), Nov. 1989, p. 9.*

[44]*Shaul Shay and Yoram Schweitzer, The "Afghan Alumni" Terrorism: Islamic Militants against the Rest of the World (Herzliya: International Institute for Counter-Terrorism, 2000), pp. 19–20.*

[45]*Abdullah Azzam, Join the Caravan, 2nd English ed. (London: Azzam Publications, 2001), p. 9; idem, Defense of Muslim Lands (London: Azzam Publications, 2001), p. 8.*

[46]*Nachman Tal, "Suicide Attacks: Israel and Islamic Terrorism," Strategic Assessment, June 2002, Jaffee Center for Strategic Studies, Tel Aviv University, p. 2.*

[47]*Ibid., p. 45.*

[48] *"Declaration of the International Islamic Front for Jihad against the Crusaders and the Jews," Al-Quds al-Arabi (London), Feb. 23, 1998.*

[49]*Marvin Zonis and Daniel Brumberg, "Ayatollah Khomeini's Ideology of Revolutionary Shi'ism," in Martin Kramer, ed., Shi'ism: Resistance and Revolution (Boulder: Westview Press, 1987), pp. 49–59.*

[50]*Ibid., p. 52.*

[51]*Zonis and Brumberg, "Ayatollah Khomeini's Ideology of Revolutionary Shi'ism," p. 56.*

[52]*Uriah Furman, Islamiyun: Dat Ve-Chevrah Be Mishnatam Shel Neemaney Ha-Islam Bney Zmaneynu (Tel Aviv: Ministry of Defense, 2002), p. 54.*

[53]*Tal, "Suicide Attacks," p. 3.*

[54]*Michael Rubin and Suzanne Gershowitz, "Political Strategies to Counterterrorism," in Nicola Pedde, ed., The Evolving Threat: International Terrorism in the Post 9–11 Era (Rome: Globe Research, 2006).*

[55]*Al-Jazeera TV (Doha), Dec. 27, 2001.*

[56]*Shaul Shay, The Shahids, pp. 126–7.*

[57]*New York: Columbia University Press, 2007.*

[58]*Farhad Khosrokhavar, Suicide Bombers: Allah's New Martyrs, David Macey, trans. (London: Pluto Press, 2005), p. 36; Pape, Dying to Win, p. 21.*

[59]*Mia Bloom, Dying to Kill: The Allure of Suicide Bombing (New York: Columbia University Press, 2005), p. 29.*

[60]*Khosrokhavar, Suicide Bombers, pp. 149–53.*

[61]*Boaz Ganor, Countering Suicide Bombing (Herzliya: International Institute for Counter-Terrorism, 2007), p. 9.*

[62]*Ibid., pp. 63, 66–7.*

[63]*Ibid.; Yair Hirschfeld, Oslo: A Formula for Peace: From Negotiation to Implementation (Tel Aviv: Am-Oved Publishing, 2000), p. 199, 248.*

[64]*Pape, Dying to Win, p. 4.*

[65]*Marc Sageman, Understanding Terror Networks (Philadelphia: University of Pennsylvania Press), p. 137, 175, 178, 181, 184.*

[66]*Guevara, Guerrilla, p. 42.*

[67]Reeve, One Day in September, pp. 47, 155–7, 294 (ftnt. 27).

[68]*Ganor, Countering Suicide Bombing, p. 6.*

[69]*Mark Jeurgensmeyer, Terror in the Mind of God: The Global Rise of Religious Violence (Berkeley: University of California Press, 2000), pp. 1–14.*

[70]*Laqueur, Guerrilla, p. 268.*

41 Is Religion the Problem?

MARK JUERGENSMEYER

Perhaps the leading scholar on global religious violence, Juergensmeyer asks whether religion is the culprit or victim of terrorism. What is his answer? And just as importantly, what is his solution?

In the rubble following the collapse of the World Trade Center towers in the violent assault of September 11 lies the tawdry remnants of religion's innocence. In those brief horrifying moments our images of religion came of age. Religion was found in bed with terrorism. Whatever bucolic and tranquil notions we may have had were rudely replaced by those that were tough, political, and sometimes violent.

Is this the fault of religion? Has its mask been ripped off and its murky side exposed—or has its innocence been abused? Is religion the problem or the victim?

The answers to these basic questions have run in extreme directions. Religion's role has been hotly debated in the public discussion after September 11 among journalists and policy makers, and among academic researchers and observers. Yet there is seldom agreement about the most basic issue, whether religion is the cause of violence or its unwilling servant. For this reason the very starting point in discussions about religious violence often contain assumptions about religion's role that should be contested. Interestingly, two of these assumptions are diametrically opposed to one another.

On the one hand, religion—Islam in particular—is often assumed to be the problem. Despite the cautionary words of President George W. Bush imploring Americans not to blame Islam for September 11, a certain Islamiphobia has crept into public conversation. The implication is that the whole of Islam has supported acts of terrorism. The inevitable attachment of Islam to terrorism in the ubiquitous phrase "Islamic terrorism" is one example

---

Source: Mark Juergensmeyer, "Is Religion the Problem?" First published in *The Hedgehog Review* 6.1 (Spring 2004): 21–33. Reprinted with permission.

of this habit of thinking. Another is the vaunting of *jihad* to a place of supreme Islamic importance—as if all Muslims agreed with the militarized usage of the term by unauthorized extremist groups. The most strident expositions of this way of thinking are found in assertions of Christian televangelists such as Pat Robertson and Jerry Falwell that the Prophet himself was a kind of terrorist. More moderate forms are the attempts by political commentators and some scholars to explain—as if there was need for it—why Islam is so political. Even Connecticut's liberal Senator Christopher Dodd, in a television interview in November 2003, cautioned Americans not to expect too much tolerance from Islam given its propensity for ideological control over public life. He referenced a recent book by historian Bernard Lewis for this point of view, a book that he recommended to the viewers.

The assumption of those who hold this "religion is the problem" position is that Islam's relationship to politics is peculiar. But this is not true. Most traditional societies have had a close tie between political leadership and religious authority, and religion often plays a role in undergirding the moral authority of public life. In Judaism the Davidic line of kingship is anointed by God; in Hinduism the kings are thought to uphold divine order through the white umbrella of *dharma*; in Christianity the political history of Europe is rife with contesting and sometimes merging lines of authority between church and state. Violent Jewish, Hindu, and Christian activists in recent years have all, like their Muslim counterparts, looked to traditional religious patterns of politicized religion to justify their own militant stance.

The public life of contemporary America is no exception. It is one in which religion is very much involved with politics and politics with religion. The evangelical professions of faith of President Bush and advisors such as Attorney General John Ashcroft fuel the impression

that U.S. foreign policy has a triumphant agenda of global Christendom. This characterization of religion's hand in US politics is often exaggerated by foreign observers in Europe and the Middle East, but the Christian rhetoric of American political leaders is undeniable and lends credibility to such a view.

Even more troubling are strands of Christian theocracy that have emerged among extreme groups in the United States. Some employ violence in their opposition to secular society and their hatred of a globalized culture and economy. A neo-Calvinist theology of a religious state lies behind the bombing of abortion clinics and the shooting of abortion clinic staff by Lutheran and Presbyterian activists in Maryland and Florida. The Christian Identity philosophy of race war and a government enshrining a White Christian supremacy lies behind the attack on the Atlanta Olympic park, the bombing of gay bars and abortion clinics, the killing of a Denver radio talk-show host, an assault on a Jewish day care center in Los Angeles, and many other incidents—including Ruby Ridge—perpetrated by Christian militia in recent years. The Christian Cosmotheism espoused by William Pierce and embraced by Timothy McVeigh was the ideological justification for McVeigh's bombing of the Oklahoma City Federal Building. In fact, there have been more attacks—far more, in fact—by Christian terrorist groups on American soil in the last fifteen years than Muslim ones. Aside from September 11 and the 1993 attempt to destroy the World Trade Center, almost all of the other terrorist acts are Christian.

Yet somehow, despite evidence to the contrary, the American public labels Islam as a terrorist religion rather than Christianity. The arguments that agree—or disagree—with this position often get mired in the tedious task of dredging up historical examples from the past to show the political and militant side of Islam (or contrarily, of other religions like Christianity,

Judaism or Hinduism, as I have just done)—and then opponents will challenge the utility of those examples, and the debate goes on and on. The arguments would not be necessary, however, if one did not assume that religion is responsible for acts of public violence in the first place.

This is exactly the position taken by the other extreme in the public discussion over religion after September 11—those who deny that religion is the problem. They see religion as a victim. The implication is that when religion enters into the public arena in a violent way it is because its innocence is exploited by nasty politicians. This is usually what is meant when reporters and other observers talk about religion being "used" for political purposes. A U.S. State Department official once told me that religion was being "used" throughout the Middle East, masking problems that were essentially economic in nature. He assured me that if jobs were to be had by unemployed Egyptians and Palestinians the problem of religious politics in these impoverished societies would quickly vanish. From his point of view it was unthinkable that religious activists would actually be motivated by religion, or at least by ideological views of the world that were framed in religious language. Similarly Michael Sells' excellent study of the role of Christian symbolism in resurgent Serbian nationalism, *The Bridge Betrayed*, was ridiculed by a reviewer for *The Economist* who saw the conflict as purely a matter of secular nationalism in which religion played no role. The assumption of the reviewer, like that of the State Department official with whom I spoke, was that religion was the dependent variable, a rhetorical gloss over the real issues that were invariable economic or political.

This position—that religion is essentially innocent—is supported by many mainstream religious leaders in the faiths in which violent occurs. In these cases they do not explain away the religious motives of the violent activists, but they deny that these extreme religious groups represent the normative traditions. Most Buddhist leaders in Japan, for instance, distanced themselves from what they regarded as the pseudo-Buddhism of the Aum Shinrikyo sect that was implicated in the nerve gas attack on the Tokyo subways. Most Muslims refused to believe that fellow members of their faith could have been responsible for anything as atrocious as they September 11 attacks—and hence the popular conspiracy theory in the Muslim world that somehow Israeli secret police had plotted the terrible deed. Most Christians in America saw the religiosity of Timothy McVeigh as anti-Christian, even anti-religious, despite the strong Christian subtext of the novel, *The Turner Diaries*, which McVeigh regarded as his Bible.

In some cases scholars have come to the defense of religion in a similar way, by characterizing the religion of activists groups as deviant from the religious norm and therefore uncharacteristic of true religion. This is essentially the stance that Bruce Lawrence takes in defending Islam in *Shattering the Myth*. The term "fundamentalism"—applied not just to Christianity but to a whole host of religious traditions—is another way of excusing "normal" religion and isolating religion's problems to a deviant form of the species. It is used sometimes to suggest an almost viral spread of an odd and dangerous mutation of religion that if left on its own naturally leads to violence, autocracy, and other extremes. Fortunately, so this line of thinking goes, normal religion is exempt. Recently, however, "Islam" and "fundamentalism" are tied together so frequently in public conversation that the term has become a way of condemning all of Islam as a deviant branch of religion. But even in this case the use of the term "fundamentalism" allows for the defenders of religion to take comfort in the notion that their kind of nonfundamentalist religion is exempt from violence or other extreme forms of public behavior.

Are they right? Is religion only an innocent victim that is misused by a small number of extremists? Or is religion itself the problem, a force for intolerance and violence around the world?

It is not easy to answer the question of religion's role in contemporary world politics by an all-or-nothing answer. As anyone who has ever taken a multiple choice test knows, there is a dilemma when presented with such absolutes. The most accurate responses are often to be found in the gray categories: c) none of the above, or d) all of the above. In the case of the question regarding the involvement of religion in contemporary public life, the answer is not simply a matter of peculiar religion gone bad or good religion being used by bad people. We know that there are strata of religious imagination that deal with all sides and moods of human existence, the peace and the perversity, the tranquility and the terror.

Hence my own answer to the question is a variation of answers c) and d), none of the above and all of the above. I do not think that religion is the problem. But I do think that the involvement of religion in public life is often problematic.

I came to this conclusion by a circuitous route. Through a series of case studies and interviews over several years, I explored the question of why religion has surfaced at this moment of late modernity as a force in public life. As the seemingly endless series of vicious attacks associated with religion around the world reveal, religion has returned with a vengeance from its banishment from public life by the European Enlightenment. Moreover its return has been curiously ubiquitous. Virtually every religious tradition in the world has been associated with a violent act or group, and both highly industrialized and underdeveloped societies have been involved. There has been Christian terrorism in the US and Ireland; Buddhist terrorism in Japan; Muslim terrorism in Indonesia, North Africa and the Middle East; Jewish terrorism in the US and Israel; and Hindu terrorism in India.

My own quest for answers to the questions of religion's political extremism began with the Sikhs. For years I had lived and taught in the Punjab region of India where most Sikhs live, and knew them to be affable, intelligent and interesting people. Thus it was with a deep sense of personal anguish as well as intellectual curiosity that I observed from afar the mounting spiral of violence between a faction of young Sikhs from the elite stratum of the rural Jat caste and the increasingly belligerent agencies of the Indian government, including its military and police. Thousands were killed yearly in terrorist acts on the part of the Sikh militants and violent encounters with the Indian police. The crisis came to a head in 1984 when Prime Minister Indira Gandhi gave the approval for the Indian government to raid the most sacred site of Sikhism, the Golden Temple in Amritsar, where the militant Sikhs' leader, Sant Jarnail Singh Bhindranwale, had sought sanctuary. Sikhs around the world were incensed at what they perceived as desecration of this holy place, and later that year Mrs. Gandhi was assassinated by her own Sikh bodyguards in an act of retaliation.

Why did the Sikh militants and the Indian government arrive at this sad confrontation, and what, if anything, did religion have to do with it? I knew enough about the Punjab to know that young rural Sikhs had perfectly good reasons for being unhappy. Economically they saw their agricultural products receiving what they thought to be less than fair market; politically they felt their own authority was being undercut by the ruling Congress party; and socially they regarded their status and influence waning in comparison with the urban castes. But none of these things explained the vitriol and religious passion with which their opposition to the government was expressed.

To understand how religion was related to these grievances I turned to the speeches of the fallen martyr, Bhindranwale. What I expected to find was an example of how religion was used by a wily politician. That is, I expected to find an example of the politicization of religion. What I discovered, however, was that Bhindrawale was essentially a country preacher. Like the legion of Protestant Christian revival speakers that traipsed through the Mid-American rural countryside where I was raised, he spoke of the struggles between good and evil, truth and falsehood, that reside within each troubled soul, and called for renunciation, dedication, and redemption. It seemed that he was speaking to young men in particular about their easy compromises with the lures of modern life.

Initially I was baffled at the apparent lack of political or social content to Bhindranwale's message. Examining closely these tapes and transcripts, however, I found an occasional aside or reference to contemporary political leaders. I realized that unlike the internal spiritual war that most Protestant Christian revival preachers proclaimed in my Midwestern rural youth, Bhindranwale's war had an external dimension. The satanic forces had somehow come to earth and were residing in the official residence of India's head of state.

What this meant was that Bhindranwale had skillfully merged the spiritual conflict that is found in every religion with the social and political tensions in modern society that young men often experience. He portrayed a sacred war, but one that could be waged in the streets as well as in the soul.

Thus it appeared that my initial conclusions about the political use of religion by Bhindranwale had to be amended. Instead of the politicization of religion, it appeared in the Sikh case that Bhindranwale was describing the religionization of politics. The social and political conflict of Sikhs with their secular government and society was seen in religious terms. The template of religious drama was imposed on social situations, and what might otherwise be seen as a secular conflict with government was lifted to the high proscenium of religious drama. Here, it seemed to me, was an interesting case of how religion was used to characterize the perceived failure of the secular state and to mobilize its opposition.

In a postmodern and post-Marxist world, it seemed that religion—at least in the Punjab—had become an ideology of protest. What I didn't know was whether this was idiosyncratic to the Sikh case, or whether it was a world-wide phenomenon. If it was a global occurrence, I wanted to know why.

For these reasons I took my thesis on the road. Beginning in the late 1980s and continuing into the 90s and after, I began looking at a variety of cases of recent religious activism. I didn't have to look far. Outside of the Punjab, elsewhere in India there was a rise of Hindu political violence, and in Kashmir there were Muslim activists. Buddhists were supporting anti-government protests in nearby Sri Lanka, and soon came word of a new religious movement in Japan with Buddhist roots that saw the government involved in an apocalyptic war. In Iran, Shi'ite Muslims had already waged their own successful revolutionary campaign. Sunni Islamic ideologies accompanied nationalist movements in Iran, Egypt, Palestine and elsewhere in the Middle East, and in Israel violent activists were motivated by Messianic Judaism. Christianity was merged with nationalism in Ireland and formed the ideologies of anti-state militia in the United States.

I found that in all of these cases an interesting replication of the main thesis that I found in the Sikh situation. Of course each group was responding to its own set of local social, economic, and political factors. But in all cases there was a common ideological component: the perception that the modern idea of secular nationalism was insufficient in moral, political and social terms. In many cases the effects of globalization were in the background as global economic and communications systems undercut the distinctiveness of nation-state identities. In some cases the hatred of the global system was overt, as in the American Christian militia's hatred of the "new world order" and the al Qaeda network's targeting the World Trade Center. In each case, religion was the ideology of protest. Particular religious images and themes were marshaled to resist the global secular systems and their secular nation-state supporters.

There were other similarities among these cases. In each case those who embraced radical anti-state religious ideologies felt personally upset with what they regarded as the oppression of the secular state. They experienced this oppression as an assault on their pride and identity, and felt humiliated as a result. The failures of the state, though economic, political and culture, were often experienced in personal ways as humiliation and alienation, as a loss of selfhood.

It is understandable then, that those men (and they were usually men) who experienced this loss of pride and identity would lash out in violence—the way that men often do when frustrated. Such expressions of power are meant to at least symbolically regain their sense of manhood. In each case, however, the activists challenged these feelings of violence through images of collective violence borrowed from their religious traditions: the idea of cosmic war.

The idea of cosmic war was a remarkably consistent feature of all of these cases. Those people whom we might think of as terrorists regarded themselves as soldiers in a what they imagined to be sacred battles. I call such notions of warfare "cosmic" because they are larger than life. They evoke great battles of the legendary past, and they relate to metaphysical conflicts between good and evil. Notions of cosmic war are intimately personal but can also be translated to the social plane. Ultimately, though, they transcend human experience. Often activists employ images of sacred warfare that are found in every religious tradi-

tion—such as the battles in the Hebrew Bible (Old Testament), the epics of Hinduism and Buddhism, and the Islamic idea of *jihad*. What makes religious violence particularly savage and relentless is that its perpetrators have placed such religious images of divine struggle—cosmic war—in the service of worldly political battles. For this reason, acts of religious terror serve not only as tactics in a political strategy but also as evocations of a much larger spiritual confrontation.

This brings us back to the question of whether religion is the problem. In looking at the variety of cases, from the Palestinian Hamas movement to al Qaeda and the Christian militia, it was clear that in most cases there were real grievances at issue—economic and social tensions that were experienced by large numbers of people. These grievances were not religious. They were not aimed at religious differences or issues of doctrine and belief. They were issues of social identity and meaningful participation in public life that in other contexts were expressed through Marxist and nationalists ideologies. Curiously in this present moment of late modernity these secular ideological expressions of rebellion have been replaced by ideological formulations that are religious. Yet the grievances—the sense of alienation, marginalization, and social frustration—are often much the same.

So religion is not the problem. Yet the fact that religion is the medium through which these issues are expressed is, as I earlier said, *problematic*. It is problematic in that religion brings new aspects to conflicts that were otherwise not a part of them.

For one thing religion personalizes the conflict. It provides *personal rewards*—religious merit, redemption, the promise of heavenly luxuries—to those who struggle in conflicts that otherwise have only social benefits. It also provides *vehicles of social mobilization* that embrace vast numbers of supporters who otherwise would not be mobilized around social or political issues. In many cases, it provides an *organizational network* of local churches, mosques, temples, and religious associations into which patterns of leadership and support may be tapped. It gives the legitimacy of *moral justification* for political encounter. Even more important, it provides *justification for violence* that challenges the state's monopoly on morally-sanctioned killing. Using Max Weber's dictum that the state's authority is always rooted in the social approval of the state to enforce its power through the use of bloodshed—in police authority, punishment, and armed defense—religion is the only other entity that can give moral sanction for violence and is therefore inherently at least potentially revolutionary.

Religion also provides the image of *cosmic war*, which adds further complications to a conflict that has become baptized with religious authority. The notion of cosmic war gives an *all-encompassing world view* to those who embrace it. Supporters of Christian militia movements, for instance, described their "aha" experience when they discovered the world-view of the Christian Identity totalizing ideology that helped them make sense of the modern world, their increasingly peripheral role in it, and the dramatic actions they can take to set the world right. It gives them roles as *religious soldiers* who can literally fight back against the forces of evil.

The image of cosmic war is a potent force. When the template of spiritual battle is implanted onto a worldly opposition it dramatically changes the perception of the conflict by those engaged in it, and it vastly alters the way that the struggle is waged. It *absolutizes the conflict* into extreme opposing positions and *demonizes opponents* by imagining them to be satanic powers. This absolutism makes compromise difficult to fathom, and holds out the promise of *total victory* through divine intervention. A sacred war that is waged in a godly span of time need not be won immediately, however. The *time line of sacred struggle is vast,* perhaps even eternal.

I once had the occasion to point out the futility—in secular military terms—of the Islamic struggle in Palestine to Dr Abdul Aziz Rantisi, the leader of the political wing of the Hamas movement. It seemed to me that Israel's military force was such that a Palestinian military effort could never succeed. Dr Rantisi assured me that that "Palestine was occupied before, for two hundred years." He explained that he and his Palestinian comrades "can wait again—at least that long." In his calculation, the struggles of God can endure for eons. Ultimately, however, they knew they would succeed.

So religion can be a problematic aspect of contemporary social conflict even if it is not *the* problem, in the sense of the root causes of discontent. Much of the violence in contemporary life that is perceived as terrorism around the world is directly related to the absolutism of conflict. The demonization of enemies allows those who regard themselves as soldiers for God to kill with no moral impunity. Quite the opposite—they feel that their acts will give them spiritual rewards.

Curiously the same kind of thinking has crept into some of the responses to terrorism. The "war on terrorism" that was launched by the United States government after September 11 is a case in point. To the degree that the war references are metaphorical, and meant to imply an all-out effort in the manner of previous administrations' "war on drugs," and "war on poverty," it is an understandable and appropriate response. The September 11 attacks were, after all, hideous acts that deeply scarred the American consciousness, and one could certainly understand that a responsible government would want to wage an all-out effort to hunt down those culpable and bring them to justice.

But among some who espouse a "war on terrorism" the militant language is more than metaphor. God's blessing is imagined to be bestowed on a view of confrontation that is, like cosmic war, all-encompassing, absolutizing, and demonizing. What is problematic about this view is that it brings an impatience with moderate solutions that require the slow procedures of systems of justice. It demands instead the quick and violent responses of war that lend simplicity to the confrontation and a sense of divine certainty to its resolution. Alas, such a position can fuel the fires of retaliation, leading to more acts of terrorism instead of less.

The role of religion in this literal "war on terrorism" is in a curious way similar to religion's role in the cosmic war imagined by those perpetrating terrorism. In both cases religion is a problematic partner of political confrontation. Religion brings more to conflict than simply a repository of symbols and the aura of divine support. It problematizes a conflict through its abiding absolutism, its justification for violence, and its ultimate images of warfare that demonize opponents and cast the conflict in transhistorical terms.

This is a dismal assessment of religion's role, and one might well wonder if religion does not, in some instances, have something positive to bring to conflict. I am happy to report that it does. Although our attention recently has been riveted on examples that display religion's dark side of justifying violence and demonizing opponents, religion can also bring more positive elements to a situation of conflict. It can offer images of a peaceful resolution, justifications for tolerating differences, and a respect for the dignity of all life. It was these images and arguments that brought Hindu values into the notion of *satyagraha*, or "truth force," the idea of conflict resolution advocated by Mohandas Gandhi. Similar concepts from Christianity informed the insights of the American theologian, Reinhold Niebuhr, who advocated countervailing power and the institutions of justice as peaceful ways of countering social evil. Niebuhr and Gandhi both influenced the thinking behind the nonviolent struggle of the American civil rights leader, Martin Luther King, Jr.

On a theoretical level, one can appreciate the long line of theorists from Émile Durkheim and Sigmund Freud up to and including such contemporary thinkers as the literary theorist René Girard. Theirs is a line of reasoning that sees religion as the cultural tool for defusing violence within a social community. They see the symbols and rituals of religion as essential in symbolically acting out violence as a way of displacing real acts of violence in the world. If this position has any utility at all—and I think that it does—what the world needs now is more ritual and symbol, not less of it.

In a curious way, then, the solution to religious violence is not more violence but more religion. That is, the solution to our current moment of religious violence may involve an understanding of religion that is not parochial and defensive, but expansive and tolerant in the manner advocated by virtually all religious scriptures and authorities. Beyond particular religions, moreover, there is a broad sense of the moral and spiritual unity of the family of humanity that can be dimly heard in the background even in the discordant moments of the 21st century's clashes of religion. It is good to be assured that there are religious resources for peace to be tapped, even as we know that religion provides the ammunition for some of our generation's most lethal acts. Though religion can be a problematic partner in confrontation it also holds the potential of providing a higher vision of human interaction than is portrayed in the bloody encounters of the present.

REFERENCES

GIRARD, RENÉ. *Violence and the Sacred.* Baltimore: Johns Hopkins University Press, 1977. (Translated from the 1972 French edition by Patrick Gregory.)

JUERGENSMEYER, MARK. *The New Cold War? Religious Nationalism Confronts the Secular State.* Berkeley: University of California Press, 1993.

JUERGENSMEYER, MARK. *Terror in the Mind of God: The Global Rise of Religious Violence.* Third edition. Berkeley: University of California Press, 2003.

LAWRENCE, BRUCE. *Shattering the Myth: Islam Beyond Violence*. Princeton, NJ: Princeton University Press, 2000.

LEWIS, BERNARD. *The Crisis of Islam: Holy War and Unholy Terror*. New York: Random House, 2003.

MACDONALD, ANDREW [pseudonym for William Pierce]. *The Turner Diaries*. Hillsboro, WV: National Vanguard Books, 1978. (Reprinted by the National Alliance, Arlington, VA, in 1985, and by Barricade Books, New York, 1996.)

NIEBUHR, REINHOLD. *Moral Man and Immoral Society*. New York: Scribner Publishing, 1932.

RANTISI, ABDUL AZIZ, co-founder and political leader of Hamas. Interview with the author, Khan Yunis, Gaza, March 1, 1998.

SELLS, MICHAEL A. *The Bridge Betrayed: Religion and Genocide in Bosnia*. Berkeley: University of California Press, 1996.

WEBER, MAX. "Politics as a Vocation." In Hans H. Gerth and C. Wright Mills, eds., *From Max Weber: Essays in Sociology*. New York: Oxford University Press, 1946.

MARK JUERGENSMEYER is a professor of sociology and religious studies and director of global and international studies at the University of California, Santa Barbara. He is author or editor of fifteen books, including *Terror in the Mind of God: The Global Rise of Religious Violence*.

42 Is Religious Violence Inevitable?

JAMES K. WELLMAN, JR. AND KYOKO TOKUNO

Continuing with our theme of whether religion is associated with violence, Wellman and Tokuno argue that we must not be surprised that religion leads to violence. Religion does not necessarily have to lead to violence, but in reality it often does. Not until we are able to understand that fact, they argue, can we make progress.

Religion kills. Religion brings peace. What is religion? The past 150 years are strewn with definitional cul-de-sacs in the study of religion in Western academia, in part because religion can never be fully explained and in part because there is no essence of religion that can finally be reified. But it is noteworthy that no definitions have put violence at the heart of religion. For Edward Tylor, religion is a false explanatory system (Tylor [1871] 1958); for Durkheim, religion is the social nexus of the group (Durkheim 1915); for Clifford Geertz, religion is meaning (Geertz 1973); for Rodney Stark, religion is the terms of exchange with the god or gods (Stark and Finke 2000); for Christian Smith, religion is a moral orientation to life (Smith 2003); for Ninian Smart, religion is an ever-evolving organism with multiple sociocultural dimensions (Smart 1969).

All these strike us as important approximations of religion, but there is something missing in them. We do not provide a full definition of religion, but we suggest that from our work on Western and Eastern religious traditions, past and present, there are patterns within religion that tend toward conflict and even violence.[1] Thus, our argument is the following. *The symbolic and social boundaries of religion (no matter how fluid or porous) mobilize individual and group identity in conflict, and sometimes violence, within and between groups.*

In the post-Cold-War era, a peace dividend appeared on the horizon. It never materialized. To the surprise of many, various religious communities moved into the new cultural and political space; they came out of relative obscurity

Source: James K. Wellman, Jr. and Kyoko Tokuno, "Is Religious Violence Inevitable?" from *Journal for the Scientific Study of Religion*, Volume 43. Copyright © 2004. Reproduced with permission of Blackwell Publishing Ltd.

to set cultural and even political agendas. We see this in Asia, Africa, Latin America, and even in the United States. In China, indigenous movements such as Falun Gong and the underground Christian churches have met with violent suppression from the Chinese government. In Japan, new religions emerged with alternative worldviews that in some cases, such as Aum Shinrikyo, adopted violence as a viable means to realize their religious goals (Reader 2000). In the Middle East and in Asia, various Islamist groups refuse to be intimidated by either the former Soviet Union or the United States (Juergensmeyer 2000). The global Christian evangelical movement is reshaping the southern hemisphere; evangelical growth has made substantial gains on the Roman Catholic Church in Latin America and has begun to transform the cultural and religious face of Africa (Jenkins 2002; Freston 2001). . . .

Theorists of secularization, many of whom are European in origin, looked at the religious world through the blinkered lenses of the Cold War (Swatos and Olson 2000). They did not see the power of religion to thrive in places of political and cultural oppression. The political ideologies of the 20th century now appear fragile against the ability of religious movements to inject their demands into the public sphere (Casanova 1994). In the post-Cold-War period, a time of great cultural and political transformation, religions have come to the fore to push their varied agendas. However, this phenomena is neither new nor should it be surprising. Indeed, we argue that religion is ideally suited to survive and thrive under difficult circumstance and, in fact, from our review of religious history and traditions, conflict tends to galvanize religious communities rather than subdue them. Our counterintuitive claim is that religion tends toward greater vitality when it is in tension with surrounding cultures. Modernity has not destroyed religion but rather become a case study in its resilience. What is behind the buoyancy of religion to thrive despite predictions to the contrary?

The symbolic boundaries of religion provide a powerful engine for individual and group identity formation. Religion has always functioned to shape individual and social identities and inspire group formation. The powerful affective events and experiences of religion, embodied in ritual action and mystical practice, formulated through systems of belief and story, have motivated human beings across time and culture. This nexus of experience, practice, and discourse are the core of religion's internal combustion engine that fuels individual leaders and their groups. It is precisely the power of this energy that creates tension, conflict, and sometimes violence with out-groups. As regards out-groups or more powerful political entities, religion provides points of moral, social, and political legitimation that are independent of typical social norms. The pattern is historically familiar. The strong communal identities of Jews and early Christians in the first centuries of the Common Era threatened the Roman empire; Muhammad and his small cadre of followers consolidated a community of the faithful that united warring tribes and became a dominant power in the Mediterranean and the Middle East; the Buddhist community in medieval China advanced its strategy to safeguard its tradition even as it was repeatedly subjected to state persecution because it was said that it threatened the indigenous cultural heritage and the state's political power (Nomura 1968); Joseph Smith and his family, who provoked and fended off various early persecutions, created a new religion that is now competitive with the growth rates of Christianity and Islam; the Sikhs, against overwhelming odds, rebelled against the Indian government in the 1980s. The symbolic and social building blocks of religion lend to groups, no matter their size, powerful mobilizing energies that are successful in part because they create tension, produce conflict, and sometimes engender violence against other religious groups, cultural powers, and global empires.

We argue, therefore, that it is a part of the nature of religious communities to gain their identity through conflict and tension with out-group cultures. Conflict, in this sense, is socially functional (Coser 1956). Identity is galvanized by the degree to which one is against the outsider, the other, whether as a competing religious community or a powerful national regime. Vital religious communities need the internal affective experience of religious transcendence (as a force or power) as well as tension or conflict with other political or cultural forces. It is against these external forces that they portray their purity, as with Protestantism; their chosenness, as with the Jews; their single-mindedness, as with Islam; or their clarity, as with the Sri Lankan Buddhists. This tension and conflict with out-groups does not always lead to violence. Forms of rhetorical and cultural conflict function to vitalize and mobilize religious identity as well. Christian Smith's work on American evangelicals shows that the evangelical groups that thrive are neither those that separate from culture (fundamentalists) nor those that accommodate (liberal Christians), but those that engage with it in conflict and competition (Smith 1998). The establishment of Indian Buddhism in medieval China offers another illustration. Even as adherents of Buddhism made efforts to narrow the cultural disparity using strategies of accommodation (skillful means), they nevertheless established Buddhism's symbolic and social identity through a series of public debates and polemical writings against Confucian and Taoist proponents. The process sharpened Buddhist rhetoric without compromising its core values.

Religions in general, and monotheisms in particular, need social conflict and competition both to hone their symbolic boundaries and to keep them from imploding internally from internecine conflict. The history of Protestantism is replete with internal strife and schisms that produced various sects' claims to purity (Ward 1992; Wuthnow 1988). The history of Catholicism is framed by Rodney Stark as an internal conflict between the church of piety and the church of power (Stark 2001). This internal conflict serves the Catholic Church by stimulating reform to restore its evangelical outreach and internal theological identity. Religions, as monopolies or as oppressed groups, use conflict to strengthen their identity and mobilize their groups to action. We have argued elsewhere that the U.S. administration formulated the second Iraq war (and the creation of an enemy) in part because it fit the logic of its evangelical base (Wellman 2004). Minority religions, including the Roman Catholics in Northern Ireland, Tamil Hindus in Sri Lanka, and the Protestants in Guatemala, use their religious traditions to energize and mobilize their cultural and political action against dominate political structures (Juergensmeyer 2000).

However, we are less persuaded that religions seek conflict because they know it is functional to their identity. Continuing the engine metaphor, one of the central pistons that motivates religions is the belief that the religions are true. Truth claims, whether implicit or explicit, act as powerful motivators to individuals and groups in expressing beliefs about their religion. Implicit truth claims imply that one's rituals and one's behavior are normal, that is, real. Truth claims, however, do not always remain embedded in religious group behavior. They often become explicit and are discursively defended as what is true about one's religion, the cosmos, and reality itself. This has been the case with the development of sophisticated religious traditions before the Common Era in classical Hinduism, Buddhism, and Taoism, which have accelerated in the Common Era with the metaphysics of Judaism, Christianity, and Islam. As the awareness and reality of cultural and religious diversity increases in the modern period, the need to defend and articulate one's religious symbol systems increases.

We believe it is folly to assert that true religion seeks peace; or that religion is somehow hijacked when it becomes implicated in conflict or even violence. Indeed, religion *does* produce conflict and, less frequently, violence. We do not believe that this is a new situation or that it will end soon. These patterns are replete in our studies throughout history. Mesopotamian religion was enormously violent, both in its symbolic cosmogonic portrayals and in its social and military actions toward others. Ancient Israel developed a concept of God that was agonistic to the extreme; it enabled the Jews to trust that God was on their side and that their cosmos reflected their earthly destiny (Niditch 1993; Collins 2003). Ancient Indian and Chinese religious beliefs and behaviors included sanctioned violence in cosmogony, sacrificial ritual, and mortuary practice (Basham 1989; Bodde 1981; Lewis 1990). Buddhists have not shunned the use of force or violence against oneself or others, especially in the sphere of religious nationalism. In medieval Japan, the Buddhist monk Nichiren (1222–1282) inaugurated an exclusivistic religious movement based on the theology of the *Lotus Sûtra* and an assertion of a nation governed by Buddhist law; the movement provoked conflict and persecution (McMullin 1984; Stone 1994); Buddhists supported Japanese imperialist aggression before and during World War II (Victoria 1997). In the contemporary period, militant political activist monks used violence for political ends in Sri Lanka (Tambiah 1992). Christians, of course, produced the crusades; killing for Christ in the medieval period became a heroic act of piety. To be sure, pious popes inspired and led these social movements (Stark 2001).

The partnership of religion and conflict is not only longstanding but new religions make a habit of creating conflict with dominant cultures. Modern examples include the self-inflicted violence of Jonestown in 1978; the mass murder in the Movement for the Restoration of the Ten Commandments in Uganda in 2000; the governmental attacks on the Branch Davidians in 1992; Scientology's battle for its public status in Europe in the 1990s; and the sarin gas attack on a Tokyo subway station by Aum Shinrikyo in 1995 that killed 12 and injured thousands (Bromley and Melton 2002).

The examples of religion and conflict could be multiplied. To say these are anomalous cases is to beg the question: Are there exceptions? We suggest no. To be sure, few new (or old) religious groups create violent goals. However, tension and conflict are inherent in all religious groups and are central to their identity formation and group mobilization. Once again, violence is not often a religion's intent, but as an outcome of its relation to culture and politics, it is certainly not an uncommon consequence. Religion, it can be said, is a nexus of independent power, which by its very nature threatens political centers, no matter their shape or size.

Religions throughout history and across cultures have formed themselves around a power or force that is experienced as within, outside, and above the sources of "normal" forms of moral authority in human societies. Religions call on sources of moral and spiritual authority that cannot be empirically disconfirmed by means of ordinary verification, whether socially, culturally, politically, or scientifically. In this way, the power and force of religion is beyond question, analysis, or inspection. This gives to religion and to leaders within religious communities enormous social and moral leverage to mobilize groups toward whatever metaphysical or political goals they experience or create. In Western religious terms, Soren Kierkegaard's description of Abraham's sacrifice of Isaac captures religion's tendency to transcend "universal" moral standards. Kierkegaard said that the sacrifice of Abraham was the "teleological suspension of the ethical." In essence, whatever is found to be persuasive by an experience of this force or power can be used to mobilize and rationalize social action, however deviant (Kierkegaard 1941).

In the case of China and, by extension, East Asia in general, the individual is less pivotal. Nevertheless, religion as a group phenomenon remains powerful in confronting state powers, as was demonstrated by frequent uprisings and rebellions throughout premodern period that were religiously motivated and sanctioned (Kamata 1990; McMullin 1984). The political institution, however, has the ultimate authority over religious institutions, in part because of the ancient Confucian ideology that mythologized the emperor as the earthly representation of the cosmic will. The situation contrasts sharply with the Indian and Southeast Asian context, where ultimate authority (at least during the premodern period) lay in the hands of the righteous king, who ruled according to religious ideals (Strong 1983; Tambiah 1976). Thus in China the power of religion to challenge political authority is checked if perceived as a threat to the social order. Consequently, we see state persecution of Buddhism in the medieval period (Nomura 1968), and suppression of smaller sectarian groups called White Lotus Teachings in the late imperial period (Haar 1992). Powerful religions such as Buddhism, therefore, had to resort to covert means (such as creating new scriptures to support its symbolic and social identity) or perform useful functions on behalf of the state, such as conducting rituals of protecting the state and its members.

Rodney Stark's work on religious conflict portrays the rational choice makeup of religions. Religions make claims and create rewards that motivate individuals to do extraordinary things in light of the truth claims and promises of the religion. Depending on the rewards promised, many people are willing to give up "normal" preferences for survival, social status, or purported universal social norms (Stark 2001). They willingly submit to religious authorities who encourage them to act in ways that are different from what they were raised to do or what many around them expect. It is empirically true that there is an endless supply of individuals who are willing to give up their lives for religious ideals. Religion, as Larry Iannaccone has argued, is

uniquely able to act as a vehicle for politically oppressed and socially marginalized groups, in this case Islamic extremists (though it is certainly not unique to Islam) (Iannaccone 2004). Religion is an ideal vehicle precisely because it creates an economy of culture that gives small groups both experiences of transcendent power and socialization that protects them from out-group exposure. These groups create a cosmic vision, offer an ideal social order, provide supernormal rewards, and produce a God that sanctifies horrific violence all in the name of religious goals.

Conflict in religion is socially functional. Moreover, it is in religion's very nature to produce tension with parent cultures. It animates followers under a system of symbols that verifies an experience of a felt power or force that not only produces truth claims but promises social and metaphysical rewards. As mentioned above, religion is not merely a vehicle; it has an engine that never runs out of fuel. The source of the fuel is exactly this power or force that cannot be disconfirmed internally or externally. This engine is precisely why nation states and modern secular elites fear religion and seek to marginalize it. For on the one hand, religion will not submit to any external authority (no matter how strong), and on the other hand, religion cannot be undercut by rational deconstruction because it has a source that rests outside of rational and empirical modes of discourse.

Religion is a tricky business for academics. Theorists of secularization thought at one time that it was doomed either to extinction or to the private world of the human heart. They were wrong (Berger 1999). The adventure of studying religion is that no one can control the subject except as they realize its power to motivate and mobilize groups. To give religion its due respect is the beginning of wisdom. So, we ask, is religious violence inevitable? Our answer is that religious conflict is predictable and should be expected. Because religion is often an independent cultural force in society, it has the tendency to become a threat to other cultural and political powers. Religious violence, we would argue, may not be inevitable, but it should surprise no one.

NOTE

1. By conflict we mean disagreement with others short of emotional or physical injury. Violence is thought of as relational and collective action that creates injury to others either emotionally or physically using words and/or actions.

REFERENCES

BASHAM, A. L. 1989. *The origins and development of classical Hinduism*, edited and annotated by K. G. Zysk. Boston, MA: Beacon Press.

BERGER, P. L., editor. 1999. *The desecularization of the world: Resurgent religion and world politics*, Grand Rapids, MI: WILLIAM B. Eerdmans Publishing Company.

BODDE, D. 1981. Harmony and conflict in Chinese philosophy. In *Essays on Chinese civilization*, edited by D. Bodde and C. LeBlanc. Princeton, NJ: Princeton University Press.

BROMLEY, D. G. and J. G. MELTON, editors. 2002. *Cults, religion and violence.* Cambridge: Cambridge University Press.

CASANOVA, J. 1994. *Public religions in the modern world.* Chicago, IL: University of Chicago Press.

COLLINS, J. J. 2003. The zeal of Phinehas: The Bible and the legitimation of violence. *Journal of Biblical Literature* 122(1):3–21.

COSER, L. 1956. *The function of social conflict.* New York: Free Press.

DURKHEIM, E. 1915. *The elementary forms of the religious life.* London: George Allen and Unwin.

FRESTON, P. 2001. *Evangelicals and politics in Asia, Africa and Latin America.* Cambridge: Cambridge University Press.

GEERTZ, C. 1973. *The interpretation of cultures.* New York: Basic Books.

HAAR, B. J. TER. 1999. *The white lotus teachings in Chinese religious history.* Leiden: E.J. Brill, 1992; repr. University of Hawaii Press.

IANNACCONE, L. R., 2004. The market for martyrs. Paper presented at the Religion, Conflict and Violence: Exploring Patterns Past and Present, East and West University of Washington Symposium. Seattle, WA.

JENKINS, P. 2002. *The next Christendom: The coming of global Christianity.* Oxford: Oxford University Press.

JUERGENSMEYER, M. 2000. *Terror in the mind of God: The global rise of religious violence.* Berkeley, CA: University of California Press.

KAMATA, S. 1990. *Chugoku bukkyoshi* [History of Buddhism in China], vol. 3. Tokyo: Tokyo daigaku shuppansha.

KIERKEGAARD, S. 1941. *Fear and trembling and the sickness unto death*, translated by W. Lowrie. Princeton, NJ: Princeton University Press.

LEWIS, M. E. 1990. *Sanctioned violence in early China.* Albany, NY: State University of New York Press.

MCMULLIN, N. 1984. *Buddhism and the state in sixteenth-century Japan.* Princeton, NJ: Princeton University Press.

NIDITCH, S. 1993. *War in the Hebrew Bible: A study in the ethics of violence.* New York: Oxford University Press.

NOMURA, Y. 1968. *Shûbu hûnan no kenkyû* [A study of the persecution of Buddhism by the Northern Chou Emperor Wu]. Tokyo: Higashi shuppan, Inc.

READER, I. 2000. *Religious violence in contemporary Japan: The case of Aum Shinrikyō.* Honolulu, HI: University of Hawaii Press.

SMART, N. 1969. *The religious experience of mankind.* New York: Charles Scribner's Sons.

SMITH, C. 1998. *American evangelicalism: Embattled and thriving.* Chicago, IL: University of Chicago Press.

———. 2003. *Moral, believing animals: Human personhood and culture.* Oxford: Oxford University Press.

STARK, R. 2001. *One true God: Historical consequences of monotheism.* Princeton, NJ: Princeton University Press.

STARK, R. and R. FINKE. 2000. *Acts of faith: Explaining the human side of religion.* Berkeley, CA: University of California Press.

STONE, J. 1994. Rebuking the enemies of the lotus: Nichirenist exclusivism in historical perspective. *Japanese Journal of Religious Studies* 21(2–3):231–59.

STRONG, J. S. 1983. *The legend of King Aśoka: A study and translation of the Aśokāvadāna.* Princeton, NJ: Princeton University Press.

SWATOS, W. H. and D. V. A. OLSON, editors. 2000. *The secularization debate.* New York: Rowman & Littlefield Publishers, Inc.

TAMBIAH, S. J. 1976. *World conqueror & world renouncer: A study of Buddhism and polity in Thailand against a historical background.* Cambridge: Cambridge University Press.

———. 1992. *Buddhism betrayed?: Religion, politics, and violence in Sri Lanka.* Chicago/London: University of Chicago Press.

TYLOR, E. B. [1871] 1958. *Religion in primitive culture.* New York: Harper and Brothers.

VICTORIA, B. (DAIZEN) A. 1997. *Zen at war.* New York/Tokyo: Weatherhill.

WARD, W. R. 1992. *The Protestant evangelical awakening.* Cambridge: Cambridge University Press.

WELLMAN Jr., J. K. 2004. War is normal: The logic of American evangelical Christian religion. Paper presented at the Religion, Conflict and Violence: Exploring Patterns Past and Present, East and West University of Washington Symposium, Seattle, WA.

WUTHNOW, R. 1988. *The restructuring of American religion: Society and faith since World War II.* Princeton, NJ: Princeton University Press.

43 Religion, Violence, and Peacemaking

SHARON ERICKSON NEPSTAD

The final reading in this Religious Violence section takes a different approach than the previous articles. Erickson explores religious peacemakers, and attempts to begin to understand why religion is sometimes used for violence, but often used for positive dialogue and nonviolent resolution of conflicts. She identifies a key distinction: truth seekers versus truth protectors. How are these terms related to understanding religious violence and peacemaking?

The recent rise of religiously inspired terrorism has revived interest in religion's darker capacities. Although the events of September 11 occurred only a few years ago, religion and political violence have been intertwined for centuries. Holy wars, forced conversions, witch hunts, and heresy executions led early social theorists to question why and how the religious imagination fosters and is fueled by cultures of violence. Although these are critical questions to revisit in light of contemporary political concerns, it is also important to recognize that religion has historically played a significant role in curbing violence, constraining aggression, and promoting reconciliation and understanding between disputing groups. Church history, for

example, demonstrates that Christianity was responsible for the brutal Crusades but has also tried to place limits on fighting through Ambrose and Augustine's Just War criteria. Furthermore, it has inspired nonviolent groups that denounce militarism and have heroically intervened in war.

Since religion can be both bellicose and pacifying, what are the conditions that, on the one hand, make it a force that foments violence or, on the other hand, promotes peace? In his book *Terror in the Mind of God*, Mark Juergensmeyer (2000) offers an answer to the first part of this question by examining the social dynamics that foster religious violence. Comparing terrorist groups in several faith traditions, he concludes

Source: Sharon Erickson Nepstad, "Religion, Violence, and Peacemaking," from *Journal for the Scientific Study of Religion*, Volume 443. Copyright © 2004. Reproduced with permission of Blackwell Publishing Ltd.

that religious terrorists share the following attributes. First, they consider contemporary forms of religion as weakened versions of the true, authentic faith. These terrorists embrace a more demanding, "hard" religion that requires sacrifice. Second, they refuse to compromise with secular institutions, critiquing "soft" religions for readily accommodating to the mainstream culture. Thus Islamic radicals call for a stronger stance against Western influence, Jewish settlers denounce Israeli politicians who are willing to negotiate over the occupied territories, and abortion clinic bombers reject U.S. Christians' complacency vis-à-vis the *Roe v. Wade* Supreme Court decision. These activists feel justified in defying laws since they view their responsibilities as citizens as secondary to their faith and religious obligations. Finally, Juergensmeyer notes that religious terrorists reject the public-private split whereby faith is considered a private matter to be kept outside the realm of politics. Some even hope that their actions will contribute to the demise of the secular state, ultimately leading to the establishment of a theocracy.

Yet these same attributes are also typical of many religious activists who aim to *stop* political violence. For example, the U.S. Catholic Left repudiates "soft Christianity" that acquiesces to expanding American militarism. This group commits radical acts of peacemaking by breaking into weapons production sites and military compounds to disarm weapons of mass destruction through sabotage. Those who participate in these "plowshares actions" face lengthy prison sentences, but this does not deter them since they believe that authentic faith yields the same consequences that Christ and the early apostles faced, namely, prison and death (Nepstad 2004). Similarly, Quakers have a longstanding tradition of rejecting compromises with secular institutions such as the government. They refused conscription and military service (which most religious groups accept) and denounced slavery. Yet Quakers did not confine their convictions to a personal refusal to own slaves or private decisions to boycott goods produced by slave labor. They actively interfered with the institution of slavery by participating in the Underground Railroad and obstructing slave hunters' efforts after the passage of the Fugitive Slave Act. Perhaps the best-known religious peacemaker, Mahatma Gandhi, also rejected a complete public-private split, stating: "I could not be leading a religious life unless I identified myself with the whole of mankind, and that I could not do unless I took part in politics... You cannot divide social, economic, political and purely religious work into watertight compartments" (Gandhi 1958:63).

If these three traits—rejection of soft religion, the public-private split, and compromises with secular society—characterize religious terrorists as well as peacemakers, then why is religion sometimes divisive and destructive and sometimes a powerful force for peace? Aside from ethical differences on the use of force, there are several factors that distinguish peaceful religious movements from violent ones. I offer some reflections on these differences by examining commonalties in the philosophy and practice of several prominent religious peacemakers of various faiths—Gandhi (Hindu), Daniel Berrigan (Catholic), Martin Luther King Jr. (Protestant), and Thich Nhat Hanh (Buddhist). Although this type of comparative analysis could include a variety of other factors, I focus on distinctions in the worldviews and religious imaginations of these groups.

DISTINCTIONS BETWEEN VIOLENT AND NONVIOLENT RELIGIOUS ACTIVISTS

Views on the Nature of Good and Evil

One notable point of divergence between radical religious peacemakers and religious activists who use violence is found in their view of good and evil. For religious terrorists, there is no ambiguity: they perceive their enemies as completely wicked and consider themselves the protectors of righteousness. James Aho (1994) argues that this tendency to view conflicting parties in Manichean terms is not unique to religious groups. In fact, he states that both religious and secular groups manufacture enemies because this provides the opportunity to valiantly battle evil, thereby establishing themselves as heroes and granting meaning and purpose to their existence. Furthermore, Aho notes that enemies function as a societal enema, allowing groups to transfer their own negative attributes to others and purifying themselves in the process.

We represent right, *Recht*, law and morality. We are righteousness; we are rigid; we are, to use a term familiar to clinical psychologies of anality, "rectal." We comprise the social rectum, as it were. The enemy is what is wrong, what is left, not right, what is left behind, that which remains. What remains is waste material, the refuse of the social body, what it refuses, that which is not permitted.... Moral campaigns purge the social body of its refuse. They represent public enemas of sorts, collective "escapes from evil." (Aho 1994:109)

When religiosity is mixed into the process of constructing an enemy, it can intensify the conflict. If people believe that they are carrying out a divine mandate, they may be less willing to negotiate, since the devout will not compromise the will of God. Furthermore, earthly struggles may take on cosmic significance, reflecting a transcendent battle between good and evil. This type of worldview often leads people to draw rigid, impermeable divisions between groups. Evil is no longer an individual trait but rather a characteristic of an entire group that is considered incapable of change. "A satanic enemy cannot be transformed," Juergensmeyer states, "it can only be destroyed" (2000:217). The only way to completely eliminate evil, therefore, is to annihilate the wicked and any means used to accomplish this are morally justified.

For religious peacemakers, the line between good and evil lies within each individual, not between groups. By acknowledging that we are all capable of evil, the basis for moral self-righteousness is removed and it becomes difficult to condemn others for weaknesses that all people possess. Thich Nhat Hanh, a Vietnamese Buddhist monk, frequently emphasizes this point. He deconstructs rigid dualisms and simplistic moral judgments as he speaks about a letter he received from a Southeast Asian refugee who recounted how he and others fled by boat, only to encounter a pirate who raped one of the refugees—a 12-year-old girl. The girl became so despondent that she threw herself into the ocean and drowned. Hanh writes:

When you first learn of something like that, you get angry at the pirate. You naturally take the side of the girl. As you look more deeply you will see it differently. If you take the side of the little girl, then it is easy. You only have to take a gun and shoot the pirate. But... in my mediation I saw that if I had been born in the same village of the pirate and raised in the same conditions as he was, there is a great likelihood that I would become a pirate. I cannot condemn myself so easily. In my meditation, I saw that many babies are born along the Gulf of Siam, hundreds every day, and if we educators, social workers, politicians, and others do not do something about the situation, in 25 years a number of them will become sea pirates.... If you take a gun and shoot the pirate, you shoot all of us, because all of us are to some extent responsible for this state of affairs. (1987:62)

Recognizing that everyone is capable of committing injustices, religious peacemakers also believe that all individuals are redeemable. Unlike the religious terrorists who argue that the wicked cannot be transformed, advocates of nonviolence assert that anyone can be converted. Rather than shunning their enemies and accentuating divisions, peacemakers intentionally traverse group boundaries to have dialogue and develop relationships with their opponents. Daniel Berrigan, a Jesuit priest who destroyed draft files during the Vietnam War and damaged missiles during the nuclear arms race, underscores this point.

[T]he Christian (if he follows Christ's example) will constantly want to cross over and be with the ex-communicated, or be with the stigmatized, or be with the so-called "enemy."...For those who belong to the radical religious community, I don't care whether it is located in the East or West, whether it is Christian or Buddhist, there is a constant insistence that...whatever judgments are rendered, they are not retributive so much as redemptive. Mercy is the point. We are trying to say even to those who in the name of law or in the name of power commit most awful actions against others—we are declaring that those people are redeemable too. (Berrigan and Coles [1971] 2001:165).

This should not be misunderstood as unrealistic optimism or naïve faith in the essential goodness of humanity. Martin Luther King Jr. called people to be realistic pacifists who would not ignore "the glaring reality of collective evil" (King 1958:99). He emphasized that all humans have the capacity for both good and evil but he argued that the use of violence expands an individual's malevolence whereas nonviolence calls forth virtuosity.

Views on the Nature of Truth

A second fundamental distinction between nonviolent and violent religious activists centers on their views of truth. Religious terrorists maintain that there is only one truth that is timeless and unchanging. Protecting this divine, absolute truth is of paramount importance and thus ideas take precedence over people. In contrast, Thich Nhat Hanh argues that this mindset is dangerous, leading to dogmatism and a readiness to kill in the name of truth. His religious principles encourage the opposite—nonattachment to ideas. He describes the first three precepts of the Tiep Hien Order of Engaged Buddhism.

First: Do not be idolatrous about or bound to any doctrine, theory, or ideology, even Buddhist ones.

All systems of thought are guiding means; they are not absolute truth.... Human life is more precious than any ideology, any doctrine.... [I]f you have an ideology and stick to it, thinking it is the absolute truth, you can kill millions. This precept includes the precept of not killing in its deepest sense. Humankind suffers very much from attachment to views. In the name of truth, we kill each other.... Second: Do not think that the knowledge you presently possess is changeless, absolute truth. Avoid being narrow-minded and bound to present views. Learn to practice non-attachment from views in order to be open to receive others' viewpoints. ... Third: Do not force others, including children, by any means whatsoever, to adopt your views, whether by authority, threat, money, propaganda, or even education. However, through compassionate dialogue, help others renounce fanaticism and narrowness. (Hanh 1987:89–91)

This alternative perspective is perhaps most clearly exemplified in Gandhi's life and work. Gandhi maintained that "Truth is God," in contrast to the more common premise that God is truth. Since humans do not know God completely and fully, then they do not possess absolute truth and hence are not in a position to punish others. Thus, rather than being protectors of the truth, Gandhi argued that we should be pursuers of it, which is tantamount to seeking God. This quest for truth requires individuals to unmask falsehoods, persistently persuading oppressors to stop perpetrating injustices. Yet it also requires truthseekers to remain unceasingly open to other views, including their opponent's. This is the heart of the Gandhian concept of *satyagraha*, translated as "holding on to truth" or "truth force." Joan Bondurant (1958) described it as a "Gandhian dialectic" since the ultimate goal of *satyagraha* is to synthesize the truths of both parties in a conflict, thereby expanding their common ground and bringing each closer to God. In practice this means that religious activists cling to their understanding of truth, aiming to resolve conflicts through persuasion of their opponents in word and action. Yet simultaneously the *satyagrahi* (truthseeker) invites the other side to demonstrate the correctness of its position. Bondurant carefully notes that this is not equivalent to compromise. She states:

[T]he Gandhian technique proceeds in a manner qualitatively different from compromise. What results from the dialectical process of conflict of opposite positions as acted upon by satyagraha, is a synthesis, not a compromise. The satyagrahi is never prepared to yield any position which he holds to be the truth. He is, however, prepared—and this is essential—to be persuaded by his opponent that the opponent's position is the true, or the more nearly true, position.... When persuasion has been effected, what was once the opponent's position is now the position of both antagonist and protagonist. There is no victory in the sense of triumph of one side over the other.... There is no "lowering" of demands, but an aiming at a "higher" level of adjustment which creates a new, mutually satisfactory, resolution. (1958:197)

Satyagraha does not mean that religious peacemakers are any less radical than religious activists who use violence. Gandhi's faith and convictions inspired him to fight for comprehensive social change in India's political, economic, and cultural realms. His movement had revolutionary goals—to free India from British colonial rule, to move toward economic self-sufficiency, and eliminate the caste system. This is not the "soft" compromising religion that religious terrorists repudiate. The Gandhian pursuit of Truth/God, the Catholic Left's efforts to abolish weapons of mass destruction, and Engaged Buddhists' efforts to stop the Vietnam War required serious sacrifice. Similar to religious terrorists, these religious peacemakers were willing to die for their faith and their cause. However, they were not willing to kill for it.

Views of Religion

The discussion of Gandhi's view of truth reveals that religious terrorists and religious peacemakers also think of faith in fundamentally different ways. For religious terrorists, *religion is an end in itself.* Often, their struggle is not only to defeat earthly evil but also to usher in an era in which their religion dominates. For some, this may take the form of a theocracy while others believe their actions will inaugurate an apocalypse that will culminate in a spiritual transformation of the world (Juergensmeyer 2000). Because religion is the end goal, people may be sacrificed in order to establish or preserve a religious foothold in society.

For religious peacemakers, *religion is viewed as a means to an end*, namely, enlightenment, truth, or spiritual fulfillment. Thich Nhat Hanh asserts that religious principles and practices are methods designed to guide individuals toward this destination. "Buddha's teaching is only a raft to help you cross the shore, a finger pointing to the moon," he states. "Don't mistake the finger for the moon. The raft is not the shore" (Hanh 1987:89). Moreover, many religious peacemakers hold that the type of vessel one uses to reach the shore is not so important. Gandhi commented:

Religions are different roads converging to the same point. What does it matter that we take different roads, so long as we reach the same goal? In reality, there are as many religions as there are individuals. If a man reaches the heart of his own religion, he has reached the heart of others too. So long as there are different religions, every one of them may need some distinctive symbol. But when the symbol is made into a fetish and an instrument of proving the superiority of one's religion over others, it is fit only to be discarded. ([1958] 1999:54)

For religious peacemakers, therefore, the goal is spiritual enlightenment and truth—not only for individuals but also for society as a whole. This is not to be confused with religious terrorists' desire to establish a religious government or culture but rather to integrate religiously inspired principles of justice and respect for all people into the fabric of society.

CONCLUSION

A comprehensive discussion of the factors that contribute to religion's capacity to promote respect, dialogue, and nonviolent resolution of conflicts—or, conversely, promote a climate of terror—requires a more systematic, in-depth investigation than I offer in this brief essay. Although I examine key differences in the worldviews of religious peacemakers and terrorists, future research ought to explore the broader structural influences on religious actors' decisions to adopt nonviolent or violent tactics. For instance, recent debates suggest that the spread of democracy may inhibit violent revolutionary movements and foster nonviolent protest as opposition groups can now work for reform within the system. Although the nature of religious terrorism is fundamentally different from political acts of violence, we do not have systematic data that determines whether or how various forms of government affect religious activists' tactical choices. Juergensmeyer (2000) also suggests that key historical developments and economic shifts have contributed to the global rise of religious violence; we need similar comparative information about the type of environmental changes that foster the emergence and vitality of faith-based peacemaking movements. Additionally, the social organization within religious groups is another factor that merits further consideration. Do hierarchical religious institutions encourage moral dualism and dogmatic views of truth more or less often than decentralized groups that determine and implement doctrine at the local level?

I have not presented a definitive theoretical account of why religion sometimes promotes violence and at other times fosters peace. Rather, I drew attention to the fact that religion is not inherently dogmatic, rigid, socially intolerant, and exclusive. It can be—and this is true for both conservative as well as progressive faiths. However, when religious teachers and practitioners reject simplistic moral dualism and define themselves as truthseekers rather than truth protectors, then religion can undercut the polarizing dynamics of conflict. It can be a potent force that encourages disputing parties to see the limitations of their own perspectives, the humanity of the opposing side, and the possibility of transforming even hardened hearts. Religion can operate as a moral compass that values human life over ideas. Those who seek fulfillment through a "hard" faith will find that many nonviolent faith traditions require resolute commitment and sacrifice, including the willingness to offer one's life as Gandhi, King, and other religious peacemakers have done. Radical religious peacemaking demands the type of altruism that accepts suffering but does not inflict it on others.

REFERENCES

AHO, J. 1994. *This thing of darkness: A sociology of the enemy.* Seattle, WA: University of Washington Press.

BERRIGAN, D. and R. COLES. [1971] 2001. *The geography of faith: Underground conversations on religious, political and social change.* Woodstock, VT: SkyLight Paths Publishing.

BONDURANT, J. V. 1958. *Conquest of violence: The Gandhian philosophy of conflict.* Princeton, NJ: Princeton University Press.

GANDHI, M. K. [1958] 1999. *All men are brothers: Autobiographical reflections.* New York: Continuum.

HANH, T. N. 1987. *Being peace.* Berkeley, CA: Parallax Press.

JUERGENSMEYER, M. 2000. *Terror in the mind of God: The global rise of religious violence.* Berkeley, CA: University of California Press.

KING Jr., M. L. 1958. *Stride toward freedom.* San Francisco, CA: HarperCollins.

NEPSTAD, S. E. 2004. Persistent resistance: Commitment and community in the Plowshares Movement. *Social Problems* 51(1):43–60.

Reading

44 Redefining the Boundaries of Belonging: The Institutional Character of Transnational Religious Life

PEGGY LEVITT

Technology allows us to go beyond our local environment, to have greater awareness and contact with the people and cultures around the world. As communication and transportation technologies advance and become more affordable, what is the impact on religion? How is religious life transnational, and what difference does it make?

INTRODUCTION

Every Sunday morning, a group of families in Governador Valadares, Brazil gather in their living rooms to watch the Catholic mass that is broadcast on their local TV. But this mass is not held in Valadares or in any other Brazilian city. Instead, it is a videotaped recording of the Portuguese mass held at St. Joseph's Church in Somerville, Massachusetts where large numbers of Brazilians have migrated. Family members still living in Brazil watch hoping they will glimpse their relatives worshipping in Boston. They pray along with the familiar liturgy while they scour the crowd for some sign that their family is okay.

This ability to bring U.S. religious life into the living rooms of Governador Valadares is one piece of a larger dynamic that this paper seeks to illustrate. Many aspects of religious life have long been global. Contemporary migrants extend and deepen these cross-border ties by transnationalizing everyday religious practice. In addition to earning their livelihoods and supporting their families by "keeping feet in two worlds," transnational migrants expand already-global religious institutions and assert their dual memberships in spiritual arenas. By doing so, they broaden and thicken the globalization of religious life.

But what is the nature of transnational religious life for ordinary individuals? How does transnational religious belonging complement or undermine other kinds of transnational membership? What difference does it make

Source: Peggy Levitt, "Redefining the Boundaries of Belonging: The Institutional Character of Transnational Religious Life." Reprinted with permission, from *Sociology of Religion*, Volume 65, © 2004.

when new migrants are integrated into receiving communities and remain connected to their sending communities through religious rather than political arenas?

The preliminary findings I present here are based on an on-going study of transnational migration among five immigrant communities in the greater Boston Metropolitan area. The larger study includes Pakistanis, and Dominicans but here I focus primarily on the experiences of Irish from the Inishowen Peninsula in County Donegal who live in the southeastern sections of Boston and its surroundings, Brazilians from the city of Governador Valadares who live in Framingham, Mass., and Indian migrants from Gujarat State who have settled in and around the city of Lowell. Over the last four years, I have worked with a team of graduate and undergraduate student researchers to interview migrants and their leaders in the U.S. We then travel to each sending country where we work with colleagues to conduct a parallel set of interviews with nonmigrant family members and organizational leaders at the local, regional, and national levels.

. . .

THEORETICAL DEBATES

. . . Researchers have only recently begun to pay attention to the relationship between transnational migration and religion (Levitt 1998; McAlister 2002; Tweed 1999). . . . Global religious institutions shape the transnational migration experience while migrants chip away at and recreate global religions by making them local and starting the process anew. Migrants' religious institutions are also sites where globally diffused models of social organization and individuals' local responses converge to produce new mixes of religious beliefs and practices. The study of transnational migration and religion, therefore, provides an empirical window onto one way in which religious globalization actually gets done.

The developing work on transnational migrants' religious practices addresses a set of common themes and questions that also drive the research presented here. Some of these studies are concerned with the institutional forms produced by transnational religious activities. Ebaugh and Chafetz (2002) used network analysis to capture these dynamics. They examined the relationship between network ties among individuals, local-level corporate bodies, and international religious bodies and found that ties frequently crossed between nodes. Yang (2002) discovered three-layered trans-Pacific networks formed by contacts between individuals, single churches, and para-Chinese Christian Churches that connected migrants in Taiwan, Hong Kong, and Mainland China to their counterparts in the U.S. and Canada. Transnational institutional connections transformed immigrant community religious life, and the political and religious life of the home country (Kurien 2001) and enabled immigrant religious communities to exert power within their global religious systems (Yang and Ebaugh 2001).

Other studies ask how religion encourages or impedes transnational membership. Wellmeier (1998) argued that Guatemalan Mayans had energy and resources to make hometown improvements because they belonged to independent storefront ministries that were ethnically homogeneous. Similarly, because many members of the Protestant churches that Menjívar (1999) studied came from the same regions of El Salvador, and they were not constrained by the institutional requirements of membership in the Catholic Church, they also engaged in home-town oriented activities with little conflict.

Some churches, however, enable transnational membership better than others. Menjívar (1999) found that Catholic Church membership was far less conducive to transnational activism because the Church wanted to emphasize pan-ethnic allegiances and feared that homeland-oriented activities might reignite schisms within the Salvadoran community. Peterson and Vásquez (2001) found that Charismatic Catholic activities encouraged individual transnational religious practices but produced few collective responses.

A third set of questions running across this literature focuses on the relationship between religion and politics and how this changes when it is enacted transnationally. Many assume, for instance, that Pentecostals would be apolitical with respect to both transnational and national concerns, but several studies find that Pentecostal communities influence the secular settings where they are located (Peterson et al. 2001; Menjívar 1999). Because members fulfill multiple roles and participate in multiple settings they influence the secular world and it continues to influence them.

The purpose of this article is to build on this incipient conversation. In the next section, I suggest an approach to the study of migrants' transnational religious practices and in the sections that follow, I present some of my research findings to date.

STUDYING TRANSNATIONAL MIGRANTS' RELIGIOUS PRACTICES

One way that migrants stay connected to their sending communities is through transnational religious practices. Some migrants sustain long-term, long-distance memberships in the religious organizations they belonged to before they migrated. They contribute financially to these groups, raise funds to support their activities, host visiting religious leaders, seek long-distance guidance from them, participate in worship and cultural events during return visits, and are the subject of nonmigrants' prayers. Other migrants participate in religious pilgrimages, worship certain saints or deities, or engage in informal, popular religious practices that affirm their enduring ties to a particular sending-country group or place.

The transnational religious practices that individuals engage in are often reinforced by the organizational contexts where they take place. For example, some migrants belong to host-country religious institutions that have formal ties to a home-country "sister congregation." They belong to groups that function like franchises or chapters of a sending-country group or they participate in religious groups that have no official affiliation with a sending-country religious community but that "brings in" religious leaders and supplies, thus linking members to their homelands. For others, the denomination that they belong to is part of a worldwide religious institution that treats them as members wherever they are.

To understand the role of religion in transnational migration, then, we must build from the ground up. We need to start by examining the ways in which ordinary individuals live their everyday religious lives across borders, explore how these activities influence their continued sending and receiving-country membership, and analyze the relationship between cross-border religious membership and other kinds of transnational belonging. We need to explore these changes in the home and host-country context and observe the ways in which they iteratively transform one another over time. Research on the religious lives of transnational migrants must also be concerned with how local sending- and receiving-country religious organizations respond to migration and with what changes, if any, these trigger at the regional, national, and international organizational levels. For example, localized connections between members and leaders of Brazilian Baptist churches in Governador Valadares in Brazil and in Framingham, Massachusetts should be analyzed within the context of the broader national and international denominational connections where they emerge.

Transnational migrants clearly live in multi-layered global worlds so that studies of their religious practices must be nested within the multi-layered social fields where migrants are embedded. Of singular importance is the role of states that regulate movement and religious expression, and thereby strongly influence the magnitude and character of migrants' transnational religious practices. Global culture and institutions also clearly shape migrants' transnational religious practices (Meyer, Boli, Thomas, and Ramirez 1997). Widely available patterns of religious institutionalization strongly influence the ways in which migrants combine host and homeland traditions. Because the "model" for prayer and administration in certain denominations is similar around the world, migrants know how to participate in any church wherever they are.

VARIATIONS IN TRANSNATIONAL RELIGIOUS LIFE

Three types of transnational religious organizations emerge thus far from our data. These are offered as heuristic devices rather than static, fixed categories. The boundaries between them are messy and organizations may move between types over time.

Extended Transnational Religious Organizations

The first type of transnational religious organization suggested by our study, exemplified by the Catholic Church, is an *extended transnational religious organization*. From the mid 1800s to the present, the Catholic Church has worked diligently to create and reinforce its role as a transnational, publicly influential institution. Vatican II furthered this by reversing a century-long trend toward centralization and acknowledging the plurality of national Catholicisms while instituting a set of liturgical changes that homogenized Catholicism throughout the world (Hervieu-Léger 1997). The same general ethos of the Church as a global institution that tolerates religious pluralism also encourages transnationalties. Because the

ethnic identity combines U.S. and homeland experiences for so many migrants, the resources and labor the Church allocates to ethnic congregations also reinforces homeland affinities.

When migrants circulate in and out of parishes or religious movement groups in the U.S., Ireland, the Dominican Republic, or Brazil, they broaden and deepen a global religious system that is already powerful and legitimate. The transnational connections that emerge grow out of relations between individuals, clergy, religious movement members and churches in both settings. For example, Father Ted, an Irish-born priest sent over by the Irish Church to work with the community in Boston, sees part of his job as enabling transnational membership. He wants "the new Irish" to integrate into the parishes where they live but to help those who so desire to continue to maintain strong ties to Ireland. "It is not my intention," he said, "to keep them away from the American Church but to meet them where they are and to help them branch out from there." The Irish Pastoral Center offers classes in Irish dance and in Gaelic. He is often asked to say mass in memory of someone in Ireland. The premarital classes he runs, required for anyone wanting a Church wedding, cover how to get life and disability insurance, a mortgage, or open a bank account in Boston and Ireland. Because so many people return to Ireland to be married, the Pastoral Center also helps them prepare all the necessary paperwork before they go.

The staffing and finances of the Irish Pastoral Program are also organized transnationally. Catholic clergy in the northeastern U.S. felt overwhelmed by the large numbers of largely illegal parishioners who arrived in the 1980s and they approached their Irish colleagues for support. The Irish Church loans these priests for five-year periods during which their salary and living costs are paid by their Archdiocese in the U.S.

These relations extend an already global religious institution in ways that allow migrants to maintain ties to their sending country while they become incorporated into the U.S. They also incorporate migrants into powerful, resource-rich networks that are potential venues for representation and protection vis-à-vis their home and host countries.

Churchgoing builds civic skills in several ways (Verba, Schlozman, and Brady 1999). Because Inishoweners attend the English-language mass, they get informal civics lessons each time they go to church. Most of the priests who serve them are native born and well-informed about local politics. Inishoweners also participate directly in parish governance rather than in the ethnic parish councils that most non-English speakers are relegated to. Inishoweners described activities such as signing petitions in favor of school vouchers or attending a candidate's night as some of the new "political" experiences they had at church. The support groups for young families that the Irish Pastoral Center organized became clearinghouses for information about jobs, housing, and schools. Though informal social networks had always played this role in Ireland, many people said they never thought of the church as a place to turn to for this kind of help.

This local-level advocacy and social service provision function has a national level equivalent in the form of the Irish Apostolate U.S. Irish clergy working around the country created this umbrella group in 1997. Father Tim, its director, got permission to establish the group from the Irish Bishops in Dublin and the National Council of Catholic Bishops (NCCB) in the U.S. He recalled,

In the early 1990s, I went back to Ireland to talk with government officials. I told them that these people are not American citizens, they still need help, without citizenship or a green card they are very vulnerable. If the Church does not help them, they will be in bad shape. I said to make no mistake, the Irish Church officials working out there (in the United States) are not there working for the American government or the American Church but for the Irish Church and government.

By 2001, the Irish Apostolate U.S. had programs all over the country. Because Father Tim worked in part for the NCCB's Office of Migrant and Refugee Services, when migrants ran into problems in places with no official program, he could ask the local priest to help out. Support for these activities came from a yearly $300,000 grant from the Irish government, to which Father Tim submitted a yearly report, and from occasional funding from the NCCB. He also raised funds from "Irish Americans who have made good," and from private foundations.

The Irish Apostolate U.S., along with a national coalition of Irish Immigration Centers, also formed an informal political action committee and lobbying group that works on immigrant rights' issues. Finally, the Irish Apostolate is the Irish governments' point of contact with the emigrant community in the U.S. When government officials needed information, they asked the priests.

The Minister of Foreign Affairs came here three years ago and the Minister for Social Welfare came last year. Any time a President comes, like Mary Robinson or Mary McAlese, they come and talk to us. Mary Robinson came and talked to us at lunch and asked us about the different issues we confront. We also visit Irish prisoners here and we keep the government informed about whether they are being treated properly, what their sentences are, whether they can be sent back home. We are the voice of the immigrant community for the Irish government (Father Mike, Boston, 2001).

Negotiated [Transnational] Religious Organizations

Brazilian Protestant churches typify a second type of negotiated transnational religious organization revealed by this study. In these contexts, relations between sending and receiving country churches evolve without a strong federated institutional structure or rules. Instead, individuals and organizations enter into informal agreements with one another that have weaker connections to political circles but are more flexibly constituted. In this section, I focus on the International Church of the Four Square Gospel to illustrate how religious participation becomes a kind of religious citizenship with its own set of norms and expectations about the collective good.

In the 1960s, less than five percent of the Brazilian population called themselves Protestant. Now, close to forty percent claims to be "born again." There are an estimated 430 Protestant churches in Governador Valadares, a city of close to 300,000 in Minas Gerais. In 1997, in one neighborhood of approximately 3,000 residents alone, we identified at least 35 churches. These congregations ranged from Mainline Protestant groups that pray in elegant, well-established churches to start-up Pentecostal congregations using living rooms and storefronts as places to pray. Even some of the most fledgling groups had plaques outside their doors indicating they had chapters in Massachusetts.

Like their Catholic counterparts, negotiated transnational religious organizations also evolve from connections between individuals and institutions. In some cases, an individual pastor maintains ties to his or her denomination in Brazil while in others, ties emerge between sending and receiving-country churches.

Aimee Semple McPherson founded the International Church of the Four Square Gospel (ICFSG) in Los Angeles in 1924. In 1951, the Church sent its first missionaries to Minas Gerais and Sao Paulo in Brazil. Though a relatively small denomination in the U.S., the ICFSG spread rapidly in Brazil. In 2001, there were an estimated 10,000 churches throughout the country. Brazilian migration to the northeast, and the United States ICFSG's subsequent decision to focus on evangelization in this region, produced a reverse missionary movement to New England.

Several layers of connections produce and reinforce the ties between Four Square members in Brazil and in Boston. Some migrants still officially belong to their church in Valadares and continue to tithe there. Pastor Luis, the senior pastor of the community, is still close to his counterpart in Valadares, the leaders of his former church in Sao Paulo, and members of the Church's national governing board. He still retains credentials from the Brazilian ICFSG though he is now an official member of the Church in the U.S.

Where Pastor Luis falls in this web of relationships, and how his work is supervised and financed, speaks to the informal, evolving character of these transnational religious ties. The Brazilian national Board of Directors had to give him permission to work in the U.S. Initially he got some funding from the U.S. Church and a one-time, $500 grant from his former church in Brazil. He now receives support from the Missions Department of the church in Brazil because the director is a personal friend. He funds most of his work on his own, using income from investments.

Although Pastor Luis no longer has any formal responsibilities in Brazil, he recognizes the importance of maintaining good relations with his colleagues. He goes back to visit at least once a year and often invites pastors to come and preach in Massachusetts. Although he submits no formal report, he keeps the national board in Brazil up-to-date about his church planting activities. Pastor Luis knows his position is somewhat unusual. Since he was a national leader, his Brazilian colleagues turn to him when they want to know what is happening in the U.S. Other preachers might have to give up their credentials if they worked outside the country but, he claims, they can rejoin the Church if they return with "no problem at all."

Brazil-to-U.S. and U.S.-to-Brazil oriented missionary efforts reinforce these transnational connections. In 2001, the new U.S.

ICFSG President initiated a series of activities designed to increase coordination between national Churches and to heighten national actors' sense of belonging to an international church. According to Pastor Dale, a U.S.-born former missionary in Massachusetts, whose church hosts a Brazilian immigrant congregation,

Last year, the American president invited all the Missions Departments that we have around the world to meet with him. I think he is trying to encourage us all to feel, whether we are Brazilian, Panamanian, or American, that we are all part of an international church that has various national parts that work together. He is trying to bring about greater coordination in the mission activities, so that we will not duplicate our efforts. All of the countries are independent, equal members of the worldwide assembly and that meets once a year but this is an effort to strengthen our international church community.

Negotiated transnational churches arise from a set of personal and institutional relationships that emerge organically, in response to the challenges posed by a particular context. Like the Catholic Church, these ties broaden and thicken what, in some cases, are already global institutions or they create new global connections. In contrast to the Catholic Church, however, they are negotiated with respect to authority, organization, and ritual. There is generally no one leader or administrative hierarchy to set policy and dictate how things are done. A more diverse, diluted set of partnerships emerges that are malleable and shift over time. These groups function like what Manuel Castells (2000) has described as a network society — decentralized, flexible yet connected networks that provide customized services and goods. Just as decentralized, adaptive modes of production are better suited to meet the challenges of global economic competition, so flexible production and dissemination of religious goods may be better suited to meeting the needs of contemporary religious consumers.

Smaller models are also more adaptable and more responsive and, therefore, more likely to endure.[1]

Negotiated transnational churches also influence political activism. Membership provides believers with tools to engage in the secular transnational public sphere or locates them within an alternative Christian landscape, that co-exists with or substitutes for its actual physical counterpart, and that comes with rights and responsibilities of its own. Four Square doctrine provides followers with clear ideas about what it means to be a good person and a good citizen. The notion of citizenship that is imparted is one that combines civic and religious elements and that is applicable to both transnational political and religious spaces. Followers become good citizens by being good Christians. The main point, Pastor Luis says, is that

... when they are good Christians, they are good citizens. So when we teach them to be consistent in their faith, they will be, at the same time, good people, good husbands, good people in the sense that they will try to help others, to try to make a difference in their neighborhoods. They will be concerned about other's well-being. So it's not necessary to become legal and become naturalized and so forth. But in the Bible itself, in the way that Christians should be, would be enough for them to be good citizens. ... There are ways of being in the world that have nothing to do with whether you are Brazilian or whether you are from the U.S. but that have more to do with faith in Christ. I teach my followers that they have a responsibility to all mankind but especially to their fellow Christians. We live in a world where Christ is the king, not George Bush or Fernando Colar.

By saying this, Pastor Luis firmly locates church members within the Kingdom of Christ. He tells them that living a good Christian life is

---

[1]Peterson and Vásquez (2001) make this same argument in their study of the Charismatic Catholic Renewal Movement (CCR). While parish life is characterized by a Fordist mode of production that results in a one size fits all product, the CCR is post-Fordist, flexibly creating a customized product that is especially successful because it does not challenge established hierarchies.

the way to achieve membership in good standing in one's local, national, and transnational communities. ICFSG members interpret this call in different ways. When they debated whether to contribute to an investment fund established to support projects in Valadares or to sign a letter opposing same sex marriages in Massachusetts, some saw themselves as using Christian principles to guide their transnational activism, in a secular space.

I know there are some people who think of themselves as living in the Kingdom of Christ. Pastor Luis talks about that a lot. But I see myself as firmly planted on the ground. My life is here and in Brazil. I feel very strongly about my church and about the lessons it teaches. But I see these lessons as telling me to get involved in the world around me. So when the police want to meet with the Brazilian community to understand us better or there are meetings to try to get people driver's licenses (which is illegal without a social security card), I go. My God tells me to be here and to help out (Umberto, 52 year old migrant, Framingham).

In contrast, the Christian landscape takes precedence for other believers. These migrants saw themselves primarily as members of a global Christendom which demanded that they act on their beliefs wherever they are called upon to do so. Their good works are motivated by their religious identity not out of a sense of patriotism or ethnic pride.

When I volunteer at the soup kitchen or at my child's school, it is because this is what God would want me to do. I am not guided by what the Worker's Party has to say about Brazil or the Democratic Party has to say about here. I live in a Christian world that just happens to have national boundaries that criss-cross it. If what good I do helps bring about political change, that's okay with me, but that is not my primary goal (Eliana, 47 year old migrant, Framingham).

Recreated Transnational Religious Organizations

The experiences of Gujarati Hindus from the Baroda district in India, suggest a third type of *recreated transnational religious organization.*

Many migrants started their own groups when they came to Massachusetts because there were few organizations when they first arrived. They either created groups with guidance from home-country leaders or Indian religious leaders came to areas where there were significant numbers of Indians and set up U.S.-based organizations with immigrant support. Some of these franchise-like groups are run by migrants who receive periodic resources, financing, and guidance from sending-country leadership while chapters are supported and supervised regularly by those who remain behind. There are also non-affiliated groups that simply bring what they need from India to carry out their religious practices but that do not belong to a particular organization.

The Devotional Associates of Yogeshwar or the Swadhyaya movement is one group that was recreated in the U.S. Swadhyaya groups are informally organized in India. Families living in the same neighborhood get together once or twice a week to chant *bhajans* (devotional hymns) and to watch and discuss videotapes of lectures by Dadaji, the group's founder. Larger, citywide meetings take place on Sundays. According to Didiji, Dadaji's daughter and successor, leadership emerges consensually; those who are the most knowledgeable and experienced become *motobhais* or elder brothers of each group. Swadhyaya is, at its core, a family. Members do what they are asked because it is their duty as part of this para-kinship group.

When people move, the family becomes transnational. It remains a close one, however, due to the strong ties linking members in the U.S., England, and India. The social lives of these individuals and the business of building Swadhyaya overlap. Leaders in Bombay said that they speak to someone from the U.S. almost every day because they are friends as well as religious co-workers. Similarly, Jitubhai, who supervises Swadhyaya activities in the university town of

Vidianagar, said he is in close touch with many former students who now live in the northeastern United States. If he hears that someone has family or financial difficulties, he calls one of the other *Moto-bhais* and asks them to intervene on his behalf.

When someone is facing divorce or a broken family, I call Dr. Bhorat and ask him to see if there is anything he can do. We stay close to our people when they face this kind of problem no matter where they are. We try to understand what they are facing, whether it be an economic, psychological or any other kind of problem. If the problem is with someone here, I will write a letter or go to see the family. If the problem is with someone in the U.S. we will call Dr. Bhorat or one of the other fellows and say please go there, contact him, and try to help him solve the problem.

Migrant Swadhyaya members have adapted Dadaji's teachings so they can still observe them despite the different demands of their lives in the U.S. They say that the principles that guide their activities are the same although their activities take different forms. For example, all followers are supposed to "devote time to God" by participating in *Yogeshwar Krishi*. In India, these are cooperative farms or fishing enterprises, created by the movement. Members donate their labor each month and then distribute their earnings to the poor. To do Yogeshwar Krishi in Chicago, Swadhayees formed a small company that made ink refills for pens that they work at in addition to their full-time jobs. In Massachusetts, groups of families get together to assemble circuit boards on contract from computer companies.

The International Swaminarayan Satsang Organization (ISSO) provides a second example of a recreated transnational organization. The ISSO in Lowell functions like a chapter of the ISSO in India. It has its own 12-member Board of Directors. There is a Massachusetts state organization as well as a national ISSO group. Again, strong social ties link members in the U.S. and India. These relationships, and the basic values espoused by the group, have transformed the national organization into something of a revolving loan and skill fund. State and local leaders meet one another constantly at regular meetings and at the yearly round of special celebrations, inaugurations, and visits by Indian leaders that they attend. When a group in one part of the country needs help building a temple or recruiting more members, leaders from other parts of the country go and help. Once that group is on its way, the national-level organization turns its attention to the next challenge. According to Ghananesh, a 43 year old migrant leader of the ISSO in Lowell,

Our group was always contributing money to other groups that were building temples. There is no set amount. Each group gives according to its own capacity. We used to give money and then when it was time for us to build our temple, those chapters supported us. Like in New Jersey, they say, "OK, we will give you $40,000." And the California chapter said they would give so much and the Chicago chapter gave us some money. And in the meantime, we were raising our own money.

Like their Catholic and Protestant counterparts, these institutional arrangements, and the theological messages they impart, also influence migrants' participation in their home and host communities. Two significant differences characterize the Gujarati case. First, recreated organizations clearly play a much greater role in reinforcing sending-country involvements than in promoting incorporation into the U.S. In fact, many respondents saw religious belonging as a way to protect themselves and their children from what they perceived as inferior Western values. Despite fairly high levels of economic and residential integration, they wanted to remain socially apart. While they had spent an average of 15 years in the U.S., they could recall few instances when they had participated in community affairs.

Certain institutional features reinforce this continuing orientation toward India at the expense of members' integration into the U.S.

First, the ISSO *Sadhus* (holy men or teachers) who are sent to lead the community know little about what goes on outside the temple walls. They speak no English. They are not allowed to interact with women and must rely on male followers to take care of their daily needs. As a result, unlike the native-born priests who work with Inishoweners, they understand little about the challenges of immigrant life. They cannot counsel their followers about the problems they face and they do little to encourage their participation in the broader community.

Both the ISSO and Swadhyaya have created new home-country based programs that formalize the ties to India already in place. Both groups have established post-secondary school training courses for the children of immigrants. Parents send their children for one to two years of additional study in India to strengthen their religious education and to ensure their full fluency in Indian culture and values.

The second difference in the way that recreated transnational religious organizations influence the transnational political activism of their members, compared to their Protestant and Catholic counterparts, is their message about good citizenship. Like many of the Irish and Brazilians in this study, most Swadhyayees and ISSO members also said that good people are those who respect and care for their neighbors and who follow the rules. In contrast, however, they said that social change is achieved through individual change. Once individuals recognize the God within themselves and in others, they become better people. Through these multiple individual transformations, a better world is achieved.

The result is civic engagement by accident. One of Dadaji's goals is to help people extricate themselves from the claims of political strongmen. He believes that the ability to solve one's own problems diminishes one's dependency on corrupt elites and government officials. He urges Swadhyayees to stay clear of politics. Although *Yogeshwar Krishi* involves participating in community development projects, the respondents who participated in them were adamantly against calling them political. They felt they would be overstepping their *dharma* or duty to become involved in politics. Their first responsibility was to their families and their neighbors and to think of changing society or leading such an effort would be presumptuous.

To some degree, this is a question of semantics. Though they would not call it political, other members felt they were setting an example for Americans that would ultimately lead to positive changes in the U.S. Avanti, a 52-year-old migrant described this as follows, "We must change ourselves before we change society as a whole. But I do think I am setting an example by my behavior. The other day, I found $200 at work. Now, I could have pocketed that money. But I gave it to my supervisor. And I felt that by doing that I was setting an example for others of the way one should act. I was teaching them about Swadhyaya through my actions." Part of Avanti's religious identity includes thinking of herself as a social change agent. It remains to be seen if this will assume a more explicit, organized form as she spends more years in the U.S.

MOVING FORWARD — THE NEED FOR ADDITIONAL RESEARCH

The institutional connections that migration engenders, and that reinforce and are reinforced by already-global aspects of religious life, transform religion into a powerful, underexplored site of transnational belonging. The extended, negotiated, and recreated transnational religious organizations in this study enable migrants to stay connected to their sending communities at the same time that they are incorporated into the U.S. They integrate migrants into cross-border institutional networks that help them gain access to services, achieve representation, and make demands vis-à-vis their sending and receiving countries.

Religious institutions become places where a common vocabulary and shared set of expectations about rights and responsibilities are worked out. In some cases, transnational religious life serves as the door through which migrants enter informal politics. In other cases, transnational religious life provides an alternative script for belonging and social change, through personal transformation and by example, or because believers see themselves as living within and responsible for improving the religiously-defined world where they situate themselves. Clearly, many religious transnational practices occur sub-nationally or between local, state, or regional sending- and receiving-country actors. The goals or targets of transnational religious activism shift and expand in ways that may make it more sustainable over time. . . .

The intensification of life across borders will only increase the numbers for whom social and political citizenship is decoupled from residence. It is time we put religion front and center in our attempts to understand how identity and belonging are redefined in this increasingly global world.

REFERENCES

CASTELLS, M. 2000. *End of millennium*. Oxford, England: Blackwell Publishers.

EBAUGH, H. R., and J. CHAFETZ. 2002. *Religion across borders: Transnational religious networks*. Walnut Creek: Altamira Press.

HERVIEU-LÉGER, D. 1997. Faces of Catholic transnationalism: In and beyond France. In *Transnational religion and fading states*, edited by S. Rudolph and J. Piscatori, 104-121. Boulder: Westview Press.

KURIEN, P. 2001. Religion, ethnicity, and politics: Hindus and Muslim Indian immigrants in the United States. *Ethnic and Racial Studies* 24:263-93.

KYLE, D. 2001. *Transnational peasants*. Baltimore, Maryland: Johns Hopkins University Press.

LEVITT, P. 1998. Local-level global religion: The case of U.S.-Dominican migration. *Journal for the Scientific Study of Religion* 3:74-89.

MCALISTER, E. 2002. *Rara! Vodou, power, and performance in Haiti and its diaspora*. Los Angeles and Berkeley: University of California Press.

MENJÍVAR, C. 1999. Religious institutions and transnationalism: A case study of Catholic and Evangelica; Salvadoran immigrants. *International Journal of Politics, Culture, and Society* 12(4):589-611.

MEYER, J., W. J. BOLI, G. M. THOMAS, and F. O. RAMIREZ. 1997. World society and the nation-state. *American Journal of Sociology* 103(1):144-181.

PETERSON, A., and M. VÁSQUEZ. 2001. Upwards: Never down: The Catholic charismatic renewal in transnational perspective. *In Christianity, Social Change, and Globalization in the Americas*, edited by A. Peterson, P. Williams, and M. Vásquez, 88-210, New Brunswick, NJ: Rutgers University Press.

TWEED, T. 1999. *Our lady of exile*. New York: Oxford University Press.

VERBA, S., K. SCHLOZMAN, and H. BRADY. 1995. *Voice and equality*. Cambridge, MA: Harvard University Press.

WELLMEIER, N. J. 1998. Santa Eulalia's people in exile: Maya religion, culture, and identity in Los Angeles. In *Gatherings in diaspora: Religious communities and the new immigration*, edited by R. S. Warner and J. Wittner, 97-123. Philadelphia: Temple University Press.

YANG, F. 2002. Chinese Christian transnationalism: Diverse networks of a Houston church. In *Religious across borders: Transnational religious networks*, edited by H. R. Ebaugh and J. Chafetz, 175-204, Maryland: Altamira Press.

YANG, F., and H. R. EBAUGH. 2001. Transformation of new immigrant religions and their global implications. *American Sociological Review* 66(2):269-288.

45 Global Religion and the Re-enchantment of the World: The Case of the Catholic Charismatic Renewal

THOMAS J. CSORDAS

Csordas focuses on one example of the globalization of religion. He studies what is called the Catholic Charismatic Renewal movement, that is, Catholic people and organizations that practice "charismatic gifts" such as speaking in tongues. He traces for us the international expansion of this movement, showing a specific case of how globalization occurs.

The Catholic Charismatic Renewal is a movement that began in the United States within the Roman Catholic Church, synthesizing elements of Catholicism and Pentecostalism with ecumenical leanings and a tropism towards development of intentional communities.... I want to focus on the Catholic Charismatic Renewal movement as a particularly apt example of globalization or re-globalization, or perhaps planetarization (Melucci, 1996) of world religions. Christianity, in its earliest phase of globalization, spread the power of a Church that was the dominant world institution of its time, and later on supported the power of the colonial empires which were the dominant institutions of their time. No such dominant institution supports the current wave of globalization of Christianity, which often takes the form of Pentecostal or Charismatic evangelization, spread rapidly and dramatically by movements, ministries, fellowships, or independent denominations taking advantage of all the available technologies of travel and communication.

To rehearse, in brief, the history of the movement, the Catholic Charismatic Renewal began in the United States in 1967, blending influences from the Cursillo movement that originated in Spain and the indigenous American enthusiasm of Protestant Pentecostalism. In the midst of the 1960s cultural ferment, it promised a dramatic renewal of Church life, based on a born-again spirituality of a 'personal relationship' with

Jesus and direct access to divine power and inspiration through 'spiritual gifts' or 'charisms', including faith-healing, prophecy and speaking in tongues. Adherents formed informal prayer groups or tightly disciplined 'covenant communities', with larger institutional structures taking the form of a National Service Committee in the United States in 1970 and an International Communications Office in 1975. The latter began under the auspices of 'The Word of God' covenant community in Ann Arbor, Michigan, subsequently moving to Brussels under the sponsorship of Cardinal Leon Joseph Suenens, and finally to the centre of the Catholic world in Rome. Pope Paul VI took note of the movement's existence as early as 1971, and publicly addressed its 1975 International Conference in Rome. Pope John Paul II continued to be generally supportive, apparently tolerating the movement's relatively radical theology for the sake of encouraging its markedly conservative politics, its militant activism for 'traditional' values, its opposition to women's rights to contraception and abortion, and its encouragement of individual spirituality and contribution to parish activities and finances.

In sum, there have been two principal modes of international expansion. Evidence suggests that the typical pattern for the movement's introduction in a Third World region was as follows: a missionary priest visited the United States, was exposed to Baptism of the Holy Spirit, organized a prayer group on his return, and subsequently called on outside help for doctrinal instruction or healing services. A class of Catholic healer-evangelists can be called on for such purposes. The International Catholic Charismatic Renewal Services (ICCRS) is an instrumental clearing house in this respect through the retreats, workshops, leadership training and newsletter that it sponsors. The second mechanism is via the communitarian branch of the movement. From very early on, some Charismatics wanted to live lives of greater commitment to spiritual ideals of

Christian community than was found in weekly prayer groups. They began to adopt formal written documents, called covenants, that established basic rules of life, and referred to the resulting groups as covenant communities. . . .

For a long time now, I have imagined a study that could examine the nature of the relation between religion and globalization, using the Catholic Charismatic Renewal as a paradigmatic empirical case. . . . In earlier writings, I have presented descriptions from available sources of the movement's development in the United States, Quebec, France, Italy, Mexico, Chile, Brazil, Nigeria, Zambia, Zaire, Indonesia, Malaysia and Japan (Csordas, 1992, 1994, 1995, 1997). In this article I will update these accounts with recent material from India, Brazil and Nigeria, then proceed to some reflections on what the Charismatic Renewal has to teach us on the theme of religion and globalization.

INDIA

As in many countries, the Charismatic Renewal was introduced to India in the early 1970s. By 1976 a national convention in Bombay attracted 1500 registered delegates, and another in 1978 attracted 3500, including Cardinal Lawrence Picachy of Calcutta, along with the archbishops of Bombay and Hyderabad, and the bishops of Quilon and Kottar. In addition to the convention, there was a leaders' conference, two priests' retreats, and a three-day leaders' seminar on healing, conducted by the renowned Francis MacNutt (at the time still a Dominican priest). A report from the movement's international newsletter in 1986 cited the spread of the movement into rural northwest India, and one in 1994 documented evangelization in tribal areas in northeast India, bordering on China.

The movement is perhaps most prominent in the south-western state of Kerala where there is a concentration of Catholics of Syro-Malabar, Syro-Malankara, and Latin rites. In

1987 a priest of the Vincentian Congregation named Mathew Naickomparambil received a divine inspiration to transform his small prayer group at Potta into a healing ministry, which has since grown into a veritable moral metropole within the movement, even bragging its own train station. Day-long healing services attract as many as 5000–10,000 people – foreigners as well as people from all across India – apparently including substantial numbers of non-Christians. Six kilometres from the church/ashram, the group has built a Divine Retreat Centre where week-long retreats are conducted for as many as 10,000 (and up to 20,000 in the summer season), with preaching from 6:30am until 10:00pm simultaneously in six auditoria: in the buildings on one side of the road services are conducted in Malayalam, Tamil and Telugu, and on the other side services are in English, Konkani, Hindi and Kannada. Mental patients are excluded from retreats, and instead their family members are instructed to attend as surrogates.

Anthropologist Murphy Halliburton visited Potta in 1997 and reported that during the week-long retreat, participants were not allowed to leave the grounds, nor were they permitted to drink or smoke. The facilities were impressive, with physicians, bookshops, snack bars and pharmacies on site, and the auditoria were large enough to hold several thousand people. He described the atmosphere as being 'like that of a major rock concert in a big stadium, only with more facilities' (2000). He was also able to see patient wards, including a locked ward for alcoholics, where television monitors constantly showed what was transpiring on stage in the auditorium. Halliburton's informant indicated that about 60 per cent of participants were patients with a variety of medical problems, including psychiatric and substance abuse issues, with many others seeking help with marital problems, infertility, or other situations, and about 10 per cent coming 'just for prayer'.

What is of critical import for our discussion is not only that Potta is a destination for foreigners and non-Christians, nor that Father Naickomparambil and his colleagues conduct retreats and services all throughout India, but that they also have an energetic presence in North America and Europe. For example, their website announced a five-week, nine-stop tour of the United States, a bible conference in Germany, and listed numerous contacts among past retreat participants from the United States, England and Germany.

Matthew Schmalz (1998, 1999, 2002) has documented a series of striking postmodern dislocations and juxtapositions of Hindu and Catholic elements on the level of personal transformation through Catholic Charismatic healing in north India. He describes the healing ministry of Jude, a lay Catholic south Indian living in a north Indian city sacred to Hindus and attracting both Catholic Charismatic and Hindu supplicants. Jude was a repentant alcoholic and womanizer who relocated following a dishonourable discharge from the military and a failed business venture selling an Ayurvedic remedy for sexual impotence, subsequently returning to the Church and joining the Charismatic Renewal on the advice of a confessor.

The cross-fertilization of Hinduism and Catholicism appears on several levels in the account of Jude's healing ministry. The forms of empowerment he deploys include the readily recognizable Charismatic 'spiritual gift' of 'discernment' – a form of divine inspiration which allows him to identify the problems of supplicants, often embodying their afflictions himself as clues to their nature. They also include an authenticating narrative of a miraculous birth in which, during a medical crisis, he was surgically removed and replaced into his mother's womb, a theme paralleled in myths of the births of Krishna, Mahavira, Buddha and Parikshit.

On the level of disjunction in practice and interpretation, Schmalz recounts the case of a female patient who experienced disturbing visions of three men that appeared to be Hindu *bhut* or *pret* spirits, brought to the Catholic healer by a Protestant lawyer convinced of the Satanic identity of the traditional spirits. The Catholic healer attributed the problem instead to the effects of sin and troubled interpersonal relations, but was understood by the patients' parents in terms of a Hindu paradigm of the body's response to purifying fluids when the patient was blessed with Catholic holy water. Homologies in ritual symbolism appear in the juxtapositions of the Christian Eucharist and the eating of *Prasad*, or food left over from offerings to the Hindu deities, of the Christian scapular and the *rakhi* or wrist string worn as protection, of Christian holy water and water or milk used to ritually cool the Hindu deities, of prayerful repetition of the name of Jesus and the Hindu use of *mantra*, of the Charismatic blowing of a blessing in a supplicant's face and the parallel Hindu practice of *duha*. Again, that such parallels can be found is predictable; what it of interest is whether, and if so how, they are thematized in practice. For instance, the healer Jude strenuously objected to equating the repetition of the name of Jesus with the 'pagan' practice of uttering *mantras*, but quite unself-consciously blew his blessings in a way that would not be recognized by Catholic Charismatics elsewhere. Finally, in several ways, Indian and non-Indian notions become inextricably conflated, as in the healer's implicit understanding of sin not necessarily as a matter of intent but as one of contamination by the acts of others, implying an Ayurvedic conception of the body in terms of vital fluids passing through channels, so that the effect of sin is that it 'occludes the flow of grace as it ripens or hardens in the body' (Schmalz, 1998: 105–6).

The outlines traced by the Potta phenomenon, and by the interface between Hinduism and Catholicism, as well as the points of both syncretism and contradiction that become highlighted in such accounts, are more than jarring anomalies. They are symptomatic of the simultaneous pull towards universal culture and postmodern cultural fragmentation that characterizes the global condition of religion. A final dimension is added by the work of anthropologist Corinne Dempsey (2001) on Christianity in Kerala, with respect to competition between indigenous Syrian Christianity purportedly introduced by Thomas the Apostle in the 1st century, and Roman Christianity forcibly imposed by Portuguese colonialists in the 16th. She recounts a conversation with a priest whose denunciation of western influences included everything from the Portuguese to contemporary culture, claiming that it was undermining the faith of young people in particular, but who was optimistic in part because of the Charismatic Renewal. She notes the irony in the fact that the movement itself is an import from the United States, but resolves the irony by suggesting that 'the Charismatic movement has been assimilated and transformed by the Kerala Catholic community . . . domestic adoption of this "Western" movement seems to have been so thorough as to enable it to be wielded by and on behalf of Malayali Christians as a means to combat what it used to be itself: "Western" influence' (2001: 32). Dempsey interprets this in the light of Babha's understanding of how hybridity reverses the effects of 'colonialist disavowal' – that is, of the rhetorical/ideological assertion of sameness that masks domination. The hybrid assertion of sameness – in this instance, participation in a purportedly universal and homogeneous international movement under allegiance to Rome – in effect is not only a strategy for autonomy, but has the potential to subtly transform the centre. In this sense, the empirical fascination of the Charismatic Renewal is that there is no bipolarity between colonist and colonizer, but a multinational religious conglomerate that invites the layering of hybridity upon syncretism upon synthesis, in a universal culture that is not polyglot but glossolalic.

BRAZIL

Our initial observation must be that Brazil, unlike India, is a predominantly Catholic country, and therefore the cultural landscape in which the Charismatic Renewal can move differs in the most significant way. The Charismatic Renewal was introduced to Brazil in São Paulo by Jesuit priests from the United States, by one account in 1969 and by another in 1972. By 1992 the movement's international office reported two million Catholic Charismatics in Brazil. The estimated number of followers in 1994, according to Pierucci and Prandi (1995), was 3,800,000. The Renewal has largely been a phenomenon of the middle class since de Oliveira's early article in 1978 (when participants numbered only in the thousands), according to the writing of Prandi (1997: 159–62). . . .

The work of Maria José de Abreu (2002) examines the manner in which Charismatic experience is understood as unmediated access to the divine, not only in relation to the Church as the traditional mediator of religious experience for its faithful, but especially in relation to the electronic media, in the manipulation of which the movement has exhibited a certain virtuosity. The issue is the possibility of 'transferring an idea concerning non-mediation to the very core of the media sphere' such that 'the TV screen is not so much about images as about revelatory communication'. This is, in effect, the question of whether televangelism is conceived in terms of transparency and immediacy or in terms of opacity and mediatization. In other words, the problem for Charismatics is how to maintain the 'principle of subjectivity', or the fundamental experiential postulate

that the imitation of Christ 'is an inward process of imitation, a spiritual resemblance, which stems from *a presence* rather than a mere representation enacted on stage'. She looks at two of the most visible Charismatic media presences in Brazil: the Cançao Nova Media System of Communication and the ministry of evangelistic healing priest Marcelo Rossi. Cançao Nova is one of the original and best-known Brazilian Charismatic communities, with 12 branches throughout Brazil, two in Portugal, and one in Rome. It has facilities on campus for retreats and services, as well as broadcasting and publishing facilities, and 150 transmission antennae across the country, as well as internet broadcasting. Marcelo Rossi is a handsome, 37-year-old priest, who has composed many devotional songs and is widely known for elaborate masses 'of cure and liberation of bad energies, during which people participated in what he called the "aerobics of Jesus" – masses that are, in effect, Charismatic pageants performed in front of large audiences. De Abreu sees both phenomena as reflecting 'the extent to which the Chrismatic Renewal has gradually moved from the intimate space of the prayer group (*grupo de oraçao*) to the big stadiums and the global media space'.

A key event in de Abreu's account (2002) is a gathering at which Rossi (regarded by some both within and outside the movement as a marginal loner who has become more of a showman than a Charismatic leader), despite consorting with celebrities and film stars, was recognized by the pre-eminent movement leader and founder of Cançao Nova, Father Jonas Abib, as having been the victim of enemies of the Renewal. As he called on the crowd, including those watching on television, to collectively pray for and lay hands on Rossi, the latter fell on his knees, awash in tears, and Abib cried out that the movement belonged to the masses and they should not be afraid to say so. De Abreu marshals several important observations to account for this event. She points out that, unlike both popular Catholicism and liberation theology, the Charismatic Renewal is 'compatible with the urban segmentation of identities and spatial fragmentation'. The Renewal also exhibits the 'idea that it is not the content per se, but the form and means of dealing with symbols and images that distinguish the movement'. The movement is in part predicated on the fundamental need to transmit the Word of God by testimony, prophecy and healing, but also 'as a result of the mass media, the gift of transmission, which should be a sign of inward spirituality, becomes an outward token of popularity'. In sum there are two contradictory effects of mediatization. In de Abreu's words:

1. While Charismatics initially wanted to change the meanings attached to sanctity by redefining the borders between this world and the other, the media has created a new divide, jeopardizing the distinction between a living icon and an icon of idolatry.
2. ... media can enhance and reproduce the logic of Charismatic embodiment and transform frozen images into 'lively' ones. Since this reformulation depends on the primacy of the Charismatic self, the dynamic character of the mass media reaffirms the notion of 'living icons' rather than that of religious representations. (de Abreu, 2002)

The famous healing priest, by falling on his knees and allowing himself to be prayed over in public, was saved for the movement from becoming a representation, a creature of the virtual reality of media stardom.

Carlos Steil (2001) takes up the encounter between the Charismatic Renewal and apparitions of the Virgin Mary, another prominent phenomenon of contemporary Catholicism. He sees this encounter in terms of a multiple intersection or syncretism between Pentecostalism and Catholicism, popular Catholicism and the Charismatic Renewal, tradition and modernity.... One might add the intersection between the local and global in the precise

sense that Steil, while placing the Brazilian apparitions firmly in the Brazilian context, recognizes the Marian apparition of 1981 in the Croatian village of Medjugorje as the transnational prototype of a new mode of performativity in the historical genre of Marian apparitions. He discusses an apparition in Taquari in 1988 and juxtaposes it with a similar recent phenomenon known as the Piedade de Gerais. In both cases, Charismatics were involved from the outset, some moving to live in the locality of the apparitions, while at the same time deploying their access to the media to transmit the message beyond the locality as one of universal significance – in Taquari they went so far as to acquire control of a local radio station. In the case of the Piedade do Gerais, the Charismatic ethos not only penetrated the community of local devotees, but the Charismatics became a network of support for disseminating the event – assisting the original visionaries in travels to other cities and even to Europe. A different outcome was at hand in Taquari, where the Franciscan friars who ran the parish developed strategies of control, suppressing the Charismatic gift of prophecy by limiting it to one individual of their choice, disallowing it in the chapel and restricting it to the sacristy, subjecting it to the scrutiny of a committee, and allowing it to be disseminated only in writing. Their rationale was protecting the faith of the poor from the implicit standpoint of a liberation theology suspect of the bourgeois Charismatics.

... Prophecy is the most typically Charismatic among Charismatic media and epitomizes the notion of transparency and immediacy of access to the divine, for it is an inspired first person utterance in which the ultimate speaker is understood to be God (note that I am referring to the genre as the medium, and not the person making the utterance, as is typically implied in referring to spirit possession).

The transmutation of the genre between the Charismatic context and the context of apparitions in popular Catholicism consists in the fact that the speaker is no longer God but the Virgin. However, the implications are far greater. Certainly one of them is the appropriation of discourse from the local visionaries by the translocal Charismatics. But on an experiential level there is a movement of revelation from the apparition in the form of an externality to the experience of prophecy as an 'inner locution', contributing to the subjectivity and reflexivity characteristic of the Charismatic sacred self. Steil reports that in Taquari, eventually even one of the original visionaries began to recast her experience in terms of such inner locutions. On the sensory level, this marks a profound shift away from a visual orientation with images of the Virgin, the dancing sun and the weeping tree as emblems for a fixed message or series of secrets to be transmitted from the virgin through the visionaries to the faithful. The shift is toward an auditory/oral modality, and moreover one that is indeterminately productive/generative as new prophecies are received. And to the extent that the prophets include members of a community not limited to the original visionaries, the revelatory inspiration is dispersed among a field of the faithful that has the potential to expand indefinitely and on a global scale. Steil summarizes nicely:

> ... insofar as the clergy seeks to define truth from outside the event, by the authority of the Church, the Charismatics want to produce a truth through the adherence of a constantly increasing that is, within a specific mode of temporality number of devotees. What is more, it is critical to observe that [ironically or not] the criterion applied by Charismatics also belongs to Catholic orthodoxy, which recognizes the *sensu fidelium* as a secure basis for defining a dogma or recognizing the authenticity of a divine manifestation. (Steil, 2001: 139)

This is the globalization of religion on a level of populations, spreading devotees in networks of communities that create styles of inter-subjectivity and inter-corporeality through adherence to common experiential modalities

and performative genres. Steil (2004) also observes that the Charismatic Renewal is not only a synthesis between Catholic and Pentecostal ritual forms, but that its activities provide a revolving door opening onto both Catholicism and Pentecostalism for participants, thus forming a threshold between the two forms of religious sociality. In this process, aspiration to a universal culture (or in indigenous terms, to the task of bringing about the kingdom of God) exists in generative tension with ... culturally distinct settings and syncretistic opportunities crisscrossed by transnational media activities of healing and evangelization (or in indigenous terms, the movement of the Holy Spirit among the people).

NIGERIA

Pentecostalism exerted an influence on the religious scene in Nigeria from very early on, taking the form of the Aladura churches described by Turner (1967) and Peel (1968), as well as the classical Pentecostal denominations. Neo-Pentecostalism or Charismatic Christianity is discussed by Ojo (1988), who observes that this wave of Pentecostalism originated in the early 1970s among college students and university graduates of various denominations. As in many settings around the globe, a primary emphasis is divine healing, but in addition there is much attention to *restitution* 'for one's past sins, mistakes, and every sort of unchristian act' (Ojo, 1988: 184), reflecting aspects of the traditional Yoruba concern for purification. Restitution often takes the form of returning stolen articles, which Ojo interprets as a reaction against the quest for material wealth following the Nigerian oil boom of the 1970s. Restitution applied to marriage assumes the greed of a polygynous man who makes amends by divorcing all but his first wife (Ojo, 1988: 184–5). According to Bastian (2002), by the late 1980s born-again neo-Pentecostalism was widespread in southern Nigeria and the notion of charisms or spiritual gifts was intriguing to many Protestants and Catholics, with numbers of adherents skyrocketing during the 1990s and the movement highly mediatized by the start of the 21st century. Particularly striking is the popularity of 'spiritual warfare' against Satan and his legion of demonic spirits – in Nigeria augmented by the seductive sea spirit Mami Wata (Queen of the Coast) and a variety of ancestral spirits – through the form of healing called 'deliverance' as popularized by North American neo-Pentecostals (Bastian, 2002).

Specifically among Catholics, by 1976 the movement's first national leadership conference in Benin City attracted 110 participants with official support from the local bishop. In 1983, a National Advisory Council was formed to oversee movement activities. Francis Mac-Nutt (1975), the first and most widely known among American Catholic Charismatic healers, recounts a Charismatic retreat in Nigeria in which traditional deities were cast out or 'delivered' as occult spirits, including the following case of a man in Benin City:

An outstanding Catholic Layman, he was a convert who had been brought up in the old religion. He discovered as a child that after certain practices of dedication his toes were affected by a divining spirit. If the day of his plans were to be propitious, one toe would pinch him; if they were to be unlucky, a different toe would pinch. Consequently, he came to plan his life around these omens, which he said always came true, even if he tried to disregard them. When he desired to pray out loud at our retreat, however, his unpropitious toe began to act up; at this point, he decided that these strange manifestations must be from an evil spirit and had to be renounced. (MacNutt, 1975: 9)

This incident – a variant of the time-honoured Catholic strategy of ritual incorporation of indigenous practices – is based on acceptance of their existential reality but negation of their spiritual value, condemning them as inspired by the demonic forces of Satan. . . .

Anthropologist Misty Bastian encountered the Catholic Charismatic Renewal during the 1980s in the ethnically Igbo southeast of Nigeria, where Catholicism is the dominant form of Christianity. Bastian (2005) describes a male healer/visionary firmly ensconced in the official Church networks and endorsed by the hierarchy, and a female healer/visionary who was both explicitly criticized by her male counterpart and marginalized by the Church hierarchy. Both healers were most active from the mid-1980s through to the early 1990s. We can interpret her account as an excellent example of how the Charismatic Renewal can be seen as being a discrete interactional milieu in which cultural tensions between tradition and modernity, and between male and female, are played out.

Father Edeh was a mainstream priest whose ministry was at least initially supported by his colleagues in the Church hierarchy, and was appreciated as an overt counter-balance against the appeal of Protestant Pentecostalism. He was academically trained at a US university and had published a book on *Igbo Metaphysics*, based on significant ethnographic fieldwork, with Loyola University Press. His ministry was highly mediatized, and he was building a cathedral and prayer compound at his home parish to accommodate the press, as well as the day trippers and campers who came to experience healing prayer, while at the same time travelling to conduct open-air rallies and healing masses throughout Igboland. His ministry was in decline by the late 1990s, because, according to Bastian, his followers did not see enough of the miracles they expected, his reputation was compromised by involvement in commercial activities, and a variety of other spiritual options had emerged to compete with him.

Sister Kate was a young woman who described herself as having the three occupations of 'housewife, hospital worker and prophet' (Bastian, 2005). She had experienced visions since her youth in the 1960s, beginning at her First Communion. Alienated from her family in part because of her spiritual characteristics, her father disinherited her and she found a haven amongst Protestant Pentecostals. Eventually she became re-involved with the Catholic Church and began exercising her spiritual gifts of healing and prophecy in the 1970s against the background of the Charismatic Renewal. She carried out her ministry entirely from home, remaining deferential to a disapproving pastor by continuing to attend mass but abstaining from the sacraments in order to avoid confrontation. During the Marian year of 1987 she heard increasingly from both Mary and the Holy Spirit and was banned from her parish and eventually excommunicated from the Church.

The contrast between these two healers plays out a variety of criss-crossing themes in the dynamics between tradition and modernity, male and female. The power manifest in Edeh's ministry could have a remote effect through notes submitted with prayer requests, or holy water blessed by the priest to protect against theft, to expose witch-craft, or to tap the healer's power, whereas Kate's power was manifest only in direct personal contact with the healer granting individualized attention to each patient. Geographically, Edeh's activities and reputation extended throughout Igboland, whereas Kate's ministry was localized in her home and parish. Edeh's group disseminated items such as bumper stickers and pre-printed prayers, engaging in a variety of commercial ventures, whereas Kate had no merchandise and merely charged a nominal fee for those who registered by number for her consultations. Edeh's activities invoked the power of literacy both through pre-printed prayers and through the submitting of written prayer requests, whereas Kate's communication with her followers was exclusively oral.

Edeh attributed his inspiration for the most part to the Holy Spirit, whereas Kate claimed inspiration from both the Spirit and the Virgin Mary. Edeh's prayers and revelations were primarily directed toward healing, whereas Kate

engaged in both healing and prophecy. Sister Kate's prophetic messages often included quite precise predictions of personal tragedy – a feature that was likely perceived by religious authorities as a focus on the negative and hence spiritually suspect – as well as predictions of the dark political times under the regime of General Abacha. Whereas Edeh gave prominence to the struggle against evil and countering witchcraft, Kate in addition placed considerable emphasis on healing barrenness among her female clients. Finally, Father Edeh preached spiritual submissiveness, while the life, work and demeanor of Sister Kate were a testimony to spiritual and personal independence.

Indeed, Sister Kate explicitly described herself as 'modern', and Bastian describes her not only as a full time career hospital worker, but in terms of her demure (although contemporary) attire, in contrast to the black clothing of the traditional Igbo visionary woman who never bathes and is either sexually submissive or celibate. It was likewise striking that during Bastian's interview with her, Sister Kate remained seated while a male follower stood in her presence, an explicit reversal of traditional gender dominance. In this context it is noteworthy that Father Edeh in public made overt attacks on Sister Kate, claiming that she was inspired by Satan and was a manifestation of Mami Wata, the archetypal urban witch. Stories of Edeh's healings include examples such as that of a rich woman who obtained her money by witching and killing her husband, and who repented when touched with holy water blessed by Edeh. Again, sick children who were in fact enchanted *dada* twins turned into serpents when sprinkled with holy water, the moral being that bringing animal spirits into a patrilineage through bestial adultery is to be condemned. For Bastian, this story bears the anti-female message that multiple births are bad, whereas for Sister Kate multiple births were signs of blessing and doubled evidence of the healer's success in relieving barrenness.

In sum, this Nigerian case outlines the convergence of Igbo culture in which it is more common to encounter male than female *dibia* or diviners, and Catholic culture characterized by an age-old tension between female visionary experience and male hierarchical control or suppression of such experience. Although males have never been excluded from such visionary experience, in the Charismatic Renewal males as well as females have relatively equal access to the 'gifts of the Spirit', or charisms, with the overall apparent result of further strengthening the framework of patriarchal domination. All of these interwoven themes and contrasts merit further examination in the Igbo context, and could well constitute an outline for a comparative examination of local instantiations of the global Charismatic renewal.

CHARISMATIC PERMUTATIONS OF TRANSNATIONAL TRANSCENDENCE

The three comparative cases I have discussed based on recently published scholarly material represent three continents, and, perhaps not coincidentally, come from populous countries, each of which is recognized as the most dynamic and diverse nation on its continent. Standing economically between the developed and developing worlds, these three crucibles of globalization may also be points of convergence between the fetishization of commodities and the fetishization of experience – ideal crucibles of religious ferment and re-enchantment. Part of this is certainly related to the technological possibilities for mediatization of spirituality in these nearly-developed nations. At the same time, specificities of the cultural milieu in these countries offer intriguing grounds for further comparison of Charismatic permutations. Brazil is a predominantly Catholic nation where the Renewal interacts with strong Marian traditions as well as Kardecist spiritism and the gamut of Afro-Brazilian religions.

Nigeria is an ethnically diverse nation where Catholicism is strongest among the Igbo and the Renewal exists in relation to traditional religion in the local setting and within the Christian/Islamic dynamic on the national scene. India's Catholic population tends to be concentrated regionally in the southwest, and the Renewal exists in relation to Hindu and Muslim traditions.

The dimensions of comparison multiply if one considers the varying contours of the movement around the globe (Csordas, 1997). The relative roles of clergy and laity participating in the movement constitute one such dimension: writing on the Renewal in Canada emphasizes its distinctiveness from the US branch of the movement by highlighting the prominent role of the clergy. The degree of US influence is varyingly acknowledged, for example in France, with the caveat that the flavour of the movement was quickly nationalized toward French sensibilities. The relative role of missionaries from various religious orders and of covenant communities from the US and France also affects the tenor of transnational transcendence within the movement. Differing patterns of penetration to ethnic Catholics in multicultural societies like the US and to indigenous groups like the Mapuche in Chile or the Navajo in the US can be traced. Some countries entertain more than one strand of what is ostensibly the same Renewal: Italy has branches associated with the international movement, including both prayer groups and communities, and another with conservative/elderly people oriented toward experiencing and documenting charisms; Zambia has a branch started by Irish missionaries and another started by the indigenous Archbishop Milingo; Zaire has *charismatiques* who participate in organized prayer groups with an identified leader and emphasis on charisms, and the *renouveau* composed of young educated urbanites whose practice emphasizes group prayer.

. . .

In 2001 I was poised to reinitiate my study of the Charismatic Renewal after a ten year hiatus. I learned that the ICCRS in Rome was planning to hold a seminar in the Mediterranean on the topic of deliverance from evil spirits, directed by a leading expert on this form of healing – a Portuguese-surnamed priest from the west of India. Intended as advanced training for those from around the world who already had experience in the deliverance ministry, this appeared to present an ideal opportunity for me to gain an initial sense of cross-cultural variation in the encounter with evil spirits, as well as to develop a set of contacts that could be pursued with subsequent visits to the field. Mobilizing some of my old contacts among movement leadership, I obtained the letter of sponsorship required to register for this seminar – this precaution was to ensure the necessary level of spiritual maturity and legitimacy among participants who were to deal with the sensitive issues of casting out demons, and was certainly necessary for a movement outsider such as myself. Then, just as the preparations were underway, I learnt that the seminar had been cancelled for lack of a sufficient number of participants. The reason, however – and this is the point of the story – was not that there was insufficient interest, and neither that the likely candidates could not afford the expense of travel, but that the Portuguese Indian priest had already presented his experiences among so many Charismatics in so many settings around the world that those who would have participated appear to have judged that the experience would be redundant. The voice for a universal culture of healing had pre-empted itself from drawing into the centre that which it had already sallied forth to touch in its indigenous setting, thus at the same time pre-empting an encounter among healers with diverse experiences that could have potentially called into question some of the homogenizing goals of the event.

The image of cultural fragmentation, on the other hand, is contained in the story of Archbishop Emmanuel Milingo of Lusaka, Zambia. Quite independently of any broader movement, he began to practise faith healing in 1973 (Milingo, 1984; Ter Haar, 1987, 1992). In 1976, however, he established a relationship with The Word of God Catholic Charismatic Community in the US and founded his own Divine Providence Community. By 1979 the archbishop was a prominent participant in a Charismatic pilgrimage to Lourdes. The Archbishop's teachings exhibited a simultaneous 'indigenization' of Charismatic ritual healing and a 'Charismatization' of a distinctly African form of Christian healing. More remarkable, however, is that within a decade, his healing ministry had created such controversy that in 1983 he was recalled to Rome. There he was detained and interrogated, and eventually relinquished his ecclesiastical post. In return he was granted an appointment as Special Delegate to the Pontifical Commission for Migration and Tourism, with the freedom to travel (except to Zambia), and was reassured by the Pope that his healing ministry would be 'safeguarded' (Milingo, 1984: 137). Ironically, given that the overt goal of his recall was in part to protect Zambian Catholics from what must have appeared to Church officials as a kind of neo-paganism, Milingo subsequently became immensely popular as a healer among Italian Catholic Charismatics. With established followings in 10 Italian cities, and already a figure on national television, in 1987 he moved his public healing service from the church of Argentini of Rome to a large room in the Ergife Hotel. Once again in 1989, his controversial ministry was temporarily suspended by the Church, and later renewed outside Rome (Lanternari, 1994). In 1994 the Bishop's conference in Tuscany issued a pastoral note on demonology and witchcraft, quite likely targeted at Milingo's ministry. The archbishop next re-emerged into the public spotlight at the turn of the millennium as a new devotee of Reverend Sun Myung Moon's Unification Church. As much of a scandal as was his apparent defection from the church – or perhaps from his own standpoint a new level of ecumenism – was his ritual marriage to a nubile Korean follower of Moon in a ceremony central to the Unification doctrine. Only after a great deal of effort that doubtless included coaxing, negotiation and threat did Milingo recant and return to the fold. Archbishop Milingo contributes to a decentring of meaning that cannot but take place in a global movement whose key symbol is, after all, speaking in tongues. Although Lanternari (1987) described the effect as a 'religious short-circuit' between Africa and Europe, there is less, not more anomaly in the Milingo case if it is acknowledged that the contemporary situation is best represented not as a modernist circuit diagram, but as a global, postmodern montage of transposable spiritualities.

Neither of these two images allows us to conclude that the global Catholic Church simply served as a kind of institutional trellis upon which the florescent Charismatic movement easily climbed. What is at stake is the fate of that particularly powerful master narrative called 'salvation history' which, rather than being undermined by the decentring force of postmodernism, is now globally promulgated in a Charismatic, sensuous immediacy and in a multiplicity of idioms.... The differences between the early globalization of Catholicism and the globalization of the contemporary Catholic Charismatic Renewal lie in changed conditions having to do with mass media and the ease of travel that dramatically affect interaction between local adherents and the central leadership, as well as in changed idioms of interaction with indigenous religions. A movement such as the Charismatic Renewal weaves the cosmic time of salvation history into the fabric of everyday life, speeding it up and lending it a sense of urgency with the notion that the movement is part of a preparation for the 'end times' before Christ's second coming, but also providing the discipline of a carefully reconstructed *habitus* that structures the rhythms of everyday life, particularly in the more highly elaborated Charismatic intentional communities.

I am convinced that consideration of this movement will allow us to pose, if not yet to answer, some of these issues central to an understanding of religion as a global phenomenon in the 21st century. In my early analysis of the global implications of the movement, I proposed three hypotheses. A cultural hypothesis was that the Charismatic Renewal was a potential vehicle of class consciousness for a transnational bourgeoisie insofar as it could be assumed that a world political-economic system must be accompanied by world religious and ideological systems. A structural hypothesis (particularly relevant to Latin America) was that the appeal of the movement leap-frogs over the working classes to link the bourgeoisie with the very poor, with the excluded middle being the group with the greatest class antagonism to the bourgeoisie and to which the appeal of both classical Pentecostalism and socialism are strongest. It thus may be an ideological articulation of pre-existing social relationships in terms of 'transcending class and cultural barriers' in the name of Christianity, and also (as appears now to have been quite true) of appealing to communitarian sentiment while advancing conservative values in opposition to liberation theology. Finally, a historical hypothesis was that the Charismatic Renewal may play a role on a global scale analogous to that played by Methodism on a national scale in 18th-century England, insofar as it can be argued that it promulgates a moral framework and motivational language for the emergence of a new socioeconomic order (Csordas, 1992).

On another level – that of bodily experience – consider only one theme reflecting consequences for the self in global religious phenomena. Charismatics place a premium on bodily events and practices ranging from reve-latory sensory imagery and the sacred swoon of being overcome by the Holy Spirit, to ritual gestures such as the laying on of hands and prostration in prayer (Csordas, 1990, 1994, 1997, 2002). To understand the central place of embodiment in the global Charismatic re-sacralization, it is useful to turn to the concept elaborated by Mellor and Schilling (1997) of the 'baroque modern body' characteristic of contemporary Western society. For Mellor and Schilling, this is characterized by a heightened sensuality, and is in addition 'internally differ-entiated, prone to all sorts of doubts and anxi-eties, and to be arenas of conflict' (1997: 47). Such a description fits the Charismatic body perfectly, and given examples such as we have seen in the above from India and Brazil, we can suggest that the Charismatic renewal, and perhaps other planetary religious forms, are promulgating this variant of embodiment in the global arena. Certainly, the tendency to associate the contemporary upsurge of sensu-ousness with that of the baroque cultures of Counter-Reformation Catholicism is telling, insofar as in much of the Third World Charis-matic healing and various spiritual manifesta-tions are likewise playing the role of a bulwark against the enthusiastic spirituality of Protes-tant Pentecostalism, to say nothing of the sen-suality of contemporary indigenous religions.

Finally, are we witnessing a re-sacralization or a re-enchantment? Are the Charismatic Renewal and similar phenomena of interest because they contribute to the constitution of an ideological/religious dimension of a global social system? Insofar as religion is a cultural component of any social system, it would be a mistake not to recognize that such develop-ments would accompany the development of other elements of a global social system, including the global economic order, global communications, global population move-ments and diasporas. Specifically, it would appear that the increasing articulation of the world social system generates an ideological impulse towards formulations of universal cul-ture such as the Catholic Charismatic move-ment. What requires empirical determination are the conditions under which global religious phenomena consciously aspire to the status of universal acceptance, in contrast to those in which they are examples of religious ideology as reflection or reflex of the global social real-ity. In either case, such religious phenomena constitute a significant part of the conscious-ness of the contemporary world system, and this can be judged to be a false consciousness in no more or less a sense than was religion in the classic era of industrializing nation states.

REFERENCES

BASTIAN, M.L. (2002) 'Take the Battle to the Enemies' Camp: Militarizing the Spirit in Nigerian Neo-Pentecostal Christianity', paper presented to the Annual Meetings of the American Anthropological Association, New Orleans, LA.

BASTIAN, M.L. (2005) 'A Tale of Two Visionaries: Father EDEH, Sister KATE, and Visions of the Everyday in Southeastern Nigeria', in R. VAN DIJK and J. Hanson (eds) *Religious Modernities in West Africa: New Moralities in Colonial and Post-Colonial Societies*. Bloomington: University of Indiana Press.

CSORDAS, T.J. (1990) 'Embodiment as a Paradigm for Anthropology' (1988 Stirling Award Essay), *Ethos* 18: 5–47.

CSORDAS, T.J. (1992) 'Religion and the World System: The Pentecostal Ethic and the Spirit of Monopoly Capital', *Dialectical Anthropology* 17: 3–24.

CSORDAS, T.J. (1994) *The Sacred Self: A Cultural Phe-nomenology of Charismatic Healing*. Berkeley: Uni-versity of California Press.

CSORDAS, T.J. (1995) 'Oxymorons and Short-Circuits in the Re-Enchantment of the World: The Case of the Catholic Charismatic Renewal', *Etnofoor* 8 ('Special issue on The Enchanted World'): 5–26.

CSORDAS, T.J. (1997) *Language, Charisma, and Creativ-ity: The Ritual Life of a Religious Movement*. Berke-ley: University of California Press.

CSORDAS, T.J. (2002) *Body/Meaning/Healing*. New York: Palgrave.

DE ABREU, M.J.A. (2002) 'On Charisma, Meditation & Broken Screens', *Etnofoor* 15(1/2): 240–58.

DEMPSEY, C.G. (2001). *Kerala Christian Sainthood: Colli-sions of Culture and Worldview in South India*. Oxford: Oxford University Press.

HALLIBURTON, M. (2000) 'Possession, Purgatives, or Prozac? Illness and the Process of Psychiatric Healing in Kerala, South India', PhD dissertation, Department of Anthropology, City University of New York.

LANTERNARI, V. 1987. Un corto-circuito religioso tra Africa e Italia: La terapia Afro-Catolica del Rev. Milingo, in *Medicina, magia, religion: Dalla culture populare alle soieta traditionali*. Rome: Libreria Internazionale Esedra.

———. (1994) *Medicina, magia, religione, valori*. Naples: Liguori.

MACNUTT, FRANCIS (1975) 'Report from Nigeria', *New Covenant* 4: 8–12.

MAUES, R.H. (1998) *O leigo catolico no movimento carismatico em belem do para anthropology*. Caxambu: UFPA.

MELLOR, P.A. and C. SCHILLING (1997) *Re-Forming the Body: Religion, Community, and Modernity*. London: Sage.

MELUCCI, A. (1996) *The Playing Self: Person and Meaning in the Planetary Society*. Cambridge: Cambridge University Press.

MILINGO, E. (1984) *The World in Between: Christian Healing and Struggle for Spiritual Survival*. Maryknoll, NY: Orbis Books.

OJO, MATTHEWS A. (1988) 'The Contextual Significance of the Charismatic Movements in Independent Nigeria', *Africa* 58(2): 175–92.

Peel, J.D.Y. (1968) *Aladura: A Religious Movement among the Yoruba*. London: Oxford University Press.

PIERUCCI, A.F. and R. PRANDI (1995) 'Religioes e voto: a eleicao presidencial de 1994', *Opiniao Publica, Campinas* 3(1): 20–43.

PRANDI, R. (1997) *Um sopro do spirito*. São Paulo: EdUSP.

SCHMALZ, M.N. (1998) *A Space for Redemption: Catholic Tactics in Hindu North India*. Chicago: University of Chicago Press.

SCHMALZ, M.N. (1999) 'Images of the Body in the Life and Death of a North Indian Catholic Catechist', *History of Religions* 39(2): 177–201.

SCHMALZ, M.N. (2002) 'The Silent Body of Audrey Santo', *History of Religions* 42(2): 116–42.

STEIL, C.A. (2001) 'Aparicoes marianas contemporaneas e carismatismo catolico', in Pierre Sanchis (ed.) *Fieis e Cidadaos: Percusos de sincretismo no Brasil*, pp. 117–46. Rio de Janeiro: EDUER.

STEIL, C.A. (2004) 'Renovacao carismatica atolica: porta de entrada ou de saida do catolicismo? uma etnografia do grupo Sao Jose, em Porto Alegre', *Religiao e Sociedade* 24: 11–36.

TER HAAR, G. (1987) 'Religion and Healing: The Case of Milingo', *Social Compass* 34: 475–93.

TER HAAR, G. (1992) *Spirit of Africa: The Healing Ministry of Archbishop Milingo of Zambia*. London: Hurst.

TURNER, H.W. (1967) *History of an African Independent Church*. Oxford: Clarendon Press.

46 Transnational Religious Connections

ROBERT WUTHNOW AND STEPHEN OFFUTT

Focusing on the activities of US congregations and their members, Wuthnow and Offutt provide an expansive view of how religion shapes and is shaped by globalization. Focus on the main argument and ask yourself if you can identify the categories of global influence.

Scholars increasingly observe that religion in the United States cannot be understood by considering only the United States. This observation has arisen from several rather disparate lines of inquiry: theoretical arguments about globalization, studies of immigrant congregations, surveys about Americans' attitudes toward the world and the world's attitude toward America, discussions of global Christianity, and missiological research, among others. From these various perspectives, religion is increasingly viewed as a transnational phenomenon. Although it exists in local communities and is distinctively influenced by a national cultural and political context, it has connections with the wider world and is influenced by these relations. . . .

We focus on the activities of churches and church members in the United States that cross U.S. borders and, where possible, situate these activities in relation to information about religious practices in other countries. Our approach follows the literature on globalization that treats transnationalism as *flows* of people, goods, information, and other resources across national boundaries (Freeman 2006; Hannerz 1996; Kellner 2002; Steger 2003; United Nations 2004). Flows that have been of interest in this literature include trade, foreign investment, capital, migration, telephone calls, remittances, music, pornography, protest networks, terrorist networks, and tourism (Asal, et al. 2007; Della Porta, et al. 2006; Harris 2005; Hjalager 2007; Page and Plaza 2006; Palm 2002; Rosecrance

Source: Robert Wuthnow and Stephen Offutt, "Transnational Religious Connections." Reprinted with permission, from *Sociology of Religion*, Volume 69, © 2008.

and Thompson 2003; Sachs 2007; Salisbury and Barnett 1999; Stallings 2007; Tarrow 2005; Zook 2003). In much of this literature, the more readily quantifiable flows have been examined not only descriptively but also with an eye toward understanding their consequences for a broad range of social phenomena, such as economic development, inequality, the authority of nation-states, and the structure of cities (Alderson and Beckfield 2004; Farrell 2006; Marcotullio 2003; Sacks, et al. 2001; Schularick 2006; Tsai 2007). However, in the case of transnational religious connections, as with many other aspects of globalization, few of the descriptive questions have been fully addressed. This is especially evident when the complexity of these flows is recognized. Not only is it necessary to take account of different kinds (e.g., people, information), but also to consider their location (many are transnational but few are truly global) and duration, as well as such aspects as speed, scope of societal involvement, and mode of organization (Steger 2003; Rosenberg 2000).

In emphasizing flows, our approach differs from that of studies in which transnationalism is taken to exist only if people develop an alternative sense of themselves as being citizens of no particular country or attach primary loyalty to a religious community that exists in several countries or engage in business activities that cause them to live and work on two sides of a border over a long period of time.[1] We understand that scholars investigating other topics have sometimes felt it necessary to define transnationlism in these ways. But for our purposes, a broader definition is essential in the same way it is for understanding the flows of people, goods, information, and resources in other spheres affected by globalization.

---

[1] Among approaches that take a different approach are treatments of religion and globalization that emphasize the theoretical implications of long-term modernization processes (Beyer 1994; Robertson 1992) and studies that consider it transnationalism only in the context of immigrant communities that sit astride political borders to such an extent that they are neither here nor there (Portes 1997, 1999; Portes, et al. 1999).

Any discussion of transnational religious connections must begin by acknowledging that relations of this kind have been around for a long time. Itinerant Buddhist monks in China and Japan, Spanish and Portuguese priests in South America, and the churching of North America by European immigrants are familiar examples. An early example that illustrates U.S. influences overseas is the American Board of Commissioners of Foreign Missions. It was founded in 1810 by Congregationalists and Presbyterians, and by 1835 had distributed 90 million pages of religious tracts, opened 63 overseas mission stations with 311 staff members, and initiated 474 schools for upwards of 80,000 pupils (Anderson 1861). Religion is transnational because human flows so often transcend arbitrary political demarcations, but also because religious teachings frequently encourage geographic expansion.

If transnational ties are not new, they have become more pronounced and of greater interest in recent decades. Technological innovations have facilitated such connections in the past. London Missionary Society founder William Carey wrote in 1792 that the invention of the mariner's compass was key to the rising missionary movement. This is no less the case at present with email, the Internet, faster aviation, and cheaper shipping making it easier to communicate and travel. The United States—which ranked fourth overall in a recent ranking of countries on measures of globalization (Kearny 2006)—is increasingly connected with other countries through trade, migration, international investment, and technology. These linkages frequently facilitate religious connections as well. . . .

FLOWS OF PEOPLE

People who cross national borders to live, work, or travel in other countries constitute one important kind of transnational connection that often has a religious dimension. Immigration has received considerable attention because of its role in the formation of new ethnically defined religious congregations. People flows also include full-time religious workers, short-term volunteers, and tourists.

Migration

The past several decades have witnessed historic movements of people across borders. Between 1965, when immigration laws changed, and 2000, an estimated 22 million people immigrated legally to the United States and between seven and ten million more may have come as undocumented workers. The impact of immigration was especially evident among young adults where the proportion of men in their twenties who were non-citizens or naturalized citizens grew from four percent in 1970 to 18 percent in 2000 (Wuthnow 2007).

Migration to the United States is part of a larger global phenomenon. Immigrants to Britain made up 7.5 percent of the population in 2000, and the resulting religious diversity is challenging some to recast Britain's national identity as one of overlapping spiritual identities (Bradley 2007). France's immigrant population in 2000 was 11 percent, and has brought Islam decisively into the French context (Bowen 2007). Across the Middle East and Asia, city-states and select countries are being completely reshaped through migration. For instance, 58 percent of those living in Kuwait, 40 percent in Bahrain and Hong Kong, and 66 percent in Macao are immigrants. Although South Africa's foreign-born population of three to five percent appears to be more modest (Schlemmer 2006), 41 percent of Botswanans and 54 percent of Mozambiquans in 2000 said their parents worked in South Africa, reflecting labor cycles that have long characterized economic life in Southern Africa (Crush, et al. 2005). Meanwhile, sending countries are also being restructured. At least 17 countries in the developing world experienced at least two percent annual

population losses in the 1990s (United Nations 2004). Even countries that continue to grow are affected by a still more quickly growing diaspora. El Salvador's population, for example, is about seven million, but an estimated 3.2 million more Salvadorans now live outside the country, with roughly 2.5 million of those living in the United States.

Immigrants not only add to the religious diversity of host societies, but also forge connections between societies. These ties emerge organically, but can generally be classified as connections between immigrants and their home country, immigrants and non-immigrants, or immigrants of different countries. Churches become intimately involved in the transnational ties of their congregants, and over time help to institutionalize and routinize these connections. Levitt (2004) notes three strategies used by churches in this endeavor—extended, negotiated, and recreated—and the different types of religious organizations that most often employ them (Catholic, Protestant, and Hindu, respectively). The level of diversity between transnational patterns is, however, somewhat limited because immigrant churches of all stripes, as Ebaugh and Chafetz (2000b) point out, tend toward the "de facto congregationalism" adopted by religious communities in America (Warner 1994).

The ties between immigrants and their home countries often allow them to participate in two communities simultaneously. Levitt (2007) has shown that immigrants frequently make return trips to their countries of origin, maintain dual residences, and even participate in elections in more than one country. Remittances tend to be dominated by flows from host to sending countries, but forms of media flow freely in both directions, including newspapers, movies, television shows, radio programs, phone calls, email, and videos. Wuthnow's (2006) New Elites Project—a study of 200 well-established, occupationally successful first-and second-generation immigrants from 35 countries—finds similar evidence of continuing transnational interaction despite these immigrants' successful assimilation into more general cultural norms within the United States. For instance, 73 percent had personally visited siblings or other immediate family members who lived outside the United States at least once a year. There is also ample evidence of the role played by transnational networks prior to their becoming permanent U.S. residents: 43 percent had previously worked in another country, 78 percent knew someone in the U.S. who helped them find a job or get settled, and 67 percent had studied abroad. In all of these ways, immigrants create and maintain ties to their countries of origin.

Besides these direct transnational ties, immigrants interact with other immigrants and with non-immigrants, often in churches. This is one way in which the impact of transnational ties extends beyond immigrant communities into the wider society. In Wuthnow's Global Issues Survey, eight percent of active U.S. church members were immigrants, but 74 percent of members attended congregations in which recent immigrants were present. Qualitative information shows that the presence of immigrants has various effects, both formal and informal, such as initiating special Bible study groups for non-English speakers and spinning off start-up ministries in predominantly immigrant neighborhoods. In addition, the presence of a few recent immigrants sometimes helps in initiating partnerships with churches in other countries and humanitarian programs. There are also increasing instances of congregations drawing together immigrants from different countries—sometimes from the same region and with the same language (Ebaugh and Chafetz 2000a, 2002), and sometimes from multiple continents (as in the case of a Philadelphia church in which members come from China, India, Kenya, and several Latin American countries).

Religious Workers

Professional and other full-time religious workers who go from one country to live and work in another country—i.e., *missionaries*—continue to be an important kind of transnational religious connection. Although casual observers often argue that the missionary era is over (e.g., MacLeod 2004; Siermon-Netto 2003), figures collected by Protestant mission agencies and denominations in 2001 show that there were 42,787 U.S. citizens working full-time as missionaries in other countries, representing an increase of approximately 16 percent over the previous decade, and significantly higher than the comparable number in the 1950s at the often assumed height of overseas missionary endeavors. Among Catholics, as of 2004, 111 American-born diocesan priests and 1,420 American-born religious priests were serving abroad. Unlike the upward trend among U.S. Protestant missionaries working abroad, this figure was approximately one-sixth the number of Catholic clergy who had served abroad in 1968. Instead, the number of foreign-born priests serving in the United States appears to be growing, judging from the fact that, in 2005, 16 percent of all U.S. priests and 27 percent of those recently ordained were foreign-born (Lefevere 2006).

While the large majority of religious workers in most countries are indigenous, foreign religious workers create important transnational linkages. According to the most comprehensive source for *global* Christian statistics, eight percent of full-time Christian workers worldwide in 2000 were non-citizens (Barrett and Johnson 2001:420–21). Non-citizens comprised nine percent of all Christian workers in Asia, 11 percent in Africa, 16 percent in Oceania, and 23 percent in Latin America, but only six percent in Europe and two percent in North America. Differences between poorer and richer parts of the world were also evident in the fact that the ratio of foreign religious workers received to religious workers sent abroad was 5.2 in Africa, 2.6 in Latin America, 2.4 in Asia, and 1.9 in Oceania, whereas it was 0.5 for Europe and 0.3 for North America.

Comparable data for other religions are unavailable; however, one estimate counted 141,630 Islamic *da'wah* groups (propagators of the faith) engaged in foreign missions worldwide (Johnson and Scoggins 2005). As another example, hundreds of Turkish imams can now be found in Germany, the vast majority of whom are funded by the Turkish government and typically serve four year terms before returning to their own country (Gibbon 2006). In the United Kingdom, estimates suggest that 90 percent of the country's 2,000 imams have been trained abroad, many at schools funded by Saudi Arabia (Klausen 2004).

Modern mission mobilization among Christian organizations involved transnational cooperation from the start, especially between agencies in the United States and England. These partnerships continued and broadened through such endeavors as the Lausanne Committee for World Evangelization and other international mission conferences in the twentieth century (Winter and Hawthorne 1999). Among U.S. agencies, mission programs have long been centrally coordinated by denominational and interdenominational boards. This pattern continues. For instance, the International Mission Board of the Southern Baptist Convention had a budget of $283 million in 2005 and supported more than 5,000 full-time foreign missionaries—a five-fold increase since 1955. The support staff in Richmond, Virginia, consists of 500 full-time employees. The board is also responsible for training and deploying approximately 30,000 short-term volunteers. Through its missionaries and volunteers, the board claims approximately 600,000 baptisms annually worldwide and assists in the work of nearly 100,000 overseas churches.

Transnational missionary efforts are also widely supported by local congregations. In the Global Issues Survey, 74 percent of U.S. church members said their congregation supported a missionary working in another country during the past year. On average, four in ten said their congregation has a committee that focuses on overseas missions or other international programs, and one in five reported that his or her congregation had a full-time staff member with special responsibility for overseas missions and other global ministries.

Short-Term Volunteers

Increasingly, people go from one country to another as amateur volunteers for what have come to be called short-term mission trips. Although hard numbers are difficult to find, an estimate from the Global Issues Survey is that 1.6 million U.S. church goers participate in short-term mission trips to other countries each year. The median length of time abroad, not counting travel is eight days, meaning that short-term volunteers contribute approximately 30,000 person-years to U.S. mission efforts abroad—about one-fourth the amount provided by professional missionaries. The dollar value of this effort, using rates established by Independent Sector, is approximately $1.1 billion. At an average cost of at least $1,000 per trip, transportation conservatively totals at least another $1.6 billion.

Forty-four percent of those surveyed said their congregation sent a group abroad in the past year to do short-term missions or relief work. An indication that the numbers of people involved in short-term missions has probably increased is that only two percent of those who had been teenagers during the 1950s, 1960s, or 1970s said they had gone to another country on a short-term mission trip while in high school, whereas this proportion increased to five percent among those who had been teenagers in the 1990s and 12 percent among those who had been teenagers since the 1990s. Although short term mission trips are primarily a U.S. phenomenon, Offutt's research uncovered teams originating in El Salvador that had visited Kosovo, Equatorial Guinea, Honduras, Niger, Nicaragua, and Vietnam. Teams originating in South Africa had gone to Greece, France, India, Lesotho, Malawi, Mozambique, Poland, and Thailand. These short-term trips are generally facilitated by preexisting transnational ties. For instance, in one case, a middle class Salvadoran immigrated to New Mexico and joined a church, which subsequently sent a team to the immigrant's previous church in San Salvador. In other cases, denominations provide a transnational link, often through congregation-to-congregation partnerships. Nongovernmental humanitarian organizations and campus-to-campus ties are also important facilitators.

When teams arrive at their destination, they engage in a wide variety of activities. Several of the churches we studied near the U.S.-Mexico border enlisted volunteer teams to collect building materials in the United States and assemble them in Mexico with local help. A congregation in Atlanta was fairly typical in sending a team to Africa for a week to investigate organizations with which the congregation would partner over a period of years to provide financial assistance. Teams of medical professionals volunteer at health clinics; groups of teachers volunteer at schools. Still other groups put on puppet shows for children, engage in evangelistic ministries, and distribute food and clothing to communities in need.

Long term transnational connections may or may not result from short term mission trips. Some medical professionals, for instance, serve in as many parts of the world as possible, and so view a trip to a specific location as a one time event. In other cases, return visits flow out of relationships that form across cultures. For example, a Seattle-based group first visited El Salvador to help build a house and to upgrade a local NGO's computer systems. A year later,

one of the team members moved to El Salvador to assist the NGO in different ways. The other team members communicate regularly and visit El Salvador about once a year.

Religious Transnationalism in Other Fields

People travel internationally and live temporarily in other countries for leisure and work-related activities that may have nothing to do with religion, and yet insofar as they are religious people, their religious beliefs and practices are sometimes involved. By narrow definitions of transnationalism that restrict its meaning to long-term, identity-changing social relationships, these ephemeral contacts may not matter. And yet an understanding of *flows* of people across borders must include such contacts and must also include the possibility that they do broaden horizons and facilitate other kinds of exchange. In the Global Issues Survey nearly two-thirds (62 percent) of active church members said they had traveled or lived in another country—a figure that of course includes short-distance visits to Canada or Mexico.[4] One in seven (14 percent) had lived in another country for at least a year. More than four in ten (43 percent) had friends or relatives who lived outside the United States. Among church members currently working, 37 percent said they routinely interact with people from other countries at work. Transnational contacts of these kinds generally do not result in discussions about religion. And yet, 10 to 15 percent of Americans do talk about

---

...

[4]This figure may be skewed by the fact that active church members tend to be better educated than the general public; nevertheless, among respondents who had not been to college, 41 percent reported having traveled or lived outside the United States. In a previous national survey (Wuthnow 2005), 57 and 58 percent of regular church attenders and non-attenders, respectively, said they have traveled or lived outside the United States; among those who had, 11 percent of both groups had been to the Middle East and 17 and 20 percent, respectively, had been to India, China, Japan, or another part of Asia.

religion with people from other religious traditions who have grown up in other countries, and, not surprisingly, Americans who have traveled abroad are more likely to have participated in diverse worship services (Wuthnow 2005).

Congregations are one of the places in which transnational contacts occur. In the Global Issues Survey, 48 percent said their congregation had hosted a guest speaker from another country in the past year. Colleges and universities are another. In 2004, the number of foreign students enrolled at American universities totaled more than 572,000, up from only 179,000 in 1975. Denominations, seminaries, and parachurch organizations are yet another source, hosting international conferences and study-abroad opportunities. One example is the triennial Urbana Missions Conference, which attracted 23,000 college-age participants in 2006. Another is Passion, a multi-day Christian music and worship fest that drew a similar number of young people to Atlanta in 2007.

Pilgrimages represent another critical component of transnational religious activity. Among Muslims, the annual *hajj* is a prominent example, drawing approximately 2.5 million visitors to Mecca each year, including an estimated 10,000 from the United States (Kahn 2005). American Hindus are among the more than 100,000 pilgrims who travel annually to Kashmir to see a symbol of Lord Shiva, one of Hinduism's three most revered gods, and are said to be increasingly represented among pilgrims to large "Hindu theme parks" in India (Rohde 2002; Kurien 2007:104). Hindus, Buddhists, Jains, and Bonpo believers all consider Mount Kailas in Tibet to be a place for pilgrimage at least once in their lifetimes, and come from all over the globe to circle its base (Henriksen 2003). For American Christians and Jews, visits to Israel frequently have meaning as religious pilgrimages. Overall, tourism to Israel (from all countries) grew from just over one million in 1990 to 2.4 million in 2000,

declined to 862,000 in 2002 after the 9/11 attacks, and thereafter rose to 1.8 million in 2006.[5] Organizations such as Taglit-Birthright Israel, Hillel, the Catholic Pilgrimage Center, the World Religious Travel Association, local congregations, and commercial travel agencies are examples of organizations that facilitate pilgrimages.

Business and professional personnel increasingly travel internationally as the global economy expands, and in some instances also use these contacts to forge religious ties (Yamamori and Eldred 2003). Offutt's research in Central America and Africa finds numerous examples. For instance, a Salvadoran visiting a plant in Honduras announces that he is an evangelical Christian and that he is interested in a potential project because he thinks it could honor and glorify God. The plant manager responds that he shares the Salvadoran's faith, and is excited about the partnership for the same reason. A South African commodities trader believes that "there are a lot of people in darkness," and he consequently tries to share his faith through his business interactions, which often cross national borders. Other examples include the international business leaders known as "boss Christians" in China (Cunfu and Tianhai 2004), and so-called "great commission companies," such as Pura Vida Coffee and Gateway Telecommunications (Rundle and Steffen 2003). Religious actors also create ties in diplomatic venues. For example, a South African Christian lawyer told Offutt she believes that God has called her to fight for social justice, and she does this by representing South Africa in committees at the United Nations and on women's issues in the Democratic Republic of Congo. She uses transnational connections, including contacts at American universities and in Washington, as resources.

---

[5]Figures from annual reports by the United Nations' World Tourism Organization, online at www.world-tourism.org.

FLOWS OF RESOURCES

Besides flows of people, transnational religious connections consist of exchanges of money, knowledge, information, and other goods and services between religious communities or between donors in one country and recipients in another. The cost of training, transporting, and maintaining religious workers abroad implies a transnational investment of resources. Others include remittances, funds for religious personnel and programs, humanitarian efforts, and flows of religious products and information.

Remittance

Global statistics for 2002, the most recent year available, shows that migrants sent nearly $80 billion home to developing countries. In Mexico alone, remittances from people working abroad totaled $9.8 billion, approximately twice the value of the country's annual agricultural exports (A.T. Kearney 2006). In El Salvador, remittances totaled nearly $2.8 billion in 2005 and an estimated 22 percent of households in El Salvador receive remittances.

Remittances primarily benefit family members, but in turn sometimes expand the possibilities for religious congregations to hire staff and run programs. Kurien's (2002) research among Indian workers in the Middle East shows how remittances affect Christian, Muslim, and Hindu communities in India. Levitt's (2007) research provides examples of remittances facilitating the activities of congregations in the Dominican Republic and Ireland. An example from Offutt's work in El Salvador also shows how churches benefit from remittances. Mario Gonzalez, the senior pastor of the Christian Community of Faith and Adoration estimates that all of his 150 members have relatives living in the U.S., and that 80 percent receive remittances. The church worships in a rented space in Zacamil, a lower middle class sector of San Salvador. Remittances

enable the very simple lifestyle to which the members aspire. Gonzalez encourages members to tithe the remittances just as they would income, and he estimated that 20 percent of them do. As it seeks to purchase a lot and erect a new church building, the added tithes from remittances will certainly help.

Religious Funding

Financial support of religious organizations and personnel in other countries represents another significant flow of resources. Studies of religious congregations in poor countries appropriately emphasize the role of indigenous leaders and local participation, and yet may underestimate the role of external funding in arguing that overseas missionaries are not involved. In 2001, approximately 65,000 non-U.S. citizens and foreign nationals were working in other countries under full financial sponsorship by a Protestant U.S. agency. Though small compared to the likely number of clergy supported through local funding, this number was larger by nearly half than the number of U.S. foreign missionaries. In total, U.S. Protestant churches contributed more than $3.7 billion for overseas ministries, an after-inflation increase of 45 percent over the previous decade (Welliver and Northcutt 2004).

Whether the labor value of short-term volunteers represents an actual financial contribution can be questioned on grounds that these volunteers also consume time and resources from their hosts and may only be replacing local labor in areas where unemployment is already high. However, short-term volunteers sometimes provide financial assistance as well. For instance, a study of four U.S. teams of high school students working with Peruvian churches showed that the 89 volunteers contributed a total of more than $25,000 in cash toward church construction and repair (Priest 2007).

Humanitarian Aid

Congregations and denominations are significantly involved in international humanitarian aid. A national poll released on January 13, 2005 showed that 36 percent of the U.S. public claimed to have donated money to their churches for tsunami victims (www.pewresearchcenter.org). The Southern Baptist Convention collected $16 million, United Methodists took in more than $6 million, the United Church of Christ contributed more than $3 million, and the Evangelical Lutheran Church in America raised $2.5 million. Catholic Relief Services alone accounted for $114 million.

In the Global Issues Survey, 76 percent of active church members said they had personally given money in the past year for international relief or hunger projects. The same percentage said their congregation had an offering in the past year to raise money for overseas hunger or relief programs. In more than 80 percent of these congregations, there had been more than one such offering in the past year. The survey also showed that 29 percent belonged to congregations that had helped support a refugee or refugee family within the past year. Qualitative interviews with pastors and lay leaders suggested that congregations usually contribute in rather small ways to humanitarian efforts. This impression is reinforced by the survey in which 70 percent of respondents said they gave less than $500 total to religious organizations during the year and, of these, the majority either did not know or assumed the amount they had given to help people in other countries was less than $100.

Individual donations, though, comprise only part of what U.S. religious organizations contribute to international humanitarian aid. Data collected in 1981 showed that many of the largest nonprofit humanitarian organizations were religious—for example, Catholic Relief Services, World Vision, Church World

Service, and the Adventist Development and Relief Agency—and that some of these organizations were receiving substantial revenue from government grants and contracts (Smith 1990). By 2003, judging from IRS 990 forms, inflation-adjusted budgets of the top 25 faith-based international aid organizations had grown 134 percent, reaching a total of $2.3 billion. Among the largest, Catholic Relief Services received 74 percent of its support from government sources. Church World Service, World Relief, the Adventist Development and Relief Agency, and World Vision received 64 percent, 50 percent, 46 percent, and 37 percent, respectively. Besides government funding, private philanthropy, such as that of the Arthur S. DeMoss Foundation, the DeVos Foundation, and the Mclellan Foundation, also played a significant role.

Religious Products and Information

One of the more important transnational flows of religious information is the production and distribution of Bibles. In 2006, approximately 24 million Bibles were distributed worldwide by United Bible Societies, a transnational organization that began in 1946 and currently includes offices in 120 countries. Bibles are printed in local languages and support in raised through local congregations. However, the effort also represents a significant investment of U.S. resources. The American Bible Society's 2006 IRS 990 form shows assets of $493.8 million and total expenses of $82.6 million, of which $37.7 million was for "overseas out-reach."

Another example is the Jesus Project, a film about the life of Jesus produced and distributed by U.S.-based Campus Crusade for Christ. From the project's inception in 1979 through 2005, an estimated 42 million video-cassettes (as well as 13 million audiocassettes) were distributed, according to the project's website (www.jesusfilm.org). The material has been translated into 1,000 different languages, and the organization claims it has reached six billion people in 105 countries.

A third example is the leadership literature produced by John C. Maxwell (e.g. Maxwell 1998). Maxwell, an Atlanta-based speaker and author, appears regularly on bestseller lists such as *The New York Times* and *Business Week*. He is aggressively reaching out around the globe, touring 12 countries in Latin America in 2006. In El Salvador he spoke to over 1,000 business and religious leaders before meeting with the country's President, Tony Saca. In 2007, Maxwell spoke to senior executives and ministry leaders in South Africa. His books are prominently displayed in Christian book stores throughout El Salvador and South Africa. When an assistant pastor in a Salvadoran megachurch of 15,000 was asked by Offutt which American authors he trusted, his first response was "John Maxwell."

Other religious products also facilitate a sense of a single faith community across borders. The second generation Swadhyayees (a Hindu movement) that Levitt studied watch videotapes (with English subtitles) of lectures by their leader. The Swadhyaya headquarters now has a unit that spends its days mailing these out around the world. Likewise in Pakistan, Farat Hashmi, a female religious scholar who is very popular with middle-class Pakistani women, is spreading her word through audiotapes, video, and books; she is gaining increasing visibility throughout South Asia and the Middle East (Levitt 2007).

THE GLOBAL POLITICAL ECONOMY

Besides the flows of people and resources that connect religious communities transnationally, religion is shaped indirectly by global economic and political relations. These economic and political relations are part of the globalization process and typically involve new market relations, rising opportunities for some and declining opportunities for others, trade agreements, and diplomatic relations. The impact of these changing dynamics of the global political economy on local religious communities is often profound. A good example of these indirect influences was the integration of northern Brazil into the global economy through the construction of the Belem-Brasilia highway and the subsequent growth of iron, timber, ranching, and hydroelectric power generation. As subsistence farmers and agricultural workers were displaced from rural areas, Belem's migrant population swelled and the shantytown population increased four- to eightfold. Pentecostal churches grew rapidly in these neighborhoods, attracting domestic servants, security guards, janitors, day laborers, and the unemployed. Without healthcare or traditional family networks, people were especially drawn to the healing services the churches offered (Chesnut 1997). In other areas, Pentecostal and evangelical churches have grown among different social strata (Martin 2002). The point is that even religious developments led by indigenous clergy and in highly specific local settings are often shaped by transnational influences. . . .

Trade and Communication

People in different parts of the world are increasingly connected through international trade and communication. As a share of Gross Domestic Product, international trade rose during the 1990s among 67 countries for which records were kept and declined among only 14, according to the World Bank (www.worldbank. org). During the same period, the United Nations tracked 1,885 changes in national regulations and found that 94 percent liberalized the flow of international trade (ww.uctad.org). International telephone traffic, as measured by minutes U.S. residents spent talking internationally, increased by 500 percent between 1990 and 2004 (A. T. Kearney 2006). The Internet, email, and satellite links to newspapers and cable television stations have also encouraged greater awareness of people and events beyond national borders. In the Global Issues Survey, 75 percent said they watched news about other parts of the world on television at least once a week, a quarter read about international news at least once a week, and four in ten obtained information about foreign events at least once a week from the Internet.

In our 300 qualitative interviews among U.S. clergy and laity, we found numerous examples of religious practices being influenced by international trade and communication. Liturgical prayers focused on late breaking news in some instances and included prayer requests received overnight from missionaries in others. A church in South Carolina started a relief project in Africa after one of its members returned there from a business trip. A lay leader in Massachusetts became interested in working with the International Justice Mission after hearing about human trafficking on a visit to Thailand. An immigrant church in Philadelphia keeps in close contact with family members in Nigeria through email.

Equality and Inequality

Free markets and increasing international trade have affected national economies nearly everywhere, bringing rising economic opportunities for some and reinforcing poverty for others. Between 1987 and 1998, the share of the world's population living in extreme poverty fell from 28 percent to 23 percent, with most of this decline occurring in China and India, while the number of poor people living in Africa increased (Dollar 2005). Income inequality *within* developing countries appears to have declined in some cases and risen in others. Other measures of development, such as expansion of primary schooling and reductions in child mortality rates, show only modest gains during the recent period of globalization (Ravallion 2003).

Ethnographic studies suggest that religious communities have responded in complex ways to these shifting economic realities. Chesnut's research in northern Brazil illustrates Pentecostalism's appeal to people in declining strata, while other research in southern Brazil suggests a different kind of Pentecostalism emerging among the rising middle class. Research among evangelicals in Ghana shows teachings that give hope and legitimacy to people with increasing economic aspirations but at the same time warn against the dangers of consumer gratification (Meyer 1998). In China, studies variously suggest that business leaders with expanding profits from international trade are involved in bankrolling new Christian churches, that the rising urban middle class is both drawn to prosperity gospel preaching and increasingly secular, that the Korean expatriate community is growing and deeply religious, that the Chinese government is more tolerant of religion in some areas and better able to suppress it in others, and that rural poverty is a source of growing spiritualism and syncretic folk religious practices (Wenger 2004; Ownby 2007). All of these developments are influenced by changes in the global economy.

Democracy

The democratic revolution that has affected many parts of the world since the end of the [colonial] era has been a transnational movement both in spreading ideas about democracy from one society to the next and in creating new political agreements (such as the European Union) that include multiple nations. As a significant feature of its foreign policy during and after the Cold War, the United States has sought to encourage democratic regimes at least in parts of the world where it was in the nation's interests to do so. One aspect of U.S. policy that dealt specifically with religion has been its attempts to promote international religious freedom as part of a broader agenda of extending human rights.

Although the implications of this democratic revolution for religion vary, three broad implications can be identified. First, democratic regimes have opened doors for foreign religious workers in many instances. Russia, other parts of Eastern Europe and central Asia, Uganda, and Indonesia are examples. Second, reactions against democratization, perceived as a westernizing and secularizing influence, have emerged in Burma, Algeria, and some parts of the Middle East, effectively reducing opportunities for foreign religious workers. And third, questions about religious pluralism and the rights of religious minority groups have risen in importance as repressive regimes have disappeared and as smaller religious communities have acquired the right to speak on their own behalf.

Cultural Influences

Transnational religious connections are also influenced by the spread of common symbols and narratives. They do not displace local traditions, but they do reflect the power of rich countries to influence global culture. The fact that so many speak English has made long- and short-term mission work easier. English is the first language of only 375 million people, but is a second language for another 375 million people as a result of colonial histories and migration, and it is estimated to be part of the repertoire of another 750 million people who have felt the need to learn English as a second language. Consumer culture is another influence. In 2000, for instance, the global market for films was estimated at one trillion dollars, of which American content comprised slightly more than half (Hamano 2004). Of the ten top-grossing films at the international box office, all originated in the United States. Although it is unclear how widespread these cultural influences may be, writers point to numerous anecdotal examples, such as "Amazonian Indians wearing Nike sneakers, denizens of the Southern Sahara

purchasing Texaco baseball caps, and Palestinian youths proudly displaying their Chicago Bulls sweatshirts in downtown Ramallah" (Steger 2003:36). Local religious organizations are influenced by these messages, sometimes incorporating them and often warning followers against them (Meyer 1998).

CONCLUSION

Globalization has been described as a culturally homogenizing force, spreading a monoculture of fast food items and western-style entertainment, and as an equalizing dynamic that reduces poverty. Both claims are disputed by scholars who argue that globalization actually facilitates diversity and perhaps increases income disparities. What is not disputed is the fact that some countries are much richer and more powerful than others. Global inequality is thus a significant reality for understanding transnational religious connections. It means that many of these connections are asymmetric.

For example, the 155 million Christians living in Brazil and the 192 million Christians living in the United States give an appearance that the two countries are nearly equivalent in religious demographics, but there are notable differences. In the United States the average Christian enjoys an annual income of $26,980, whereas the annual income of Christians in Brazil is $3,640. Not surprisingly, Christian organizations are much more numerous and better supported in the United States than in Brazil. Brazil has more than twice as many Catholics as the United States, but the United States has more than twice as many Catholic parishes as Brazil and the ratio of priests to parishioners is six times higher in the United States than in Brazil (Froehle and Gautier 2003). Overall, Catholic and Protestant churches take in approximately nine times more money annually than churches in Brazil. The point is not to diminish the importance of indigenous churches in Brazil, many of which have experienced explosive growth in recent decades, but that churches in the United States have enormous *capacity* to support programs both at home and abroad.

These asymmetries notwithstanding, symmetric links and counter-flows are also evident. For example, Pentecostal missionaries and telecasts from the United States to Brazil are now reversed through programming from the Universal Church of the Kingdom of God in Brazil, which is reproduced for the New York City Spanish language media market (Mora 2007). Similarly, black gospel music once imported in Ghana from the United States is more recently joined by holy hip hop music from Ghana being popular in Atlanta. Symmetry is encouraged by norms of reciprocity, by rising interest in cultural diversity, and in some instances by contact with visitors from rich countries conferring prestige on pastors and lay leaders in poor countries.

. . .

Counter flows and multilateral connections are not ahistorical. Rather, they exist in the world created by the flows, counter flows, and multilateral connections that went before them. The culture that flowed through these connections yesterday is often repackaged and sent on again, picking up the local flavors of each stop in its transnational journey. Cultural echoes often reverberate back through the transnational connections to the senders, influencing those communities yet again, while the cultural artifacts go on to new places and take on unanticipated forms. In a remote section of Papua New Guinea that had never been missionized, Robbins (2004) observed apocalyptic rumors of Christ's imminent return that betrayed a remarkable awareness of the wider world. The European Union was thought to be a harbinger of a world government, turmoil in the Middle East signaled the end times, a new world order was in the making, and Satan was behind the universal product code and the spread of ATM machines. Further investigation traced the rumors through local networks

among the villagers and their pastor to several outside sources, including a New Zealand-based evangelist who had become popular in Papua New Guinea and who, in turn, had been heavily influenced by the American writer Hal Lindsey, author of the best-selling *Late Great Planet Earth*.

Clearly, the existence and probable increase of transnational religious connections poses new opportunities and challenges for scholars of religion. Besides chronicling the existence of these connections, future studies will need to consider the organizational mechanisms through which they are refracted, the ways in which easier travel and communication increase the chances of local congregations in different parts of the world supporting one another and working cooperatively, and how these possibilities affect local congregations and their choice of partners. As with other relationships involving power differences, those between religious organizations in rich and poor countries merit special consideration.

REFERENCES

A. T. KEARNEY. 2006. "The Global Top 20." *Foreign Policy* (November/December): 74-81.

ALDERSON, ARTHUR S., and JASON BECKFIELD. 2004. "Power and Position in the World City System." *American Journal of Sociology* 109:811-51.

ANDERSON, RUFUS. 1861. *Memorial Volume of the First Fifty years of the American Board of Commissioners for Foreign Missions*. Boston, MA: ABCFM.

ASAL, VICTOR, BRIAN NUSSBAUM, and D. WILLIAM HARRINGTON. 2007. "Terrorism as Transnational Advocacy: An Organizational and Tactical Examination." *Studies in Conflict & Terrorism* 30:15-39.

BARRETT, DAVID B., and TODD M. JOHNSON. 2001. *World Christian Trends, A.D 30 – A.D 2200: Interpreting the Annual Christian Megacensus*. Pasadena, CA: William Carey Library.

BEYER, PETER. 1994. *Religion and Globalization*. Thousand Oaks, CA: Sage.

BOWEN, J. R. 2007. *Why the French Don't Like Headscarves: Islam, the State, and Public Space*. Princeton, NJ: Princeton University Press.

BRADLEY, IAN. 2007. *Believing in Britain: The Spiritual Identity of 'Britishness'*. New York, NY: I.B. Tauris.

CHAVES, MARK. 2004. *Congregations in America.* Cambridge, MA: Harvard University Press.

CHESNUT, R. ANDREW. 1997. *Born Again in Brazil: The Pentecostal Boom and the Pathogens of Poverty.* New Brunswick, NJ: Rutgers University Press.

CRUSH, JONATHAN, VINCENT WILLIAMS, and SALLY PEBERDY. 2005. "Migration in Southern Africa: A Paper Prepared for the Policy Analysis and Research Programme of the Global Commission of International Migration." Geneva: Global Commission on International Migration.

CUNFU, CHEN, and HUANG TIANHAI. 2004. "The Emergence of a New Type of Christians in China Today." *Review of Religious Research* 46:183-200.

DELLA PORTA, DONATELLA, MASSIMILLANO ANDRETTA, LORENZO MOSCA, AND HERBERT REITER. 2006. *Globalization from Below: Transnational Activists and Protest Networks.* Minneapolis, MN: University of Minnesota Press.

DOLLAR, DAVID. 2005. "Globalization, Poverty, and Inequality." Pp. 96-128 *Globalization: What's New?* edited by M.M. Weinstein. New York, NY: Columbia University Press.

EBAUGH, HELEN ROSE, and JANET SATLZMAN CHAFETZ. 2000a. "Dilemmas of Language in Immigrant Congregations: The Tie the Binds or the Tower of Babel?" *Review of Religious Research* 41:432-52.

———. 2000b. "Structural Adaptations in Immigrant Congregations." *Sociology of Religion* 61:135-53.

———. 2002. *Religion across Borders: Transnational Immigrant Networks.* Walnut Creek, CA: AltaMira Press.

FARRELL, HENRY JOHN. 2006. "Regulating Information Flows: States, Private Actors, and [E-commerce.]" *Annual Review of Political Science* 9:353-74.

FREEMAN, RICHARD B. 2006. "People Flows in Globalization." *Journal of Economic Perspectives* 20:145-70.

FROEHLE, BRYAN T., and MARY L. GAUTIER. 2003. *Global Catholicism: Portrait of a World Church.* Maryknoll, NY: Orbis.

GIBBON, JAMES. 2006. "Religion, Migrants, and the Turkish Government in Germany." Working Paper, Princeton University, Center for the Study of Religion.

GREEN, JOHN C. 2003. "Evangelical Protestants and Civic Engagement: An Overview." Pp. 11-30 in *A Public Faith: Evangelicals and Civic Engagement,* edited by M. CROMARTIE. Lanham, MD: Rowman & Littlefield.

HANNERZ, ULF. 1996. *Transnational Connections: Culture, People, Places.* London: Routledge.

HAMANO, YASUKI. 2004. "Building the Content Industry." *Japan Plus: Asia-Pacific Perspectives* (May). Retrieved 17 December 2007 (*http://www.jijigaho.or.jp/old/app/0405/eng/sp12.html*).

HARRIS, RACHEL. 2005. "Reggae on the Silk Road: The Globalization of Uyghur Pop." *China Quarterly* 183:627-43.

HENRIKSEN, ALEXANDER. 2003. "Trekking Towards Enlightenment." *Geographical.* 75(11): 22-29.

HJALAGER, AENNE-METTE. 2007. "Stages in the Economic Globalization of Tourism." *Annals of Tourism Research* 34:437-57.

JOHNSON, TODD M., and DAVID R. SCOGGINS. 2005. "Christian Missions and Islamic *Da'wah:* A Preliminary Quantitative Assessment," *International Bulletin of Missionary Research* 29:8-11.

KAHN, AFZAL. 2005. "American Muslims Perform Hajj, Celebrate Eid-ul Adha." *Current Issues* (January 21). Retrieved 17 December 2007 (*http://usinfo.state.gov/xarchives/display.html?p=washfile-english&y=2005&m=January&x=20050121173803cpataruk0.6693384*)

KELLNER, DOUGLAS. 2002. "Theorizing Globalization." *Sociological Theory* 20:285-305.

KLAUSEN, JYTTE. 2004. "Is There an Imam Problem?" Prospect 98 (May). Retrieved 17 December 2007. (*http://www.prospect-magazine.c o.uk/article_details. php?id=5945*)

KURIEN, PREMA. 2002. *Kaleidoscopic Ethnicity: International Migration and the Reconstruction of Community Identities in India.* New Brunswick, NJ: Rutgers University Press.

———. 2007. *A Place at the Multicultural Table: The Development of an American Hinduism.* New Brunswick, NJ: Rutgers University Press.

LEFEVERE, PATRICIA. 2006. "Study Looks at Foreign-born Priests Serving in U.S." *National Catholic Reporter* (February 24). Retrieved 17 December 2007. (*http://findarticles.com/p/articles/mi_m1141/is_17_42 /ai_n16107683*).

LEVITT, PEGGY. 2004. "Redefining the Boundaries of Belonging: The Institutional Character of Transnational Religious Life." *Sociology of Religion:* 65:1-18.

———. 2007. *God Needs No Passport.* New York, NY: New Press.

MACLEOD, ALEX. 2004. "A New Reformation is Happening in Global Christianity." *Presbyterian Record* 128:44-45.

MARCOTULLIO, PETER J. 2003. "Globalisation, Urban Form and Environmental Conditions in Asia-Pacific Cities." *Urban Studies* 40:219-47.

MARTIN, DAVID. 2002. *Pentecostalism: The World Their Parish.* Oxford: Blackwell.

MAXWELL, JOHN. C. 1998. *The 21 Irrefutable Laws of Leadership.* Nashville, TN: Thomas Nelson.

MEYER, BIRGIT. 1998. "Commodities and the Power of Prayer: Pentecostalist Attitudes Towards Consumption in Contemporary Ghana" *Development and Change* 29: 751-76.

MORA, CRISTINA. 2007. "Transnational Religious Organizations and the Production of 'Made for TV' Conversion Narratives in the US and Brazil," Working Paper, Princeton University, Center for the Study of Religion.

OWNBY, DAVID. 2007. "China, Religion, and Human Rights: Social Change and State Response." Working Paper, Georgetown University, Berkley Center for Religion, Peace, and World Affairs.

PAGE, JOHN, and SONIA PLAZA. 2006. "Migration Remittances and Development: A Review of Global Evidence." *Journal of African Economies* 15:245-336.

PALM, RISA. 2002. "International Telephone Calls: Global and Regional Patterns." *Urban Geography* 23:750-70.

PORTES, ALEJANDRO. 1997. Transnational communities: Their emergence and significance in the contemporary world-system. In *Latin America in the World Economy*, edited by R. P. Korzeniewicz and W.C. Smith, pp. 151–68. Westport, CT: Greenwood Press.

———. 1999. Globalization from below: The rise of transnational communities. In *The Ends of Globalization: Bringing Society Back In*, edited by D. Kalb, M. van der Land, and R. Staring, pp. 253-70. Boulder, CO: Rowman & Littlefield.

PRIEST, ROBERT J. 2007. "Peruvian Protestant Churches Seek Linking Social Capital." Working Paper, Trinity Evangelical Divinity School, Deerfield, IL.

RAVALLION, MARTIN. 2003. "The Debate on Globalization, Poverty and Inequality: Why Measurement Matters." World Bank Policy Research Working Paper No. 3038. Retrieved 17 December 2007 (*http://ssm.com/abstract =636400*).

ROBBINS, JOEL. 2004. *Becoming Sinners: Christianity and Moral Torment in a Papua New Guinea Society*. Berkeley, CA: University of California Press.

ROBERTSON, ROLAND. 1992. *Globalization: Social Theory and Global Culture*. Thousand Oaks, CA: Sage.

ROHDE, DAVID. 2002. "Braving Nature and Militants: Hindus Trek for a Peek at God's Icy Symbol." *New York Times* (August 5). Retrieved 17 December 2007 (*http:// query.nytimes.com/gst/fullpage.html?res=9C01EED813 3BF936A3575BC0A9649C8B63&sec=&spon=*).

ROSENBERG, JUSTIN. 2000. *The Follies of Globalisation Theory*. London: Verso.

ROSECRANCE, RICHARD, and PETER THOMPSON. 2003. "Trade, Foreign Investment, and Security." *Annual Review of Political Science* 6:377-98.

RUNDLE, STEVE, and TOM STEFFEN. 2003. *Great Commission Companies*. Downers Grove, IL: InterVarsity Press.

SACHS, CAROLYN E. 2007. "Going Public: Networking Globally and Locally." *Rural Sociology* 72:2-24.

SACKS, MICHAEL ALLEN, MARC J. VENTRESCA, and BRIAN UZZI. 2001. "Global Institutions and Networks: Contingent Change in the Structure of World Trade Advantage, 1965-1980." *American Behavioral Scientist* 44:1579-601.

SALISBURY, JOSEPH G. T., and GEORGE A. BARNETT. 1999. "The World System of International Monetary Flows: A Network Analysis." *Information Society* 15:31-49.

SCHLEMMER, LAWRENCE. 2006. "Immigrants in South Africa: Perceptions and Reality in Witbank, a Medium-Sized Industrial Town." *CDE Focus*, Number 9 (May). Johannesburg: Centre for Development and Enterprise.

SCHULARICK, MORITZ. 2006. "A Tale of Two 'Globalizations': Capital Flows from Rich to Poor in Two Eras of Global Finance." *International Journal of Finance & Economics* 11:339-54.

SIERMON-NETTO, UWE. 2003. "Surprise: Resilient Christianity." *World & 1* 18:29-31.

SMITH, BRIAN H. 1990. *More Than Altruism: The Politics of Private Foreign Aid*. Princeton, NJ: Princeton University Press.

STALLINGS, BARBARA. 2007. "The Globalization of Capital Flows: Who Benefits?" *Annals of the American Academy of Political and Social Science* 610:202-16.

STEGER, MANFRED B. 2003. *Globalization: A Very Short Introduction*. New York, NY: Oxford University Press.

TARROW, SIDNEY. 2005. *The New Transnational Activism*. New York, NY: Cambridge University Press.

TSAI, MING CHANG. 2007. "Does Globalization Affect Human Well-Being?" *Social Indicators Research* 81:103-26.

United Nations. 2004. *Human Development Report*. New York, NY: United Nations.

WARNER, R. Stephen. 1994. "The Place of the Congregation in the American Religious Configuration." Pp. 54-99 in *American Congregations*, Volume 2, edited by J.P. WIND and J.W. LEWIS. Chicago, IL: University of Chicago Press.

WELLIVER, DOTSEY, and MINNETTE NORTHCUTT. 2004. *Mission Handbook, 2004-2006: U.S. and Canadian Protestant Ministries Overseas*. Wheaton, IL: Billy Graham Center.

WENGER, JACQUELINE E. 2004. "Official vs. Underground Protestant Churches in China: Challenges for Reconciliation and Social Influence." *Review of Religious Research* 46:169-82.

WINTER, RALPH D., and STEVEN C. HAWTHORNE, eds. 1999. *Perspectives on the World Christian Movement*. Pasadena, CA: William Carey Library.

WUTHNOW, ROBERT. 2005. *America and the Challenges of Religious Diversity*. Princeton, NJ: Princeton University Press.

———. 2006. *American Mythos: Why Our Best Efforts to Be a Better Nation Fall Short*. Princeton, NJ: Princeton University Press.

———. 2007. *After the Baby Boomers: How Twenty- and Thirty-somethings are Shaping the Future of American Religion*. Princeton, NJ: Princeton University Press.

YAMAMORI, TETSUNAO, and KENNETH A. ELDRED, eds. 2003. *On Kingdom Business: Transforming Missions Through Entrepreneurial Strategies*. Wheaton, IL: Crossway.

ZOOK, MATTHEW A. 2003. "Underground Globalization: Mapping the Space of Flows of the Internet Adult Industry." *Environment and Planning* A 35: 1261-86.